Children, Adolescents, and the Media

THIRD EDITION

Children, Adolescents, and the Media

THIRD EDITION

Victor C. Strasburger
University of New Mexico School of Medicine

•

Barbara J. Wilson
*Department of Communication at the
University of Illinois at Urbana-Champaign*

•

Amy B. Jordan
*The Annenberg Public Policy Center,
University of Pennsylvania*

⑤SAGE

Los Angeles | London | New Delhi
Singapore | Washington DC

Los Angeles | London | New Delhi
Singapore | Washington DC

FOR INFORMATION:

SAGE Publications, Inc.
2455 Teller Road
Thousand Oaks, California 91320
E-mail: order@sagepub.com

SAGE Publications Ltd.
1 Oliver's Yard
55 City Road
London EC1Y 1SP
United Kingdom

SAGE Publications India Pvt. Ltd.
B 1/I 1 Mohan Cooperative Industrial Area
Mathura Road, New Delhi 110 044
India

SAGE Publications Asia-Pacific Pte. Ltd.
3 Church Street
#10-04 Samsung Hub
Singapore 049483

Acquisitions Editor: Reid Hester
Assistant Editor: Eve Oettinger
Editorial Assistant: Sarita Sarak
Production Editor: Brittany Bauhaus
Copy Editor: Rachel Keith
Typesetter: C&M Digitals (P) Ltd.
Proofreader: Joyce Li
Indexer: Kathy Paparchontis
Cover Designer: Bryan Fishman
Marketing Manager: Lisa Sheldon Brown
Permissions Editor: Adele Hutchinson

Copyright © 2014 by SAGE Publications, Inc.

Printed in the United States of America

Library of Congress Cataloging-in-Publication Data

Strasburger, Victor C., 1949-

Children, adolescents, and the media / Victor C. Strasburger, University of New Mexico School of Medicine, Barbara J. Wilson, Department of Communication at the University of Illinois at Urbana-Champaign, Amy B. Jordan. — Third Edition.

pages cm
Includes bibliographical references and index.

ISBN 978-1-4129-9926-7 (pbk. : alk. paper)

1. Mass media and children—United States. 2. Mass media and teenagers—United States. I. Wilson, Barbara J. II. Jordan, Amy B. (Amy Beth) III. Title.

HQ784.M3S78 2013
302.23083—dc23   2012046292

This book is printed on acid-free paper.

14 15 16 17 10 9 8 7 6 5 4 3 2

Brief Contents

Detailed Contents

Preface

American youth spend the vast majority of their leisure time with the media. They laugh with television characters who are funny; they viciously attack and destroy evil videogame creatures; they see advertising for candy, makeup, and even liquor; they listen to rap lyrics about sex and violence; and they interact with people all over the world online. The social world these "digital natives" experience is very different from the one their parents and grandparents faced during childhood.

The purpose of this book is to provide an overview of what is known about the impact of the media on youth in the 21st century. The goal is to provide a comprehensive, research-oriented treatment of how children and adolescents interact with the media and of the role it has assumed in their everyday lives. In each chapter, we review the latest findings as well as seminal studies that have helped frame the issues. Because research alone can often be dry and difficult to follow, we have sprinkled each chapter with illustrations, examples from the media, public debates, and real-life instances of media impact. Our intent is to show the relevance of social science research to media-related issues involving youth.

One of the unique features of this book is its developmental focus. In Chapter 1, we begin with a discussion of how children and teens are unique audiences of the media, and we outline developmental differences in how young people process and make sense of media content and form. We also discuss how babies increasingly are interacting with media. Our developmental framework is used throughout the remainder of the book to help readers appreciate how, for example, a 5-year-old might respond differently to a media message than a 10-year-old or a 15-year-old would. In subsequent chapters, we examine the impact of media content in distinct areas, including advertising (Chapter 2); educational and prosocial content (Chapter 3); violence (Chapter 4); sexuality (Chapter 5); drugs, alcohol, and tobacco (Chapter 6); obesity and eating disorders (Chapter 7); and the family (Chapter 11). An important strength of this book is the inclusion of chapters written by leading experts in the topic, including Ed Donnerstein, who writes about revolutionary ways in which the Internet has changed the landscape of content available to children (Chapter 8); Megan Moreno, who presents cutting-edge research on youth engagement with social media (Chapter 9); and Jeanne Funk Brockmyer, who writes about the positive and negative outcomes of video game playing (Chapter 10). Finally, Robert McCannon has provided a thorough review of studies and a guide for media literacy and media education as a strategy for inoculating youth against the negative effects of antisocial content (Chapter 12). The book concludes with a consideration of U.S. media policies and their effectiveness at improving the media environment in which children live and learn.

Two other features make this book unique. First, the book covers the entire developmental period ranging from infancy to childhood to adolescence. Other media-related books have been limited to addressing only children or only teens, but to our knowledge, this is the first media book of its kind that deals with the entire age span that characterizes youth. Second, the three authors bring very different backgrounds to the issues at hand. Victor C. Strasburger is a Distinguished Professor of Pediatrics who has spent most of his career looking at the impact of the mass media on children's health. Barbara J. Wilson is the Kathryn Lee Baynes Dallenbach Professor of Communication who conducts research on child development and the media. Amy B. Jordan is the Director of the Media and the Developing Child sector of the Annenberg Public Policy Center at the University of Pennsylvania, where she studies the impact of media policy on children and families. Together we have identified the media topics that are most pressing to parents, health care practitioners, educators, and policymakers today. As coauthors, we bring our rich and diverse experiences in medicine, social science, child development, and public policy to the issue of youth and media. We also all are parents, which of course gives us firsthand experience with many of the issues we raise.

The approach we have taken is grounded in the media effects tradition. Where appropriate, we have highlighted other perspectives and readings that take a more cultural or critical approach to the study of media and youth. Those perspectives sensitize us to the importance of considering children and teens as active and powerful agents of their media experiences. Youth cannot be shielded from the media, nor should they be. Clearly, children use the media to learn about their culture as well as about childhood itself. In fact, several chapters in this edition of our book focus exclusively on the positive effects of exposure to the media on children's development. Still, there is much we can do to help children and teens approach the media as critical consumers. Readers will notice that we have selected some of the most controversial topics about the media for several chapters of this book. Our aim is not to be one-sided but instead to target the areas at the heart of debates in the United States about the media and public health. Where relevant, we also introduce how other countries are grappling with these issues. We hope we have highlighted the importance of considering the content of the messages to which children are exposed. For today's young people, there are tremendous benefits as well as serious hazards of spending time with media.

This book is designed to serve as a core text for courses in communication, psychology, education, and public health where content covers children and the media. It could also serve as supplemental reading in courses on child and adolescent development, issues in child development, or issues in the media. The book is most appropriate for an upper-level or advanced undergraduate course or even a beginning graduate seminar in the area. We assume some basic knowledge of research methods in social science, but we also provide background to help readers distinguish and compare different research traditions and methodologies. As a way to engage students, we provide a series of exercises at the end of each chapter. The exercises are meant to stimulate debate and can serve as paper assignments or small-group discussion activities. To our minds, the exercises illustrate just how complex and engaging the media environment is for today's youth.

Acknowledgments

Dr. Strasburger would like to thank his colleagues in the Council of Communications of the American Academy of Pediatrics, who have supported his interest in the media, and his colleagues at the University of New Mexico School of Medicine, who have allowed him time to write this book. In particular, he would like to thank Dr. Loretta Cordova de Ortega, Chair of the Department of Pediatrics, and Dr. Paul Roth, Chancellor of the UNM Health Sciences Center.

Dr. Wilson would like to thank two industrious doctoral students, Julius M. Riles (MA, University of Illinois at Urbana-Champaign) and Kira Varava (MA, University of Illinois at Urbana-Champaign), for their persistent efforts to track down journal articles, online references, and terrific examples of media content popular with youth.

Dr. Jordan would like to thank Michael Delli Carpini, Dean of the Annenberg School for Communication, and Kathleen Hall Jamieson, Director of the Annenberg School for Communication, for their unfailing support in her teaching and research in the field of children, adolescents, and the media.

Victor C. Strasburger
Barbara J. Wilson
Amy B. Jordan

CHAPTER 1

Children and Adolescents

Unique Audiences

Sometimes wise and disconcertingly like adults, children are nonetheless children. To the wonder, joy, and vexation of adults, they are different. As they grow older, they become increasingly like us and therefore intelligible to us, but at each age or stage of development there is something for adults to learn more about, to be amused by, and to adjust to.

—Professor Aimee Dorr
Television and Children: A Special Medium for a Special Audience (1986, p. 12)

Over the past twenty or thirty years, the status of childhood and our assumptions about it have become more and more unstable. The distinctions between children and other categories—"youth" or "adults"—have become ever more difficult to sustain.

—Professor David Buckingham
After the Death of Childhood: Growing Up in the Age of Electronic Media (2000, p. 77)

Children and young people are a distinctive and significant cultural grouping in their own right—a sizeable market share, a subculture even, and one which often "leads the way" in the use of new media.

—Professor Sonia Livingstone
Young People and New Media: Childhood and the Changing Media Environment (2002, p. 3)

Unlike the children of the 1950s, 1960s, and 1970s, whose media choices were limited and stood out like isolated, familiar landmarks in communal life, kids today inhabit an environment saturated and shaped by a complex "mediascape" that envelops and bombards them day and night.

—James P. Steyer
The Other Parent: The Inside Story of Media's Effect on Our Children (2002, p. 4)

Because it was one of her favorite movies, Louise decided to rent a DVD of the film *Monsters, Inc.* to share with her two children, a 4-year-old and a 10-year-old. The 10-year-old immediately liked the blue-furred Sulley and his one-eyed sidekick Mike, laughing at the monsters as they scared children and collected their screams to power their factory in the city of Monstropolis. The 4-year-old, on the other hand, tensed up the first time she saw Sulley's hulking frame and Mike's bulging eyeball. The young child asked several nervous questions: "What are they?" "Why are they trying to scare those kids?" Shortly thereafter, the 4-year-old announced that she did not like this "show" and that she wanted to change the channel. When a young girl named Boo accidentally entered the factory, the 4-year-old let out a yelp and buried her face in her blanket (see Figure 1.1). Louise was dismayed at her young child's reaction, wondering how anyone could be frightened by such funny and benign monsters.

Although this example involves a fictitious family, the incident is likely to resonate with parents who are often perplexed by their children's responses to the media. Indeed, a great

Figure 1.1 Image from the film *Monsters, Inc.*

many parents have reported that their preschool children were unexpectedly frightened by the gentle but strange-looking alien in the movie *E.T. the Extra-Terrestrial* (Cantor, 1998). Likewise, G-rated movies such as *Bambi* and *Beauty and the Beast* have provoked fear in younger children (Hoekstra, Harris, & Helmick, 1999). One study even found that younger children were frightened by Michael Jackson's music video "Thriller," which featured the popular singer transforming into a werewolf (Sparks, 1986).

These reactions are not unique to a few films or videos. Research has documented strong differences in the types of media themes that frighten people across age (Harrison & Cantor, 1999). The types of stories that most often upset children younger than 7 involve animals or distorted-looking characters such as ghosts and witches (see Figure 1.2). The impact of such themes greatly diminishes by the time people reach adolescence and adulthood. In older viewers, portrayals involving blood and physical injury are most likely to trigger negative emotions.

From an adult perspective, a young child's fears of monsters and ghosts are difficult to explain. But they signal the importance of considering children's unique orientation to the world in trying to understand how the media can affect younger audiences. In this chapter, we will explore how children and adolescents interact with the media, concentrating on the crucial role human development plays in the process. As background, we will first give an overview of the media environment and media habits of today's youth. Next, we will explore several major principles or ideas that can be gleaned from child development research: Children are different from adults, children are different from each other, and adolescents are different from children. We will conclude the chapter with a focused look at specific cognitive skills that emerge during childhood and adolescence that are relevant to making sense of the mass media.

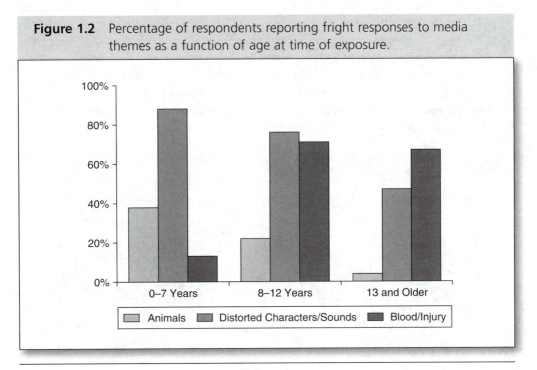

Figure 1.2 Percentage of respondents reporting fright responses to media themes as a function of age at time of exposure.

SOURCE: Adapted from Harrison and Cantor (1999).

The Media Environment and Habits of Today's Youth

A recent headline in the *Detroit Free Press* warned, "More Kids Vulnerable to Sexual Exploits Online" (Baldas, 2012). The article described an incident in which a 14-year-old boy visited an online chat room and interacted with a stranger who convinced him to expose himself on a webcam. According to research cited in the article, nearly half of American children (48%) between the ages of 10 and 17 say they have visited chat rooms, and one in 11 children (9%) has received an unwanted sexual solicitation online. Such statistics help to stir a sense of panic about the impact of media technologies on youth. But even more traditional forms of media can raise concerns. Reality programs on television feature the lives of teenage moms as they juggle adolescence with parenthood, and those of "real" housewives who seem obsessed with physical appearance and money. Rap artists such as Eminem and Lil Wayne celebrate hatred, revenge, and violence in their music. And video games have become increasingly violent. A popular video game series called *Call of Duty* allows the player to take on the role of a soldier battling increasing levels of enemy violence, which occasionally results in the death of innocent parents and children.

There is no doubt that today's youth are confronted with a media environment very different from the one faced by their grandparents or even their parents (see Figure 1.3). Terms such as *digital television*, *texting*, and *Google* did not even exist 20 or 30 years ago. One of the most profound changes concerns the sheer proliferation of media outlets and technologies. Children today live in a "multidevice, multiplatform, multichannel world" (Carr, 2007). The advent of cable and satellite television has dramatically increased the number of channels available in most homes today. Digital cable is multiplying this capacity. Many homes in the United States are also equipped with CD players, DVD players, personal computers, wireless Internet access, and digital cameras. At a very young age, then, children are learning about keypads, e-readers, touch screens, and remote controls.

As these technologies proliferate, they are changing the nature of more traditional media. The TV screen, which once provided a way to watch broadcast television, is now being used for a much wider range of activities, including online shopping, video-on-demand, and viewing digitally recorded photographs and home movies. Newspapers can still be delivered to the doorstep, but they can also be received online. In other words, old distinctions between the television screen and the computer screen or between print and broadcast are becoming less meaningful.

Figure 1.3

SOURCE: *Baby Blues* by Rick Kirkman and Jerry Scott. © 2006 Reprinted with permission of King Features Syndicate.

As media technologies are converging, so are the corporations that own them. In January 2011, the Federal Communications Commission (FCC) and the Justice Department approved the merger of Comcast, the largest cable operator in the United States, and NBC Universal, the well-known broadcasting company. Together, these two media giants own 10 TV and movie production studios; a number of national cable networks, including USA, MSNBC, Oxygen, and Bravo; over two dozen local NBC and Telemundo broadcast stations; two pro sports teams, four theme parks; and several digital media properties, including NBC.com and iVillage. All of this, plus the merger, means access to more than 23 million video subscribers and nearly 17 million Internet subscribers. The deal represents a powerful integration of content and delivery, meaning that programming can be created, promoted, and delivered by a single corporation. This $30 billion megamerger is one of many examples of corporate synergy and partnership.

Such mergers have sparked heated debates in the United States about the dangers of monopolistic growth (Hiltzik, 2011; Silver, 2011). Furthermore, media corporations that were once primarily American-based now have major stakes in the international market. So our capitalistic, privately owned media system and the cultural messages we produce are being exported worldwide. And as these media industries grow, they are becoming increasingly commercial in nature. For example, advertising is now a regular part of the Internet (see Chapters 2 and 8) and is creeping into cable television and even movie theaters.

In the relentless search for new markets, media corporations are increasingly recognizing and targeting youth as a profitable group of consumers (see Chapter 2). Television networks such as Nickelodeon and the Cartoon Network are designed for young viewers; magazines such as *J-14*, *Teen Vogue*, *American Cheerleader*, and *Teen Voices* are targeted to adolescents, particularly girls; and many websites are aimed specifically at children and adolescents. Poptropica, a site targeting 6- to 15-year-olds, allows children to create a "Poptropican" character to travel the many islands of Poptropica, solve mysteries at each location, and interact with other players in "multiplayer" rooms. Of course, there are game cards and toys available for purchase. Even technologies are being marketed to youth. Handheld gadgets such as the VTech MobiGo and the LeapFrog Leapster Explorer are popular among younger children, an age group that is also the target for specially designed smartphones (see Figure 1.4). By 2010, one in five (20%) American children between the ages of 6 and 11 had their own cell phone (American Kids Study, 2010). Ownership

Figure 1.4 Technologies for young children.

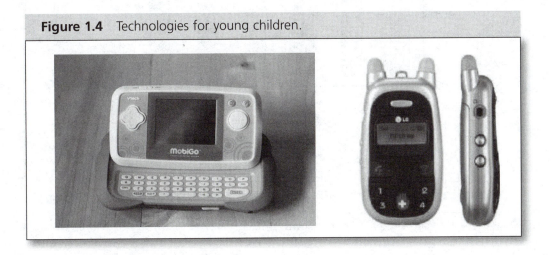

increases dramatically by age; roughly 77% teens between the ages of 12 and 17 own a cell phone (Lenhart, 2012). And two out of three (67%) teens have a mobile device capable of connecting to the Internet (Rideout, 2012). The proliferation of such handheld devices means that children can experience media around the clock, seven days a week.

Finally, digital technology is altering the very nature of media experiences. Images and sounds are more realistic than ever, further blurring the distinction between real-world and media events. By entering virtual worlds while riding on a school bus or sitting in their bedrooms, children can travel to different places, encounter strange creatures, and play adventurous and often violent games. And these new media are far more interactive, allowing youth to become participants in their quest for information, action, and storytelling.

How are the youth of today responding to this modern and complex media environment? A recent national study took an in-depth look at the media habits of American children (Rideout, Foehr, & Roberts, 2010). Surveying more than 2,000 children ages 8 to 18, the study documented that youth today are surrounded by media. The average child in the United States lives in a home with four TVs, two CD players, two radios, three DVD/VCR players, two console video game players, and two computers. More telling, the media have penetrated young people's bedrooms. A full 71% of American children between the ages of 8 and 18 have a television in their room. Moreover, 49% have access to cable or satellite TV and 50% have a video game console in their room (see Figure 1.5). And one-third (33%) of these young people have Internet access in their bedroom, up from 20% in 2005. Having a TV as well as a video game console in the bedroom is more common among both African American and Hispanic youth than among White and Asian youth (Rideout, Lauricella, & Wartella, 2011).

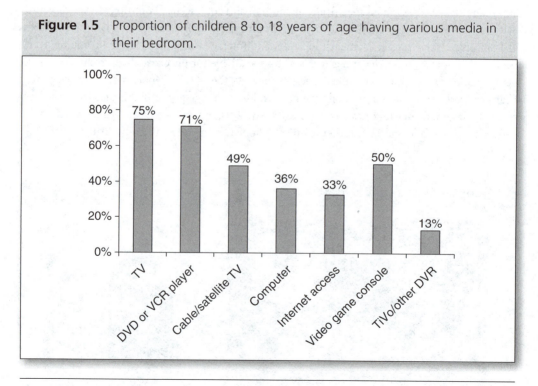

Figure 1.5 Proportion of children 8 to 18 years of age having various media in their bedroom.

SOURCE: Adapted from Rideout, Foehr, and Roberts (2010).

In terms of exposure, the average U.S. child between the ages of 8 and 18 spends seven and a half hours a day consuming media (Rideout et al., 2010). As noted by Rideout and her colleagues, the typical young person in this country spends roughly the same amount of time with media as most adults spend at work each day. Moreover, time spent with media keeps increasing. In 2005, youth spent an average of six and a half hours a day consuming media—a full hour less than in 2010. Even more critical is that most youth today engage in multitasking—using more than one medium at a time. When multitasking is taken into account, youth today consume a total of 10 hours and 45 minutes' worth of media content during those seven and a half hours per day.

Despite all the technologies available, most of this time is spent watching television (see Figure 1.6). On average, American children watch four and a half hours of TV content per day. Notably, "television" today is no longer just regularly scheduled programs on broadcast TV. It now includes DVDs of popular TV series and movies, on-demand TV, prerecorded content on TiVo and other digital recorders, and classic and current TV programs watched online using a laptop, iPad, or cell phone.

As it turns out, media use differs by race and ethnicity. Black, Hispanic, and Asian youth consistently spend more time consuming media each day than do White youth (Babey, Hastert, & Wolstein, 2013; Rideout et al., 2011). The biggest differences are in TV viewing: Black and Hispanic youth spend at least one hour more a day watching TV than White youth do (Rideout et al., 2011). In contrast, Asian youth spend about an hour more a day using the computer than do the other three groups. These differences hold up even after controlling for parents' socioeconomic status and whether the child is from a single- or two-parent home.

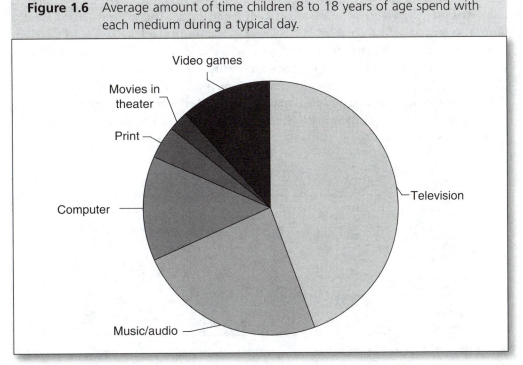

Figure 1.6   Average amount of time children 8 to 18 years of age spend with each medium during a typical day.

SOURCE: Adapted from Rideout, Foehr, and Roberts (2010).

The national study by Rideout and her colleagues (2010) also revealed that parents typically do not exercise much control over their children's media experiences. Less than half (46%) of the children reported that there were rules in their home about what they could watch on TV, and less than one-third (30%) said there were rules concerning which video games they could play. In general, children more often have rules about the specific types of content they may consume than about the amount of time they may spend consuming it. In addition, the likelihood of having media rules decreases with age—30% of 15- to 18-year-olds reported having no rules at all about any type of media use, whereas only 3% of 8- to 10-year-olds reported no rules. Of course, when parents themselves are queried, they report supervising their children's media use to a greater extent than their offspring report (Gentile, Nathanson, Rasmussen, Reimer, & Walsh, 2012). Underscoring the importance of parental oversight is the fact that children and teens who have a TV set in their bedroom spend substantially more time watching television than do those without a set in their room (Jordan et al., 2010; Rideout et al., 2010).

Computers are rapidly spreading in American homes, and so is Internet access. Today the vast majority of young people have a computer at home regardless of their parents' education or race (Rideout et al., 2010). However, Internet access, especially high-speed wireless, still varies by demographics: White youth and youth whose parents are college educated are more likely to have high-speed access. The most popular computer activities for young people are visiting a social networking site such as Facebook, playing a computer game, and watching a video on a site such as YouTube.

Of course, one of the most dramatic changes in the media landscape is the explosion of mobile devices. Roughly two-thirds of young people between the ages of 8 and 18 own a cell phone, and nearly one-third have their own laptop (Rideout et al., 2010). It is rare these days to spend time with any teen who is not carrying a phone. And texting is a big part of teen communication (see Figure 1.7). One recent study found that the typical teen sends an average of 167 text messages a day (Lenhart, 2012). Older girls in particular have embraced this form of communication; girls between 14 and 17 years of age send an average of almost 200 texts a day, or 6,000 texts a month. Heavy texters are more likely to talk on their cell phones, more likely to spend time with friends outside of school, and more likely to use a social networking site than are their light-texting peers (Lenhart, 2012). In other words, heavy texters are socially active teens. Yet despite all these gadgets, teens report that they prefer using old-fashioned face-to-face communication to talk with friends (Rideout, 2012). Moreover, in a recent

Figure 1.7

SOURCE: *Zits* © 2005 Zits Partnership. Reprinted with permission of King Features Syndicate.

national survey of 1,000 13- to 17-year-olds, 43% agreed strongly or somewhat that they wished they could "unplug" sometimes (Rideout, 2012). In addition, 41% reported that they would describe themselves as "addicted" to their cell phone.

Most of the tracking of media habits has focused on older children and teens. However, infants and preschoolers are spending a fair amount of time with media as well. One national study surveyed over 1,000 parents of children ages 6 months to 6 years (Vandewater et al., 2007), age groups that many assume are too young to be involved much with media. Contrary to this assumption, the average American child between the ages of 6 months and 6 years spends about an hour and a half a day using media. Again, most of this time is spent watching television or videos and DVDs (see Figure 1.8). In fact, children younger than age 6 spend more time watching TV and videos than they do reading (or being read to) or playing outside. Perhaps most surprising, nearly 20% of children younger than age 3 have a TV set in their bedroom; roughly 40% of 3- to 6-year-olds have a TV in their room (see Figure 1.9). In a recent large-scale study of over 600 preschoolers, those who had a TV in their bedroom were significantly more likely to suffer from sleep problems, including daytime tiredness and difficulty falling asleep at night (Garrison, Liekweg, & Christakis, 2011).

American children are not so different from some of their counterparts abroad. One early study of more than 5,000 children living in 23 different countries found that the average 12-year-old spent three hours a day watching television (Groebel, 1999), a figure remarkably comparable to that found in the United States at the time. A more recent study of five Nordic countries (Denmark, Finland, Iceland, Norway, and Sweden) found that 95% of young people in this region have Internet access in the home, but that television viewing remains the single most prominent leisure activity (Carlsson, 2010).

To summarize, youth today are confronted with a media environment that is rapidly changing. Technologies are proliferating, merging, more interactive, and mobile. Furthermore, the content featured in these technologies is increasingly graphic, realistic, and commercial in

Figure 1.8 Children spend a great deal of time watching television each day.

Figure 1.9 Television sets are common in American children's bedrooms.

nature. At the same time, media use is at an all-time high. Youth today spend anywhere from one-third to one-half of their waking hours with some form of media (see Figure 1.10). Preteens and teens frequently are engaging in more than one media activity at a time, making estimates of overall exposure more challenging. And much of this media use is becoming more private as children carry smartphones throughout their daily activities and then retreat to their bedrooms to watch TV, play video games, listen to music, or text their friends. We will now highlight several developmental principles that underscore the need to consider youth as a special audience in today's media environment.

Figure 1.10

SOURCE: *Zits* © 2005 Zits Partnership. Reprinted with permission of King Features Syndicate.

Children Are Different From Adults

Most adults believe that they personally are not affected much by the media. In a well-documented phenomenon called the "third-person effect," people routinely report that others are more strongly influenced by the media than they themselves are (Perloff, 2009). As an example, a recent study found that undergraduates perceived themselves to be less likely to be harmed by Facebook use in terms of privacy and future employment opportunities than were their closest friends, friends in their Facebook network, and even Facebook users in general (Paradise & Sullivan, 2012). This difference in perceived impact gets larger as the age of the "other" person decreases. In other words, adults perceive that the younger the other person is, the stronger the effect of the media will be (Eveland, Nathanson, Detenber, & McLeod, 1999). Interestingly, even children endorse a kind of third-person effect, claiming that only "little kids" imitate what they see on TV (Buckingham, 2000).

Are children more susceptible to media influence than adults are? At the extremes, there are two radically different positions on this issue (see Buckingham, 2011). One view is that children are naive and vulnerable and thus in need of adult protection. This stance sees the media as inherently problematic and in some cases evil because they feature material that children are simply not yet ready to confront. Buckingham (2000) points out that "media panics" have been with us a long time, especially those concerning the impact of sex and violence on children. Such panics gain steam any time a public crisis occurs, such as the massacre at Columbine High School, or any time a new and unknown form of media technology is developed (Wartella & Reeves, 1985).

A contrasting view is that children are increasingly sophisticated, mature, and media savvy (Livingstone, 2002). According to this position, efforts to shield youth from media are too protectionist in nature, smack of paternalism, and construe children as acted upon instead of actors. Instead, children should be empowered to take control of their own media experiences, negotiating and learning along the way. Buckingham (2000) noted that this position is widely shared among those who see children as independent consumers who should be able to spend their own money and buy what they want.

These very different perspectives illustrate that notions of childhood are constantly being defined, debated, and renegotiated over the course of history (James, Allison, Jenks, & Prout, 1998). In truth, neither of these extreme positions seems very satisfying. Children are not entirely passive in the face of the media, nor are they extremely worldly and discriminating. The reality is probably somewhere in between. Nevertheless, most parents, developmental psychologists, policymakers, and educators would agree that children are not the same as adults (see Figure 1.11).

Several features of childhood support this distinction. First, children bring less real-world knowledge and experience to the media environment (Dorr, 1986). Every aspect of the physical and social world is relatively new to a young child, who is busy discovering what people are like, how plants grow, what animals eat, and where one neighborhood is located relative to another. As they get older, children explore increasingly abstract concepts and ideas such as the social norms of their culture, what prejudice is, and how life begins. In almost every arena, though, children possess a more limited knowledge base compared to adults.

One implication of this is that children can fail to understand a media message if they lack the background knowledge needed to make sense of the information. As an illustration,

Figure 1.11

SOURCE: *Baby Blues* © 2007 Baby Blues Partnership. Reprinted with permission of King Features Syndicate.

in 1996, researchers at the Children's Television Workshop (now called Sesame Workshop) wanted to produce a *Sesame Street* segment about visiting the doctor. On the basis of preliminary interviews, the researchers discovered that preschoolers mostly associated doctor visits with getting shots and that they had little knowledge of the importance of such vaccinations ("Feeling Good," 1996). Had the producers not discovered this, they might have created a script that focused too much on getting shots, inadvertently reinforcing children's negative and limited impressions of the purpose of going to a physician.

As another example, researchers working on the *Sesame Street* website wanted to create an activity that would help preschoolers learn about email. In developing the "*Sesame Street* Post Office," the researchers discovered that preschool children have little, if any, experience with email or with composing letters (Revelle, Medoff, & Strommen, 2001). In other words, the children's background knowledge was quite limited. Taking this into account, the post office activity was designed to be very concrete by having the child choose a Muppet to email from a set of pictures of Muppets and then choose questions to ask from a set tailored to each Muppet. The child's message was displayed on the screen before it was sent so that children could see how their choices influenced the composed letter. Researchers also determined that adding a "Dear [name of Muppet]" to the beginning of the email and a "Your friend, [name of child]" to the end of it helped children understand the conventions of letter writing.

The lack of real-world knowledge can also make children more willing to believe the information they receive in the media. It is difficult to evaluate a story for accuracy or truthfulness in the face of no alternative data. An adult watching a TV advertisement is able to evaluate that message in the context of knowledge about the television industry as well as a vast array of personal experiences with purchasing products. A child, on the other hand, rarely has this rich set of knowledge structures on which to rely. As an illustration, Figure 1.12 presents children's perceptions of how truthful advertisements are (Chan, 2001). In a sample of over 400 children ages 5 to 12, a full 42% reported that television advertising is "mostly true." Given this level of trust, a young child seems fairly defenseless when confronted with a slick TV ad that costs thousands of dollars to produce and may yield millions of dollars in sales profit.

A second feature that distinguishes childhood from adulthood is the strong eagerness to learn that marks the early years (Dorr, 1986). Parents find this tendency exhausting sometimes,

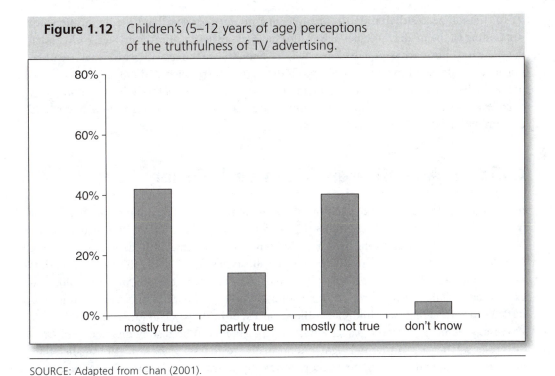

Figure 1.12 Children's (5–12 years of age) perceptions of the truthfulness of TV advertising.

SOURCE: Adapted from Chan (2001).

as their infant daughter puts one more object in her mouth or their preschool son asks for the 20th time, "What's that?" or "Why?" Such curiosity is a hallmark of childhood and is celebrated by educators. But it means that children are as open to learn from the mass media as from other sources, particularly in situations where firsthand experience is not possible. For example, most American children are not able to visit Japan, but they can learn about the country by reading a book or viewing a TV documentary. A preschooler can even watch *Big Bird in Japan*, a Sesame Workshop production available on DVD or even YouTube. These examples show the educational benefits of the media. Unfortunately, a child could also learn about Japan by visiting a website created by a hate group that disparages people of Asian descent.

A third feature that characterizes childhood is a relative lack of experience with the media. Admittedly, these days some children are actually more media savvy than their parents are. Indeed, many children know how to take and store photos on a smartphone or program the digital video recorder while their parents still fumble with these technologies. One study found that 19% of children younger than age 6 were able to turn on the computer by themselves (Rideout & Hamel, 2006). But with most media, it is still the case that adults have spent more time with the technology. Adults readily appreciate, for example, that the placement of a story in a newspaper signals something about its importance, that public television is a noncommercial channel in contrast to the broadcast networks, and that there are different genres and subgenres of movies. In contrast, children often show an incomplete understanding of production techniques such as dissolves and split screens (Beentjes, deKoning, & Huysmans, 2001), have difficulty distinguishing nightly news programs from tabloid news shows such as *Inside Edition* and *Current Affair* (Wilson & Smith, 1995), and do not fully appreciate the commercial nature of most media in the United States (Dorr, 1980). This lack of familiarity with the technical forms and structure of the media makes a child less able to critically evaluate the content presented.

To summarize, children differ from adults in a number of ways that have implications for responding to the media. Younger age groups have less experience with the real world and at the same time possess a strong readiness to learn about those things with which they are unfamiliar. They also tend to be less savvy about the nature, intricacies, and potential distortions of the media. Such naïveté makes a preschooler and even an elementary schooler more likely to believe, learn from, and respond emotionally to media messages than is a more mature and discriminating adult.

Children Are Different From Each Other

It may be easier to recognize that children are different from adults than it is to appreciate how much children differ from one another. In some ways, the label *children* itself is misleading because it encourages us to think of a fairly homogeneous group of human beings. As the *Monsters, Inc.* example at the start of this chapter illustrates, a 4-year-old thinks and responds to the world very differently than a 10-year-old does. But even a group of 4-year-olds will exhibit marked differences in how they respond to the same situation. In fact, sometimes it is difficult to believe that two children are the same age or in the same grade level.

On any elementary school playground, kindergartners can be readily distinguished from 5th graders—they are shorter in height and normally weigh less. Their heads are smaller, they dress differently, and they tend to be more physically active. But even more profound differences exist in their cognitive functioning. Younger children attend to and interpret information in different ways than do their older counterparts. Several influential perspectives on children's development support this idea, including Piaget's (1930, 1950) theory of cognitive development as well more recent models of information processing (Flavell, Miller, & Miller, 2002; Siegler, 2005).

Age is often used as a marker of these differences in cognitive abilities, although there is tremendous variation in how and when children develop. Still, most research reveals major differences between preschoolers and early elementary schoolers (3–7 years of age) on the one hand and older elementary school children (8–12 years of age) on the other, in terms of the strategies they use to make sense of the world (Flavell et al., 2002). These strategies have important implications for how children respond to mass media, as will be discussed below in the section titled "Developmental Differences in Processing the Mass Media."

Cognitive development is not the only factor that distinguishes children from each other. Personality differences also set children apart. For instance, some children are withdrawn or inhibited in unfamiliar situations, whereas others are not (Kagan & Snidman, 2004). Children also differ in the degree to which they possess prosocial dispositions toward others (Eisenberg, Fabes, & Spinrad, 2006), the degree to which they are capable of regulating their emotions (Stegge & Terwogt, 2007), and the degree to which they enjoy novel or stimulating situations (Zuckerman, 1994).

Research consistently shows sex differences among children, too. For example, girls tend to prefer activities that are less vigorous than the ones boys tend to choose (Eaton & Enns, 1986), and boys typically are more physically aggressive (Kistner et al., 2010). In terms of cognitive skills, girls generally obtain higher grades in school and do better on tests involving writing, whereas boys do better on visual-spatial tasks (Halpern, 2004).

The fact is that children, even those who share biological parents and are raised in the same environment, differ on many dimensions. And children themselves recognize these differences early in development. For example, children become aware of their own gender by around age 2 (Berk, 2000). During the preschool years, they begin formulating mental conceptions of activities, norms, attributes, and scripts that are associated with being male or female (Ruble et al., 2007). Young children's initial understanding of gender as a social category is often based on superficial qualities such as hair length and dress. As they enter elementary school, children's conceptions grow more sophisticated, and they become keenly interested in gender role information in the culture. They actively search for cultural meanings about gender in their homes, on the playground, and in the media (see Bussey & Bandura, 1999). In other words, the unique characteristics that differentiate children in turn get represented and reinforced in the culture.

All of these unique characteristics make it difficult to come up with a single prototype for what a child is like. Therefore, when we make generalizations about children and the media, we must be careful to take into account the developmental, personality, and gender characteristics of the individuals involved.

Adolescents Are Different From Children

Although we cannot generalize about all children, we can clearly differentiate them as a group from their older counterparts—teenagers. Parents certainly appreciate this transformation as they watch their warm, cuddly 12-year-old turn into an emotionally distant and independent 13-year-old. Of course, this developmental progression does not happen evenly or all at once. But the changes are reflected in a variety of activities and interests that a young person has, including media preferences. For example, children under the age of 12 prefer watching cartoons and animated movies on television, many of which involve fantasy themes (see Table 1.1). In contrast, viewers between the ages of 12 and 17 prefer reality shows and sitcoms that focus on teenage issues. There is some overlap in the list of top 10 TV programs for these two age groups, but the differences are striking.

Adolescence is often characterized as a time of challenge and turbulence (Roth & Brooks-Gunn, 2000). Along with bodily changes that can be quite dramatic, teens are faced with increased independence and growing self-discovery. Scholars of adolescent development refer to these changes as developmental transitions or passages between childhood and adulthood (Arnett, 1992a). In other words, the sometimes stormy periods are a necessary and normal part of growing up (Gondoli, 1999).

Unfortunately, parents and even the general public often view the teenage years with some trepidation. One national poll revealed that 71% of adults described teenagers negatively, using terms such as *irresponsible* and *wild* (Public Agenda, 1999). Some of this public opinion is likely fueled by the media's preoccupation with high-profile cases of troubled teens who become violent. Contrary to public opinion, though, most teens are able to navigate adolescence in a socially responsible way, learning new competencies and new roles on the path to adulthood (Graber, Brooks-Gunn, & Petersen, 1996).

What are some of the developmental hallmarks of adolescence? One of the main challenges a teen faces is identity formation (Klimstra, Hale, Raaijmakers, Branje, & Meeus, 2010). During the teenage years, boys and girls alike begin to ask questions about who they are and how they

Table 1.1 Top 10 Programs for the 2010–2011 Season

Viewers Ages 2–11

Rank	Program	Channel	Genre
1	*Phineas and Ferb*	Disney Channel	Animated movie
2	*Toy Story 2*	Disney Channel	Animated movie
3	*Bolt*	Disney Channel	Animated movie
4	*American Idol – Wednesday*	FOX	Reality
5	*A Fairly Odd Movie: Grow Up, Timmy Turner!*	Nickelodeon	Movie
6	*SpongeBob SquarePants*	Nick at Nite	Cartoon
7	*Big Time Rush*	Nick at Nite	Teen sitcom
8	*American Idol – Thursday*	FOX	Reality
9	*The SpongeBob SquarePants Movie*	Nickelodeon	Animated movie
10	*The Adventures of Sharkboy and Lavagirl*	Disney Channel	Movie

Viewers Ages 12–17

Rank	Program	Channel	Genre
1	*American Idol – Wednesday*	FOX	Reality
2	*American Idol – Thursday*	FOX	Reality
3	*Glee*	FOX	Musical comedy-drama
4	*America's Got Talent – Tuesday*	NBC	Reality
5	*The Voice*	NBC	Reality
6	*America's Got Talent – Wednesday*	NBC	Reality
7	*Family Guy*	FOX	Animated sitcom
8	*Big Time Rush*	Nick at Nite	Teen sitcom
9	*iCarly: iParty With Victorious*	Nickelodeon	Teen sitcom
10	*The Game Plan*	Disney	Movie

SOURCE: Copyrighted information of Nielsen, licensed for use herein.

differ from their parents. This emerging sense of the self is fragile and malleable as teens "try on" different appearances and behaviors. An article in *Newsweek* magazine described the teen years like this: "From who's in which clique to where you sit in the cafeteria, every day can be a struggle to fit in" (Adler, 1999, p. 56). As this quote suggests, the process of identity formation is highly social in nature, with teens working to integrate different facets of themselves as they encounter others at school, at work, and during leisure activities (Crosnoe & Johnson, 2011). Today's youth even use the media to grapple with their identities. For example, one study of

20 female teen bloggers found that the girls used LifeJournal as a digital space for self-expression and "self-theorizing" (Davis, 2010). Another study found that 50% of 9- to 18-year-olds who used the Internet had pretended to be somebody else while communicating by email, instant messaging (IM), or chat (Valkenburg, Schouten, & Peter, 2005). Teens also spend a great deal of time posting photographs, videos, and personal information on popular websites such as Facebook, YouTube, and Twitter. As they experiment with ways of expressing themselves online, teens may be working through the psychosocial process of understanding who they are and how they feel about their emerging identity (Valkenburg & Peter, 2011).

A second challenge of adolescence is increased independence. Parents naturally feel less need to supervise a 13-year-old who, unlike a 5-year-old, can dress, study, and even go places alone. Teens often have jobs outside the home and by age 16 can typically drive a car, furthering their autonomy. In one study, the percentage of waking hours that teens spent with their families fell from 33% to 14% between the 5th and 12th grade (Larson, Richards, Moneta, Holmbeck, & Duckett, 1996).

Time away from parents can provide teens with opportunities to make independent decisions. It also can allow for experimentation with a variety of behaviors, some of which are not very healthy. A large national study involving more than 90,000 adolescents in Grades 6 to 12 found strong differences between teens who regularly ate dinner with a parent and those who did not (Fulkerson et al., 2006). In particular, teens who spent less dinner time with parents showed significantly higher rates of smoking, drinking, depression, violence, and school problems, even after controlling for family support and family communication. The direction of causality is difficult to pinpoint here because it may be that troubled teens simply choose to spend less time at home. However, other studies have also documented the importance of parent involvement as a buffer against unhealthy behaviors during the teenage years (Cookston & Finlay, 2006).

This point leads us to a third feature of adolescence—risk taking. Today's teens face tough decisions regarding a number of dangerous behaviors such as smoking, drug use, and sexual activity. And there is no doubt that adolescence is a time of experimentation with reckless activities (Santelli, Carter, Orr, & Dittus, 2009). For example, 1.4 million American youth under the age of 18 started smoking cigarettes for the first time in 2010 (National Survey on Drug Use and Health, 2010). Furthermore, a recent national survey revealed that 47% of 9th through 12th graders reportedly have had sexual intercourse (Centers for Disease Control and Prevention, 2011). The same study found that 17% of the teens had carried a weapon (i.e., gun, knife, or club) during the 30 days preceding the survey, 39% had drunk alcohol, 23% had used marijuana, and 40% of sexually active students had not used a condom (see Figure 1.13). Moreover, 24% had ridden in a vehicle in the last 30 days that was driven by someone who had been drinking.

Some of this risk taking may be a function of what scholars have labeled "adolescent egocentrism" (Elkind, 1967, 1985; Schwartz, Maynard, & Uzelac, 2008). In particular, teenagers often seem preoccupied with their own thoughts and appearance and assume others are equally interested in their adolescent experiences. This view of the self as unique and exceptional can in turn lead to a feeling of invulnerability to negative consequences (Greene, Krcmar, Walters, Rubin, & Hale, 2000). In other words, self-focused teens think they are different from everyone else and that tragedies occurring to others "won't happen to me." Indeed, studies show that teens routinely underestimate their own personal chances of getting into a car accident compared with the risks they assume others face (Finn & Bragg, 1986). Similar misjudgments have been found among sexually active young girls who underestimate the likelihood that they themselves might

Figure 1.13 Percentage of U.S. high school students who reported engaging in risk-related behaviors over the last two decades.

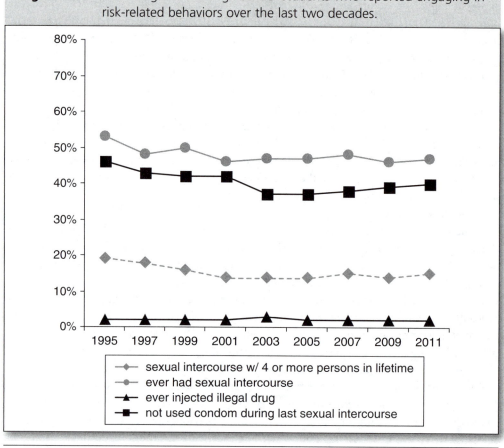

SOURCE: Adapted from Centers for Disease Control and Prevention (2012).

get pregnant (Gerrard, McCann, & Fortini, 1983). One study linked this type of optimistic bias to teen smoking. Song, Glantz, and Halpern-Felsher (2009) surveyed over 300 ninth graders every six months for two years. They found that adolescents who perceived low risk associated with being exposed to secondhand smoke were more likely to start smoking in subsequent months than were those who perceived secondhand smoke to be risky. Risk taking can also be viewed as an adolescent's effort to assert independence from parents and to achieve adult status (Jessor, 1992). However, not all teens engage in reckless behaviors, and even the ones who do seldom limit their activities to those legally sanctioned for adults. Arnett (1995) argued that risk taking must be viewed in the larger context of an adolescent's socialization. Some teens experience *narrow socialization*, which he characterized as involving strong allegiance to the family and community, clear expectations and responsibilities, unambiguous standards of conduct, and swift sanctions for any deviation from those standards. Other teens are raised in an environment of *broad socialization*, where independence and autonomy are encouraged, standards of conduct are loose or even self-determined, and enforcement of standards is lenient and uneven. Arnett argued that in addition to parents, the schools, the legal system, and even the media contribute to these overarching patterns of socialization. As might be expected, risk taking is more prevalent in cultures in which socialization is broad rather than narrow (see Arnett, 1999, for a review).

A fourth feature of adolescence is the importance of peers. Teens spend a great deal of time with friends and place a high value on these relationships (Rubin, Bukowski, & Parker, 2006). On average, teens spend up to one-third of their waking hours with friends (Hartup & Stevens, 1997). In her controversial book *The Nurture Assumption: Why Children Turn Out the Way They Do*, Judith Harris argued that parents have a minimal influence on their child's development other than to nurture and shape the child's peer group (Harris, 1998). Peer groups certainly do make a difference during adolescence. Studies have documented the role of peers in the initiation and continuation of behaviors such as cigarette smoking (Scherrer et al., 2012), drug use (Creemers et al., 2009), and sexual intercourse (Whitbeck, Yoder, Hoyt, & Conger, 1999). Engaging in reckless behavior often helps a teen become a member of a peer group, and the group itself can foster a sense of collective rather than individual invincibility (Arnett, 1992a).

But peer influence is not as straightforward and not necessarily as negative as some might assume. Friends actually can be a source of support for teens and can also increase self-esteem (Wilkinson, 2004). Generally, adolescents are more susceptible to *antisocial* peer pressure when they have more delinquent than nondelinquent friendships (Haynie, 2002), when they have poorer relationships with their parents (Dishion, 1990), and when they are alienated from community support structures such as schools (Arnett, 1992b; Resnick et al., 1997).

Last but not least, puberty and sexual development are hallmarks of adolescence. Body hair, acne, muscle growth, and weight gain are only a few manifestations of the dramatic physical changes that occur during the teenage years. Puberty typically begins during early adolescence, around age 9 or 10 for girls and roughly one to two years later for boys (Archibald, Graber, & Brooks-Gunn, 2003), although there are large individual variations. As their bodies change, many teens also experience an increased energy level as a function of significant changes in their endocrine system (Petersen & Taylor, 1980). Furthermore, increased production of androgens and estrogens stimulates the growth of reproductive organs (see Rekers, 1992).

As might be expected, the hormonal and physical changes associated with puberty are accompanied by an increased interest in sexuality. In one study, for example, 12- to 15-year-old girls who were more physically mature (i.e., had experienced earlier puberty) reported a greater interest in seeing sexual content in the movies, television, and magazines than did those who were less mature (J. D. Brown, Halpern, & L'Engle, 2005). Thus, at some point during adolescence, most teens will become intensely curious about sex and will seek information about sexual norms, attitudes, and practices in their culture. It is no accident, then, that popular teen magazines devote a great deal of space to sexual issues and relationships (Walsh-Childers, 1997).

Whether the teenage years are characterized as tempestuous or transitional, there is no doubt that significant developmental changes occur during this period. Adolescents spend more time alone or with friends and less time with parents. This growing independence comes at the same time that teens are exploring their identities and their sexuality. The challenge is to provide these young people with enough latitude as well as guidance so that the decisions they make will result in a healthy rather than risky lifestyle.

Developmental Differences in Processing the Mass Media

So far, we have focused on broad developmental features that characterize childhood and adolescence and that differentiate these periods from adulthood. Now we will turn our attention more directly to young people's interactions with the media. Any individual who confronts a mediated message must make sense of and interpret the information presented. Like adults, children and adolescents construct stories or readings of media messages that they encounter (Dorr, 1980). Given some of the pronounced differences in experience and maturation described above, we can expect that interpretations of the same content will vary across the life span. That is, a young child is likely to construct a different story from a TV program than an older child or teenager will.

These different interpretations may seem "incorrect" or incomplete to an adult viewer. But even among mature adult viewers, there are differences in how people make sense of stories. For example, one early study looked at people's reactions to the 1970s TV sitcom *All in the Family*, featuring a bigoted character named Archie Bunker (Vidmar & Rokeach, 1974). The research revealed that interpretations of the program varied widely based on individual attitudes about race. Viewers who held prejudiced attitudes identified with Archie Bunker and saw nothing wrong with his racial and ethnic slurs (see Figure 1.14). In contrast, viewers who were less prejudiced evaluated Archie in negative ways and perceived the program to be a satire on bigotry.

What cognitive activities are involved when a young person watches a television program, enjoys a movie, or plays a video game? In general, five mental tasks are involved (Calvert, 1999; Collins, 1983). First, the child needs to select important information for processing. When viewing television, for example, a multitude of auditory and visual signals are presented in a particular program or advertisement. Moreover, there are cues in the environment that often compete with the television, such as family members talking in the background or loud music from another room. A viewer must allocate attention to these myriad cues, consciously or unconsciously filtering out what is not essential and instead focusing on what is important in the situation.

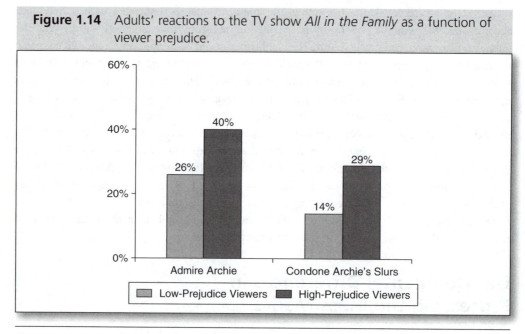

Figure 1.14 Adults' reactions to the TV show *All in the Family* as a function of viewer prejudice.

SOURCE: Adapted from Vidmar and Rokeach (1974).

Second, the child needs to sequence the major events or actions into some kind of story. Most media messages feature a narrative or storyline (Grossberg, Wartella, & Whitney, 1998). Television plots are the easiest example of this, but even an advertisement, a video game, a song, or a radio program conveys a story.

Third, the child needs to draw inferences from implicit cues in the message. The media do not have the space or the time to explicitly present all aspects of a story. Television programs jump from one location to another, characters in movies have dreams or experience flashbacks, and even characters in video games travel in ways that are not always orderly or linear. A sophisticated consumer recognizes the need to "read between the lines" to fill in the missing information. But a young child may fail to recognize that time has passed between scenes (Smith, Anderson, & Fischer, 1985), that the events depicted are only part of a dream (Wilson, 1991), or that a flashback to earlier events in the plotline has occurred (Durkin & Lowe, 1999).

Fourth, to make sense of both explicit and implicit cues in the message, a child must draw on the rich database of information he or she has stored in memory that relates to the media content. For instance, a child who lives in a rural community will have an easier time making sense of a movie about a family that loses a farm to bank foreclosure than will a child who lives in an apartment complex in New York City. This rich set of past experiences and acquired knowledge forms a mental database that helps a child interpret new messages.

Fifth, the child will typically evaluate the message in some way. The simplest evaluation pertains to liking or not liking the message. Children as young as 2 years of age already show preferences for certain types of TV programs, such as those featuring puppets and young characters (Lemish, 1987; Rideout & Hamel, 2006). One mother described her preschool daughter's attachment to a televised purple dinosaur in the following way: "She played the Barney tape every single hour that she was awake the entire weekend. And if we tried to turn it off, she'd be screaming, yelling, crying" (Alexander, Miller, & Hengst, 2001, p. 383). As children grow older, they become increasingly sophisticated and critical of media messages (Potter, 2010). Not only are they capable of evaluating the content, but they also begin to appreciate the forms, economic structure, and institutional constraints that characterize different media (Dorr, 1980). An adolescent, for example, may reject all mainstream American television programming because of its inherent commercialism.

Given this set of tasks, we can expect that children will process media messages in different ways across development. We now describe some of the major shifts in cognitive processing that occur during the transition from early to middle childhood and during the transition from late childhood to adolescence. By no means is this list exhaustive; instead, it reflects some of the skills that are most relevant to interacting with the media (for further reading, see Dorr, 1980; Flavell et al., 2002; Wilson & Drogos, 2009). We will end this chapter with a topic receiving a great deal of interest these days: How do infants and toddlers interact with the media?

Two caveats need to be noted here. First, most of the changes highlighted below occur gradually rather than abruptly during development (Flavell et al., 2002). Piaget (1950, 1952) argued that younger children's thinking is qualitatively different from that of older children, such that their cognitive systems progress through distinct stages (i.e., sensorimotor, approximately 0–2 years of age; preoperational, 2–7 years; concrete operational, 7–11 years; formal operational, 11 years and older). However, research indicates that cognitive performance can be uneven across different types of tasks and that children exhibit varied skill levels even within a particular domain (Siegler, 2005). Thus, it is widely believed that development is far less stagelike or abrupt than Piaget's theory would have us believe.

Second, the ages during which these shifts occur vary markedly across children. For rough approximations, we define younger children as those between 2 and 7, older children as those between 8 and 12, and adolescents as those between 13 and 18.

Younger Children Versus Older Children

From Perceptual to Conceptual Processing. Preschoolers pay close attention to how things look and sound. This focus on salient features has been referred to as *perceptual boundedness* (Bruner, 1966). Perceptual boundedness is defined as an overreliance on perceptual information at the expense of nonobvious or unobservable information that may be more relevant (Springer, 2001). For example, preschoolers frequently group objects together based on shared perceptual features such as color or shape (Bruner, Olver, & Greenfield, 1966; Melkman, Tversky, & Baratz, 1981). In contrast, by age 6 or 7, children have begun sorting objects based on conceptual properties such as the functions they share (Tversky, 1985). With regard to the media, studies show that younger children pay strong visual attention to perceptually salient features such as animation, sound effects, and lively music (Anderson & Levin, 1976; Calvert & Gersh, 1987; Schmitt, Anderson, & Collins, 1999). Older children, on the other hand, tend to be more selective in their attention, searching for cues that are meaningful to the plot rather than those that are merely salient (Calvert, Huston, Watkins, & Wright, 1982).

One creative experiment involving television revealed this distinction quite clearly. Hoffner and Cantor (1985) exposed children to a television character who was either attractive or ugly and who acted kind toward others or was cruel (see Figure 1.15). Preschoolers generally rated the ugly character as mean and the attractive character as nice, independent of the character's actual behavior. In other words, their evaluations were strongly affected by the character's physical appearance. Older children's judgments, in contrast, were influenced more by the character's behavior than her looks.

Why are younger children so perceptual in their focus? Tversky (1985) has argued that all children can be swayed by strong perceptual cues in a situation, but that as they develop children come to suppress immediate, salient responses in favor of slower, more thoughtful ones. This shift is undoubtedly fostered by the acquisition of knowledge that is conceptual in nature, such as the idea that motives are an important predictor of behavior. Children of all ages, and even adults, are also less likely to be swayed by perceptual cues when they are dealing with situations and tasks that are familiar (Springer, 2001).

We can apply this developmental trend in perceptual boundedness to the example at the beginning of this chapter. The preschool child is transfixed by the monsters' strange physical appearance, reacting with fright when she sees their distorted forms. In contrast, the older child is able to minimize the characters' looks and instead focus on the creatures' behavior and motivation.

From Centration to Decentration. As noted above, children and even adults can respond strongly to salient features in a message. But another characteristic of younger children's thinking is that they often focus on a single striking feature to the exclusion of other, less striking features. This tendency has been called *centration* and is illustrated in some of Piaget's classic liquid conservation tasks (see Ginsburg & Opper, 1979). In these tasks, a child is shown

Figure 1.15   Four characters differing in appearance and behavior.

SOURCE: From Hoffner and Cantor (1985). Copyright ©American Psychological Association. Reprinted with permission.

two glasses containing identical amounts of water. Once the child agrees that the amounts are identical, the experimenter pours the water from one glass into a third glass, which is taller and thinner (see Figure 1.16). The experimenter then asks the child whether the two amounts of liquid are still identical or whether one glass now contains more water. The typical pre-schooler concludes that the taller glass has more liquid in it. Why? Because the taller glass *looks* as if it has more in it. In other words, the differential height of the liquids captures most of the preschooler's attention.

In contrast, older children are increasingly able to "decenter" their attention and take into account the full array of perceptual cues. The liquid in one glass is higher, but that glass also has a different shape to it. It is taller and thinner. Also, pouring the liquid from one container to another does not change the quantity. The amount of liquid stays the same. By recognizing that the liquid is the same, the older child is able to *conserve* continuous quantities.

The same developmental differences are found with other types of conservation tasks. For example, two rows of six pennies can be laid out next to one another in one-to-one correspondence. If one row is then compressed, a younger child is likely to perceive it as containing fewer coins because it is now shorter (Ginsburg & Opper, 1979). In contrast, the older child notes all the perceptual data in the situation and recognizes that the number of pennies is unchanged or "conserved" despite appearances.

Figure 1.16 A typical Piagetian conservation task.

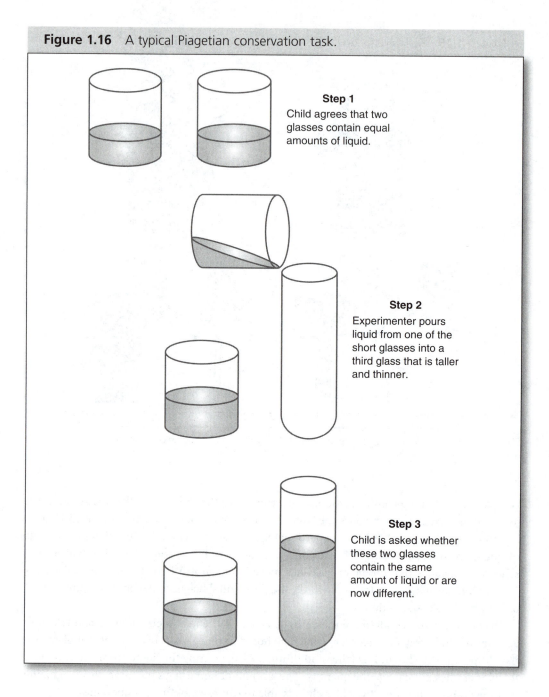

Step 1
Child agrees that two glasses contain equal amounts of liquid.

Step 2
Experimenter pours liquid from one of the short glasses into a third glass that is taller and thinner.

Step 3
Child is asked whether these two glasses contain the same amount of liquid or are now different.

O'Bryan and Boersma (1971) documented these differences further by examining children's eye movements during conservation tasks. They found that younger children who are unable to conserve or master the task correctly tend to fixate on a single dimension, such as the height of the liquid in a glass. Older children who are able to conserve show more varied eye movements, shifting their gaze over many parts of the testing display.

Applying the idea of centration to the media, younger children are likely to respond strongly to a single feature in a television or movie scene, such as a character's red dress or a hero's shiny weapon. The prominence of the cues as well as the child's own interests will help determine what is most salient. Other perceptual cues such as the character's hair color, name, physical size, and even certain overt behaviors may go unnoticed. In emotional stories, for example, a character's feelings are often conveyed through facial expressions as well as situational information in the plot. Younger children will be more likely to fixate on one or the other of these sets of cues, even when they conflict (Wiggers & van Lieshout, 1985). Thus, in some cases, we can expect that this centration will interfere with a young child's comprehension of the storyline (see Figure 1.17).

From Perceived Appearance to Reality. Another important cognitive skill during childhood concerns the ability to distinguish fantasy from reality. Much to a parent's amazement, a 3-year-old child may attribute life to an inanimate object such as a rock, have an invisible friend, and want Dora from *Dora the Explorer* to come over to the house for a play date. All of these tendencies reflect a fuzzy separation between what is real and what is not.

Numerous studies have found strong developmental differences in children's perceived reality of television (see Dorr, 1983; Wright, Huston, Reitz, & Piemyat, 1994). Younger children between the ages of 2 and 3 show little understanding of the boundary between television and the real world (Jaglom & Gardner, 1981). In fact, at this age, children routinely talk to the television set and wave at the characters (Noble, 1975). For example, in one study, many 3-year-olds reported that a bowl of popcorn shown on TV would spill if the television set were turned upside down (Flavell, Flavell, Green, & Korfmacher, 1990).

By around age 4, the young child begins to appreciate the representational nature of television but still tends to assume that anything that *looks* real is real (M. H. Brown, Skeen, & Osborn, 1979). This literal interpretation has been called the "magic window" perspective, reflecting the idea that young children naively assume that television provides a view of the real world. Gradually, children come to appreciate that some of what is shown on television is not real, although most of this centers first on perceptual cues. For example, 5-year-olds typically judge cartoons as not real because they feature physically impossible events and characters (Wright et al., 1994). In other words, the young child assesses content by looking for striking violations of physical reality (Dorr, 1983). It is important to note, though, that these emerging distinctions are initially quite fragile. Young children may be able to report that an animated character is "not real" yet still become quite frightened of it (Cantor, 1998). In one study

Figure 1.17

SOURCE: PEANUTS reprinted by permission of United Features Syndicate, Inc.

(Woolley, Boerger, & Markman, 2004), preschoolers were introduced to a novel fantasy creature named the "Candy Witch," and even 5-year-olds believed she was real and not "pretend," particularly if the witch purportedly visited their homes at night and left candy. In a more recent study, 5-year-olds were just as willing to follow advice from a computer-generated TV character as from a live person, whereas 7- and 9-year-olds responded only to the person (Claxton & Ponto, 2013).

As children mature, they begin to use multiple criteria for judging reality in the media (Hawkins, 1977). Not only do they notice marked perceptual cues, but they also take into account the genre of the program, production cues, and even the purpose of the program. Most important, older children begin to judge content based on how similar it is to real life (M. H. Brown et al., 1979). Although they recognize that much of television is scripted, older children are likely to judge a scene or a program as realistic if it depicts characters and events that are *possible* in the real world (Dorr, 1983; Hawkins, 1977). In one survey, 28% of 2nd and 3rd graders and 47% of 6th graders spontaneously referred to "possibility" criteria in judging whether a series of characters and events on television were realistic (Dorr, 1983). In contrast, only 17% of kindergartners used this type of criteria. These trends are congruent with research on language comprehension, which suggests that the concept of possibility is not fully understood until around 8 years of age (Hoffner, Cantor, & Badzinski, 1990; Piaget & Inhelder, 1975).

Obviously, a child's personal experiences will place a limit on how sophisticated these reality judgments can be. As an illustration, Weiss and Wilson (1998) found that elementary schoolers rated the TV sitcom *Full House* as very realistic, indicating on average that "most" to "all" real-life families are like the family featured in this program. These perceptions seem a bit naive given that the program was about a widowed father raising his three daughters with live-in help from his brother-in-law and his best friend.

Additionally, the nature of the media will have an impact. Computer games and other technologies that employ virtual reality can simulate the perceptual and social features of the real world. Interacting in such environments may tax a young person's cognitive capacity, making it difficult even for an older child to distinguish fantasy from reality.

From Concrete to Inferential Thinking. A final cognitive trend during childhood that has implications for the media is the shift from concrete to inferential thinking. As we have mentioned above, a young child's thinking is very tangible, focusing closely on what can be seen and heard (Bruner, 1966). For a 2- or 3-year-old, this means that attention can be swayed by highly salient cues that may actually be extraneous to the plot (Schmitt et al., 1999). For example, a bright red costume may get more attention than the actions of the character who is wearing this garment.

By age 4, children can begin to focus more on information that is central to the plot than on incidental details (Lorch, Bellack, & Augsbach, 1987). Of course, younger children do best with age-appropriate content, programs that are relatively short in duration, and comprehension tests that assess forced-choice recognition rather than spontaneous recall (Campbell, Wright, & Huston, 1987). With development, children become increasingly able to extract events that are central to the storyline in a program (Collins, 1983; Durkin & Lowe, 1999). Yet the information younger children focus on is still likely to be fairly explicit in nature. For example, one study found that 4- and 6-year-olds most often recalled actions after watching televised stories, whereas adults most often recalled information about characters' goals and motives (van den Broek, Lorch, & Thurlow, 1996). Actions are typically concrete and fairly vivid in television programming, making them easy to understand and represent in memory. Another study found that a majority of kindergartners thought an episode of *Clifford the Big Red Dog* was a story about dogs interacting, which meant they took the story quite literally (Mares & Acosta, 2008). At this young age, they missed the overarching moral lesson about social tolerance and inclusiveness. As discussed above, full comprehension involves apprehending not only explicit content but also implicit information in the unfolding narrative. For instance, in one scene, a protagonist might discover that a "friend" is trying to steal his money. In a later scene, the protagonist might hit the friend. The viewer must deduce that the protagonist's aggression, which in isolation might appear unprovoked, is actually motivated by a desire to protect personal property. In other words, the viewer must link scenes together and draw causal inferences about content that is not explicitly presented. Studies show that older children are better able than their younger counterparts to draw different types of inferences from verbally presented passages (Ackerman, 1988; Pike, Barnes, & Barron, 2010). The same pattern emerges in the context of mediated messages. By roughly age 8 or 9, children show substantial improvements in their ability to link TV scenes together and draw connections between characters' motives, behaviors, and consequences (Collins, Berndt, & Hess, 1974; Collins, Wellman, Keniston, & Westby, 1978; Kendeou, Bohn-Gettler, White, & van den Broek, 2008). This shift from concrete to inferential processing has implications for other forms of media as well. A video game and even a website require the user to make connections across space and time.

To summarize, a number of important cognitive shifts occur between early and middle childhood. A preschooler watching screen media is likely to focus on the most striking perceptual features in a program. This child may comprehend some of the plot, especially when the program is brief and age appropriate. Yet comprehension will be closely tied to concrete actions and behaviors in the storyline. In addition, the preschooler is likely to have difficulty distinguishing reality from fantasy in the portrayals. As this same child enters elementary school, she will begin to focus more on conceptual aspects of the content such as the characters' goals and motives. She increasingly will be able to link scenes together, drawing causal connections in the narrative. And her judgments of reality will become more accurate and discriminating as she compares media content with that which could possibly occur in the real world. Clearly, her overall understanding of a media message is quite advanced compared with what she was capable of as a preschooler. Nevertheless, her skills are continuing to develop even during her later elementary school years. Next we will explore some of the cognitive shifts that occur between late childhood and adolescence.

Older Children Versus Adolescents

From Real to Plausible. As described above, older children use a variety of cues to judge the reality of media content. One of the most important yardsticks for them is whether the characters or events depicted in the media are possible in real life (Morison, Kelly, & Gardner, 1981). Adolescents become even more discriminating on this dimension, judging content as realistic if it is likely or *probable* in real life (Dorr, 1983; Morison et al., 1981). In Dorr's (1983) research, almost half of adolescents defined real television events as those that were probable or plausible in real life. In contrast, probability rationales were seldom used by older elementary school children. To illustrate this distinction, a movie featuring an evil stepfather who is trying to poison his stepchildren may be very upsetting to a 9- or 10-year-old because this scenario *could* happen in real life. A teenager, on the other hand, is less likely to be disturbed by such content, reasoning that the vast majority of stepfathers in the world are not murderers. The movement to probabilistic thinking is consistent with studies of language comprehension that indicate that the ability to differentiate probability from possibility crystallizes during early adolescence (Piaget & Inhelder, 1975; Scholz & Waller, 1983).

From Empirical to Hypothetical Reasoning. A related development that occurs between late childhood and early adolescence is the shift from empirical to hypothetical reasoning (Flavell et al., 2002). Adolescents become increasingly able to understand abstract concepts, use formal logic, and think hypothetically (Byrnes, 2003). Along with this abstract thinking comes an ability to engage in inductive and deductive reasoning (Keating, 2004) as well as conditional reasoning (Gauffroy & Barrouillet, 2011). An older child is able to reason conceptually too, but much of this process is based on collecting empirical evidence. A 5th or 6th grader, for example, may watch a person's behavior across several situations and infer from these actions what the person's motives are. In contrast, an adolescent might begin with a theory or hypothetical set of motives for a person and then observe behaviors to see if the theory is correct. In other words, the teenager is capable of more abstract thinking that need not be tied too closely to observable data.

Adolescents are also increasingly capable of suspending their own beliefs to evaluate the reasoning of someone else (Moshman, 1998). Put another way, teens can sometimes reason about arguments at an objective level.

The ability to think hypothetically means that a teenager can anticipate different plot events and predict logical outcomes as a storyline unfolds. The teen is also able to critique the logic and causal structure of different media messages. As abstract thought flourishes, the adolescent may also consider the meaning behind the message (e.g., "Who is the source of this website, and why is it constructed this way? How would the content differ if it were designed by someone else with different motives?").

Metacognitive Thinking. *Metacognition* refers to the ability to understand and manipulate one's own thought processes (Metcalfe & Shimamura, 1994). It is called *meta*cognition because it refers to second-order mental activities: A person thinks about his or her own thinking. Adults routinely reflect on their own cognitive processing, especially during situations that highlight the need to do so. For instance, studying for a test or actually taking one requires a person to concentrate carefully on cognitive enterprises such as attention, comprehension, and memory.

Flavell and his colleagues (2002) have distinguished between two types of metacognition: metacognitive *knowledge* and metacognitive *monitoring and self-regulation*. Metacognitive knowledge refers to a person's knowledge and beliefs about the human mind and how it works. For example, most adults realize that short-term memory is of limited capacity (see section below on processing capacity), that it is generally easier to recognize something when you see it than to recall it outright, and that certain tasks are more difficult and demanding of the human mind than others. But young children do not necessarily possess such metacognitive knowledge. In one study, for example, Lovett and Flavell (1990) presented 1st graders, 3rd graders, and undergraduates with three tasks: a list of words to be memorized, a list of words to match up with a picture, and a list of words to memorize and match. Unlike the 1st graders, the 3rd graders and the undergraduates were able to select which strategy—rehearsal, word definition, or both—would work best for each task. Yet only the undergraduates understood that the tasks would be more difficult with longer lists and unfamiliar words. Thus, as children develop, they become increasingly aware that the mind engages in a range of activities, including memory, comprehension, and inference (Flavell et al., 2002).

The second type of metacognition involves monitoring and readjusting one's ongoing thinking. Consider the test taking instance, for example. An adult who is having difficulty with a certain section on a test might decide to jump ahead to an easier part for efficiency's sake and to build confidence before returning to the harder material. Research suggests that this type of self-monitoring is difficult during early childhood (see Flavell et al., 2002). In one study, preschoolers and elementary schoolers were instructed to examine a set of objects until they were sure they could recall them (Flavell, Friedrichs, & Hoyt, 1970). Older children examined the objects for a period of time, determined they were ready, and typically recalled all the items correctly. In contrast, the preschoolers examined the items, thought they were ready, and generally failed on the recall test. In other words, the preschoolers were not capable of monitoring their memory processes very accurately.

How do metacognitive knowledge and monitoring relate to the media? We can expect that as children approach adolescence, they will be better able to analyze the cognitive demands of different media and even different messages within a particular medium. According to Salomon (1983), some media require more nonautomatic mental elaborations or more AIME (amount of invested mental effort) than others. In general, television requires less effort and concentration than reading, for example, because the former is highly visual and relies less on language skills (Salomon & Leigh, 1984). Thus, a teenager is more likely than a young child to recognize that a difficult book or a television documentary requires higher concentration than watching a music video. Their awareness of different media will affect the depth of processing they use, which in turn should enhance comprehension and learning. Interestingly, when children are instructed to pay attention to and learn from TV, their mental effort and performance increase compared to what they do without such instruction (Salomon, 1983).

Nevertheless, the trend toward multitasking with media may make it difficult for even the most sophisticated teen to recognize the cognitive overload in such situations (see Cantor, 2009). Recent research indicates that people experience substantial declines in performance when they try to do more than one thing at a time (Bowman, Levine, Waite, & Gendron, 2010). For example, driving performance suffers when people simultaneously text on their cell phones (Owens, McLaughlin, & Sudweeks, 2011). Despite their metacognitive abilities, teens and young adults alike are fairly naive about how well they can study for an exam while monitoring Facebook, texting on their phones, and listening to music all at the same time.

Last, as children reach the teenage years, they should increasingly be able to monitor their own affective reactions to the media, for example, avoiding classical music they do not like or reminding themselves that "it's only a movie" when they feel scared. In one illustration of this, preschoolers and 9- to 11-year-olds were given different types of instructions on how to think about a frightening program they were about to watch on television (Cantor & Wilson, 1984). Children were told either to imagine themselves as the protagonist (role taking set) or to remember that the story and the characters were make-believe (unreality set). The cognitive-set instructions had no appreciable effect on the preschoolers' emotional reactions to the program. In other words, they showed little ability to use the information to alter how they perceived the program. In contrast, older children in the role taking condition were more frightened by the program, and those in the unreality condition were less frightened, compared with a control group that received no instructions at all (see Figure 1.18). The findings are consistent with the idea that as children develop, they are increasingly able to modify their thought processes while watching television.

Regulatory Competence. Adults have long assumed that much of cognitive growth occurs during the childhood years. Recent research on the brain contradicts this view. With better measurement tools such as magnetic resonance imaging (MRI), we are beginning to realize that there are substantial changes in brain development during adolescence (Spear, 2010). Much of this development occurs in the prefrontal cortex region of the brain, which is crucial to the regulation of behavior and emotion (Sowell, Trauner, Gamst, & Jernigan, 2002). Until this area of the brain is fully developed, which may not occur until the mid-20s, young people often have difficulty regulating and controlling their moods and responses to different situations. This development of an "executive suite" or executive function is receiving considerable attention these days (Steinberg, 2005), in part because it signals that our conception of "adulthood" may need to be adjusted. Consistent with this idea, scholars have now adopted the term "emerging adulthood" to characterize young people between the ages of 18 and 25 (Arnett, 2007).

Executive functioning appears to play a crucial role in how young people respond to risk. One recent study found that teens who scored low on a battery of tests that measured executive control engaged in significantly more risky behavior than did those with higher executive control, even after controlling for risky personality traits, sex, and age (Pharo, Sim, Graham, Gross, & Hayne, 2011). Executive functioning not only varies individually but

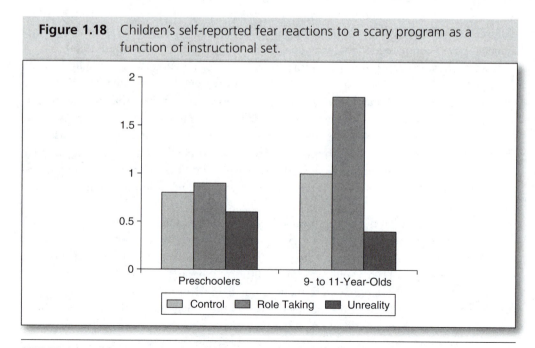

Figure 1.18 Children's self-reported fear reactions to a scary program as a function of instructional set.

SOURCE: Adapted from Cantor and Wilson (1984).

also across adolescence, generally showing gradual improvement with age (Watson, Lambert, Miller, & Strayer, 2011). Therefore, younger adolescents will typically show less maturity and more risk taking when they confront various dilemmas in life, including those mediated by technologies. For example, younger teens are more likely than older ones to play with their identity in Internet communications (Valkenburg et al., 2005). Younger teens are also more likely than older teens to talk with strangers on the Internet (Jochen, Valkenburg, & Schouten, 2006).

Two Overall Developmental Trends

Two other important trends occur continuously throughout childhood and adolescence and are not specific to particular age groups: (a) increasing knowledge about the social, physical, and mediated world in which we live and (b) increasing processing capacity.

Increase in Domain-Specific Knowledge. It may seem obvious to state that children gain increasing amounts of knowledge across different domains as they grow. But the point is still worth making because it has such important implications for interacting with the media. With each new experience, a child stores more and more information in highly organized ways in memory. The resulting knowledge structures, sometimes called mental templates or *schemas*, are powerful organizers that help children anticipate and assimilate new information (Fiske & Taylor, 1991). Research suggests that children as young as 3 years of age possess well-developed schemas or scripts for familiar events, such as getting ready for bed and taking a bath (Hudson, Sosa, & Shapiro, 1997). As evidence of the power of these mental organizers, a young child is likely to protest quite strongly if someone tries to alter these routines.

Young children also develop schemas for stories that include information about the typical structure and components of a narrative (Mandler, 1998). Research suggests that a well-developed story schema can help a child to organize and interpret television programming (Meadowcroft & Reeves, 1989). In addition, children can form schemas about the social and physical world in which they live. In the social realm, for example, children develop templates for emotions that include information about expressive signals, situational causes, and display rules associated with each affect (e.g., Campos & Barret, 1984). These schemas undoubtedly assist a child in making sense of an emotional scene on television. In turn, such schemas can be shaped and modified by exposure to the media (see Wilson & Smith, 1998).

Not surprisingly, children develop schemas about the media as well (Calvert, 1999). Each form of the media has its own special audiovisual techniques and codes, which at least in the case of television have been referred to as "formal features" (Bickham, Wright, & Huston, 2001; Huston & Wright, 1983). Television and film, for example, use production techniques such as cuts, zooms, fades, and special effects to signal shifts in time and changes in setting. Video games and computers have their own technological conventions. A user of the World Wide Web, for example, needs some understanding of search engines and hypertext. Knowing what to expect from each medium greatly increases a child's sophistication in using it (Calvert, 1999; Smith et al., 1985). For this reason, efforts to teach youth to become critical consumers of the media often include instruction on the conventions of different technologies (see Chapter 13).

In addition to developing schemas *about* the media, children can actually enhance their cognitive thinking by spending time with certain technologies (see Subrahmanyam & Greenfield, 2008).

For example, studies show that practicing certain types of video games can improve dynamic spatial skills in both children (Subrahmanyam & Greenfield, 1996) and adults (Feng, Spence, & Pratt, 2007). There is also evidence that video game playing improves strategies for dividing visual attention, presumably because players must cope with events that occur simultaneously at different places on the screen (Greenfield, deWinstanley, Kilpatrick, & Kaye, 1996). In addition, listening to a song seems to stimulate imagination more than watching a music video of the same song does (Greenfield et al., 1987). All of these studies suggest a kind of interactive relationship between media exposure and schematic processing and development.

To summarize here, children can call on larger stores of remembered information across a variety of domains as they grow. In addition, they can integrate and combine information in more complex ways, forming more elaborate connections with what they already know (Siegler, 2005). In other words, their schemas become more elaborate and differentiated, and thus their interpretations of media content become richer and more complex.

Having a great deal of knowledge and experience in a given area has all kinds of benefits for cognitive processing. Compared to a beginner, a veteran has familiar concepts and ready-made strategies to apply to a problem (Siegler, 2005). Given that the terrain is familiar, the expert expends less cognitive energy and is free to apply mental workspace to high-order activities such as metacognition (Flavell et al., 2002). Consider for a moment how a 6-year-old might respond to a cigarette advertisement in a magazine compared with how a 16-year-old would process the same message. The 6-year-old presumably has never smoked, has little knowledge of how the lungs work, is unaware of the legal battles being waged against the tobacco industry, is not cognizant of who paid for the placement of the ad in the magazine, and has little experience with the cost of various products in a grocery store. The teenager certainly has less experience than an adult would have in this domain, but compared with the grade schooler, the adolescent brings a much broader knowledge base from which to draw in interpreting and evaluating such an ad.

Increase in Processing Capacity. Regardless of age or level of development, all humans experience limits in the capacity of their working memory (Fougnie & Marois, 2006). In other words, certain situations and tasks are so demanding that they exceed a person's available cognitive resources. One way this has been demonstrated is through reaction time studies that show that people perform slowly or poorly on secondary tasks when their mental energies are consumed by a primary task (Kail, 1991; Lang, 2000).

Developmental research demonstrates that as children mature, they are able to hold increasing amounts of information in working memory (Cowan, Nugent, Elliott, Ponomarev, & Saults, 1999; Gathercole, 1998). For example, a 5-year-old is typically able to deal with only four or five bits of information at once (e.g., digits, letters), whereas the average adult can handle seven (Dempster, 1981). There are differing theoretical accounts for this increased processing capacity. Some have argued that the structure or size of one's memory space actually increases with development (Cowan et al., 1999). Others have argued that the size remains fixed, but the functional use or efficiency of the space increases (Kail, 1993). As certain tasks become familiar, they are easily categorized into preexisting schemas. This categorization and routinization mean that fewer demands are placed on the cognitive system, and hence space is freed up for other cognitive processing.

Regardless of which view is correct, the implications are the same. Younger children have difficulty considering multiple pieces of information in working memory (see Figure 1.19). In addition, their capacities may be taxed quickly by a single cognitive activity that is somewhat novel and thus cannot be easily schematized. As children mature and gain experience in certain arenas, they can more quickly classify new information into preexisting schemas. This schematization allows them to consider and interrelate more bits of information at once and to engage in concurrent cognitive tasks. In other words, they become more efficient information processors.

How does processing capacity affect children's interactions with the media? Research suggests that older children are better able than younger children to consider multiple cues within a scene or across several scenes when interpreting a television portrayal (Collins et al., 1974; Hoffner, Cantor, & Thorson, 1989). Likewise, older children are able to track the main plot of a television story even when there is a subplot interspersed throughout, whereas younger children's comprehension suffers in the face of a distracting subplot (Weiss & Wilson, 1998). Older children are also better equipped to handle fast-paced programming that involves the integration of information across rapid changes in time and place (Wright et al., 1984). As discussed above, older children are also better able to consider their own thought processes while attending to a television program (Cantor & Wilson, 1984).

Any time a media message is complex, lengthy, fast paced, or delivered in a distracting environment, it is likely to present a cognitive challenge to younger children because of their more limited processing capacities. Extending these ideas to online or digital technologies, we might also expect that interactive media such as fast-paced computer games will quickly tax the mental resources of a young child because of the need to simultaneously comprehend content and respond cognitively and physically to it. As processing capacity increases throughout childhood and adolescence, these once very difficult types of media interactions will become increasingly routinized.

Figure 1.19

SOURCE: *Baby Blues* © 2005 Baby Blues Partnership. Reprinted with permission of King Features Syndicate.

Infants and Baby Media

Video products designed and marketed specifically for infants first appeared in the late 1990s, starting with the Baby Einstein series. Today, the marketplace is exploding with such products, including DVDs, websites, flashcards, and even video games. Parents eager to have their

6-month-old interact with new technologies can buy a Fisher-Price Laugh & Learn Smilin' Smart Phone that activates music and fun phrases at the push of a button, or a VTech Baby's Learning Laptop with a colorful keyboard and a movable mouse. There is even a TV network called BabyFirstTV that features round-the-clock programming for infants. Many of these products are marketed to parents who are keen to enhance the cognitive development of their very young children. Critics have charged that this "genius baby" industry is unfair and misleading (Linn, 2009). In fact, the company behind the Your Baby Can Read products recently announced it was going out of business, citing the high cost of legal battles it was fighting in trying to defend its advertising claims about helping infants to read (Crary, 2012).

As indicated earlier in this chapter, American babies do spend a fair amount of time with screen media—on average, about one and a half hours a day (Vandewater et al., 2007). Scholars have argued that several factors contribute to the rise in babies' exposure to television and DVDs compared to a generation ago (Wartella, Richert, & Robb, 2010). First, families in the 21st century are accustomed to having television turned on throughout the day as a backdrop to all kinds of activities, including mealtimes. Obviously, this practice enhances exposure to screen media among children of all age groups. Second, families are moving older television sets into children's rooms, including those of their infants. And third, parents today are more accustomed to sending young children to preschool, and anything that can better prepare their offspring for such educational experiences is likely to be attractive (see Figure 1.20).

Surveys indicate that many parents do indeed believe that videos and DVDs can foster their infants' intellectual development (for a review, see Wartella et al., 2010). Yet the American Academy of Pediatrics (AAP) (2011) recently issued a recommendation that *discourages* media use for children younger than 2 years. The AAP also cautions against the use of background television intended for adults when an infant or baby is in the room. The AAP policy statement goes on to say, "Although infant/toddler programming might be entertaining, it should not marketed as or presumed by parents to be educational" (p. 4).

Figure 1.20 Babies with screen media.

Which view is accurate? Are media products good for infants or are they problematic? The research is still accumulating on this topic, but emerging findings suggest we need to be cautious about the educational merits of screen media for babies. For one thing, infants have difficulty orienting to the television screen and paying sustained visual attention to it until they are 3 to 6 months old (Courage & Setliff, 2010). Even after that, what captures their attention are salient cues such as laughter, music, peculiar sounds, and rapid character action (Valkenburg & Vroone, 2004). Clearly, the industry has figured this out in designing video content for babies. But paying attention to salient formal features on the screen does not mean that a baby comprehends the content (Courage & Setliff, 2010).

In fact, there are a growing number of studies indicating that before the age of roughly 3, babies learn better from watching a live person than from watching the same type of material enacted on television (see Barr, 2010). This phenomenon has been called the "video deficit" effect (Anderson & Pempek, 2005), and it has been demonstrated for a range of activities, such as teaching infants to imitate novel behaviors, search for a hidden object, and respond to emotional cues (Barr, 2010). The superiority of live action over TV is likely due to several factors, including younger children's difficulty in translating information from a two-dimensional to a three-dimensional format and their difficulty in appreciating the symbolic nature of what is on the screen (Barr, 2010).

Nevertheless, by about 18 months of age, babies are capable of learning some things from screen media, including simple vocabulary (Vandewater, 2011) and novel action sequences (Simcock, Garrity, & Barr, 2011). However, such learning is more apt to occur under the following conditions:

- when the video material is repeatedly viewed (Barr, Muentener, Garcia, Fujimoto, & Chavez, 2007)
- when popular characters are used (Lauricella, Gola, & Calvert, 2011)
- when an adult is in the room reinforcing the material (Barr, Zack, Garcia, & Muentener, 2008)
- when the material is developmentally appropriate (Linebarger & Walker, 2005)

Given all of these caveats, one might argue that spending time interacting with family members is better for babies than being plopped down in front of a screen. Indeed, developmental psychologists long have held that babies need rich social interactions with caregivers in order for healthy development to occur. Even in this context, screen media can be a challenge. Research shows that parents are less likely to interact with their babies when the television is turned on in the background (Christakis et al., 2009), and babies themselves spend less time playing with toys when the television is turned on compared to when it is off (Schmidt, Pempek, Kirkorian, Lund, & Anderson, 2008). As we develop more sophisticated ways of assessing brain development in babies, surely screen media will factor in to how we understand their growth.

Conclusion

The purpose of this chapter has been to underscore the fact that children are very different from adults and from each other when they interact with the media. Children are eager to learn, have less real-world experience, and have less developed cognitive skills, making them ultimately more vulnerable to media messages. The remainder of this book will explore how children and teens respond to different types of media content, such as violence and sexual messages, as well as to different media technologies, such as video games and the Internet. We will continually draw on the concepts and developmental trends presented in this chapter to explain how children deal with the stimulating media world that confronts them. Clearly, there are robust developmental differences in children's attention to and comprehension of media messages. These cognitive processes in turn have implications for emotional responding as well as behavioral reactions to the media.

Exercises

1. Think about your childhood. What is the first experience you remember having with the media? How old were you? What medium was involved? What type of content was involved? What was your reaction or response to the experience? Did your parents know about it? Could a child today have a similar experience? Why or why not?

2. For one day, chart the time you spend with the media (e.g., television, radio, books, cell phone, Internet). Note which media you are using and what type of content you are experiencing. Also note when you are "media multitasking," or using two or more media at once (e.g., reading a book and listening to music). How much of your day did you spend with the media? Is your media use similar to that of the typical American child, as described in this chapter? How is it similar and how is it different? Do you perceive that you are effective or ineffective when media multitasking? Provide justification for your response.

3. Watch an episode of a TV sitcom that is popular with children. Think about the main theme of the program, the sequence of events in the storyline, and the nature of the characters. Based on developmental differences in cognitive processing, describe three ways in which a 4-year-old's interpretation of the episode would differ from that of a 10-year-old. How would a 10-year-old's interpretation differ from that of a teenager? What type of viewer do you think the program is targeted toward? Think about the program itself as well as the commercial breaks in addressing this question.

4. Some scholars argue that childhood is disappearing in today's modern society. They maintain that children are dressing more like adults, talking like them, and experiencing adult activities and even adult media content. Can you think of examples to support this thesis? Can you think of examples that challenge it? How is childhood changing in the 21st century? Do you agree that childhood is vanishing? How crucial are the media in debates about these issues?

5. When you were a child, did your parents have rules about what you could do with the mass media? Did they have rules when you were a teenager? Did you have a TV set in your bedroom? Do you think parents should exercise control over their children's media experiences? Why or why not?

6. Compare and contrast three rating systems designed to inform parents about media content: (a) the Motion Picture Association of America's ratings for movies (see http://www.mpaa.org/ratings/what-each-rating-means), (b) the TV Parental Guidelines for

television shows (see http://www.tvguidelines.org/), and (c) the Entertainment Software Rating Board's ratings for computer and video games (see www.esrb.org/ratings/ratings_guide.jsp). Evaluate the three systems in terms of what we know about child development, as discussed in this chapter. Do the systems seem accurate? Are they likely to be helpful to parents? How could they be improved? Can you think of a movie, TV show, or video game that you think is rated inappropriately?

7. Watch a program targeted to children that airs on public broadcasting (e.g., *Sesame Street, Arthur, WordGirl*). Now compare it with a cartoon that airs on Cartoon Network, ABC Kids, or Nickelodeon. Compare and contrast the two programs in terms of plot, characters, formal features, and degree of realism. Which program seems better suited to the developmental capabilities of a 4- or 5-year-old? Why?

8. Find the lyrics to a song from a genre of music that is popular among young people today (e.g., hip-hop, rap). Now compare the lyrics to those from a Beatles' song of the 1960s or 1970s. What do the songs say about adolescence? How are the songs similar in their representation of adolescent themes such as risk taking, social identity, peer relations, and sexuality? How are they different? Think about the social and political context in which these songs were written in addressing these issues.

9. Are you surprised by the amount of time that babies spend with media each day? What do you think about the AAP guidelines that discourage media use for children under the age of 2? Are the guidelines reasonable? Are they based on sound evidence? Should companies in the U.S. be allowed to market media products to very young children? Why or why not?

References

Ackerman, B. P. (1988). Reason inferences in the story comprehension of children and adults. *Child Development, 59,* 1426–1442.

Adler, J. (1999, May 10). Beyond Littleton: The truth about high school. *Newsweek,* pp. 56–58.

Alexander, K. J., Miller, P. J., & Hengst, J. A. (2001). Young children's emotional attachments to stories. *Social Development, 10*(3), 374–398.

American Academy of Pediatrics, Council on Communications and Media. (2011). Media use by children younger than 2 years. *Pediatrics, 128*(5), 1–6.

American Kids Study. (2010, January 4). *Kids' cell phone ownership has dramatically increased in past five years.* Retrieved from http://www.gfkmri.com/PDF/MRIPR_010410_KidsAndCellPhones.pdf

Anderson, D. R., & Levin, S. R. (1976). Young children's attention to *Sesame Street. Child Development, 47,* 806–811.

Anderson, D. R., & Pempek, T. A. (2005). Television and very young children. *American Behavioral Scientist, 48*(5), 505–522.

Archibald, A. B., Graber, J. A., & Brooks-Gunn, J. (2003). Pubertal processes and physiological growth in adolescence. In G. R. Adams & M. D. Berzonsky (Eds.), *Blackwell handbook of adolescence* (pp. 24–47). Malden, MA: Blackwell.

Arnett, J. J. (1992a). Reckless behavior in adolescence: A developmental perspective. *Developmental Review, 12,* 339–373.

Arnett, J. J. (1992b). Socialization and adolescent reckless behavior: A reply to Jessor. *Developmental Review, 12,* 391–409.

Arnett, J. J. (1995). Broad and narrow socialization: The family in the context of a cultural theory. *Journal of Marriage and Family, 57*(3), 617–628.

Arnett, J. J. (1999). Adolescent storm and stress, reconsidered. *American Psychologist, 54*(5), 317–326.

Arnett, J. J. (2007). Emerging adulthood: What is it, and what is it good for? *Child Development Perspectives, 1*(2), 68–73.

Babey, S. H., Hastert, T. A., & Wolstein, J. (2013). Adolescent sedentary behaviors: Correlates differ for television viewing and computer use. *Journal of Adolescent Health, 52,* 70-76.

Baldas, T. (2012, May 28). Dander in the chat room: More kids vulnerable to sexual exploits online. *Detroit Free Press.* Retrieved from http://www.freep.com

Barr, R. (2010). Transfer of learning between 2D and 3D sources during infancy: Informing theory and practice. *Developmental Review, 30,* 128–154.

Barr, R., Muentener, R., Garcia, A., Fujimoto, M., & Chavez, V. (2007). The effect of repetition on imitation from television during infancy. *Developmental Psychology, 49,* 196–207.

Barr, R., Zack, E., Garcia, A., & Muentener, P. (2008). Infants' attention and responsiveness to television increases with prior exposure and parental interaction. *Infancy, 13,* 30–56.

Beentjes, J., deKoning, E., & Huysmans, F. (2001). Children's comprehension of visual formal features in television programs. *Journal of Applied Developmental Psychology, 22*(6), 623–638.

Berk, L. E. (2000). *Child development* (5th ed.). Boston, MA: Allyn & Bacon.

Bickham, D. S., Wright, J. C., & Huston, A. C. (2001). Attention, comprehension, and the educational influences of television. In D. G. Singer & J. L. Singer (Eds.), *Handbook of children and the media* (pp. 101–119). Thousand Oaks, CA: Sage.

Bowman, L. L., Levine, L. E., Waite, B. M., & Gendron, M. (2010). Can students really multitask? An experimental study of instant messaging while reading. *Computers and Education, 54*(4), 927–931.

Brown, J. D., Halpern, C. T., & L'Engle, K. L. (2005). Mass media as a sexual super peer for early maturing girls. *Journal of Adolescent Health, 36,* 420–427.

Brown, M. H., Skeen, P., & Osborn, D. K. (1979). Young children's perception of the reality of television. *Contemporary Education, 50,* 129–133.

Bruner, J. S. (1966). On cognitive growth (I & II). In J. S. Bruner, R. R. Olver, & P. M. Greenfield (Eds.), *Studies in cognitive growth* (pp. 1–67). New York, NY: John Wiley.

Bruner, J. S., Olver, R., & Greenfield, P. (1966). *Studies in cognitive growth.* New York, NY: John Wiley.

Buckingham, D. (2000). *After the death of childhood: Growing up in the age of electronic media.* Cambridge, UK: Polity.

Buckingham, D. (2011). *The material child: Growing up in consumer culture.* Cambridge, UK: Polity.

Bussey, K., & Bandura, A. (1999). Social cognitive theory of gender development and differentiation. *Psychological Review, 106,* 676–713.

Byrnes, J. P. (2003). Cognitive development during adolescence. In G. R. Adams & M. D. Berzonsky (Eds.), *Blackwell handbook of adolescence* (pp. 227–246). Malden, MA: Blackwell.

Calvert, S. L. (1999). *Children's journeys through the information age.* Boston, MA: McGraw-Hill.

Calvert, S. L., & Gersh, T. L. (1987). The selective use of sound effects and visual inserts for children's story comprehension. *Journal of Applied Developmental Psychology, 8,* 363–374.

Calvert, S. L., Huston, A. C., Watkins, B. A., & Wright, J. C. (1982). The relations between selective attention to television forms and children's comprehension of content. *Child Development, 53,* 601–610.

Campbell, T. A., Wright, J. C., & Huston, A. C. (1987). Form cues and content difficulty as determinants of children's cognitive processing of televised educational messages. *Journal of Experimental Child Psychology, 43,* 311–327.

Campos, L. A., & Barret, K. C. (1984). Toward a new understanding of emotions and their development. In C. E. Izard & R. B. Zajonc (Eds.), *Emotion, cognition, and behavior* (pp. 229–263). Cambridge, UK: Cambridge University Press.

Cantor, J. (1998). *"Mommy, I'm scared": How TV and movies frighten children and what we can do to protect them.* San Diego, CA: Harcourt Brace.

Cantor, J. (2009). *Conquer cyberoverload: Get more done, boost your creativity, and reduce stress.* Madison, WI: CyberOutlook Press.

Cantor, J., & Wilson, B. J. (1984). Modifying fear responses to mass media in preschool and elementary school children. *Journal of Broadcasting, 28,* 431–443.

Carlsson, U. (2010). Young people in the digital media culture: Global and Nordic perspectives: An introduction. In U. Carlsson (Ed.), *Children and youth in the digital media culture: From a Nordic horizon* (pp. 9–22). Goteborg, Sweden: Nordicom.

Carr, D. (2007, March 29). Do they still want their MTV? *New York Times.* Retrieved from http://www .nytimes.com/2007/02/19/business/media/19carr.html

Centers for Disease Control and Prevention. (2011). Teenagers in the United States: Sexual activity, contraceptive use, and childbearing, 2006–2010 national survey on family growth. *Vital and Health Statistics, 23*(31). Retrieved June 16, 2012, from http://www.cdc.gov/nchs/data/series/sr_23/ sr23_031.pdf

Centers for Disease Control and Prevention. (2012, July 27). *Trends in HIV-related risk behaviors among high school students – United States, 1991–2001.* Retrieved from http://www.cdc.gov/mmwr/preview/ mmwrhtml/mm6129a4.htm?s_cid=mm6129a4_w

Chan, K. (2001). Children's perceived truthfulness of television advertising and parental influence: A Hong Kong study. *Advances in Consumer Research, 28,* 207–212.

Christakis, D. A., Gilkerson, J., Richards, J. A., Zimmerman, F. J., Garrison, M. M., Xu, D., . . . Yapanel, U. (2009). Audible television and decreased adult words, infant vocalizations, and conversational turns: A population-based study. *Archives of Pediatrics and Adolescent Medicine, 163*(6), 554–558.

Claxton, L. J., & Ponto, K. C. (2013). Understanding the properties of interactive characters. *Journal of Applied Developmental Psychology,* http://dx.doi.org/10.1016/j.appdev.2012.11.007

Collins, W. A. (1983). Interpretation and inference in children's television viewing. In J. Bryant & D. R. Anderson (Eds.), *Children's understanding of television* (pp. 125–150). New York, NY: Academic Press.

Collins, W. A., Berndt, T. J., & Hess, V. L. (1974). Observational learning of motives and consequences for television aggression: A developmental study. *Child Development, 45,* 799–802.

Collins, W. A., Wellman, H., Keniston, A., & Westby, S. (1978). Age-related aspects of comprehension and inference from a televised dramatic narrative. *Child Development, 49,* 389–399.

Cookston, J. T., & Finlay, A. K. (2006). Father involvement and adolescent adjustment: Longitudinal findings from Add Health. *Fathering: A Journal of Theory, Research, and Practice About Men as Fathers, 4*(2), 137–158.

Courage, M. L., & Setliff, A. E. (2010). When babies watch television: Attention getting, attention holding, and implications for learning. *Developmental Review, 30,* 220–238.

Cowan, N., Nugent, L. D., Elliott, E. M., Ponomarev, I., & Saults, J. S. (1999). The role of attention in the development of short-term memory: Age differences in the verbal span of apprehension. *Child Development, 70,* 1082–1097.

Crary, D. (2012, June 16). Your Baby Can Read company going out of business. *Huffington Post.* Retrieved from http://www.huffingtonpost.com/2012/07/16/your-baby-can-read_n_1677465.html

Creemers, H. E., Korhonen, T., Kaprio, J., Vollebergh, W. A. M., Ormel, J., Verhulst, F. C., & Huizink, A. C. (2009). The role of temperament in the relationship between early onset of tobacco and cannabis use: The TRAILS study. *Drug and Alcohol Dependence, 104,* 113–118.

Crosnoe, R., & Johnson, M. K. (2011). Research on adolescence in the twenty-first century. *Annual Review of Sociology, 37,* 439–460.

Davis, K. (2010). Coming of age online: The developmental underpinnings of girls' blogs. *Journal of Adolescent Research, 25*(1), 145–171.

Dempster, F. N. (1981). Memory span: Sources of individual and developmental differences. *Psychological Bulletin, 89,* 63–100.

Dishion, T. J. (1990). The family ecology of boys' peer relations in middle childhood. *Child Development, 61,* 874–892.

Dorr, A. (1980). When I was a child, I thought as a child. In S. B. Withey & P. P. Abeles (Eds.), *Television and social behavior: Beyond violence and children* (pp. 191–230). Hillsdale, NJ: Lawrence Erlbaum.

Dorr, A. (1983). No shortcuts to judging reality. In J. Bryant & D. R. Anderson (Eds.), *Children's understanding of television* (pp. 199–220). New York, NY: Academic Press.

Dorr, A. (1986). *Television and children: A special medium for a special audience.* Thousand Oaks, CA: Sage.

Durkin, K., & Lowe, P. J. (1999). The effect of flashback on children's understanding of television crime content. *Journal of Broadcasting and Electronic Media, 43*(1), 83–97.

Eaton, W. O., & Enns, L. R. (1986). Sex differences in human motor activity level. *Psychological Bulletin, 100,* 19–28.

Eisenberg, N., Fabes, R. A., & Spinrad, T. L. (2006). Prosocial development. In N. Eisenberg, W. Damon, & R. M. Lerner (Eds.), *Handbook of child psychology: Vol. 3. Social, emotional, and personality development* (pp. 646–718). Hoboken, NJ: John Wiley.

Elkind, D. (1967). Egocentrism in adolescence. *Child Development, 38,* 1025–1034.

Elkind, D. (1985). Egocentrism redux. *Developmental Review, 5,* 218–226.

Eveland, W. P., Nathanson, A. I., Detenber, A. I., & McLeod, D. M. (1999). Rethinking the social distance corollary: Perceived likelihood of exposure and the third-person perception. *Communication Research, 26,* 275–302.

Feeling good about visiting the doctor. (1996). *Research Roundup, 5,* 1.

Feng, J., Spence, I., & Pratt, J. (2007). Playing an action video game reduces gender difference in spatial cognition. *Psychological Science, 18,* 850–855.

Finn, P., & Bragg, B. W. (1986). Perception of risk of an accident by young and older drivers. *Accident Analysis and Prevention, 18,* 289–298.

Fiske, S. T., & Taylor, S. E. (1991). *Social cognition* (2nd ed.). New York, NY: McGraw-Hill.

Flavell, J. H., Flavell, E. R., Green, F. L., & Korfmacher, J. E. (1990). Do young children think of television images as pictures or real objects? *Journal of Broadcasting and Electronic Media, 34,* 399–417.

Flavell, J. H., Friedrichs, A. G., & Hoyt, J. (1970). Developmental changes in memorization processes. *Cognitive Psychology, 1,* 324–340.

Flavell, J. H., Miller, P. H., & Miller, S. A. (2002). *Cognitive development* (4th ed.). Englewood Cliffs, NJ: Prentice Hall.

Fougnie, D., & Marois, R. (2006). Distinct capacity limits for attention and working memory: Evidence from attentive tracking and visual working memory paradigms. *Psychological Science, 17,* 526–534.

Fulkerson, J. A., Story, M., Mellin, A., Leffert, N., Neumark-Sztainer, D., & French, S. A. (2006). Family dinner meal frequency and adolescent development: Relationships with developmental assets and high-risk behaviors. *Journal of Adolescent Health, 39,* 337–345.

Garrison, M. M., Liekweg, K., & Christakis, D. A. (2011). Media use and child sleep: The impact of content, timing, and environment. *Pediatrics, 128*(1), 29–35.

Gathercole, S. E. (1998). The development of memory. *Journal of Child Psychology and Psychiatry, 39*(1), 3–27.

Gauffroy, C., & Barrouillet, P. (2011). The primacy of thinking about possibilities in the development of reasoning. *Developmental Psychology, 47*(4), 1000–1011.

Gentile, D. A., Nathanson, A. I., Rasmussen, E. E., Reimer, R. A., & Walsh, D. A. (2012). Do you see what I see? Parent and child reports of parental monitoring of media. *Family Relations, 61*(3), 470–487.

Gerrard, M., McCann, L., & Fortini, M. (1983). Prevention of unwanted pregnancy. *American Journal of Community Psychology, 11,* 153–167.

Ginsburg, H., & Opper, S. (1979). *Piaget's theory of intellectual development* (2nd ed.). Englewood Cliffs, NJ: Prentice Hall.

Gondoli, D. M. (1999). Adolescent development and health. In T. L. Whitman, T. V. Merluzzi, & R. D. White (Eds.), *Life-span perspectives on health and illness* (pp. 147–163). Mahwah, NJ: Lawrence Erlbaum.

Graber, J. A., Brooks-Gunn, J., & Petersen, A. C. (Eds.). (1996). *Transitions through adolescence: Interpersonal domains and context.* Mahwah, NJ: Lawrence Erlbaum.

Greene, K., Krcmar, M., Walters, L. H., Rubin, D. L., & Hale, J. (2000). Targeting adolescent risk-taking behaviors: The contributions of egocentrism and sensation-seeking. *Journal of Adolescence, 23,* 439–461.

Greenfield, P. M., Bruzzone, L., Koyamatsu, K., Satuloff, W., Nixon, K., Brodie, M., & Kingsdale, D. (1987). What is rock music doing to the minds of our youth? A first experimental look at the effects of rock music lyrics and music videos. *Journal of Early Adolescence, 7,* 315–329.

Greenfield, P. M., deWinstanley, P., Kilpatrick, H., & Kaye, D. (1996). Action video games and informal education: Effects on strategies for dividing visual attention. In P. M. Greenfield & R. R. Cocking (Eds.), *Interacting with video* (pp. 187–205). Norwood, NJ: Ablex.

Groebel, J. (1999). Media access and media use among 12-year-olds in the world. In C. von Feilitzen & U. Carlsson (Eds.), *Children and media: Image, education, participation* (pp. 61–68). Goteborg, Sweden: UNESCO International Clearinghouse on Children and Violence on the Screen.

Grossberg, L., Wartella, E., & Whitney, D. C. (1998). *Media making: Mass media in a popular culture.* Thousand Oaks, CA: Sage.

Halpern, D. F. (2004). A cognitive-process taxonomy for sex differences in cognitive abilities. *Current Directions in Psychological Science, 13*(4), 135–139.

Harris, J. R. (1998). *The nurture assumption: Why children turn out the way they do.* New York, NY: Free Press.

Harrison, K., & Cantor, J. (1999). Tales from the screen: Enduring fright reactions to scary media. *Media Psychology, 1,* 97–116.

Hartup, W. W., & Stevens, N. (1997). Friendships and adaptation in the life course. *Psychological Bulletin, 121,* 355–370.

Hawkins, R. P. (1977). The dimensional structure of children's perceptions of television reality. *Communication Research, 7,* 193–226.

Haynie, D. L. (2002). Friendship networks and delinquency: The relative nature of peer delinquency. *Journal of Quantitative Criminology, 18*(2), 99–134.

Hiltzik, M. (2011, January 1). Comcast-NBC merger does nothing to enhance the public interest. *Los Angeles Times.* Retrieved from http://articles.latimes.com/2011/jan/01/business/la-fi-hiltzik-20110101

Hoekstra, S. J., Harris, R. J., & Helmick, A. L. (1999). Autobiographical memories about the experience of seeing frightening movies in childhood. *Media Psychology, 1,* 117–140.

Hoffner, C., & Cantor, J. (1985). Developmental difference in responses to a television character's appearance and behavior. *Developmental Psychology, 21,* 1065–1074.

Hoffner, C., Cantor, J., & Badzinski, D. M. (1990). Children's understanding of adverbs denoting degree of likelihood. *Journal of Child Language, 17,* 217–231.

Hoffner, C., Cantor, J., & Thorson, E. (1989). Children's responses to conflicting auditory and visual features of a televised narrative. *Human Communication Research, 16,* 256–278.

Hudson, J. A., Sosa, B. B., & Shapiro, L. R. (1997). Scripts and plans: The development of preschool children's event knowledge and event planning. In S. L. Friedman & E. K. Scholnick (Eds.), *The developmental psychology of planning: Why, how, and when do we plan?* (pp. 77–102). Mahwah, NJ: Lawrence Erlbaum.

Huston, A. C., & Wright, J. C. (1983). Children's processing of television: The informative functions of formal features. In J. Bryant & D. R. Anderson (Eds.), *Children's understanding of television: Research on attention and comprehension* (pp. 35–68). New York, NY: Academic Press.

Jaglom, L. M., & Gardner, H. (1981). The preschool television viewer as anthropologist. In H. Kelly & H. Gardner (Eds.), *New directions for child development: Viewing children through television* (pp. 9–30). San Francisco, CA: Jossey-Bass.

James, A., Allison, J., Jenks, C., & Prout, A. (1998). *Theorizing childhood.* New York, NY: Teachers College Press.

Jessor, R. (1992). Risk behavior in adolescence: A psychosocial framework for understanding and action. *Developmental Review, 12,* 374–390.

Jochen, P., Valkenburg, P. M., & Schouten, A. P. (2006). Characteristics and motives of adolescents talking with strangers on the internet. *CyberPsychology and Behavior, 9*(5), 526–530.

Jordan, A., Bleakley, A., Manganello, J., Hennessy, M., Steven, R., & Fishbein, M. (2010). The role of television access in the viewing time of US adolescents. *Journal of Children and Media, 4*(4), 355–370.

Kagan, J., & Snidman, N. C. (2004). *The long shadow of temperament.* Cambridge, MA: Harvard University Press.

Kail, R. (1991). Developmental changes in speed of processing during childhood and adolescence. *Psychological Bulletin, 109,* 490–501.

Kail, R. (1993). The role of a global mechanism in developmental change in speed of processing. In M. L. Howe & R. Pasnak (Eds.), *Emerging themes in cognitive development, Vol. 1: Foundations* (pp. 97–119). New York, NY: Springer-Verlag.

Keating, D. P. (2004). Cognitive and brain development. In R. M. Lerner & L. Steinberg (Eds.), *Handbook of adolescent psychology* (2nd ed., pp. 45–84). Hoboken, NJ: John Wiley.

Kendeou, P., Bohn-Gettler, C., White, M., & van den Broek, P. (2008). Children's inference generation across different media. *Journal of Research in Reading, 31*(3), 259–272.

Kistner, J., Counts-Allan, C., Dunkel, S., Drew, C.H., David-Ferdon, C., & Lopez, C. (2010). Sex differences in relational and overt aggression in the late elementary school years. *Aggressive Behavior, 36*(5), 282–291.

Klimstra, T. A., Hale, W. W., Raaijmakers, Q. A. W., Branje, S. J. T., & Meeus, W. H. J. (2010). Identity formation in adolescence: Change or stability? *Journal of Youth and Adolescence, 39*(2), 150–162.

Lang, A. (2000). The limited capacity model of mediated message processing. *Journal of Communication, 50*(1), 46–70.

Larson, R., Richards, M. H., Moneta, G., Holmbeck, G., & Duckett, E. (1996). Changes in adolescents' daily interactions with their families from ages 10 to 18: Disengagement and transformation. *Developmental Psychology, 32,* 744–754.

Lauricella, A. R., Gola, A. A. H., & Calvert, S. (2011). Toddlers' learning from socially meaningful video characters. *Media Psychology, 14,* 216–232.

Lemish, D. (1987). Viewers in diapers: The early development of television viewing. In T. R. Lindlof (Ed.), *Natural audiences: Qualitative research of media uses and effects* (pp. 33–57). Norwood, NJ: Ablex.

Lenhart, A. (2012). *Teens, smartphones, & texting.* Retrieved from http://pewinternet.org/Reports/2012/Teens-and-smartphones.aspx

Linebarger, D. L., & Walker, D. (2005). Infants' and toddlers' television viewing and language outcomes. *American Behavioral Scientist, 48,* 624–645.

Linn, S. (2009). *The case for make believe: Saving play in a commercialized world.* New York, NY: New Press.

Livingstone, S. (2002). *Young people and new media: Childhood and the changing media environment.* Thousand Oaks, CA: Sage.

Lorch, E. P., Bellack, D. R., & Augsbach, L. H. (1987). Young children's memory for televised stories: Effects of importance. *Child Development, 58,* 453–463.

Lovett, S. B., & Flavell, J. H. (1990). Understanding and remembering: Children's knowledge about the differential effects of strategy and task variables on comprehension and memorization. *Child Development, 61,* 1842–1858.

Mandler, J. M. (1998). Representation. In W. Damon (Series Ed.) & D. Kuhn & R. Siegler (Vol. Eds.), *Handbook of child psychology: Vol. 2. Cognition, perception, and language* (pp. 255–308). New York, NY: John Wiley.

Mares, M. L., & Acosta, E. E. (2008). Be kind to three-legged dogs: Children's literal interpretations of TV's moral lessons. *Media Psychology, 11,* 377–399.

Meadowcroft, J. M., & Reeves, B. (1989). Influence of story scheme development on children's attention to television. *Communication Research, 16,* 352–374.

Melkman, R., Tversky, B., & Baratz, D. (1981). Developmental trends in the use of perceptual and conceptual attributes in grouping, clustering, and retrieval. *Journal of Experimental Child Development, 31,* 470–486.

Metcalfe, J., & Shimamura, A. P. (Eds.). (1994). *Metacognition: Knowing about knowing.* Cambridge, MA: MIT Press.

Morison, P., Kelly, H., & Gardner, H. (1981). Reasoning about the realities of television: A developmental study. *Journal of Broadcasting, 25,* 229–242.

Moshman, D. (1998). Cognitive development beyond childhood. In W. Damon (Series Ed.) & D. Kuhn & R. Siegler (Vol. Eds.), *Handbook of child psychology: Vol. 2. Cognition, perception, and language* (5th ed., pp. 947–978). New York, NY: John Wiley.

National Survey on Drug Use and Health. (2010). *Results from the 2010 National Survey on Drug Use and Health: Summary of national findings.* Retrieved from http://www.samhsa.gov/data/NSDUH/2k10NSDUH/2k10Results.htm

Noble, G. (1975). *Children in front of the small screen.* Thousand Oaks, CA: Sage.

O'Bryan, K. G., & Boersma, F. J. (1971). Eye movements, perceptual activity, and conservation development. *Journal of Experimental Child Psychology, 12,* 157–169.

Owens, J. M., McLaughlin, S. B., & Sudweeks, J. (2011). Driver performance while text messaging using handheld and in-vehicle systems. *Accident Analysis and Prevention, 43*(3), 939–947.

Paradise, A., & Sullivan, M. (2012). (In)visible threats? The third-person effect in perceptions of the influence of Facebook. *Cyberpsychology, Behavior, and Social Networking, 15*(1), 55–60.

Perloff, R. M. (2009). Mass media, social perception, and the third-person effect. In J. Bryant & M. B. Oliver (Eds.), *Media effects: Advances in theory and research* (pp. 252–268). New York, NY: Routledge.

Petersen, A. C., & Taylor, B. (1980). The biological approach to adolescence: Biological change and psychological adaptation. In J. Adelson (Ed.), *Handbook of adolescent psychology* (pp. 117–155). New York, NY: John Wiley.

Pharo, H., Sim, C., Graham, M., Gross, J., & Hayne, H. (2011). Risky business: Executive function, personality, and reckless behavior during adolescence and emerging adulthood. *Behavioral Neuroscience, 125*(6), 970–978.

Piaget, J. (1930). *The child's conception of the world.* New York, NY: Harcourt, Brace & World.

Piaget, J. (1950). *The psychology of intelligence.* New York, NY: International Universities Press.

Piaget, J. (1952). *The origins of intelligence in children.* New York, NY: International Universities Press.

Piaget, J., & Inhelder, B. (1975). *The origin of the idea of chance in children.* New York, NY: W. W. Norton.

Pike, M. M., Barnes, M. A., & Barron, R. W. (2010). The role of illustrations in children's inferential comprehension. *Journal of Experimental Child Psychology, 105*(3), 243–255.

Potter, W. J. (2010). The state of media literacy. *Journal of Broadcasting and Electronic Media, 54*(4), 675–696.

Public Agenda. (1999). *Kids these days '99: What Americans really think about the next generation.* Retrieved from http://www.publicagenda.org/specials/kids/kids.htm

Rekers, G. A. (1992). Development of problems of puberty and sex roles in adolescence. In C. E. Walker & M. C. Roberts (Eds.), *Handbook of clinical child psychology* (pp. 607–622). New York, NY: John Wiley.

Resnick, M. D., Bearman, P. S., Blum, R. W., Bauman, K. E., Harris, K. M., Jones, J., . . . Udry, J. R. (1997). Protecting adolescents from harm: Findings from the national longitudinal study on adolescent health. *Journal of the American Medical Association, 278,* 823–832.

Revelle, G. L., Medoff, L., & Strommen, E. F. (2001). Interactive technologies research at the Children's Television Workshop. In S. M. Fisch & R. T. Truglio (Eds.), *"G" is for growing: Thirty years of research on* Sesame Street (pp. 215–230). Mahwah, NJ: Lawrence Erlbaum.

Rideout, V. J. (2012). *Social media, social life: How teens view their digital lives.* Retrieved from http://vjrconsulting.com/storage/socialmediasociallife-final-061812.pdf

Rideout, V. J., Foehr, U. G., & Roberts, D. F. (2010). *Generation M2: Media in the lives of 8- to 18-year-olds.* Menlo Park, CA: Kaiser Family Foundation.

Rideout, V., & Hamel, E. (2006). *The media family: Electronic media in the lives of infants, toddlers, preschoolers and their parents.* Menlo Park, CA: Kaiser Family Foundation.

Rideout, V., Lauricella, A., & Wartella, E. (2011). *Children, media, and race: Media use among white, black, Hispanic and Asian American children.* Retrieved from http://web5.soc.northwestern.edu/cmhd/wp-content/uploads/2011/06/SOCconfReportSingleFinal-1.pdf

Roth, J., & Brooks-Gunn, J. (2000). What do adolescents need for healthy development? Implications for youth policy. *Social Policy Report, 14,* 3–19.

Rubin, K. H., Bukowski, W., & Parker, J. G. (2006). Peer interactions, relationships, and groups. In W. Damon & N. Eisenberg (Eds.), *Handbook of child psychology: Social, emotional, and personality development* (5th ed., pp. 619–700). Hoboken, NJ: John Wiley.

Ruble, D. N., Taylor, L. J., Cyphers, L., Greulich, F. K., Lurye, L. E., & Shrout, P. E. (2007). The role of gender constancy in early gender development. *Child Development, 78*(4), 1121–1136.

Salomon, G. (1983). Television watching and mental effort: A social psychological view. In J. Bryant & D. R. Anderson (Eds.), *Children's understanding of television: Research on attention and comprehension* (pp. 181–198). New York, NY: Academic Press.

Salomon, G., & Leigh, T. (1984). Predispositions about learning from print and television. *Journal of Communication, 34*(2), 119–135.

Santelli, J., Carter, M., Orr, M., & Dittus, P. (2009). Trends in sexual risk behaviors, by nonsexual risk behavior involvement, U.S. high school students, 1991–2007. *Journal of Adolescent Health, 44*(4), 372–379.

Scherrer, J. F., Xian, H., Pan, H., Pergadia, M. L., Madden, P. A., Grant, J. D., Sartor, C. E., . . . Bucholz, K. K. (2012). Parent, sibling and peer influences on smoking initiation, regular smoking and nicotine dependence: Results from a genetically informative design. *Addictive Behavior, 37*(3), 240–247.

Schmidt, M. E., Pempek, T. A., Kirkorian, H. L., Lund, A. F., & Anderson, D. R. (2008). The effect of background television on the toy play behavior of very young children. *Child Development, 79,* 1137–1151.

Schmitt, K. L., Anderson, D. R., & Collins, P. A. (1999). Form and content: Looking at visual features of television. *Developmental Psychology, 35,* 1156–1167.

Scholz, R. W., & Waller, M. (1983). Conceptual and theoretical issues in developmental research on the acquisition of the probability concept. In R. W. Scholz (Ed.), *Decision making under uncertainty* (pp. 291–311). New York, NY: North Holland.

Schwartz, P. D., Maynard, A. M., & Uzelac, S. M. (2008). Adolescent egocentrism: A contemporary view. *Adolescence, 43,* 441–448.

Siegler, R. S. (2005). Children's learning. *American Psychologist, 60,* 769–778.

Silver, J. (2011, January 18). Comcastrophe: Comcast/NBC merger approved. *Huffington Post.* Retrieved from http://www.huffingtonpost.com/josh-silver/comcastrophy-comcastnbc-m_b_810380.html

Simcock, G., Garrity, K., & Barr, R. (2011). The effect of narrative cues on infants' imitation from television and picture books. *Child Development, 82*(5), 1607–1619.

Smith, R., Anderson, D. R., & Fischer, C. (1985). Young children's comprehension of montage. *Child Development, 56,* 962–971.

Song, A. V., Glantz, S. A., Halpern-Felsher, B. L. (2009). Perceptions of second-hand smoke risks predict future adolescent smoking initiation. *Journal of Adolescent health, 45*(6), 618–625.

Sowell, E. R., Trauner, D. A., Gamst, A., & Jernigan, T. L. (2002). Development of cortical and subcortical brain structures in childhood and adolescence: A structural MRI study. *Developmental Medicine and Child Neurology, 44*(1), 4–16.

Sparks, G. G. (1986). Developmental difference in children's reports of fear induced by the mass media. *Child Study Journal, 16,* 55–66.

Spear, L. P. (2010). *Behavioral neuroscience of adolescence.* New York, NY: W. W. Norton.

Springer, K. (2001). Perceptual boundedness and perceptual support in conceptual development. *Psychological Review, 108*(4), 691–708.

Stegge, H., & Terwogt, M. M. (2007). Awareness and regulation of emotion in typical and atypical development. In J. J. Gross (Ed.), *Handbook of emotion regulation* (pp. 269–286). New York, NY: Guilford.

Steinberg, L. (2005). Cognitive and affective development in adolescence. *Trends in Cognitive Sciences, 9*(2), 69–74.

Steyer, J. P. (2002). *The other parent: The inside story of the media's effect on our children.* New York, NY: Atria Books.

Subrahmanyam, K., & Greenfield, P. (2008). Media symbol systems and cognitive processes. In S. Calvert & B. J. Wilson (Eds.), *The Blackwell handbook of children, media, and development* (pp. 166–187). London, UK: Blackwell.

Tversky, B. (1985). Development of taxonomic organization of named and pictured categories. *Developmental Psychology, 21,* 1111–1119.

Valkenburg, P., & Peter, J. (2011). Online communication among adolescents: An integrated model of its attraction, opportunities, and risks. *Journal of Adolescent Health, 48*(2), 121–127.

Valkenburg, P., Schouten, A., & Peter, J. (2005). Adolescents' identity experiments on the Internet. *New Media and Society, 7*(3), 383–402.

Valkenburg, P., & Vroone, M. (2004). Developmental changes in infants' and toddlers' attention to television entertainment. *Communication Research, 31*(1), 288–311.

van den Broek, P., Lorch, E. P., & Thurlow, R. (1996). Children's and adults' memory for television stories: The role of causal factors, story-grammar categories, and hierarchical level. *Child Development, 67,* 3010–3028.

Vandewater, E. A. (2011). Infant word learning from commercially available video in the US. *Journal of Children and Media, 5*(3), 248–266.

Vandewater, E. A., Rideout, V. J., Wartella, E. A., Huang, X., Lee, J. H., & Shim, M. (2007). Digital childhood: Electronic media and technology use among infants, toddlers and preschoolers. *Pediatrics, 119,* e1006–e1015. Retrieved from www.pediatrics.org

Vidmar, N., & Rokeach, M. (1974). Archie Bunker's bigotry: A study in selective perception and exposure. *Journal of Communication, 24*(1), 36–47.

Walsh-Childers, K. (1997). *A content analysis: Sexual coverage in women's, men's, teen and other specialty magazines.* Menlo Park, CA: Kaiser Family Foundation.

Wartella, E., & Reeves, B. (1985). Historical trends in research on children and the media: 1900–1960. *Journal of Communication, 35*(2), 118–132.

Wartella, E., Richert, R. A., & Robb, M. B. (2010). Babies, television, and videos: How did we get here? *Developmental Review, 30,* 116–127.

Watson, J. M., Lambert, A. E., Miller, A. E., & Strayer, D L. (2011). The magical letters P, F, C, and sometimes U: The rise and fall of executive attention with the development of prefrontal cortex. In K. L. Fingerman, C. A. Berg, J. Smith, & T. C. Antonucci (Eds.), *Handbook of life-span development* (pp. 407–436). New York, NY: Springer.

Weiss, A. J., & Wilson, B. J. (1998). Children's cognitive and emotional responses to the portrayal of negative emotions in family-formatted situation comedies. *Human Communication Research, 24,* 584–609.

Whitbeck, L., Yoder, K. A., Hoyt, D. R., & Conger, R. D. (1999). Early adolescent sexual activity: A developmental study. *Journal of Marriage and the Family, 61,* 934–946.

Wiggers, M., & van Lieshout, C. F. (1985). Development of recognition of emotions: Children's reliance on situational and facial expressive cues. *Developmental Psychology, 21*(2), 338–349.

Wilkinson, R. B. (2004). The role of parental and peer attachment in the psychological health and self-esteem of adolescents. *Journal of Youth and Adolescence, 33*(6), 479–493.

Wilson, B. J. (1991). Children's reactions to dreams conveyed in mass media programming. *Communication Research, 18,* 283–305.

Wilson, B. J., & Drogos, K. L. (2009). Children and adolescents: Distinctive audiences of media content. In M. B. Oliver & R. L. Nabi (Eds.), *The SAGE handbook of media processes and effects* (pp. 469–485). Thousand Oaks, CA: Sage.

Wilson, B. J., & Smith, S. L. (1995, May). *Children's comprehension of and emotional reactions to TV news.* Paper presented at the annual conference of the International Communication Association, Albuquerque, NM.

Wilson, B. J., & Smith, S. L. (1998). Children's responses to emotional portrayals on television. In P. Anderson & L. Guerrero (Eds.), *Handbook of communication and emotion: Research, theory, applications, and contexts* (pp. 533–569). New York, NY: Academic Press.

Woolley, J. D., Boerger, E. A., & Markman, A. B. (2004). A visit from the Candy Witch: Factors influencing young children's belief in a novel fantastical being. *Developmental Science, 7*(4), 456–468.

Wright, J. C., Huston, A. C., Reitz, A. L., & Piemyat, S. (1994). Young children's perceptions of television reality: Determinants and developmental differences. *Developmental Psychology, 30,* 229–239.

Wright, J. C., Huston, A. C., Ross, R. P., Calvert, S. L., Rolandelli, D., Weeks, L. A., . . . Potts, R. (1984). Pace and continuity of television programs: Effects on children's attention and comprehension. *Developmental Psychology, 20,* 653–666.

Zuckerman, M. (1994). *Behavioral expressions and biosocial bases of sensation seeking.* New York, NY: Cambridge University Press.

CHAPTER 2

Advertising

Children's social worlds are increasingly constructed around consuming, as brands and products have come to determine who is "in" or "out," who is hot or not, who deserves to have friends or social status.

—Juliet B. Schor
*Born to Buy: The Commercialized Child and the
New Commercial Culture* (2004, p. 11)

Keeping brands young is critical for the long-term health of the brands. Businesses need to plan ahead and nurture the brands and customers of the future.

—Anne Autherland and Beth Thompson
*Kidfluence: The Marketer's Guide to Understanding and
Reaching Generation Y—Kids, Tweens, and Teens* (2003, p. 149)

Children are seen by some as commodities—as products to be sold to advertisers.

—Michael J. Copps, Federal Communications Commissioner
Children Now's conference on "The Future of
Children's Media: Advertising" (2006, p. 5)

Marketing to children is by no means new, but children now play an increasingly important role, both as consumers in their own right and as influences on parents. They are exposed to a growing number and range of commercial messages, which extend far beyond traditional media advertising.

—David Buckingham
*The Material Child: Growing Up
in Consumer Culture* (2011, p. 5)

Eight-year-old Grace came home from 3rd grade one day and announced to her mother, "I need a *Monster High* doll, Mom. The one I like is named Draculaura." Her mother was a bit surprised, given that, to her knowledge, Grace had not expressed any interest in such a doll before and none of her friends had one.

"What's a *Monster High* doll?" her mother asked.

"They're cool, Mom. They all have monster names like Frankie Stein and Clawdeen Wolf. But I like Draculaura. She has long black hair and pink boots and a pet bat. I love her outfits," replied Grace.

"How do you know about these dolls?" her mother continued.

"Maddi told me about them. We watched some of their videos on YouTube at Maddi's house and we even played a computer game. Mom, Draculaura has her own website!"

"What do the dolls do in these videos?" probed her mother.

"They put on makeup and write in their diaries. They all go to Monster High together," Grace replied.

On the next trip to Target, Grace spotted a display of *Monster High* dolls in one of the aisles and shrieked, "Mom, can I have one, *pleeeeeease*?"

Grace's mom checked the price, weighed this struggle against all the others she might encounter that day, and reluctantly put one of the $21.99 dolls into the shopping cart. Along with millions of other parents, she caved in to what has been called the "nag factor" in the world of advertising. As it turns out, Grace's mom got away pretty cheaply that day. Anyone searching Amazon.com can find 517 different toy products and apparel items associated with *Monster High* dolls. Children and their parents can purchase, for example, sundry dolls and accessories, a *Monster High* roadster and scooter for the dolls, a high school doll playhouse, wide-ruled notebooks, pencil sets, nail polish, hairclips, and even a digital video recorder (see Figure 2.1). And all of this is marketed without the typical TV cartoon series! Instead, Mattel has created a financially successful brand that is now sold in 35 countries—all based on a website, a few TV specials on Nickelodeon, a set of videos on YouTube, and a chapter book series. A full-length movie titled *Monster High: Ghouls Rule* was released on DVD in late 2012, coinciding with Halloween.

It is estimated that more than $17 billion a year is now spent on advertising and marketing to children (Lagorio, 2009), representing almost three times the amount spent just 20 years ago

Figure 2.1   *Monster High* merchandise.

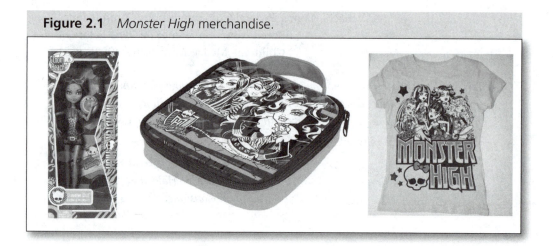

(McNeal, 1999). Marketers are paying more attention to young consumers these days for at least three reasons. First, American children today have a great deal of their own money to spend. Consumers younger than age 12 spent $2.2 billion in 1968; roughly 35 years later, this amount had risen dramatically to $42 billion (McNeal, 2007). As seen in Figure 2.2, children's spending power has steadily risen over the years. Much of this increase comes from children earning more money for household chores and receiving more money from relatives on holidays (McNeal, 1998). As might be expected, teens spend even more than children—teens spent roughly $200 billion in the year 2011 alone (Business Wire, 2011). In fact, the average American teenager spends nearly $100 a week on such products as clothes, candy, soft drinks, and music (Teenage Research Unlimited, 2004).

Second, in addition to spending their own money, young people influence their parents' consumer behaviors. At an early age, children give direction to daily household purchases such as snacks, cereals, toothpaste, and even shampoos. As they get older, teens often voice opinions about what type of car to buy, what new media equipment is needed, and even where to go on vacation. And this influence has grown over the years. In the 1960s, children influenced about $5 billion of their parents' purchases. By 1984, that figure had increased to $50 billion, and by 2005, it had leaped to $700 billion (McNeal, 2007). Relaxed parenting styles, increased family incomes, higher divorce rates, and more parents working outside the home are some of the historical changes that may account for children's increased economic influence in the family (see Valkenburg & Cantor, 2001).

Third, marketers recognize that the children of today represent adult consumers of tomorrow. Children develop loyalties to particular brands of products at an early age, and these preferences often persist into adulthood (Moschis & Moore, 1982). Many companies today, such as McDonald's and Coca-Cola, engage in what is called "cradle-to-grave" marketing in an effort to cultivate consumer allegiance at a very early age (McNeal, 1998).

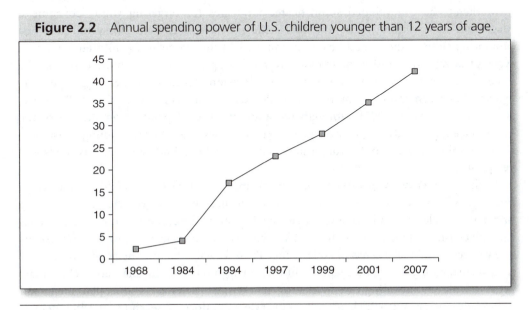

Figure 2.2   Annual spending power of U.S. children younger than 12 years of age.

SOURCE: Adapted from McNeal (1998, 2007).

Figure 2.3

Marketers have developed sophisticated strategies for targeting young consumers. Magazines such as *Teen Vogue* and *Sports Illustrated Kids* contain glossy full-page ads promoting clothes, shoes, and beauty products. Websites targeted to children feature all types of advertising, and even schools are marketing products to children. By far, the easiest way to reach young people is through television. Recent estimates suggest that the average American child sees more than 25,000 television ads per year (Gantz, Schwartz, Angelini, & Rideout, 2007), although the amount varies depending on the age of the viewer (see Figure 2.3). But marketers are exploring new ways to reach young consumers through online sources and through personal, handheld technologies such as iPods and cell phones.

In this chapter, we will explore advertising messages targeted to children and teens. First, we will examine how marketing to children has changed over the years, focusing primarily on television advertising. Then we will look at the amount and nature of television advertising targeted to youth. Next we will give an overview of how children cognitively process and make sense of advertising. Then we will examine the persuasive impact of advertising on youth. The chapter will then turn to more recent marketing efforts targeted to children, including viral marketing, marketing in schools, product placement, and online advertising. We will close with an overview of efforts to teach advertising literacy. Regulation of advertising is covered in Chapter 13 on children's media policy. It should be noted that two other chapters in this book deal with advertising as it relates to specific health hazards. Chapter 6 examines the advertising of cigarettes and alcohol, and Chapter 7 looks at the impact of food advertising on nutrition. The focus here is primarily on the advertising of toys, clothes, and other consumer goods, although food products will be referenced occasionally as well.

Historical Changes in Advertising to Children

Efforts to advertise products to children date back to the 1930s, the early days of radio. Companies such as General Mills, Kellogg's, and Ovaltine routinely pitched food products during child-oriented radio shows such as *Little Orphan Annie* and *Story Time* (Pecora, 1998). Household products such as toothpaste and aspirin were also marketed during children's programming. In these earliest endeavors, children were considered important primarily because they were capable of influencing their parents' consumer behavior.

In the 1950s, children gradually became recognized as consumers in their own right (Pecora, 1998). The sheer number of children increased so dramatically during this decade that it is now referred to as the baby boomer period. In addition, parents who had lived through the Depression and World War II experienced a new level of economic prosperity that they wanted to share with their offspring (Alexander, Benjamin, Hoerrner, & Roe, 1998). As noted by Kline (1993), "the 1950s' family became preoccupied with possession and consumption and the satisfaction that goods can bring" (p. 67). And of course, the advent of television offered new ways to demonstrate products to captive audiences of parents and children (Pecora, 1998).

The earliest television advertising looked very different than it does today. At first, programmers were more interested in getting people to buy television sets than in attracting advertisers (Adler, 1980). Some programs were offered by the broadcast networks themselves with no commercial sponsorship at all. Other programs had a single sponsor that would underwrite the entire cost of the 30-minute or 60-minute time slot. Consequently, there were fewer interruptions, and the sponsors sometimes pitched the company rather than any specific product. As more and more American homes purchased sets, the focus shifted toward attracting this large potential audience to one program or network over others. Programs also became more expensive to produce, thereby increasing the cost of advertising time so that more sponsors were necessary to share the burden.

In one of the only systematic studies of early TV advertising, Alexander and colleagues (1998) assessed 75 commercials that aired during children's shows in the 1950s. The researchers found that the average length of a commercial was 60 seconds, considerably longer than the 15- and 30-second ads of today. In addition, less overall time was devoted to advertising—only 5 minutes per hour in the 1950s compared with roughly 11 minutes per hour today (Gantz et al., 2007). Reflecting the fact that ads were directed more at families than specifically at children, household products such as appliances, dog food, and even staples such as peanut butter were commonly pitched. Nearly all ads were live action rather than animated. And the practice of host selling—using a character from the interrupted program to endorse a product in the commercial segment—was quite common. In fact, 62% of the ads featured some form of host selling, which has since been banned.

In his book *Out of the Garden: Toys, TV, and Children's Culture in the Age of Marketing*, Kline (1993) argued that 1955 was a turning point in television advertising to children. That year marked the debut of the highly successful TV show *The Mickey Mouse Club*. In great numbers, children rushed out to buy Mickey Mouse ears, guitars, and other paraphernalia, demonstrating their own purchasing power. Shortly thereafter, the toy industry moved aggressively into television.

In the 1960s, the broadcast networks also recognized the revenue potential of targeting children. However, adults continued to be the most profitable consumers to reach. Children's programs still airing in the valuable prime-time period were therefore shifted to Saturday morning, when large numbers of children could be reached efficiently and cost-effectively with cartoons. Throughout the 1970s, the networks increased the number of Saturday morning hours they devoted to children's programming in response to marketers' increasing interest in young consumers.

The 1980s saw the birth of toy-based programs (Pecora, 1998). Creating spin-off toys based on popular children's shows is a practice that dates back to the early days of radio. Toy-based programs are slightly different, however, because they are conceived for the sole purpose of promoting new toys. Hence, critics have charged that the shows themselves are actually half-hour commercials. In an unusual twist, toy manufacturers and producers come together at the earliest stage of program development. Shows are created with the consultation and often the financial backing of a toy company. In her book *The Business of Children's Entertainment*, Pecora (1998) argued that, in the 1980s,

> the line between sponsorship and program became blurred as producers, looking to spread the risk of program production costs, turned to toy manufacturers, and toy manufacturers, wanting to stabilize a market subject to children's whim and fancy, turned to the media. (p. 34)

The first example of such a partnership occurred in 1983, when Mattel joined together with the Filmation production house to create *He-Man and the Masters of the Universe*. In the deregulated era of the 1980s, these mutually beneficial arrangements proliferated. In 1980, there were no toy-based programs; by 1984, there were 40 of them on the air (Wilke, Therrien, Dunkin, & Vamos, 1985). According to Pecora (1998), the success of toy-based shows such as *The Smurfs* meant that "neither toy nor story is now considered without thought of its market potential" (p. 61). She went on to argue that by the 1990s, programming was evolving "not from the rituals of storytelling but rather the imperative of the marketplace" (p. 59).

Today, the proliferation of cable and independent networks has opened up new avenues for reaching children. Disney has its own television network, and others such as Nickelodeon and Cartoon Network have been tremendously successful in targeting the child audience. Recognizing the economic benefits, marketers are now segmenting the child audience into different age groups. Teenage consumers are widely recognized for their spending power, as evidenced by the creation of MTV, Black Entertainment Television (BET), ABC Family, TeenNick, the CW Network (a merger of the WB and UPN networks), and other specialized channels devoted to attracting adolescents and young adults. And advertisers are responsible for coining the term *tweens* to refer to 8- to 12-year-olds who are on the cusp of adolescence, are deeply interested in brand names and fashion, and spend a lot of time at shopping malls (Wells, 2011). Even the youngest age groups are being targeted. In 2006, a 24-hour cable channel called BabyFirstTV was launched to provide television programming for babies and toddlers. The network airs no commercials, but there is a link on its website that allows parents to buy BabyFirst DVDs, plush toys, and home decor. Infant videos and DVDs accrue more than $100 million in sales a year (Shin, 2007).

Thus, the current market is far different from the market of the 1950s, when the broadcast networks dominated television and there were only a few other media options. Today, licensed characters such as Dora the Explorer and SpongeBob SquarePants routinely cross over from television to other media such as books, DVDs, film, electronic games, and computer software. And numerous media outlets actually specialize in child- and teen-oriented content in an effort to attract affluent young consumers.

Content Analyses of Television Advertising

What do ads that are targeted to children look like? Most of the research has focused on television advertising, in part because children continue to spend so much time with this medium. In one early content analysis, Barcus (1980) looked at advertising during children's shows in 1971 and in later samples of programming from 1975 and 1978. In 1971, roughly 12 minutes of each broadcast hour were devoted to commercials, a marked jump from the 5 minutes documented in the 1950s (Alexander et al., 1998). Given that the typical ad had shrunk to 30 seconds, children on average were exposed to 26 different commercials each hour. The time devoted to advertising dropped in 1975 to roughly nine minutes per hour (Barcus, 1980). This shift reflects pressure on the industry in the mid-1970s from child advocacy groups and the federal government to reduce advertising to children (see Chapter 13).

What products were being pitched? In the 1978 sample, Barcus (1980) found that most advertisements were for cereal, candy, toys, and fast food restaurants. In fact, food ads generally accounted for nearly 60% of all commercials targeted to children (cereal, 24%; candy, 21%; fast foods, 12%). Barcus also found that the appeals used in children's ads were mostly psychological rather than rational. Instead of giving price, ingredient, or quality information, ads typically focused on how fun the product was or how good it tasted.

By the 1980s, commercials had been shortened even more so that many lasted only 15 seconds (Condry, Bence, & Scheibe, 1988). Although the total time devoted to ads remained somewhat constant, the briefer messages meant that children were exposed to a greater number of ads during any given hour of broadcast television.

Using a more comprehensive sample than in earlier research, Kunkel and Gantz (1992) examined a composite week of child-oriented programming during February and March 1990. Programming was sampled from seven different channels: the three major broadcast networks, two independent stations, and two cable channels (Nickelodeon and USA). The researchers found more advertising on the networks (10 minutes/hour) than on the independents (9 minutes/hour) or cable (6 minutes/hour). Consistent with earlier research, the same types of products dominated commercials during children's programming. Roughly 80% of

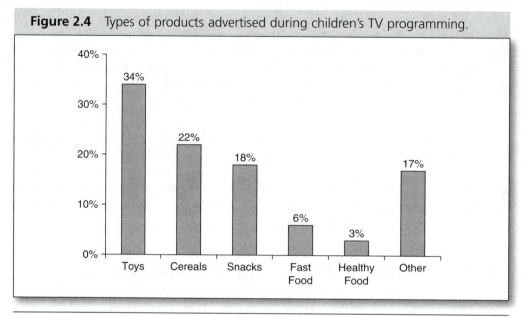

Figure 2.4 Types of products advertised during children's TV programming.

SOURCE: Adapted from Kunkel and Gantz (1992).

all ads were for toys, cereals, snacks, and fast food restaurants (see Figure 2.4). Interestingly, only 3% of all ads were for healthy foods. When the researchers compared channel types, they found that toy ads were most prevalent on independent channels, whereas ads for cereals and snacks were most common on the broadcast networks. Cable channels offered the most diverse range of products, with 35% of the ads falling into the "other" category. Kunkel and Gantz (1992) reasoned that toy ads, which have been consistently criticized for deceptive practices, may show up less often on the broadcast networks because of their more rigorous self-regulatory standards.

The researchers also coded the primary persuasive appeal used in each ad. The most prevalent theme was fun/happiness, which accounted for 27% of all ads. Two other common appeals were taste/flavor (19%) and product performance (18%). In contrast, appeals based on price, quality of materials, nutrition, and safety each accounted for less than 1% of the ads.

Rather than focusing just on programs targeted to children, the Kaiser Family Foundation sponsored a comprehensive study of all advertising content on the channels that children watched most (Gantz et al., 2007). The study looked at a composite week of programming airing in 2005 across 13 networks channels, including Nickelodeon, Disney, Cartoon Network, the four major broadcast networks (ABC, NBC, CBS, and FOX), PBS, BET, and MTV. There was considerable variation in the amount of advertising and promotional messages across the channels; PBS (1 minute/hour) and Disney (20 seconds/hour) had the least amount of such content, whereas ABC, CBS, and FOX had the most (roughly 14 minutes/hour). On average, the broadcast networks devoted more time to advertising than did the cable networks, a finding consistent with the earlier Kunkel and Gantz (1992) study.

The study looked closely at food advertising in particular. Although food commercials are common on television, food is marketed even more to children than to adults. Food ads constituted 13% of the ads on the four major broadcast networks, but they constituted 32% of the ads on three of the top children's networks (ABC Family, Nickelodeon, and Cartoon Network). In fact, half of all advertising time during children's shows was devoted to food commercials. And most of these food ads were for cereal (31%), candy and snacks (30%), and fast food (11%). Commercials for healthy foods were very rare in the 2005 sample. Of the 8,854 food commercials analyzed in the Kaiser Family Foundation study, there were no ads for fruits or vegetables targeted at children or teens. Consistent with the low nutritional value of the products, most food ads emphasized taste and fun as the main persuasive appeals (see Figure 2.5). All of these patterns are comparable to what Kunkel and Gantz (1992) had found 15 years previously. Similar findings have been documented by other researchers as well (Warren, Wicks, Wicks, Fosu, & Chung, 2008).

Therefore, despite the proliferation of channels on television, it seems that advertising to children has not changed much over the years. The same products dominate commercials, and the selling appeals continue to focus more on fun, happiness, and taste than on actual information about the product.

Content analyses have also looked at other qualities inherent in children's advertising, such as how gender is portrayed. In a study of nearly 600 commercials targeted to children, Larson (2001) compared ads featuring only girls or only boys with those featuring both girls and boys. She found that girls-only ads were far more likely to feature a domestic setting such as a bedroom or a backyard than were boys-only or mixed-gender ads. Boys-only ads seldom occurred around the house and instead featured settings such as restaurants, video arcades, and baseball fields. The types of interactions that occurred also differed across ads. More than 80% of the girls-only ads portrayed cooperation, whereas less than 30% of the boys-only ads did. Consistent with gender stereotypes, nearly 30% of the boys-only ads featured competitive interactions, but none of the girls-only ads did. Finally, there were gender differences across the types of products being pitched. Food commercials

Figure 2.5   Examples of food ads emphasizing taste and fun.

were most likely to feature girls and boys together, whereas toy ads typically were single gender in nature. Commercials targeted to boys were frequently for video games or action figures, and those targeted to girls were often for Barbie dolls. A more recent study looking just at toy ads on Nickelodeon confirmed these patterns (Kahlenberg & Hein, 2010).

Gender stereotypes exist in commercials targeted toward teens, too. In one study, ads aimed at male teens emphasized competition, having the best, and achievement in their persuasive appeals, whereas ads targeted to female teens emphasized romance, sexuality, and belonging to a group (Buijzen & Valkenburg, 2002).

Commercials can convey stereotypes in more subtle ways as well. One study examined the production techniques used in toy ads directed to boys versus girls (Welch, Huston-Stein, Wright, & Plehal, 1979). Toy ads for boys were faster in pace, used more abrupt transitions such as cuts, and had more sound effects and other types of noise. In contrast, toy ads directed at girls used smoother transitions, such as fades and dissolves between scenes, and had more background music. Such gender stereotypes in production techniques have been found in children's ads in the UK too (Lewin-Jones, & Mitra, 2009). Interestingly, elementary schoolers readily identify these different production techniques as being associated with a "boy's toy" or a "girl's toy" (Lewin-Jones & Mitra, 2009), even when the toy itself is gender neutral (e.g., a mobile) (see Huston, Greer, Wright, Welch, & Ross, 1984). There are also stereotypes about race and ethnicity in commercial messages targeted to children. Advertisements featuring White children are far more common than ads featuring children of color are (Bramlett-Solomon & Roeder, 2008; Larson, 2001). Furthermore, ads featuring Black children are more likely to sell convenience foods, especially fast foods, than are ads featuring no Black children (Harrison, 2006). Indeed, marketers target African American consumers with ads for high-calorie and low-nutrient foods and beverages (Institute of Medicine, 2006). Asians are also stereotyped in children's ads, and are commonly shown using computers and other technologies, for example (Bramlett-Solomon & Roeder, 2008).

Commercials for children have also been analyzed for violence. Palmerton and Judas (1994) looked at ads featured during the 21 top-rated children's cartoons in 1993. One-third of the ads contained overt displays of physical aggression, most commonly found in toy commercials. Furthermore, ads that were clearly targeted to boys were far more likely to feature violence than were ads targeted to girls. Literally every commercial for action figures in the sample contained violence. This link between violence and ads directed at boys has been documented in more recent research (Larson, 2001).

In summary, the typical hour of television features anywhere from 10 to 14 minutes of advertising on the channels that youth watch most (Gantz et al., 2007). A majority of the commercial messages targeted to children market toys or food products that are not particularly healthy. In fact, the average tween (8–12 years of age) in this country sees 21 food ads a day on TV (Gantz et al., 2007), most of which feature candy, snacks, and fast foods. The commercials designed for youth do not offer much in the way of "hard" information about products, such as what they are made of or how much they cost. Instead, the appeals are largely emotional ones based on fun or good taste. Toy ads in particular are fairly stereotyped in terms of gender. Ads targeted to boys typically sell violent toys that are demonstrated through action, force, and noise. Ads for girls, in contrast, sell dolls, which are featured in a quieter, slower, and more domestic environment. Commercials targeted to teens show similar gender stereotypes; ads for males tend to focus on competition, whereas ads for females focus more on relationships. The next section addresses how young people respond cognitively to these messages.

Cognitive Processing of Advertising

In the United States, policies dating back to the Communications Act of 1934 stipulate that advertising must be clearly identifiable to its intended audience (Wilcox & Kunkel, 1996). In other words, commercials should be recognized by the target audience as obvious attempts to persuade. If a viewer is unaware of or incapable of recognizing an ad, then she or he is presumably more vulnerable to its persuasive appeals. Under such circumstances, commercial messages are thought to be inherently unfair and even deceptive. Because of the potential for unfairness, researchers as well as policymakers have focused on how children of different ages make sense of advertising.

Attention to Advertising

One of the first questions to ask is whether children pay any attention to advertising. Marketers use sound effects, bright colors, jingles, animated characters, and a variety of other production techniques to attract consumers. In fact, ads are typically louder in volume than accompanying programs. All of these techniques are perceptually salient and, as we learned in Chapter 1, likely to capture the attention of younger children in particular.

Certainly many adults use commercial time to leave the room, engage in other activities, or even to change the channel. With digital video recording devices, consumers can record their favorite programs and skip over the advertising. Based on in-home observation, one study found that adults pay visual attention to programming 62% of the time and to ads only 33% of the time (Krugman, Cameron, & White, 1995). As it turns out, children's attention depends on the age of the viewer. In one early study, mothers of 5- to 12-year-olds were trained to observe their children's attention to commercials aired during different types of TV programming (Ward, Levinson, & Wackman, 1972). All children exhibited a drop in attention when a commercial was shown, and attention also decreased over the course of several ads shown in a series. However, the youngest children (5–7 years) generally displayed higher levels of attention to both commercials and programs, whereas the 11- and 12-year-olds were most likely to stop looking when an ad came on. A more recent study that videotaped families while they watched television found that 2-year-olds paid just as much attention to ads as to programs (Schmitt, Woolf, & Anderson, 2003). In contrast, 5-, 8-, and 12-year-olds looked more at programs than ads, with the difference increasing by age (see Figure 2.6). These findings suggest that older children, like adults, screen out advertisements. The data also suggest that very young children may not make clear distinctions between program and nonprogram content, an issue we will turn to in the next section.

Similar age differences have been found in laboratory research. Zuckerman, Ziegler, and Stevenson (1978) videotaped 2nd through 4th graders while they watched a brief program with eight cereal commercials embedded in it. Overall, children paid less attention to the ads than to the program, but once again, attention to the commercials decreased with age.

Younger children's heightened attention to ads may be due in part to attention-getting techniques such as jingles, animation, and slogans used to pull in the audience. Greer, Potts, Wright, and Huston (1982) found, for example, that preschoolers paid more attention to advertisements that contained high action, frequent scene changes, and numerous cuts than to ads without these production features. Likewise, Wartella and Ettema (1974) found that compared with kindergarten and 2nd-grade children, preschoolers' level of attention to ads

Figure 2.6   Percentage of time looking at TV screen during commercials and programs as a function of age of child.

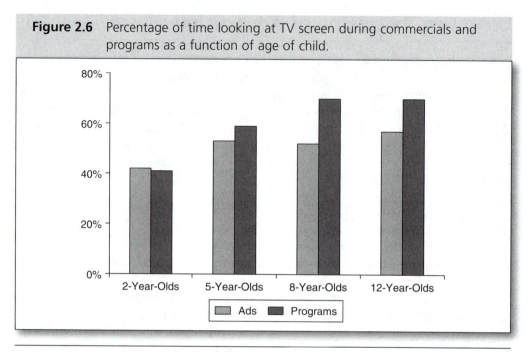

SOURCE: Adapted from Schmitt, Woolf, and Anderson (2003).

varied more as a function of visual and auditory attributes of the message. Such patterns are consistent with younger children's tendency to focus on and be swayed by perceptually salient cues in the media, as discussed in Chapter 1.

Overall, then, preschoolers and early elementary schoolers pay more attention to television advertising than older children do. In part, this may be due to the strong perceptual attributes commonly found in commercials. However, the relatively steady attention patterns during transitions from programming to advertising also suggest that younger children may not distinguish these two types of messages very clearly.

Discrimination Between Ads and Programming

Discrimination can be tested by showing different types of television content and asking children to identify what they are watching. For example, Palmer and McDowell (1979) stopped a videotape of Saturday morning content at preselected points and asked kindergartners and 1st graders whether they had just seen "part of the show" or a "commercial." The young elementary schoolers were able to accurately identify commercials only 53% of the time, which is roughly equivalent to chance guessing.

In other studies employing similar techniques, young children's discrimination skills have sometimes been better and are often above chance levels (Butter, Popovich, Stackhouse, & Garner, 1981; Levin, Petros, & Petrella, 1982). Nevertheless, age differences are consistently found through the preschool years; 3- and 4-year-olds are less able to make these distinctions than are 5-year-olds (Butter et al., 1981; Levin et al., 1982).

Once children learn to differentiate a TV ad from a program, they often do so on the basis of perceptual features rather than more conceptual properties of the two messages. For instance, when Palmer and McDowell (1979) asked kindergartners and 1st graders how they knew a particular segment was a commercial, the predominant reason cited was the length of the message ("because commercials are short"). Other studies that have interviewed children about ads versus programs without showing television content support this finding (Blatt, Spencer, & Ward, 1972; Ward, Wackman, & Wartella, 1977).

We should point out that the television industry employs separation devices to help signal to child viewers that a commercial break is occurring. These devices vary considerably in degree, from the simple insertion of several seconds of blank screen between a program and an ad to a more complex audiovisual message indicating that a program "will be right back after these messages." As it turns out, these types of separators do not help young children much. Studies comparing blank screens, audio-only messages, visual-only messages, and audiovisual separators have found little improvement in young children's discrimination abilities with any of these devices (Butter et al., 1981; Palmer & McDowell, 1979; Stutts, Vance, & Hudleson, 1981). One possible reason for the ineffectiveness of such separators is that they may be too brief to be noticed. Another possibility is that they look too much like adjacent programming. In many cases, visuals of the characters or part of the soundtrack from the show are actually featured in the separators. A more effective device may be one that is far more obvious. For example, a child or adult spokesperson who has no affiliation with the programming could state, "We are taking a break from the program now in order to show you a commercial."

To summarize, the research shows that a substantial number of preschoolers do not recognize a commercial message on TV as distinctly different from programming. By age 5, most children are capable of making this distinction, although it is typically based on somewhat superficial qualities of the messages, such as how long they are. Still, being able to identify and accurately label a commercial does not necessarily mean that a child fully comprehends the nature of advertising, a topic we turn to next.

Comprehension of Advertising

Adult consumers realize that advertisements exist to sell product and services. This realization helps a person to interpret a commercial as a persuasive form of communication. According to Roberts (1982), an "adult" understanding of advertising entails four ideas or realizations: (a) the source has a different perspective (and thus other interests) than that of the receiver, (b) the source intends to persuade, (c) persuasive messages are biased, and (d) biased messages demand different interpretive strategies than informational messages do. Most research dealing with children has focused on the first two ideas, encompassed in studies of how and when young viewers understand the selling intent of ads. Less attention has been given to children's recognition of bias in advertising, relating to the last two ideas. Not reflected in Roberts's list is the notion that other facets of advertising require understanding too, such as disclaimers. This section will consider all three topics: children's comprehension of selling intent, of advertiser bias, and of disclaimers such as "parts sold separately."

Understanding Selling Intent. Recognizing the selling motive that underlies advertising is not a simple task. For one thing, the actual source of a commercial is rarely identified explicitly.

A television commercial, for example, might show children playing with a toy or eating a type of cereal, and yet the company that manufacturers these products is invisible. It is easy to assume that the "source" of the message is the child, the celebrity, or the animated character, who in fact is merely demonstrating a new product that is available.

Research suggests that younger children's views are just this naive. In one early study, Robertson and Rossiter (1974) asked 1st-, 3rd-, and 5th-grade boys a series of open-ended questions, such as, "What is a commercial?" and "What do commercials try to get you to do?" First graders often described commercials as informational messages that "tell you about things." Although older children did this too, they were far more likely to describe advertising as persuasive in nature (i.e., "Commercials try to make you buy something"). In fact, the attribution of selling intent increased dramatically with age: Only 53% of the 1st graders mentioned selling intent, whereas 87% of 3rd graders and 99% of 5th graders did so.

Almost 20 years later, a similar study found the same pattern (Wilson & Weiss, 1992). When asked what commercials "want you to do," only 32% of 4- to 6-year-olds mentioned the selling intent of ads. Instead, this youngest age group was far more likely to cite an entertainment (e.g., "they want you to watch them," "make you laugh") or informational ("show you stuff") function for commercials. In contrast, 73% of 7- to 8-year-olds and a full 94% of 9- to 11-year-olds spontaneously mentioned the selling intent of commercials. A host of other studies using similar interviewing techniques support these age trends (Batada & Borzekowski, 2008; Blatt et al., 1972; Ward et al., 1977).

Given variations in development, it is difficult to pinpoint the specific age at which the idea of selling intent is mastered. Nevertheless, most studies suggest that children begin to develop an understanding of the persuasive purpose of advertising around the age of 8 (for reviews, see Kunkel et al., 2004; Smith & Atkin, 2003).

Some scholars have argued that the reliance on verbal measures can mask younger children's true abilities, which may be hampered by language difficulties (Macklin, 1987; Martin, 1997). To test this notion, Donohue, Henke, and Donohue (1980) devised a nonverbal measure to assess 2- to 6-year-olds' understanding of selling intent. After watching a Froot Loops commercial, children were asked to choose which of two pictures—one of a mother and child picking out a box of cereal at a supermarket and the other of a child watching television— illustrated what the commercial wanted them to do. A full 80% of the young children selected the correct picture, well above chance level with two options. However, as seen in Table 2.1, several efforts to replicate this finding with younger children have been unsuccessful (Macklin, 1985, 1987). For example, Macklin (1985) used a set of four pictures, reasoning that the two used by Donohue and his colleagues were too easy (i.e., only one of the pictures featured cereal, which made it obviously more relevant). When four pictures were shown, 80% of 3- to 5-year-olds could *not* select the correct one.

Theoretically, it makes sense that comprehension of selling intent might be difficult for younger children. Certain cognitive skills seem to be required first, such as the ability to recognize the differing perspectives of the seller and receiver. In support of this idea, one study found that the ability to role-take was a strong and significant predictor of elementary schoolers' understanding of the purpose of advertising (Faber, Perloff, & Hawkins, 1982). Interestingly, exposure to television did not correlate with comprehension of selling intent, suggesting that viewing numerous television ads is not enough to help a child recognize the purpose of commercials.

Table 2.1 Comparison of Preschoolers' Correct Responses Across Studies Using Different Nonverbal Measures of Comprehension of Selling Intent

Nature of Nonverbal Task	Incorrect	Correct
Select from two pictures (Donohue, Henke, & Donohue, 1980)	20%	80%
Select from four pictures (Macklin, 1985)	80%	20%
Select from 10 sketches in a game (Macklin, 1987)	91%	9%
Enact selling intent in creative play (Macklin, 1987)	87%	13%
Select from five pictures (Carter, Patterson, Donovan, Ewing, & Roberts, 2011)	87%	13%

SOURCE: Adapted from Macklin (1985, 1987).

In addition to role taking ability, comprehension of selling intent seems to depend on the ability to think abstractly about what persuasion is and who the true source of the message is. Consistent with this idea, one study found that the ability to identify the source of advertising and the awareness of the symbolic nature of commercials were two skills that helped differentiate children who understood the purpose of ads from those who did not (Robertson & Rossiter, 1974).

To summarize, a large body of research suggests that very young children do not comprehend the purpose of advertising and often view it as informational in nature. The ability to role-take and the ability to think conceptually have been identified as important precursors to being able to appreciate advertising as a form of persuasion. Given that such skills do not emerge until the later elementary school years (see Chapter 1), it stands to reason that understanding the selling intent of commercials does not occur much before the age of 8.

As a final issue, we might ask why comprehending the purpose of advertising is so important. Perhaps the naive view of a young child is just that—a naive view, with little or no consequence. Several studies suggest otherwise. Comprehension of selling intent seems to alter a child's reactions to advertising (Robertson & Rossiter, 1974; Ward & Wackman, 1973). For example, Robertson and Rossiter (1974) found that elementary schoolers who understood the persuasive intent of commercials were less likely to trust ads, more likely to dislike them, and less likely to want advertised products. In other words, recognizing the motives behind commercials may help trigger a cognitive defense or shield against such messages. Interestingly, the opposite pattern was found among children who viewed ads as informational—they expressed higher trust and more liking of such messages.

However, some have maintained that comprehension of selling intent may not be enough to safeguard children from ads (Rozendaal, Buijzen, & Valkenburg, 2009). After all, even adults who presumably appreciate the intent of commercials are influenced routinely by persuasive tactics. In a survey of nearly 300 8- to 12-year-olds, Rozendaal and her colleagues (2009) found that understanding the persuasive intent of advertising was effective in reducing the impact of ads on children's desire for products, but only among 10- to 12-year-olds. The opposite effect occurred for children under 10—understanding intent actually increased product desire, although comprehension was lower overall. The researchers argued that in order to defend themselves against ads, children may need even more sophisticated cognitive strategies, such as understanding particular persuasive tactics and recognizing bias in messages. The next section will explore these more advanced skills.

Recognition of Bias. Appreciating that advertising is inherently one sided and therefore biased is another facet of sophisticated consumerism (Roberts, 1982). In fact, Kunkel (2010) has argued that understanding selling intent (i.e., that an ad is trying to sell a product) is conceptually distinct from the more sophisticated understanding of *persuasive intent*, which entails a recognition that sales messages are slanted and require skeptical evaluation. As it turns out, this more advanced realization is also age related in its development. In a large-scale study, Carter and his colleagues (2011) compared comprehension of selling intent versus persuasive intent among nearly 600 children (ages 4–12) after they watched a McDonald's commercial. The researchers found that by age 8, a majority of children understood that the ad for a Happy Meal toy was trying to sell the product. However, the more sophisticated understanding of persuasive intent did not emerge until several years later, around age 11 or 12.

One challenge for children in recognizing bias is to overcome their tendency toward trusting messages. In interview situations, younger children are more likely to report that they believe what commercials say than older children are (Bever, Smith, Bengen, & Johnson, 1975; Robertson & Rossiter, 1974). For instance, Ward and his colleagues (1977) found that 50% of kindergartners said yes when asked, "Do commercials always tell the truth?" Only 12% of 3rd graders and 3% of 6th graders responded affirmatively to this question.

Similarly, Wilson and Weiss (1995) asked 4- to 11-year-olds a series of questions about advertising, including how much commercials tell you about a toy and how often commercials tell the truth. As seen in Figure 2.7, strong age trends were found on three different measures, all indicating growing skepticism of advertising across the childhood years. Even while watching television, older children spontaneously express more negative comments and criticisms of ads than younger children do (Ward, Levinson, et al., 1972).

Several factors contribute to younger children's trust in advertising. First, younger children have more difficulty differentiating appearance from reality, as discussed in Chapter 1 (see Figure 2.8). They rely heavily on perceptual cues in judging an ad (Ward & Wackman, 1973) and thus are likely to believe that products look and perform the way they are depicted in commercials. Second, younger children have less experience as consumers. One way to learn expeditiously that ads can be deceptive is to experience disappointment over a purchase. By 6th grade, the vast majority of children can describe a product they bought that turned out to be worse than what was depicted in an ad (Ward et al., 1977). As children grow older, they are more likely to cite their own consumer experiences as reasons for not trusting ads (Ward & Wackman, 1973). Third, the failure to understand selling intent makes a young child more trusting. In one study, a full 100% of older, cognitively mature children referred to advertisers'

Figure 2.7 Age differences in children's trust in advertising.

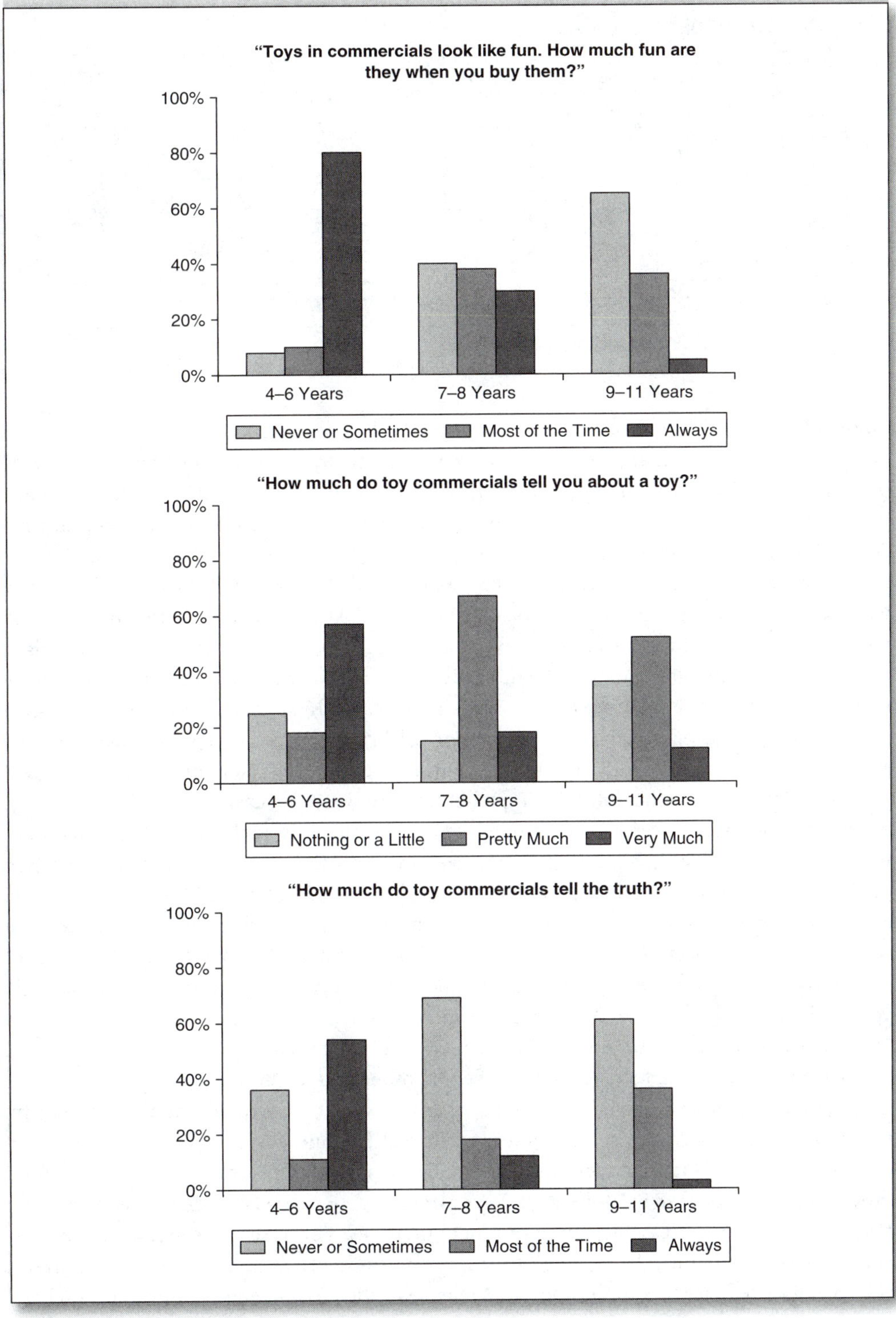
"Toys in commercials look like fun. How much fun are they when you buy them?"
100%
80%
60%
40%
20%
0%
4–6 Years
7–8 Years
9–11 Years
Never or Sometimes
Most of the Time
Always
"How much do toy commercials tell you about a toy?"
100%
80%
60%
40%
20%
0%
4–6 Years
7–8 Years
9–11 Years
Nothing or a Little
Pretty Much
Very Much
"How much do toy commercials tell the truth?"
100%
80%
60%
40%
20%
0%
4–6 Years
7–8 Years
9–11 Years
Never or Sometimes
Most of the Time
Always

SOURCE: Adapted from Wilson and Weiss (1995).

Figure 2.8

SOURCE: ©1995 Universal Press Syndicate.

motives when asked to explain why commercials do not always tell the truth (Ward & Wackman, 1973). For example, older children based their assessments of bias on the fact that advertisers "want you to buy their product" and want you to think their product is good."

It makes sense that skepticism would help children to be less gullible when they confront commercial messages. One study found that 8- to 12-year-olds who felt distrustful and negative toward advertising evaluated particular commercials less favorably than did those who were more trusting of advertising (Derbaix & Pecheux, 2003). Unfortunately, the study did not measure how much children wanted to buy the products in the commercials. Some scholars have speculated, though, that even the most savvy child consumer can be misled by powerful or seductive persuasive tactics (Derbaix & Pecheux, 2003). In support of this idea, children's understanding of advertising tactics (e.g., humor, celebrity endorsement, premiums) increases steadily between the ages of 8 and 12 (Rozendaal, Buijzen, & Valkenburg, 2011). Yet even 12-year-olds do not match adultlike comprehension for every persuasive ploy.

Skepticism toward advertising continues to develop into early adolescence. One longitudinal study found relatively high levels of mistrust in commercial claims as well as advertiser motives in a large sample of middle schoolers (Boush, Friestad, & Rose, 1994). On a five-point scale, the students' average ratings were all around four. (Zero indicated strong agreement with statements such as, "Advertisers care more about getting you to buy things than what is good for you" and "TV commercials tell only the good things about a product; they don't tell you the bad things.") Yet skepticism did not increase much within a single school year, nor were there any significant differences between 6th and 8th graders in these beliefs.

As a child reaches the teen years, then, factors other than cognitive development may be important in predicting who is most critical of advertising. One study found that skepticism toward advertising was higher among teens who watched more television, who came from families that stressed independent thinking, and who relied on peers for information about products (Mangleburg & Bristol, 1999). In contrast, skepticism was lower among teens who reported trying to impress peers with product purchases. This research suggests that once a young person is cognitively capable of recognizing the motives and tactics of advertisers, socializing forces such as parents and peers may be needed to make such information salient on a regular basis.

Comprehension of Disclaimers. Disclaimers are warnings or disclosures about a product, intended to prevent possible deception caused by an ad. "Batteries not included," "Parts sold separately," and "Part of a balanced breakfast" are examples of disclaimers that are quite common in advertising to children. Kunkel and Gantz (1992) found that more than half of the commercials targeted to children contained at least one disclaimer, and 9% featured two or more.

Disclaimers are very common in commercials for food. In fact, about half of all food ads contain some type of disclaimer (Wicks, Warren, Fosu, & Wicks, 2009). Nearly three-fourths of all cereal ads feature such a message (Gantz et al., 2007)—typically, indicating that the advertised product is only "part of a nutritious/balanced breakfast." Disclaimers are also frequently included in ads for pastries and bread (Gantz et al., 2007). Interestingly, food ads targeted to children and teens are more likely to contain disclaimers than are food ads targeted to adults (Gantz et al., 2007).

Typically, disclaimers are conveyed by an adult voiceover or by inserting the words in small print at the bottom of the screen (Muehling & Kolbe, 1999). It is rare for a disclaimer to be presented both auditorily and visually (Kunkel & Gantz, 1992; Wicks et al., 2009), even though the Federal Trade Commission recommends this practice to help children more easily detect such messages. Even young adults are better able to detect and remember disclaimers when they are presented in dual modalities (Morris, Mazis, & Brinberg, 1989).

Disclosures exist because of consumer pressure to ensure that advertisements give accurate information about products (Barcus, 1980). Yet disclaimers have been criticized as "jargon" because the wording is often fairly obscure (Atkin, 1980). In fact, research indicates that young children do not comprehend disclaimers very well. One study found that preschoolers exposed to a disclaimer in a toy ad were no better able to understand the workings of the toy than were those who saw the same ad with no disclaimer (Stern & Resnik, 1978). Another study revealed that kindergarten and 1st-grade children had little understanding of what a "balanced breakfast" means and were far more likely to remember the Rice Krispies cereal in an ad than the milk, orange juice, or strawberries that accompanied it on the table (Palmer & McDowell, 1981). Cognitive as well as language development should help to make these disclaimers more accessible with age. One study found that 85% of 10-year-olds understood "Partial assembly required" in a toy ad, whereas only 40% of 5-year-olds did (Liebert, Sprafkin, Liebert, & Rubinstein, 1977).

Yet disclaimers could be designed in a more straightforward way even for younger children. In an innovative experiment, Liebert and colleagues (1977) exposed kindergartners and 2nd graders to a toy commercial under one of three conditions: no disclaimer at all, a standard disclaimer ("Partial assembly required"), or a modified disclaimer that contained simpler wording ("You have to put it together"). Regardless of age, children who heard the simplified disclaimer were significantly more likely to understand that the toy required assembly than were those who heard the standard disclaimer (see Figure 2.9). Interestingly, the standard wording was no more effective in helping children understand that the toy needed assembly than was having no disclaimer at all; less than 25% of children in either condition understood this idea. As a comparison, commercials targeting children in Turkey regularly feature child-friendly vocabulary rather than adult language in their disclaimers (Bakir, 2009).

To recap how children process advertising, most preschoolers have difficulty differentiating a television commercial from programming, and they do not comprehend the standard

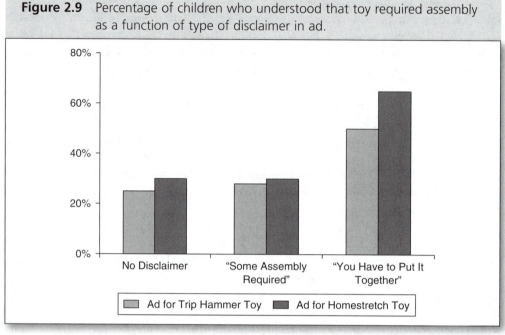

Figure 2.9 Percentage of children who understood that toy required assembly as a function of type of disclaimer in ad.

SOURCE: Adapted from Liebert, Sprafkin, Liebert, and Rubinstein (1977).

wording used in disclaimers in advertising. Thus, for this age group in particular, advertising may be unfair, given the legal principle that the audience must be capable of recognizing such content. By age 5 or 6, most children have mastered the distinction between a TV ad and a program, although it is based primarily on perceptual cues such as the length of the messages. As commercials get shorter and as they increasingly resemble adjacent programming, a kindergartner or 1st grader may have more difficulty making this distinction. Further complicating matters for younger children is the nature of advertising in newer media. Websites flash ads and banners, for example, that are mixed in seamlessly with content. In fact, some websites are entirely commercial in nature, as we will discuss below, although they may appear to be informational. The Internet requires even higher levels of cognitive sophistication to disentangle what is commercial from what is not.

Nevertheless, a young child's ability to identify an ad still does not mean she or he comprehends its purpose. Initially, ads are viewed as informational or entertaining in nature, and young children express a high degree of trust in such messages. It is not until roughly 8 years of age that a child begins to understand the selling intent of such messages. This transition is facilitated by the development of role taking skills and conceptual thinking. By age 12 or so, most children are able to recognize the source of the message, the biased nature of commercials, and typical strategies that are used to persuade. This level of awareness, coupled with a rich base of consumer experience, means that by the teenage years, most youth are fairly critical and skeptical of advertising. The only caveat here is that all of this research has been done with television and not with newer media. Even so, children of all ages, like many adults, can still be persuaded by commercials, as we will discover next.

The Persuasive Impact of Advertising

The most direct effect of an advertisement is to convince a consumer to purchase a new product. Advertisers and companies alike believe in the power of advertising to do just that. There is no other way to explain the fact that companies paid $4 million for a 30-second commercial during the 2013 Super Bowl. But there are more subtle consequences of advertising too. For example, commercials can influence family interactions. Whenever a child tries to get a parent to buy something or a parent tries to resist that effort, conflict can occur. Researchers have looked at how often this occurs and with what consequences. In addition, extensive exposure to advertising may affect more general attitudes or values that youth hold regarding consumption, money, and even physical appearance. We discuss each of these potential influences in this section.

Brand Loyalty

One of the goals of advertising is to create brand loyalty. Creating branded characters that appeal to children is a crucial component of successful marketing (Institute of Medicine, 2006). Tony the Tiger was created in 1951 to promote Kellogg's Frosted Flakes, and although he has become slimmer and more muscular, he is still used in advertising today. Ronald McDonald is recognized by nearly 96% of American children and is used to sell fast food internationally in more than 25 languages (Enrico, 1999). Through licensing agreements, popular television characters such as SpongeBob SquarePants are used to sell products as well.

It is not surprising that children are highly aware of brand names, jingles, and slogans associated with commercials and of the celebrities who endorse certain products (Burr & Burr, 1977; Fox, 1996). One study revealed that children between the ages of 8 and 12 could name five brands of beer but only four American presidents (Center for Science in the Public Interest, 1988). Another study found that teens remember brand names and recognize ad content better than adults do (Dubow, 1995).

Even preschoolers show awareness of brands and brand loyalty. One study asked 3- to 6-year-olds to match 22 brand logos to 12 different products pictured on a game board (Fischer, Schwartz, Richards, Goldstein, & Rojas, 1991). The children showed high rates of logo recognition (see Figure 2.10). More than 90% recognized the logo for the Disney Channel, but children even recognized logos for many adult products. More than 90% of the 6-year-olds in particular were able to match Old Joe (the cartoon character promoting Camel cigarettes) to a picture of a cigarette. Even when preschoolers cannot name a particular logo, they often recognize products associated with the brand. For example, in one study very few preschoolers were able to identify the Home Depot logo, but many of them knew that you could buy tools, wood, and paint there (Kinsky & Bichard, 2011). Another study found that children as young as 2 years of age can recognize many brand logos for products (Valkenburg & Buijzen, 2005). In this same study, preschoolers who watched a great deal of television were more familiar with brand names than were preschoolers who watched little television.

Brand recognition seems to breed brand preference. One study had preschool children select which product they preferred from a series of eight choices involving a branded option and a carefully chosen nonbranded one (Pine & Nash, 2003). The nonbranded options were pretested to ensure that they matched the branded ones in size, color, and other perceptual

Figure 2.10 Popular brand logos.

qualities. Children chose the branded products 68% of the time. Preschool girls showed stronger brand loyalty than preschool boys did. Among the eight types of products presented (e.g., toy, cereal, chocolate bar, T-shirt), the only product that did not generate brand loyalty was training/running shoes. Using a slightly different approach, Robinson, Borzekowski, Matheson, and Kramer (2007) presented preschoolers with two samples each of five different fast food items (e.g., hamburger, French fries, milk). For each pair of items, one was packaged in McDonald's wrapping and the other was packaged in plain paper. The foods or drinks inside the wrappings were identical, however. Children were asked to taste each sample and decide if the two were the same or if one tasted better. The preschoolers showed a strong preference for the foods and drinks they thought were from McDonald's. In other words, the simple branding of the food items significantly influenced children's taste perceptions.

Desire for Products

Asking whether advertising creates a desire for products may seem like a ridiculous question to some. American children wear T-shirts emblazoned with *Pokémon* characters, carry lunch boxes decorated with Disney images, wear designer jeans and Nike athletic shoes, and love anything with the word *Abercrombie* on it (see Figure 2.11). Adolescents seem even more conscious of brand names as well as the latest fads in clothing and technology. Where does all this consumer desire come from? When asked, most children report that they bought something because "you see it a lot" or "everybody has one" (Fox, 1996). As noted above, advertising often conveys the idea that a product will bring fun and happiness to a youngster's life. Images of other children playing with a toy or eating at a fast food restaurant reinforce the notion that everyone else is doing it too.

But does exposure to advertising create desire? A number of surveys show that children who watch a lot of television want more advertised toys and actually consume more advertised foods than children with lighter TV habits do (Atkin, 1982; Goldberg, 1990; Robertson & Rossiter, 1977; Robertson, Ward, Gatignon, & Klees, 1989). As an example, one study asked 250 children in the Netherlands to list their Christmas wishes and then compared them with the commercials that were being aired on TV at the time (Buijzen & Valkenburg, 2000). More than half the children requested at least one advertised product. Moreover, heavy exposure to television significantly predicted requests for more advertised products, even after controlling for age and gender of the child (see Figure 2.12). Another study of more than 900 5th and 6th graders found that those who watched a great deal of television had a more positive attitude toward junk food, such as sugared cereals and fast food items, than light viewers did (Dixon, Scully, Wakefield, White, & Crawford, 2007). Heavy TV viewers also perceived that other children ate junk food more often, and they perceived junk food to be healthier and reportedly ate more junk food themselves. These patterns held up even after controlling for gender, grade level, and socioeconomic status of the family.

Figure 2.11 Branded items marketed to youth.

Figure 2.12

SOURCE: *Baby Blues* © 1997 Baby Blues Partnership. Reprinted with permission of King Features Syndicate.

Among adolescents too, exposure to television has been linked to increased desire for products and brand names (Moschis, 1978; Moschis & Moore, 1979). However, evidence suggests that the strength of this relationship may decrease somewhat with age (Buijzen & Valkenburg, 2000; Robertson & Rossiter, 1977), consistent with children's growing awareness of the purpose of advertising as well as increased skepticism about such messages.

Clearly, correlational evidence reveals that there is a relationship between TV advertising and product desire, but it is difficult to establish causality in such studies. It is possible that youth who are eager to buy toys, games, clothes, and snacks actually seek out television more often to find out about new products, a reverse direction in this relationship. Thus, researchers have turned to experiments to more firmly establish the impact of advertising.

In the typical experiment, children are randomly assigned to either view or not view an advertisement for a particular product. Afterward, children are allowed to select the advertised product from a range of other choices, or they are asked a series of questions about how much they like or want that product compared to others. Experiments generally show that commercials are indeed effective. In one study, preschoolers exposed to a single ad for a toy were more likely than those not exposed to (a) choose the toy over the favorite activity at the school, (b) select the toy even if it meant playing with a "not so nice boy," and (c) choose the toy despite their mother's preference for a different toy (Goldberg & Gorn, 1978). In a study of older children, exposure to a single ad for acne cream caused 4th and 5th graders to worry more about skin blemishes and want to buy the cream (Atkin, 1976).

Although one ad can increase desire for a product, multiple exposures may be even more influential. Gorn and Goldberg (1977) found that viewing one versus three commercials was equally effective in increasing positive attitudes toward a new toy compared to a no-exposure control group, but only the three-exposure condition made children try harder to win the toy. Other research supports the idea that a single ad can increase awareness and liking of a product, but multiple exposures to varied commercials are most effective in changing consumer behavior (Gorn & Goldberg, 1980; Resnik & Stern, 1977).

Beyond repetition, there are other ways to enhance the impact of an advertisement. One tactic is to include a premium or prize with the product. In 1975, premiums were offered in nearly 50% of cereal ads targeted to children (Barcus, 1980). This practice is less common today in cereal ads, but fast food commercials routinely entice children with small toys that come with kids' meals (Kunkel & Gantz, 1992). In 1997, McDonald's had difficulty keeping Teenie Beanie Babies in stock once it began offering them as premiums in kids' Happy Meals. Research suggests that premiums in commercials can significantly increase children's desire for a product (Miller & Busch, 1979) and can actually affect children's requests for cereals in a supermarket (Atkin, 1978).

Another strategy involves the use of a celebrity or a popular character to endorse a product in an ad. Professional athlete Michael Jordan has long been associated with Nike and even had athletic shoes (Air Jordans) named after him. There are countless other examples. Teen pop star Selena Gomez has her own clothing line, called Dream Out Loud, which is sold exclusively at Kmart (see Figure 2.13). Ellen DeGeneres is a spokesperson for JCPenney, and TV show *Glee* star Lea Michele was named 2012 Candie's Girl to market a brand of shoes and apparel sold at Kohl's. Even animated TV characters sell products—Bart Simpson claims to love Butterfinger candy bars.

Research supports the idea that popular figures can be effective sources of persuasion. One study found that teens perceived celebrities as more trustworthy, competent, and attractive than noncelebrity endorsers featured in nearly identical ads (Atkin & Block, 1983). Furthermore, the featuring of celebrities resulted in more favorable evaluations of a product. In a controlled experiment, Ross and her colleagues (1984) exposed 8- to 14-year-old boys to a commercial for a race car set but systematically varied whether a celebrity endorser was included in the ad. The researchers found that exposure to the celebrity significantly enhanced boys' liking of the racing set and increased their belief that the celebrity was an expert about the toy. In a more recent experiment, associating a healthy snack (i.e., fruit) with the TV character SpongeBob or Dora enhanced its appeal among preschoolers, up to the same level as that of candy (DeDroog, Valkenburg, & Buijzen, 2011).

Figure 2.13 Sample celebrity endorsement.

Taken as a whole, the research demonstrates that commercials can have quite powerful effects on children's desires. Even a single ad can change the way a child perceives a toy or a game. Ads can also persuade young viewers to eat foods that are not very nutritious (see Chapter 7) and to try drugs such as tobacco (see Chapter 6). As it turns out, even a bland ad can make a product appealing (Resnik & Stern, 1977), but incorporating tactics such as premiums and celebrity endorsements can make a pitch even more effective. Next we will consider effects of advertising that are more indirect and not necessarily intentional on the part of advertisers: increased family conflict and changes in youth values.

Parent-Child Conflict

Most advertising agency executives believe that TV commercials do not contribute to family conflict (Culley, Lazer, & Atkin, 1976). Yet research suggests otherwise (see Figure 2.14). One study presented stories to elementary schoolers about a child who sees a TV commercial for an attractive product (Sheikh & Moleski, 1977). When asked if the child in the story would ask a parent to buy the product, nearly 60% of the children responded affirmatively. When asked what would happen if the parent said no, 33% of the children said the child in the story would feel sad, 23% said the child would be angry or hostile, and 16% said the child would persist in requesting the product. Only 23% indicated the child would be accepting of the decision.

Figure 2.14

According to mothers, children's attempts to influence purchasing occur with regularity, and this "nag factor" is perceived as stressful (Henry & Borzekowski, 2011). Mothers report that children ask most often for food items, especially cereals, snacks, and candy (Ward & Wackman, 1972). Coincidentally, those same products are among the most heavily advertised to children. Requests for a parent to purchase something does seem to decrease with age (Ward & Wackman, 1972), in part because as children get older, they have more of their own money to make independent decisions. Yet for expensive items, even adolescents can pester parents. One national survey found that 40% of 12- to 17-year-olds had asked for an advertised product they thought their parents would disapprove of, and most of these young people said they were persistent (New American Dream, 2002). In fact, the teens estimated that they had had to ask an average of nine times before their parents gave in and made the purchase.

Several studies have actually observed parents and children shopping together in an effort to assess conflict more directly. In an early study, Galst and White (1976) observed 41 preschoolers with their mothers in a grocery store. The researchers documented an average of 15 purchase influence attempts (PIAs) by the child in a typical shopping trip, or one every two minutes! Most of the PIAs were for cereals and candy, and 45% of them were successful. In other words, the mothers acquiesced to nearly half of the children's requests. In another observational study, Atkin (1978) found that open conflict occurred 65% of the time that a parent denied a child's request for a cereal in a supermarket.

One experiment creatively linked PIAs directly to advertising. Stoneman and Brody (1981) randomly assigned preschoolers to view a cartoon that contained either six food commercials or no commercials at all. Immediately afterward, mothers were told to take their preschoolers to a nearby grocery store to buy a typical week's worth of groceries, purportedly as part of another study. Posing as clerks in the store, research assistants surreptitiously coded the interactions that occurred. Children who had been exposed to the food commercials engaged in significantly more PIAs than children in the control group did. Children exposed to the commercials also made more requests for the foods featured in the ads. In addition, the mothers' behavior was influenced by the commercials. Mothers of children who had seen the ads engaged in significantly more control strategies during the shopping trip, such as putting the item back on the shelf and telling the child no.

In sum, advertising can produce pressure on parents to buy products, which in turn can cause family conflict when such requests are denied. Younger children who confront parental resistance are likely to whine, become angry, and even cry (Williams & Burns, 2000). Older children, in contrast, tend to use more sophisticated persuasion tactics, such as negotiation and white lies. There is some evidence of gender differences in this nag factor (Buijzen & Valkenburg, 2003a). Boys are more forceful and demanding in their requests than girls are, and boys also tend to be less compliant. Finally, research suggests that parent-child discord is not just an American phenomenon. One cross-cultural study found that heavy television viewing among children is linked to higher parent-child conflict about purchases in Japan and Great Britain as well as in the United States (Robertson et al., 1989).

Materialism and Value Orientations

Critics worry that in addition to creating demand for certain products, advertising may contribute more generally to materialistic attitudes in our youth. Materialism refers to the idea that money and possessions are important and that certain qualities such as beauty and success can be obtained from having material property. Fox (1996) argued that "when kids are saturated in advertising, their appetites for products are stimulated. At the same time, kids desire the values that have been associated with those products—intangible values that, like sex appeal, are impossible to buy" (p. 20). The popular Bratz dolls, for example, were marketed to tween girls as a "lifestyle brand" that revolved around makeup, sexualized clothing, and communal shopping and congregating at the mall (McAllister, 2007). In support of this materialism, or hyperconsumption, one national poll found that 53% of teens said that buying certain products made them feel better about themselves (New American Dream, 2002). Other critics argue that advertising should not be singled out for attack and that youthful consumerism is part of children's participation in a larger culture that has become rooted in commodities and capitalism (Buckingham, 2011).

Disentangling advertising from all the other forces that might foster materialism is difficult, especially because nearly all children are exposed to a world filled with toy stores, fast food restaurants, movies, peer groups, and even schools, all of which promote consumer goods. Several correlational studies have looked to see if there is a relationship between media habits and materialism in youth. To measure materialism, students are typically asked to agree or disagree with statements such as, "It is really true that money can buy happiness" and "My dream in life is to be able to own expensive things" (see Table 2.2). One early survey of more than 800 adolescents found that heavy exposure to television was positively correlated with buying products for social acceptance, even after controlling for age, sex, socioeconomic status,

Table 2.2   Sample Measure of Materialistic Orientation in Children

Instruction: We would like to ask you how you think about having and buying things. Below you will find a number of questions. Please check the box with the answer that suits you best.

1. Do you think it is important to have a lot of money?
   ☐ no, not at all   ☐ no, not so much   ☐ yes, a little bit   ☐ yes, very much

2. Do you think it is important to own a lot of things?
   ☐ no, not at all   ☐ no, not so much   ☐ yes, a little bit   ☐ yes, very much

3. Would you like to be able to buy things that cost a lot of money?
   ☐ no, not at all   ☐ no, not so much   ☐ yes, a little bit   ☐ yes, very much

4. Would you like to earn a lot of money when you grow up?
   ☐ no, not at all   ☐ no, not so much   ☐ yes, a little bit   ☐ yes, very much

5. Would you like to have more money to buy things for yourself?
   ☐ no, not at all   ☐ no, not so much   ☐ yes, a little bit   ☐ yes, very much

SOURCE: Adapted from Buijzen and Valkenburg (2003b). See http://www.ccam-ascor.nl/index.php/en/research-measures?id=106:materialism&catid=52

and amount of family communication about consumption (Churchill & Moschis, 1979). In this same study, teens who reported watching a lot of TV were also more likely to associate possessions and money with happiness. Another survey found a similar pattern for tweens (Buijzen & Valkenburg, 2003b). That is, 8- to 12-year-olds who frequently watched television commercials were more materialistic than were their peers who seldom watched commercials were. This was true regardless of the child's age, gender, or socioeconomic status. More recently, a survey of 10- to 14-year-olds found that both heavy television exposure and high recognition of brand logos were independent predictors of higher materialism (Vega & Roberts, 2011). Trust in advertising also predicted more materialism among these preteens and teens.

Such patterns are certainly suggestive, but they do not permit firm causal conclusions. Materialistic youth could seek out advertising, advertising might cause materialism, or both. Clearly, longitudinal research is needed to ascertain whether heavy exposure to advertising during early childhood leads to more materialistic attitudes over time. As an example, Moschis and Moore (1982) surveyed 6th through 12th graders twice, across 14 months, about their exposure to television commercials and their materialistic attitudes. At Time 1, there was a significant association between exposure to ads and materialism, as has been found in other studies. Looking over time, exposure to advertising at Time 1 also predicted higher scores on materialism 14 months later at Time 2, but *only* among those youth who were initially low in materialism. In other words, television seemed to have its greatest impact on those who were not already highly materialistic. More longitudinal research of this sort is needed, particularly with younger children whose values are still developing. Obviously, studies also need to explore other relevant socialization factors, such as parents' and peers' values regarding material goods (Chia, 2010).

Another concern is whether advertising contributes to a preoccupation with physical appearance, especially among female adolescents. Teen magazines, in particular, are rife with ads featuring thin, attractive models (see Figure 2.15). Studies have found that female adolescents and college students do compare their physical attractiveness to models featured in advertising (Martin & Kennedy, 1993; Richins, 1991). Moreover, looking at ads of highly attractive models can temporarily affect self-esteem and even body image (Stice & Shaw, 1994), especially

Figure 2.15   Covers of popular teen magazines.

among girls who are encouraged to evaluate themselves (Martin & Gentry, 1997). In one experiment, adolescent girls who were exposed to a heavy dose of commercials emphasizing physical appearance were more likely to believe that being beautiful is an important character-istic and is necessary to attract men than were those in a control group exposed to other types of ads (Tan, 1979).

Longitudinal evidence is beginning to emerge here as well, suggesting that early television and magazine exposure increases young girls' desire to have a thin body (Harrison & Hefner, 2006) and young boys' desire to have a muscular body (Harrison & Bond, 2007) when they grow up.

Phases of Consumer Behavior During Childhood

Valkenburg and Cantor (2001) outlined four phases of consumer development in child-hood, which provide a nice overview of much of the material covered in this chapter so far. The first phase, which they call "Feeling Wants and Preferences," characterizes infants and toddlers. During this phase, young children show distinct preferences for smells, colors, sounds, and objects, an important component of consumer behavior. Still, at this young age, children are primarily reactive rather than goal directed, so they are not capable of acting like true consumers.

The second phase, "Nagging and Negotiating," captures the preschool years. As we have noted above, preschoolers have difficulty distinguishing ads from programs and do not fully comprehend the intent of commercials. Consequently, Valkenburg and Cantor (2001) argue, marketing efforts have a strong impact on this age group. Because of preschoolers' tendency toward centration (see Chapter 1), they are likely to gravitate toward products that are visually striking. They also immediately want what they see, so they are most likely to pester parents and to exhibit noncompliant and emotional behavior when they are denied something.

Phase 3, "Adventure and the First Purchase," characterizes the early elementary school years, between the ages of 5 and 8. Cognitive abilities are in transition here as children gradu-ally consider more conceptual information, become more responsive to information pre-sented verbally, and increase their attention span. But this age group can still be confused about the purpose of ads and can still respond strongly to perceptual cues. Children typically make their first solo purchase during this phase, thus becoming a bona fide consumer inde-pendent of a parent.

Phase 4, "Conformity and Fastidiousness," marks the tween years, from 8 to 12. The ability to critically evaluate information, compare products, and appreciate the selling intent of ads develops during this time. Because of their attention to detail and quality, many children become serious collectors of objects during this period. Tweens show a strong sensitivity to the norms and values of their peers as well as to what older adolescents are buying and doing. Most tweens regularly visit different types of stores, making independent purchases and influ-encing household buying practices. In other words, by late elementary school, all the funda-mentals of consumer behavior are in place (i.e., the child shows preferences, can evaluate options, and can choose and purchase a product).

Although Valkenburg and Cantor (2001) did not identify a Phase 5, they noted that con-sumer skills continue to develop during adolescence, which is consistent with research described earlier in this chapter. In particular, teens are increasingly able to recognize bias, and they are more skeptical of commercial messages. However, their preoccupation with identity development means that they pay close attention to self-presentation and peer acceptance, which in turn can make them susceptible to brand-related social status messages in the commercialized world (Buijzen, Van Reijmersdal, & Owen, 2010).

Marketing Strategies in the 21st Century

As children's and teens' spending power increases, marketers are continually experimenting with new ways to reach young consumers. Large corporations such as Coca-Cola, McDonald's, and KFC are developing a variety of digital marketing tactics to reach tweens and teens as they spend countless hours with screen media. The idea is to capitalize on the fact that young people today are constantly connected to devices, yearn for personalized messages, prioritize opportunities to network with peers, and enjoy immersive digital environments (Montgomery & Chester, 2009). In this section, we will examine five techniques that are burgeoning in the 21st century: character merchandising, product placement, viral marketing, online marketing, and marketing in schools.

Character Merchandising

Character merchandising refers to the licensing of popular characters to promote many types of products (Institute of Medicine, 2006). Using characters to build brand loyalty is not a new phenomenon. Mickey Mouse was created in 1928 by Walt Disney, and today the anthropomorphized creature is an international icon. Similarly, the promotion of toys that are based on popular programs is a marketing strategy that has been around for a while, as discussed earlier in this chapter. As early as 1969, the cartoon *Hot Wheels* was criticized as nothing more than a 30-minute commercial for Hot Wheels toys (Colby, 1993). Roughly 20 years later, the *Teenage Mutant Ninja Turtles* cartoon helped to sell more than $500 million worth of toy merchandise in 1990 alone (Rosenberg, 1992).

Nowadays, however, characters are being used in a more integrated fashion across media platforms. Consider the *Pokémon* craze (see Figure 2.16). The cute pocket-sized monsters originated in 1996 in Japan as characters in a Nintendo video game. In 1998, U.S. marketers simultaneously launched a TV cartoon series, trading cards, a video game, and toy merchandise. Later came party products, a Warner Brothers motion picture, a CD, children's apparel sold at JCPenney, kids' meal premiums at Burger King, and even *Pokémon* tournament leagues that met weekly at Toys'R'Us to play the video game (Annicelli, 1999; Brass, 1999; Jones, 2000). The *Pokémon* franchise explicitly reinforces the idea that the best way to become cool is to collect as many monsters as possible. Apparently, children have been convinced. Within the first 10 years after its 1996 launch, the franchise generated $26 billion in retail sales and sold more than 155 million *Pokémon* video games worldwide (Graft, 2007). And there is no end in sight to the pocket monsters' popularity. In 2010, 153 new characters were unveiled as Nintendo released its fifth generation of games, *Pokémon Black* and *Pokémon White*, designed for the Nintendo DS. On the first day of availability in the U.S., more than 1.08 million copies were sold (Pereira, 2011). In 2012,

Figure 2.16 Character merchandising: The *Pokémon* craze.

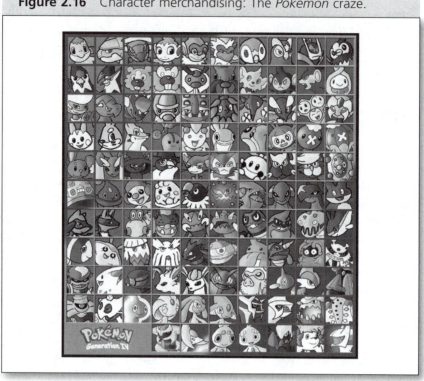

Nintendo released the very popular sequels *Pokémon Black 2* and *Pokémon White 2*. Films, music recordings, and trading cards have accompanied each of these game releases.

Such tactics do seem to blur the differences between advertising and entertainment content. Toy-based cartoons, for example, have been criticized as "animated sales catalogs masquerading as entertainment" (Waters & Uehling, 1985, p. 85). One of the challenges for young viewers is that toy-based cartoons feature the same popular characters, slogans, and sound effects that are employed in related commercials for the toys. Several studies reveal that the combination of a cartoon and related advertising can be very confusing for young children (Hoy, Young, & Mowen, 1986; Kunkel, 1988). For example, Wilson and Weiss (1992) found that 4- to 6-year-olds were less able to recognize an ad for a *Beetlejuice* toy or comprehend its selling intent when it was shown with a *Beetlejuice* cartoon than when it was shown with an unrelated *Popeye* cartoon. Moreover, the confusion occurred regardless of whether the related *Beetlejuice* cartoon was immediately adjacent to the ad or separated from it by five minutes of filler material. This finding is consistent with younger children's perceptual dependence, as discussed in Chapter 1.

Interestingly, the evidence is mixed on whether airing ads together with related programming is a good marketing strategy. Some studies have found that this technique enhances children's desire for a product (Kunkel, 1988; Miller & Busch, 1979), whereas others have not (Hoy et al., 1986; Wilson & Weiss, 1992). Success presumably depends in part on the nature of the product as well as the popularity of the related character.

Thus, as commercials increasingly resemble TV programs and popular characters appear in movies, on cereal boxes, as toys, on websites, in CDs, and in video games, the young child is likely to become even more confused about what advertising actually is. On occasion, even sophisticated consumers may feel bewildered or perhaps overwhelmed by these multimedia character merchandising endeavors.

Product Placement

Product placement is a promotional tactic used by marketers whereby a commercial product is placed in a visible setting outside a typical marketing context. The most common product placement occurs in movies, where a corporation will typically pay to have its product used by the characters. Candy sales shot up by 66%, for example, when Spielberg's movie character E.T. was shown eating Hershey's Reese's Pieces (Mazur, 1996). Product placement on television has become popular in recent years too, especially because consumers are using newer digital recording technologies such as TiVo to skip over commercials. Reality TV shows in particular have become known for their use of brand-name products in helping people to redesign their homes, their gardens, and even their love lives. For example, the Coca-Cola Company paid $10 million in 2002 to have Coke served to the judges on *American Idol* (Howard, 2002).

Unlike reality shows, children's programs have avoided product placement so far, presumably because of the separation principle. This principle, established by the Federal Communications Commission (FCC) in 1974, mandates that there must be a clear distinction between program and advertising content during shows targeted to children (see discussion on advertising policy in Chapter 13).

The idea behind product placement is to have a product fit seamlessly into the context of a story or program. This subtle technique is an effort to build brand loyalty without calling attention to the persuasive intent of the strategy. Some have referred to these types of tactics as "stealth marketing" because the consumer is unaware that it is an attempt to influence purchasing behaviors (Institute of Medicine, 2006).

Product placement also occurs when websites have sponsors that place their logos on the page. The TeenNick website (teennick.com), for example, has a box or banner on the top of the homepage that is used for rotating commercial messages. Recently, for example, there was an image of Clearasil products prominently placed at the top, with the accompanying message "Click to Learn More." The link was not explicitly labeled or identified as an advertisement.

Advertisers have also developed "advergames," which are online video games with a subtle or overt commercial message. For example, Candystand.com, a website hosted by various candy companies, features dozens of games, including one called Gummi Grab involving Gummi Bears and another called Trident Layers Factory involving stacks of chewing gum. While playing these games, the user is exposed to multiple images of such candy, purportedly helping to build brand loyalty. In fact, the brands are often used as tools or equipment for playing the game, making the commercial nature of the game imperceptible or somewhat concealed (Lee, Choi, Cole, Quilliam, & Cole, 2009). Moreover, games on for-profit websites rarely contain nutritional or health-related information (Cicchirillo & Lin, 2011; Culp, Bell, & Cassady, 2010). One study of 77 food-related websites targeted to children found a total of 546 different games containing food brands on these sites (E. S. Moore, 2006).

Like character merchandising, product placement blurs the traditional distinction between commercial content and entertainment content. Individuals confronted with these types of embedded messages need to comprehend the film's storyline or learn to play the game, so they have fewer cognitive resources available to process the coexisting commercial branding

(Owen, Hang, Lewis, & Auty, 2012). Even adults are not always aware of such brand exposure (Yang, Roskos-Ewoldsen, Dinu, & Arpan, 2006). As we have discussed above, such covert strategies are likely to make it even more challenging for young children who already struggle to identify and comprehend advertising. Because such tactics are subtle, they may also go unnoticed by older children and teens who ordinarily could muster their cognitive defenses in the face of overt commercial persuasion. As a demonstration of impact, a recent experiment found that children who played Pop-Tarts and Oreo advergames were more likely to select unhealthy snack foods than were those who played either Dole-sponsored ("healthy") games or nonfood games (Harris, Speers, Schwartz, & Brownell, 2012). Moreover, no age differences were observed among the 7- to 12-year-olds in the study. In other words, both younger and older children were affected by the placement of unhealthy food products in the advergames. Another recent experiment confirms the idea that food images in advergames can increase unhealthy snacking in children (Folkvord, Anschutz, Buijzen, & Valkenburg, 2013).

Viral Marketing

Viral marketing is another form of "under-the-radar" or stealth marketing (Institute of Medicine, 2006). This term refers to the "buzz" or "word of mouth" about a product that occurs when people talk about it. Marketers use various techniques to stimulate buzz about a product, from paying trendsetters to use a product and talk about it to creating a blog to encourage online chat about a product (Calvert, 2008). For example, music industry marketers have used this approach by sending attractive young consumers into music stores to talk about a new CD to each other, knowing that unsuspecting customers will overhear the conservation (Kaikati & Kaikati, 2004).

Stimulating buzz is not an accident—such campaigns are meticulously engineered and the results are carefully measured (Khermouch & Green, 2001). In 2007, Webbed Marketing, an agency specializing in viral marketing, announced the release of the Webbed-O-Meter ("Viral Marketing Agency," 2007). The tool measures the amount of buzz surrounding any website, which consists of all the online references made to that site by Internet consumers, bloggers, analysts, reviewers, and reporters. Today, there are many agencies as well as software and dashboards (e.g., Trendiction, HootSuite) that can track the success of viral marketing (J. Wethall, personal communication, September 10, 2012).

Viral marketing is thought to be particularly effective with young, trend-conscious consumers who want to be first among their peers to have new products and wear new fashions (Khermouch & Green, 2001). Finding the right individuals to stimulate the buzz, then, is part of the challenge. Companies often recruit popular teens, called "connectors," through a company website, through YouTube videos, through Twitter, or by monitoring online chat rooms related to teen culture (Dunnewind, 2004). Sometimes marketers "seed" an idea or a brand in targeted blogs, videos, or tweets with the hope that these seeds will be picked up by other bloggers/video channels/tweeters and blossom into a message that goes viral. Downloadable widgets are also popular with adolescents—they can be used to personalize a webpage, but they also allow marketers to track user responses (Montgomery & Chester, 2009).

An offshoot of viral marketing is called "guerrilla marketing" (Levinson, 2007), which is typically a low-cost, unconventional strategy designed to capture people's attention, create buzz, and hopefully turn viral. Flash mobs are one example of this technique. The lap dance that Eninem received during the MTV Movie Awards in 2009 is another example. Companies can engage in guerrilla marketing too. To advertise Super Glue-3, marketers glued coins on various city sidewalks. When people tried to pick up the coin, they saw a small logo for the product glued next to the irremovable coin. This street marketing tactic was later picked up on YouTube (see http://www.youtube.com/watch?v=6O-Q4TVH808).

Viral marketing is frequently one component of an integrated marketing communications campaign. But many believe it will become increasingly more common as marketers struggle to reach consumers in a media landscape composed of hundreds of television channels. In addition, marketers recognize that young people use the Internet a great deal, frequently download applications on their smartphones, are often cynical about 30-second TV ads, and are greatly influenced by peers.

Yet viral marketing is also controversial. Critics charge that it is an insidious form of commercialism because marketers are working at the grassroots level, manipulating people's social relationships with these relatively inexpensive ploys (Khermouch & Green, 2001; Minow, 2004). There is also concern that such techniques may come under regulatory scrutiny because consumers can be misled about the commercial relationship that often exists between the connectors and the corporations sponsoring their activities (Creamer, 2005). According to the basic principle of advertising, people should know they are being solicited for commercial purposes.

Online Marketing to Youth

Millions of American children and teens go online each week, and there are countless websites to attract them (see Chapter 8). In fact, several lists exist to help parents and children identify websites designed just for young people, including KidSites.com, More4Kids.info, and CommonsenseMedia.org. Interestingly, the five most popular websites among children revolve around television: Nick.com, NickJr .com, PBSKids.org, Disney.com (Club Penguin), and CartoonNetwork.com (see Table 2.3).

As anyone who goes online knows, the Internet is filled with advertising. In fact, Internet ad spending worldwide is projected to be $98 billion for 2012, representing a 16% increase from the year before (Hof, 2012). Moreover, in the first quarter of 2012, the growth rate for ad spending on the Internet surpassed that for other forms of media, which for the most part also showed an increase (see Table 2.4). Magazines are the only medium where ad spending dropped compared to the year prior.

Many online commercial messages are targeted directly to children. Banners lure children to commercial websites to advertise

Table 2.3 Most Popular Kids' Websites in September 2012

Rank	Website	Estimated Unique Monthly Visitors
1	Nick	4,800,000
2	PBSKids	4,600,000
3	Nick Jr.	4,500,000
4	Club Penguin	4,400,000
5	Cartoon Network	4,300,000
6	Yahoo! Kids	4,100,000
7	Poptropica	2,750,000
8	Moshi Monsters	2,700,000
9	Webkinz	2,600,000
10	Stardoll	2,520,000
11	FunBrain	2,500,000
12	Cool Math Games	1,950,000
13	Neopets	1,800,000
14	Primary Games	1,400,000
15	Fantage	550,000

SOURCE: The 15 most popular kids' websites per eBizMBA's ranking, which is a constantly updated average of each website's Alexa Global Traffic Rank and the U.S. Traffic Rank from both Compete and Quantcast (http://www.ebizmba.com/articles/kids-websites).

Table 2.4 Change in Global Spending on Advertising by Media From 2011 to 2012

Medium	Change in Spending
Television	2.8%
Radio	7.9%
Newspapers	3.1%
Magazines	−1.4%
Internet	12.1%
Cinema	4.1%

SOURCE: Nielsen Global AdView Pulse report, 2012, Q1, from Hof (2012).

and sell products. And websites for children often blend commercialism with content in ways that make them indistinguishable from each other (Cai & Zhao, 2010). For example, one study found that over 80% of popular children's websites featured character spokespersons on their homepages, in ads, and/or in the games that could be played (Bucy, Kim, & Park, 2011). In addition, only about one in four of the websites that employed such characters in advertising explicitly labeled the content as commercial in nature. Many branded products targeted to youth have websites that are created to supplement traditional forms of advertising. These "branded environments" are relatively cheap to maintain and typically feature a range of activities, such as games, polls, quizzes, and guestbooks. For example, the Crayola website offers the child user a variety of games to play, crafts to make, and links to Crayola applications that can be downloaded to mobile devices. Of course, the site also sells Crayola products.

Several websites entice children to enter virtual worlds that involve products. The Webkinz website is an example of this craze (www.webkinz.com). One journalist has likened it to "Beanie Beanies in cyberspace" (Hawn, 2007). The company sells Webkinz plush animals and the newer, smaller Lil'Kinz animals for anywhere between $10 and $25 apiece. Each animal comes with a "secret code" that allows the child to enter the Webkinz website, where the animal comes to life and can be adopted, named, exercised, and fed (see Figure 2.17). The child can also play games to earn "KinzCash," which can be used to buy the animal toys, clothes, and furniture. Children can even talk online with their friends using KinzChat. When the toys were first introduced in 2005, retailers had difficulty keeping them in stock. In 2008, e-commerce data revealed that the term "Webkinz" was searched more than 3.5 million times in a single month, making it the top product searched for during September, ahead of "Wii" and even "Halloween costumes" (Deatsch, 2008). Suffice it to say that children are likely to have trouble discerning what is and is not advertising in these online environments. In one creative study, researchers designed a variety of webpages that included commercial content and asked over 400 children to point to whatever they thought was an advertisement (Ali, Blades, Oates, & Blumberg, 2009). As a comparison, adults were almost perfectly accurate in identifying all the ads on the pages. In contrast, 6-year-olds recognized only 25% of the ads, 8-year-olds recognized about 50%, and 10- to 12-year-olds recognized 75% of the ads. The inclusion of price information in some of the ads did little to help the two younger groups, demonstrating how confusing website commercialism can be. Some critics have called for limiting ads to fixed positions (e.g., upper right corner) or including bridge windows or pages to "physically" separate ads from content on webpages designed for children (Cai & Zhao, 2010).

Unlike other media, the Internet also allows marketers to collect personal information from individuals to be used in promotional efforts, market research, and electronic commerce. And this worries parents. According to a national survey, 73% of parents with home Internet connections

Figure 2.17 Homepage for the Webkinz website.

are nervous about websites having their personal information, and 95% believe that teenagers should have to get their parents' consent before giving out information online (Turow, 2003). Research suggests that parents need to be vigilant. One study of 133 websites popular with children found that 87% collected personal information from the user such as name, e-mail address, birth date, and postal address (Cai & Zhao, 2010). In an earlier study of over 160 websites for kids, roughly 15% of the sites that requested personal information asked for a credit card number (Cai, Gantz, Schwartz, & Wang, 2003). Most alarming, two-thirds of the sites requesting information made no effort to persuade the child to obtain parental permission first.

Recognizing these problems, Congress passed the Children's Online Privacy Protection Act (COPPA) in 1998, to be enforced by the Federal Trade Commission (FTC). The law requires that all websites targeted to children younger than 13 must have a prominent link to a privacy policy that clearly identifies how personal information is collected and used. Despite this ruling, some children's websites still do not post a privacy policy, and many that have one do not make the link very prominent or the policy itself very accessible or readable for parents (Cai & Zhao, 2010; Turow, 2001). In the content analysis of popular children's websites described above (Cai et al., 2003), only 4 of the 162 websites were in full compliance with COPPA. It should be noted that COPPA does not apply to websites targeted to youth over the age of 12, even though parents are concerned about privacy protection for teens as well (Turow, 2003).

Even with explicit policies in place, one of the challenges is that marketing strategies keep changing. Recently, a number of child advocacy groups filed a complaint with the FTC, asserting that several well-known websites aimed at children, such as HappyMeal.com and Nick. com, were encouraging children to provide a friend's email address—without seeking parental consent (Singer, 2012). Such "Tell a friend" or "Play this game and share it with your friends" messages are a powerful form of viral marketing using an online platform. As new tactics evolve, the FTC will have to determine how to apply COPPA rules to these innovations.

Even still, a privacy policy such as COPPA may not be enough to protect families. In a national survey of 10- to 17-year-olds, 31% reported that they had given out personal information to a website (Turow & Nir, 2000). Moreover, 45% of the youngsters said they would exchange personal information on the Web for a free gift, and 25% reported never having read a site's privacy policy. In addition, there is some evidence that a warning about age restrictions for membership on a website may actually increase preteens' willingness to disclose personal information (Miyazaki, Stanaland, & Lwin, 2009). Thus, it seems reasonable to conclude that as long as marketers are free to collect information about users regardless of age, the Internet will be a relatively easy way to discover and try to influence the consumer preferences of youth.

Marketing in Schools

Commercialism in schools has soared in recent years, spurring much public debate about the ethics of such practices (Molnar, Boninger, & Fogarty, 2011). Corporations are eager to partner with schools as a way to reach young consumers, who spend almost 20% of their time in the classroom. In turn, public schools often feel desperate to augment tight budgets, and corporate support offers one way to do so.

Four types of commercial practices can be found in various degrees across American schools (Consumers Union Education Services, 1995; Wartella & Jennings, 2001). First, marketers often advertise directly to students by placing ads on school billboards, buses, or athletic scoreboards, and even in student newspapers and yearbooks (see Figure 2.18). Second, corporations occasionally give away products or coupons to expose children to different brand names. For example, Minute Maid, McDonald's, and Pizza Hut have offered food coupons to students who meet their teachers' reading goals.

Third, corporations frequently sponsor fund-raisers to help schools afford new equipment, uniforms, or class trips. Students themselves become marketers in these efforts, approaching aunts and uncles, neighbors, and even parents' work colleagues. Pitching anything from poinsettia plants to gift wrap to frozen pizzas, students can earn prizes for themselves and money for their school. In a particularly troubling example, Kohl's department stores ran a "Kohl's Cares for Schools" contest during the summer and fall of 2010 (Molnar et al., 2011). To win the race for a $500,000 prize, schools engaged in a variety of activities to gather votes on Facebook, including setting up booths at local community events and creating YouTube videos. The 20 schools with the most votes won the contest, and everyone who voted was put on Kohl's mailing list to receive advertisements and promotional messages.

Fourth, marketers often create educational materials such as workbooks, brochures, and videos on specific curriculum topics. For instance, Shell recently partnered with Scholastic Inc. to produce an "Energize Your Future" curriculum that focused on the importance of producing multiple energy sources and linked Shell to such activities (Molnar et al., 2011). Unfortunately, one study found that nearly 80% of these corporate-sponsored materials contained biased or incomplete information (Consumers Union Education Services, 1995).

A fifth and more controversial form of commercialism in schools is Channel One, a 12-minute daily news program designed for middle and high school students. Introduced in 1990 by Whittle Communications, the program includes 10 minutes of originally produced

Figure 2.18 Advertising in schools.

news for teens and two minutes of advertising. Schools sign a three-year contract that provides them with a dedicated satellite transmission system, a satellite dish, television sets and other display converters in certain classrooms, a preview monitor, and all wiring and maintenance for the equipment. In exchange, a school agrees to show Channel One News on at least 90% of the days that the school is in session. Roughly 7,000 American middle and high schools have entered into this contractual arrangement (Channel One News, n.d.).

Channel One has been challenged on several fronts. Critics have charged that the arrangement cedes control of the curriculum to outside parties, requires students to be a captive audience to ads, and exposes students to messages that run counter to nutritional lessons taught in school (Consumers Union Education Services, 1995). Amid the controversy, several advertisers, such as PepsiCo and Cingular, decided to pull their advertising from the newscast, and the network has struggled financially in recent years (Atkinson, 2007).

Research supports some of the criticisms that have been lodged against Channel One. A study by Brand and Greenberg (1994) found that, compared with nonviewers, students exposed to Channel One gave more favorable ratings to products that were advertised during the newscast. Viewers also expressed more materialistic attitudes than nonviewers did. On the positive side, viewers did seem to learn more about news, particularly those events covered in the daily programs (Greenberg & Brand, 1993).

A similar initiative in Canada, called Youth News Network (YNN), had minimal success. This corporate initiative promised audiovisual and computer equipment to schools in exchange for showing a 12.5-minute newscast that included 2.5 minutes of ads. The service was banned in every Catholic school in Canada and in 6 of the 13 provinces. A report by the Canadian Centre for Policy Alternatives concluded that

> having a corporate presence in the classroom is tantamount to giving such companies school time—and the public money which pays for that time—in which to advertise their products to kids. Our taxes are literally paying for the commercial targeting of our students, and diverting time and money from their education. (Shaker, 2000, p. 19)

Today, nearly 5 million American teens watch advertising on television each day in the classroom ("Who Are We?" 2012). Other students enter contests, receive curriculum materials, and are exposed to hallway ads that promote products. Some believe these arrangements represent innovative ways to support struggling schools (see Richards, Wartella, Morton, & Thompson, 1998). Others view this growing trend as a violation of "the integrity of education" (Consumers Union Education Services, 1995). Regardless of which view is taken, such practices are likely to continue as marketers search for creative ways to reach youth.

Teaching Advertising Literacy

Recognizing the difficulty of changing the advertising environment in the United States, some have called for efforts to teach children how to be more critical consumers. As it turns out, even older children who clearly recognize the selling intent of ads do not typically critique commercials spontaneously while viewing them (Brucks, Armstrong, & Goldberg, 1988; Derbaix & Bree, 1997). In other words, their general skepticism toward advertising is not always activated when they actually encounter commercial messages. One study suggests that a simple cue or reminder can trigger a viewer's cognitive defenses, raising the number of counterarguments that older children produce during exposure to commercials (Brucks et al., 1988).

Other studies have explored more formal training procedures to help children deal with advertising. Roberts, Christenson, Gibson, Mooser, and Goldberg (1980) compared two 15-minute instructional films designed to teach children about commercials: *The Six Billion $$$ Sell*, which focused on tricks and appeals used in ads, and *Seeing Through Commercials*, which focused on how ads are made. Second, third, and fifth graders were randomly assigned to view one of the two films or a control film unrelated to advertising. Results revealed that the treatment films increased children's general skepticism toward advertising as well as their ability to be critical of specific ads. The strongest effects were observed for *The Six Billion $$$ Sell*, the film that detailed specific strategies and showed ad examples. Moreover, the youngest participants, who initially were far more accepting of advertising, learned the most from the films.

Christenson (1982) used excerpts from *The Six Billion $$$ Sell* to create a three-minute public service announcement (PSA) about the nature of advertising. One group of children saw the PSA before watching cartoons embedded with ads, whereas another group simply watched the content without the PSA. The insertion of the PSA increased 1st and 2nd graders' comprehension of the selling intent of ads, and it enhanced skepticism about ads among this younger age group as well as among 5th and 6th graders. Furthermore, the PSA actually lowered children's taste ratings of two food products advertised during the cartoons.

Instruction that is more traditional can teach children about advertising as well. One study found that half-hour training sessions over the course of several days were effective in teaching children as young as 6 how to detect persuasive tricks and strategies in ads (Peterson & Lewis, 1988). In another study, Donohue, Henke, and Meyer (1983) compared two types of instruction: role playing, which had children assume the role of an advertiser to create a commercial, and traditional, which had children watch TV ads and discuss the purpose and nature of commercials. Compared with a control group, both treatments helped 1st graders to better discriminate ads from programs and to be more skeptical of commercials. However, only the traditional instruction increased children's understanding of the persuasive intent of advertising.

Conceptual knowledge of advertising, however, does not necessarily mean that children *use* this information when they are confronted with a highly attractive commercial message. Rozendaal, LaPierre, van Reijmersdal, and Buijzen (2011) point out that children typically process ads under conditions of "low elaboration," meaning that they do not critically evaluate the content of the message. In fact, because most commercial messages contain little information and instead are high in emotional appeal, they actually foster shallow processing. Under such conditions, children have difficulty engaging in the "stop-and-think" response that is needed to defend oneself against a persuasive message (Rozendaal, LaPierre, et al., 2011). In other words, children who are still maturing lack the ability to retrieve their advertising-related knowledge and apply it to a commercial message while they are simultaneously trying to make sense of the message. Such reasoning is consistent with the growth in processing capacity and executive functioning that occurs during childhood and adolescence, as described in Chapter 1.

In support of this idea, the researchers conducted a study in which 8- to 12-year-old children watched a brief TV show that contained a commercial for Lays potato chips (Rozendaal, Buijzen, & Valkenburg, 2012). Children were told either to think aloud while watching the video, stating everything that came to mind, or to write down all the thoughts they had after watching. There was no difference between the two conditions in terms of the number of critical thoughts children had about the commercial. However, the think-aloud method was more effective in decreasing children's desire for the advertised product. The researchers argued that both groups possessed the knowledge about advertising (based on the number of critical thoughts produced), but that only the think-aloud procedure help children *apply* that critical stance while viewing.

In addition to formal and informal instruction, it turns out that parents can help in a number of ways, too (see Figure 2.19). One experiment found that simply reducing grade school children's television and video game use for six months decreased their toy purchase requests compared to those of a control group that did not change media habits (Robinson, Saphir, Kraemer, Varady, & Haydel, 2001). Parents also can talk to their children about the nature of commercials and how to evaluate them. Such discussion can improve younger children's understanding of the purpose of advertising (Ward et al., 1977). Critically discussing commercials with a parent can also reduce children's consumption of advertised foods (Buijzen, 2009) and is associated with fewer purchase requests and less materialism in elementary schoolers (Buijzen & Valkenburg, 2005). One caveat is in order here: Parents need to take into account the difficulty children have in applying what they know when faced with an onslaught of emotionally appealing commercial messages. Parents who watch TV or surf the Internet *with* their children can help activate such critical thinking.

Parental discussion even seems to benefit adolescents. Teens who talk with their parents about consumption show a higher knowledge of prices (R. L. Moore & Stephens, 1975) and more discriminating behavior when making purchases (Moschis & Churchill, 1978). Teens whose parents encourage critical thinking also show more concern about divulging

Figure 2.19

WALL STREET JOURNAL

"...No, he can't really fly...no, the bad guys don't really have a ray gun...no, this cereal really isn't the best food in the whole world...no, it won't make you as strong as a giant..."

SOURCE: Reprinted with permission from Tribune Media Services.

privacy information on the Internet (Moscardelli & Divine, 2007). As with other types of media content (see Chapter 12), parental mediation can play an important role in preparing youth for daily encounters with commercial messages.

Conclusion

Children are born to become consumers in the United States. They typically visit their first store at the tender age of 2 months, and by the time they reach 2 years, most have made a request for a product (McNeal, 2007). Their bedrooms are filled with Disney characters, designer crib sheets, and Baby Gap clothes, and their playrooms are stuffed with all kinds of toys. By the time children reach preschool, they are watching their favorite toy-based cartoons, seeing several hours' worth of TV advertising each week, and making regular trips with a parent to the grocery store, fast food restaurants, and Toys'R'Us. All of this exposure comes at a time when children are very naive about commercial messages and trusting of their content.

As children reach the early elementary school years, they gradually learn about the motives behind advertising and the tactics used in commercials. Some of this knowledge helps them to become more skeptical of such messages. Yet keeping these cognitive defenses in mind is not always easy for them when they confront a slick and highly entertaining commercial suggesting that everyone else has a particular new toy. Certainly, television is not the only source of these desires. School-aged children may be most vulnerable when commercialism invades their classroom, becoming part of the decor or even the curriculum itself. And spending time online and with mobile devices such as smartphones may confuse children even more, as marketing becomes intimately intertwined with noncommercial content.

In the face of all this commercialism, some critics have argued that advertising is inherently unfair to young children and ought to be eliminated from content targeted to those younger than age 8. An opposite position holds that children will never learn to be consumers unless they are exposed to commercial messages. A third intermediary position is that parents and educators need to develop ways to help youth become more critical consumers. As children's discretionary income grows and they spend more time surfing websites, wandering in shopping malls, and watching TV on personal laptops and alone in their bedrooms, early training in critical consumer skills seems crucial.

Exercises

1. Find a magazine advertisement targeted to children. What type of product is being advertised? Does it fit into one of the top four categories of children's ads found on television (see the Kunkel & Gantz, 1992, study above)? What is the main appeal used in this ad to persuade children? Is there any disclaimer offered in the ad? If so, is it likely to be noticed or understood by a child? Is there anything in the ad that might be misleading or confusing for a 5-year-old child? For a 10-year-old child?

2. Find a magazine ad targeted to teens. What type of product is being advertised? Do you see evidence of gender or racial stereotyping in the ad? What is the main appeal used in the ad? Is there anything about the ad that might make teens feel self-conscious about their own physical appearance?

3. Think about your childhood. What is the first toy purchase you remember feeling disappointed about? How old were you? Did you buy the toy with your own money? Did advertising have anything to do with your disappointment? How did your mother or father respond to your disappointment? Did your parents discuss advertising with you?

4. Since the late 1990s, Sweden has not allowed advertisements to air immediately before, during, or after a television program oriented primarily to children under 12 years of age. Do you think such a ban is a good idea in the United States? Why or why not? Instead of an all-out ban, can you think of any other types of regulation of children's advertising that might be easier to enact in the United States?

5. Find two popular websites for children, one that is highly commercialized and one that is not. For example, you could compare the Barbie site (www.barbie.com) with a site called Math for Kids (www.math-exercises-for-kids.com), which is designed to teach children math lessons. Design a coding scheme that allows you to answer the following: How much advertising is on each website? Are there features of the sites that look like content but are actually ads? Do the sites ask children for personal information? If so, is there a privacy policy? Critique each site, thinking about a 9-year-old user without a parent in the room.

6. Harry Potter is an example of a remarkably successful brand story. A total of seven books have been published about the boy wizard, and eight live-action movies have been made. In addition, there have been hundreds of tie-in products made available for purchase, from candy to computer games. List as many examples as you can that reflect how this book series has been commercialized across different media. Have you ever spent any money on Harry Potter products? When you were a child, was there any movie you can remember that was similarly successful? What has changed in the past 20 years regarding the promotion of media stories and their characters? Find a current successful brand story and compare it to the Harry Potter franchise in terms of commercialization, success, and target audience.

7. You are a principal of a large high school in a rural area. Your school band has been invited to perform in Washington, DC, and your basketball team is ranked highly in the state. But the band desperately needs new uniforms, and the basketball team needs new athletic equipment, both of which are not in your budget. You are approached by the head of B&W Marketing, who offers you $100,000 in exchange for placing a select number of advertisements in school hallways. What should you do? What factors should you consider in making your decision?

8. Using all the research cited in this chapter, design a video that would help teach a 6-year-old about commercial advertising in today's society. What skills should you focus on? How will your video cover different media (e.g., television, Internet)? How will you help children to apply what they learn when they actually encounter commercial messages? Now imagine that you need to design a video for 10-year-olds. How will the content of your video change?

References

Adler, R. (1980). Children's television advertising: History of the issue. In E. L. Palmer & A. Dorr (Eds.), *Children and the faces of television: Teaching, violence, selling* (pp. 237–248). New York, NY: Academic Press.

Alexander, A., Benjamin, L. M., Hoerrner, K., & Roe, D. (1998). "We'll be back in a moment": A content analysis of advertisements in children's television in the 1950s. *Journal of Advertising, 27*(3), 1–9.

Ali, M., Blades, M., Oates, C., & Blumberg, F. (2009). Young children's ability to recognize advertisements in web page designs. *British Journal of Developmental Psychology, 27,* 71–83.

Annicelli, C. (1999, June). *Monster cash;* Pokémon *has made a fortune; Prepare for the second wave.* Retrieved from http://www.findarticles.com/cf_0/m3196/6_97/55084237/p1/article.jhtml.

Atkin, C. K. (1976). Children's social learning from television advertising: Research evidence on observational modeling of product consumption. *Advances in Consumer Research, 3,* 513–519.

Atkin, C. K. (1978). Observation of parent-child interaction in supermarket decision-making. *Journal of Marketing, 42*(4), 41–45.

Atkin, C. (1980). Effects of television advertising on children. In E. L. Palmer & A. Dorr (Eds.), *Children and the faces of television: Teaching, violence, selling* (pp. 287–305). New York, NY: Academic Press.

Atkin, C. (1982). Television advertising and socialization to consumer roles. In D. Pearl, L. Bouthilet, & J. Lazar (Eds.), *Television and behavior: Ten years of scientific progress and implications for the eighties* (Vol. 2, pp. 191–200). Washington, DC: Government Printing Office.

Atkin, C., & Block, M. (1983). Effectiveness of celebrity endorsers. *Journal of Advertising Research, 23*(1), 57–61.

Atkinson, C. (2007, April 23). *Kicked out of class: Primedia sheds in-school net.* Retrieved from http://www.commercialalert.org/news

Autherland, A., & Thompson, B. (2003). *Kidfluence: The marketer's guide to understanding and reaching Generation Y—kids, tweens, and teens.* New York, NY: McGraw-Hill.

Bakir, A. (2009). "Some assembly required": Comparing disclaimers in children's TV advertising in Turkey and the United States. *Journal of Advertising Research, 49*(1), 93–103.

Barcus, F. E. (1980). The nature of television advertising to children. In E. L. Palmer & A. Dorr (Eds.), *Children and the faces of television: Teaching, violence, selling* (pp. 273–285). New York, NY: Academic Press.

Batada, A., & Borzekowski, D. (2008). Snap! Crackle! What? Recognition of cereal advertisements and understanding of persuasive intent among urban, minority children in the US. *Journal of Children and Media, 2*(1), 19–36.

Bever, T. G., Smith, M. L., Bengen, B., & Johnson, T. G. (1975). Young viewers' troubling response to TV ads. *Harvard Business Review, 53,* 109–120.

Blatt, J., Spencer, L., & Ward, S. (1972). A cognitive development study of children's reactions to television advertising. In G. Comstock, J. Murry, & E. A. Rubinstein (Eds.), *Television and social behavior* (Vol. 4, pp. 452–467). Washington, DC: Government Printing Office.

Boush, D. M., Friestad, M., & Rose, G. M. (1994). Adolescent skepticism toward TV advertising and knowledge of advertiser tactics. *Journal of Consumer Research, 21*(1), 165–175.

Bramlett-Solomon, S., & Roeder, Y. (2008). Looking at race in children's television. *Journal of Children and Media, 2*(1), 56–66.

Brand, J. E., & Greenberg, B. S. (1994). Commercials in the classroom: The impact of Channel One advertising. *Journal of Advertising Research, 34*(1), 18–27.

Brass, K. (1999, November 21). Pokemon *fad at a fever pitch—and what a pitch indeed.* Retrieved from http://www.findarticles.com/cf_0/m0VPW/47_27/ 58047459/p1/article.html

Brucks, M., Armstrong, G. M., & Goldberg, M. (1988). Children's use of cognitive defenses against television advertising: A cognitive response approach. *Journal of Consumer Research, 14,* 471–482.

Buckingham, D. (2011). *The material child: Growing up in consumer culture.* Cambridge, UK: Polity Press.

Bucy, E. P., Kim, S. C., & Park, M. C. (2011). Host selling in cyberspace: Product personalities and character advertising on popular children's websites. *New Media Society, 13*(8), 1245–1264.

Buijzen, M. (2009). The effectiveness of parental communication in modifying the relation between food advertising and children's consumption behaviour. *British Journal of Developmental Psychology, 27,* 105–121.

Buijzen, M., & Valkenburg, P. (2000). The impact of television advertising on children's Christmas wishes. *Journal of Broadcasting and Electronic Media, 44,* 456–470.

Buijzen, M., & Valkenburg, P. M. (2002). Appeals in television advertising: A content analysis of commercials aimed at children and teenagers. *Communications, 27,* 349–364.

Buijzen, M., & Valkenburg, P. M. (2003a). The effects of television advertising on materialism, parent-child conflict, and unhappiness: A review of research. *Applied Developmental Psychology, 24,* 437–456.

Buijzen, M., & Valkenburg, P. M. (2003b). The unintended effects of television advertising. *Communication Research, 30,* 483–503.

Buijzen, M., & Valkenburg, P. M. (2005). Parental mediation of undesired advertising effects. *Journal of Broadcasting and Electronic Media, 49,* 153–165.

Buijzen, M., Van Reijmersdal, E. A., & Owen, L. H. (2010). Introducing the PCMC model: An investigative framework for young people's processing of commercialized media content. *Communication Theory, 20,* 427–450.

Burr, P., & Burr, R. M. (1977). Product recognition and premium appeal. *Journal of Communication, 27,* 115–117.

Business Wire. (2011, September 7). *Research and markets: Teen spending & behavior – 30 million U.S. teens aged 13–19 wielding more than $200 billion in buying power.* Retrieved from http://www.businesswire .com/news/home/20110927005677/en/Research-Markets-Teen-Spending-Behavior---30

Butter, E. J., Popovich, P. M., Stackhouse, R. H., & Garner, R. K. (1981). Discrimination of television programs and commercials by preschool children. *Journal of Advertising Research, 21*(2), 53–56.

Cai, X., Gantz, W., Schwartz, N., & Wang, X. (2003). Children's website adherence to the FTC's online privacy protection rule. *Journal of Applied Communication Research, 31,* 346–362.

Cai, X., & Zhao, X. (2010). Click here, kids! Online advertising practices on popular children's websites. *Journal of Children and Media, 4*(2), 135–154.

Calvert, S. L. (2008). The children's television act. In S. L. Calvert & B. J. Wilson (Eds.), *Blackwell handbook of child development and the media* (pp. 455–478). New York, NY: Blackwell.

Carter, O. B. J., Patterson, L. J., Donovan, R. J., Ewing, M. T., & Roberts, C. M. (2011). Children's understanding of the selling versus persuasive intent of junk food advertising: Implications for regulation. *Social Science & Medicine, 72,* 962–968.

Center for Science in the Public Interest. (1988, September 4). *Kids are aware of booze as presidents, survey finds* [Press release]. Washington, DC: Author.

Channel One News. (n.d.). *Who are we?* Retrieved from http://www.channelone.com/about/

Chia, S. C. (2010). How social influence mediates media effects on adolescents' materialism. *Communication Research, 37*(3), 400–419.

Children Now. (2006). *The future of children's media: Advertising* [Conference report]. Oakland, CA: Author.

Christenson, P. G. (1982). Children's perceptions of TV commercials and products: The effects of PSA's. *Communication Research, 9,* 491–524.

Churchill, G., Jr., & Moschis, G. P. (1979). Television and interpersonal influences on adolescent consumer learning. *Journal of Consumer Research, 5*(1), 23–35.

Cicchirillo, V., & Lin, J. (2011). Stop playing with your food: A comparison of for-profit and non-profit food-related advergames. *Journal of Advertising Research, 51*(3), 484-498.

Colby, P. A. (1993, April). *From* Hot Wheels *to* Teenage Mutant Ninja Turtles*: The evolution of the definition of program length commercials on children's television.* Paper presented at the annual meeting of the Broadcast Education Association, Las Vegas, NV.

Condry, J. C., Bence, P. J., & Scheibe, C. L. (1988). Nonprogram content of children's television. *Journal of Broadcasting and Electronic Media, 32,* 255–270.

Consumers Union Education Services. (1995). *Captive kids: A report on commercial pressures on kids at school.* Yonkers, NY: Author.

Creamer, M. (2005). Foul mouth: Stealth marketers flirt with law. *Advertising Age, 76*(40), 6.

Culley, J., Lazer, W., & Atkin, C. (1976). The experts look at children's television. *Journal of Broadcasting, 20,* 3–20.

Culp, J., Bell, R. A., & Cassady, D. (2010). Characteristics of food industry web sites and "advergames" targeting children. *Journal of Nutrition Education and Behavior, 42*(3), 197–201.

Deatsch, K. (2008). *EBay and Webkinz once again top most-searched terms.* Retrieved from http://www .internetretailer.com/2008/10/28/ebay-and-webkinz-once-again-top-most-searched-terms

DeDroog, S. M., Valkenburg, P. M., & Buijzen, M. (2011). Using brand characters to promote young children's liking of and purchase requests for fruit. *Journal of Health Communication, 16,* 79–89.

Derbaix, C., & Bree, J. (1997). The impact of children's affective reactions elicited by commercials on attitudes toward the advertisement and the brand. *International Journal of Research in Marketing, 14,* 207–229.

Derbaix, C., & Pecheux, C. (2003). A new scale to assess children's attitude toward TV advertising. *Journal of Advertising Research, 43,* 390–399.

Dixon, H. G., Scully, M. L., Wakefield, M. A., White, V. M., & Crawford, D. A. (2007). The effects of television advertisements for junk food versus nutritious food on children's food attitudes and preferences. *Social Science and Medicine, 65,* 1311–1323.

Donohue, T. R., Henke, L. L., & Donohue, W. A. (1980). Do kids know what TV commercials intend? *Journal of Advertising Research, 20*(5), 51–57.

Donohue, T. R., Henke, L. L., & Meyer, T. P. (1983). Learning about television commercials: The impact of instructional units on children's perceptions of motive and intent. *Journal of Broadcasting, 27,* 251–261.

Dubow, J. S. (1995). Advertising recognition and recall by age—including teens. *Journal of Advertising Research, 35*(5), 55–60.

Dunnewind, S. (2004, November 20). Teen recruits create word-of-mouth "buzz" to hook peers on products. *Seattle Times.* Retrieved from http://www.seattle times.nwsource.com

Enrico, D. (1999). Top 10 advertising icons. *Advertising Age, 70*(14), 42–46.

Faber, R. J., Perloff, R. M., & Hawkins, R. P. (1982). Antecedents of children's comprehension of television advertising. *Journal of Broadcasting, 26,* 575–584.

Fischer, P. M., Schwartz, M. P., Richards, J. W., Goldstein, A. O., & Rojas, T. H. (1991). Brand logo recognition by children aged 3 to 6 years: Mickey Mouse and Old Joe the Camel. *Journal of the American Medical Association, 266,* 3145–3148.

Folkvord, F., Anschutz, D. J., Buijzen, M., & Valkenburg, P. (2013). The effect of playing advergames that promote energy-dense snacks or fruit on actual food intake among children. *The American Journal of Clinical Nutrition, 97,* 239–245.

Fox, R. F. (1996). *Harvesting minds: How TV commercials control kids.* Westport, CT: Praeger/Greenwood.

Galst, J. P., & White, M. A. (1976). The unhealthy persuader: The reinforcing value of television and children's purchase-influencing attempts at the supermarket. *Child Development, 47,* 1089–1096.

Gantz, W., Schwartz, N., Angelini, J. R., & Rideout, V. (2007). *Food for thought: Television food advertising to children in the United States.* Menlo Park, CA: Kaiser Family Foundation.

Goldberg, M. E. (1990). A quasi-experiment assessing the effectiveness of TV advertising directed to children. *Journal of Marketing Research, 27,* 445–454.

Goldberg, M. E., & Gorn, G. J. (1978). Some unintended consequences of TV advertising to children. *Journal of Consumer Research, 5*(1), 22–29.

Gorn, G. J., & Goldberg, M. E. (1977). The impact of television advertising on children from low income families. *Journal of Consumer Research, 4*(2), 86–88.

Gorn, G. J., & Goldberg, M. E. (1980). Children's responses to repetitive television commercials. *Journal of Consumer Research, 6,* 421–424.

Graft, K. (2007, April 22). *This week: The real Pokemon hits US.* Retrieved from http://www.next-gen .biz.com

Greenberg, B. S., & Brand, J. E. (1993). Television news and advertising in schools: The "Channel One" controversy. *Journal of Communication, 43,* 143–151.

Greer, D., Potts, R., Wright, J. C., & Huston, A. C. (1982). The effects of television commercial form and commercial placement on children's social behavior and attention. *Child Development, 53,* 611–619.

Harris, J. L., Speers, S. E., Schwartz, M. B., & Brownell, K. D. (2012). US food company branded advergames on the Internet: Children's exposure and effects on snack consumption. *Journal of Children and Media, 6,* 51–68.

Harrison, K. (2006). Fast and sweet: Nutritional attributes to television food advertisements with and without Black characters. *Howard Journal of Communication, 17,* 249–264.

Harrison, K., & Bond, B. J. (2007). Gaming magazines and the drive for muscularity in preadolescent boys: A longitudinal examination. *Body Image, 4,* 269–277.

Harrison, K., & Hefner, V. (2006). Media exposure, current and future body ideals, and disordered eating among preadolescent girls: A longitudinal panel study. *Journal of Youth and Adolescence, 35,* 153–163.

Hawn, C. (2007, March 23). Time to play, money to spend. *CNN Money.* Retrieved from http://money .cnn.com/magazines/business2

Henry, H. K. M., & Borzekowski, D. L. G. (2011). The nag factor: A mixed-methodology study in the US of young children's requests for advertised products. *Journal of Children and Media, 5*(3), 298–317.

Hof, M. (2012). Internet ad spending bucks economy to grow 12% in Q. *Forbes*. Retrieved from http://www.forbes.com/sites/roberthof/2012/07/10/internet-ad-spending-bucks-economy-to-grow-12-in-q1/

Howard, T. (2002, September 9). Real winner of "American Idol": Coke. *USA Today*, p. 6B.

Hoy, M. G., Young, C. E., & Mowen, J. C. (1986). Animated host-selling advertisements: Their impacts on young children's recognition, attitudes, and behavior. *Journal of Public Policy and Marketing, 5*, 171–184.

Huston, A. C., Greer, D., Wright, J. C., Welch, R., & Ross, R. (1984). Children's comprehension of televised formal features with masculine and feminine connotations. *Developmental Psychology, 20*, 707–716.

Institute of Medicine. (2006). *Food marketing to children and youth: Threat or opportunity?* Washington, DC: National Academy of Sciences.

Jones, R. (2000). *Kids are target of* Pokemon's *shrewd marketing effort*. Retrieved from http://abcnews.go.com/sections/business/thestreet/pokemon_991117.html

Kahlenberg, S. G., & Hein, M. M. (2010). Progression on Nickelodeon? Gender-role stereotypes in toy commercials. *Sex Roles, 62*, 830–847.

Kaikati, A. M., & Kaikati, J. G. (2004). Stealth marketing: How to reach consumers surreptitiously. *California Management Review, 98*, 48–58.

Khermouch, G., & Green, J. (2001, July 30). Buzz marketing: Suddenly this stealth strategy is hot—but it's still fraught with risk. *BusinessWeek*. Retrieved from http://www.businessweek.com

Kinsky, E. S., & Bichard, S. (2011). "Mom! I've seen that on a commercial!" US preschooler's recognition of brand logos. *Young Consumers, 12*(2), 145–156.

Kline, S. (1993). *Out of the garden: Toys, TV, and children's culture in the age of marketing*. New York, NY: Verso.

Krugman, D. M., Cameron, G. T., & White, C. M. (1995). Visual attention to programming and commercials: The use of in-home observations. *Journal of Advertising, 24*(1), 1–12.

Kunkel, D. (1988). Children and host-selling television commercials. *Communication Research, 15*, 71–92.

Kunkel, D. (2010). Mismeasurement of children's understanding of the persuasive intent of advertising. *Journal of Children and Media, 4*(1), 109–117.

Kunkel, D., & Gantz, W. (1992). Children's television advertising in the multichannel environment. *Journal of Communication, 42*(3), 134–152.

Kunkel, D., Wilcox, B. L., Cantor, J., Palmer, E., Linn, S., & Dowrick, P. (2004). *Report of the APA Task Force on Advertising and Children*. Washington, DC: American Psychological Association. Retrieved from http://www.apa.org/releases/childrenads.pdf

Lagorio, C. (2009, February 11). Resources: Marketing to kids. *CBS News*. Retrieved from http://www.cbsnews.com/2100-500823_162-2798401.html

Larson, M. S. (2001). Interactions, activities and gender in children's television commercials: A content analysis. *Journal of Broadcasting and Electronic Media, 45*, 41–56.

Lee, M., Choi, Y., Quilliam, E. T., & Cole, R. T. (2009). Playing with food: Content analysis of food advergames. *The Journal of Consumer Affairs, 43*(1), 129–154.

Levin, S. R., Petros, T. V., & Petrella, F. W. (1982). Preschoolers' awareness of television advertising. *Child Development, 53*, 933–937.

Levinson, J. C. (2007). *Guerrilla marketing* (4th ed.). New York, NY: Houghton Mifflin.

Lewin-Jones, J., & Mitra, B. (2009). Gender roles in television commercials and primary school children in the UK. *Journal of Children and Media, 3*(1), 35–50.

Liebert, D. E., Sprafkin, J. N., Liebert, R. M., & Rubinstein, E. A. (1977). Effects of television commercial disclaimers on the product expectations of children. *Journal of Communication, 27,* 118–124.

Macklin, M. C. (1985). Do young children understand the selling intent of commercials? *Journal of Consumer Affairs, 19,* 293–304.

Macklin, M. C. (1987). Preschoolers' understanding of the informational function of television advertising. *Journal of Consumer Research, 14,* 229–239.

Mangleburg, T. F., & Bristol, T. (1999). Socialization and adolescents' skepticism toward advertising. In M. C. Macklin & L. Carlson (Eds.), *Advertising to children: Concepts and controversies* (pp. 27–48). Thousand Oaks, CA: Sage.

Martin, M. C. (1997). Children's understanding of the intent of advertising: A meta-analysis. *Journal of Public Policy and Marketing, 16,* 205–216.

Martin, M. C., & Gentry, J. W. (1997). Stuck in the model trap: The effects of beautiful models in ads on female pre-adolescents and adolescents. *Journal of Advertising, 26*(2), 19–33.

Martin, M. C., & Kennedy, P. F. (1993). Advertising and social comparison: Consequences for female pre-adolescents and adolescents. *Psychology and Marketing, 10,* 513–530.

Mazur, L. A. (1996, May/June). Marketing madness. *E Magazine: The Environmental Magazine, 7*(3), 36–42.

McAllister, M. P. (2007). "Girls with a passion for fashion": The Bratz brand as integrated spectacular consumption. *Journal of Children and Media, 1,* 244–258.

McNeal, J. U. (1998). Tapping the three kids' markets. *American Demographics, 20*(4), 36–41.

McNeal, J. U. (1999). *The kids' market: Myths and realities.* Ithaca, NY: Paramount Market.

McNeal, J. U. (2007). *On becoming a consumer: Development of consumer behavior patterns in childhood.* Burlington, MA: Butterworth-Heinemann.

Miller, J. H., & Busch, P. (1979). Host selling vs. premium TV commercials: An experimental evaluation of their influence on children. *Journal of Marketing Research, 16,* 323–332.

Minow, N. (2004, September 21). "Have you heard?" Stealth advertising puts products and pitches everywhere . . . and you may never know. *Chicago Tribune.* Retrieved from http://proquest.umi.com

Miyazaki, A. D., Stanaland, A. J. S., & Lwin, M. O. (2009). Self-regulatory safeguards and the online privacy of preteen children: Implications for the advertising industry. *Journal of Advertising, 38*(4), 79–91.

Molnar, A., Boninger, F., & Fogarty, J. (2011). *The educational cost of schoolhouse commercialism—the fourteenth annual report on schoolhouse commercializing trends: 2010–2011.* Boulder, CO: National Education Policy Center. Retrieved from http://nepc.colorado.edu/publication/schoolhouse-commercialism-2011

Montgomery, K. C., & Chester, J. (2009). Interactive food and beverage marketing: Targeting adolescents in the digital age. *Journal of Adolescent Health, 45,* S18–S29.

Moore, R. L., & Stephens, L. F. (1975). Some communication and demographic determinants of adolescent consumer learning. *Journal of Communication, 29,* 197–201.

Moore, E. S. (2006). *It's child's play: Advergaming and the online marketing of food to children.* Menlo Park, CA: Kaiser Family Foundation.

Morris, L. A., Mazis, M. B., & Brinberg, D. (1989). Risk disclosures in televised drug advertising to consumers. *Journal of Public Policy and Marketing, 8,* 64–80.

Moscardelli, D. M., & Divine, R. (2007). Adolescents' concern for privacy when using the Internet: An empirical analysis of predictors and relationships with privacy-protecting behaviors. *Family and Consumer Sciences Research Behavior, 35,* 232–252.

Moschis, G. P. (1978). Teenagers' responses to retailing stimuli. *Journal of Retailing, 54,* 80–93.

Moschis, G. P., & Churchill, G. A. (1978). Consumer socialization: A theoretical and empirical analysis. *Journal of Marketing Research, 15,* 599–609.

Moschis, G. P., & Moore, R. L. (1979). Decision making among the young: A socialization perspective. *Journal of Consumer Research, 6,* 101–112.

Moschis, G. P., & Moore, R. L. (1982). A longitudinal study of television advertising effects. *Journal of Consumer Research, 9,* 279–286.

Muehling, D. D., & Kolbe, R. H. (1999). A comparison of children's and prime-time fine-print advertising disclosure practices. In M. C. Macklin & L. Carlson (Eds.), *Advertising to children: Concepts and controversies* (pp. 143–164). Thousand Oaks, CA: Sage.

New American Dream. (2002). *Thanks to ads, kids won't take no, no, no, no, no, no, no, no, no for an answer.* Retrieved from http://www.newdream.org/kids/poll.php

Owen, L., Hang, H., Lewis, C., & Auty, S. (2012). Children's processing of embedded brand messages: Product placement and the role of conceptual fluency. In L. J. J. Shrum (Ed.), *The psychology of entertainment media* (2nd ed., pp. 65–92). New York, NY: Routledge.

Palmer, E. L., & McDowell, C. N. (1979). Program/commercial separators in children's television programming. *Journal of Communication, 29,* 197–201.

Palmer, E. L., & McDowell, C. N. (1981). Children's understanding of nutritional information presented in breakfast cereal commercials. *Journal of Broadcasting, 25,* 295–301.

Palmerton, P. R., & Judas, J. (1994, July). *Selling violence: Television commercials targeted to children.* Paper presented at the annual meeting of the International Communication Association, Sydney, Australia.

Pecora, N. O. (1998). *The business of children's entertainment.* New York, NY: Guilford.

Pereira, C. (2011). Pokemon Black & White *day one sales exceed 1 million.* Retrieved from http://www.1up.com/news/pokemon-black-white-day-one-sales-1-million

Peterson, L., & Lewis, K. E. (1988). Preventive intervention to improve children's discriminating of the persuasive tactics in televised advertising. *Journal of Pediatric Psychology, 3,* 163–170.

Pine, K. J., & Nash, A. (2003). Barbie or Betty? Preschool children's preference for branded products and evidence for gender-linked differences. *Developmental and Behavioral Pediatrics, 24,* 219–224.

Resnik, A., & Stern, B. L. (1977). Children's television advertising and brand choice: A laboratory experiment. *Journal of Advertising, 6*(3), 11–17.

Richards, J. I., Wartella, E. A., Morton, C., & Thompson, L. (1998). The growing commercialization of schools: Issues and practices. *Annals of the American Academy of Political and Social Science, 557,* 148–163.

Richins, M. L. (1991). Social comparison and the idealized images of advertising. *Journal of Consumer Research, 18,* 71–83.

Roberts, D. F. (1982). Children and commercials: Issues, evidence, interventions. *Prevention in Human Services, 2*(1/2), 19–35.

Roberts, D. F., Christenson, P., Gibson, W. A., Mooser, L., & Goldberg, M. E. (1980). Developing discriminating consumers. *Journal of Communication, 30*(3), 94–105.

Robertson, T. S., & Rossiter, J. R. (1974). Children and commercial persuasion: An attribution theory analysis. *Journal of Consumer Research, 1,* 13–20.

Robertson, T. S., & Rossiter, J. R. (1977). Children's responsiveness to commercials. *Journal of Communication, 27,* 101–106.

Robertson, T. S., Ward, S., Gatignon, H., & Klees, D. M. (1989). Advertising and children: A cross-cultural study. *Communication Research, 16,* 459–485.

Robinson, T. N., Borzekowski, D. L., Matheson, D. M., & Kramer, H. C. (2007). Effects of fast food branding on young children's taste preferences. *Archives of Pediatrics and Adolescent Medicine, 161,* 792–797.

Robinson, T. N., Saphir, M. N., Kraemer, H. C., Varady, A., & Haydel, K. F. (2001). Effects of reducing television viewing on children's requests for toys: A randomized controlled trial. *Journal of Developmental and Behavioral Pediatrics, 22*(3), 185–187.

Rosenberg, J. M. (1992, February 18). Toymaker upbeat about coming year. *Santa Barbara News Press,* p. C4.

Ross, R. P., Campbell, T. A., Wright, J. C., Huston, A. C., Rice, M. L., & Turk, P. (1984). When celebrities talk, children listen: An experimental analysis of children's responses to TV ads with celebrity endorsement. *Journal of Applied Developmental Psychology, 5*(3), 185–202.

Rozendaal, E., Buijzen, M., & Valkenburg, P. (2009). Do children's cognitive advertising defenses reduce their desire for advertised products? *Communications, 34,* 287–303.

Rozendaal, E., Buijzen, M., & Valkenburg, P. (2011). Children's understanding of advertisers' persuasive tactics. *International Journal of Advertising, 30*(2), 329–350.

Rozendaal, E., Buijzen, M., & Valkenburg, P. (2012). Think-aloud process superior to thought-listing in increasing children's critical processing of advertising. *Human Communication Research, 38,* 199–221.

Rozendaal, E., LaPierre, M. A., van Reijmersdal, E. A., & Buijzen, M. (2011). Reconsidering advertising literacy as a defense against advertising effects. *Media Psychology, 14*(4), 333–354.

Schmitt, K. L., Woolf, K. D., & Anderson, D. K. (2003). Viewing the viewers: Viewing behaviors by children and adults during television programs and commercials. *Journal of Communication, 53,* 265–281.

Schor, J. B. (2004). *Born to buy: The commercialized child and the new commercial culture.* New York, NY: Scribner's.

Shaker, E. (Ed.). (2000, July). *In the corporate interest: The YNN experience in Canadian schools.* Ottawa, Ontario: Canadian Centre for Policy Alternatives. Retrieved from http://policyalternatives.ca/documents/National_Office_Pubs/ynnexperience.pdf

Sheikh, A. A., & Moleski, L. M. (1977). Conflict in the family over commercials. *Journal of Communication, 27,* 152–157.

Shin, A. (2007, April 8). TV shows targeting the diaper demographic. *Washington Post.* Retrieved from http://www.nashuatelegraph.com

Singer, N. (2012, August 22). Web sites accused of collecting data on children. *New York Times.* Retrieved from http://www.nytimes.com/2012/08/22/business/media/web-sites-accused-of-collecting-data-on-children.html?_r=0

Smith, S. L., & Atkin, C. (2003). Television advertising and children: Examining the intended and unintended effects. In E. L. Palmer & B. M. Young (Eds.), *The faces of televisual media: Teaching, violence, selling to children* (pp. 301–326). Mahwah, NJ: Lawrence Erlbaum.

Stern, B. L., & Resnik, A. J. (1978). Children's understanding of a televised commercial disclaimer. In S. C. Jain (Ed.), *Research frontiers in marketing: Dialogues and directions* (pp. 332–336). Chicago, IL: American Marketing Association.

Stice, E., & Shaw, H. E. (1994). Adverse effects of the media portrayed thin-ideal on women and linkages to bulimic symptomatology. *Journal of Social and Clinical Psychology, 13,* 288–308.

Stoneman, Z., & Brody, G. H. (1981). The indirect impact of child-oriented advertisement on mother-child interactions. *Journal of Applied Developmental Psychology, 2,* 369–376.

Stutts, M. A., Vance, D., & Hudleson, S. (1981). Program-commercial separators in children's television: Do they help a child tell the difference between Bugs Bunny and the Quik Rabbit? *Journal of Advertising, 10*(2), 16–25.

Tan, A. S. (1979). TV beauty ads and role expectations of adolescent female viewers. *Journalism Quarterly, 56,* 283–288.

Teenage Research Unlimited. (2004). *Teens spent $175 billion in 2003.* Retrieved from http://www.teenresearch.com/PRview.cfm?edit_id=168

Turow, J. (2001). *Privacy policies on children's websites: Do they play by the rule?* Washington, DC: Annenberg Public Policy Center of the University of Pennsylvania.

Turow, J. (2003). *Americans & online privacy: The system is broken.* Washington, DC: Annenberg Public Policy Center of the University of Pennsylvania.

Turow, J., & Nir, L. (2000). *The Internet and the family 2000: The view from parents; the view from kids.* Washington, DC: Annenberg Public Policy Center of the University of Pennsylvania.

Valkenburg, P. M., & Buijzen, M. (2005). Identifying determinants of young children's brand awareness: Television, parents and peers. *Journal of Applied Developmental Psychology, 4,* 456–468.

Valkenburg, P. M., & Cantor, J. (2001). The development of a child into a consumer. *Journal of Applied Developmental Psychology, 22*(1), 61–72.

Vega, V., & Roberts, D. F. (2011). Linkages between materialism and young people's television and advertising exposure in a US sample. *Journal of Children and Media, 5*(2), 181–193.

Viral marketing agency releases tool to track online buzz. (2007, April 14). Retrieved from http://www .promotionworld.com/news/press/070416WebbedMarketing.html

Ward, S., Levinson, D., & Wackman, D. (1972). Children's attention to advertising. In E. A. Rubinstein, G. A. Comstock, & J. P. Murray (Eds.), *Television and social behavior* (Vol. 4, pp. 491–515). Washington, DC: Government Printing Office.

Ward, S., & Wackman, D. (1972). Family and media influences on adolescent consumer learning. In E. A. Rubinstein, A. Comstock, & J. P. Murray (Eds.), *Television and social behavior* (Vol. 4, pp. 554–565). Washington, DC: Government Printing Office.

Ward, S., & Wackman, D. B. (1973). Children's information processing of television advertising. In P. Clarke (Ed.), *New models for mass communication research* (pp. 119–146). Beverly Hills, CA: Sage.

Ward, S., Wackman, D. B., & Wartella, E. (1977). *How children learn to buy: The development of consumer information-processing skills.* Beverly Hills, CA: Sage.

Warren, R., Wicks, R. H., Wicks, J. L., Fosu, I., & Chung, D. (2008). Food and beverage advertising on US television: A comparison of child-targeted versus general audience commercials. *Journal of Broadcasting and Electronic Media, 52*(2), 231–246.

Wartella, E., & Ettema, J. S. (1974). A cognitive developmental study of children's attention to television commercials. *Communication Research, 1,* 69–88.

Wartella, E., & Jennings, N. (2001). Hazards and possibilities of commercial TV in the schools. In D. G. Singer & J. L. Singer (Eds.), *Handbook of children and the media* (pp. 557–570). Thousand Oaks, CA: Sage.

Waters, H. F., & Uehling, M. D. (1985, May 13). Toying with kids' TV. *Newsweek, 105,* 85.

Welch, R. L., Huston-Stein, A., Wright, J. C., & Plehal, R. (1979). Subtle sex-role cues in children's commercials. *Journal of Communication, 29,* 202–209.

Wells, T. (2011). *Chasing youth culture and getting it right.* Hoboken, NJ: John Wiley.

Wicks, J. L., Warren, R., Fosu, I., & Wicks, R. H. (2009). Dual-modality disclaimers, emotional appeals, and production techniques in food advertising airing during programs rated for children. *Journal of Advertising, 38*(4), 93–105.

Wilcox, B. L., & Kunkel, D. (1996). Taking television seriously: Children and television policy. In E. F. Zigler & S. L. Kagan (Eds.), *Children, families, and government: Preparing for the twenty-first century* (pp. 333–352). New York, NY: Cambridge University Press.

Wilke, J., Therrien, L., Dunkin, A., & Vamos, M. N. (1985, March 25). Are the programs your kids watch simply commercials? *BusinessWeek,* p. 53.

Williams, L. A., & Burns, A. C. (2000). Exploring the dimensionality of children's direct influence attempts. *Advances in Consumer Research, 27,* 64–71.

Wilson, B. J., & Weiss, A. J. (1992). Developmental differences in children's reactions to a toy advertisement linked to a toy-based cartoon. *Journal of Broadcasting and Electronic Media, 36,* 371–394.

Wilson, B. J., & Weiss, A. J. (1995, May). *Children's reactions to a toy-based cartoon: Entertainment or commercial message?* Paper presented to the International Communication Association, Albuquerque, NM.

Yang, M., Roskos-Ewoldsen, D. R., Dinu, L., & Arpan, L. M. (2006). The effectiveness of "in-game" advertising comparing college students' explicit and implicit memory for brand names. *Journal of Advertising, 35,* 143–152.

Zuckerman, P., Ziegler, M., & Stevenson, H. W. (1978). Children's viewing of television and recognition memory of commercials. *Child Development, 49,* 96–104.

CHAPTER 3

Educational and Prosocial Media

Children spend more time engaged with media than they spend doing any other activity besides sleeping.[1] Over the course of their childhood, they will also spend more time watching television than they will in the classroom (Hearold, 1986). We know from several chapters of this book that there are many potential negative effects of watching television shows and movies, playing video and computer games, reading magazines, and surfing the Web. But is there anything positive that can come from the important and extensive role of media in children's lives? Can media use be intellectually and cognitively beneficial? Can children's exposure to enriching content enhance children's social and emotional well-being?

In this chapter, we consider the economic and regulatory forces that shape the availability of positive media for children today. We examine different ways in which media have been found to be "educational" for children—specifically, the media's contribution to academic knowledge, creativity, and language development. From there, we consider whether there are contextual or medium-related differences in *how* children learn from media and *what* they can learn. Finally, we examine the category of media and outcomes that are labeled "prosocial." The focus of this chapter is on the benefits of television for children's healthy development, in part because this tends to be the medium of choice for most children and in part because this is the most thoroughly studied medium. When possible, we also consider the growing body of research on newer media, including computer-based media and video games.

Economic and Regulatory Forces That Affect Media Offerings for Children

Most companies that make media, including prosocial and educational media for children, are part of mega-conglomerates that often own numerous media types (e.g., magazines, movie production houses, television networks, music recording studios, websites) and sometimes numerous nonmedia companies. As of this writing, the Walt Disney Company, for example, owns the Disney Channel, the ABC television network, Touchstone, Pixar Animation, and Marvel Worldwide. It also owns the Disney Interactive Media Group, Disney theme and water parks, and many kids' TV properties, including *Schoolhouse Rock* (http://www.freepress.net/ownership/chart/). The driving force behind all media companies is the economic bottom line and accountability to company shareholders. As such, the marketplace economy for children's media does not always work in the best interests of the developing child (McIntyre, 2013). For this reason, the U.S. system of public broadcasting, like noncommercial television in countries around the world, carves out portions of its broadcast day to ensure that the needs children are met through prosocial and educational content.

Regulation

Turow (1981) has observed that the early days of television saw plenty of programs geared to children with the hope that child viewers would badger their parents into buying TV sets. Over the years, child-oriented programs were slowly replaced with programs for adults, in the expectation that adult audiences could lure in more advertising dollars. By the 1970s, the lack of quality and quantity in children's programming led public and advocacy groups, such as Action for Children's Television (ACT), to pressure the Federal Communications Commission (FCC)—the U.S. regulatory agency in charge of television broadcasters—to step in (Kunkel & Wilcox, 2001) (see Chapter 13). The FCC responded in 1974 by issuing guidelines calling for broadcasters to make a "meaningful effort" to provide a "reasonable amount" of educational programming for children (Kunkel & Canepa, 1994). Regulators hoped that broadcasters would improve the quantity and quality of children's programming voluntarily, although the FCC warned broadcasters that if they did not do so, stricter rules would be forthcoming.

The result? By 1978, children's programming had not improved. ACT petitioned the FCC to conduct an inquiry into compliance with the 1974 policy statement, and within the year, the FCC concluded that broadcasters had not met their obligations and recommended regulatory action. The commission proposed a minimum weekly requirement of children's programming (five hours of educational programming for preschoolers and two and a half hours of educational programming for school-aged children). It also proposed defining "educational" programs as those addressing "history, science, literature, the environment, drama, music, fine arts, human relations, other cultures and languages, and basic skills such as reading and mathematics" (FCC, 1979). The proposal languished.

Undeterred, advocates took up the cause with congressional leaders and ultimately gained passage of a piece of legislation known as the Children's Television Act of 1990 (CTA). This bill emerged from Congress as an amendment to the Communications Act and implementation was left to the FCC, although the language was significantly modified (and watered down) from what advocates were pressing for (Kunkel, 1998). Essentially, the CTA mandated that broadcasters serve the "educational/informational needs of children through the licensee's overall programming, including programming specifically designed to serve such needs" (CTA, 2006). Educational/informational programming was broadly defined as content that will "further the positive development of the child in any respect, including the child's cognitive/intellectual or emotional/social needs" (CTA, 2006). Left undefined, however, were issues such as how much programming is enough, how age specific the programming needs to be, when the programming needs to air, and how the programming should be identified.

The Children's Television Act of 1990 did not dramatically change the landscape of children's television. As noted in Chapter 13, Kunkel and Canepa (1994) found inconsistencies in how licensees submitted their applications and dubious claims of educational value for programs such as *Teenage Mutant Ninja Turtles* and *G. I. Joe.* Lawmakers were ready to tighten the loopholes. By 1997, the FCC had adopted a processing guideline wherein broadcasters would be fined for making false claims about their educational efforts on behalf of children (FCC, 1996).[2] In addition, the FCC processing guideline specified how much, when, and to whom such "core" educational programming must be directed to qualify for an expedited license renewal. (See Figure 3.1 for a summary of the "three-hour rule" guidelines for educational programming.)

Despite a government mandate to provide informational/educational material to children over the public airwaves, analyses show that in the U.S. there few high-quality educational programs on commercial broadcast stations (Wilson, Kunkel, & Drogos, 2008). Why are there not more high-quality programs available, and why are those that are available widely seen as less profitable for the networks than the lower-quality programs? Clearly, these concerns go hand in hand. If broadcasters could make more money on the high-quality, educational programs, they would be more likely to air them.

Economics

Television programs have traditionally received the bulk of their profits from advertising revenue (Jordan, 2004). Historically, companies that advertised to children through the medium of television were most interested in reaching the largest possible number of children between the ages of 2 and 12. Competition for advertisers' dollars in an ever more crowded field led broadcasters to keep a close eye on the ratings. If the programs don't reach ratings expectations, networks must "make good" by providing free airtime elsewhere in their schedule (Jordan, 1996).

Prior to the proliferation of cable access, most broadcast networks aimed for the largest possible audience of 6- to 11-year-olds. The widespread adoption of cable and satellite television has created a "niche programming" model, where narrower slices of the audience allow for a more focused tailoring of advertising messages. One example of this is the

Figure 3.1 Core educational programming requirements.

Has education as a significant purpose

Specifically addresses the needs of a child audience wherein children are defined as 16 and under

Is labeled as educational on the air and in printed listings

Airs between the hours of 7 a.m. and 10 p.m.

Is regularly scheduled

Is at least 30 minutes in length

SOURCE: Federal Communications Commission MM Docket No. 93-48.

Disney Channel's discovery of the "tween" audience—children (primarily girls) who are not yet teenagers but are no longer interested in cartoons.

Television shows, video games, websites, and other platforms have increasingly been merging into a form that Henry Jenkins describes as "transmedia storytelling" in his book *Convergence Culture* (2006, p. 20). "Transmedia" can be thought of as a franchise property, title, or set of characters that "live" on multiple media platforms such as DVDs, television channels, video games, and websites. As Phillips (2012) writes, "the stories in these projects are interwoven, but lightly; each piece can be consumed on its own, and you'll still come away with the idea that you were given a complete story" (p. 13). An example of franchise transmedia is the Disney property *High School Musical* (HSM), which is a collection of titles with a group of characters designed to appeal to tween girls. HSM began as a made-for-TV movie on the Disney Channel and quickly extended to music CDs, theatrical release films, a Wii dance game and a Nintendo handheld video game, and a book series featuring East High (see Figure 3.2.). A more complex way of thinking about transmedia, however, focuses less on the windowing of a property and more on the narrative experience of the user. In Jenkins's definition, transmedia storytelling

> represents a process where integral elements of a fiction get dispersed systematically across multiple delivery channels for the purpose of creating a unified and coordinated entertainment experience. Ideally, each medium makes its own unique contribution to the unfolding of the story. (quoted in Phillips, 2012, p. 15)

Examples of this way of thinking about transmedia include the *Star Wars* media property, the *Harry Potter* phenomenon, and the *Batman* franchise. From this perspective, an economically successful children's media property will be one that "has legs"; in other words, it has the potential for longevity and it provides opportunities to extend the story and the audience's experience of it into multiple media and nonmedia domains.

Figure 3.2   Disney's transmedia property *High School Musical*.

SOURCE: Disney Channel (left); Nintendo Wii game (right).

Children's media properties can also make money through international distribution channels (Jordan, 2004; Pecora, 1998). A property that is appealing to an international audience, for example, can not only sell advertising on the television program but also extend the profits to be made from licensing fees. Sesame Workshop, a nonprofit production company based in New York, has agreed to license the use of its name and its characters to a for-profit educational company that offers preschool education in India. *Galli Galli Sim Sim*, the Hindi version of *Sesame Street*, has been popular in this country and its characters are well-known to Indian schoolchildren and their parents. For the right to use the brand and materials, franchisees will pay Sesame Workshop a fee and a cut of tuition revenue (Garrison, 2012).

The opportunities presented by cultivating international audiences come with challenges too. Though animated cartoons with a lot of action sequences can be dubbed easily and have storylines that are universally understandable, narrowly tailored and culturally specific educational or prosocial content may be less appealing to worldwide audiences. The Warner Bros. program *Histeria!,* which focused on teaching history lessons through humor and animation, used contained content (e.g., details about the American Revolutionary War) that would not be of much interest abroad. The program lasted only a few seasons.

Children's Educational Learning From Media

Most programs that air on broadcast stations to fulfill FCC requirements are what we might consider "prosocial"—programs that address children's ability to feel good about themselves and get along well with others (Jordan, 2004; Wilson et al., 2008). Such content is important, and will be addressed later in the chapter. In this section, however, we explore the relationship between children's media use and their cognitive, intellectual, and academic skills. Though many have argued that entertainment media use is antithetical to learning (because it displaces time spent in more intellectually stimulating activities; see Healy, 1990), many have also linked children's media use to creativity, language development, school-related learning, and more (D. R. Anderson, Huston, Schmitt, Linebarger, & Wright, 2001). Research reveals that it is critical to consider not whether or how much television children are exposed to in the early years, but rather what kind of television is on in the household. Barr and her colleagues (2010) followed 60 children between the ages of 1 and 4 and found that high levels of exposure to television programs designed for adults during the preschool years were associated with poorer executive functioning skills, such as attention and working memory, and other cognitive outcomes at age 4 (see Chapter 1 for a lengthier discussion of executive functioning). Of note, however, there was no relationship between exposure to child-oriented television and these outcomes. As discussed in Chapter 11, parents may be less likely to interact with their children when the television is constantly on (Christakis et al., 2001; Kirkorian, Pempek, Murphy, Schmidt, & Anderson, 2009), and children's play may be disrupted by the constant barrage of noises from adult TV that they don't understand (Schmidt, Pempek, Kirkorian, Lund, & Anderson, 2008).

The Lessons of *Sesame Street* and Children's Educational Media

Far and away, the majority of studies on preschool children's learning from television have involved *Sesame Street* (Fisch, Truglio, & Cole, 1999) (see Figure 3.3). The program, launched

Figure 3.3   PBS's *Sesame Street*.

SOURCE: © Sesame Workshop.

in 1969, was designed by producer and founder Joan Ganz Cooney to address the gap between children who had access to preschool and other economic advantages and those who did not (Fisch & Truglio, 2001). In Cooney's words, "it's not whether children learn from television, it's what they learn" (Knowlton & Costigan, 2006). From the beginning, a research team was in place to ensure that children not only liked the characters and the programs but also learned from them. The data suggest that the program did—and still does—achieve its mission of making children more "ready to learn" (Fisch & Bernstein, 2001).

Through his research on *Sesame Street* and other programs such as *Gullah Gullah Island* and *Blue's Clues,* Daniel Anderson has provided convincing evidence that children are active and engaged viewers. In one clever study, Anderson and his colleagues replaced the *Sesame Street* soundtrack with Greek (D. R. Anderson, Lorch, Field, & Sanders, 1981). They found that children paid less attention when they could not understand what they were watching. In another, Anderson mixed up the narratives so that the bits did not make sense. Again, children paid less attention (D. R. Anderson et al., 1981). Anderson argues that children bring their learning skills to bear when they watch television, and if they determine that a program is nonsensical, they stop attending. This is a far different argument from that of social critics who have asserted that television's fast cuts and funny voices are solely responsible for driving children's attention (Healy, 1990). Children want to understand television, and if they do not, they stop watching.

Sesame Street research has also indicated that children learn most when a parent is involved in the viewing. In fact, even if a mother is simply in the room coviewing and not saying anything, children learn more than if she is not present (although they learn most when the mother is actively engaged, talking and pointing things out) (Wright, St. Peters, & Huston, 1990). For this reason, the creators of *Sesame Street* intentionally inserted content that only adults would understand or find funny, such as the takeoff on the opera singer Placido Domingo (on the show he is Placido Flamingo) or the inclusion of adult celebrities (such movie stars as Glenn Close or the rock band R.E.M.). Despite this, parents' coviewing of *Sesame Street* has declined significantly over the years, to the point where producers determined that the adult-oriented portions of the program were providing few benefits to the majority of the viewing audience. Most of the adult-oriented content has therefore been stripped from the program (Fisch & Truglio, 2001).

Research on preschoolers' viewing of educational programming beyond *Sesame Street* also suggests learning benefits. Studies have shown that multiple viewings of the program *Blue's Clues,* in which a host encourages child viewers to help solve puzzles posed by his sidekick dog Blue, lead to a greater increase in engagement with the program, an increase in specific attention skills, and more use of problem solving strategies when compared to a single viewing (Crawley, Anderson, Wilder, Williams, & Santomero, 1999) or the viewing of a noninteractive children's educational program (Crawley et al., 2002) (see Figure 3.4).

Media and Make-Believe

Television and other entertainment media use—such as video game playing—is sometimes blamed for stifling children's creativity, imagination, and make-believe (or pretend) play.

Figure 3.4   Nickelodeon's *Blue's Clues.*

Because these are cognitive activities that are linked to language development, critical thinking, and abstract thinking, such an accusation should be taken seriously (Bellin & Singer, 2006). Certainly, children's imaginative play is influenced by their environment, including the presence or absence of electronic media, as well as their developmental stages. Valkenburg (2001) suggests that there are contradictory opinions about the influence of media, in particular television, on play and creativity. One line of thinking, which Valkenburg labels the "stimulation hypothesis," suggests that media enrich the store of ideas from which children can draw when engaged in imaginative play or creative tasks (p. 123). TV content may be incorporated into pretend play, computer game settings may spark curiosity about other people and places, and music may set off images and emotions that might otherwise lie dormant. At least two preschool educational programs have been linked with increased imaginative play and creative thinking: *Mister Rogers' Neighborhood* (which includes a clear transition from the real-world setting for Fred Rogers's home to the Land of Make-Believe via trolley) (D. R. Anderson et al., 2001; Singer & Singer, 1976) and *Barney & Friends* (which has imagination—led by a big purple dinosaur—as a central tenet of the core curriculum) (Singer & Singer, 1998) (see Figure 3.5). Research on the viewing of these programs shows significant gains in creative and imaginative play when compared with the viewing of other children's programs (Singer & Singer, 1976). Importantly, however, gains are greatest when viewing is facilitated by adults, either parents or teachers (Hogan, 2012a).

An alternative hypothesis, which Valkenburg (2001) calls the "reduction hypothesis," suggests that media stifle children's creative capacities by replacing more cognitively stimulating

Figure 3.5 *PBS's Barney & Friends.*

activities (such as reading or playing with friends) with passive viewing and mindless surfing. In addition, some media (particularly those that have both audio and visual components) might be seen as supplanting children's imaginings with prefabricated pictures from which children have trouble disassociating (Runco & Pezdek, 1984; Valkenburg & Beentjes, 1997). Researchers looking specifically at the content of media have also argued that media violence adversely affects imaginative play, although it is not clear whether this is because children become more impulsive (Singer, Singer, & Rapaczynski, 1984) or more anxious (Fein, 1981), or whether some other mechanism is at work.

Although there is little evidence that screen media use stimulates children's imaginative play and creativity (with the exception of a few preschool programs), there is some suggestion that audiovisual media interventions can be designed to encourage play. *My Magic Story Car*, a video-based series designed to enhance children's play with the goal of building their early literacy skills, found quite positive effects when used in a classroom setting (Bellin & Singer, 2006). In this series, low-income, at-risk children and their caregivers are given explicit ideas for engaging in make-believe play. For example, adults help children assemble their own "magic story cars" (chairs, cushions, or cardboard boxes decorated with alphabet letters) with a "license plate" on which children are assisted in writing their names or initials. Child viewers drive their magic story cars to play learning games with make-believe narratives designed to strengthen specific emergent literacy skills, such as conceptions about print, and socioemotional skills, such as cooperative play. Bellin and Singer found that, when compared to a control group, children who were exposed to the intervention showed significant gains in virtually all aspects of emergent literacy. The brilliance of this program is in the recognition that parents and caregivers have, in many ways, forgotten how to "play" in ways that are developmentally constructive. In addition, *My Magic Story Car* capitalizes on the ubiquity of the medium and children's affinity for it. Although similar claims have been made about the potential for video and computer games to stimulate creativity and imagination (Johnson, 2005; McGonigal, 2011), and although many of the games themselves claim to boost children's make-believe skills (Valkenburg, 2001), research in this area is lacking.

Media and Language Learning

Several studies have argued that DVDs with titles like *Baby Einstein* mislead parents into thinking they will be educational for their infants. Research suggests that claims of the educational efficacy of such products are baseless. Separate studies by DeLoache and her colleagues (2010) and Krcmar (2011) found that children who watched a DVD designed for infants "12 months and up" learned virtually no words featured in the video. However, at least one study found evidence for a possible role of age-appropriate media in encouraging verbal interactions, particularly for infants living in low-income, immigrant families (Mendolsohn et al., 2010). In this longitudinal study, children whose parents coviewed educational television programs with them and interacted with them around the program content showed gains in language development at 14 months (Mendolsohn et al., 2010).

Media may contribute to children's academic achievement by acting as an "incidental language teacher" (Naigles & Mayeux, 2001). In the course of a study of families' use of television, researchers at the Annenberg Public Policy Center employed the Peabody Picture Vocabulary Test (PPVT) to assess vocabulary (Scantlin & Jordan, 2006). One 9-year-old boy was given the word *cascade* and asked to point to the picture that represented the word. The boy immediately did so correctly, asserting that he had learned the word from his favorite video game! Indeed, for decades, researchers (Rice, 1984, 1990) have asserted that television programs have the potential to encourage children to understand and use new words, although it is unclear whether media can effectively teach more complex language acquisition skills such as grammar (Naigles & Mayeux, 2001).

Program complexity and age appropriateness of the verbal content of media both play an important role in language development. Linebarger and Walker (2004) examined the relationship between children's television viewing and their expressive language and vocabulary. Unlike most studies, which look cross-sectionally at children's cognitive abilities and their viewing patterns (making it difficult to establish causality), this study collected data on children's viewing every three months, beginning at 6 months of age and ending at about 30 months of age. Even when parent's education, child's home environment, and child's cognitive performance were statistically controlled, watching *Dora the Explorer, Blue's Clues, Arthur, Clifford the Big Red Dog*, or *Dragon Tales* resulted in a larger vocabulary and higher expressive language scores (see Figure 3.6); watching *Teletubbies* was related to a smaller vocabulary and lower expressive language scores; watching *Sesame Street* was related only to lower expressive language scores; and watching *Barney* was related to a smaller vocabulary and more expressive language. What is interesting about this study is the notion that the type of educational program children watched resulted in different cognitive outcomes. *Blue's Clues* and *Dora* are "interactive" shows, where children are encouraged to talk to the screen. *Sesame Street* is not (potentially explaining why there was less gain in expressive language). *Barney* aims to engage children in creative and imaginative play but keeps its language fairly simple and straightforward (potentially explaining the gap in vocabulary building).

Lasting Effects of Exposure to Educational Media

In a 10-year longitudinal study that followed children from preschool to high school, researchers in Massachusetts and Kansas found that children who watch educational television

Figure 3.6 Nickelodeon's *Dora the Explorer* and PBS's *Clifford the Big Red Dog*.

in the early years perform better some 10 years later, even when other important variables (such as family socioeconomic and the availability of books) are factored in (D. R. Anderson et al., 2001). The researchers found that viewing educational versus entertainment programs was associated with greater gains, but some programs encouraged the development of skills more than others did. A similar study, which tracked two cohorts of German children over a four-year period, also found that although educational program viewing was positively correlated with reading achievement, relationships between entertainment program viewing and reading performance were negative (Ennemoser & Schneider, 2007). These important and ground-breaking studies ultimately concluded that McLuhan (1964) was wrong when he wrote, "The medium is the message." Rather, they argue, "the message is the message" (D. R. Anderson et al., 2001, p. 134).

When the Medium Is the Message

Despite what Daniel Anderson and his colleagues (2001) argue, however, there are properties of media that seem to encourage the use of some cognitive skills and academic pursuits. Studies of computer and video games suggest that visual attention, peripheral vision, and spatial reasoning can be improved by game play (see, e.g., McGonigal, 2011; Okagaki & Frensch, 1994; Subrahmanyam & Greenfield, 1994). Jackson and her colleagues (2006) found that children who were struggling as readers were helped by at-home use of the Internet (presumably because it encouraged the use of text-based information). Literacy has also been improved for at-risk children when television captions have been made available onscreen, helping children to recognize and read more words, identify the meanings of those words, generate inferences regarding program content, and transfer those skills to other settings (Linebarger, Piotrowski, & Greenwood, 2010). Beal and Arroyo (2002) provided evidence that a user-driven computer game can effectively encourage the integration of math and science concepts above and beyond what a teacher alone can do within a classroom.

Figure 3.7

Children's Social Learning From Media

Though the term *prosocial* is often bandied about by the media industry, federal regulators, academics, and advocates, there is not necessarily a shared definition within or among these groups. Most writers suggest that prosocial media content is somehow socially helpful (such as that which promotes altruism, friendliness, acceptance of diversity, and cooperation). Others would include content that is more personally helpful (calming fears, engaging in safer sex practices, eating healthfully). In this chapter, we use the definition provided in one of the first comprehensive reports of the positive effects of the media, written in the 1970s, titled "Television and Behavior." The authors define *prosocial* as that which is "socially desirable and which in some way benefits other persons or society at large" (quoted in Lowery & DeFleur, 1995, p. 354).

Any definition of *prosocial* involves some level of value judgment. Some might argue that a program that emphasizes "looking out for #1" prepares a child better for a competitive world than one that instills values of "cooperation." Despite this caveat, we examine studies that have explored the benefits of prosocial media using the definition cited above: content which in some way benefits other persons or society at large. Most of the landmark studies were conducted in the 1970s, in response to increased federal funding to investigate the positive role of television in children's lives (this came on the heels of the surgeon general's report outlining the negative role of television—particularly the deleterious consequences of TV violence) (Lowery & DeFleur, 1995). The studies reviewed in this chapter are mainly focused on television content, though by extension, many of the findings would hold true for DVD and videotape viewing of the programs. Less clear is the impact of other electronic media—including computer and video games, Internet social websites (including networking sites), music, and magazines.

Many studies have found that children's emotional and social skills are linked to their early academic standing (e.g., Wentzel & Asher, 1995). Children who have difficulty paying attention in class, getting along with their peers, and controlling their own negative emotions of anger and distress do less well in school (Arnold et al., 1999; McLelland, Morrison, & Holmes, 2000). What is more, longitudinal studies suggest that this link may be causal: "For many children, academic achievement in their first few years of schooling appears to be built on a firm foundation of children's emotional and social skills" (Raver, 2002, p. 3). Specifically, research on early schooling suggests that the relationships that children build with peers and teachers are (a) based on children's ability to regulate emotions in prosocial versus antisocial ways, and (b) a "source of provisions" that either help or hurt children's chances of doing well, academically, in school (Ladd, Birch, & Buhs, 1999, p. 1375).

Developmental psychologists believe that children have a set of "emotional competencies" that determine how they think about and handle their own and others' emotions (Saarni, 1990). For example, a child's ability to recognize and label different emotions gives him or her powerful social tools. Children's emotional styles are thought to be influenced not only by their temperament but also by their environments. Certainly, the ways in which parents use warmth, control, and harshness in the home matter (see Chapter 11). Media may matter too. As we shall see in a moment, media have been shown to be effective at developing skills such as altruism and cooperation in young viewers.

Prosocial Media Content for Children

In the early days of television, the networks featured many "family-friendly" prosocial programs such as *Lassie, Captain Kangaroo,* and *The Waltons.* Through the 1970s and early 1980s, content analyses revealed that children's favorite programs often featured portrayals of empathy, altruism, and an exploration of feelings (Palmer, 1988). Networks soon discovered, however, that more money could be made on so-called program-length commercials—cartoons that were mainly vehicles for selling toys such as action figures (Kunkel, 1998). As a consequence, prosocial television declined through the 1980s and mid-1990s (Calvert & Kotler, 2003). The Children's Television Act of 1990 aimed to reverse that trend, but it really was not until the FCC processing guideline went into effect—explicitly stating a minimum requirement of three hours per week of educational television—that the landscape of children's television began to include more prosocial television. Despite this legislation, there is conflicting evidence about the extent to which prosocial content is available. One analysis of the top 20 shows for children and teens ages 2 to 17 found that only two contained themes of altruism, antiviolence, or friendliness in the episodes analyzed (Mares & Woodard, 2005). However, a broader analysis of 2,227 programs on 18 different channels found that 73% of the programs featured altruistic acts, with a rate of 2.92 incidents per hour (Smith et al., 2006). As described below, many studies find positive effects of prosocial content on children's beliefs and behaviors. However, a meta-analysis of 35 prosocial studies found that the impact of prosocial television content seems to peak at age 7 and fall off rapidly after that (Mares & Woodard, 2005, 2012). For this reason, we look separately at content aimed at children versus that aimed at adolescents.

Do Prosocial Media Affect Youth?

Researchers who study children's prosocial learning from media typically work under the assumption that characters who behave kindly, cooperatively, responsibly, and altruistically are providing models that children can learn from and subsequently imitate. Much of this research is grounded in Bandura's social cognitive theory, which originally explored how televised aggression might be imitated under certain conditions (see Chapter 4), but it has also looked at prosocial behavior that might result from media exposure. Generally speaking, the mechanism goes like this: Children observe a character behave in a positive manner. That behavior is more likely to be imitated if the character (a) is perceived as realistic, (b) is similar to the child (for example, in age or gender), (c) receives positive reinforcement, and (d) carries out an action that is imitable by the child (Thomas, 2005). Other theorists have argued that as children develop moral reasoning, they become better able to understand the motives of characters, judge the value of their actions, and assess the relevance of what they see, hear, and read for their own contexts and interpersonal relationships (Glover, Garmon, & Hull, 2011).

Prosocial content may also be providing children with skills for dealing with their emotions and managing their moods. As noted in Chapter 1, children are born with temperament but look to their environments to learn emotional competencies—for example, ways to feel better about themselves or get through a bad day. *Sesame Street*, in its four decades on the air, has taught children about emotional coping as one of its curricular goals. It has addressed the scariness of hurricanes, the jealousy that arrives with a new sibling, and even the uncertainty that came after the 2001 terrorist attacks. However, we know very little about the efficacy of these storylines.

Similarly, *Mister Rogers' Neighborhood* produced many episodes for children on topics that scared them or made them uncomfortable. (Indeed, there is a large body of research on children's management of their fright reactions to media. See, for example, Cantor, 2012.)

Another potential mechanism underlying the relationship between media content and prosocial behavior may be that prosocial content offers children "scripts" for dealing with unfamiliar situations. According to schema or script theory, a schema is an organized structure of knowledge about a topic or event that is stored in memory and helps a person assimilate new information (Mandler, 1984). Schema theory suggests that people possess schemas for emotions, which include information about facial expressions, the cause of feelings, and the appropriate ways of expressing feelings. Children use schemas to help them interpret what they encounter in the media. In turn, media content can contribute to a child's schemas. Cultivation theory, described in Chapter 5, has found that, over time, heavy TV viewers tend to adopt beliefs about the world that are consistent with television's portrayal of the world. In other words, children who watch a lot of TV featuring crime or hospitals may come to see the world as a mean and scary place (Gerbner, Gross, Signorielli, & Morgan, 1986). Mares, Braun, and Hernandez (2012) have found that media are particularly powerful for adolescents who have little exposure to the contexts they will eventually encounter. In one study, 5th graders were randomly assigned to watch a tween television episode that was high or low in social conflict and then asked questions about their future middle school, as well as about their typical TV diet. They found that children who were heavy viewers of tween-oriented television—which is rife with stereotypical cliques and interpersonal hostility—expected less friendliness and more bullying and had greater anxiety about attending their future school than did light viewers of such fare. The researchers also found that children who did not typically view this content but who saw the high-conflict episode in the experimental setting had lower expectations of friendliness and heightened expectations of hostility compared to those who saw the low-conflict episode.

The Research Evidence

Empathy

Social learning theory, cultivation theory, and schema theory might all be used to understand children's development of empathy, or the ability of children to understand and relate to another's feelings by taking his or her perspective. Many would argue that the ability of humans to empathize with others is both hardwired and learned. Developmental psychologists who follow the Piagetian tradition would argue that it is not until children are 6 or 7 years old that they are "sociocentric" enough to understand that not everyone sees the world or events as they do. In one famous experiment, children were put in front of a constructed three-dimensional mountain with different objects placed on it. Piaget asked the child to choose, from four pictures, which view the experimenter would see (the experimenter was standing on the opposite side of the mountain). Younger children selected the picture of the view that they themselves saw (Thomas, 2005). From this experiment and others, Piaget argued that children have difficulty understanding others' perspectives, including how they might feel. By the time children reach school age, they have become more attuned to the feelings and needs of others.

Research suggests that child audiences can recognize the feelings of media characters, though it appears that younger children are less likely to experience the character's feelings (that is, empathize with them) than older children are. In one study, 3- to 5-year-olds and 9- to 11-year-olds watched a scary movie clip. For one clip, a threatening "stimulus" was shown. For the other, a character's fear in response to the threatening stimulus was shown. Older children were more frightened and physiologically aroused by the character's fear than the younger children were, although all children recognized the character as frightened (Wilson & Cantor, 1985).

Calvert and Kotler (2003) examined prosocial programs for elementary school–aged youth airing on commercial broadcast, cable, and public television. Their two-pronged study involved 2nd to 6th graders in both a naturalistic reporting methodology (in which children logged onto a website and reported on what they were watching and what they learned) and an experimental methodology (in which children were shown programs in the classroom and asked about them afterward). Their research suggests that school-aged children learn from prosocial programs even more than from traditional, school-related educational shows. Moreover, much of what the children seemed to be learning was how to identify the emotions of characters and apply what they learned to their own lives. As one 6th-grade girl in the experimental condition wrote about the program *Anatole*,

> This program was about a little mouse that tried her hardest in singing but just couldn't do it. The mouse gave up and ripped her opera notes up because of her frustration. When her dad (Papa) met an Opera singer named Renee, he knew that if his daughter heard her singing, she would have kept her confidence. And she did. She learned that just because you are not good at something doesn't mean you have to give up. And that is the lesson that I will keep in mind when I get frustrated with something I am not good at. (quoted in Calvert & Kotler, 2003, p. 316)

Altruism/Helping

One of the first studies of the impact of prosocial television came with the program *Lassie*, which ran from 1954 to 1974 on commercial broadcast TV. The show featured an extraordinary collie, who was devoted to her family and, in particular, her boy owner (Jeff). Because of her devotion and intelligence, Lassie often helped the family out of dangerous situations. In the experiment (Sprafkin, Liebert, & Poulos, 1975), 1st-grade children saw one of three TV shows. In one condition, they saw a prosocial episode of *Lassie* in which Jeff rescues a puppy. In the second, they viewed a "neutral" episode of Jeff trying to avoid taking violin lessons. In the third, the children watched a "competitive" episode of the *Brady Bunch*. After viewing the television program, children were told to play a game to win points and prizes. They were also told that if they needed assistance, they could press a "help" button, though that would mean they would need to stop playing the game and presumably would be less likely to win a prize. Children could hear dogs barking with increasing intensity and distress through the experimental period (the barking was, of course, prerecorded). Children who saw the prosocial episode of *Lassie* were nearly twice as likely to seek help as children in the neutral condition. Children in the competitive condition were the least likely to seek help.

Jane McGonigal, author of the book *Reality is Broken: Why Games Make Us Better and How They Can Change the World*, has argued that young people who play video and computer games are given opportunities to work collectively and altruistically in the games they play. She cites the example of FreeRice.com, an online game used by teachers to help children learn vocabulary and spelling and which donates rice through the World Food Programme to help end hunger (www.freerice.com). As of August, 2012, over 96 billion grains of rice had been donated. Even with competitive games, there is an expectation of cooperation and collaboration. McGonigal writes,

> Good games don't just happen. Gamers work to make them happen. Any time you play a game with someone else, unless you're just trying to spoil the experience, you are actively engaged in highly coordinated, prosocial behavior. No one forces gamers to play by the rules, to concentrate deeply, to try their best, to stay in the game, or to act as if they care about the outcome. They do it voluntarily, for the mutual benefit of everyone playing, because it makes a better game. (p. 269)

Social Interaction

In a 1979 study, Friedrich-Cofer, Huston-Stein, Kipnis, Susman, and Clewett explored the effects of daily exposure to *Mister Rogers' Neighborhood* (see Figure 3.8), over a two-month period, on preschool children's social interactions with one another. All of the children were enrolled in Head Start programs. In one classroom, children watched *Mister Rogers*, and teachers were trained and relevant play material was provided. In a second classroom, children watched *Mister Rogers*, but teachers had no training. However, relevant play material was provided. In the third, children viewed *Mister Rogers*, but there was neither teacher training nor program-related play material provided. In the final condition, children watched "neutral" films in classrooms containing irrelevant play material. Researchers observed

Figure 3.8 PBS's *Mister Rogers' Neighborhood.*

SOURCE: ©2001 Family Communications, Inc., and PBS.

children's natural social behaviors in the classroom and on the playground before and after the two months of viewing. They found that positive interactions with peers increased the most in the condition where children had exposure to prosocial programming, teachers were trained, and relevant play material was provided. Prosocial television alone, however, led to few differences in children's behavior, at least in this early study.

A second program that has been extensively studied is *Barney & Friends*. This program, which features a big purple dinosaur and emphasizes kindness and good manners, has been found to have a positive effect on children from diverse regions in the United States (Singer & Singer, 1998). Similar to the *Mister Rogers* study described above, day care centers were assigned to a viewing or a viewing-plus-lessons condition or a no-viewing control group. Even without the accompanying lessons, children who viewed *Barney* were rated as more civil and having better manners.

Acceptance of Others/Acceptance of Diversity

A major goal of the program *Sesame Street* has been to highlight the diversity of American life and to model racial harmony. Program characters include African Americans, Latino Americans, White Americans, American Indians, and Asian Americans. Even its Muppets are different colors! In 1989, in response to increasing racial unrest in the U.S., the producers and researchers at Sesame Workshop (the nonprofit production company that makes the program) designed a curriculum to encourage friendship among people of different races and cultures. Preschool viewers were encouraged to perceive people who look different from themselves as possible friends and to bring a child who had been rejected because of physical or cultural differences into the group. Truglio, Lovelace, Segui, and Schneider (2001) write that initially, there was some doubt as to whether race relations was truly an issue for preschoolers. However, a review of the literature, along with meetings with experts, revealed that preschoolers were aware of racial differences. Truglio and her colleagues' formative research suggested that ethnic minority children felt less good about themselves and that White children were more likely to segregate African American children in an imaginary neighborhood they were asked to create. However, most of the children were open to the idea of being friends with children of different races.

One very interesting study analyzed two segments of *Sesame Street* that were created to address racial harmony and interaction. In one, "Visiting Ieshia," a White girl visits an African American girl in her home. The other, "Play Date," shows a similar visit that a White boy makes to his African American friend's home. Researchers at Sesame Workshop found that children liked the segments and identified with and remembered them. Most of the children who viewed the episodes stated that the White girl felt positive about being at Ieshia's home (70%) and the White boy felt positive about being at Jamal's home (58%). However, less than half of the children who viewed "Play Date" felt that the African American mother in the program (48%) and the White mother of the visiting boy (39%) felt happy about the visit. Why? Preschoolers perceived their own mothers as not feeling positive about other-race friendships, even after viewing friendly and inviting images of parents in "Play Date." From these findings, the researchers recommended that in future segments, mothers and fathers have a more prominent role in expressing support about the child character's friendships with children of different races before, during, and after the visits. They also suggested that the segments show the parents of the different-race children interacting and expressing the positive value of making good friends (Truglio et al., 2001).

The Limitations of Research on Prosocial Content for Children

It is unfortunate that so few studies have investigated the potential benefits of prosocial programming for children, particularly when there are so many programs now being offered by commercial broadcasters to satisfy the three-hour rule. As Mares and Woodard (2012) point out, there are still many unanswered questions about how best to design prosocial content for children. First, does children's exposure to a specific prosocial portrayal (such as a character donating money) translate into more "general kindness" or "goodness"? They argue that such a link has been found in exposure to antisocial models (with, of course, the opposite effect), and that despite the fact that the research could be carried out fairly easily, it never has. The popular series *American Idol*, for example, televised a double episode called "Idol Gives Back" in which the judges spotlighted the ravages of poverty, including the desperate plight of AIDS-afflicted mothers and children in Africa. By modeling charitable behavior (one of the episode's hosts, Ellen DeGeneres, donated $100,000, and the program's host, Ryan Seacrest, went to Africa and cared for dying women and children), the hosts (or program) raised a total of $60 million. Children watching the program asked their parents to give and pledged their own allowances. But is this generosity fleeting, or have children's beliefs and behaviors been affected in the longer term?

There is also a question about what kind of prosocial portrayal is most effective for different ages. For example, Mares and Woodard (2012) argue that

> the combination of aggression and a prosocial theme may be particularly pernicious. That is, showing violence and mayhem in the cause of social justice may be more deleterious to children's prosocial interactions than showing violence unadulterated by any prosocial theme. (p. 195)

A study by Krcmar and Valkenburg (1999) found that 6- to 12-year-olds could easily reason that "unjustified violence" is wrong in an abstract, hypothetical situation. However, children who were heavy viewers of the fantasy violence program *Power Rangers* were more likely than light viewers of this show to judge "justified" aggression in the hypothetical scenarios as morally correct. One might argue that children who see the world in this way (that is, that justified violence is morally right) are drawn to superhero-type shows such as *Power Rangers*. Krcmar and Curtis (2003) conducted an experiment in which 5- to 14-year-olds were randomly assigned to one of three conditions: One watched an action cartoon that featured characters arguing and eventually engaging in violence; another watched a similar clip involving an argument, but the characters walked away instead of fighting; and a control group did not watch television. Afterward, the subjects listened to and judged four hypothetical stories involving violence. Children who had watched the violent program were subsequently more likely than those in the control group to judge the violence as morally acceptable. They also exhibited less sophisticated moral reasoning in their responses (for example, they relied on punishment as a rationale—"Don't hit or you'll get in trouble").

Not only is much of children's superhero programming portrayed with conflicting pro- and antisocial messages; so too is the adult programming popular with young audiences. The FOX TV series *24* was roundly criticized for having its hero, Jack Bauer, use torture against his enemies (including his bad-guy brother) to save the world from disaster (Moritz, 2007). Similarly, if one aim is to have children imitate constructive, prosocial behavior, what is the best way to promote that? Should the reward be intrinsic or extrinsic? Should children be shown precisely how to carry this behavior over into their own lives? The program *Captain Planet* highlighted the ecological problems facing the world—problems that were solved by superheroes called "planeteers." At the end of the program, however, children were shown exactly what they could do in their own homes and communities to be a "planeteer" too. Behaviors included recycling newspapers, making birdhouses, and picking up litter.

It is clear that research needs to account for the developmental differences of audiences when examining the potential benefits of prosocial content. As Mares and Woodard (2012) point out, "Judgments about what is bad and why it is bad are not the same for a 4 year old and a 10 year old or an adult" (p. 200). Researchers Calvert and Kotler (2003) argue that at least for school-aged children, prosocial program content is even more "educational" than academic-oriented shows that feature science, literature, or math. As Jordan (2003) points out, however, it is difficult to know whether the children remember the lessons better because they have been ingrained in them since they were toddlers (share, be nice, etc.) or whether it is because the narrative structure is more entertaining and engaging. Children's interpretations of content, as well as the capacity of such content to be assimilated into existing cognitive schemes, are critical factors in understanding the effects of prosocial media.

Prosocial Media for Adolescents

The great majority of research on prosocial effects of media has involved children, especially very young children (Hogan, 2012b; Hogan & Strasburger, 2008). Only a handful of studies and experiments have specifically examined the possibility of prosocial effects of media on adolescents (Mares & Woodard, 2005). As noted earlier, a meta-analysis of studies examining the effects of prosocial television content found that effects of prosocial television dropped off after the age of 7 (Mares & Woodard, 2005). However, new technology is bringing a whole variety of new ways to reach teenagers with prosocial content, and evaluations suggest that such content may have beneficial effects on adolescent health and well-being.

Prosocial Messages and Outcomes in New Media Technologies

Research with interactive media shows great promise for the positive benefits of media use by adolescents in both the short term and long term (C. A. Anderson, Gentile, & Dill, 2012; Gentile et al., 2009; Greitemeyer & Osswald, 2010; Prot, McDonald, Anderson, & Gentile, 2012). Recently, the Robert Wood Johnson Foundation funded an $8.25 million initiative to advance the research and design of digital games that promote health (http://www.healthgamesresearch.org). A number of new video and computer games have been developed with applications for adolescents with the goal of increasing their physical health and social well-being. Examples include the following:

- *Packy and Marlon* is a video game in which two diabetic elephants stroll through the jungle, trying to pick the right foods, checking their blood glucose levels, and giving themselves insulin shots. A six-month study of 60 diabetic children and teens found that those who used the video game were four times less likely to require urgent care visits than were those who played another popular video game ("Managing Ailments," 1999). Some health care organizations, like Kaiser, actually pay for such games for their patients.

- A computer-based intervention that pairs adolescent users' self-concept with images of warm social acceptance has been shown to temper adolescents' tendency to react to social rejections with aggressiveness, particularly for subjects with low self-esteem (Baldwin, Baccus, & Milyavskaya, 2010).
- A video game titled *Re-Mission* (HopeLab, Palo Alto, CA) has been developed for cancer patients and features a "nanobot" named Roxxi, an attractive character who travels through the body blasting away at cancer cells. In a study of 375 cancer patients (ages 13 to 29 years) at 34 different medical centers, those who played the game were more compliant with chemotherapy and antibiotic treatments (Beale, Kato, Marin-Bowling, Guthrie, & Cole, 2007).
- *Dance Dance Revolution* (see Figure 3.9) is a popular video game that encourages exercise at home and can double energy expenditure (Lanningham-Foster et al., 2006). While some researchers found no reduction in body mass index among children who used it (Madsen, Yen, Wlasiuk, Newman, & Lustig, 2007), others found that exergames can increase energy expenditure four to eight times over resting levels among adolescents who engage in moderate to vigorous participation (Bailey & McInnis, 2011; Smallwood, Morris, Fallows, & Buckley, 2012). The key may be the intensity level of physical exercise (O'Loughlin, Dugas, Sabiston, & O'Loughlin, 2012). Other games, like *Body Mechanics*, teach children to avoid becoming obese by allying themselves with a team of superheroes to battle villains such as Col Estorol and Betes II (Ellis, 2007).
- An in-home virtual reality video game has been shown to improve hand function and forearm bone health in adolescents with hemiplegic cerebral palsy (Golomb et al., 2010). Similarly, a breath-controlled video game that uses biofeedback has been used to promote better breathing in children with cystic fibrosis (Bingham, Bates, Thompson-Figueroa, & Lahiri, 2010).

Figure 3.9   *Dance Dance Revolution* for PlayStation.

- Video games like *The Baby Game* and *It's Your Game: Keep It Real* have potential to decrease teen pregnancy by changing attitudes about unsafe sex (Hogan, 2012b).
- An extensive review of the literature found 38 studies that used video games to provide physical therapy, psychological therapy, improved disease self-management, or increased physical activity. The range of success was 37% to 69% improvement in outcomes. However, the authors point out that many of the studies in the review used methodology that was not rigorous, and unfortunately had limited follow-up periods (Primack et al., 2012).

Beyond gaming, digital technology is also increasingly being used in Web-based platforms, cell phone texting, and social networking sites (Boyar, Levine, & Zensius, 2011; Ybarra, 2013, in press). For example, using digital technology has been shown in small studies to delay initiation of sex, remove sexual references from social network profiles, and alter attitudes about condom use among teens and young adults (Collins, Martino, & Shaw, 2011; Guse et al., 2012; Moreno & Kolb, 2012). Other examples include the following:

- A 16-week online intervention succeeded in producing weight loss and a reduction in binge eating for a small group of adolescents (Jones et al., 2008).
- A randomized controlled trial of 170 adolescents with depression found that a computerized intervention—an interactive fantasy game called *SPARX* (Smart, Positive, Active, Realistic, X-factor thoughts)—reduced depressive symptoms as much as or more than face-to-face treatment (Merry et al., 2012). College freshmen whose Facebook profiles reference depression want their friends to respond in person, according to another study (Whitehill, Brockman, & Moreno, 2013).
- *Puff City*, a Web-based asthma intervention for urban teens, improved symptoms and decreased school absences in a year-long study of 422 students (Joseph et al., 2012).
- A randomized clinical trial using an Internet obesity prevention program for adolescents decreased sedentary behavior and increased healthy eating and activity in a six-month study of 384 teenagers (Whittemore, Jeon, & Grey, 2012).
- A text message reminder has been used to increase the rate of influenza vaccination in a low-income, urban pediatric population (Stockwell et al., 2012).
- In San Francisco, the Department of Public Health has become the first in the country to begin sending safer-sex text messages to young people who request them (Allday, 2006).
- More recently, in California, more than 3,000 teens signed up for Hook Up (Carroll & Kirkpatrick, 2011), which provides facts about reproductive health and referrals to youth-oriented clinical medical services.
- Delivering sexually transmitted infection (STI) prevention messages via Facebook actually increased condom use over two months in a recent study of 1,578 teens (Bull, Levine, Black, Schmiege, & Santelli, 2012).
- A computer-delivered HIV/AIDS program resulted in increased condom use in a randomized trial with 157 college students (Kiene & Barta, 2006).
- A Web-based program to help teens suffering from chronic fatigue syndrome showed success in treating symptoms. In a randomized controlled trial of 135 teens, 85% of the teens who used the Web-based program reported their fatigue was gone after six months compared with 27% of the control subjects (Nijhof, Bleijenberg, Uiterwaal, Kimpen, & van de Putte, 2012).

A number of private and federally funded programs have incorporated Web-based and online approaches for sex education and prevention of HIV and other STIs (Delgado & Austin, 2007; Whiteley, Mello, Hunt, & Brown, 2012). In particular, using cell phones and texting may represent an important and innovative way to reach teens with preventive health information (Perry et al., 2012). As part of its "Staying Alive" campaign, MTV developed an iPhone app that searches via GPS for the nearest place that sells condoms (Sniderman, 2011). MTV has also developed a "GYT" (Get Yourself Tested) campaign that uses text messaging to locate nearby clinics for testing and a website with videos that promote and normalize open communication with partners and providers about sexually transmitted diseases (STDs) and testing (www.gytnow.org) (Kaiser Family Foundation, 2012) (see Figure 3.10). Some experts think that an app will soon be developed for Facebook that will

Figure 3.10 Get Yourself Tested website (GYT.org).

notify users about their risk of a sexually transmitted infection based on their friend's status updates (Clark-Flory, 2012). Researchers are already using Facebook for partner notification in HIV infections (Clark-Flory, 2012).

National and International Prosocial Efforts

Evidence is increasing that well-conceived health campaigns involving the media can have a demonstrable impact (Noar, 2006). One of the earliest prosocial experiments was conducted in Mexico by Miguel Sabido. His telenovela, *Acompáñame* (Accompany Me), featured a young woman with two children who decided that she did not want any more pregnancies and therefore needed contraception. The show was immensely popular, and sales of contraceptives increased 23% in the first year the show aired, compared with 7% the year before the show began (Brink, 2006). Radio soap operas, in which characters discuss the problems of dealing with the risk of AIDS, have also been used to convey public health messages in India, China, and Africa (Singhal & Rogers, 1999). In Zambia, a media campaign to reduce the risk of HIV resulted in a doubling of condom use among those teenagers who viewed at least three TV ads from the campaign (Underwood, Hachonda, Serlemitsos, & Bharath-Kumar, 2006). In 2006, the African Broadcast Media Partnership Against HIV/AIDS began a three- to five-year campaign involving a series of PSAs on radio and TV in 25 African countries (Kaiser Family Foundation, 2006). The goal of the campaign, bearing the slogan "An HIV-free generation . . . It begins with you," is to educate people in Africa about what they can do to stop the spread of HIV. And in China, students have been successfully given sex education via the Internet (Lou, Zhao, Gao, & Shah, 2006).

In the United States, the Kaiser Family Foundation began partnering with MTV in 1997 to produce a total of 62 different PSAs and 19 full-length shows dealing with HIV/ AIDS (Rideout, 2003). Kaiser joined with Viacom to get HIV/AIDS storylines incorporated into shows such as *Becker, Touched by an Angel*, and *Queer as Folk* (Kaiser Family Foundation, 2004). A RAND study of 506 regular viewers of the hit sitcom *Friends* found that more than one-fourth could recall seeing one particular episode in which Rachel became pregnant despite the use of a condom. Of those who had viewed the show, 40% had watched the episode with an adult, and 10% had talked with an adult about condom use as a direct result of the show (Collins, Elliott, Berry, Kanouse, & Hunter, 2003). Similarly, a Kaiser survey of more than five hundred 15-to 17-year-olds found that one-third had had a conversation with a parent about a sexual matter because of something they saw on television (see Figure 3.11). In the same survey, 60% of teens said they had learned how to say no to sex by seeing something on TV, and nearly half said that TV had helped them talk to a partner about safe sex (Kaiser Family Foundation, 2002). In 2008, a study showed that viewers of a *Grey's Anatomy* episode had learned that HIV-positive mothers could still have HIV-negative babies (Rideout, 2008) (see Figure 3.12).

Other national media campaigns have also tried to increase parent-teen communication about sex (Evans, Davis, Ashley, & Khan, 2012; Palen et al., 2011). For example, an innovative campaign in North Carolina used TV and radio PSAs and billboards to encourage parents to talk to their teenagers about sex. "Talk to your kids about sex. Everyone else is," was the primary message, and a subsequent survey of 1,132 parents found that the campaign had indeed been effective (DuRant, Wolfson, LaFrance, Balkrishnan, & Altman, 2006).

Community-based campaigns have been effective in reducing the risk of repeated STDs in adolescents who initially test positive for one (Sznitman et al., 2011). Both the

Figure 3.11 Results of study on conversations with parents about sex as a result of watching television.

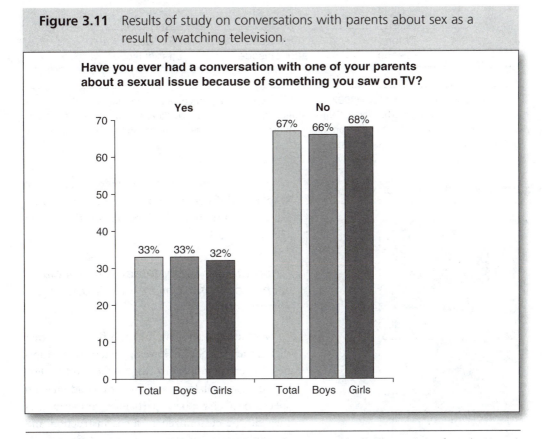

SOURCE: Kaiser Family Foundation (2002). This information was reprinted with permission from the Henry J. Kaiser Family Foundation. The Kaiser Family Foundation, based in Menlo Park, California, is a nonprofit, private operating foundation focusing on the major health care issues facing the nation and is not associated with Kaiser Permanente or Kaiser Industries.

Figure 3.12 A study of *Grey's Anatomy* viewers after an episode involving a pregnant woman who initially thinks she must have an abortion because she is HIV positive (Rideout, 2008). After the doctors educate her, she changes her mind.

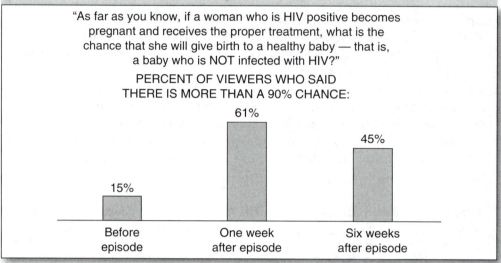

"As far as you know, if a woman who is HIV positive becomes pregnant and receives the proper treatment, what is the chance that she will give birth to a healthy baby — that is, a baby who is NOT infected with HIV?"

PERCENT OF VIEWERS WHO SAID
THERE IS MORE THAN A 90% CHANCE:

	61%	
15%		45%
Before episode	One week after episode	Six weeks after episode

SOURCE: Kaiser Family Foundation (2002). This information was reprinted with permission from the Henry J. Kaiser Family Foundation. The Kaiser Family Foundation, based in Menlo Park, California, is a nonprofit, private operating foundation focusing on the major health care issues facing the nation and is not associated with Kaiser Permanente or Kaiser Industries.

Figure 3.13 Advocates for Youth ad.

SOURCE: Advocates for Youth (www.advocatesforyouth .org). Reprinted with permission.

National Campaign to Prevent Teen and Unplanned Pregnancy and Advocates for Youth have run similar campaigns across the nation (see Figure 3.13).

Opportunities Presented by New Media Technologies for Children With Learning Differences

New technologies such as the iPad and other digital learning devices have opened up opportunities for learning and growing in the modern era. The educational tools available for children with special needs have been particularly important, as they can be customized to focus instruction and curriculum on those areas where a student needs the greatest amount of assistance (Ayres, Maguire, & McClimon, 2009). Children with dyslexia, for example, have been found to benefit from computer software that recodes words into multisensory representations comprising visual and auditory codes (Kast, Baschera, Gross, Jancke, & Meyer, 2011). In one study, low-performing kindergart-ners made significantly greater gains in early literacy skills when using computer-assisted instruction to supplement a phonics-based reading curriculum compared to children in typical classrooms (Macaruso & Rodman, 2011).

Autism presents unique issues for educators and parents, and media can help to support efforts at instruction in both the cognitive and social realms. A systematic review of the use of computer-based interventions (CBI) to teach communication skills to children with autism sug-gests that initial studies are promising (Ramdoss et al., 2011). Studies have shown that autistic children can learn from computer-based video instruction (CBVI) that leads them through social protocols, such as turn taking (Simpson, Langone, & Ayres, 2004), as well as functional life skills, such as making a sandwich or setting the table (Ayres et al., 2009). Video games that are popular with neurotypical children have also been found to benefit children with autism. In one study, researchers taught children with autism to play *Guitar Hero II*, and this game playing helped keep children on task. The authors of the study argue that the ability to play games like *Guitar Hero* can also translate into greater social engagement (Blum-Dimaya, Reeve, Reeve, & Hoch, 2010).

Learning to Learn From Media

Children are not born using media. Indeed, as much as children are socialized by media, they are socialized to use media in particular ways. Social psychologist Gavriel Salomon system-atically explored how children's preconceptions about a medium—for example, that print is "hard" and television is "easy"—shape the amount of mental effort they will invest in process-ing the medium. This amount of invested mental effort, or AIME, is defined as "the number of non-automatic mental elaborations applied to the material" (Salomon, 1984). AIME, in turn, shapes how much children will take away from the medium; that is, how much they might learn. The contexts of a child's life will contribute to how "shallowly" or "deeply" he or she will process mediated information (Cohen & Salomon, 1979). For example, comparisons of Israeli children and American children during the 1970s showed that, even when IQ was accounted for, Israeli children learned more from television programming than their American counterparts did. He reasoned that this was because at the time of his studies, Israelis used television primarily as a news source. Salomon also found that the perceived demand characteristics (PDCs) of a medium could be altered. Children who were told that they would be asked questions about what they viewed, or who were told to pay attention because the material was hard, did in fact pay more attention and did in fact learn more (Salomon, 1983).

AIME theory raises the question of how children come to think about media as fulfilling particular uses or gratifying particular needs. Van Evra (1998) suggests that since much of television is entertainment, children develop a particular schema for how much processing is required—a schema that will drive viewing of even educational programming. While pre-school programming, particularly that which airs on PBS, has historically had a mission to educate, the past decade has seen a virtual explosion of educational offerings for children—and novel approaches for getting children engaged with the material. Research with the pro-gram *Blue's Clues* has been an interesting case study. The producers of the program designed the series to be "interactive," mimicking Mr. Rogers's (*Mister Rogers' Neighborhood*) style of speaking and pausing as though he were talking with the young viewers themselves. Assessments of viewers' reactions to the series indicate that the program encouraged a novel style of TV watching—one in which preschoolers talk to characters, shout out solutions to problems, and generally "interact" with what is on the screen. These *Blue's Clues*–induced viewing styles, moreover, translated to the viewing of other programs, including noninteractive ones such as Cartoon Network's *Big Bag* (Crawley et al., 2002).

Conclusion

As the amount of content aimed at children proliferates, and as media become connected as transmedia properties, producers have an opportunity to make the most of the "best" of what is available and leverage it for learning. As Lauricella, Gola, and Calvert (2011) have found, media content that contains a socially meaningful character (in their study, the *Sesame Street* character Elmo) can enhance children's learning and attention. Children form relationships with onscreen characters, come to trust that they are socially relevant and meaningful, and trust them to be reliable sources of information (Richert, Robb, & Smith, 2011). To be sure, most children learn best from real, live human beings (Krcmar, 2011). Nevertheless, the stresses facing modern families and the fact that many of our schools are resource poor means that much of childhood learning may occur in front of a screen. Educationally beneficial media characters, stories, and curricula can supplement teaching and parenting, encourage toddlers' exploration, and accommodate children with special learning needs.

Exercises

1. Watch television on Saturday mornings and see if you can find the educational shows commercial broadcast stations are offering to children (you can tell by the "e/i" symbol that is on the screen throughout the show). Can you tell what the "lesson" of the show is?

2. *Sesame Street* is the most researched show on television—and also the most enduring. If you haven't watched it for a while, tune in and see if you can figure out the ways that it has changed.

3. Go to a store or go online to view the kinds of baby-oriented DVDs that are being sold. What are the implicit or explicit educational claims that are being made about the product? As a researcher, how would you test whether there is any evidence to support these claims?

4. One study found that children who were below grade level in reading significantly improved their reading skills by having access to the Internet at home. Think about your own Internet use. How much of the time would you say you spend reading (vs. watching television episodes or movie trailers!)?

5. Design an educational media product for children that you think fills the gap in the current landscape of offerings for children. The product should be theoretically driven and empirically justified. What does it look like?

6. Where do you draw the line between prosocial messages and what George Orwell described as "mind control" in his novel *Nineteen Eighty-Four* (Orwell, 1949)? For example, most people agree that, in general, war is bad. Should prime-time shows contain messages about the recent war in Iraq, or would that be "crossing the line"? Should children's shows such as *Sesame Street* contain antiwar messages? Messages about terrorism? Where do you draw the line between public health and moralizing?

7. Imagine a version of *Sesame Street* designed and produced by (a) the Chinese government, (b) Al Jazeera TV, (c) the former Soviet Union, and (d) the state of California. Who would the main characters be? What would some of the main themes be? Try watching *The World According to Sesame Street,* a documentary showing coproductions from China, Israel/Palestine, and Russia. Are there differences between these shows and the American version?

8. As regular viewers of *The Simpsons* know, *The Itchy & Scratchy Show* is a parody of violent children's cartoons. Like Wile E. Coyote and the Roadrunner, Itchy and Scratchy do little more than pummel each other constantly. After Marge writes a letter to the producer of the show, however, the tone becomes much more prosocial— and dull. Kids began turning off their TV sets and heading outdoors. Can prosocial programming be entertaining as well as educational? Do you think Web-based programs, video games, or social networking sites will be able to make significant improvements in (a) child and adolescent obesity, (b) adolescent drug use, or (c) teen sexual activity?

Notes

1. Every day, on average, children spend nearly four hours (3:51) watching television (including videos and DVDs); one and three-quarters hours (1:44) listening to the radio or to CDs, tapes, or MP3s; just over one hour (1:02) on the computer outside of schoolwork; and just under one hour (0:49) playing video games. By contrast, children say they read for pleasure (books, magazines, newspapers) 43 minutes a day. These data, collected in 2005 by the Kaiser Family Foundation and based on a national sample of 3rd to 12th graders (Rideout, Roberts, & Foehr, 2005), suggest the vast potential of media for contributing to children's cognitive development. This seems particularly true when one contrasts children's media time with the amount spent hanging out with parents (2:17), doing homework (0:50), or doing chores (0:32) (Rideout et al., 2005).

2. In 2007, Univision received a record fine for labeling a telenovela (Spanish-language soap opera for adults) as educational for children (Ahrens, 2007).

References

Ahrens, F. (2007, February 25). FCC expected to impose record $24 million fine against Univision. *Washington Post.* Retrieved from http://www.washingtonpost.com/wp-dyn/content/article/2007/02/24/AR2007022401453.html

Allday, E. (2006, April 26). Safer sex info goes high-tech. *San Francisco Chronicle,* p. B-1.

Anderson, C. A., Gentile, D. A., & Dill, K. E. (2012). Prosocial, antisocial, and other effects of recreational video games. In D. G. Singer & J. L. Singer (Eds.), *Handbook of children and the media* (2nd ed., pp. 249–272). Thousand Oaks, CA: Sage.

Anderson, D. R., Huston, A. C., Schmitt, K. L., Linebarger, D. L., & Wright, J. C. (2001). Early childhood television viewing and adolescent behavior. *Monographs of the Society for Research in Child Development, 68*(Serial No. 264), 1–143.

Anderson, D. R., Lorch, E. P., Field, D. E., & Sanders, J. (1981). The effects of TV program comprehensibility on preschool children's visual attention to television. *Child Development, 52,* 151–157.

Arnold, D. H., Ortiz, C., Curry, J. C., Stowe, R. M., Goldstein, N. E., Fisher, P. H., . . . Yershova, K. (1999). Promoting academic success and preventing disruptive behavior disorders through community partnership. *Journal of Community Psychology, 5,* 589–598.

Ayres, K. M., Maguire, A., & McClimon, D. (2009). Acquisition and generalization of chained tasks taught with computer based video instruction to children with autism. *Education and Training in Developmental Disabilities, 44*(4), 493–508.

Bailey, B. W., & McInnis, K. (2011). Energy cost of exergaming: A comparison of the energy cost of 6 forms of exergaming. *Archives of Pediatrics and Adolescent Medicine, 165,* 597–602.

Baldwin, M. W., Baccus, J. R., & Milyavskaya, M. (2010). Computer game associating self-concept to images of acceptance can reduce adolescents' aggressiveness in response to social rejection. *Cognition and Emotion, 24*(5), 855–862.

Barr, R., Lauricella, A., Zack, E., & Calvert, S. (2010). Infant and early childhood exposure to adult-directed and child-directed television programming: Relations with cognitive skills at age four. *Merill-Palmer Quarterly, 56*(1), 21–48.

Beal, C., & Arroyo, I. (2002). The AnimalWatch project: Creating an intelligent computer mathematics tutor. In S. Calvert, A. Jordan, & R. Cocking (Eds.), *Children in the digital age: Influences of electronic media on development* (pp. 183–198). Westport, CT: Praeger.

Beale, I. L., Kato, P. M., Marin-Bowling, V. M. Guthrie, N., & Cole, S. W. (2007). Improvement in cancer-related knowledge following use of a psychoeducational video game for adolescents and young adults with cancer. *Journal of Adolescent Health, 41,* 263–270.

Bellin, H., & Singer, D. (2006). My Magic Story Car: Video-based play intervention to strengthen emergent literacy of at-risk preschoolers. In D. Singer, R. Golinkoff, & K. Hirsh-Pasek (Eds.), *Play = learning: How play motivates and enhances children's cognitive and social-emotional growth* (pp. 101–123). Oxford, UK: Oxford University Press.

Bingham, P. M., Bates, J. H. T., Thompson-Figueroa, J., & Lahiri, T. (2010). A breath biofeedback computer game for children with cystic fibrosis. *Clinical Pediatrics, 49,* 337–342.

Blum-Dimaya, A., Reeve, S. A., Reeve, K. F., & Hoch, H. (2010). Teaching children with autism to play a video game using activity schedules and game-embedded simultaneous video modeling. *Education and Treatment of Children, 33*(3), 351–370.

Boyar, R., Levine, D., & Zensius N. (2011). *TECHsex: Youth sexuality and reproductive health in the digital age.* Oakland, CA: ISIS.

Brink, S. (2006, November 13). Prime time to learn. *Los Angeles Times.* Retrieved from http://www.latimes.com/features/health/la-he-media13nov13,1,5874234.story

Bull, S. S., Levine, D. K., Black, S. R., Schmiege, S. J., & Santelli, J. (2012). Social media–delivered sexual health intervention: A cluster randomized controlled trial. *American Journal of Preventive Medicine, 43,* 467–474.

Calvert, S., & Kotler, J. (2003). Lessons from children's television: The impact of the Children's Television Act on children's learning. *Applied Developmental Psychology, 24,* 275–335.

Cantor, J. (2012). The media and children's fears, anxieties, and perceptions of danger. In D. Singer & J. Singer (Eds.), *Handbook of children and the media* (2nd ed.). Thousand Oaks, CA: Sage.

Carroll, J. A., & Kirkpatrick, R. L. (2011). *Impact of social media on adolescent behavioral health in California.* Oakland, CA: Adolescent Health Collaborative.

Children's Television Act of 1990, Pub. L. No. 101-437, 104 Stat. 996 (codified at 47 U.S.C. 303a-303b (2006)).

Christakis, D. A., Gilkerson, J., Richards, J. A., Zimmerman, F. J., Garrison, M. M., Xu, D., . . . Yapanel, U. (2001). Audible television and decreased adult words, infant vocalizations, and conversational turns. *Archives of Pediatrics and Adolescent Medicine, 163*(6), 554–558.

Clark-Flory, T. (2012, March 31). Facebook: The next tool in fighting STDs. *Salon.* Retrieved from http://www.salon.com/2012/04/01/facebook_the_next_tool_in_fighting_stds/

Cohen, A., & Salomon, G. (1979). Children's literate television viewing: Surprises and possible explanations. *Journal of Communication, 29*(3), 156–163.

Collins, R. L., Elliott, M. N., Berry, S. H., Kanouse, D. E., & Hunter, S. B. (2003). Entertainment television as a healthy sex educator: The impact of condom-efficacy information in an episode of *Friends. Pediatrics, 112,* 1115–1121.

Collins, R. L., Martino, S. C., & Shaw, R. (2011). *Influence of new media on adolescent sexual health: Evidence and opportunities.* Santa Monica, CA: RAND.

Crawley, A. M., Anderson, D. R., Santomero, A., Wilder, A., Williams, M., Evans, M. K., & Bryant, J. (2002). Do children learn how to watch television? The impact of extensive experience with *Blue's Clues* on preschool children's television viewing behavior. *Journal of Communication, 52*(2), 264–279.

Crawley, A. M., Anderson, D. R., Wilder, A., Williams, M., & Santomero, A. (1999). Effects of repeated exposures to a single episode of the television program *Blue's Clues* on the viewing behaviors and comprehension of preschool children. *Journal of Educational Psychology, 91,* 630–637.

Delgado, H. M., & Austin, S. B. (2007). Can media promote responsible sexual behaviors among adolescents and young adults? *Current Opinion in Pediatrics, 19,* 405-410.

DeLoache, J. S., Chiong, C., Sherman, K., Islam, N., Vanderborght, M., Troseth, G. L., . . . O'Doherty, K. (2010). Do babies learn from baby media? *Psychological Science, 21*(11), 1570–1574.

DuRant, R. H., Wolfson, M., LaFrance, B., Balkrishnan, R., & Altman, D. (2006). An evaluation of a mass media campaign to encourage parents of adolescents to talk to their children about sex. *Journal of Adolescent Health, 38,* 298.e1–299.e9.

Ellis, J. (2007, February 21). *New DVD game battles childhood obesity.* Retrieved from http://abcnews.go.com/Business/print?id=2892244.

Ennemoser, M., & Schneider, W. (2007). Relations of television viewing and reading: Findings from a 4-year longitudinal study. *Journal of Educational Psychology, 99*(2), 349–368.

Evans, W. D., Davis K. C., Ashley, O. S., & Khan, M. (2012). Effects of media messages on parent-child sexual communication. *Journal of Health Communication, 17,* 498–514.

Federal Communications Commission. (1979). *Television programming for children: A report of the children's task force* (Vol. 1, at 3).

Federal Communications Commission. (1996). In the matter of policies and rules concerning children's television programming: Report and order. *Federal Communications Commission Record, 11,* 10660–10778.

Fein, G. G. (1981). Pretend play in childhood: An integrative review. *Child Development, 52,* 1095–1118.

Fisch, S., & Bernstein, L. (2001). Formative research revealed: Methodological and process issues in formative research. In S. Fisch & R. Truglio (Eds.), *"G" is for growing* (pp. 39–60). Mahwah, NJ: Lawrence Erlbaum.

Fisch, S., & Truglio, R. (Eds.). (2001). *"G" is for growing.* Mahwah, NJ: Lawrence Erlbaum.

Fisch, S., Truglio, R., & Cole, C. (1999). The impact of *Sesame Street* on preschool children: A review and synthesis of 30 years' research. *Media Psychology, 1,* 165–190.

Friedrich-Cofer, L. K., Huston-Stein, A., Kipnis, D. M., Susman, E. J., & Clewett, A. S. (1979). Environmental enhancement of prosocial television content: Effect on interpersonal behavior, imaginative play, and self-regulation in a natural setting. *Developmental Psychology, 15,* 637–646.

Garrison, M. (July 24, 2012). Sesame Street *steps into Indian education business.* Retrieved from http://www.marketplace.org/topics/business/education/sesame-street-steps-indian-education-business

Gentile, D. A., Anderson, C.A., Yukawa, S., Ihori, N., Saleem, M., Ming, L. K., . . . Sakamoto, A. (2009). The effects of prosocial video games on prosocial behaviors: International evidence from correlational, longitudinal, and experimental studies. *Personality and Social Psychology Bulletin, 35,* 752–763.

Gerbner, G., Gross, L., Signorielli, N., & Morgan, M. (1986). *Television's mean world: Violence profiles No. 14–15.* Philadelphia: University of Pennsylvania, Annenberg School of Communications.

Glover, R. J., Garmon, L. C., & Hull, D. M. (2011). Media's moral messages: Assessing perceptions of moral content in television programming. *Journal of Moral Education, 40*(1), 89–104.

Golomb, M. R., McDonald, B. C., Warden, S. J., Yonkman, J., Saykin, A. J., Shirley, B., . . . Burdea, G. C. (2010). In-home virtual reality videogame telerehabilitation in adolescents with hemiplegic cerebral palsy. *Archives of Physical Medicine and Rehabilitation, 91,* 1–8.

Greitemeyer, T., & Osswald, S. (2010). Effects of prosocial video games on prosocial behavior. *Journal of Personality and Social Psychology, 98,* 211–221.

Guse, K., Levine, D., Martins, S., Lira, A., Gaarde, J., Westmorland, W., & Gilliam M. (2012). Interventions using new digital media to improve adolescent sexual health: A systematic review. *Journal of Adolescent Health.* doi:10.1016/j.jadohealth.2012.03.014

Healy, J. (1990). *Endangered minds: Why our children don't think.* New York, NY: Simon & Schuster.

Hearold, S. (1986). A synthesis of 1043 effects of television on social behavior. In G. Comstock (Ed.), *Public communication and behavior* (Vol. 1, pp. 65–133). Orlando, FL: Academic Press.

Hogan, M. (2012a). Parents and older adults: Models and monitors of healthy media habits. In D. G. Singer & J. L. Singer (Eds.), *Handbook of children and the media* (2nd ed., pp. 661–680). Thousand Oaks, CA: Sage.

Hogan, M. (2012b). Prosocial effects of media. *Pediatric Clinics of North America, 59,* 635–645.

Hogan, M. J., & Strasburger, V. C. (2008). Media and prosocial behavior in children and adolescents. In L. Nucci & D. Narvaez (Eds.), *Handbook of moral and character education.* Mahwah, NJ: Lawrence Erlbaum.

Jackson, L. A., von Ey, A., Biocca, F., Barbatsis, G., Zhao, Y., & Fitzgerald, H. (2006). Does home Internet use influence the academic performance of low-income children? *Developmental Psychology, 42,* 429–435.

Jenkins, H. (2006). *Convergence culture: Where old and new media collide.* New York, NY: New York University Press.

Johnson, S. (2005). *Everything bad is good for you: How today's popular culture is actually making us smarter.* New York, NY: Riverhead.

Jones, M., Luce, K. H., Osborne, M. I., Taylor K., Cunning, D., Celio Doyle, A., . . . Taylor, B. (2008). Randomized, controlled trial of an Internet-facilitated intervention for reducing binge eating and overweight in adolescents. *Pediatrics, 121,* 453–462.

Jordan, A. (1996). *The state of children's television: An examination of quantity, quality and industry beliefs* (Report No. 2). Philadelphia: University of Pennsylvania, Annenberg Public Policy Center.

Jordan, A. (2003). Children remember prosocial program lessons but how much are they learning? [Commentary]. *Journal of Applied Developmental Psychology, 24,* 341–345.

Jordan, A. (2004). The three-hour rule and educational television for children. *Popular Communication, 2*(2), 103–119.

Joseph, C. L. M., Ownby, D. R., Havstad, S. L., Saltzgaber, M. S., Considine, S., Johnson, D., . . . Cole Johnson, C. (2012). Evaluation of a Web-based asthma management intervention program for urban teenagers: Reaching the hard to reach. *Journal of Adolescent Health.* doi: 10.1016/j.jado health.2012.07.009

Kaiser Family Foundation. (2002). *Teens, sex and TV.* Menlo Park, CA: Author.

Kaiser Family Foundation. (2004). *Entertainment education and health in the United States.* Menlo Park, CA: Author.

Kaiser Family Foundation. (2006, November 30). African Broadcast Media Partnership Against HIV/ AIDS launches coordinated, multi-year media campaign in 25 countries [News release]. Menlo Park, CA: Author.

Kaiser Family Foundation. (2012, April 9). MTV audience encouraged to "GYT" [News release]. Menlo Park, CA: Author.

Kast, M., Baschera, G.M., Gross, M., Jancke, L., & Meyer, M. (2011). Computer-based learning of spelling skills in children with and without dyslexia. *Annals of Dyslexia, 61,* 177–200.

Kiene, S. M., & Barta, W. D. (2006). A brief individualized computer-delivered sexual risk reduction intervention increases HIV/AIDS preventive behavior. *Journal of Adolescent Health, 39,* 404–410.

Kirkorian, H. L., Pempek, T. A., Murphy, L. A., Schmidt, M. E., & Anderson, D. (2009). The impact of background television on parent-child interaction. *Child Development, 80*(5), 1350–1359.

Knowlton, L., & Costigan, L. (Producers/Directors). (2006). *The world according to* Sesame Street [Documentary]. United States: Participant Productions.

Krcmar, M. (2011). Word learning in very young children from infant-directed DVDs. *Journal of Communication, 61,* 780–794.

Krcmar, M., & Curtis, S. (2003). Mental models: Understanding the impact of fantasy violence on children's moral reasoning. *Journal of Communication, 53*(3), 460–478.

Krcmar, M., & Valkenburg, P. (1999). A scale to assess children's moral interpretations of justified and unjustified violence and its relationship to television viewing. *Communication Research, 26,* 608–634.

Kunkel, D. (1998). Policy battles over defining children's educational television. *Annals of the American Academy of Political and Social Sciences, 557,* 39–53.

Kunkel, D., & Canepa, J. (1994). Broadcasters' license renewal claims regarding children's educational programming. *Journal of Broadcasting and Electronic Media, 38,* 397–416.

Kunkel, D., & Wilcox, B. (2001). Children and media policy. In D. Singer & J. Singer (Eds.), *Handbook of children and the media* (pp. 589–604). Thousand Oaks, CA: Sage.

Ladd, G. W., Birch, S. H., & Buhs, E. S. (1999). Children's social and scholastic lives in kindergarten: Related spheres of influence? *Child Development, 70,* 1373–1400.

Lanningham-Foster, L., Jensen, T. B., Foster, R. C., Redmond, A. B., Walker, B. A., Heinz, D., & Levine, J. A. (2006). Energy expenditure of sedentary screen time compared with active screen time for children. *Pediatrics, 118,* e1831–e1835.

Lauricella, A., Gola, A. A., & Calvert, C. (2011). Toddlers' learning from socially meaningful video characters. *Media Psychology, 14*(2), 216–232.

Linebarger, D., Piotrowski, J. T., & Greenwood, C. (2010). On-screen print: The role of captions as a supplemental literacy tool. *Journal of Research in Reading, 33*(2), 148–167.

Linebarger, D., & Walker, D. (2004). Infants' and toddlers' television viewing and language outcomes. *American Behavioral Scientist, 46,* 1–22.

Lou, C.-H., Zhao, Q., Gao, E.-S., & Shah, I. H. (2006). Can the Internet be used effectively to provide sex education to young people in China? *Journal of Adolescent Health, 39,* 720–728.

Lowery, S. A., & DeFleur, M. L. (1995). *Milestones in mass communication research.* White Plains, NY: Longman.

Macaruso, P., & Rodman, A. (2011). Efficacy of computer-assisted instruction for the development of early literacy skills in young children. *Reading Psychology, 32,* 172–196.

Madsen, K. A., Yen, S., Wlasiuk, L., Newman, T. B., & Lustig, R. (2007). Feasibility of a dance videogame to promote weight loss among overweight children and adolescents. *Archives of Pediatrics and Adolescent Medicine, 161,* 105–107.

Managing ailments through video games. (1999, April 6). *New York Times.* Retrieved from http://www .nytimes.com/1999/04/06/health/managing-ailments-through-video-games.html?pagewanted=print &src=pm

Mandler, J. M. (1984). *Stories, scripts and scenes: Aspects of schema theory.* Hillsdale, NJ: Lawrence Erlbaum.

Mares, M. L., Braun, M. T., & Hernandez, P. (2012). Pessimism and anxiety: Effects of tween sitcoms on expectations and feelings about peer relationships in school. *Media Psychology, 15,* 121–147.

Mares, M.-L., & Woodard, E. (2001). Prosocial effects on children's social interactions. In D. G. Singer & J. L. Singer (Eds.), *Handbook of children and the media* (pp. 183–206). Thousand Oaks, CA: Sage.

Mares, M.-L., & Woodard, E. (2005). Positive effects of television on children's social interactions: A meta-analysis. *Media Psychology, 7,* 301–322.

McGonigal, J. (2011). *Reality is broken: Why games make us better and how they can change the world.* New York, NY: Pengu.

McIntyre, Jeff J. (2013). The political narrative of children's media research. In K. Dill (Ed.) *The Oxford Handbook of Media Psychology* (pp. 462–473). New York, NY: Oxford University Press.

McLelland, M. M., Morrison, F. J., & Holmes, D. L. (2000). Children at risk for early academic problems: The role of learning-related social skills. *Early Childhood Research Quarterly, 15,* 307–329.

McLuhan, M. (1964). *Understanding media: The extension of man.* New York, NY: McGraw-Hill.

Mendolsohn, A. L., Brockmeyer, C. A., Dreyer, B. P., Fierman, A. H., Serkule-Silberman, S. B., & Tomopoulos, S. (2010). Do verbal interactions with infants during electronic media exposure mitigate adverse impacts on their language development as toddlers? *Infant and Child Development, 19*(6), 577–593.

Merry, S. N., Stasiak, K., Shepherd, M., Frampton, C., Fleming, T., & Lucassen, M. F. G. (2012). The effectiveness of SPARX, a computerized self help intervention for adolescents seeking help for depression: Randomized controlled non-inferiority trial. *British Medical Journal, 344,* e2598.

Moreno, M. A., & Kolb, J. (2012). Social networking sites and adolescent health. *Pediatric Clinics of North America, 59,* 601–612.

Moritz, O. (2007, February 10). Defense bigs ask "24" to cool it on torture. *New York Daily News,* Sports Final Edition, p. 3.

Naigles, L., & Mayeux, L. (2001). Television as incidental language teacher. In D. Singer & J. Singer (Eds.), *Handbook of children and the media* (pp. 135–152). Thousand Oaks, CA: Sage.

Nijhof, S. L., Bleijenberg, G., Uiterwaal, C. S. P. M., Kimpen, J. L. L., & van de Putte, E. M. (2012). Effectiveness of Internet-based cognitive behavioural treatment for adolescents with chronic fatigue syndrome (FITNET): A randomized controlled trial. *Lancet, 379,* 1412–1418.

Noar, S. M. (2006). A 10-year retrospective of research in health mass media campaigns: Where do we go from here? *Journal of Communication, 11,* 21–42.

Okagaki, L., & Frensch, P. (1994). Effects of video game playing on measures of spatial performance: Gender effects in late adolescence. *Journal of Applied Developmental Psychology, 15,* 33–58.

O'Loughlin, E. K., Dugas, E. N., Sabiston, C. M., & O'Loughlin, J. L. (2012). Prevalence and correlates of exergaming in youth. *Pediatrics, 130,* 1–9.

Orwell, G. (1949). *Nineteen eighty-four.* London, UK: Secker and Warburg.

Palen, L. A., Ashley, O. S., Gard, J. C., Kan, M. L., Davis, K. C., & Evans, W.D. (2011). Effects of media campaign messages targeting parents on adolescent sexual beliefs: A randomized controlled trial with a national sample. *Family and Community Health, 34,* 28–38.

Palmer, E. (1988). *Television and America's children: A crisis of neglect.* New York, NY: Oxford University Press.

Pecora, N. (1998). *The business of children's entertainment.* New York, NY: Guilford.

Perry, R. C. W., Kayekjian, K.C., Braun, R.A., Cantu, M., Sheoran, B., & Chung, P. J. (2012). Adolescents' perspectives on the use of a text messaging service for preventive sexual health promotion. *Journal of Adolescent Health.* doi:10.1016/j.jadohealth.2011.11.012

Phillips, A. (2012). *A creator's guide to transmedia storytelling: How to captivate and engage audiences across multiple platforms.* New York, NY: McGraw-Hill.

Primack, B. A., Carroll, M. V., McNamara, M., Klem, M. L., King, B., Rich, M.,. . . . Nayak, S. (2012). Role of video games in improving health-related outcomes: A systematic review. *American Journal of Preventive Medicine, 42,* 630–638.

Prot, S., McDonald, K. A., Anderson, C. A., & Gentile D. A. (2012). Video games: Good, bad, or other? *Pediatric Clinics of North America, 59,* 647–658.

Ramdoss, S., Lang, R., Mulloy, A., Franco, J., O'Reilly, M., Didden, R., & Lancioni, G. (2011). Use of computer-based interventions to teach communication skills to children with autism spectrum disorders: A systematic review. *Journal of Behavioral Education, 20,* 55–76.

Raver, C. C. (2002). Emotions matter: Making the case for the role of young children's emotional development for early school readiness. *Social Policy Report, 16*(3), 1–18.

Rice, M. (1984). The words of children's television. *Journal of Broadcasting, 28,* 445–461.

Rice, M. (1990). Preschoolers' QUIL: Quick incidental learning of words. In G. Conti-Ransden & C. Snow (Eds.), *Children's language* (Vol. 7, pp. 171–194). Hillsdale, NJ: Lawrence Erlbaum.

Richert, R. A., Robb, M. B., & Smith, E. I. (2011). Media as social partners: The social nature of young children's learning from screen media. *Child Development, 82*(1), 82–95.

Rideout, V. J. (2003). *Reaching the MTV generation: Recent research on the impact of the Kaiser Family Foundation/MTV Public Education Campaign on Sexual Health.* Menlo Park, CA: Kaiser Family Foundation.

Rideout, V. (2008). *Television as a health educator: A case study of* Grey's Anatomy. Menlo Park, CA: Kaiser Family Foundation.

Rideout, V., Roberts, D., & Foehr, U. (2005). *Generation M: Media in the lives of 8–18 year-olds.* Menlo Park, CA: Kaiser Family Foundation.

Runco, M. A., & Pezdek, K. (1984). The effect of television and radio on children's creativity. *Human Communication Research, 11,* 109–120.

Saarni, C. (1990). Emotional competence: How emotions and relationships become integrated. In R. Thompson (Ed.), *Nebraska Symposium on Motivation 1988: Socioemotional development* (pp. 115–182). Lincoln: University of Nebraska Press.

Salomon, G. (1983). Television watching and mental effort: A social psychological view. In D. Anderson & J. Bryant (Eds.), *Children's understanding of television: Research on attention and comprehension* (pp. 181–198). New York, NY: Academic Press.

Salomon, G. (1984). Television is "easy" and print is "tough": The differential investment of mental effort as a function of perceptions and attributions. *Journal of Educational Psychology, 76,* 647–658.

Scantlin, R., & Jordan, A (2006). Families' experiences with the V-chip: An exploratory study. *Journal of Family Communication, 6*(2), 139–159.

Schmidt, M. E., Pempek, H. L., Kirkorian, H. L., Lund, A. F., & Anderson, D. R. (2008). The effects of background television on the toy play behavior of very young children. *Child Development, 79*(4), 1137–1151.

Simpson, A., Langone, J., & Ayres, K. M. (2004). Embedded video and computer-based instruction to improve social skills for students with autism. *Education and Training in Developmental Disabilities, 39,* 240–252.

Singer, J. L., & Singer, D. G. (1976). Can TV stimulate imaginative play? *Journal of Communication, 26*(3), 74–80.

Singer, J. L., & Singer, D. G. (1998). *Barney & Friends* as entertainment and education: Evaluating the quality and effectiveness of a television series for preschool children. In J. K. Asamen & G. Berry (Eds.), *Research paradigms, television, and social behavior* (pp. 305–367). Beverly Hills, CA: Sage.

Singer, J. L., Singer, D. G., & Rapaczynski, W. S. (1984). Family patterns and television viewing as predictors of children's beliefs and aggression. *Journal of Communication, 34*(2), 73–89.

Singhal, A., & Rogers, E. M. (1999). *Entertainment-education: A communication strategy for social change.* Mahwah, NJ: Lawrence Erlbaum.

Smallwood, S. R., Morris, M. M., Fallows, S. J., & Buckley, J. P. (2012). Physiologic responses and energy expenditure of Kinect active video game play in schoolchildren. *Archives of Pediatrics and Adolescent Medicine, 166,* 1005–1009.

Smith, S. W., Smith, S. L., Pieper, K. M., Yoo, J. H., Ferris, A. L., Downs, E., & Bowden, B. (2006). Altruism on American television: Examining the amount of, and context surrounding, acts of helping and sharing. *Journal of Communication, 56*, 707–727.

Sniderman, Z. (2011, August 9). *MTV app locates places to get condoms.* Retrieved from http://mashable .com/2011/08/09/mtv-condom-app/

Sprafkin, J. N., Liebert, R. M., & Poulos, R. W. (1975). Effects of a prosocial televised example on children's helping. *Journal of Experimental Child Psychology, 20*, 119–126.

Stockwell, M.S., Olshen Kharbanda, E., Andres Martinez, R., Vargas, C. Y., Vawdrey, D. K., & Camargo, S. (2012). Effect of a text messaging intervention on influenza vaccination in an urban, low-income pediatric and adolescent population: A randomized controlled trial. *Journal of the American Medical Association, 307*, 1702–1708.

Subrahmanyam, K., & Greenfield, P. (1994). Effect of video game practice on spatial skills in girls and boys. *Journal of Applied Developmental Psychology, 15*, 13–32.

Sznitman, S., Stanton, B. F., Vanable, P. A., Carey, M. P., Valois, R. F., Brown, L. K., . . . Romer, D. (2011). Long term effects of community-based STI screening and mass media HIV prevention messages on sexual risk behaviors of African American adolescents. *AIDS and Behavior, 15*, 1755–1763.

Thomas, R. M. (2005). *Comparing theories of child development* (6th ed.). Belmont, CA: Thomson Wadsworth.

Truglio, R. T., Lovelace, V. O., Segui, I., & Schneider, S. (2001). The varied role of formative research: Case studies from 30 years. In R. Truglio & S. Fisch (Eds.), *"G" is for growing.* Mahwah, NJ: Lawrence Erlbaum.

Turow, J. (1981). *Entertainment, education and the hard sell: Three decades of network children's television.* New York, NY: Praeger.

Underwood, C., Hachonda, H., Serlemitsos, E., & Bharath-Kumar, U. (2006). Reducing the risk of HIV transmission among adolescents in Zambia: Psychosocial and behavioral correlates of viewing a risk-reduction media campaign. *Journal of Adolescent Health, 38*, 55e1–55e13.

Valkenburg, P. (2001). Television and the child's developing imagination. In D. Singer & J. Singer (Eds.), *Handbook of children and the media* (pp. 121–134). Thousand Oaks, CA: Sage.

Valkenburg, P., & Beentjes, J. (1997). Children's creative imagination in response to radio and television stories. *Journal of Communication, 47*(2), 21–38.

Van Evra, J. (1998). *Television and child development.* Mahwah, NJ: Lawrence Erlbaum.

Wentzel, K. R., & Asher, S. R. (1995). The academic lives of neglected, rejected, popular, and controversial children. *Child Development, 66*, 754–763.

Whitehill, J. M., Brockman, L. N., & Moreno, M. A. (2013). "Just talk to me": Communicating with college students about depression disclosures on Facebook. *Journal of Adolescent Health, 52*, 122–127.

Whiteley, L. B., Mello, J., Hunt, O., & Brown, L. K. (2012). A review of sexual health Web sites for adolescents. *Clinical Pediatrics, 51*, 209–213.

Whittemore, R., Jeon, S., & Grey, M. (2012). An Internet obesity prevention program for adolescents. *Journal of Adolescent Health.* doi: 10.1016/j.jadohealth.2012.07.014

Wilson, B. J., & Cantor, J. (1985). Developmental differences in empathy with a television protagonist's fear. *Journal of Experimental Child Psychology, 39*, 284–299.

Wilson, B. J., Kunkel, D., & Drogos, K. L. (2008). *Educationally insufficient? An analysis of the availability and educational quality of children's E/I programming.* Retrieved from http://www.childrennow.org/ uploads/documents/eireport_2008.pdf

Wright, J., St. Peters, M., & Huston, A. (1990). Family television use and its relation to children's cognitive skills and social behavior. In J. Bryant (Ed.), *Television and the American family* (pp. 227–251). Hillsdale, NJ: Lawrence Erlbaum.

Ybarra, M. (2013, in press). Technology and public health interventions. In A. Jordan & D. Romer (Eds.). *Media and the well-being of children and adolescents.* New York: Oxford University Press.

CHAPTER 4

Media Violence

True, media violence is not likely to turn an otherwise fine child into a violent criminal. But, just as every cigarette one smokes increases a little bit the likelihood of a lung tumor someday, every violent show one watches increases just a little bit the likelihood of behaving more aggressively in some situation.

—Psychologists Brad J. Bushman and L. Rowell Huesmann
in *Handbook of Children and the Media* (2001, p. 248)

It's easy to fall into the trap of thinking that young people emulate literally what they see in entertainment. That if they like a rapper who insults gays, then they must be learning hostility to gays, and if they love a movie hero who defeats villainy with a gun, then they must be learning to solve problems with violence. Anthropologists and psychologists who study play, however, have shown that there are many other functions as well—one of which is to enable children to pretend to be just what they know they'll never be.

—Gerard Jones
*Killing Monsters: Our Children's Need for Fantasy,
Heroism, and Make-Believe Violence* (2002, p. 11)

We find it harder, though, to shield our children from the relentless, in-your-face glorification of violence promoted on our TV screens and in the movies. It's every-where, and you can't seem to find the remote fast enough.

—Representative Kevin Brady (R-TX.)
as quoted in the *New York Times* (Lichtblau, 2013)

Media violence isn't going to disappear and most current efforts to stop it are unlikely to succeed. Like displays of material excess and gratuitous sex, violence exists within a commercial structure predicated on a powerful system of fantasies.

—David Trend
*The Myth of Media Violence:
A Critical Introduction* (2007, p. 10)

Violence in America threatens the very fabric of contemporary society. In 2010 alone, over 1.2 million violent crimes occurred in this country, which breaks down into one murder every 35 minutes, one forcible rape every six minutes, one robbery every minute, and one aggravated assault every 40 seconds (U.S. Department of Justice, 2011). Looking just at young people, homicide is the second leading cause of death among 10- to 24-year-olds (Centers for Disease Control and Prevention [CDC], 2010). Every day, 16 children in this country are murdered, and 82% of these youth are killed with firearms (CDC, 2006). Despite a drop in violent crime since the 1990s, the United States still ranks first among industrialized nations in homicides (United Nations Office on Drugs and Crime, 2012). The statistics are certainly troubling, but so are the national tragedies involving homicide. The Newtown, Connecticut, massacre of 20 young children and 6 school staff members is only one recent incident in a deluge of shootings in America over the past decade. The fact that several of these shootings have occurred in schools heightens our sense of vulnerability for our youth (Toppo, 2007). Responding to the 2012 movie theater killings in Aurora, Colorado, Chicago-based journalist Robert Koehler (2012) argued,

> The U.S. is far more violent than other developed countries, for reasons seldom addressed or even looked at in anything like a holistic way. The root of the matter, as I see it, is our false distinction between "good violence" and "bad violence." We don't address the issue systemically because of our social investment in "good violence" and the enormous payoff it delivers to some. But good violence—the authorized, glorified, "necessary" kind—inevitably morphs into bad violence from time to time, and thus we are delivered jolts of headline-grabbing horror on a regular basis.

As violence continues to permeate our society, government officials, health professionals, educators, and scientists struggle to understand the complex causes of human aggression. To be sure, no single factor propels a person to become violent. Neurological and hormonal abnormalities (Carré, McCormick, & Hariri, 2011), deficiencies in cognitive functioning (Dodge & Pettit, 2003), and even parental violence (Moretti, Obsuth, Odgers, & Reebye, 2006) have been linked to aggression. So have social forces such as poverty, drugs, and the availability of guns (Archer, 1994; Vaughn et al., 2012). Another factor that continually emerges in public debates about violence is the role of the media. Public opinion polls over the years indicate that most American adults believe that TV and movie violence contributes to real-world crime and aggression (Common Sense Media/Center for American Progress, 2013), and that Hollywood should do more to reduce violence in entertainment programming (Lowry, 1997). Being a parent seems to heighten these concerns. In one poll, 90% of parents with children younger than age 7 believed that TV violence had a serious negative impact on their children (Benton Foundation, 2005).

Are the media part of the problem, or do they merely reflect the violence that is occurring in society? Is media violence chiefly a form of entertainment that dates back to the ancient Greeks, or is it a cultural tool that serves to legitimate violent means of power and social control? There are many opinions about the topic of media violence, and we cannot possibly resolve all of the issues in a single chapter. Consistent with the approach taken throughout this book, we will focus primarily on social scientific research regarding media violence and youth.

There are hundreds of published studies on the impact of media violence. Researchers who have comprehensively reviewed these studies argue quite conclusively that media violence can have antisocial effects (Anderson et al., 2003; Comstock & Powers, 2012; Huesmann, 2007). A 2001 report on youth violence by the surgeon general stated that "research to date justifies sustained efforts to curb the adverse effects of media violence on youths" (U.S. Department of Health and Human Services, 2001). In recent years, several professional organizations have also examined the evidence and concurred that screen violence is harmful to children (e.g., American Academy of Pediatrics, 2009; American Medical Association, 2008).

This chapter begins by addressing the issue of how much violence exists in American media. Then we turn to the question of whether media violence appeals to young people. Next we will give an overview of the research regarding three potential harmful effects of exposure to media violence: (a) the learning of aggressive attitudes and behaviors, (b) desensitization, and (c) fear. As an important contrast, we will present some of the views of critics who disagree with this research. We will conclude with brief sections on guns and the media, suicide and the media, violence in Japan for cross-cultural comparison, and the prosocial effects of media violence on youth.

How Violent Are American Media?

American television and movies provide young people with a relentless diet of violent content. Conservative estimates have indicated that the average child or teenager in this country views 1,000 murders, rapes, and aggravated assaults per year on television alone (Rothenberg, 1975). A review by the American Psychological Association put this figure at 10,000 per year—or approximately 200,000 by the time a child reaches the teenage years (Huston et al., 1992). This statistic is likely to be even higher if a child concentrates her or his viewing on certain channels and types of programming, as we will see below.

In one of the earliest efforts to quantify violence on television, George Gerbner and his colleagues analyzed a week of programming each year from 1967 until the late 1980s (e.g., Gerbner, Gross, Morgan, & Signorielli, 1980; Gerbner, Signorielli, Morgan, & Jackson-Beeck, 1979). Looking at the three major broadcast networks, the researchers found a great deal of consistency over time, with roughly 70% of prime-time programs and 90% of children's programs containing some violence (see Signorielli, 1990). The rate of violence was fairly steady, too, with 5 violent actions per hour featured in prime time and 20 actions per hour in children's shows (see Figure 4.1).

In the late 1990s, the National Television Violence Study (NTVS) assessed violence on broadcast as well as cable television (Smith et al., 1998; Wilson et al., 1997, 1998). In this large-scale content analysis, researchers randomly selected programming during a nine-month period across 23 channels from 6:00 a.m. to 11:00 p.m., seven days a week. This method produced a composite week of television consisting of more than 2,500 hours of content each year. For three consecutive years (1996–1998), the researchers found that a steady 60% of all programs contained some violence. However, violence varied a great deal by channel type. More than 80% of the programs on premium cable channels featured violence, whereas fewer than 20% of the programs on public broadcasting did (see Figure 4.2). More recent studies continue to confirm the overall NTVS finding that a majority of television programs feature some physical aggression (Glascock, 2008; Linder & Lyle, 2011). But violence in the media is not all the same. To illustrate, compare a film

Figure 4.1 Violence in prime-time and children's programming based on annual content analyses by George Gerbner and colleagues.

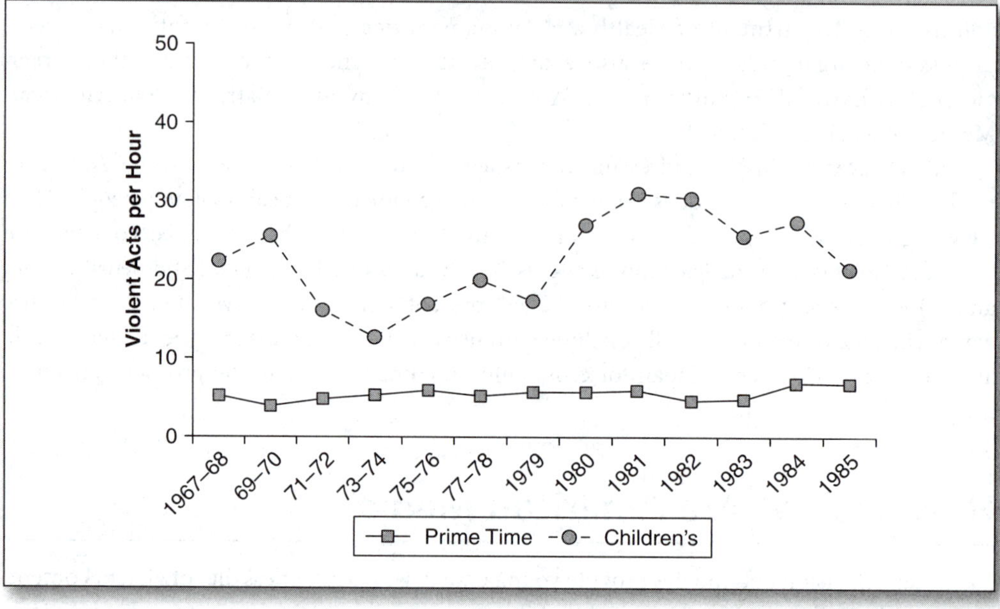

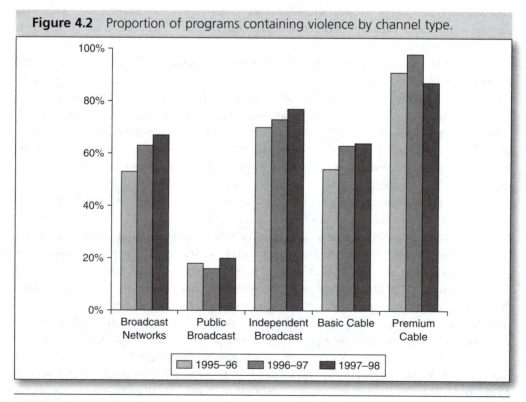

SOURCE: Adapted from Signorielli (1990).

Figure 4.2 Proportion of programs containing violence by channel type.

SOURCE: Adapted from Smith et al. (1998).

such as *Schindler's List,* about the brutality of the Holocaust, with a movie such as *300,* a box office hit featuring a group of buffed-up Spartan soldiers in prolonged, blood-spraying battles against a Persian army. One movie shows the tragic consequences of brutality, whereas the other seems to celebrate or at least condone violence. The NTVS assessed how often violence is shown in a way that can be educational to viewers. Despite the overall pervasiveness of violence, less than 5% of violent programs featured an antiviolence theme across the three years of the study (Smith et al., 1998).

The researchers also examined contextual features of violence, such as who commits the aggression, whether the violence is rewarded or punished, and whether it results in negative consequences. The study drew several conclusions from the findings:

Violence on television is frequently glamorized. Nearly 40% of the violent incidents were perpetrated by "good" characters who can serve as role models for viewers. In addition, a full 71% of violent scenes contained no remorse, criticism, or penalty for violence.

Violence on television is frequently sanitized. Close to half of the violent incidents on television showed no physical harm or pain to the victim. Furthermore, less than 20% of the violent programs portrayed the long-term negative repercussions of violence for family and friends of the victim.

Violence on television is often trivialized. More than half of the violent incidents featured intense forms of aggression that would be deadly if they were to occur in real life. Yet despite such serious aggression, 40% of the violent scenes on television included some type of humor.

As we will see below, all of these contextual features increase the chances that media violence will have a harmful effect on the audience.

Of course, the patterns outlined here characterize all programming taken together, not necessarily the shows that young people spend most of their time viewing. In subsequent analyses of the NTVS sample, researchers looked specifically at two genres that are popular among youth: programs targeted specifically to children younger than 12 (Wilson, Smith, et al., 2002) and music videos (Smith & Boyson, 2002).

In programs targeted to children, nearly all of which are cartoons, violence is far more prevalent. For example, roughly 7 out of 10 children's shows contained some violence, whereas 6 out of 10 nonchildren's shows did (Wilson, Smith, et al., 2002). Furthermore, a typical hour of children's programming contained 14 different violent incidents, or one incident every four minutes. In contrast, nonchildren's programming featured about six violent incidents per hour, or one every 12 minutes. The researchers also found that children's programs were substantially more likely than other types of programming to depict unrealistically low levels of harm to victims compared with what would happen in real life. This pattern is particularly problematic for children younger than age 7, who have difficulty distinguishing reality from fantasy (see Chapter 1) and may assume such aggression is harmless. Finally, when children's shows were divided into categories, superhero cartoons such as *Exosquad* and *Spider-Man* as well as slapstick cartoons such as *Animaniacs* and *Road Runner* were far more saturated with violence than were social relationship cartoons such as *Care Bears* and *Rugrats* (Wilson, Smith, et al., 2002). Magazine-formatted shows such as *Barney & Friends*, *Blue's Clues*, and *Bill Nye the Science Guy* rarely contained any violence at all.

Looking at music videos, which are popular with preteens and teens, the overall prevalence of violence is quite low (Smith & Boyson, 2002). In one study, only 15% of all videos featured in a typical week of television on BET, MTV, and VH1 contained violence. However, violence varied by music genre. As seen in Figure 4.3, rap and heavy metal videos were more likely to contain violence than other genres were. In fact, nearly one in three rap videos featured physical aggression. The violence in rap videos was also more likely to involve repeated acts of aggression against the same target. More recently, Hunnicutt and Andrews (2009) analyzed the lyrics of 329 rap songs that were popular from 1989 to 2000. Overall, about a third of the songs contained at least one reference to homicide. Notably, homicide-related lyrics increased over time; by 1998, homicide was mentioned in 42% of the popular songs. The researchers also analyzed the way in which homicide was portrayed. They found that rap lyrics portrayed violent death as a common occurrence and often depicted it in a glorified way.

What about violence in other media? Chapter 10 focuses on video games, so we will not include that medium here. Two studies focused particularly on movies marketed to children. Yokota and Thompson (2000) analyzed G-rated animated films released between 1937 and 1999. All 74 movies in the sample contained at least one act of physical aggression. Furthermore, there was a significant increase in the duration of screen violence over the 40-year period. A classic theme in many of the movies was the good guy triumphing over the bad guy by using physical force. A subsequent study by the same authors revealed that G-rated films that were animated actually contained more violence than those that were not animated did (Thompson & Yokota, 2004). For both television and movies, then, animated content is some of the most violent fare on the market.

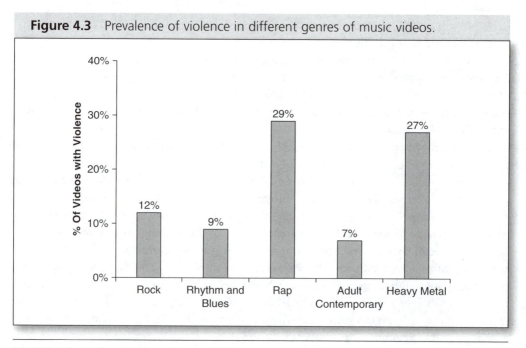

Figure 4.3 Prevalence of violence in different genres of music videos.

SOURCE: Adapted from Smith and Boyson (2002).

A recent study has looked at movies for all ages, not just children. Bleakley, Jamieson, and Romer (2012) analyzed over 800 top-grossing films from 1950 to 2006. The researchers found that a whopping 89% contained violence and that the proportion of characters, both male and female, involved in violence steadily increased over time. Similarly, a study of 77 top PG-13 movies found that 90% were "permeated" with violence, and yet two-thirds of these films were assigned the rating of PG-13 for reasons other than violence (Webb, Jenkins, Browne, Afifi, & Kraus, 2007).

The statistics presented here demonstrate what many people increasingly recognize—there is a great deal of violence in screen entertainment (see Figure 4.4). And today, there are numerous television networks and other screen-based technologies (e.g., computers, iPods) available for young people to find and experience such content. Furthermore, much of this violence is portrayed in formulaic ways that glamorize, sanitize, and trivialize aggression. Finally, violence is particularly prevalent in many of the very products that are targeted to younger audiences. Indeed, a recent study found that even best-selling novels for teens are ripe with violence (Coyne et al., 2011)!

Figure 4.4   Violence in screen media targeted to youth.

Does Media Violence Attract Youth?

Writers and producers often claim that there would be less violence in the media if people would stop being attracted to it. Certainly we can think of many films and television shows that have drawn huge audiences and are brimming with violence. Horror films such as *Scream* and the sequels of *Paranormal Activity* are examples that have been extremely popular among teenagers. And the success of *Lego Ninjago: Masters of Spinjitzu*, *The Legend of Korra*, and *Looney Tunes* demonstrates that violent programming can be popular with children too.

But does violence ensure that a movie or TV show will be appealing? One way to answer this question is to look at viewership statistics. Hamilton (1998) analyzed Nielsen ratings for more than 2,000 prime-time TV movies airing on the four major broadcast networks between 1987 and 1993. After controlling for factors such as the channel and the time the movie aired, the popularity of the program preceding the movie, and the amount of advertising in *TV Guide*, he found that movies about murder or about family crime did in fact have higher household ratings. He also found that films explicitly described in *TV Guide* as "violent" attracted higher viewership as measured by household ratings. Yet despite all the factors Hamilton controlled for, there are still many differences among movies that could account for their varying popularity.

Other researchers have exposed viewers to different programs to determine whether those with violence are rated as more appealing (Diener & Woody, 1981; Greenberg & Gordon, 1972). Even with this methodology, it is difficult to tease out the role that violence plays in enhancing appeal, given that programs differ on so many other dimensions. What is needed is a controlled study that varies the level of violence while holding all other program features constant. Berry, Gray, and Donnerstein (1999) did just that. In a series of three experiments, the researchers left a movie intact or cut specific scenes of graphic violence from it. Across all three studies, undergraduates rated the cut versions as less violent than the uncut versions. The presence of violence also influenced enjoyment, but the findings differed by the sex of the student. Cutting violence from a full-length movie actually increased women's enjoyment of the content, but it decreased men's ratings of enjoyment.

Yet two more recent studies involving television programming contradict this pattern. In a large-scale experiment, Weaver and Wilson (2009) edited episodes from five different prime-time TV dramas (e.g., *The Sopranos*, *Oz*, *24*) to create three versions of each: a version with graphic violence, a version with sanitized violence, and a version with no violence. Across all five episodes, undergraduates enjoyed the nonviolent version significantly more than either of the violent ones. This pattern held true for both males and females, regardless of the graphicness of the content or the participants' preexisting aggressive tendencies.

In a follow-up experiment, Weaver, Jensen, Martins, Hurley, and Wilson (2011) decided to test whether it might be action rather than violence that viewers find most appealing. The researchers created four different versions of an original, slapstick cartoon using animation software: one low in both action and violence, one low in action but high in violence, one high in action but low in violence, and one high in both action and violence. A total of 128 elementary school children were randomly assigned to watch one of the four versions. The researchers found that violence had no impact on children's liking of the cartoon. Instead, action increased liking of the cartoon, but only for boys and not for girls. In other words, boys liked the high-action versions better than the low-action versions of the same cartoon. The findings challenge the idea that violence in and of itself is appealing to children.

Other evidence pertaining to children corroborates this idea. In an early random survey of parents in Madison, Wisconsin, nearly 30% named the *Mighty Morphin Power Rangers* as their elementary schoolers' favorite TV show (Cantor & Nathanson, 1997). Nevertheless, the family situation comedy *Full House* was more often cited as a favorite. A look at more recent Nielsen ratings reveals that violent cartoons such as *Planet Sheen* and *T.U.F.F. Puppy* are quite popular among 2- to 11-year-olds, especially during the Saturday morning time block (see Table 4.1). However, family movies such as *Tinker Bell and the Great Fairy*

Table 4.1 Top Programs Among Children Ages 2–11: 2010–2011 Season

	SATURDAY MORNING		
Rank	Program	Channel	Genre
1	SpongeBob SquarePants	Nickelodeon	cartoon
2	Penguins of Madagascar	Nickelodeon	cartoon
3	T.U.F.F. Puppy	Nickelodeon	cartoon
4	Fish Hooks	Disney Channel	cartoon
5	Phineas and Ferb	Disney Channel	cartoon
6	Good Luck Charlie	Disney Channel	teen sitcom
7	A.N.T. Farm	Disney Channel	teen sitcom
8	Planet Sheen	Nickelodeon	cartoon
9	Shake It Up	Disney Channel	teen sitcom
10	Jake and the Never Land Pirates	Disney Channel	cartoon
	PRIME TIME		
Rank	Program	Channel	Genre
1	Phineas and Ferb: The Movie	Disney Channel	movie
2	iCarly: iParty With Victorious	Nickelodeon	teen sitcom
3	SpongeBob SquarePants	Nick at Nite	cartoon
4	iCarly: iStart a Fan War	Nickelodeon	teen sitcom
5	American Idol – Wednesday	FOX	reality
6	Big Time Rush	Nick at Nite	teen sitcom
7	American Idol – Thursday	FOX	reality
8	Tinker Bell and the Great Fairy Rescue	Disney Channel	animated movie
9	Sharpay's Fabulous Adventure	Disney Channel	movie
10	Sky High	Disney Channel	animated movie

SOURCE: Rankings are based on national ratings from Nielsen Media Research for the 2010–2011 season. Copyrighted information of Nielsen, licensed for use herein.

Adventure, teen sitcoms such as *iCarly*, and reality shows such as *American Idol* rank high when the prime-time hours are considered.

These types of divergent patterns have led several researchers to conclude that violence is not necessarily always attractive (Cantor, 1998; Goldstein, 1999; Zillmann, 1998). Instead, the appeal of violence seems to depend on several factors, including the nature of the aggression involved. For example, undergraduates who were exposed to a graphic documentary-style film portraying the bludgeoning of a monkey's head or the slaughtering of steer uniformly found the content disgusting, and most chose to turn the television off before the program ended (Haidt, McCauley, & Rozin, 1994). More recently, Weaver and Wilson (2009) found that graphic violence produced greater feelings of disgust and other negative emotions among undergraduates than sanitized violence did. On the other hand, brutal violence against a vicious villain who deserves to be punished can be enjoyable (see Zillmann, 1998).

The appeal of violence not only depends on its form but also on the type of viewer involved. A large body of research documents that there are sex differences in attraction to violence (see Cantor, 1998). Compared with girls, boys are more likely to select violent fairytale books (Collins-Standley, Gan, Yu, & Zillmann, 1996), seek out violent movies at the theater (Sargent et al., 2002), play violent video games (Funk, Buchman, & Germann, 2000), and play with violent toys (Servin, Bohlin, & Berlin, 1999). Various theories have been posited for these patterns, some focusing on gender-role socialization and others on biological differences between the sexes (see Oliver, 2000). Nevertheless, greater attraction to media violence among males is not merely a childhood phenomenon—it persists into adolescence and adulthood (Hamilton, 1998; Johnston, 1995).

Certain viewers possess personalities that seem to draw them to media violence as well. Zuckerman (1979) has argued that individuals vary in their need for arousal and that those high on "sensation seeking" will generally seek out novel and stimulating activities. Indeed, studies show that sensation seeking does predict exposure to violent television shows, movies, and even violent websites among adolescents and adults (Aluja-Fabregat, 2000; Slater, 2003; Xie & Lee, 2008). Moreover, sensation seeking is positively related to the enjoyment of graphic horror films (Tamborini & Stiff, 1987; Zuckerman & Litle, 1986). High sensation seeking among teens has even been linked to a preference for listening to heavy metal music (Arnett, 1995).

Finally, children who are more aggressive themselves seem to prefer violent television. In one survey, parents who rated their children as aggressive also rated them as more interested in violent cartoons (Cantor & Nathanson, 1997). A similar pattern has been documented among adolescents (Selah-Shayovits, 2006). In a study of 8th graders, for example, boys who were rated as more aggressive by teachers also watched more violent films (Aluja-Fabregat, 2000). Huesmann, Moise-Titus, Podolski, and Eron (2003) have found longitudinal evidence showing that aggressive children seek out more violent television programs over time. Fenigstein (1979) and others (Cantor & Nathanson, 1997) speculate that aggressive people use violent scenes in the media to understand and justify their own behaviors.

One final caveat concerns conceptual confusion about the term *attraction*. Several scholars have begun to recognize that there may be a distinction between being drawn to content that is violent, often called "selective exposure," and actually enjoying that experience (Cantor, 1998; Weaver & Kobach, 2012). There seems to be growing empirical support for the idea that people may select violent over nonviolent material, but afterward they do not always like it better (Weaver & Kobach, 2012). In fact, Weaver (2011) recently separated the eight published studies that have assessed selective exposure to media violence from the 18 published studies that have looked at enjoyment after viewing screen violence. His meta-analysis (see definition of this term below) of these two groups of studies shows that violence affects selective exposure and liking in very different and opposite ways. That is, violence increases people's desire to see a movie or TV show, but actually decreases their enjoyment after viewing. Clearly, unpacking these two concepts will help us to better understand the role that violence plays in media entertainment.

To summarize, there is a fair amount of evidence supporting the idea that violence sells. But a closer look at the data suggests that it is not that simple. For one thing, violence may be attractive to viewers because it is associated with action, suspense, or conflict. In this way, violence might serve as a proxy for other appealing plot features. It must be acknowledged, however, that nonviolent themes in programming can attract large audiences too. Nevertheless, the sheer prevalence of violence on television and in movies means that there are simply fewer options available if someone is seeking nonviolent content. Still, it may not be accurate to think of violence in a unidimensional way as either present or absent. Certain forms of violence seem to be more popular than others. In addition, particular individuals enjoy aggressive portrayals more than others do. To complicate matters further, Cantor (1998) speculates that there may be a relationship between an individual's personality and the types of violence that are most appealing. For example, highly anxious children may seek out portrayals in which good wins over evil, whereas an aggressive bully may enjoy a good TV battle regardless of the characters involved or the outcome. In other words, more research is needed on the types of violent messages that are most appealing, on the types of youth who seek out this content, and on the distinction between selective exposure and enjoyment of violent entertainment.

Can Media Violence Lead to Aggression?

Undoubtedly, the single issue that has received most attention with regard to the media is whether violent content can lead to aggressive behavior. No researcher today would argue that the media are the sole or even the most important cause of aggressive behavior in youth. Yet there is strong agreement among many social scientists that exposure to media violence can *contribute* to aggressiveness in individuals (see Bushman, Huesmann, & Whitaker, 2009; Comstock & Powers, 2012; Murray, 2008). This section will begin with an overview of the research evidence that has been brought to bear on this issue. Next we will present three theoretical perspectives that can help explain the relationship between media violence and aggression. The section will conclude with a discussion of who is most at risk for learning aggressive attitudes and behaviors from the media.

Experimental Studies

Some of the earliest evidence linking media violence to aggression comes from laboratory studies of children in controlled settings. In a series of classic experiments, Bandura and his colleagues exposed nursery school children to a filmed model who engaged in violent behaviors, often directed against a plastic, inflatable Bobo doll or punching bag (Bandura, Ross, & Ross, 1961, 1963a, 1963b). Afterward, children were taken to a playroom that contained a number of toys, including a Bobo doll, and their own behaviors were observed from behind a one-way mirror.

The purpose of such research was to investigate the circumstances under which children would learn and imitate novel aggressive acts they had seen on film. The researchers consistently found that children who were exposed to a violent model were more likely to act aggressively than were children in control groups who had not viewed such violence (Bandura et al., 1961, 1963b). Furthermore, children were more likely to imitate a violent model who had been rewarded with cookies than one who had been punished. In fact, children generally imitated the model so long as no punishment occurred, suggesting that the absence of punishment can serve as a tacit reward or sanction for such behavior (Bandura, 1965).

Bandura and his colleagues also found that children could learn novel aggressive responses as easily from a cartoonlike figure, a "Cat Lady," for example, as from a human adult (Bandura et al., 1963a). This finding clearly implicates Saturday morning TV as an unhealthy reservoir of violence. Subsequent studies using similar procedures revealed other aspects of imitation. For example, children exposed to televised aggressive sequences could reproduce the behaviors they had seen up to six to eight months later (Hicks, 1965). In addition, preschoolers would aggress against a human adult dressed as a clown just as readily as they would a Bobo doll (Hanratty, O'Neal, & Sulzer, 1972; Savitsky, Rogers, Izard, & Liebert, 1971). This finding helped to undercut the criticism that attacking an inflatable doll is merely play behavior and not akin to real aggression.

Experimental studies have looked at older age groups, too. For instance, research shows that older adolescents and even adults who are exposed to television violence in laboratory settings will engage in increased aggression (Coyne et al., 2008; Scharrer, 2005).

However, the experimental evidence has been criticized on methodological grounds (Fowles, 1999; Freedman, 2002). Laboratory studies often (a) employ unrealistic or "play" measures of aggression, (b) are conducted in artificial viewing situations, (c) involve adult experimenters who willingly show violence on TV in a way that may seem to be condoning aggression, and (d) are able to assess only short-term effects of exposure. According to Fowles (1999), "Viewing in the laboratory setting is involuntary, public, choiceless, intense, uncomfortable, and single-minded. . . . Laboratory research has taken the viewing experience and turned it inside out so that the viewer is no longer in charge" (p. 27).

To overcome some of these limitations, researchers have conducted field experiments in nonlaboratory settings with more realistic measures of aggression (Friedrich & Stein, 1973; Josephson, 1987). For example, in one early study, 3- to 5-year-old children were randomly assigned to watch violent or nonviolent TV shows for 11 days at their school (Steuer, Applefield, & Smith, 1971). Children in the violent viewing condition displayed significantly more physical aggression against their peers (e.g., hitting, kicking, throwing objects) during play periods than children in the nonviolent TV group did.

In a study 20 years later, researchers exposed elementary schoolers to a single episode of the *Mighty Morphin Power Rangers* and then observed verbal and physical aggression in the classroom (Boyatzis, Matillo, & Nesbitt, 1995). Compared with a control group, children and particularly boys who had watched the violent TV program committed significantly more intentional acts of aggression inside the classroom, such as hitting, kicking, shoving, and insulting a peer. In fact, for every aggressive act perpetrated by children in the control group, there were seven aggressive acts committed by children who had seen the *Power Rangers*. Notably, these types of bullying behaviors are no longer seen as part of normal development and have been linked to high levels of psychological distress, poor social and emotional adjustment, failure in school, and even long-term health difficulties among victims (Nansel et al., 2001; Rigby, 2003).

With regard to the *Power Rangers*, the Boyatzis and colleagues (1995) study reveals that the prosocial message delivered at the end of each episode in this TV series is not nearly as salient to children as the perpetual violence that the superheroes commit (see Figure 4.5). At least one other study has demonstrated that moral lessons on television are relatively ineffective when they are couched in violence (Liss, Reinhardt, & Fredriksen, 1983).

In general, controlled experiments dating back to the 1960s clearly demonstrate that exposure to screen violence can *cause* some children to behave aggressively immediately after viewing (for a review, see Huesmann, 2007). Moreover, this effect has been found with various age groups and in laboratory as well as more naturalistic studies. But such evidence is still limited in that it points only to immediate effects that may not persist much beyond the viewing situation. In addition, most experiments involve small samples of children or teens who may or may not be representative of young people in general.

Correlational Studies

In the 1970s, a number of investigators surveyed large populations of children and teenagers to determine if those who were heavy viewers of TV violence were also more aggressive. As an example, one study surveyed 2,300 junior and senior high school students in Maryland and asked them to list their four favorite programs, which were then analyzed for violent content (McIntyre & Teevan, 1972). Measures of aggression were compiled from a self-reported checklist of activities, using five scales that ranged from aggressive acts (e.g., fighting

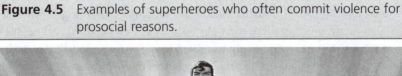
Figure 4.5 Examples of superheroes who often commit violence for prosocial reasons.

at school) to serious delinquency (involvement with the law). Results revealed that children whose favorite programs were more violent were also higher in overall aggressive and delinquent behavior.

Other studies used slightly different measures of aggression, including peer ratings (McLeod, Atkin, & Chaffee, 1972a, 1972b) and self-reports of willingness to use violence in hypothetical situations (Dominick & Greenberg, 1972). Across different samples in different regions of the United States, the findings were remarkably consistent. Higher exposure to TV violence was positively associated with higher levels of aggressive behavior (Belson, 1978; Dominick & Greenberg, 1972; McLeod et al., 1972a, 1972b; Robinson & Bachman, 1972). Furthermore, the relationship held up even after controlling for factors such as parental education, school achievement, socioeconomic status, and overall amount of television viewing (McLeod et al., 1972a, 1972b; Robinson & Bachman, 1972).

The relationship between TV violence and aggressive behavior has been documented in other nations as well. In a survey of more than 30,000 adolescents from eight different countries (Kuntsche et al., 2006), heavy television viewing was significantly associated with increased verbal aggression and verbal bullying. This finding held up in all eight countries, even after controlling for gender and age. In three of the countries in which teens spent a lot of time watching TV on weekends (i.e., the United States, Poland, Portugal), there was also a significant relationship between television viewing and physical forms of bullying (e.g., kicking, pushing).

More recently, Ybarra and her colleagues (2008) found that exposure to violence on the Internet is associated with youth aggression. The researchers randomly sampled over 1,500 American 10- to 15-year-olds and used an online survey to ask them about their media exposure, their home situation, their peer group, and their own violent behavior (defined in this case as aggravated assault, robbery, sexual assault, or stabbing or shooting someone). Those who indicated that many, most, or all of the websites they visited depicted real people engaging in violence were five times more likely to report engaging in seriously violent behavior than were those who never visited such sites. This relationship held up even after controlling for household income, alcohol use, trait aggression, having delinquent friends, and exposure to violence in the community. The websites defined as violent in this study included hate sites, sites showing satanic rituals, sites depicting war or terrorism, and sites showing dead people or people dying. The large and often representative samples in these studies suggest that the causal effects documented in experimental studies can be generalized to the real world. However, the problem with correlational studies is that we cannot be certain about which variable came first. Screen violence could be causing an increase in aggression. Alternatively, youth who are already aggressive could be seeking out violent content. To disentangle the direction of causality, longitudinal studies are needed.

Longitudinal Studies

In the past several decades, social scientists have increasingly moved toward longitudinal studies, which involve surveying the same group of individuals at repeated intervals over time. This type of design permits a researcher to test the cumulative effects of exposure to the media. It also provides a test of the "chicken and egg" quandary: Does violence in the media lead to aggression, or do aggressive people seek out such content?

In one of the most impressive longitudinal studies, Leonard Eron, Rowell Huesmann, and their colleagues tested the same sample of children, originally from upstate New York, over a 22-year period (Eron, Huesmann, Lefkowitz, & Walder, 1972; Huesmann, 1986; Huesmann, Eron, Lefkowitz, & Walder, 1984; Lefkowitz, Eron, Walder, & Huesmann, 1972). The researchers measured television viewing habits and aggressive behavior at three different points in time: when the participants were 8, 19, and 30 years of age. As seen in Figure 4.6, the results revealed that among boys, the relationship between viewing TV violence in the 3rd grade and aggressive behavior 10 years later was positive and highly significant. In other words, exposure to TV violence during early childhood was predictive of higher levels of aggression at age 19. This relationship persisted even after controlling for IQ, socioeconomic status (SES), and overall exposure to television. In contrast, aggressive behavior in the 3rd grade was *not* predictive of violent TV consumption at age 19. Thus, the idea that being aggressive can lead a child to watch more TV violence did not receive support. Interestingly, neither of the cross-lagged correlations from Time 1 to Time 2 was significant for girls.

The researchers followed up on these same individuals another 10 years later, most of them now age 30 (Huesmann, 1986). In some of the most compelling evidence to date, the data revealed a link between exposure to TV violence at age 8 and self-reported aggression at age 30 among males (Huesmann & Miller, 1994). Moreover, violent TV habits in childhood were a significant predictor of the seriousness of criminal acts performed at age 30 (see Figure 4.7). Once again, this relationship held up even when childhood aggression, IQ, SES, and several parenting variables were controlled. Huesmann (1986) concluded that "early childhood television habits are correlated with adult criminality independent of other likely causal factors" (p. 139).

Using a similar longitudinal approach, these same researchers conducted a three-year study of more than 1,000 children in five countries: Australia, Finland, Israel, Poland, and the United States (Huesmann & Eron, 1986a). Despite very different crime rates and television

Figure 4.6 TV violence watched in 3rd grade correlates with aggressive behavior at age 19 for boys.

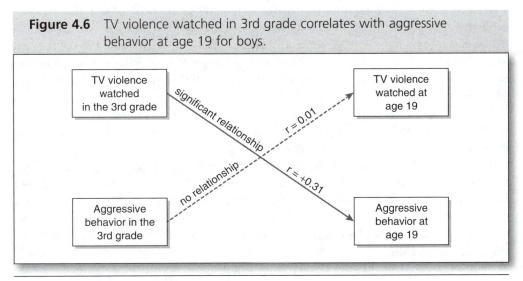

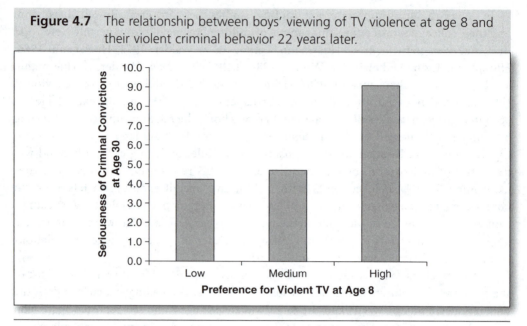

Figure 4.7 The relationship between boys' viewing of TV violence at age 8 and their violent criminal behavior 22 years later.

SOURCE: Adapted from Huesmann (1986).

programming in these nations, early childhood exposure to television violence significantly predicted subsequent aggression in every country except Australia. Furthermore, the relationship was found just as often for girls as for boys in three of the countries, including the United States. Finally, although the relationship between early TV habits and later aggression was always stronger, there was some evidence for the reverse direction: Early aggression led to higher levels of violent viewing. Based on this pattern, Huesmann and his colleagues argued that pinning down the precise direction of causality between TV violence and aggression is not so crucial because the relationship is probably reciprocal: Early violent viewing stimulates aggression, and behaving aggressively then leads to a heightened interest in violent TV content (Huesmann, Lagerspetz, & Eron, 1984). Likewise, Slater (2003) has posited that the relationship between TV violence and aggressive behavior becomes mutually reinforcing over time, resulting in what he calls a "downward spiral model."

The most recent longitudinal research by Huesmann and his colleagues continues to support the idea that both boys and girls are influenced by television violence (Huesmann et al., 2003). In this study, the researchers interviewed more than 500 elementary school children and then surveyed them again 15 years later. Again, they found that heavy exposure to television violence in childhood predicted increased aggressive behavior in adulthood. Unlike their earliest work, their more current evidence reveals the same pattern for both boys and girls. The researchers have speculated that the shift in findings pertaining to girls is due to increased societal acceptance of assertive behavior for females as well as an increase in aggressive female characters on television.

With one exception (Milavsky, Kessler, Stipp, & Rubens, 1982), other longitudinal evidence corroborates these patterns. For example, in one 5-year study, children who had watched the most television during preschool, particularly action adventure shows, were also the most aggressive at age 9 (Singer, Singer, & Rapaczynski, 1984). Early viewing of violence in the preschool years also predicted more behavioral problems in school. These relationships remained just as strong after the effects of parenting style, IQ, and initial aggressiveness were statistically removed. More recently, a large-scale longitudinal study of German teens found the same over-time connection between early exposure to violent screen media and aggressive behavior one year later (Krahe & Moller, 2010), even after controlling for preexisting trait aggression, academic achievement, and nonviolent media use.

To summarize, longitudinal studies provide powerful evidence that television violence can have a cumulative effect on aggression over time. Childhood exposure to such content has been shown to predict aggression in later years and even serious forms of criminal behavior in adulthood. Some of the earliest research indicated that these effects held true only for boys, but more recent studies have found significant relationships over time for girls too. Finally, the relationship between TV violence and aggressive behavior may be cyclical in nature, such that each reinforces and encourages more of the other.

Meta-analyses

When researchers conclude that media violence can increase aggressive attitudes and behaviors, they typically look at all the evidence collectively. Lab experiments provide convincing evidence of causal effects, but they may be detecting outcomes that would not occur in everyday life, and they assess short-term effects only. Field experiments increase our confidence that real aggression is involved; correlational studies show that there is a positive relationship between TV violence and aggression in large, often representative samples of youth; and longitudinal studies suggest a cumulative effect of TV violence over time, even after controlling for other potential causal variables. In other words, each method has its strengths and weaknesses, but collectively the research shows a consistent pattern.

Another way to detect patterns is to conduct a meta-analysis. A meta-analysis is the statistical analysis of a large collection of results from individual studies. In this case, each study becomes a data point in a new, combined "super-study" (Mullen, 1989). The goal of a meta-analysis is to synthesize findings from a large body of studies but to do so in a statistical rather than a descriptive way (Cooper & Hedges, 1994). Meta-analyses produce numerical estimates of the size of an effect across all studies on a particular topic.

Several meta-analyses have been conducted on the research regarding media violence and aggression. In the earliest one, Hearold (1986) looked at 230 studies of the impact of TV on both prosocial and antisocial behavior. Antisocial behavior consisted mostly of physical aggression but also included other outcomes such as theft and rule breaking. Hearold found an average effect size of 0.30 (similar to a correlation) between violent TV content and the broad category of antisocial behavior. According to scientific conventions, any effect around 0.1 is considered to be "small," around 0.3 to be "medium," and around 0.5 to be "large" (Cohen, 1988).

In a much smaller meta-analysis, Christensen and Wood (2007) examined only those experiments that observed children's aggressive behavior in unconstrained situations, after viewing violence. The goal was to isolate the studies that used realistic settings and realistic measures of aggression in order to respond to the criticism that laboratory studies are artificial. Across a total of 29 experiments, the researchers found a significant aggregate effect of media violence on aggression. They concluded that "media violence enhances children's and adolescents' aggression in interactions with strangers, classmates, and friends" (p. 164).

Updating the Hearold (1986) study, Paik and Comstock (1994) analyzed 217 studies of the impact of television violence on antisocial behavior (the researchers did not include studies of prosocial behavior, as Hearold did). Paik and Comstock found that the overall effect size between TV violence and antisocial behavior was 0.31, surprisingly consistent with that found by Hearold. Another way to interpret this statistic is that roughly 10% of the individual variation (0.31^2) in antisocial behavior can be accounted for by exposure to TV violence.

More recently, Bushman and Anderson (2001) limited their meta-analysis to studies looking at aggression as an outcome rather than the broader category of antisocial behavior. Across 212 different samples, the researchers found a positive and significant relationship between media violence and aggression. In addition, the study found that since 1975, the effect sizes in media violence research have increased in magnitude, suggesting that the media are becoming more violent and/or that people are consuming more of this type of content.

Bushman and Anderson (2001) also compared the overall effect of media violence with other types of effects found in scientific research. As it turns out, the link between media violence and aggression is much stronger than several effects that today go unquestioned, such as the link between ingesting calcium and increased bone mass or the link between exposure to asbestos and laryngeal cancer (see Figure 4.8). Furthermore, the correlation between media violence and aggression (0.31) is only slightly smaller than that between smoking and lung cancer (nearly 0.40). Obviously, not everyone who smokes will develop lung cancer, but the risk is real and significant. The analogy to media violence is clear; not

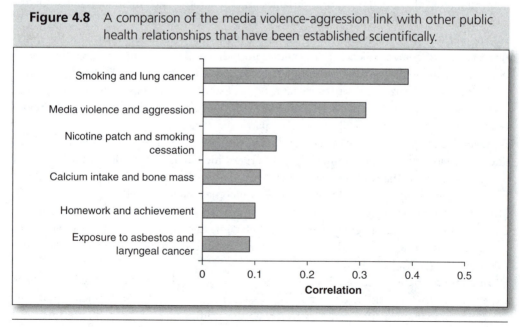

Figure 4.8 A comparison of the media violence-aggression link with other public health relationships that have been established scientifically.

SOURCE: Adapted from Bushman and Huesmann (2001).

every child or teen who watches a heavy dose of violent programming will become aggressive, but some young people are certainly at risk of doing so.

Despite these large-scale meta-analyses, there are still a few researchers who raise doubts about the evidence. Gunter (2008) offers an in-depth critique of the shortcomings of the research, including the fact that effect sizes are small, and cautions against accepting "blanket conclusions about harmful effect of media violence" (p. 1061). Instead, he calls for a more refined approach that focuses on the types of people who are most at risk for harmful effects and the types of media depictions that are most problematic. Even more critical, Ferguson and Kilburn (2009, 2010) have conducted their own meta-analyses and argue that once unpublished studies and studies with poor measures of aggression are removed, there is little evidence that media violence increases aggressive behavior. Ferguson and Kilburn's work has been criticized vigorously by some of the most renowned media scholars in the field (Bushman, Rothstein, & Anderson, 2010; Huesmann, 2010). The debate, published in the journal *Psychological Bulletin*, illustrates how complex the issues are and how heated the topic can get, even in the academic community. Still, after reviewing the accumulated evidence from the last 50 years, the majority of media effects researchers and the major health-related professional associations in the United States (e.g., American Medical Association, American Psychological Association, American Academy of Pediatrics) assert that exposure to screen violence increases the risk of aggressive behavior among youth.

Why Does Exposure to Violence Encourage Aggression?

Many theories have been offered to account for the relationship between media violence and aggression. Catharsis theory was first proposed by Aristotle, who argued that good drama offers audience members a way to purge their negative feelings of emotion. Extended to media violence, the idea is that exposure to such content can cleanse one's feelings of anger and frustration, resulting in a therapeutic *reduction* in aggression. There is very little empirical support for catharsis theory. In fact, most data suggest an opposite, instigational effect of media violence on aggression (see Huesmann, Dubow, & Yang, 2013). Yet catharsis theory continues to be cited today, especially by some members of the media industry. Another theory called excitation transfer posits that any type of media content can enhance aggression so long as the material is arousing (Zillmann, 1991). According to excitation transfer theory, an erotic film is more likely to enhance aggression in an angered individual than a violent film is, so long as the erotic material is more arousing (Zillmann, 1971).

In this section, we will review three major perspectives, all of which focus on the content of media portrayals rather than their arousal properties. Each perspective has generated much research and made significant contributions to our understanding of how media violence might facilitate aggression.

Cognitive Priming

Cognitive priming is a perspective developed by Berkowitz and his colleagues to explain short-term reactions to media violence (Berkowitz, 1984; Jo & Berkowitz, 1994). According to the theory, violent stimuli in the media can activate or elicit aggressive thoughts in a viewer. These thoughts can then "prime" other closely related thoughts, feelings, and even motor tendencies stored in memory. For a short time after exposure, then, a person is in a state of activation whereby hostile thoughts and action tendencies are at the forefront of the mind. Research supports the idea that violent media content can "prime" aggressive thoughts in people (Bushman & Geen, 1990). For example, in a study by Berkowitz, Parker, and West (cited in Berkowitz, 1973, pp. 125–126), children who read a war comic book were more likely to select aggressive words when asked to complete a series of sentences than were children who read a neutral comic book.

Several conditions can encourage these aggressive thoughts and feelings to unfold into aggressive behavior. One such condition is the person's emotional state. Berkowitz (1990) argued that individuals who are experiencing a negative affect, particularly anger or frustration, are more likely to be primed to act aggressively by the media because they are in a state of readiness to respond in a fight-or-flight manner. Indeed, angered individuals do seem to be more strongly influenced by media violence (Paik & Comstock, 1994).

Another condition that helps encourage individuals to act out their aggressive thoughts is justification (Jo & Berkowitz, 1994). If media violence is portrayed as morally proper, it can help to reduce a person's inhibitions against aggression for a short time afterward, making it easier to act out such behavior. Justified violence in the media may even help a person rationalize her or his own aggression (Jo & Berkowitz, 1994). There is a great deal of evidence indicating that justified violence can facilitate aggression (Paik & Comstock, 1994).

Finally, cues in the environment that remind people of the media violence they have just seen can trigger aggressive behavior (Jo & Berkowitz, 1994). Such cues help to reactivate and sustain the previously primed aggressive thoughts and tendencies, thereby prolonging the influence of the violent media content. In a classic study that demonstrates such cuing, 2nd- and 3rd-grade boys were exposed to either a violent or a nonviolent TV show (Josephson, 1987). The violent program prominently featured walkie-talkies in the plot. Immediately afterward, the boys were taken to a school gymnasium to play a game of floor hockey. At the start of the game, an adult referee interviewed each boy using a walkie-talkie or a microphone. Results revealed that aggression-prone boys who had viewed the violent program and then saw the real walkie-talkie were more aggressive during the hockey game than were those in any other condition, including boys who had seen the violent show but no real walkie-talkie. According to priming theory, the walkie-talkie served as a cue to reactivate aggressive thoughts and ideas that had been primed by the earlier violent program.

A recent meta-analysis by Roskos-Ewoldsen, Klinger, and Roskos-Ewoldsen (2007) demonstrated that exposure to violent media images and even violence-related concepts such as weapons can prime aggressive thoughts and behaviors. Primes that are intense or repeated have the strongest effects, as do primes that have recently occurred (Roskos-Ewoldsen, Roskos-Ewoldsen, & Carpentier, 2009). The research also suggests that the effects of a prime will fade over time (see Roskos-Ewoldsen et al., 2009).

Cognitive priming theory helps to explain how media violence can have short-term effects by triggering already learned aggressive thoughts and behaviors. But where do these aggressive tendencies come from originally? Social learning theory focuses on how the media can help children acquire aggressive attitudes and behaviors in the first place.

Social Learning

Developed by Bandura (1965), social learning theory posits that children can learn new behaviors in one of two ways: by direct experience through trial and error, or by observing and imitating others in their social environment. Bandura (2009) has pointed out that observational learning is ultimately more efficient than trying to discover everything on your own. Children can and do learn from other people in their environment, including parents, siblings, peers, and teachers. Children can also learn from characters and people featured in the media (see Figure 4.9).

According to social learning theory, a child observes a model enact a behavior and also witnesses the reinforcements that the model receives. In a sense, the child experiences those reinforcements vicariously. If the model is rewarded, the child too feels reinforced and will imitate or perform the same behavior. If the model is punished, the child is unlikely to perform the behavior, although the actions may still be stored in memory and performed at a later date (Bandura, 1965).

Early experiments supported social learning theory and demonstrated that children could learn just as easily from a filmed model as from a real person (Bandura, 1965; Bandura et al., 1963a, 1963b; Walters & Parke, 1964). In addition to imitation, early research showed that the media could encourage children to act aggressively in ways that differed from the precise behaviors seen in a portrayal. In one study, nursery school children viewed either a violent or a nonviolent cartoon and then were given two toys to play with (Lovaas, 1961). One toy had a lever that caused a doll to hit another doll over the head with a stick; the other toy consisted of a wooden ball that maneuvered through obstacles inside a cage.

Figure 4.9

"I don't place much credence in the effects of TV violence on children."

SOURCE: *New Breed* © 1991 Bob Ting. Dist. by King Features Syndicate.

Compared with those in the nonviolent condition, children who had seen the violent cartoon used the hitting doll more frequently. Bandura and his colleagues (1963b) called this process "disinhibition," whereby exposure to media violence can weaken a child's normal inhibitions or restraints against behaving aggressively, resulting in acts of violence that are similar but not identical to what was seen in a program. More recently, Bandura (2009) has labeled this process "abstract modeling" because an observer extracts a general rule or concept from watching a specific modeled action and then generates a new behavior that goes beyond what was observed.

Today, certain models in the media can have remarkable effects on young people. Consider the thousands of preteen and teen girls who donned chains and skimpy clothes in an effort to emulate Madonna during her Material Girl phase. More recently, Miley Cyrus, Selena Gomez, and Justin Bieber are some of the stars that seem to be captivating American youth. One survey of Los Angeles teens found that nearly 40% of the 12- to 17-year-olds named a media figure as their role model—roughly the same percentage (42%) that named a parent or relative (Yancey, Siegel, & McDaniel, 2002). As a well-known Hollywood producer once stated,

> I'd be lying if I said that people don't imitate what they see on the screen. I would be a moron to say they don't, because look how dress styles change. We have people who want to look like Julia Roberts and Michelle Pfeiffer and Madonna. Of course we imitate. It would be impossible for me to think they would imitate our dress, our music, our look, but not imitate any of our violence or our other actions. (quoted in Auletta, 1993, p. 45)

In the 1980s, Bandura (1986) reformulated his theory because it had been criticized as too behavioristic, focusing mostly on reinforcements and how people act. Now called social cognitive theory, the newer perspective acknowledges that cognitive processes such as attention and retention are involved in observational learning (Bandura, 2009). These mental activities place more emphasis on how children symbolically construe or make sense of a model's behavior. Children selectively pay attention to different features of a model's behavior, they bring forth different experiences to interpret and evaluate the model's actions, and they store different information in memory. These types of cognitive processes can be used to help explain why some children might imitate a model but others do not.

Social learning and social cognitive theory are useful frameworks for understanding how children can learn new behaviors from media violence. But they tend to focus most on short-term learning. The final theory we will discuss takes observational learning a bit further and provides a perspective to account for cumulative or long-term effects of media violence on a child's behavior.

Social Informational Processing Theory

Huesmann (1998) proposed an information processing model that deals with how aggressive behaviors are both developed and maintained over time. The model focuses on scripts, which are mental routines for familiar events that are stored in memory (Abelson, 1976). A script typically includes information about what events are likely to happen, how a person should behave in response to these events, and what the likely outcome of these behaviors will be. Consequently, scripts are used to guide behavior and social problem solving. For example, young children possess scripts for common activities such as going to the doctor and getting ready for bed.

Scripts can be acquired through personal experience as well as through exposure to the media (Krcmar & Hight, 2007). Huesmann (1998) has argued that a child's early learning experiences play a critical role in the development of scripts. According to the theory, a child who is exposed to a great deal of violence, either in real life or through the media, is likely to develop scripts that encourage aggression as a way of dealing with problems (Huesmann, 1988).

Once scripts are learned, they can be retrieved from memory and tried out in social situations (see Figure 4.10). Some scripts are easier to retrieve than others. Those that are rehearsed by the child, through simple recall, through fantasizing, or even through playacting, will be more accessible in memory. In addition, cues in the environment that are similar to those present when the script was first developed can encourage retrieval of that script (Tulving & Thomson, 1973). Similar to priming, then, a situational cue can prompt an aggressive memory based on a previously seen violent TV show or film.

Regardless of how a script is retrieved, once an aggressive strategy is employed, it can be reinforced and elaborated by new information in a given situation, and eventually the script becomes applicable to a wider set of circumstances (Geen, 1994). According to this perspective, the aggressive child is one who has developed from an early age a network of stable and enduring cognitive scripts that emphasize aggression as a response to social situations. Consistent and repeated exposure to violent messages in the media can contribute to the creation of these scripts and to the retrieval of already learned ones (Krcmar & Hight, 2007).

Huesmann's theory incorporates ideas from observational learning and from priming but takes a broader view of how the media can contribute to aggression over time. This perspective reminds us that media violence is only one of many environmental influences that can foster habitual

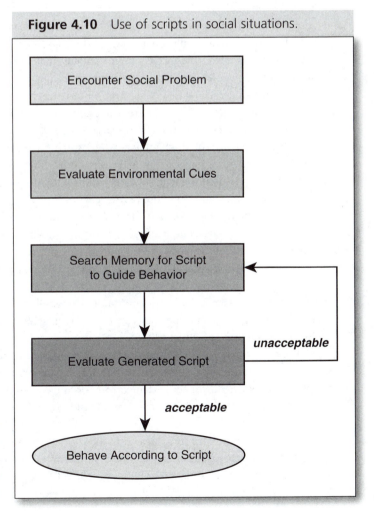

Figure 4.10   Use of scripts in social situations.

forms of aggression in some children. Yet according to a U.S. surgeon general's report, media violence is as great a risk factor as other commonly known predictors of youth violence, such as low IQ, hyperactivity, poor parenting, and lack of social ties (U.S. Department of Health and Human Services, 2001). Next, we turn to the types of media portrayals that are most likely to teach aggressive patterns of behavior and the types of individuals who are most at risk for this learning.

Types of Portrayals That Encourage the Learning of Aggression

As discussed earlier, violence can be portrayed in a variety of ways. For instance, the same act of aggression looks very different when it is perpetrated by a law officer trying to save lives than by a thief trying to steal something. As it turns out, the way in which violence is portrayed may be even more important than the sheer amount of it when trying to assess its likely impact on a viewer. Research has identified seven contextual features of violence that affect the likelihood that a viewer will learn aggressive attitudes and behaviors from a portrayal (see Wilson et al., 1997).

First, an *attractive perpetrator* increases the risk of learning aggression. In accordance with social learning theory, children as well as adults are more likely to attend to, identify with, and learn from attractive role models than they are unattractive ones (Bandura, 1986, 2009). The most obvious way to make a perpetrator appealing is to make her or him a hero (Calvert, Murray, & Conger, 2004; Liss et al., 1983). But even characters who act in benevolent ways can be attractive to young people (Hoffner & Cantor, 1985). Moreover, characters who are similar to the self can be potent role models. Research suggests that children, for example, pay more attention to younger than older characters when watching television (Schmitt, Anderson, & Collins, 1999) and are more likely to imitate peer models than they are adult models (Hicks, 1965). Viewers also pay attention to and identify more with same-sex characters than opposite-sex ones (Hoffner & Buchanan, 2005; Jose & Brewer, 1984).

Second, the motive or *reason for violence* is important. Consistent with cognitive priming, violent actions that seem justified or morally defensible can facilitate viewer aggression, whereas unjustified violence can actually diminish the risk of learning aggression (Berkowitz & Powers, 1979; Hogben, 1998). Third, the *presence of weapons* in a portrayal, particularly conventional weapons such as guns and knives, can enhance aggressive responding among viewers (Berkowitz, 1990; Carlson, Marcus-Newhall, & Miller, 1990). Weapons are assumed to function as a violent cue that can prime aggressive thoughts in a viewer (Subra, Muller, Begue, Bushman, & Delmas, 2010).

Fourth, violence that seems *realistic* can promote greater learning of aggressive attitudes and behaviors among viewers (Atkin, 1983; Krcmar, Farrar, & McGloin, 2011). From this finding, it is tempting to conclude that cartoon or fantasy violence in the media is relatively harmless. However, research with very young children, to be discussed below, challenges such an assumption.

Fifth, we know from social learning theory that violence that is explicitly *rewarded* or that simply goes *unpunished* increases the risk of imitative aggression, whereas violence that is condemned decreases that risk (Bandura, 1965; Carnagey & Anderson, 2005). Sixth, the *consequences* of violence for the victim are an important contextual cue; explicit portrayals of a victim's physical injury and pain can actually decrease or inhibit the learning of aggression among viewers (Baron, 1971a, 1971b; Wotring & Greenberg, 1973). Finally, violence that is portrayed as *humorous* can increase aggression in viewers (Baron, 1978; Berkowitz, 1970). Part of the reason for this effect is that humor can trivialize the seriousness of violence (Gunter & Furnham, 1984). Researchers have speculated that humor may also serve as a positive reinforcement or reward for violence (Berkowitz, 1970).

Taken as a whole, the research clearly suggests that there are risky and not-so-risky ways of portraying violence. If a parent is concerned about a child learning aggressive behaviors from the media, then programs that feature heroes or good characters engaging in justified violence that is not punished and results in minimal consequences should be avoided (see Table 4.2). As it turns out, this formula is very common in animated programming, especially superhero and slapstick cartoons (Wilson, Smith, et al., 2002). On the other hand, portrayals that feature less attractive perpetrators who are punished in the plot and whose violence results in serious negative consequences can actually teach youth that aggression is not necessarily a good way to solve problems.

Types of Youth Most at Risk

Not only do certain messages pose more risk, but certain young people are more susceptible to violent content. In their meta-analysis, Paik and Comstock (1994) found that viewers of all age groups can be influenced by television violence but that preschoolers showed the strongest effect size. This is consistent with Huesmann's (1998) argument that early childhood learning is critical. It also reflects the fact that younger children are least likely to have developed and internalized strong social norms against aggression. Younger children also have difficulty

---

Table 4.2 Risky Versus Educational Depictions of Violence

Media themes that *encourage* the learning of aggression

- ✓ "Good guys" or superheroes as perpetrators
- ✓ Violence that is celebrated or rewarded
- ✓ Violence that goes unpunished
- ✓ Violence that is portrayed as defensible or justified
- ✓ Violence that results in no serious harm to the victim
- ✓ Violence that is made to look funny

Media themes that *discourage* the learning of aggression

- ✓ Evil or bad characters as perpetrators
- ✓ Violence that is criticized or penalized
- ✓ Violence that is portrayed as unfair or morally unjust
- ✓ Violence that causes obvious injury and pain to the victim
- ✓ Violence that results in anguish and suffering for the victim's loved ones

distinguishing reality from fantasy on television (see Chapter 1 and discussion below), making them prone to imitating even the most fantastic presentations.

The heightened vulnerability that characterizes the preschool years means that parents should be especially cautious about mindlessly using television as a babysitter for their young children. Indeed, studies indicate that babies as young as 18 months old are capable of imitating and remembering what they see on television (Brito, Barr, McIntyre, & Simcock, 2012). Fortunately, when busy parents need a break, public broadcast channels contain very little violence and feature educational programs such as *Sesame Street* that are truly enriching for children (Fisch & Truglio, 2001).

Research also indicates that at any age, children who perceive television as realistic and who identify strongly with violent characters are most likely to learn from violent content (Huesmann et al., 2003; Konijn, Nije Bijvank, & Bushman, 2007). In a tragic case in 1999, a 12-year-old fan of TV wrestling claimed he was simply imitating his favorite heroes when he threw a 6-year-old playmate into a metal staircase, killing her (see box below). It seems that even some older children can be confused by highly scripted and unrealistic portrayals of violence.

Being in a particular emotional state can also make a child more vulnerable. Numerous studies reveal that viewers who are made to feel angry or frustrated are more likely to behave aggressively after exposure to media violence than nonangered persons are (see Paik & Comstock, 1994). According to priming theory, angered individuals are in a state of readiness to respond that facilitates aggressive actions (Berkowitz, 1990). It is important to note, however, that a child does not have to be angry to learn aggression from the media (see Hearold, 1986).

Being unpopular with peers and doing poorly in school also place a child at greater risk for learning aggression from media violence (see Huesmann, 1986). Social and academic failures can be frustrating experiences that instigate aggression (Huesmann, 1988). Such experiences in turn can lead to more social withdrawal and more television viewing, making the process a vicious cycle. Finally, children raised in homes characterized by parental rejection and parental aggression show stronger effects of media violence (Bauer et al., 2006; Singer & Singer, 1986).

TELEVISION ON TRIAL FOR MURDER?

Lionel Tate at age 14

On July 28, 1999, a 12-year-old boy named Lionel Tate beat to death his 6-year-old playmate, Tiffany Eunick. The two were playing in the Florida home that Lionel shared with his mother, who was babysitting the girl. The mother was asleep at the time.

An autopsy showed that Tiffany had suffered a fractured skull, lacerated liver, internal hemorrhaging, and more than 30 other injuries. The 170-pound boy allegedly had punched, kicked, and thrown the 48-pound girl around the room. When questioned by authorities, Lionel claimed to have accidentally thrown Tiffany into a metal staircase and a wall while trying to toss her onto a sofa.

During the murder trial, defense attorney Jim Lewis argued that Lionel was an avid fan of pro wrestling who was imitating moves he had seen on TV without realizing the damage that could occur. He claimed that Lionel was too immature to understand that pro wrestlers are not actually hurting one another. "He wanted to emulate them," attorney Jim Lewis said (Spencer, 2001). "Like Batman and Superman, they were his heroes. He loved to play." Earlier, Lewis had tried unsuccessfully to subpoena professional wrestlers to testify at the trial.

Prosecutor Ken Padowitz argued that television violence was not on trial and that the boy knew he was savagely beating Tiffany.

After only three hours of deliberation, a Florida jury found Lionel guilty of first-degree murder. Pointing to the cruelty and callousness of Lionel's acts, Judge Joel T. Lazarus sen-

Lionel Tate at 14.

tenced the boy to life in prison without the possibility of parole. Tate was one of the youngest defendants in the United States to be sentenced to spend the rest of his life in prison.

In 2004, a state appeals court overturned Tate's conviction. The appeals court ruled that it was not clear whether Tate had understood the charges against him. He was freed from prison after he agreed to plead guilty to second-degree murder and was sentenced to time already served and 10 years' probation.

Tate has been in and out of court since then. In 2005, he was arrested and accused of robbing a pizza delivery person at gunpoint. In 2006, he pled guilty to gun possession, which violated his probation, and is now serving 30-year prison sentence. In 2008, he pled no contest to the robbery charge and was sentenced to 10 years, to be served concurrently with his 30-year sentence.

It is important to remember that no single factor will propel a child from nonviolence to violence. Instead, each risk factor increases the chances that a child will internalize and act out the violence that she or he witnesses in the media. Huesmann and Eron (1986b) summarize risk in the following way: "For most children, aggressiveness seems to be determined mostly by the extent to which their environment reinforces aggression, provides aggressive role models, frustrates and victimizes the child, and instigates aggression" (p. 4).

Developmental Differences in Processing Media Violence

Chapter 1 describes several ways in which younger and older children differ in their processing of media messages. At least three of these have important implications for how young people are likely to interpret media violence. First, children differ markedly in their cognitive ability to distinguish reality from fantasy (see Dorr, 1983; Wright, Huston, Reitz, & Piemyat, 1994). Preschoolers often assume that anything that looks or sounds real *is* real (Brown, Skeen, & Osborn, 1979). Consistent with this tendency, studies show that preschoolers and even young elementary schoolers will readily imitate violent cartoon characters such as the ThunderCats and even Bugs Bunny (Bandura et al., 1963a; Friedrich & Stein, 1973; Steuer et al., 1971). Such portrayals are likely to be discounted as fantasy by older, more sophisticated viewers who are far more responsive to portrayals of violence involving events and characters that are possible in the real world (Atkin, 1983; Scharrer, 2005; Thomas & Tell, 1974).

The television rating system takes this developmental consideration into account with its "TVY7" label. Programs rated TVY7 are designed for children 7 years of age and older who have "acquired the developmental skills needed to distinguish between make-believe and reality" (*TV Parental Guidelines*, n.d.).

A second relevant cognitive skill concerns the shift from perceptual to conceptual processing (Fisher, 2011). Younger children pay close attention to perceptually salient features in a program, such as what characters look like and what they do (Gibbons, Anderson, Smith, Field, & Fischer, 1986; Hoffner & Cantor, 1985; van den Broek, Lorch, & Thurlow, 1996). Older children and teens, on the other hand, can consider more conceptual or abstract information in a plot (Collins, 1975; van den Broek et al., 1996). In the realm of violence, this means that younger children are most likely to comprehend and learn from those violent behaviors and consequences that are explicitly portrayed on screen in concrete ways. When events are implied or not visually depicted, they will be more difficult for a young child to discern. In support of this idea, Krcmar and Cooke (2001) found that younger children focused more on the punishments that a character received in judging whether an aggressive behavior was right or wrong, whereas older children focused more on the character's motives, which are typically depicted in more subtle ways.

A third important skill is the ability to draw inferences. As seen in Chapter 1, younger children are less able than their older counterparts to link scenes together, integrate information, and draw causal conclusions from the plot (Kendeou, Bohn-Gettler, White & van den Broek, 2008). Therefore, contextual cues that are separated from the violence itself will be more difficult for younger children to appreciate. Collins (1973) demonstrated this in an intriguing study involving 3rd, 6th, and 10th graders. Children viewed a violent scene in which the perpetrator was punished either immediately after engaging in violence or after a four-minute commercial break. The results revealed that 3rd graders gave more aggressive responses themselves in the separation than in the no-separation condition (see Figure 4.11). In other words, the commercial break interfered with younger children's ability to connect the punishment to the violence—the violence stood alone as a model for behavior. In contrast, older children's responses were unaffected by the separation manipulation, suggesting that they appreciated the punishment even when it occurred at a different point in the storyline.

Unfortunately, television supplies numerous instances in which aggressive behavior goes unpunished, at least in the short run; if punishment is delivered, it typically happens toward the end of the plot (Wilson, Smith, et al., 2002). A child younger than age 7 or 8 is not capable of connecting this delayed consequence back to an earlier transgression. Therefore, if punishment is temporally separated from the act, it will seem to a younger viewer as if the perpetrator "got away" with violence.

Young children are also likely to have trouble deducing or inferring the moral of a televised story (Mares &Acosta, 2008). Moreover, their grasp of a moral lesson may be particularly

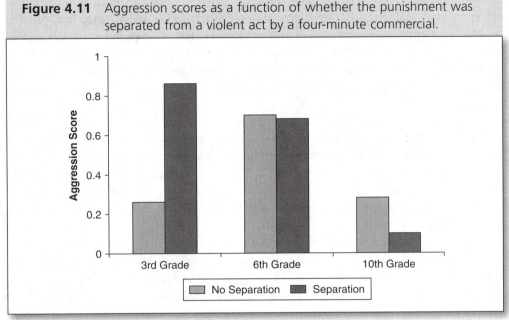

Figure 4.11   Aggression scores as a function of whether the punishment was separated from a violent act by a four-minute commercial.

SOURCE: Adapted from Collins (1973).

challenging if there are negative emotions portrayed in the plot, which is often the case with media violence. Hence, even if a movie concludes with an overall message that violence is not a good solution, the lesson is unlikely to be grasped by younger viewers, who will be absorbed in the violent actions and emotions throughout the storyline. Repeated viewing of the same program can help overall comprehension of the plot, but even then, the moral is difficult for children under 8 to extract (Mares, 2006).

One last developmental consideration is the age of the perpetrator. As discussed above, people tend to like characters in the media who are most like themselves. It stands to reason, then, that young people will be most attracted to younger characters. Studies support this; children's visual attention to the television screen increases when a child character appears (Schmitt et al., 1999). Moreover, children typically choose characters who are about their own age as their favorites (Cohen, 1999; Hoffner, 1996). Although there are far fewer child and teen perpetrators than adult ones on television (Wilson, Colvin, & Smith, 2002), these young aggressors are particularly salient for a younger viewer. Movies such as *Super 8* or *The Karate Kid*, which feature young characters engaging in justified violence, are likely to be very appealing to children. Likewise, music videos, which often feature teen perpetrators (Wilson, Colvin, et al., 2002), can be potent messages for preadolescent and adolescent audiences.

Relational or Social Aggression

Up to this point, we have focused primarily on physical aggression as a possible outcome of exposure to media violence. Yet in the past decade or so, developmental psychologists have come to recognize that there are other, less overt ways to engage in aggression (Ostrov &

Godleski, 2010). Relational or social aggression involves acts that are intended to harm others emotionally rather than physically. Examples include gossiping, spreading rumors, socially isolating others, or engaging in insulting or mean talk. These types of socially aggressive behaviors can occur in face-to-face situations, and they can even be perpetrated using the Internet. In recent national surveys, 17% of American youth report that they have been electronically bullied through instant messaging, in a chat room, or by email within the last year (Jayson, 2012).

Like physical aggression, social aggression emerges early in development, by age 3 or so (Crick, Ostrov, & Werner, 2006). However, unlike physical aggression, social aggression seems to be more common among girls than boys (Spieker et al., 2012). Public concern about this type of behavior has spawned a number of popular books with titles such as *Queen Bees and Wannabes: Helping Your Daughter Survive Cliques, Gossip, Boyfriends, and the New Realities of Girl World*. Popular movies such as *Mean Girls* and *Diary of a Wimpy Kid* also illustrate this type of behavior.

A handful of recent studies suggest that the media may be contributing to social aggression. One content analysis of the 50 most watched programs among 2- to 11-year-olds found that 92% of the shows contained social aggression (Martins & Wilson, 2012a). Moreover, an average of 14 different incidents of social aggression occurred per hour in these shows, or one every four minutes. The vast majority of these incidents (78%) were verbal in nature, with insults and name calling being the most common types (see Figure 4.12). Fewer of the incidents were nonverbal, and most of these involved making a mean facial expression at someone or laughing at someone. Similarly high levels of social aggression have been documented in prime-time programs (Glascock, 2008) and in programs popular with adolescents (Coyne & Archer, 2004). Research also suggests that adolescents are exposed to far more indirect and social aggression on television than they are in school (Coyne, Archer, & Eslea, 2006).

But is there any evidence for a link between media exposure and relational aggression? One study of preschoolers found that media exposure was positively associated with physical aggression for boys and with relational aggression for girls (Ostrov, Gentile, & Crick, 2006). Unfortunately, the study did not cleanly assess the content of what children were watching. More recently, a longitudinal study of over 400 grade school children found that heavy exposure to media violence at the beginning of the school year predicted higher levels of both physical and relational aggression later in the year (Gentile, Coyne, & Walsh, 2011), even after controlling for age, sex, race, and parental involvement. However, the link between media violence and aggression was stronger for physical than for relational forms of this behavior. The researchers speculated that their measure of media violence exposure was too broad and might not have captured programs high in relational aggression in particular.

Addressing this issue, Martins and Wilson (2012b) looked specifically at children's viewing of programs high in social aggression, as documented by their content analysis (Martins & Wilson, 2012a). Examples of such shows included *American Idol, Suite Life of Zach & Cody*, and *Drake & Josh*. Surveying over 500 children (K–5th grade), Martins and Wilson found that heavy exposure to televised social aggression was significantly related to greater social aggression in school, but only for girls and not for boys. The researchers speculated that the lack of findings for boys might be due to the popularity of socially aggressive programming with girls and to sex differences in types of aggressive behavior. Interestingly, exposure to programs high in physical violence was not linked to social

Figure 4.12 Types of verbal and nonverbal social aggression in programs popular among children.

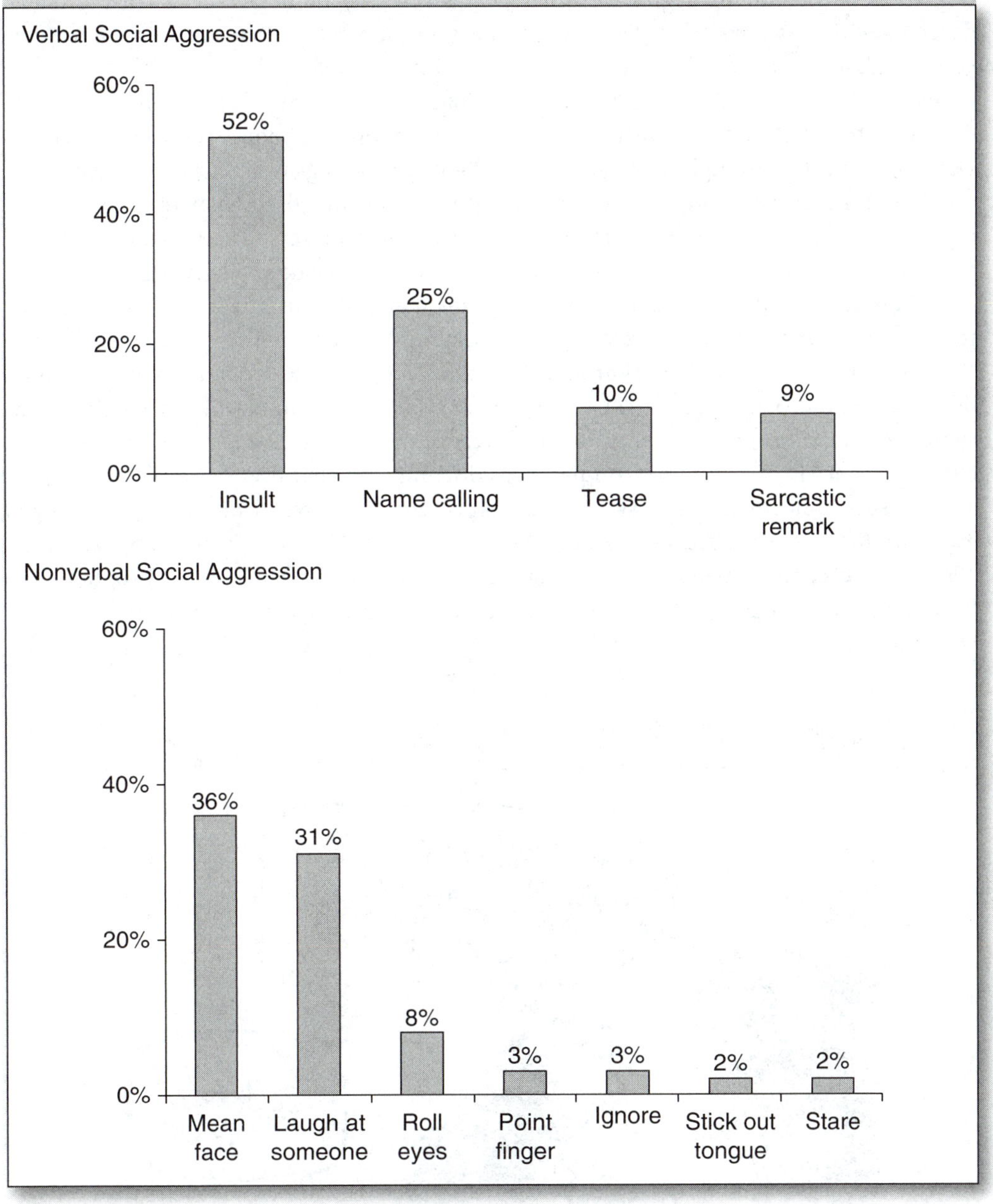

Verbal Social Aggression

Insult 52%, Name calling 25%, Tease 10%, Sarcastic remark 9%

Nonverbal Social Aggression

Mean face 36%, Laugh at someone 31%, Roll eyes 8%, Point finger 3%, Ignore 3%, Stick out tongue 2%, Stare 2%

SOURCE: Adapted from Martins and Wilson (2012a).

aggression (for girls or for boys), suggesting that the specific nature of the content and role modeling in violent programming is crucial.

Clearly, more research is needed on this provocative topic. It may be that our historical preoccupation with physical aggression has caused us to overlook other types of harmful outcomes of media violence, especially those that may be more prominent among girls.

Can Media Violence Desensitize Young People?

Concern about children's aggressive behavior has certainly dominated most of the public debates and the research on media violence. However, an outcome that may be far more pervasive is desensitization (see Figure 4.13). Desensitization refers to the idea that extensive exposure to a stimulus can lead to reduced emotional responsiveness to it. In clinical settings, desensitization techniques have been used to treat people's phobias (Olatunji, Cisler, & Deacon, 2010). For example, a person who is frightened of dogs is gradually exposed under nonthreatening circumstances to a variety of these types of animals, often with cognitive coping skills accompanying the exposure treatment. Eventually, the person acclimates to dogs and the fear is eliminated. Can repeated exposure to media violence be similarly therapeutic?

We do know that repeated viewing of violent materials can affect a person's arousal responses. For example, an early study found that boys who were heavy viewers of television exhibited less physiological arousal during selected scenes from a violent film than light viewers did (Cline, Croft, & Courrier, 1973). Likewise, adults who are habitual consumers of violent screen media show low levels of arousal while watching a violent film clip (Krahe et al., 2011). Other studies have documented that even within a single program, people's heart rate and skin conductance go down over time during prolonged exposure to violence (Lazarus & Alfert, 1964; Speisman, Lazarus, Davison, & Mordkoff, 1964). Some critics have speculated that American films and television programs are becoming increasingly graphic and violent because audiences are desensitized to tamer versions of such content (Farr, 2012).

Figure 4.13

SOURCE: Reprinted with permission of Mike Luckovich and Creators Syndicate, Inc.

If repeated exposure to media violence merely resulted in decreased arousal, there might be little cause for concern. In fact, one could argue that a reduction in arousal is even functional, given that being in a heightened state of arousal for too long can be taxing to the body (Ursin & Eriksen, 2001). What alarms people is the possibility that desensitization to entertainment violence will in turn affect responses to real-life violence. In their book *High Tech, High Touch: Technology and Our Search for Meaning,* Naisbitt, Naisbitt, and Philips (1999) wrote,

> In a culture of electronic violence, images that once caused us to empathize with the pain and trauma of another human being excite a momentary adrenaline rush. To be numb to another's pain—to be acculturated to violence—is arguably one of the worst consequences our technological advances have wrought. That indifference transfers from the screen, TV, film, Internet, and electronic games to our everyday lives through seemingly innocuous consumer technologies. (pp. 90–91)

Research suggests that there is some merit to this concern. For example, one study found that both children and adults were less physiologically aroused by a scene of real-life aggression if they had previously watched a violent drama on TV than if they had watched a nonviolent program (Thomas, Horton, Lippincott, & Drabman, 1977). In other words, the fictional portrayal produced an indifference to real-life violence. Violent video games can have a similar effect (see Chapter 10). In one recent experiment, college students who played a violent game for 20 minutes subsequently displayed less physiological arousal (i.e., heart rate and galvanic skin response) while watching a graphic videotape of real violence than did those who had played a nonviolent game (Carnagey, Anderson, & Bushman, 2007).

Even more troubling, can desensitization affect people's willingness to intervene or take action on behalf of a victim? In one experiment (Thomas & Drabman, 1975), 1st and 3rd graders were shown either a violent or a nonviolent TV program and then placed in charge of monitoring the behavior of two preschoolers at play. Older children who viewed the violent TV show were significantly slower in seeking help when the preschoolers broke into a fight than were those who viewed the nonviolent show. In fact, more than half the older children in the violent TV condition never left the room even though they had been told to get an adult if trouble erupted. This type of callousness to real violence has been replicated in other media studies involving children (Drabman & Thomas, 1974; Molitor & Hirsch, 1994) and even adults (Bushman & Anderson, 2009).

Desensitization can also cause callousness to real-world crime. In a pair of studies, Linz, Donnerstein, and Penrod (1984, 1988) exposed male undergraduates over a two-week period to five full-length "slasher" films depicting violence against women, such as *The Texas Chain Saw Massacre* and *The Toolbox Murders.* After each film, emotional reactions, perceptions of violence in the films, and attitudes toward the women in the films were measured. Supporting the idea of desensitization, males perceived less violence in the films and evaluated the films as less degrading to women over the course of the exposure period. At the end of the viewing period, participants were asked to evaluate a videotaped enactment of a legal trial involving a rape victim. Compared with various control groups, males who had been exposed to a heavy dose of slasher films were less sympathetic toward a rape victim and more inclined to hold her responsible.

One critical question is whether desensitization is a transitory effect or a more permanent state that persists beyond the exposure period. That is, can people become *resensitized* to real-world violence? Mullin and Linz (1995) tested this idea by varying the amount of time that lapsed between exposure to fictional violence and evaluations of real victims of violence. In this experiment, male college students were exposed to three slasher films over a six-day period. In a supposedly unrelated context, they were asked either three, five, or seven days later to watch a documentary about domestic abuse. The researchers found that three days after exposure, males expressed less sympathy for domestic violence victims and rated their injuries as less severe than did a no-exposure control group (see Figure 4.14). However, five and seven days later, levels of sympathy had rebounded to the baseline level of the control group. In other words, the desensitization effect seemed to diminish after about a three-day period.

Of course, resensitization requires that a person no longer be exposed to entertainment violence during the "recovery" period. As we have seen, most children watch between four and five hours of television per day, and many watch a great deal more. Given the pervasiveness of violence in this medium, heavy viewers are presumably exposed to a fairly constant diet of aggressive behaviors. If these same children also play violent video games, listen to violent music, and go to a violent film or two a month, there are ample occasions for desensitization to occur and not much of an opportunity to reestablish sensitivity to aggression.

Because desensitization is construed as an automatic process similar to habituation, it can happen without a person's awareness. Furthermore, unlike aggression, which is easy to see, there are fewer outward manifestations of this type of effect.

Thus, large numbers of young people in our society may be gradually becoming desensitized by media violence without us ever knowing. The popularity in recent years of graphically violent movie series such as *Rambo* and *Kill Bill* and graphic TV series such as *The Walking Dead* suggests that we are already experiencing a cultural shift in our acceptance of violence

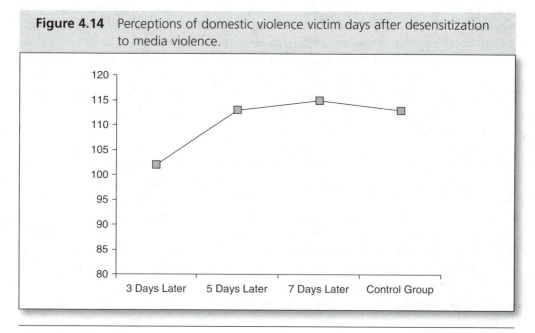

Figure 4.14   Perceptions of domestic violence victim days after desensitization to media violence.

SOURCE: Adapted from Mullin and Linz (1995).

in the media (Hayes, 2007). The danger, of course, is in the possibility that such an effect will spill over into real life, resulting in a society that is increasingly tolerant of aggression and indifferent to its victims.

Can Media Violence Produce Fear?

The third potential effect of media violence is to create fear in audiences (see Figure 4.15). Many of us can remember a movie or TV show that frightened us as a child. In one study, more than 90% of college students could vividly describe a film or television program that caused intense fear when they were younger (Harrison & Cantor, 1999). *Psycho, Jaws,* and *The Exorcist* were just a few of the more common movies cited (see Figure 4.16). Amazingly, one-fourth of these students said they were still bothered by what they had seen. And even though many of these movies are fictional, adults often report seemingly irrational long-term anxieties, such as fear of walking in the woods after seeing *The Blair Witch Project* (Cantor, 2004).

Such patterns are consistent with research involving children, too. Surveys indicate that a majority of preschoolers and elementary schoolers have experienced fright reactions to media programming, much of which is violent (Cantor, Byrne, Moyer-Gusé, & Riddle, 2010; Wilson, Hoffner, & Cantor, 1987). Furthermore, many of these reactions have endured beyond the viewing experience, resulting in nightmares, sleep disturbances, and even acute fears in some cases (see Cantor, 2009). In fact, studies have documented symptoms of post-traumatic stress disorder in young people as a result of media exposure to violent news

Figure 4.15

SOURCE: Jeff Stahler: © Columbus Dispatch/Dist. by Newspaper Enterprise Association, Inc.

Figure 4.16 Examples of movies that frighten children and teens.

events, such as the Oklahoma City bombing and the terrorist attacks on September 11, 2001 (Otto et al., 2007; Pfefferbaum et al., 2000).

The types of images that frighten children change as a function of age or developmental level (for reviews, see Cantor, 2009; Valkenburg & Buijzen, 2011). Preschoolers and younger elementary schoolers respond most to characters and scenes that *look* scary, consistent with the idea of perceptual dependence discussed in Chapter 1. Therefore, younger children are often frightened by programs that feature monsters, gory-looking characters, and witches. *The Wizard of Oz* and even certain Disney films are examples of upsetting content for this age group. In contrast, older elementary school children are less upset by surface features and more concerned about whether a violent portrayal could happen in real life. Again, this is consistent with the gradual understanding of reality-fantasy distinctions. Thus, more realistic programs that involve harm to human beings, especially family members, are often cited as frightening by 8- to 12-year-olds. Interestingly, this age group is also more likely to be scared by TV news stories of violent crime than their younger counterparts are (Riddle, Cantor, Byrne, & Moyer-Gusé, 2012; Smith & Wilson, 2002). Adolescents respond to realistic depictions too, but their abstract thinking skills also allow them to imagine implausible and inconceivable events (see Chapter 1). Therefore, teens are far more susceptible than children to intangible threats in the media, such as global conflict, nuclear war, and political attacks (Cantor, Wilson, & Hoffner, 1986).

Gerbner and his colleagues took the idea of fear one step further, arguing that extensive exposure to media violence can lead to a greater sense of apprehension, mistrust, and insecurity about the real world (Gerbner & Gross, 1976; Gerbner, Gross, Morgan, & Signorielli, 1994). In other words, violence in the media can cultivate a "mean world syndrome" in viewers (Morgan, Shanahan, & Signorielli, 2009). According to cultivation theory, heavy exposure to television can alter a person's perceptions of social reality in a way that matches the TV world. Given that television features so much violence, heavy viewers should come to see the world as more violent. In numerous studies with samples of all different ages, Gerbner and his colleagues consistently found that frequent viewers of television perceive the world as a more violent place and perceive themselves as more likely to become a victim of violence than light viewers do (see Morgan et al., 2009).

Cultivation theory has been rigorously critiqued by other researchers (Hawkins & Pingree, 1981; Hirsch, 1980; Hughes, 1980; Potter, 1993). One of the most widespread concerns is that most of the findings that support the theory are correlational. The cultivation effect does typically hold up even after controlling for demographic variables as well as other factors that could explain the relationship between TV and perceptions of reality (see Shanahan & Morgan, 1999). But even after controlling for "third" variables, it is difficult to determine the direction of causality from correlational data. Does television cause fear, or are frightened people drawn to watching more TV, in part because such content allows them to work out their fears? In support of cultivation theory, experimental evidence shows that repeated exposure to television violence, for as little as one week or as much as six weeks, under controlled conditions can heighten fear and anxiety in viewers (Bryant, Carveth, & Brown, 1981; Ogles & Hoffner, 1987). However, research also shows that crime-apprehensive people seek out violent drama, especially that which features the restoration of justice (Zillmann & Wakshlag, 1985). As with aggression, then, the relationship between entertainment violence and anxiety may be cyclical in nature.

A second criticism of the theory is that it assumes all television content is alike and that what matters most in predicting cultivation is the sheer amount of exposure to TV. We have already seen that PBS features relatively little violence (Wilson et al., 1998), so it stands to reason that if a child selectively watches that channel, there will be less likelihood of enhanced fear. Research also suggests that cultivation is heightened among those who watch a great deal of news content (Romer, Jamieson, & Aday, 2003). Thus, a person's television habits and favorite genres seem to be important factors to consider. Furthermore, technological developments such as cable and satellite networks, DVRs, pay-per-view, and the Internet have changed the face of "television" so that it is no longer a uniform experience. Yet despite all these innovations, Morgan (2009) argues that TV content and people's habits have not changed much over the years.

A third criticism is that the theory is too simplistic because it predicts an effect for anyone who watches a lot of television. In fact, not all of the subgroups in Gerbner's studies show a cultivation effect (Gerbner et al., 1980), suggesting that intervening variables are at work. Some studies indicate that cultivation is more likely to occur among those who perceive television as realistic (e.g., Busselle, 2001). Also, research suggests that personal experience with crime and one's motivation for viewing television (i.e., to learn versus to escape) may be important mediating factors (Gross & Aday, 2003; Perse, 1990). In addition, the cognitive abilities of the viewer may make a difference. Preschoolers, for example, lack the ability to distinguish reality from fantasy and the ability to integrate information from a program, so their perceptions may be less influenced by media content (Hawkins & Pingree, 1980). However, studies have found that by the elementary school years, exposure to news programming on TV is associated with exaggerated perceptions of murder and even child kidnapping (Smith & Wilson, 2002; Wilson, Martins, & Marske, 2005).

Finally, the theory has paid little attention to the cognitive processes that underlie cultivation. Shrum (2009) has argued that cultivation is a result of heuristic processing. Compared with more careful, systematic processing, heuristic processing is characterized by rapid and less careful thinking as well as the reliance on cognitive shortcuts and readily available or salient information. According to Shrum, most people engage in heuristic processing when asked to make judgments. Moreover, heavy viewers of television have numerous salient examples of violence stored in their memory. The more a person watches violent programming, the more accessible these exemplars are and the more likely they will be used in making judgments about social reality (see Shrum & Lee, 2012). In support of this model, one study found that college students who were encouraged to think carefully and accurately in answering questions about the incidence of crime in the world were *less* likely to show a cultivation effect than students who were encouraged to make rapid judgments or students who were given no instructions about how to answer the questions (Shrum, 2001). In other words, careful, systematic processing truncated the cultivation effect. In further support of heuristic processing, a recent experiment by Riddle (2010) found that people are more likely to show a cultivation effect after viewing repeated violence on television that is vivid (e.g., close-up shots of violence, blood, gore) compared to nonvivid. Here, the vividness presumably enhances memory and accessibility of those images when making subsequent judgments. Altogether, this newer research suggests that cultivation is a function of the extent to which people engage in heuristic processing and have lots of vivid instances of screen violence stored in memory.

Despite the criticisms of cultivation theory, there is still a great deal of evidence supporting the idea that media violence can make children, teens, and even adults feel more anxious about the real world. The challenge for the future is to better understand how and when these fear effects occur. Also, research needs to explore the relationship between fear and desensitization, which seem like contradictory outcomes. Perhaps repeated exposure to media violence frightens some and numbs others, depending on the nature of the content that is sought as well as the type of individual who seeks it.

Cultural Debates About Media Violence

Despite all the evidence presented here, there are critics who do not agree that media violence is harmful. Some of the most vocal opponents are people who work in the industry. To many of them, media violence has become a convenient scapegoat for politicians who refuse to grapple with more deep-seated causes of violence, such as gun access and poverty (Bradshaw, 2012). Another argument often made is that good drama requires conflict and conflict means violence (Braxton, 1991). Others in the industry argue that media violence will disappear if people simply quit watching it and paying for it (Pool, 1991). In other words, in the marketplace of American culture, consumers are ultimately responsible for the violence that surrounds us. Violence does seem to attract audiences, as we discussed above. Yet there are many examples of good storytelling with little or no physical aggression. Cartoon series such as *Doc McStuffins*, situation comedies such as *Modern Family*, and even movies such as *Dolphin Tale* and *The Help* illustrate this point. One of the problems is that violence is relatively easy and cheap to produce and has a strong international market (Groebel, 2001). Action movies seem to translate fairly easily across cultural, national, and linguistic borders.

There are also scholars who challenge the research, as noted earlier in this chapter. Some are social scientists themselves, and they critique the validity and reliability of the studies. For example, Freedman (2002) points out the limitations of laboratory studies, field experiments, and correlational research and concludes that the evidence does not yet support a causal relationship between TV violence and aggression. Similarly, Ferguson and Kilburn (2009) and Savage and Yancey (2008) question the existence of effects, based on their own statistical analyses of the research. Other scholars argue that focusing on the "effects" of media violence on children is too simplistic and unidimensional, ignoring how young people choose, interpret, and negotiate violent media texts in their lives (Buckingham, 2000). Still others believe that social science research obfuscates larger issues, such as how media violence as a cultural institution legitimizes power and control in our society (Ball-Rokeach, 2000). A more radical view is represented by Fowles (1999), who believes that media violence is therapeutic for people. At least in the social science arena, though, there is little evidence to support this position.

Obviously, there are many points of view regarding media violence. The debates are often intense, and given the stakes involved, there are no easy solutions. Social scientists are increasingly joining the public discussions and grappling with the politics of their work (Bushman & Anderson, 2001; Huesmann, Dubow, & Yang, 2013). The challenge, it seems, is to stay focused on children in the midst of these political and scholarly disputes.

Guns and the Media

Firearms play a leading role in mortality and morbidity among American youth (Children's Defense Fund [CDF], 2012). In fact, the leading cause of death among African American males between the ages of 15 and 19 is gun homicide. Moreover, the death rate due to firearms among U.S. teens and young adults is 43 times higher than among young people in 23 other industrialized countries *combined* (CDF, 2012). In 2008 and 2009 alone, a total of 5,740 children and teens died from guns in the U.S., which translates to one child or teen every three hours, or eight youth a day (CDF, 2012). During this same two-year period, over 34,000 American youth suffered nonfatal gun injuries.

There is little doubt that the United States is "the most heavily armed nation on earth" (O. G. Davidson, 1993), with approximately one-third of homes with children younger than 18 years of age having at least one firearm (Johnson, Coyne-Beasley, & Runyan, 2004). In a good number of these homes, especially homes with teens, the firearms are unlocked and either loaded or stored near ammunition (Johnson, Miller, Vriniotis, Azrael, & Hemenway, 2006). And young people seem to know it. In one national survey, 24% of adolescents reported that they had "easy access" to a gun in their home (Swahn, Hammig, & Ikeda, 2002). In another national study, 16% of American youth (and 25% of males) reported that they had carried a handgun by the age of 17 (Snyder & Sickmund, 2006).

Unfortunately, guns kept at home can be more dangerous to the people who live there than to any criminal intruder (Kellermann et al., 1993; Kellermann, Somes, Rivara, Lee, & Banton, 1998). In one 5-year study of youth brought to a medical trauma center, 75% of the guns used in suicide attempts and unintentional injuries came from the victim's home or the home of a relative or friend (Grossman, Reay, & Baker, 1999). In another study in New Mexico, 25 unintentional firearm deaths and 200 woundings were identified within a four-year period, mostly involving children playing with loaded guns at home (Martin, Sklar, & McFeeley, 1991).

Large epidemiological studies show that keeping a gun in the home increases the risk of suicide and homicide among the adults who reside there (Miller, Lippmann, Azrael, & Hemenway, 2007) and even increases the risk of suicidal tendencies and violence among teen residents (Resnick et al., 1997). One study found that the odds of a depressed teenager successfully committing suicide increase 75-fold if there is a gun kept at home (Rosenberg, Mercy, & Houk, 1991). Yet nearly 2 million children and youth in the United States are living in homes with loaded and unlocked firearms (Okoro et al., 2005). Furthermore, 23% of gun-owning parents believe that their child can be trusted with a loaded gun (Farah, Simon, & Kellermann, 1999).

One study graphically demonstrates just how naive children can be about firearms. Jackman, Farah, Kellermann, and Simon (2001) observed more than 60 boys between the ages of 8 and 12 as they played in a room full of toys. The room also contained an unloaded .380-caliber handgun concealed in a drawer. Within 15 minutes of play, the vast majority of boys (75%) discovered the gun. More disturbing, 63% of the boys who found the gun handled it, and 33% actually pulled the trigger. When questioned afterward, almost half of the boys who found the gun thought it was a toy or were not sure whether it was real. Children from gun-owning families behaved no differently than children from non-gun-owning families.

Despite all the risks, many Americans seem to have a long-standing love of guns, and this passion is frequently played out in the movies and on television. A recent study of 100 top-grossing movies between 1995 and 2004 found that a full 70% featured at least one scene with a firearm (Binswanger & Cowan, 2009). Furthermore, firearm depictions accounted for 17% of the screen time in these movies, and messages about gun safety were "exceedingly rare." The majority of the films featuring firearms were rated PG-13 and could be viewed readily by older children and teens. But such images are not limited to the movies (see Figure 4.17). Young children can witness laser guns and a variety of other types of firearms being used in cartoons such as *Green Lantern* and even *Looney Tunes*. Using data from the National Television Violence Study described above, Smith, Boyson, Pieper, and

Wilson (2001) found that 26% of all violent incidents in a composite week of television involved the use of a gun. Three types of programming accounted for most of this gun violence: movies (54%), dramatic series (19%), and children's shows (16%). In terms of rate, a child viewer will see, on average, nearly two gun-related violent incidents every hour that she or he watches TV. That rate goes up if the child selectively watches gun-filled genres such as movies or children's shows.

According to cognitive priming theory, images of guns in the media can trigger aggressive thoughts and ideas in young viewers. In one experiment, just flashing pictures of guns and other weapons on a computer screen served to prime aggressive-related thoughts in college students (Anderson, Benjamin, & Bartholow, 1998). In other words, a gun need not even be fired to incite aggression. In support of this idea, a meta-analysis of 56 experiments found that the mere presence of weapons, either pictorially or in the natural environment, significantly enhanced aggression among angered as well as nonangered adults (Carlson et al., 1990).

Clearly, the portrayal of guns in entertainment media is a public health concern. For many young children, television will be the first place they encounter such weapons. Repeated exposure to images of heroes and other attractive role models using firearms will at the very least help to glorify these deadly devices. Even the news can draw attention to gun use. Some have criticized the television networks for airing graphic images of the

Figure 4.17 Images of guns in television, films, and video games.

gunmen and their weapons in stories about the massacres at Virginia Tech and Aurora, Colorado, in part because such publicity gives undue notoriety to deranged individuals (Bauder, 2012; Klimkiewicz, 2007).

Suicide and the Media

Suicide is the third leading cause of death among youth between the ages of 10 and 24 (CDC, 2011). However, many teens consider suicide without attempting it or attempt it without being successful. Suicidal thoughts are alarmingly common among teenagers. In a recent national survey, 16% of all high schoolers reported having seriously considered attempting suicide in the previous 12 months, and 13% had actually made a plan about how they would do it (Youth Risk Behavior Surveillance System, 2012). Given such statistics, having firearms in the home and making firearms a common feature in the media both seem like dangerous practices.

In addition to glorifying guns, the media may contribute to adolescent suicide by highlighting such behavior in public cases (Phillips, Carstensen, & Paight, 1989). On April 5, 1994, lead singer Kurt Cobain of the popular rock group Nirvana put a shotgun to his head and pulled the trigger. This highly publicized suicide prompted a great deal of public concern about the potential of the event to spark copycat behaviors among anguished teen fans (Jobes, Berman, O'Carroll, Eastgard, & Knickmeyer, 1996). In fact, a large number of studies, both in the United States and Europe, have demonstrated a link between media coverage of suicide and subsequent increases in such behavior among teens (for reviews, see Pirkis & Nordentoft, 2011; Sisask & Varnik, 2012). This contagion effect has been found for both TV news coverage and newspaper coverage of stories (Romer, Jamieson, & Jamieson, 2006). The effect is enhanced by prominent coverage and repetition of the news stories (Etzersdorfer, Voracek, & Sonneck, 2004). Furthermore, the impact is strongest within the first three days of media coverage and then seems to level off after about two weeks (Phillips & Carstensen, 1986), although it can last longer (Fu & Yip, 2007).

One key factor in this phenomenon may be the extent to which a susceptible teen identifies with the publicized suicide victim (L. E. Davidson, Rosenberg, Mercy, Franklin, & Simmons, 1989). In support of this idea, a meta-analysis of 55 studies on the effect of suicide stories in the news found that the risk of contagion was significantly greater when a celebrity was involved (Stack, 2005). However, because the studies to date have all involved large numbers of young people, it is difficult to know precisely which factors influenced any particular individual. In addition, although such research typically controls for factors such as time of year and yearly trends in suicide, the data are still only correlational, so they are always subject to alternative explanations.

Fictional media content can also portray suicide stories. Popular films such as *The Virgin Suicides* and *A Beautiful Mind* focus on characters struggling with mental illness and suicidal tendencies. Other films such as *Romeo and Juliet* almost seem to celebrate suicide by depicting it as a heroic act. There is some evidence to suggest that the depiction of suicidal themes in feature-length films has increased over the years (see Jamieson & Romer, 2011). Furthermore, exposure to such films has been linked to particular beliefs about mental illness. One national survey found that among adolescents and young adults identified as depressed/suicidal, frequent viewing of films with mentally disturbed characters was associated with less confidence in the effectiveness of mental health treatments (Jamieson, Romer, & Jamieson, 2006). Among nontroubled youth, however, there was no relationship between film exposure and treatment beliefs. The researchers speculated that movies that glorify suicide and fail to model successful coping techniques may be teaching young people about the futility of seeking help. Because these data are correlational, it could also be that troubled youth who are already skeptical about treatment are seeking out these types of films.

Newer media also present information about suicide for the curious or depressed young person. There are websites that can be characterized as "prosuicidal," online chat rooms and virtual bulletin boards that provide digital spaces for users to discuss suicidal ideations, and even YouTube videos that demonstrate self-injury techniques such as cutting and burning (see Luxton, June, & Fairall, 2012). A recent national study of 14- to 24-year-olds found that most youth (64%) had "heard or seen a story about someone who committed suicide in the past few months" in a newspaper, but 24% reported that they had been exposed to a suicide story on a social networking site and 15% said they had learned of a suicide case from an online forum or self-help website (Dunlop, More, & Romer, 2011). Thus, concerns about contagion effects increasingly need to consider social media rather than just traditional news outlets.

Clearly, the causes of suicidal behaviors are complex and multifold (Amitai & Apter, 2012). Nevertheless, research supports the above-mentioned idea known in the medical field as suicide "contagion" (Insel & Gould, 2008), whereby exposure to the suicide of one person encourages others to attempt such behavior. The contagion effect appears to be stronger among adolescents than adults (Gould, Wallenstein, Kleinman, O'Carroll, & Mercy, 1990), which is quite consistent with the idea that suicidal tendencies might be learned and/or primed by observing the behavior of others. Given that troubled teens do seem to take notice of public suicides, the CDC and the American Association of Suicidology have issued guidelines for reporting suicide in the media (see www.suicidology.org/c/document_library/get_file?folderId=236&name=DLFE-336.pdf). They recommend that news stories avoid sensationalizing the act, glorifying the person involved, or providing how-to details. Recent evidence indicates that U.S. newspapers are not doing a very good job of following these guidelines (Tatum, Canetto, & Slater, 2010). Such guidelines could apply just as readily to entertainment programs that feature suicide in the plot or to websites that focus on suicide information.

Japan Versus the United States: A Cross-Cultural Comparison

The only country in the world with nearly as much entertainment violence as the United States is Japan. Yet Japanese society is far less violent than American society (United Nations Office on Drugs and Crime, 2012). If media violence contributes to real-life aggression, why is Japan not more affected? There are several important differences between the two countries. First, the portrayal of violence is different in Japan. Compared with American television, programming in Japan more heavily emphasizes the negative consequences of violence in the storyline (Iwao, Pool, & Hagiwara, 1981; Kodaira, 1998). Interestingly, in Japan, the "bad guys" commit much of the TV violence, with the "good guys" suffering the consequences—a pattern opposite to what is found in American programming (Smith et al., 1998). As discussed earlier, featuring unattractive perpetrators and showing victim pain both reduce the risk that a portrayal will encourage aggression in viewers.

Second, children are raised in fairly traditional family structures with a strong emphasis on discipline and control. Third, Japan has very strict gun control laws. Individuals are not allowed to own guns, and very few exceptions are allowed. The only type of firearm a citizen may acquire is a shotgun, for hunting purposes only, and only after a lengthy licensing procedure involving classes, a written exam, and medical certification of mental health (Kopel, 1993). After a wave of shootings by gangs in 2007, Japan strengthened its already-strict gun control laws by imposing a 1- to 15-year prison sentence or a fine of up to 5 million yen ($46,100) for possession of a gun as part of organized crime (Nishiyama, 2007).

Despite these cultural differences, teen violence in Japan is on the rise. By U.S. standards, the figures are still low. But the number of minors younger than age 14 who committed violent crimes increased 47% from 2002 to 2003 (Faiola, 2004). The recent surge in youth violence has led some to point fingers at the increasingly violent nature of Japanese media (Faiola, 2004). Often quite graphic, Japanese *anime* or animation is exported worldwide in the form of comic books, cartoons, short films, and video games (Bosker, 2007). Others have blamed the escalation of violence in Japan on an intensive educational system and a breakdown in traditional values (Lies, 2001). Japan can still be considered a relatively peaceful country relative to the United States, but the celebration of violence in popular culture there is giving rise to public concern. Indeed, a longitudinal study of Japanese and American youth found that playing violent video games predicted increased physical aggression three to six months later in both countries, even after controlling for gender and initial aggressiveness (Anderson et al., 2008). Moreover, the size of the effect was similar for the two countries, despite Japan's being a "low-violence" culture. The researchers concluded,

> That both cultures yielded significant longitudinal effects of approximately the same magnitude illustrates the power of violent video games to affect children's developmental trajectories in a harmful way. These findings also further suggest that common social learning processes underlie media violence effects across cultures, and contradict another popular alternative hypothesis: that only highly aggressive children (either by nature, culture, or other socialization factors) will become more aggressive if repeatedly exposed to violent video games. (p. e1070)

Can Media Violence Have Positive Effects?

Much of this chapter has focused on the negative effects of exposure to media violence. However, violent portrayals can have prosocial effects as well. In 1998, Court TV (now called truTV) commissioned a study to assess whether television violence could help teach young people to be *less* aggressive (Wilson et al., 1999). In the study, 513 young adolescents from three different middle schools in California were randomly assigned to receive or not receive an antiviolence curriculum in school. The *Choices and Consequences* curriculum was presented by the regular teachers during normal class time. The three-week curriculum involved watching videotaped court cases about real teens who had engaged in risky behavior that resulted in someone dying. In one case, for example, a group of teens pushed a young boy off a railroad trestle and he drowned.

Each week, students watched portions of the videotaped trial, discussed them in class, engaged in role playing activities, and completed homework assignments based on the trial case. Compared with the no-curriculum control group, the intervention significantly reduced middle schoolers' verbal aggression and curbed their physical aggression. The curriculum also increased empathic skills and knowledge of the legal system. In other words, exposure to programming that emphasized the lifelong negative consequences of antisocial behavior had prosocial effects on teens.

Other types of critical viewing curricula have been tested as well. For example, Huesmann, Eron, Klein, Brice, and Fischer (1983) had 2nd and 4th graders write essays about the harmful effects of television violence and the unrealistic nature of particular violent shows. Then the children were videotaped while they read their essays; the footage was purportedly to be used to create a film about the problems of media violence. Compared with a control group that wrote essays about hobbies, the intervention group showed several positive effects. The intervention significantly altered children's attitudes about TV violence, decreased their aggressive behavior, and eliminated the relationship between TV violence and aggressive behavior. Most of these effects were measured four months after the intervention, suggesting that a rather simple treatment can produce lasting changes.

In support of this earlier work, a recent meta-analysis of nine studies found that media literacy programs can be effective in changing how people respond to screen violence (Jeong, Cho, & Hwang, 2012). Such efforts are consistent with more broad-based curricular programs designed to teach media literacy to children (see Chapter 12).

Even in the absence of instructions or structured lessons plans, though, programs that treat violence in a sensitive manner can have a positive impact on audience members. One large-scale experiment found that a made-for-TV movie about acquaintance rape increased adults' concern about the societal problems associated with rape and also reduced their acceptance of rape myths (Wilson, Linz, Donnerstein, & Stipp, 1992). Another study documented similar educational benefits of watching a TV movie about date rape among high schoolers (Filotas, 1993). However, both of these studies found that among some people, the intervention actually had a "boomerang" effect. In other words, teaching about the perils of media violence *enhanced* aggressive attitudes among certain groups. Such findings serve as a caution for those who wish to design such interventions. Knowing the audience and their preexisting attitudes is a first step. In addition, a recent experiment suggests that showing violent clips, even in the context of instructions that attempt to educate about violence, may inadvertently prime aggressive thoughts and attitudes among children (Byrne, Linz, & Potter, 2009). Thus, visual images that glamorize violence need to be used with care. Although no empirical tests have confirmed this, movies such as *Hotel Rwanda*, *Mystic River*, and *Blood Diamond* that portray the realistic consequences of violence may be less likely to prime aggression in viewers and therefore could be more effective in educating youth about the personal and societal costs associated with aggression.

Conclusion

Today there is strong consensus among most researchers that exposure to aggressive messages on television and in movies can have harmful effects on youth (Report of the Media Violence Commission, 2012). The most well-documented effect concerns aggression. Experimental studies, correlational research, longitudinal studies, and meta-analyses of published data all point to the same conclusion: Aggression is a learned behavior that can be acquired, reinforced, and primed by media messages. Young children are particularly vulnerable, as are children who strongly identify with violent characters, who are doing poorly in school, who perceive television as realistic, and who are unpopular with peers. The evidence does not suggest that media violence is the major cause of violence in society, but it is a socially significant one. The media are part of a complex web of cultural and environmental factors that can teach and reinforce aggression as a way of solving problems.

Yet aggression is not the only possible outcome. Extensive exposure to media violence can also desensitize some young people and make them more callous toward real-world violence. In others, it can lead to exaggerated concern and fear of becoming a victim of violence. None of these outcomes is straightforward and universal. Instead, certain children and teens are more vulnerable depending on their cognitive development, the types of media violence they like, and the amount of exposure they have to media violence in relation to other types of messages.

Given all these potential risks, one could advocate the elimination of violence from the media. But violence does seem to turn a profit, at least with some audiences, so it is unlikely that it will ever go away in a free-market society. Nor should we necessarily try to make it do so. As we see in Chapter 13, policymakers walk a fine line between respecting the First Amendment rights of media makers and attempting to protect special audiences, like children, who may be vulnerable to the negative effects of exposure to violent media. Additionally, research shows quite clearly that certain portrayals are less harmful than others and that some depictions can actually have educational or prosocial effects on youth. The challenge for parents and educators is to ensure that youth are exposed to these alternative messages that accurately portray the seriousness of violence in society. The challenge to the media industry is to create more of these alternative messages and to ensure that they are just as appealing as those that glorify violence.

Exercises

1. Suppose you were asked to monitor the amount of violence on television. How would you define *violence?* What types of issues would need to be considered in crafting your definition? Would you include fantasy violence? Would you include slapstick violence? How might your definition differ if you were a media researcher versus an executive in the television industry? What channels would you include in your study? What challenges, if any, would technologies such as TiVo and other digital video recording (DVR) devices pose for your study?

2. What is the most violent movie or television program you have ever seen? What made it so violent? Did you enjoy the program? Why or why not? If you were a parent, would you let your 6-year-old watch this program? Your 10-year-old? Your 15-year-old? Think about cognitive development as well as the nature of the content in addressing these questions.

3. Watch a popular cartoon and an evening crime drama on television. Compare the two in terms of *how* violence is portrayed. Think about contextual features such as the

nature of the perpetrators, whether violence is rewarded or punished, and the consequences of violence. According to the research cited in this chapter, which program poses more risk to a young child viewer? Why?

4. In 1999, Mario Padilla and Samuel Ramirez, two teenage cousins, said the movie *Scream* inspired them to kill one of their mothers. That same year, two troubled teens who were obsessed with violent video games walked into Columbine High School and started shooting. Media violence is often blamed in these and many other "copycat" behaviors. Should the media be placed on trial? Divide into groups and develop arguments that might be used in a criminal case against such youth. Who or what is responsible for violence in these instances? Should writers and producers be held to any standards regarding the violent material they create?

5. Critics charge that television news is more violent than ever, often relying on the "If it bleeds, it leads" rule of practice. Is TV news too violent? Should news be treated differently than fictional content in the debates about media violence? In addressing this issue, consider what constitutes news versus entertainment programming. Is there a difference? Where do reality-based programs such as *Cops* and *Police POV* fit in?

6. Bullying is receiving a great deal of attention in America these days. Do you think media violence is contributing to this problem among youth? Why or why not? Can you think of instances of bullying that are portrayed in popular media? Are there ways we could use the media to teach children about the seriousness of bullying? Based on the research cited in the section titled "Can Media Violence Have Positive Effects?" as well as on other studies you can find, design an intervention program that could help reduce bullying among youth. Make sure you use the media in your intervention program.

7. In his provocative book *Channeling Violence: The Economic Market for Violent Television Programming*, James Hamilton (1998) argues that television violence, like pollution, generates negative externalities or costs that are shouldered by others rather than the people who produce the material. Using pollution as an analogy, he goes on to say that restrictions should be devised that place more responsibility on the TV industry while still protecting artistic freedom. For example, a violence tax could be imposed on those responsible for aggressive portrayals. How might such a tax work? Who should pay, and how should the amount be determined? Can you think of other approaches that could be implemented, using the pollution comparison? Would such efforts be constitutional?

8. Think back to your childhood. Can you remember a TV program or movie that really frightened you? How old were you? How long did your fear last? What aspect of the show frightened you? Did you change your behavior in any way as a result of seeing this show? Analyze your reaction in light of what we know about cognitive development and children's fear reactions to media, as discussed in this chapter.

9. In the debates about media violence, much less attention has been paid to desensitization as a harmful outcome than to aggression. Can you think of an occasion during which you felt desensitized to media violence? If our society gradually becomes desensitized to media violence, what are some of the possible outgrowths of this? Will it affect

parenting? Will it affect the legal system? Explore some of the ways desensitization could affect individuals as well as our culture. You should look at a recent study by Engelhardt, Bartholow, Kerr, and Bushman (2011) that connects desensitization to aggressive behavior.

10. America is a violent country. Do you believe that the media have been unfairly blamed in public debates about this problem? Think about how you would respond to such a question if you worked in the media industry. Now think about how you would respond if you were a parent of a young child who had been seriously injured by a friend on the playground who was imitating a cartoon superhero. Defend your responses from these two different perspectives, using strong arguments based on research evidence to support your positions.

References

Abelson, R. P. (1976). Script processing in attitude formation and decision-making. In J. Carroll & J. Payne (Eds.), *Cognition and social behavior* (pp. 33–45). Hillsdale, NJ: Lawrence Erlbaum.

Aluja-Fabregat, A. (2000). Personality and curiosity about TV and films violence in adolescents. *Personality and Individual Differences, 29,* 379–392.

American Academy of Pediatrics. (2009). Policy statement—media violence. *Pediatrics, 124*(5), 1495–1503.

American Medical Association. (2008). *National Advisory Council on Violence and Abuse: Policy compendium.* Retrieved from http://www.ama-assn.org//resources/doc/violence/vio_policy_comp.pdf

Amitai, M., & Apter, A. (2012). Social aspects of suicidal behavior and prevention in early life: A review. *International Journal of Environmental Research and Public Health, 9*(3), 985–994.

Anderson, C. A., Benjamin, A. J., Jr., & Bartholow, B. D. (1998). Does the gun pull the trigger? Automatic priming effects of weapon pictures and weapon names. *American Psychological Society, 9,* 308–314.

Anderson, C. A., Berkowitz, L., Donnerstein, E., Huesmann, L. R., Johnson, J. D., Linz, D., . . . Wartella, E. (2003). The influence of media violence on youth. *Psychological Science in the Public Interest, 4*(3), 81–110.

Anderson, C. A., Sakamoto, A., Gentile, D.A., Ihori, N., Shibuya, A., Yukawa, S., . . . Kobayashi, K. (2008). Longitudinal effects of violent video games aggression in Japan and the United States. *Pediatrics 122,* 1067–1072.

Archer, D. (1994). American violence: How high and why? *Law Studies, 19,* 12–20.

Arnett, J. J. (1995). The soundtrack of recklessness: Musical preferences and reckless behavior among adolescents. *Journal of Adolescent Research, 7,* 313–331.

Atkin, C. (1983). Effects of realistic TV violence vs. fictional violence on aggression. *Journalism Quarterly, 60,* 615–621.

Auletta, K. (1993, May 17). Annals of communication: What they won't do? *New Yorker, 69,* 45–53.

Ball-Rokeach, S. J. (2000, June). *The politics of studying media violence: Reflections thirty years after the violence commission.* Paper presented at the annual meeting of the International Communication Association, Acapulco, Mexico.

Bandura, A. (1965). Influence of models' reinforcement contingencies on the acquisition of imitative response. *Journal of Personality and Social Psychology, 1,* 589–595.

Bandura, A. (1986). *Social foundations of thought and action: A social cognitive theory.* Englewood Cliffs, NJ: Prentice Hall.

Bandura, A. (2009). Social cognitive theory of mass communication. In J. Bryant & M. B. Oliver (Eds.), *Media effects: Advances in theory and research* (pp. 94–124). New York, NY: Routledge.

Bandura, A., Ross, D., & Ross, S. A. (1961). Transmission of aggression through imitation of aggressive models. *Journal of Abnormal and Social Psychology, 63,* 575–582.

Bandura, A., Ross, D., & Ross, S. A. (1963a). Imitation of film-mediated aggressive models. *Journal of Abnormal and Social Psychology, 66,* 3–11.

Bandura, A., Ross, D., & Ross, S. A. (1963b). Various reinforcement and imitative learning. *Journal of Abnormal and Social Psychology, 67,* 601–607.

Baron, R. A. (1971a). Aggression as a function of magnitude of victim's pain cues, level of prior anger arousal, and aggressor-victim similarity. *Journal of Personality and Social Psychology, 18,* 48–54.

Baron, R. A. (1971b). Magnitude of victim's pain cues and level of prior anger arousal as determinants of adult aggressive behavior. *Journal of Personality and Social Psychology, 17,* 236–243.

Baron, R. A. (1978). The influence of hostile and nonhostile humor upon physical aggression. *Personality and Social Psychology Bulletin, 4,* 77–80.

Bauder, D. (2012, July 24). *Aurora shooting: Victims' families urge television networks to use James Holmes' name less.* Retrieved from http://www.huffingtonpost.com/2012/07/25/aurora-shooting-victims-tv-networks-name_n_1701093.html

Bauer, N. S., Herrenkohl, T. I., Lozano, P., Rivara, F. P., Hill, K. G., & Hawkins, J. D. (2006). Childhood bullying involvement and exposure to intimate partner violence. *Pediatrics, 118*(2), e235–e242.

Belson, W. A. (1978). *Television violence and the adolescent boy.* Westmead, UK: Saxon House, Teakfield.

Benton Foundation. (2005, October 11). *New poll finds escalating violence in children's TV now a crisis for parents.* Retrieved from http://benton.org/node/323

Berkowitz, L. (1970). Aggressive humor as a stimulus to aggressive responses. *Journal of Personality and Social Psychology, 2,* 359–369.

Berkowitz, L. (1973). Words and symbols as stimuli to aggressive responses. In J. F. Knutson (Ed.), *Control of aggression: Implications from basic research* (pp. 113–143). Chicago, IL: Aldine-Atherton.

Berkowitz, L. (1984). Some effects of thoughts on anti- and prosocial influences of media events: A cognitive-neoassociation analysis. *Psychological Bulletin, 95,* 410–427.

Berkowitz, L. (1990). On the formation and regulation of anger and aggression: A cognitive neoassociationistic analysis. *American Psychologist, 45,* 494–503.

Berkowitz, L., & Powers, P. C. (1979). Effects of timing and justification of witnessed aggression on the observers' punitiveness. *Journal of Research in Personality, 13,* 71–80.

Berry, M., Gray, T., & Donnerstein, E. (1999). Cutting film violence: Effects on perceptions, enjoyment, and arousal. *Journal of Social Psychology, 139,* 567–582.

Binswanger, I. A., & Cowan, J. A. (2009). Firearms in major motion pictures, 1995–2004. *Journal of Trauma Injury, Infection, and Critical Care, 66*(3), 906–911.

Bleakley, A., Jamieson, P., & Romer, D. (2012). Trends of sexual and violent content by gender in top-grossing U.S. films, 1950–2006. *Journal of Adolescent Health, 51,* 73–79.

Bosker, B. (2007, August 31). Manga mania. *Wall Street Journal.* Retrieved from http://online.wsj.com/article/SB118851157811713921.html

Boyatzis, J., Matillo, G. M., & Nesbitt, K. M. (1995). Effects of the *Mighty Morphin Power Rangers* on children's aggression with peers. *Child Study Journal, 25,* 45–55.

Bradshaw, P. (2012, July 21). *Will the* Dark Knight Rises *shootings revive the debate on "copycat" crimes?* Retrieved from http://www.guardian.co.uk/film/filmblog/2012/jul/21/dark-knight-rises-shootings-copycat-crimes

Braxton, G. (1991, July 31). Producers defend violence as honest. *Los Angeles Times,* pp. F1, F14.

Brito, N., Barr, R., McIntyre, P., & Simcock, G. (2012). Long-term transfer of learning from books and video during toddlerhood. *Journal of Experimental Child Psychology, 111*(1), 109–119.

Brown, M. H., Skeen, P., & Osborn, D. K. (1979). Young children's perception of the reality of television. *Contemporary Education, 50,* 129–133.

Bryant, J., Carveth, R. A., & Brown, D. (1981). Television viewing and anxiety: An experimental examination. *Journal of Communication, 31*(1), 106–109.

Buckingham, D. (2000). *After the death of childhood: Growing up in the age of electronic media.* Cambridge, UK: Polity.

Bushman, B. J., & Anderson, C. A. (2001). Media violence and the American public: Scientific facts versus media misinformation. *American Psychologist, 56*, 477–489.

Bushman, B. J., & Anderson, C. A. (2009). Comfortably numb: Desensitizing effects of violent media on helping others. *Psychological Science, 20*(3), 273–277.

Bushman, B. J., & Geen, R. G. (1990). Role of cognitive-emotional mediators and individual differences in the effects of media violence on aggression. *Journal of Personality and Social Psychology, 58*, 156–163.

Bushman, B. J., & Huesmann, L. R. (2001). Effects of televised violence on aggression. In D. G. Singer & J. L. Singer (Eds.), *Handbook of children and the media* (pp. 223–254). Thousand Oaks, CA: Sage.

Bushman, B. J., Huesmann, L. R., & Whitaker, J. L. (2009). Violent media effects. In R. L. Nabi & M. B. Oliver (Eds.), *Media processes and effects* (pp. 361–376). Thousand Oaks, CA: Sage.

Bushman, B. J., Rothstein, H. R., & Anderson, C. A. (2010). Much ado about something: Violent video game effects and a school of red herring: Reply to Ferguson and Kilburn (2010). *Psychological Bulletin, 136*(2), 182–187.

Busselle, R. W. (2001). The role of exemplar accessibility in social reality judgments. *Media Psychology, 3*, 43–68.

Byrne, S., Linz, D., & Potter, J. (2009). A test of competing cognitive explanations for the boomerang effect in response to the deliberate disruption of media-induced aggression. *Media Psychology, 12*(3), 227–248.

Calvert, S. L., Murray, K. J., & Conger, E. E. (2004). Heroic DVD portrayals: What US and Taiwanese adolescents admire and understand. *Journal of Applied Developmental Psychology, 25*(6), 699–716.

Cantor, J. (1998). Children's attraction to violent television programming. In J. H. Goldstein (Ed.), *Why we watch: The attractions of violent entertainment* (pp. 116–143). New York, NY: Oxford University Press.

Cantor, J. (2004). "I'll never have a clown in my house": Why movie horror lives on. *Poetics Today, 25*(2), 283–304.

Cantor, J. (2009). Fright reactions to mass media. In J. Bryant & M. B. Oliver (Eds.), *Media effects: Advances in theory and research* (3rd ed., pp. 287–303). Hillsdale, NJ: Lawrence Erlbaum.

Cantor, J., Byrne, S., Moyer-Gusé, E., & Riddle, K. (2010). Descriptions of media-induced fright reactions in a sample of US elementary school children. *Journal of Children and Media, 4*, 1–17.

Cantor, J., & Nathanson, A. I. (1997). Predictors of children's interest in violent television programs. *Journal of Broadcasting and Electronic Media, 41*, 155–167.

Cantor, J., Wilson, B. J., & Hoffner, C. (1986). Emotional responses to a televised nuclear holocaust film. *Communication Research, 13*, 257–277.

Carlson, M., Marcus-Newhall, A., & Miller, N. (1990). Effects of situational aggression cues: A quantitative review. *Journal of Personality and Social Psychology, 58*, 622–633.

Carnagey, N. L., & Anderson, C. A. (2005). The effects of reward and punishment in violent videogames on aggressive affect, cognition, and behavior. *Psychological Science, 16*, 882–889.

Carnagey, N. L., Anderson, C. A., & Bushman, B. J. (2007). The effect of video game violence on physiological desensitization to real-life violence. *Journal of Experimental Social Psychology, 43*, 489–496.

Carré, J. M., McCormick, C. M., & Hariri, A. R. (2011). The social neuroendocrinology of human aggression. *Psychoneuroendocrinology, 36*(7), 935–944.

Centers for Disease Control and Prevention. (2006). *Understanding youth violence* (Fact sheet). Retrieved from http://www.cdc.gov/ncipc/pub-res/ YVFactSheet.pdf

Centers for Disease Control and Prevention. (2010). *Youth violence.* Retrieved from http://www.cdc.gov/violenceprevention/pdf/yv-datasheet-a.pdf

Centers for Disease Control and Prevention. (2011). *Suicide prevention.* Retrieved from http://www.cdc.gov/violenceprevention/pub/youth_suicide.html

Children's Defense Fund. (2012). *Protect children, not guns 2012.* Retrieved from http://www.childrens defense.org/child-research-data-publications/data/protect-children-not-guns-2012.pdf

Christensen, P. N., & Wood, W. (2007). Effects of media violence on viewers' aggression in unconstrained social situations. In R. W. Preiss, B. M. Gayle, N. Burrell, M. Allen, & J. Bryant (Eds.), *Mass media effects research: Advances through meta-analysis* (pp. 145–168). Mahwah, NJ: Lawrence Erlbaum.

Cline, V. B., Croft, R. G., & Courrier, S. (1973). Desensitization of children to television violence. *Journal of Personality and Social Psychology, 35,* 450–458.

Cohen, J. (1988). *Statistical power analysis for the behavioral sciences* (2nd ed.). Hillsdale, NJ: Lawrence Erlbaum.

Cohen, J. (1999). Favorite characters of teenage viewers of Israeli serials. *Journal of Broadcasting and Electronic Media, 43,* 327–345.

Collins, W. A. (1973). Effect of temporal separation between motivation, aggression, and consequences: A developmental study. *Developmental Psychology, 8,* 215–221.

Collins, W. A. (1975). The developing child as viewer. *Journal of Communication, 25,* 35–44.

Collins-Standley, T., Gan, S., Yu, H. J., & Zillmann, D. (1996). Choice of romantic, violent, and scary fairy-tale books by preschool girls and boys. *Child Study Journal, 26,* 279–302.

Common Sense Media/Center for American Progress (2013, January 10). *National survey reveals parents' deep concern about protecting kids from violence.* Retrieved from http://www.commonsense media.org/about-us/news/press-releases/national-survey-reveals-parents-deep-concern-about -protecting-kids-from

Comstock, G., & Powers, J. (2012). Paths from television violence to aggression: Reinterpreting the evidence. In L. J. Shrum (Ed.), *The psychology of entertainment media*: Blurring the lines between entertainment and persuasion (2nd ed., pp. 305–328). New York, NY: Routledge.

Cooper, H., & Hedges, L. V. (Eds.). (1994). *The handbook of research synthesis.* New York, NY: Russell Sage.

Coyne, S. M., & Archer, J. (2004). Indirect aggression in the media: A content analysis of British television programs. *Aggressive Behavior, 30,* 254–271.

Coyne, S. M., Archer, J., & Eslea, M. (2006). "We're not friends anymore!" Unless . . . : The frequency and harmfulness of indirect, relational, and social aggression. *Aggressive Behavior, 32,* 294–307.

Coyne, S. M., Callister, M., Pruett, T., Nelson, D. A., Stockdale, L., & Wells, B. M. (2011). A mean read: Aggression in adolescent English literature. *Journal of Children and Media, 5,* 411–425.

Coyne, S. M., Nelson, D. A., Lawton, F., Haslam, S., Rooney, L., Titterington, L., . . . Ogunlaja, L. (2008). The effects of viewing physical and relational aggression in the media: Evidence for a cross-over effect. *Journal of Experimental Psychology, 44*(6), 1551–1554.

Crick, N. R., Ostrov, J. M., & Werner, N. E. (2006). A longitudinal study of relational aggression, physical aggression, and children's social-psychological attachment. *Journal of Abnormal Child Psychology, 34,* 127–138.

Davidson, L. E., Rosenberg, M. L., Mercy, J. A., Franklin, J., & Simmons, J. T. (1989). An epidemiologic study of risk factors in two teenage suicide clusters. *Journal of the American Medical Association, 262,* 2687–2692.

Davidson, O. G. (1993). *Under fire: The NRA and the battle for gun control.* New York, NY: Holt, Rinehart, & Winston.

Diener, E., & Woody, L. W. (1981). TV violence and viewer liking. *Communication Research, 8,* 281–306.

Dodge, K. A., & Pettit, G. S. (2003). A biopsychosocial model of the development of chronic conduct problems in adolescence. *Developmental Psychology, 39*(2), 349–371.

Dominick, J. R., & Greenberg, B. S. (1972). Attitudes toward violence: The interaction of television exposure, family attitudes, and social class. In G. A. Comstock & E. A. Rubinstein (Eds.), *Television and social behavior: Vol. 3. Television and adolescent aggressiveness* (pp. 314–335). Washington, DC: Government Printing Office.

Dorr, A. (1983). No shortcuts to judging reality. In J. Bryant & D. R. Anderson (Eds.), *Children's understanding of television: Research on attention and comprehension* (pp. 199–220). New York, NY: Academic Press.

Drabman, R. S., & Thomas, M. H. (1974). Does media violence increase children's toleration of real-life aggression? *Developmental Psychology, 10,* 418–421.

Dunlop, S. M., More, E., & Romer, D. (2011). Where do youth learn about suicides on the Internet, and what influence does this have on suicidal ideation? *Journal of Child Psychology and Psychiatry, 52*(10), 1073–1080.

Engelhardt, C. R., Bartholow, B. D., Kerr, G. T., & Bushman, B. J. (2011). This is your brain on violent video games: Neural desensitization to violence predicts increased aggression following violent video game exposure. *Journal of Experimental Social Psychology, 47,* 1033–1036.

Eron, L. D., Huesmann, L. R., Lefkowitz, M. M., & Walder, L. O. (1972). Does television violence cause aggression? *American Psychologist, 27,* 253–263.

Etzerdorfer, E., Voracek, M., & Sonneck, G. (2004). A dose-response relationship between imitational suicides and newspaper distribution. *Archives of Suicide Research: Official Journal of the International Academy for Suicide Research, 8*(2), 137–145.

Faiola, A. (2004, August 9). Youth violence has Japan struggling for answers: 11-year-old's killing of classmate puts spotlight on sudden acts of rage. *Washington Post,* p. A01. Retrieved from http://www.washingtonpost.com/wp-dyn/articles/A50678-2004Aug8.html

Farah, M. M., Simon, H. K., & Kellermann, A. L. (1999). Firearms in the home: Parental perceptions. *Pediatrics, 104,* 1059–1063.

Farr, J. (2012, July 21). When movie violence helps inspire real violence, isn't it time to tone it down? *Huff Post Entertainment.* Retrieved from http://www.huffingtonpost.com/john-farr/when-movie-violence-inspi_b_1692208.html

Fenigstein, A. (1979). Does aggression cause a preference for viewing media violence? *Journal of Personality and Social Psychology, 37,* 2307–2317.

Ferguson, C. J., & Kilburn, J. (2009). The public health risks of media violence: A meta-analytic review. *Journal of Pediatrics, 154*(5), 759–763.

Ferguson, C. J., & Kilburn, J. (2010). Much ado about nothing: The misestimation and overinterpretation of violent video game effects in Eastern and Western nations: Comment on Anderson et al. (2010). *Psychological Bulletin, 136*(2), 174–178.

Filotas, D. Y. (1993). *Adolescents' rape attitudes: Effectiveness of rape prevention in high school classrooms.* Unpublished master's thesis, University of California, Santa Barbara.

Fisch, S. M., & Truglio, R. T. (2001). *"G" is for growing: Thirty years of research on children and* Sesame Street. Mahwah, NJ: Lawrence Erlbaum.

Fisher, A. (2011). Processing of perceptual information is more robust than processing of conceptual information in preschool-age children: Evidence from costs of switching. *Cognition, 119,* 253–264.

Fowles, J. (1999). *The case for television violence.* Thousand Oaks, CA: Sage.

Freedman, J. L. (2002). *Media violence and its effect on aggression: Assessing the scientific evidence.* Toronto, Ontario, Canada: University of Toronto Press.

Friedrich, L. K., & Stein, A. H. (1973). Aggressive and prosocial television programs and the natural behavior of preschool children. *Monographs of the Society for Research in Child Development, 38*(4, Serial No. 151), 63.

Fu, K., & Yip, P. S. (2007). Long-term impact of celebrity suicide on suicidal ideation: Results from a population-based study. *Journal of Epidemiology and Community Health, 61*(6), 540–546.

Funk, J. B., Buchman, D. D., & Germann, J. N. (2000). Preference for violent electronic games, self-concept, and gender differences in young children. *American Journal of Orthopsychiatry, 70,* 233–241.

Geen, R. G. (1994). Television and aggression: Recent developments in research and theory. In D. Zillmann, J. Bryant, & A. C. Huston (Eds.), *Media, children, and the family: Social, scientific, psychodynamic, and clinical perspectives* (pp. 151–162). Hillsdale, NJ: Lawrence Erlbaum.

Gentile, D. A., Coyne, S., & Walsh, D. A. (2011). Media violence, physical aggression, and relational aggression in school age children: A short-term longitudinal study. *Aggressive Behavior, 37,* 193–206.

Gerbner, G., & Gross, L. (1976). Living with television: The violence profile. *Journal of Communication, 26,* 172–199.

Gerbner, G., Gross, L., Morgan, M., & Signorielli, N. (1980). The "mainstreaming" of America: Violence profile No. 11. *Journal of Communication, 30*(3), 10–29.

Gerbner, G., Gross, L., Morgan, M., & Signorielli, N. (1994). Growing up with television: The cultivation perspective. In J. Bryant & D. Zillmann (Eds.), *Media effects: Advances in theory and research* (pp. 17–41). Hillsdale, NJ: Lawrence Erlbaum.

Gerbner, G., Signorielli, N., Morgan, M., & Jackson-Beeck, M. (1979). The demonstration of power: Violence profile No. 10. *Journal of Communication, 29,* 177–196.

Gibbons, J., Anderson, D. R., Smith, R., Field, D. E., & Fischer, C. (1986). Young children's recall and reconstruction of audio and audiovisual narratives. *Child Development, 57,* 1014–1023.

Glascock, J. (2008). Direct and indirect aggression on prime-time network television. *Journal of Broadcasting and Electronic Media, 52,* 268–281.

Goldstein, J. (1999). The attraction of violent entertainment. *Media Psychology, 1,* 271–282.

Gould, M. S., Wallenstein, S., Kleinman, M. H., O'Carroll, P., & Mercy, J. (1990). Suicide cluster: An examination of age-specific effects. *American Journal of Public Health, 80,* 211–212.

Greenberg, B. S., & Gordon, T. F. (1972). Perceptions of violence in television programs: Critics and the public. In G. A. Comstock & E. A. Rubinstein (Eds.), *Television and social behavior: Vol. 1. Media content and control* (pp. 244–258). Washington, DC: Government Printing Office.

Groebel, J. (2001). Media violence in cross-cultural perspective: A global study on children's media behaviors and some educational implications. In D. G. Singer & J. L. Singer (Eds.), *Handbook of children and the media* (pp. 255–268). Thousand Oaks, CA: Sage.

Gross, K., & Aday, S. (2003). The scary world in your living room and neighborhood: Using local broadcast news, neighborhood crime rates, and personal experience to test agenda setting and cultivation. *Journal of Communication, 53,* 411–426.

Grossman, D. C., Reay, D. T., & Baker, S. A. (1999). Self-inflicted and unintentional firearm injuries among children and adolescents: The source of firearms. *Archives of Pediatrics and Adolescent Medicine, 153,* 875–878.

Gunter, B. (2008). Media violence: Is there a case for causality? *American Behavioral Scientist, 51*(8), 1061–1122.

Gunter, B., & Furnham, A. (1984). Perceptions of television violence: Effects of programme genre and type of violence on viewers' judgements of violent portrayals. *British Journal of Social Psychology, 23,* 155–164.

Haidt, J., McCauley, C., & Rozin P. (1994). Individual differences in sensitivity to disgust: A scale sampling seven domains of disgust elicitors. *Personality and Individual Differences, 16,* 701–713.

Hamilton, J. T. (1998). *Channeling violence: The economic market for violent television programming.* Princeton, NJ: Princeton University Press.

Hanratty, M. A., O'Neal, E., & Sulzer, J. L. (1972). The effect of frustration upon imitation of aggression. *Journal of Personality and Social Psychology, 21,* 30–34.

Harrison, K., & Cantor, J. (1999). Tales from the screen: Enduring fright reactions to scary media. *Media Psychology, 1*(2), 97–116.

Hawkins, R. P., & Pingree, S. (1980). Some processes in the cultivation effect. *Communication Research, 7,* 193–226.

Hawkins, R. P., & Pingree, S. (1981). Uniform messages and habitual viewing: Unnecessary assumptions in social reality effects. *Human Communication Research, 7,* 291–301.

Hayes, J. (2007, January 19). Films and TV up the ante on graphic torture scenes. *Pittsburgh Post-Gazette.* Retrieved from http://www.post-gazette.com/stories/ae/movies/films-and-tv-up-the-ante-on-graphic-torture-scenes-468338/

Hearold, S. (1986). A synthesis of 1045 effects of television on social behavior. In F. Comstock (Ed.), *Public communication and behavior* (Vol. 1, pp. 65–133). New York, NY: Academic Press.

Hicks, D. J. (1965). Imitation and retention of film-mediated aggressive peer and models. *Journal of Personality and Social Psychology, 2,* 97–100.

Hirsch, P. (1980). The "scary world" of the nonviewer and other anomalies: A reanalysis of Gerbner et al.'s findings of cultivation analysis (Part I). *Communication Research, 7,* 403–456.

Hoffner, C. (1996). Children's wishful identification and parasocial interaction with favorite television characters. *Journal of Broadcasting and Electronic Media, 40,* 389–402.

Hoffner, C., & Buchanan, M. (2005). Young adults' wishful identification with television characters: The role of perceived similarity and character attributes. *Media Psychology, 7*(4), 325–351.

Hoffner, C., & Cantor, J. (1985). Developmental differences in responses to a television character's appearance and behavior. *Developmental Psychology, 21,* 1065–1074.

Hogben, M. (1998). Factors moderating the effect of televised aggression on viewer behavior. *Communication Research, 25,* 220–247.

Huesmann, L. R. (1986). Psychological processes promoting the relation between exposure to media violence and aggressive behavior by the viewer. *Journal of Social Issues, 42,*125–139.

Huesmann, L. R. (1988). An information processing model for the development of aggression. *Aggressive Behavior, 14,* 13–24.

Huesmann, L. R. (1998). The role of social information processing and cognitive schemas in the acquisition and maintenance of habitual aggressive behavior. In R. G. Geen & E. Donnerstein (Eds.), *Human aggression: Theories, research, and implications for social policy* (pp. 1120–1134). San Diego, CA: Academic Press.

Huesmann, L. R. (2007). The impact of electronic media violence: Scientific theory and research. *Journal of Adolescent Health, 41*(6), S6–S13.

Huesmann, L. R. (2010). Nailing the coffin shut on doubts that violent video games stimulate aggression: Comment on Anderson et al. (2010). *Psychological Bulletin, 136*(2), 179–181.

Huesmann, L. R., Dubow, E. F., & Yang, G. (2013). Why it is hard to believe that media violence causes aggression. In K. E. Dill (Ed.), *The Oxford Handbook of Media Psychology* (pp. 159–171). New York, NY: Oxford University Press.

Huesmann, L. R., & Eron, L. D. (1986a). The development of aggression in American children as a consequence of television violence viewing. In L. R. Huesmann & L. D. Eron (Eds.), *Television and the aggressive child: A cross national comparison* (pp. 45–80). Hillsdale, NJ: Lawrence Erlbaum.

Huesmann, L. R., & Eron, L. D. (1986b). The development of aggression in children of different cultures: Psychological processes and exposure to violence. In L. R. Huesmann & L. D. Eron (Eds.), *Television and the aggressive child: A cross national comparison* (pp. 1–27). Hillsdale, NJ: Lawrence Erlbaum.

Huesmann, L. R., Eron, L. D., Klein, R., Brice, P., & Fischer, P. (1983). Mitigating the imitation of aggressive behaviors by changing children's attitudes about media violence. *Journal of Personality and Social Psychology, 44,* 899–910.

Huesmann, L. R., Eron, L. D., Lefkowitz, M. M., & Walder, L. O. (1984). Stability of aggression over time and generations. *Developmental Psychology, 20,* 1120–1134.

Huesmann, L. R., Lagerspetz, K., & Eron, L. D. (1984). Intervening variables in the TV violence-aggression relation: Evidence from two countries. *Developmental Psychology, 20,* 746–775.

Huesmann, L. R., & Miller, L. S. (1994). Long-term effects of repeated exposure to media violence in childhood. In L. R. Huesmann (Ed.), *Aggressive behavior: Current perspectives* (pp. 153–186). New York, NY: Plenum.

Huesmann, L. R., Moise-Titus, J., Podolski, C., & Eron, L. D. (2003). Longitudinal relations between children's exposure to TV violence and their aggressive and violent behavior in young adulthood: 1977–1992. *Developmental Psychology, 39,* 2001–2021.

Hughes, M. (1980). The fruits of cultivation analysis: A re-examination of television in fear of victimization, alienation, and approval of violence. *Public Opinion Quarterly, 44,* 287–302.

Hunnicutt, G., & Andrews, K. H. (2009). Tragic narratives in popular culture: Depictions of homicide in rap music. *Sociological Forum, 24*(3), 611–630.

Huston, A. C., Donnerstein, E., Fairchild, H. H., Feshbach, N. D., Katz, P. A., Murray, J. P., . . . Zuckerman, D. (1992). *Big world, small screen: The role of television in American society.* Lincoln: University of Nebraska Press.

Insel, B. J., & Gould, M. S. (2008). Impact of modeling on adolescent suicidal behavior. *Psychiatric Clinics of North America, 31*(2), 293–316.

Iwao, S., Pool, I., & Hagiwara, S. (1981). Japanese and U.S. media: Some cross-cultural insights into TV violence. *Journal of Communication, 31*(2), 29–36.

Jackman, G. A., Farah, M. M., Kellermann, A. L., & Simon, H. K. (2001). Seeing is believing: What do boys do when they find a real gun? *Pediatrics, 107*, 1247–1250.

Jamieson, P. E., & Romer, D. (2011). Trends in explicit portrayal of suicidal behavior in popular U.S. movies, 1950–2006. *Archives of Suicide Research, 15*(3), 277–289.

Jamieson, P. E., Romer, D., & Jamieson, K. H. (2006). Do films about mentally disturbed characters promote ineffective coping in vulnerable youth? *Journal of Adolescence, 29*, 749–760.

Jayson, S. (2012, August 8). Studies show cyberbullying concerns have been overstated. *USA Today.* Retrieved from http://www.usatoday.com/news/health/story/2012-08-01/research-cyberbullying -prevalent/56724200/1

Jeong, S., Cho, H., & Hwang, Y. (2012). Media literacy interventions: A meta-analytic review. *Journal of Communication, 62*(3), 454–472.

Jo, E., & Berkowitz, L. (1994). A priming effect analysis of media influences: An update. In J. Bryant & D. Zillmann (Eds.), *Media effects: Advances in theory and research* (pp. 43–60). Hillsdale, NJ: Lawrence Erlbaum.

Jobes, D. A., Berman, A. L., O'Carroll, P. W., Eastgard, S., & Knickmeyer, S. (1996). The Kurt Cobain suicide crisis: Perspectives from research, public health, and the news media. *Suicide and Life Threatening Behavior, 26*, 260–269.

Johnson, R. M., Coyne-Beasley, T., & Runyan, C. W. (2004). Firearm ownership and storage practices, US households, 1992–2002: A systematic review. *American Journal of Preventative Medicine, 27*(2), 173–182.

Johnson, R. M., Miller, M., Vriniotis, M., Azrael, D., & Hemenway, D. (2006). Are household firearms stored less safely in homes with adolescents? *Archives of Pediatrics and Adolescent Medicine, 160*, 788–792.

Johnston, D. D. (1995). Adolescents' motivations for viewing graphic horror. *Human Communication Research, 21*, 522–552.

Jones, G. (2002). *Killing monsters: Our children's need for fantasy, heroism, and make-believe violence.* New York, NY: Basic Books.

Jose, P. E., & Brewer, W. F. (1984). Development of story liking: Character identification, suspense, and outcome resolution. *Developmental Psychology, 20*, 911–924.

Josephson, W. L. (1987). Television violence and children's aggression: Testing the priming, social script, and disinhibition predictions. *Journal of Personality and Social Psychology, 53*, 882–890.

Kellermann, A. L., Rivara, F. P., Rushforth, N. B., Banton, J. G., Reay, D. T., Francisco, J. T., . . . Somes, G. (1993). Gun ownership as a risk factor for homicide in the home. *New England Journal of Medicine, 329*, 1084–1091.

Kellermann, A. L., Somes, G., Rivara, F. P., Lee, R. K., & Banton, J. G. (1998). Injuries and deaths due to firearms in the home. *Journal of Trauma, Injury Infection and Critical Care, 45*, 263–267.

Kendeou, P., Bohn-Gettler, C., White, M. J., & van den Broek, P. (2008). Children's inference generation across different media. *Journal of Research in Reading, 31*(3), 259–272.

Klimkiewicz, J. (2007, April 20). The making of an abhorrent icon. *Hartford Courant.* Retrieved from http://articles.courant.com/2007/apr/20

Kodaira, S. I. (1998). A review of research on media violence in Japan. In U. Carlsson & C. von Feilitzen (Eds.), *Children and media violence* (pp. 81–105). Goteborg, Sweden: UNESCO International Clearinghouse on Children and Violence on the Screen.

Koehler, R. (2012, July 25). *Good violence, bad violence.* Retrieved from http://commonwonders.com/ ourselves/good-violence-bad-violence/

Konijn, E. A., Nije Bijvank, M., & Bushman, B. J. (2007). I wish I were a warrior: The role of wishful identification in the effects of violent video games on aggression in adolescent boys. *Developmental Psychology, 43*, 1038–1044.

Kopel, D. B. (1993). Japanese gun control. *Asia Pacific Law Review, 2*(2), 26–52. Retrieved from http://www.2ndlawlib.com/journals/dkjgc.html

Krahe, B., & Moller, I. (2010). Longitudinal effects of media violence on aggression and empathy among German adolescents. *Journal of Applied Developmental Psychology, 31*, 401–409.

Krahe, B., Moller, I., Huesmann, L. R., Kirwil, L., Felber, J., & Berger, A. (2011). Desensitization to media violence: Links with habitual media violence exposure, aggressive cognitions, and aggressive behavior. *Journal of Personality and Social Psychology, 100*(4), 630–646.

Krcmar, M., & Cooke, M. C. (2001). Children's moral reasoning and perceptions of television violence. *Journal of Communication, 51*, 300–316.

Krcmar, M., Farrar, K., & McGloin, R. (2011). The effects of video game realism on attention, retention and aggressive outcomes. *Computers in Human Behavior, 27*(1), 432–439.

Krcmar, M., & Hight, A. (2007). The development of aggressive mental models in young children. *Media Psychology, 10*, 250–269.

Kuntsche, E., Pickett, W., Overpeck, M., Craig, W., Boyce, W., & deMatos, M. G. (2006). Television viewing and forms of bullying among adolescents from eight countries. *Journal of Adolescent Health, 39*, 908–915.

Lazarus, R. S., & Alfert, E. (1964). Short-circuiting of threat by experimentally altering cognitive appraisal. *Journal of Abnormal and Social Psychology, 69*, 195–205.

Lefkowitz, M. M., Eron, L. D., Walder, L. O., & Huesmann, L. R. (1972). Television violence and child aggression: A follow-up study. In G. A. Comstock & E. A. Rubinstein (Eds.), *Television and social behavior: Vol. 3. Television and adolescent aggressiveness* (pp. 33–135). Washington, DC: Government Printing Office.

Lichtblau, E. (2013, January 11). Makers of violent video games marshal support to fend off regulation. *New York Times*, retrieved from http://www.nytimes.com/2013/01/12/us/politics/makers-of-violent-video-games-marshal-support-to-fend-off-regulation.html

Liebert, R. M., & Sprafkin, J. (1988). *The early window: Effects of television on children and youth.* New York, NY: Pergamon.

Lies, E. (2001, June 8). *Random violence on the rise in Japan.* Retrieved from http://cbsnews.com/now/story/0%2c1597%2c295560-412%2c00.html

Linder, J., & Lyle, K. (2011). A content analysis of indirect, verbal, and physical aggression in television programs popular among school-aged girls. *American Journal of Media Psychology, 4*, 24–42.

Linz, D. G., Donnerstein, E., & Penrod, S. (1984). The effects of multiple exposures to filmed violence against women. *Journal of Communication, 34*, 130–147.

Linz, D. G., Donnerstein, E., & Penrod, S. (1988). Effects of long-term exposure to violent and sexually degrading depictions of women. *Journal of Personality and Social Psychology, 55*, 758–768.

Liss, M. B., Reinhardt, L. C., & Fredriksen, S. (1983). TV heroes: The impact of rhetoric and deeds. *Journal of Applied Developmental Psychology, 4*, 175–187.

Lovaas, O. I. (1961). Effect of exposure to symbolic aggression on aggressive behavior. *Child Development, 32*, 37–44.

Lowry, B. (1997, September 21). The times poll: TV on decline, but few back U.S. regulation. *Los Angeles Times*, p. A01.

Luxton, D. D., June, J. D., & Fairall, J. M. (2012). Social media and suicide: A public health perspective. *American Journal of Public Health, 102*(s2), s195–s200.

Mares, M. L. (2006). Repetition increases children's comprehension of television content—up to a point. *Communication Monographs, 73*(2), 216–241.

Mares, M. L., & Acosta, E. E. (2008). Be kind to three-legged dogs: Children's literal interpretations of TV's moral lessons. *Media Psychology, 11*(3), 377–399.

Martin, J. R., Sklar, D. P., & McFeeley, P. (1991). Accidental firearm fatalities among New Mexico children. *Annals of Emergency Medicine, 20*, 58–61.

Martins, N., & Wilson, B. J. (2012a). Mean on the screen: Social aggression in programs popular with children. *Journal of Communication, 62,* 991-1009.

Martins, N., & Wilson, B. J. (2012b). Social aggression on television and its relationship to children's aggression in the classroom. *Human Communication Research, 38,* 48–71.

McIntyre, J. J., & Teevan, J. J., Jr. (1972). Television violence and deviant behavior. In G. A. Comstock & E. A. Rubinstein (Eds.), *Television and social behavior: Vol. 3. Television and adolescent aggressiveness* (pp. 383–435). Washington, DC: Government Printing Office.

McLeod, J. M., Atkin, C. K., & Chaffee, S. H. (1972a). Adolescents, parents, and television use: Adolescent self-report measures from Maryland and Wisconsin samples. In G. A. Comstock & E. A. Rubinstein (Eds.), *Television and social behavior: Vol. 3. Television and adolescent aggressiveness* (pp. 173–238). Washington, DC: Government Printing Office.

McLeod, J. M., Atkin, C. K., & Chaffee, S. H. (1972b). Self-report and other-report measures from the Wisconsin sample. In G. A. Comstock & E. A. Rubinstein (Eds.), *Television and social behavior: Vol. 3. Television and adolescent aggressiveness* (pp. 239–313). Washington, DC: Government Printing Office.

Milavsky, J. R., Kessler, R., Stipp, H. H., & Rubens, W. S. (1982). *Television and aggression: A panel study.* New York, NY: Academic Press.

Miller, M., Lippmann, S. J., Azrael, D., & Hemenway, D. (2007). Household firearm ownership and rates of suicide across the 50 United States. *Journal of Trauma – Injury, Infection, and Critical Care, 62*(4), 1029–1034.

Molitor, F., & Hirsch, K. W. (1994). Children's toleration of real-life aggression after exposure to media violence: A replication of the Drabman and Thomas studies. *Child Study Journal, 24,* 191–207.

Moretti, M. M., Osbuth, C. L., Odgers, P., & Reebye, P. (2006). Exposure to maternal vs. paternal partner violence, PTSD, and aggression in adolescent girls and boys. *Aggressive Behavior, 4,* 385–395.

Morgan, M. (2009). Cultivation analysis and media effects. In R. Nabi & M. Oliver (Eds.), *Handbook of media effects* (pp. 69–82). Thousand Oaks, CA: Sage.

Morgan, M., Shanahan, J., & Signorielli, N. (2009). Growing up with television: Cultivation processes. In J. Bryant & M. Oliver (Eds.), *Media effects: Advances in theory and research* (3rd ed., pp. 34–49). Hillsdale, NJ: Erlbaum.

Mullen, B. (1989). *Advanced basic meta analysis.* Hillsdale, NJ: Lawrence Erlbaum.

Mullin, C. R., & Linz, D. (1995). Desensitization and resensitization to violence against women: Effects of exposure to sexually violent films on judgments of domestic violence victims. *Journal of Personality and Social Psychology, 69,* 449–459.

Murray, J. P. (2008). Media violence: The effects are both real and strong. *American Behavioral Scientist, 51*(8), 1212–1230.

Naisbitt, J., Naisbitt, N., & Philips, D. (1999). *High tech, high touch: Technology and our search for meaning.* New York, NY: Broadway Books.

Nansel, T. R., Overpeck, M., Pilla, R. S., Ruan, W. J., Simons-Morton, B., & Scheidt, P. (2001). Bullying behaviors among US youth: Prevalence and association with psychosocial adjustment. *Journal of the American Medical Association, 285,* 2094–2100.

New poll finds escalating violence in children's TV now a crisis for parents. (2005). Retrieved from http://www.fradical.com/New_poll_finds_violence.htm

Nishiyama, G. (2007, November 26). Japan tightens gun control after spate of shootings. *Reuters.* Retrieved from http://www.reuters.com/article/2007/11/26/idUST262994

Ogles, R. M., & Hoffner, C. (1987). Film violence and perceptions of crime: The cultivation effect. In M. L. McLaughlin (Ed.), *Communication yearbook* (Vol. 10, pp. 384–394). Newbury Park, CA: Sage.

Okoro, C. A., Nelson, D. E., Mercy, J. A., Balluz, L. S., Crosby, A. E., & Mokdad, A. H. (2005). Prevalence of household firearms and firearm-storage practices in the 50 states and the District of Columbia: Findings from the behavioral risk factor surveillance system, 2002. *Pediatrics, 116*(3), e370–e376.

Olatunji, B. O., Cisler, J. M., & Deacon, B. J. (2010). Efficacy of cognitive behavioral therapy for anxiety disorders: A review of meta-analytic findings. *Psychiatric Clinics of North America, 33*(3), 557–577.

Oliver, M. B. (2000). The respondent gender gap. In D. Zillmann & P. Vorderer (Eds.), *Media entertainment: The psychology of its appeal* (pp. 215–234). Mahwah, NJ: Lawrence Erlbaum.

Ostrov, J. M., Gentile, D. A., & Crick, N. R. (2006). Media exposure, aggression and prosocial behavior during early childhood: A longitudinal study. *Social Development, 15,* 612–627.

Ostrov, J. M., & Godleski, S. A. (2010). Toward an integrated gender-linked model of aggression subtypes in early and middle childhood. *Psychological Review, 117*(1), 233–242.

Otto, M. W., Henin, A., Hirshfeld-Becker, D. R., Pollack, M. H., Biederman, J., & Rosenbaum, J. F. (2007). Posttraumatic stress disorder symptoms following media exposure to tragic events: Impact of 9/11 on children at risk for anxiety disorders. *Journal of Anxiety Disorders, 21,* 888–902.

Paik, H. J., & Comstock, G. (1994). The effects of television violence on antisocial behavior: A meta-analysis. *Communication Research, 21,* 516–546.

Perse, E. M. (1990). Cultivation and involvement with local television news. In N. Signorielli & M. Morgan (Eds.), *Cultivation analysis: New directions in media effects research* (pp. 51–69). Newbury Park, CA: Sage.

Pfefferbaum, B., Seale, T. W., McDonald, N. B., Brandt, E. N., Jr., Rainwater, S. M., Maynard, B. T., . . . Miller, P. D. (2000). Posttraumatic stress two years after the Oklahoma City bombing in youths geographically distant from the explosion. *Psychiatry, 63,* 358–370.

Phillips, D. P., & Carstensen, L. L. (1986). Clustering of teenage suicides after television-news stories about suicide. *New England Journal of Medicine, 315*(11), 685–689.

Phillips, D. P., Carstensen, L. L., & Paight, D. J. (1989). Effects of mass media news stories on suicide, with new evidence on the role of story content. In C. R. Pfeffer (Ed.), *Suicide among youth: Perspectives on risk and prevention* (pp. 101–116). Washington, DC: American Psychiatric Press.

Pirkis, J., & Nordentoft, M. (2011). Media influences on suicide and attempted suicide. In R. C. O'Connor, S. Platt, & J. Gordon (Eds.), *International handbook of suicide prevention: Research, policy and practice*. Malden, MA: John Wiley.

Pool, B. (1991, November 3). Screen violence would stop if it didn't sell tickets, filmmakers say. *Los Angeles Times*, pp. B1, B6.

Potter, W. J. (1993). Cultivation theory and research: A conceptual critique. *Human Communication Research, 19,* 564–601.

Report of the Media Violence Commission. (2012). *Aggressive Behavior, 38*(5), 335–341.

Resnick, M. D., Bearman, P. S., Blum, R. W., Bauman, K. E., Harris, K. M., Jones, J., . . . Udry, J. R. (1997). Protecting adolescents from harm: Findings from the National Longitudinal Study on Adolescent Health. *Journal of the American Medical Association, 278,* 823–832.

Riddle, K. (2010). Always on my mind: Exploring how frequent, recent, and vivid television portrayals are used in the formation of social reality judgments. *Media Psychology, 13,* 155–179.

Riddle, K., Cantor, J., Byrne, S., & Moyer-Gusé, E. (2012). "People killing people on the news": Young children's descriptions of frightening television news content. *Communication Quarterly, 60*(2), 278–294.

Rigby, K. (2003). Consequences of bullying in schools. *Canadian Journal of Psychiatry, 48,* 583–590.

Robinson, J. P., & Bachman, J. G. (1972). Television viewing habits and aggression. In G. A. Comstock & E. A. Rubinstein (Eds.), *Television and social behavior: Vol. 3. Television and adolescent aggressiveness* (pp. 173–238). Washington, DC: Government Printing Office.

Romer, D., Jamieson, K. H., & Aday, S. (2003). Television news and the cultivation of fear of crime. *Journal of Communication, 53,* 88–104.

Romer, D., Jamieson, P. E., & Jamieson, K. H. (2006). Are news reports of suicide contagious? A stringent test in six U.S. cities. *Journal of Communication, 56,* 253–270.

Rosenberg, M. L., Mercy, J. A., & Houk, V. N. (1991). Guns and adolescent suicides. *Journal of the American Medical Association, 266,* 3030.

Roskos-Ewoldsen, D. R., Klinger, M. R., & Roskos-Ewoldsen, B. (2007). Media priming: A meta-analysis. In R. W. Preiss, B. M. Gayle, N. Burrell, M. Allen, & J. Bryant (Eds.), *Mass media effects research: Advances through meta-analysis* (pp. 53–80). New York, NY: Routledge.

Roskos-Ewoldsen, D. R., Roskos-Ewoldsen, B. B., & Carpentier, F. D. (2009). Media priming: An updated synthesis. In J. Bryant & M. B. Oliver (Eds.), *Media effects: Advances in theory and research* (pp. 74–93). New York, NY: Routledge.

Rothenberg, M. B. (1975). Effect of television violence on children and youth. *Journal of the American Medical Association, 234,* 1043–1046.

Sargent, J. D., Heatherton, T. F., Ahrens, M. B., Dalton, M. A., Tickle, J. J., & Beach, M. L. (2002). Adolescent exposure to extremely violent movies. *Journal of Adolescent Health, 31,* 449–454.

Savage, J., & Yancey, C. (2008). The effects of media violence exposure on criminal aggression: A meta-analysis. *Criminal Justice and Behavior, 35*(6), 772–791.

Savitsky, J. C., Rogers, R. W., Izard, C. E., & Liebert, R. M. (1971). Role of frustration and anger in the imitation of filmed aggression against a human victim. *Psychological Reports, 29,* 807–810.

Scharrer, E. (2005). Hypermasculinity, aggression, and television violence: An experiment. *Media Psychology, 7,* 353–376.

Schmitt, K. L., Anderson, D. R., & Collins, P. A. (1999). Form and content: Looking at visual features of television. *Developmental Psychology, 35,* 1156–1167.

Selah-Shayovits, R. (2006). Adolescent preferences for violence in television shows and music video clips. *International Journal of Adolescence and Youth, 13,* 99–112.

Servin, A., Bohlin, G., & Berlin, L. (1999). Sex differences in 1-, 3-, and 5-year-olds' toy-choice in a structured play-session. *Scandinavian Journal of Psychology, 40,* 43–48.

Shanahan, J., & Morgan, M. (1999). *Television and its viewers: Cultivation theory and research.* London, UK: Cambridge University Press.

Shrum, L. J. (2001). Processing strategy moderates the cultivation effect. *Human Communication Research, 27,* 94–120.

Shrum, L. J. (2009). Media consumption and perceptions of social reality: Effects and underlying processes. In J. Bryant & M. Oliver (Eds.), *Media effects: Advances in theory and research* (3rd ed., pp. 50–73). Hillsdale, NJ: Erlbaum.

Shrum, L. J., & Lee, J. (2012). Multiple processes underlying cultivation effects: How cultivation works depends on the types of beliefs being cultivated. In M. Morgan, J. Shanahan, & N. Signorielli (Eds.), *The cultivation differential: State of the art research in cultivation theory.* New York, NY: Peter Lang.

Signorielli, N. (1990). Television and health: Images and impact. In C. Atkin & L. Wallack (Eds.), *Mass communication and public health: Complexities and conflicts* (pp. 96–113). Newbury Park, CA: Sage.

Singer, J. L., & Singer, D. G. (1986). Family experiences and television viewing as predictors of children's imagination, restlessness, and aggression. *Journal of Social Issues, 42,* 107–124.

Singer, J. L., Singer, D. G., & Rapaczynski, W. (1984). Family patterns and television viewing as predictors of children's beliefs and aggression. *Journal of Communication, 34,* 73–89.

Sisask, M., & Varnik, A. (2012). Media roles in suicide prevention: A systematic review. *International Journal of Environmental Research and Public Health, 9,* 123–138.

Slater, M. D. (2003). Alienation, aggression, and sensation seeking as predictors of adolescent use of violent film, computer, and website content. *Journal of Communication, 53,* 105–121.

Smith, S. L., & Boyson, A. R. (2002). Violence in music videos: Examining the prevalence and context of physical aggression. *Journal of Communication, 52,* 61–83.

Smith, S. L., Boyson, A. R., Pieper, K. M., & Wilson, B. J. (2001, May). *Brandishing guns on American television: How often do such weapons appear and in what context?* Paper presented at the annual meeting of the International Communication Association, Washington, DC.

Smith, S. L., & Wilson, B. J. (2002). Children's comprehension of and fright reactions to television news. *Media Psychology, 4,* 1–26.

Smith, S. L., Wilson, B. J., Kunkel, D., Linz, D., Potter, W. J., Colvin, C., & Donnerstein, E. (1998). Violence in television programming overall: University of California, Santa Barbara study. In *National television violence study: Vol. 3* (pp. 5–220). Thousand Oaks, CA: Sage.

Snyder, H. N., & Sickmund, M. (2006). *Juvenile offenders and victims: 2006 national report.* Washington, DC: U.S. Department of Justice, Office of Juvenile Justice and Delinquency Prevention.

Speisman, J. C., Lazarus, R. S., Davison, L., & Mordkoff, A. M. (1964). Experimental analysis of a film used as a threatening stimulus. *Journal of Consulting Psychology, 28,* 23–33.

Spencer, T. (2001, January 25). Wrestling death case deliberated. *Los Angeles Times.* Retrieved from www.latimes.com/wires/20010125/tCB00V0225.html

Spieker, S. J., Campbell, S. B., Vandergrift, N., Pierce, K. M., Caufmann, E., Susman, E. J., & Roisman, G. I. (2012). Relational aggression in middle childhood: Predictors and adolescent outcomes. *Social Development, 21*(2), 354–375.

Stack, S. (2005). Suicide in the media: A quantitative review of studies based on nonfictional stories. *Suicide and Life-Threatening Behavior, 35,* 121–133.

Steuer, F. B., Applefield, J. M., & Smith, R. (1971). Televised aggression and interpersonal aggression of preschool children. *Journal of Experimental Child Psychology, 11,* 442–447.

Subra, B., Muller, D., Begue, L., Bushman, B. J., & Delmas, F. (2010). Automatic effects of alcohol and aggressive cues on aggressive thoughts and behaviors. *Personality and Social Psychology Bulletin, 36*(8), 1052–1057.

Swahn, M. H., Hammig, B. J., & Ikeda, R. M. (2002). Prevalence of youth access to alcohol or a gun in the home. *Injury Prevention, 8,* 227–230.

Tamborini, R., & Stiff, J. (1987). Predictors of horror film attendance and appeal: An analysis of the audience for frightening films. *Communication Research, 14,* 415–436.

Tatum, P. T., Canetto, S. S., & Slater, M. D. (2010). Suicide coverage in U.S. newspapers following the publication of the media guidelines. *Suicide and Life-Threatening Behavior, 40*(5), 524–534.

Thomas, M. H., & Drabman, R. S. (1975). Toleration of real life aggression as a function of exposure to televised violence and age of subject. *Merrill-Palmer Quarterly, 21,* 227–232.

Thomas, M. H., Horton, R. W., Lippincott, E. C., & Drabman, R. S. (1977). Desensitization to portrayals of real-life aggression as a function of exposure to television violence. *Journal of Personality and Social Psychology, 35,* 450–458.

Thomas, M. H., & Tell, P. M. (1974). Effects of viewing real versus fantasy violence upon interpersonal aggression. *Journal of Research in Personality, 8,* 153–160.

Thompson, K. T., & Yokota, F. (2004). Violence, sex, and profanity in films: Correlation of movie ratings with context. *Medscape General Medicine, 6*(3), 3–11.

Toppo, G. (2007). Experts ponder patterns in school shootings. *USA Today.* Retrieved from http://www.usatoday.com/news/education/2007-04-18-schoolshooters_N.htm

Trend, D. (2007). *The myth of media violence: A critical introduction.* Malden, MA: Blackwell.

Tulving, E., & Thomson, D. M. (1973). Encoding specificity and retrieval processes in episodic memory. *Psychological Review, 80,* 359–380.

TV parental guidelines. (n.d.). Washington, DC: The TV Parental Guidelines Monitoring Board. Retrieved from http://www.tvguidelines.org/guidelin.htm

United Nations Office of Drugs and Crime. (2012). *United Nations Office of Drugs and Crime homicide statistics* (Fact sheet). Retrieved from http://www.unodc.org/ documents/data-and-analysis/statistics/crime/Homicide_statistics2012.xls

Ursin, H., & Eriksen, H. R. (2001). Sensitization, subjective health complaints, and sustained arousal. *Annals of the New York Academy of Sciences, 933,* 119–129.

U.S. Department of Health and Human Services, Office of the Surgeon General. (2001). *Youth violence: A report of the surgeon general.* Retrieved from http://www.ncbi.nlm.nih.gov/books/NBK44294/

U.S. Department of Justice, Federal Bureau of Investigation. (2011). *Uniform Crime Report: Crime in the United States, 2010*. Retrieved from http://www.fbi.gov/about-us/cjis/ucr/crime-in-the-u.s/2010/crime-in-the-u.s.-2010/2010%20CIUS%20Summary.pdf

Valkenburg, P. M., & Buijzen, M. (2011). Fear responses to media entertainment. In S. L. Calvert & B. J. Wilson (Eds.), *The handbook of children, media and development* (pp. 334–352). Oxford, UK: Blackwell.

van den Broek, P., Lorch, E. P., & Thurlow, R. (1996). Children's and adults' memory for television stories: The role of causal factors, story-grammar categories, and hierarchical level. *Child Development, 67,* 3010–3028.

Vaughn, M. G., Perron, B. E., Abdon, A., Olate, R., Groom, R., & Wu, L. (2012). Correlates of handgun carrying among adolescents in the United States. *Journal of Interpersonal Violence, 27*(10), 2003–2021.

Walters, R. H., & Parke, R. D. (1964). Influence of response consequences to a social model on resistance to deviation. *Journal of Experimental Child Psychology, 1,* 269–280.

Weaver, A.J. (2011). A meta-analytical review of selective exposure to and the enjoyment of media violence. *Journal of Broadcast and Electronic Media, 55,* 232–250.

Weaver, A. J., Jensen J. D., Martins N., Hurley R., & Wilson, B. J. (2011). Liking violence and action: An examination of gender differences in children's processing of animated content. *Media Psychology, 14,* 49–70.

Weaver, A. J., & Kobach, M. J. (2012). The relationship between selective exposure and the enjoyment of television violence. *Aggressive Behavior, 38,* 175–184.

Weaver, A. J., & Wilson, B. J. (2009). The role of graphic and sanitized violence in the enjoyment of television dramas. *Human Communication Research, 35*(3), 442–463.

Webb, T., Jenkins, L., Browne, N., Afifi, A. A., & Kraus, J. (2007). Violent entertainment pitched to adolescents: An analysis of PG-13 films. *Pediatrics, 119*(6), e1219–e1229.

Wilson, B. J., Colvin, C. M., & Smith, S. L. (2002). Engaging in violence on American television: A comparison of child, teen, and adult perpetrators. *Journal of Communication, 52*(1), 36–60.

Wilson, B. J., Hoffner, C., & Cantor, J. (1987). Children's perceptions of the effectiveness of techniques to reduce fear from mass media. *Journal of Applied Developmental Psychology, 8,* 39–52.

Wilson, B. J., Kunkel, D., Linz, D., Potter, W. J., Donnerstein, E., Smith, S. L., . . . Gray, T. (1997). Violence in television programming overall: University of California, Santa Barbara study. In *National television violence study* (Vol. 1, pp. 3–268). Thousand Oaks, CA: Sage.

Wilson, B. J., Kunkel, D., Linz, D., Potter, W. J., Donnerstein, E., Smith, S. L., . . . Berry, M. (1998). Violence in television programming overall: University of California, Santa Barbara study. In *National television violence study* (Vol. 2, pp. 3–204). Thousand Oaks, CA: Sage.

Wilson, B. J., Linz, D., Donnerstein, E., & Stipp, H. (1992). The impact of social issue television programming on attitudes towards rape. *Human Communication Research, 19,* 179–208.

Wilson, B. J., Linz, D., Federman, J., Smith, S., Paul, B., Nathanson, A., . . . Lingsweiler, R. (1999). *The Choices and Consequences evaluation: A study of Court TV's anti-violence curriculum.* Santa Barbara: University of California, Santa Barbara, Center for Communication and Social Policy.

Wilson, B. J., Martins, N., & Marske, A. L. (2005). Children's and parents' fright reactions to kidnapping stories in the news. *Communication Monographs, 72,* 46–70.

Wilson, B. J., Smith, S. L., Potter, W. J., Kunkel, D., Linz, D., Colvin, C. M., & Donnerstein, E. (2002). Violence in children's television programming: Assessing the risks. *Journal of Communication, 52*(1), 5–35.

Wotring, C. E., & Greenberg, B. S. (1973). Experiments in televised violence and verbal aggression: Two exploratory studies. *Journal of Communication, 23,* 446–460.

Wright, J. C., Huston, A. C., Reitz, A. L., & Piemyat, S. (1994). Young children's perceptions of television reality: Determinants and developmental differences. *Developmental Psychology, 30,* 229–239.

Xie, G.-X., & Lee, M. (2008). Anticipated violence, arousal, and enjoyment of violent movies: Viewers' reactions to violent previews based on arousal-seeking tendency. *Journal of Social Psychology, 148*(3), 277–292.

Yancey, A. K., Siegel, J. M., & McDaniel, K. L. (2002). Role models, ethnic identity, and health-risk behaviors in urban adolescents. *Archives of Pediatrics and Adolescent Medicine, 156,* 55–61.

Ybarra, M. L., Diener-West, M., Markow, D., Leaf, P. J., Hamburger, M., & Boxer, P. (2008). Linkages between Internet and other media violence with seriously violent behavior by youth. *Pediatrics, 122*(5), 929–937.

Yokota, F., & Thompson, K. M. (2000). Violence in G-rated animated films. *Journal of the American Medical Association, 283,* 2716–2720.

Youth Risk Behavior Surveillance System. (2012). Youth risk behavior surveillance—United States, 2011. *Morbidity and Mortality Weekly Report, Surveillance Summaries, 61*(4).

Zillmann, D. (1971). Excitation transfer in communication-mediated aggressive behavior. *Journal of Experimental Social Psychology, 7,* 419–434.

Zillmann, D. (1991). Television viewing and physiological arousal. In J. Bryant & D. Zillmann (Eds.), *Responding to the screen: Reception and reaction processes* (pp. 103–133). Hillsdale, NJ: Lawrence Erlbaum.

Zillmann, D. (1998). The psychology of the appeal of portrayals of violence. In J. H. Goldstein (Ed.), *Why we watch: The attractions of violent entertainment* (pp. 179–211). New York, NY: Oxford University Press.

Zillmann, D., & Wakshlag, J. (1985). Fear of victimization and the appeal of crime drama. In D. Zillmann & J. Bryant (Eds.), *Selective exposure to communication* (pp. 141–156). Hillsdale, NJ: Lawrence Erlbaum.

Zuckerman, M. (1979). *Sensation-seeking: Beyond the optimal level of arousal.* Hillsdale, NJ: Lawrence Erlbaum.

Zuckerman, M., & Litle, P. (1986). Personality and curiosity about morbid and sexual events. *Personality and Individual Differences, 7,* 49–56.

CHAPTER 5

Sex, Sexuality, and the Media

Today's first base is kissing . . . plus fondling this and that. Second base is oral sex. Third base is going all the way. Home plate is learning each other's names.

—Tom Wolfe
Hooking Up (2001)

Pornography is now our most prominent sex educator.

—Youth services worker as quoted in
The Sydney Morning Herald (Ryan, 2012)

[My doctor's] only gone to one medical school, but if you go online, you can get advice from all over the world.

—Teenager as quoted in *TECHsex USA: Youth Sexuality and Reproductive Health in the Digital Age* (Boyar, Levine, & Zensius, 2011, p. 17)

Something's in the air, and I wouldn't call it love. Like never before, our kids are being bombarded by images of oversexed, underdressed celebrities who can't seem to step out of a car without displaying their well-waxed private parts to photographers.

—Lead article, *Newsweek*, February 12, 2007
(Deveny & Kelley, 2007, p. 40)

By baring a single breast in a slam-dunk publicity stunt of two seconds' duration, [Janet Jackson] also exposed just how many boobs we have in this country. We owe her thanks for a genuine public service.

—*New York Times* critic Frank Rich
(2004, p. 1)

One erect penis on a U.S. screen is more incendiary than a thousand guns.

—*Newsweek* critic David Ansen
(1999, p. 66)

In 1976, the NBC Standards and Practices Department (the network censors) refused to let writer Dan Wakefield use the word *responsible* when James, at 15, and his girlfriend were about to have sexual intercourse for the first time and wanted to discuss birth control (Wakefield, 1987). To date, the networks still reject most public service announcements (PSAs) and advertisements about contraception, fearing that they would offend some unknown population (Strasburger, 2012a). If an occasional ad for a birth control product does make it to the air, it is because of its noncontraceptive properties (e.g., Ortho Tri-Cyclen is usually advertised as a treatment for acne, not as a means of preventing pregnancy).

Sex (the commercial networks seem to be telling us) is good for selling everything from shampoo, office machinery, hotel rooms, and beer to prime-time series and made-for-TV movies, but a product that would prevent the tragedy of teenage pregnancy—condoms—must never darken America's television screens (Strasburger, 2012a). Other media have become increasingly sexually explicit as well, particularly in the past two decades, without much regard for discussing either contraception or sexually transmitted diseases (STDs). "Sexting" and "sextortion"— terms that were completely unknown a decade ago—now put teenagers at risk. Meanwhile, a certain "raunchiness" has crept into mainstream American media, with four-letter words showing up even on prime-time television (Rice, 2000) and celebrity role models such as Paris Hilton, the Kardashians, and Lindsay Lohan engaging in increasingly outrageous and provocative behavior (Deveny & Kelley, 2007). Only AIDS has begun to threaten the conspiracy of silence about the health consequences of sexual activity and to free up the flow of useful and factual information to teenagers, who need it most.

Why and how has this paradox occurred, and what effect does it have on teenage sexual activity? The amount of sexual suggestiveness in the media has increased dramatically in the past two decades (Kunkel, Eyal, Finnerty, Biely, & Donnerstein, 2005). Although the data are not quite as convincing as those for media violence (see Chapter 4), an increasing number of studies now show that media sex warrants considerable concern (Wright, 2011; Strasburger 2012a).

In the absence of widespread, effective sex education at home or in schools, television and other media have arguably become the leading source of sex education in the United States today (Ballam & Granello, 2011; J. D. Brown, 2008; Strasburger, 2012a). As one noted researcher observes, "Long before many parents begin to discuss sex with their children, answers to such questions as 'When is it OK to have sex?' and 'With whom does one have sexual relations?' are provided by messages delivered on television" (Kunkel, Cope, & Biely, 1999, p. 230) (see Figure 5.1). This is a rather sad commentary, considering that American media are arguably the most sexually suggestive and irresponsible in the world. Although other countries may show more nudity, only American media titillate their viewers with countless jokes and innuendoes about all aspects of human sexuality. Yet ironically, while advertisers are using sex to sell virtually everything from hotel rooms to shampoo to drugs for erectile dysfunction, the national networks remain reluctant to air advertisements for birth control products.

The body of research about how children and teenagers learn about sexuality from the media and whether it affects their behavior has increased dramatically in the past five years (Strasburger, Jordan, & Donnerstein, 2012; Wright, 2011; Wright, Malamuth, & Donnerstein, 2012). There are now 18 studies using longitudinal data (some use the same data sets) that potentially allow cause-and-effect conclusions to be drawn (Ashby, Arcari, & Edmonson, 2006; Bersamin, Bourdeau, Fisher, & Grube, 2010; Bersamin et al., 2008; Bleakley, Hennessy, Fishbein, & Jordan, 2008; J. D. Brown & L'Engle, 2009; J. D. Brown, L'Engle, et al., 2006; Chandra et al., 2008; Collins et al., 2004; Delgado, Austin, Rich, & Bickham, 2009; Gottfried, Vaala, Bleakley, Hennessy, & Jordan, 2011; Hennessy, Bleakley, Fishbein, & Jordan, 2009; L'Engle & Jackson, 2008; Martino et al., 2006; Martino, Collins, Kanouse, Elliott, & Berry, 2005; O'Hara, Gibbons, Gerrard, Li, & Sargent, 2012; Peter & Valkenburg, 2008; Wingood et al., 2003; Ybarra, Mitchell, Hamburger, Diener-West, & Leaf, 2011), and virtually all of them show a significant impact of sexual content in the media on adolescents' sexual behavior (Wright, 2011). In addition, dozens of older studies document how the media can shape children's and adolescents' beliefs and attitudes about sex and sexuality (J. D. Brown & Strasburger, 2007; Strasburger, 2012a; Strasburger & Council on Communications and Media, 2010; Wright et al., 2012). Nearly all of the studies deal with traditional media; only a few very recent studies have examined the impact of new technology on sexual attitudes and behavior.

Figure 5.1

SOURCE: Jeff Stahler, Newspaper Enterprise Association, Inc. Reprinted with permission.

Why Is This an Issue?

From a public health perspective, sexual content in the media and its impact on adolescent sexual behavior have become an increasingly important issue. Many teenagers actively seek out sexual content in the media (Bleakley, Hennessy, & Fishbein, 2011), and one large international study found that most teenagers are more comfortable finding information about birth control online than they are from their doctors (Bayer HealthCare Pharmaceuticals, 2011). Given the risks involved in early sexual intercourse—pregnancy and sexually transmitted infections (STIs) most notably—one might think that *any* factor that could affect early sexual activity and prevent harmful consequences would be closely scrutinized. Sadly, that is not the case: Research into sex and the media has lagged behind research on media violence, obesity, and substance use and remains extremely difficult to do because of lack of funding and difficulty obtaining research approval (Strasburger, 2009).

Although the teenage pregnancy rate in 2010 reached an all-time low, the lowest rate in seven decades—34.3 births per 1,000 women 15- to 19-years-old (Hamilton &Ventura, 2012)—the U.S. continues to have the highest teen pregnancy rate in the Western world and one of the highest rates in the entire world (Centers for Disease Control and Prevention [CDC], 2012a; Martinez, Copen, & Abma, 2011) (see Figure 5.2). The U.S. rate is 10 to 15 times higher than the rate in other developed countries (United Nations, 2011). By contrast, the teen birth rate in Canada was 14 births per 1,000 (about one-third the U.S. rate), the rate in Germany was 10, and the rate in Italy was 7 (less than one-quarter the U.S. rate) (United Nations, 2011). In 2009, more than 400,000 teens 15 to 19 years old gave birth, which was 4% of all women in that age group (CDC, 2011a). Most of these were unintended pregnancies (Kaiser Family Foundation, 2011), and the total cost of all unintended pregnancies in women of childbearing age is an estimated $11 billion a year (Monea & Thomas, 2011). In a unique analysis of data from 86,000 women who gave birth in 2006, researchers found that 40% of pregnancies in the U.S. are either unwanted or mistimed (Finer & Kost, 2011). Contrary to popular belief, young adults have more abortions than teenagers do: 57% of all women having abortions are 20 to 29 years old, and only 16% are teenagers (Pazol et al., 2011).

Similarly, rates of teenage sexual activity have leveled off from the early 1990s but remain problematic. Unfortunately, the Youth Risk Behavior Survey (YRBS)—a biennial survey of high school students nearly nationwide—does not give a complete picture of adolescent sexual activity. Only 7 questions on the national survey deal with sex, compared to 32 questions about drugs and 20 about diet and physical activity. Nevertheless, the survey's large numbers (it samples more than 16,000 students in 9th through 12th grade every two years in 47 different states) and widespread use make it the most widely quoted source of information. According to the CDC's 2011 Youth Risk Behavior Surveillance survey (CDC, 2012b) (see Table 5.1):

- In 2011, nearly half (47%) of all high school students reported (ever) having had sexual intercourse. This represents a decline from 54% in 1991.
- One-third had had sex in the previous three months. Six percent said that they had first had sex before age 13. Fifteen percent reported having had four or more sexual partners.
- Condom use at last intercourse had increased since 1991 but plateaued at 61%; birth control pill use had decreased to 20%.

Figure 5.2   U.S. teen births highest of all industrialized countries.

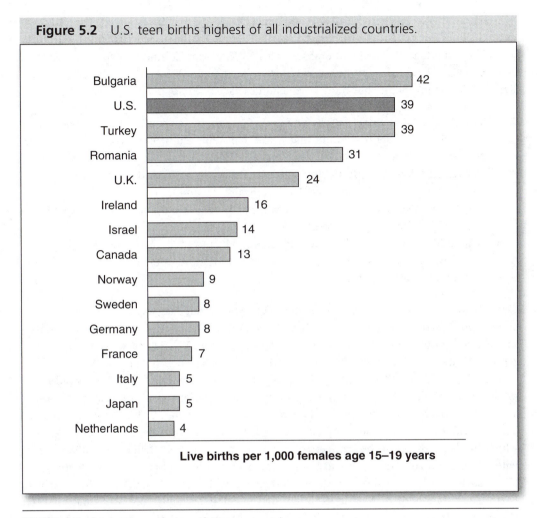

Live births per 1,000 females age 15–19 years

SOURCE: http://www.cdc.gov/features/dsteenpregnancy/

Table 5.1   Sexual Behavior Among U.S. High School Students, 2011 (in percentages) (*N* = 15,424)

Grade	Ever Had Sexual Intercourse		First Sex Before Age 13		Four or More Lifetime Sex Partners		Condom Use at Last Sex	
	Female	Male	Female	Male	Female	Male	Female	Male
9	28	38	4	13	5	12	56	67
10	43	45	4	9	9	15	57	70
11	52	55	3	7	15	19	56	67
12	64	63	2	6	22	26	49	65
Total	46	49	3	9	13	18	54	67

SOURCE: Data from Centers for Disease Control and Prevention (2012b).

Rates of other sexual activities, especially oral sex, are less well investigated. The YRBS, for example, does not ask about oral sex. A large 2002 study that included 10,000 teens 15 to 19 years old found that 55% had had oral sex (Mosher, Chandra, & Jones, 2005). Another older study of 580 students in 9th grade found that 20% had had oral sex (Halpern-Felsher, Cornell, Kropp, & Tschann, 2005). Four more recent studies have been done:

- The 2006–2008 National Survey of Family Growth, which surveyed more than 21,000 teens 15 to 19 years old, found that nearly half reported having had oral sex (Abma, Martinez, & Copen, 2010).
- In a recent study of nearly 14,000 high school students nationwide, two-thirds reported having engaged in oral sex by age 18 (Halpern & Haydon, 2012).
- Less than 10% of older teens report having had oral sex only, apart from sexual inter-course (Chandra, Mosher, Copen, & Sionean, 2011).
- A large 2012 study of nearly 6,500 teenagers and young adults, ages 15 to 24 years, found that about two-thirds had engaged in oral sex at some point in their lives (Copen, Chandra, & Martinez, 2012).

With sexual activity obviously comes the risk of STIs, and teenagers and young adults have a disproportionate percentage of these infections. Of the 18 million STIs diagnosed annually in the U.S., approximately half occur in young people ages 15 to 24 years, even though they represent only 25% of the sexually experienced population (CDC, 2011a).

One might think that with all of these risks to young people's health, there would be a public health impetus to educate teenagers in an intensive and comprehensive way about sex. In the U.S., however, that has not been the case (Quindlen, 2009; Strasburger, 2012a). The first eight years of the new millennium were devoted to abstinence-only sex education, which has been shown to be ineffective (Kirby & Laris, 2009; Santelli et al., 2006), except with 12-year-old African American boys in inner-city Philadelphia (Jemmott, Jemmott, & Fong, 2010). Comprehensive sex education does work (Cavazos-Rehg et al., 2012; Kirby & Laris, 2009; Lindberg & Maddow-Zimet, 2012), but it arguably has been marginalized (Lindberg, Santelli, & Singh, 2006). For example, although most of the nearly 2,800 fifteen-to nineteen-year-olds surveyed in the 2006–2008 National Survey of Family Growth reported having received sex education, 30% of females and 38% of males reported having received no information on methods of birth control (Martinez, Abma, & Copen, 2010). A comprehensive survey of sex ed programs in 45 states found that less than half taught 11 comprehensive sex ed topics (Kann, Brener, McManus, & Wechsler, 2012). Ironically, at the same time that abstinence-only sex education was being promulgated, the media were becoming much more sexually suggestive (Strasburger, 2012a). Yet time and again, compre-hensive sex education has been shown to be effective: A recent study of 4,691 males and females ages 15 to 26 found that the protective influence extended to when and whether to have sex, contraception, partner selection, and reproductive health outcomes (Lindberg & Maddow-Zimet, 2012). It may even lower teen pregnancy rates, although other factors (e.g., religiosity, abortion policies, sociodemographic characteristics) may play an important role as well (Cavazos-Rehg et al., 2012).

Research shows that parent-child communication can also be effective in preventing early sexual activity among teenagers (Martino, Elliott, Corona, Kanouse, & Schuster, 2008). When surveyed, parents overwhelmingly state that they want their children to receive most of their information about sex from them (Lagus, Bernat, Bearinger, Resnick, & Eisenberg, 2011). But while the majority of parents also favor sex education in schools (Bleakley, Hennessy, & Fishbein, 2006)—90% said it was very or somewhat important in one national survey of parents (National Public Radio, Kaiser Family Foundation, & Kennedy School of Government, 2004)—half of parents of 10- to 12-year-olds have not talked about peer pressure to have sex or how to prevent pregnancy and STIs (Kaiser Family Foundation & Children Now, 1999). Another, more recent study found that more than 40% of teens have had sexual intercourse before any discussion with their parents about birth control (Beckett et al., 2010).

In a separate Kaiser survey, two-thirds of parents said they were very concerned about their children being exposed to too much inappropriate content in the media, and 55% said that sex in the media was contributing a lot to teenagers' behavior (Rideout, 2007). As the senior vice president of the Kaiser Family Foundation noted, "The 'big talk' isn't what it used to be. It now needs to be 'supersized'" (Kaiser Family Foundation & Children Now, 1999). And the media have picked up the slack (J. D. Brown, 2008; Strasburger, 2012a).

Where's the Sex?

In any given society, at any given moment in history, people become sexual the same way they become anything else. Without much reflection, they pick up directions from their social environment. They acquire and assemble meanings, skills, and values from the people around them. Critical choices are often made by going along and drifting. People learn when they are quite young the few things they are expected to be, and continue slowly to accumulate a belief in who they are and ought to be throughout the rest of childhood, adolescence, and adulthood.

—John Gagnon, social science researcher
as quoted in *Television and Children* (E. Roberts, 1983, p. 9)

Traditional Media

Television

Prime Time TV. Despite the advent of new technology, prime-time television remains very popular with teenage viewers. What has changed is that TV shows may now be viewed on a laptop, iPad, or cell phone rather than the family's TV set in the den (Battaglio, 2010; Worden, 2011). About 60% of young people's TV viewing consists of live TV on a TV set, but the other 40% is now either time-shifted or watched online, on mobile devices, or DVDs (Rideout, Foehr, & Roberts, 2010). In fact, Nielsen reports that TV and video viewing are actually at an all-time high (Nielsen Company, 2011a). Although teenagers watch less TV than adults, they still average nearly 24 hours per week (Nielsen Company, 2011b). Much of what they see contains appreciable sexual content, especially on cable TV and sitcoms. Remarkably, one recent study found that exposure to sexual material is actually highest with TV, followed by music at 69%. In the most recent Growing Up With Media survey, Ybarra (2011) surveyed more than 1,500 youth 10 to 15 years old and found that the Internet was actually the least common way that young people are exposed to sexual material, at 16% to 25%.

As much as 15 years ago, one-fourth of all verbal interactions on prime-time series watched by teens contained sexual content (Ward, 1995). A subsequent analysis of the sexual messages in the top 15 shows according to Nielsen ratings of teenage viewers found that two-thirds contained sexual talk or behavior, with intercourse depicted in 7% of the programs (Cope-Farrar & Kunkel, 2002). The most comprehensive content analysis of television found that more than 75% of prime-time shows on the major networks contained sexual content, but only 14% of incidents included any mention of the risks or responsibilities of sexual activity or the need for contraception (Kunkel et al., 2005) (see Figure 5.3). This figure rose to 27% for shows depicting or implying intercourse, however (Kunkel et al., 2005). Following the 1997–1998 season, the amount of prime-time sexual content increased from 67% to 77%, but there was only a slight increase in the responsible content figure (Eyal, Kunkel, Biely, & Finnerty, 2007; Kunkel et al., 1999). Movies and sitcoms contain the most sexual content (Kunkel et al., 2005). In fact, talk about sex or sexual behavior can occur as often as 8 to 10 times per hour of prime-time television (Kunkel, Cope, & Colvin, 1996). Unfortunately, only one content analysis exists past 2005 (Parents Television Council, 2010). Not only are these studies expensive and time consuming, but there is very little government or private funding for doing them. In 2010, the Kaiser Family Foundation—which had previously funded the content analyses of sexual material on TV—closed its Media and Health section.

What has been demonstrated so far, however, is that American television largely consists of unrealistic, unhealthy, suggestive sexual behavior or sexual innuendoes (Strasburger & Council on Communications and Media, 2010; Strasburger, 2012a; Van Damme & Van Bauwel, 2013, in press; Wright et al., 2012). It is sex as a casual pastime, a romp in the hay, with little or no consequences. What is meant by content that is sexually suggestive? A few examples will suffice:

- In the late 1990s, a rash of teenage sitcoms appeared on prime-time TV. In *Popular*, a mother confronts her daughter and stepdaughter: "One of you is thinking of Doing It, if not already Doing It." In *That '70s Show*, one dim teenager asks, "Why cuddle when you can Do It?" This began the current generation of shows for teenagers that has been termed "Happy Days With Hormones" (K. Tucker, 1999).
- More recently, the MTV series *Skins* has featured teen girls having sex with each other and teen boys taking erectile dysfunction drugs; CW's *Gossip Girl* has featured a threesome; and Showtime's *Shameless* has depicted both teenage boys as being sexually active—one of them with a married man (Tomashoff, 2011).
- Children and teens watch a lot of prime-time and adult programming, which similarly has expanded the boundaries of what is permissible. *The Good Wife*—a Nielsen Top 20 show—featured oral sex in the 2010–2011 season. Showtime series like *Spartacus*, *Californication*, and *Secret Diary of a Call Girl* are filled with sex and nudity (Strauss, 2010).
- One survey actually found that in the 25 highest-rated prime-time series among teenagers, teen female characters were engaged in sexual behavior 47% of the time whereas adult women were engaged in sexual behavior only 29% of the time (Parents Television Council, 2010).
- Both network and cable TV have seemingly become obsessed with genitalia. MTV's series *The Hard Times of RJ Berger* began the trend in 2010 with a series about an unpopular high school sophomore who nevertheless has an exceptionally large penis. HBO's *Hung* followed with a series about a male prostitute with a similar endowment.

Figure 5.3 Content analyses of sexual content on TV, 1998–2005.

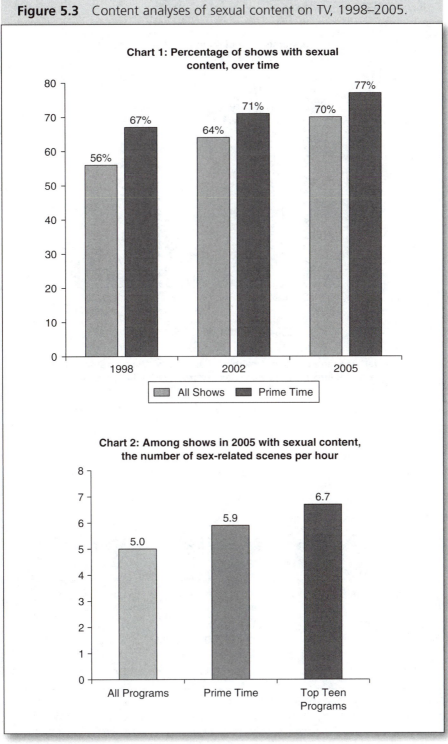

Chart 1: Percentage of shows with sexual content, over time

Chart 2: Among shows in 2005 with sexual content, the number of sex-related scenes per hour

(Continued)

Figure 5.3   (Continued)

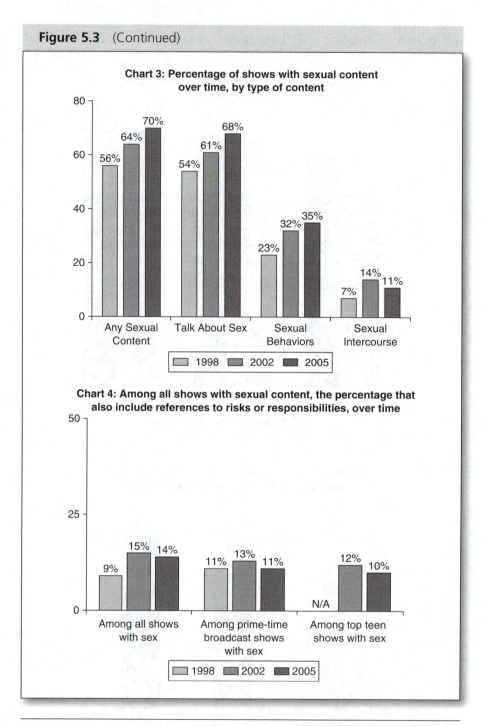

SOURCE: Kunkel, Eyal, Finnerty, Biely, and Donnerstein (2005). This information was reprinted with permission from the Henry J. Kaiser Family Foundation. The Kaiser Family Foundation, based in Menlo Park, California, is a nonprofit, private operating foundation focusing on the major health care issues facing the nation and is not associated with Kaiser Permanente or Kaiser Industries.

NOTE: Not only is there a lot of sexual content on mainstream American television, but most of it does not deal with the risks and responsibilities of sexual activity.

And most recently, CBS replaced Charlie Sheen on *Two and a Half Men* with Ashton Kutcher's character, who displays his large appendage on the very first show. Meanwhile, female anatomy has not been shortchanged: On CBS's hit show *2 Broke Girls*, waitress Max tries to cool off annoying customers with "That's the sound of my vagina drying up"; her roommate criticizes her sexual relationships with "What'd you do, shine a bat symbol on your vagina?"; and *Whitney*'s main character wonders aloud, "When did vaginas get so boring?" (Carter, 2011a; M. E. Williams, 2011).

- Discussion of contraception remains rare among shows popular with teens. *Glee* never mentions birth control, one of the *Gossip Girl* characters has had sex with at least eight different men without mention of contraception, and *90210* has had an HIV-positive storyline but rarely mentions safe sex. Only *The Secret Life of the American Teenager* has discussed both birth control pills and condoms and ends with a PSA directing teens to health care resources (Tuck, 2011).

A distinct minority of TV shows in the past 10 to 15 years have wrestled successfully with sexual responsibility. Beginning with *Beverly Hills, 90210*, the character of Donna (played by Tori Spelling) maintained her virginity throughout high school, when everyone else was losing theirs. At the end of the decade, during the 1999–2000 season of *Dawson's Creek*, the two major characters, Dawson and Joey, remained virgins as they approached their senior year in high school (Jacobs & Shaw, 1999). One research group notes that this is the one encouraging sign in all of the recent content analyses of mainstream television—that shows popular with teens may be more willing to address risks and responsibilities of early sex (Eyal et al., 2007). However, the actual percentage of such shows remains surprisingly low: 14% of any shows with sexual content in 2005, but 23% of shows where teens talk about or engage in sex (Kunkel et al., 2005) (see Figure 5.4). In one interesting twist, the hit show *Modern Family* featured an episode in which the Dunphy children walk in on their parents having sex. As it turned out, the kids were more comfortable talking about the situation than their parents were (Tomashoff, 2011).

Where the new shows on teen pregnancy fit in is anybody's guess. MTV's *Teen Mom* and *16 and Pregnant* have been criticized for glamorizing teen pregnancy, but many organizations are using discussion guides distributed by the National Campaign to Prevent Teen and Unplanned Pregnancy to make the shows positive learning experiences (Hoffman, 2011a). The risk, of course, is analogous to that of other health-related concerns and the media—do these shows make teen pregnancy seem like normative behavior? In one study, a survey of 162 teens associated with Boys & Girls Clubs of America found that 60% had watched *16 and Pregnant*, 82% felt that the show helped them understand the challenges of teen pregnancy and parenthood, and only 15% thought it glamorized teen pregnancy (Suellentrop, Brown, & Ortiz, 2010) (see Figure 5.5). However, this was a very small study, and the bias of social desirability cannot be excluded. A much better, controlled study of 126 teenagers found that viewers of the show had a lower perception of their own pregnancy risk and a greater perception that the benefits of teen pregnancy outweigh the risks (Aubrey, Behm-Morawitz, & Kim, 2013, in press).

MTV is unique among the major networks in having dealt substantively with the issue of teenage abortion, a subject which virtually every other major network—and Hollywood in general—has ignored in years gone by (Navarro, 2007). It aired "No Easy Decision" in 2010 following an episode of *16 and Pregnant* and included Dr. Drew Pinsky discussing abortion with several teenagers (Fisher, 2010). In the past few years, *The Secret Life of the American Teenager* and *Make It or Break It* on ABC Family have dealt with the topic head on.

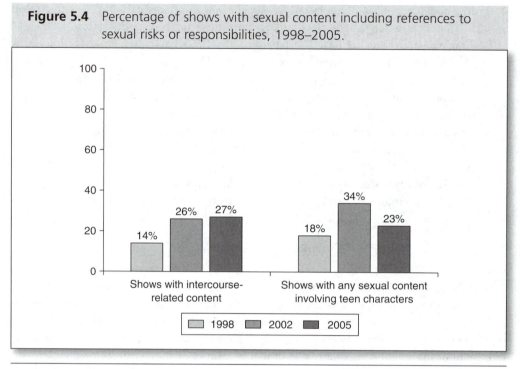

Figure 5.4 Percentage of shows with sexual content including references to sexual risks or responsibilities, 1998–2005.

SOURCES: Kunkel, Eyal, Finnerty, Biely, and Donnerstein (2005).

NOTE: Programs that depict teen characters in sexual situations are more likely to include references to the risks and responsibilities of sexual intercourse.

Soap Operas. As with prime-time programming, soap operas have become even more sexually oriented and sexually explicit since the 1980s. Even as far back as the 1990s, there was an average of 6.6 sexual incidents per hour, sex was visually depicted twice as often as it was talked about, and half of the sexual incidents involved sexual intercourse, usually between unmarried partners (Greenberg & Busselle, 1994; Heintz-Knowles, 1996). Surprisingly, rape was the second most frequently depicted sexual activity, with a total of 71 incidents, or 1.4 per hour. Contraception or "safe sex" was mentioned only 5 times out of 333 sexual incidents. The only mention of AIDS among the 50 episodes studied concerned the risk associated with intravenous drug use, not sex. And there was a single episode where a parent discussed sex with her teenage daughter. British soap operas popular with teenagers have also contained a lot of relational aggression (Coyne & Archer, 2004).

But more recently, soap opera producers have actually been more responsive to national health issues than prime-time producers (Huntemann & Morgan, 2012; Stern, Russell, & Russell, 2005). As one commentary notes, "the once-staple story, popular on shows such as *Beverly Hills 90210* and daytime soap operas, of a lone gay male dying of AIDS in a cold hospital room or the young teenager coming out to his homophobic parents has receded" (Huntemann & Morgan, 2012, p. 310). For example, *General Hospital* (ABC) was the first to feature a character with HIV who at one point discusses with her partner the need to use condoms if they have intercourse. On *The Young and the Restless* (CBS), a woman decides to get tested for HIV after learning about her husband's affairs. Internationally, soap operas have

Figure 5.5 Proportion of teens who agreed or strongly agreed with survey statements.

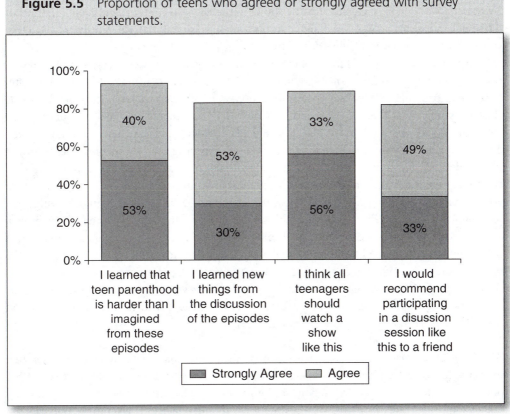

SOURCE: Suellentrop, Brown, and Ortiz (2010). Reprinted by permission of The National Campaign to Prevent Teen and Unplanned Pregnancy, Washington, DC.

been used prosocially to foster healthier attitudes about sex, sexuality, and particularly HIV (Howe, Owen-Smith, & Richardson, 2002; Rivadeneyra & Ward, 2005; Weinberg, 2006).

Reality TV. Despite its name, reality TV is anything but real—as any communications student, teacher, or parent well knows (Brenton & Cohen, 2003; Hill, 2005; Murray & Ouellette, 2004). Reality shows seem to appeal to people because they provide both instant gratification and a vicarious sense of self-importance (Kubey, Banerjee, & Donovan, 2012; Nabi, Stitt, Halford, & Finnerty, 2006). But in the early 2000s, reality TV suddenly became immensely popular. In the Nielsen ratings for June 26 to July 2, 2006, for example, 5 of the top 20 shows were reality shows ("Nielsen Ratings," 2006). Reality shows can vary from talent shows (*American Idol, So You Think You Can Dance, The X Factor, America's Got Talent*) to adventure dramas (*Survivor, Amazing Race, Fear Factor*) to the most common type—sexually oriented shows. These vary from all-out voyeurism (*Big Brother, The Real World, Are You Hot?, Jersey Shore*) (Bagdasarov et al., 2010) to dating shows such as *The Bachelorette* and MTV's *Next* and *Parental Control.* The BBC reality show *The Baby Borrowers*, which premiered in 2007, had parents "donating" their children to teenagers so that they could practice being parents. The announcer opens the show with the statement, "With the highest rate of teen pregnancy in Europe, Britain's teenagers are breeding like rabbits" ("Teens 'Borrow' Babies," 2007). NBC tried to duplicate the show in 2008, but it was quickly canceled. Reality shows in the UK also contain significant amounts of relational and verbal aggression (Coyne, Robinson, & Nelson, 2010). Currently, only one U.S. show, *Extreme Makeover: Home Edition*, fits into the prosocial category.

The overriding messages of many of these shows are that appearance, money, power, and success are paramount and that "you've got to be 'hot'" (Christenson & Ivancin, 2006; Ferris, Smith, Greenberg, & Smith, 2007). They may appeal to viewers' sense of self-importance and provide "instant gratification" (Kubey et al., 2012). Reality TV has become extremely popular—*Jersey Shore* has more than 4 million viewers ages 18 to 49—but its popularity may be waning (Carter, 2010b). To date, only three studies have explored the impact of such shows on adolescents and young adults. A study of 197 young adults found that males and viewers who perceived the shows to be real were more likely to share the attitudes displayed in reality dating shows (Ferris et al., 2007). In a study of 334 college students, Zurbriggen and Morgan (2006) found viewing such programming to be correlated with belief in a double standard, the belief that men are sex driven, and the belief that men and women are sexual adversaries. But the researchers also found that those students who tended to be less sexually experienced were actually watching more of the reality dating shows, which may signify the importance of such programs in sexual socialization. And a study of 1,141 preteen and teen girls found that viewing reality shows increased their expectations of respect in dating relationships but also increased their focus on appearance and desire for fame (Ferguson, Salmond, & Modi, 2013).

A Broader Definition of Sex. Sex on television is much more than sexual intercourse or sexual intimacy, however. Children and adolescents can also learn a great deal about sex roles: What does it mean to be a man or a woman? To be gay or straight, bisexual or transgender? What makes someone "cool"? Attractive? Successful? How should one behave around the opposite sex (Signorielli, 2001; Steele, 1999; Strasburger, 2012a)? How should society treat sexual minorities?

Mainstream television is not kind to adolescent girls, for example (Parents Television Council, 2010; Pipher, 1997; Zurbriggen et al., 2010; Smith, Choueiti, Prescott, & Pieper, 2013). The television world is disproportionately White and male, and female characters are much more likely to be attractive and provocatively dressed than male characters (Zurbriggen et al., 2010). Nearly one-fourth of sexual remarks made on prime-time comedies involve catcalling, leering, ogling, or staring at female characters; another 17% of the sexual remarks concern either body parts or nudity (Lampman et al., 2002). Similarly, a content analysis of workplace situation comedies found an average of 3.3 incidents per episode of joking about women's sexuality or their bodies, usually accompanied by laugh tracks (Montemurro, 2003). Numerous analyses from the 1990s reported similar findings (Zurbriggen et al., 2010). Whether the new female writers (e.g., *2 Broke Girls*, *Whitney*, *New Girl*) will be able to change this is or will simply add fuel to the fire is unknown.

On the positive side, the portrayal of sexual minorities *has* changed dramatically. When Rickie Vasquez came out to his family in a 1994 episode of *My So-Called Life*, he was bruised and battered, ostracized from his family and living in an abandoned warehouse, and afraid to even utter the word *gay*. Sixteen years later, it took only four episodes of *Glee* for Kurt Hummel to tell his father "I'm gay," to which his father shrugs and responds, "If that's who you are, there's nothing I can do about it. And I love you just as much" (Armstrong, 2011). This may be the prime example of Hollywood "leading" society rather than merely "mirroring" it (as producers typically assert). Increased portrayals may lead to a mainstreaming effect on the public's attitudes toward sexual minorities (Calzo & Ward, 2009; Huntemann & Morgan, 2012).

More than two dozen gay teens are currently or recently depicted on cable and network shows, ranging from *Glee* to *90210*, *Shameless*, *Skins*, and *Pretty Little Liars* (Armstrong, 2011). Unlike the "gay friends" episodes of the 1990s, gay characters on TV now can have children (e.g., *Six Feet Under*, *Modern Family*), be professionals (e.g., *Project Runway*), or even compete on game shows (*Survivor*, *Amazing Race*). Compared with even 5 to 10 years ago (Fouts & Inch, 2005), adolescents can now see happy, well-adjusted, professionally successful gay men on TV, although they are still predominantly White (Huntemann & Morgan, 2012) (see Figure 5.6). *Glee*, with its 14 million viewers, has broken ground not only with its mainstream gay character but with its second-season bullying storyline. Yet gay characters are still absent from most prime-time sitcoms and tween networks, like the Disney Channel and Nickelodeon.

Advertising

In 1967, the Noxzema girl asked male viewers to "take it off, take it all off." In 1980, Brooke Shields looked seductively at the camera and purred, "Nothing comes between me and my Calvins" (Calvin Klein jeans). Women's sexuality has always been exploited by Madison Avenue (see Figure 5.7). But now, seemingly, anything goes: Couples in adjoining bathtubs extol the virtues of erectile dysfunction drugs (L. Carroll, 2010), and Super Bowl ads for Budweiser show a three-armed man grabbing a women's rear and two men ogling women's crotches in a yoga

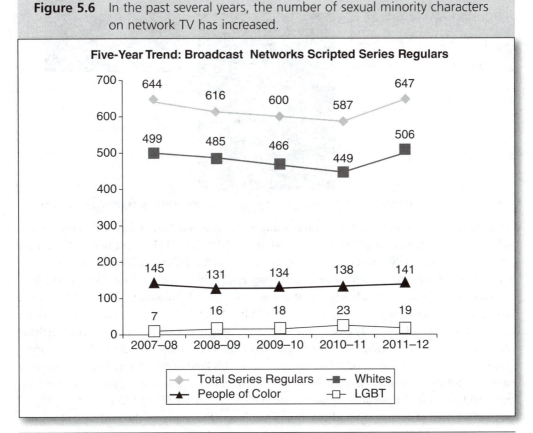

Figure 5.6 In the past several years, the number of sexual minority characters on network TV has increased.

SOURCE: Gay & Lesbian Alliance Against Defamation (2011). Reprinted with permission.

Figure 5.7   Exploiting women's sexuality in advertising.

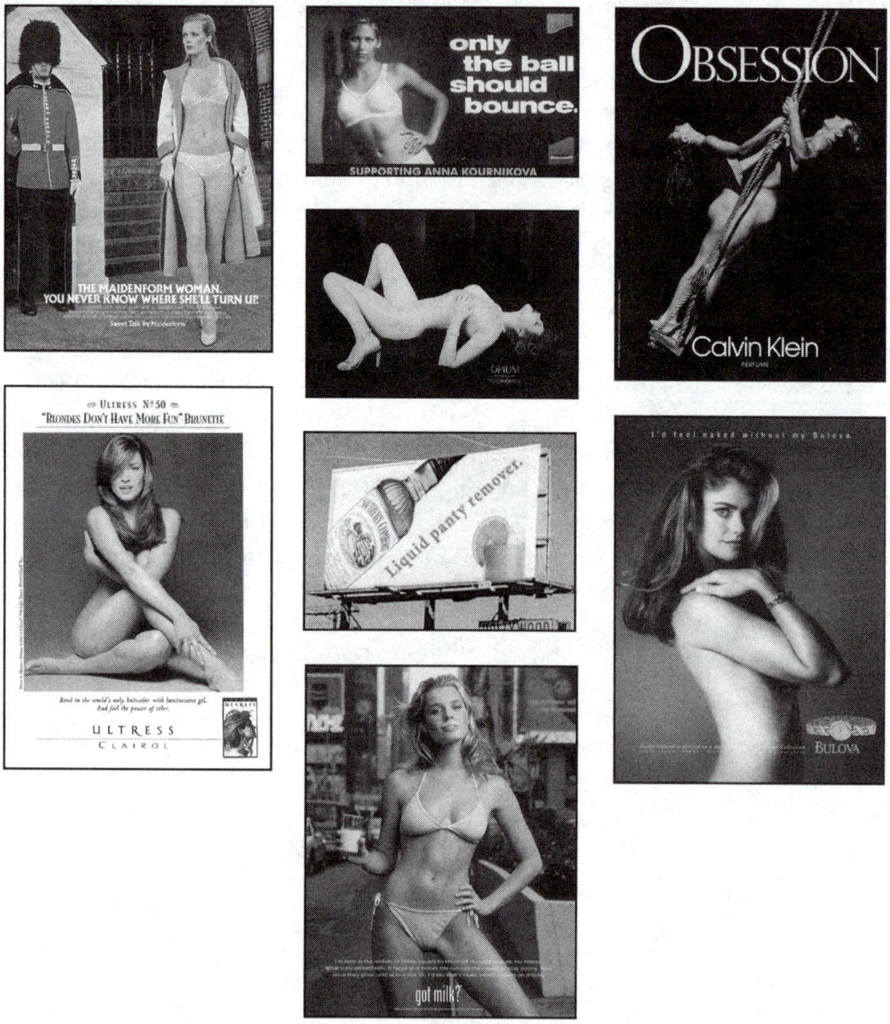

class (Bennett, 2003). In mainstream advertising, women are most often depicted as sex objects, as likely to be shown in suggestive clothing (30%), partially clothed (13%), or nude (6%) as they are to be fully clothed (Reichert & Carpenter, 2004; Stankiewicz & Rosselli, 2008). Young teenagers are likely to be exposed to a variety of sexual imagery (Pardun & Forde, 2006) (see Table 5.2).

Increasingly, little girls are being sexualized as well (Levin & Kilbourne, 2009). Abercrombie & Fitch advertises thongs bearing the words "Wink Wink" and "Eye Candy" and push-up bras for 7-year-olds (Lo, 2011) (see Figure 5.8). According to one observer, modern advertising often features women's bodies that have been "dismembered"—just the legs or breasts appear (Kilbourne, 1999) (see Figure 5.9). One by-product of this kind of advertising is that women are subtly taught that their main goal in life is to attract men or serve as sexual prizes. If a woman is successful, how can she possibly say no to a man when he wants sex (J. D. Brown & Steele, 1995)?

Critics have not been blind to these trends; but instead of changing the portrayal of women in advertising, Madison Avenue responded by increasingly exploiting men for their sex appeal, as if that would balance things out (Mager & Helgeson, 2011) (see Figure 5.10).

Table 5.2 Type and Proportion of Sexual Content in Commercials Aired During Programs Most Watched by Early Adolescents (N = 3,250 seventh and eighth graders surveyed and 1,783 commercials examined)

Type of Sexual Content	Percentage of Total Sexual Content in Commercial
Sexual emphasis on body	61.8
Light romantic touch	17.6
Dating and relationships	11.5
Sexual innuendo (verbal)	5.1
Marriage	3.6
Passionate kissing	2.3
Reference to sexual intercourse	1.2
Public health messages (sex related)	0.6
Crushes or flirting	0.3

SOURCE: Pardun and Forde (2006). Reprinted with permission.

Movies

As a medium, movies are probably less significant than television because they command much less time from the average teenager and are usually viewed with friends, thus allowing the process of socialization to temper whatever potential effects may exist. If teenagers see two movies per week on their computer or iPad, that still represents only 10% to 15% of the time they spend with all media in an average week. This does not imply that movies are not important, however (Steele, 2002). As many as 80% of all movies later shown on network or cable TV contain sexual content (Kunkel et al., 1999), and that content may be considerably more explicit in the initial theatrical release. There has also been a consistent trend toward the presentation of more sexually suggestive and sexually graphic

Figure 5.8 Originally Abercrombie & Fitch marketed these bras for 7-year-olds, but in response to a firestorm of criticism, they changed the age range to 8 to 10 years old. The bras were priced at $24.50, then placed on sale for $18.38.

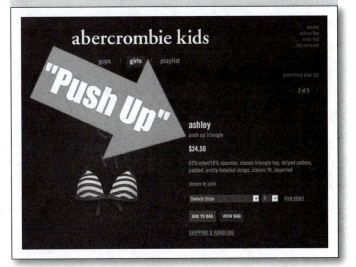

Figure 5.9 Advertisements featuring women's "dismembered" bodies.

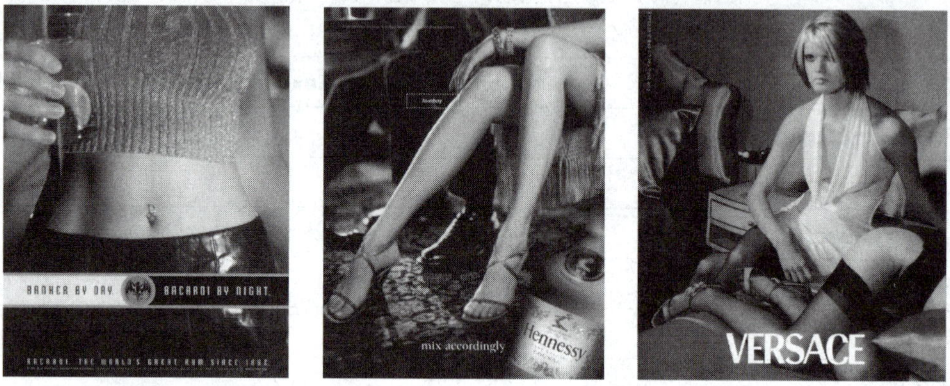

SOURCE: ©1995 Universal Press Syndicate.

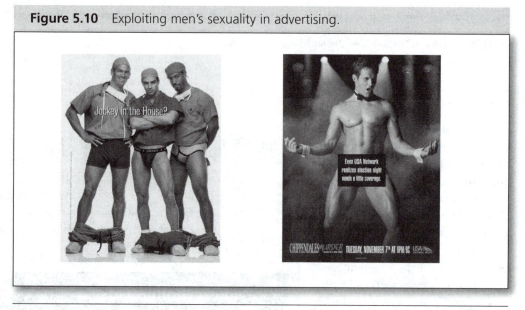

Figure 5.10 Exploiting men's sexuality in advertising.

SOURCE: ©2008 Jockey International, Inc. All rights reserved; CHIPPENDALES®, THE ULTIMATE GIRLS NIGHT OUT®, and the Cuffs & Collars Trade Dress are registered trademarks owned by Chippendales USA, LLC., and may not be used or reproduced without permission from Chippendales. ©2000–2007 Chippendales USA, LLC. All rights reserved.

material in movies (Escobar-Chaves et al., 2005; M. Rich, 2008). At the same time, there is a considerable gender imbalance in G-rated films: Female characters are outnumbered three to one by male characters (J. Kelly & Smith, 2006).

Even 25 years ago, more than half of 15- to 16-year-olds surveyed in three Michigan cities had seen the majority of the most popular R-rated movies (Greenberg, Siemicki, Dorfman, Heeter, & Stanley, 1993). Compared with prime-time television, these movies have a frequency of sexual acts or references that is seven times higher, with a much franker depiction than on television (Greenberg, Siemicki, et al., 1993). Moreover, for a society concerned with abstinence, it seems curious that there was an average of eight acts of sexual intercourse between unmarried partners per R-rated film analyzed, or nearly half of all the sexual activity depicted. The ratio of unmarried to married intercourse was 32 to 1 (Greenberg, Siemicki, et al., 1993). As Greenberg (1994) notes, "What television suggests, movies and videos do" (p. 180).

The years 1970 through 1989 represented the era of teenage "sexploitation" films. Hollywood pandered to the adolescent population, presumably because of demographic considerations: Teenagers constitute the largest moviegoing segment of the population. Such movies as *Porky's* (*I, II,* and *III*), *The Last American Virgin, Going All the Way, The First Time, Endless Love, Risky Business, Bachelor Party,* and *Fast Times at Ridgemont High* have dealt with teenage sex. Since the 1980s, virtually every R-rated teen movie has contained at least one nude scene, and some, such as *Fast Times at Ridgemont High* and *Porky's,* contain up to 15 instances of sexual intercourse (Greenberg, Siemicki, et al., 1993; Strasburger, 2012a).

With the baby boom generation and Generation Y having come of age and produced children and grandchildren of their own, Hollywood seems to continue to target the teen audience. Beginning in 1999, the *American Pie* series updated *Porky's* for the next generation. As one movie critic noted, the film was "pitched to the first generation of male and female adolescents who have been taught, from birth (mostly by MTV), to act as sex objects for each other" (Glieberman, 1999, p. 43). Several *American Pie* sequels exist. One review cited *American Pie 2* as being about "breasts, genitalia, 'potential' lesbianism, blue silicone sex toys, crude methods of seduction, 'the rule of three' (just watch the movie), a shower of 'champagne,' phone sex, tantric sex, and oh yeah . . . superglue" ("*American Pie 2,*" n.d.). Other researchers feel that the distorted view of romance in contemporary movies popular with teens is at least as problematic as the overt sex (Pardun, 2002). Or that frank portrayals of adolescent sexuality are incredibly rare (C. Kelly, 2005). Sex in many teen-oriented films seems to occur between people who have only recently met (Gunasekera, Chapman, & Campbell, 2005). As in mainstream TV, depictions of sex in popular movies tend to lack safe-sex messages—in one 2005 review of the top 200 movies of the past 20 years, one-third had sex scenes, yet there was only one suggestion of condom use (Gunasekera et al., 2005).

In the past decade, Hollywood films have kept all of their increasingly suggestive and explicit sex and sexuality, and predominantly male orientation, but added a few new twists:

- Sex is still seen most often from the (horny) teenage male's point of view. In *The Girl Next Door* (2004), a virginal male's dreams come true when a former porn star moves in next door. In *I Love You, Beth Cooper* (2009), a nerdy male valedictorian declares his love during graduation for the hottest girl in school, who then shows up on his doorstep that night. *Sex Drive* (2008) features a high school senior who steals his brother's car because a girl whom he's met online from a neighboring state has agreed to hook up with him. In *The Virginity Hit* (2010), Matt is the last virgin in his circle of friends, who celebrate having sex for the first time by smoking marijuana on a special bong shaped like a naked woman and discussing all the details.
- From 1950 to 2006, female characters continued to be underrepresented, yet their depiction in explicit sexual content has increased. A study of 855 of the top-grossing movies over 57 years found that male characters outnumber female characters two to one but female characters are twice as likely to be involved in sex (Bleakley, Jamieson, & Romer, 2012).

- A study of 122 family films (rated G, PG, and PG-13) between 2006 and 2009 found that one in four female characters was depicted in "sexy, tight, or alluring attire," compared with 4% of male characters (Smith & Choueti, 2010). A similar study found that women in G-rated films wear the same amount of skimpy clothing as women in R-rated films, and 25% of the women were shown with a waist so small that it left "little room for a womb or any other internal organs" (Baird, 2010).

- Judd Apatow has brought new raunch into romantic comedies, with films like *The 40 Year Old Virgin* (2005), *Knocked Up* (2007), and *Bridesmaids* (2011). Both *Knocked Up* and *Juno* (2010) assiduously avoided any serious discussion of teenage abortion (see Rickey, 2007). However, *Juno* was successful in portraying two intelligent, caring, and thoughtful parents of a teenage girl—a distinct rarity in teen films.

A few films have tackled sex and sexuality from a teenage girl's perspective, most notably *Thirteen* (2003), *Juno*, and *Easy A* (2010). But the abstinence-only movement in the early 2000s seems to have impacted *Easy A* in an unfavorable way—the movie concerns a 17-year-old girl named Olive who lies about losing her virginity, pretends to have sex with a gay male friend to "protect" his reputation, and turns into a "skank" to impress her peers (Doyle, 2010). So, through the decades, the pattern in Hollywood movies has been to titillate and try to entertain rather than to educate or try to be accurate. This seems unlikely to change in the near future, but what will continue to change are the boundaries of good taste and explicitness.

Print Media

Contemporary magazines reflect the same trend seen in television and movies—a shift away from naive or innocent romantic love in the 1950s and 1960s to increasingly clinical concerns about sexual functioning (Planned Parenthood Federation of America, 2006; Treise & Gotthoffer, 2001; Walsh-Childers, Gotthoffer, & Lepre, 2002). Content analyses of men's magazines show a decided concentration on female nudity and male sexual pleasure (Coy & Horvath, 2011). In magazines for females, one of the most dominant themes is being attractive and therefore sexually desirable to men. Looking "hot" and "sexy" and "costuming for seduction" are all important features of the articles, ads, and photographs (Duffy & Gotcher, 1996; Zurbriggen et al., 2010). Both men's and women's magazines tend to focus on "great sex" (Menard & Kleinplatz, 2008). In magazines like *Glamour* and *Cosmopolitan*, STDs are portrayed as being ubiquitous, dangerous, and disgusting; yet most of the stories promote casual sex for women's pleasure (Clarke, 2010).

The number of teen magazines has decreased dramatically—only *Seventeen* still exists in print—but a number of magazines have reemerged online, and most teens read magazines (Case, 2007; D. Roberts, Foehr, & Rideout, 2005; Zurbriggen et al., 2010). In one of the handful of studies of print media that adolescents read, Klein and his colleagues (1993) found that *Seventeen, Sports Illustrated, Teen, Time, Ebony, Young Miss, Jet, Newsweek,* and *Vogue* accounted for more than half of all reported reading. Adolescents who read sports or music magazines were more likely to report engaging in risky behaviors. Many teenagers, especially girls, have reported that they rely on magazines as an important source of information about sex, birth control, and health-related issues (Kaiser Family Foundation, 1999; Treise & Gotthoffer, 2001; Wray & Steele, 2002); unfortunately, no studies on the subject have been done in the last decade. A 2004 content analysis of British magazines for teens found that girls' magazines tended to focus on romance, emotions, and female responsibility for contraception, whereas boys' magazines were more visually suggestive and assumed that all males were heterosexual (Batchelor, Kitzinger, & Burtney, 2004).

A content analysis of teen magazines found that they devoted an average of two and a half pages per issue to sexual matters (Walsh-Childers, 1997), but the primary focus seems to be on when to lose one's virginity (Walsh-Childers et al., 2002). Indeed, a content analysis of 627 sex-related feature stories in three U.S. magazines (*Seventeen*, *CosmoGirl!*, and *Teen*) from 2006 to 2008 compared with three Dutch teen girl magazines found that teenage girls' sexual desires are more prominently depicted in the American magazines (Joshi, Peter, & Valkenburg, 2011). Nearly everything that teenage girls are encouraged to do in a variety of different media is geared toward gaining the attention of boys (Zurbriggen et al., 2010).

Kilbourne (1999) points out the trivialization of sex that occurs in women's magazines, both in their content and their advertising. For example, one print ad for jeans says, "You can learn more about anatomy after school" and shows a teenage guy groping a girl. According to Kilbourne, the print media give adolescent girls impossibly contradictory messages: Be innocent, but be sexually experienced too. Teen magazines such as *Jane* (which ended publication in 2007) were filled with articles such as "How Smart Girls Flirt," "Sex to Write Home About," "15 Ways Sex Makes You Prettier," and "Are You Good in Bed?" (Kilbourne, 1999).

In their defense, however, the print media are also far more likely to discuss contraception and advertise birth control products than broadcast media are (Walsh-Childers et al., 2002). As stated above, a 1997 study found that teen magazines devoted an average of two and a half pages per issue to sexual matters, and nearly half (42%) of sexual articles in teen magazines concerned health issues (Walsh-Childers, 1997). In fact, the October 2005 issue of *Seventeen* featured a very frank, two-page discussion of gynecological health, titled "Vagina 101," which won a Maggie Award from the Planned Parenthood Federation of America (2006). However, in general, much of the health coverage in teen magazines is in the form of advice columns, and the overarching focus seems to be on deciding when to lose one's virginity (Huston, Wartella, & Donnerstein, 1998). A number of studies have now included sexual content in magazines in their assessment of whether sexy media lead to earlier intercourse (Bleakley et al., 2008; J. D. Brown, 2008; J. D. Brown, L'Engle, et al., 2006; Hennessy et al., 2009; Ybarra, Mitchell, et al., 2011).

Music and Music Videos

What else can you rap about but money, sex, murder or pimping? There isn't a whole lot else going on in our world.

—Rapper Ja Rule
as quoted in *Newsweek* (October 9, 2000)

Music. When Little Richard sang, "Good golly, Miss Molly / Sure likes to bawl / When you're rockin' and rollin' / You can't hear your mama call!" in 1959, he was not singing about a young woman with hay fever and middle ear problems. Nor was the Rolling Stones' 1960s hit "Let's Spend the Night Together" about a vacationing family planning to stay at a Motel 6. Of course, suggestive song lyrics did not originate with 1950s rock 'n' roll. From Cole Porter ("The Lady Is a Tramp," "Let's Do It") to 1930s country music singer Jimmy Rodgers ("If you don't wanna smell my smoke / Don't monkey with my gun"), classic blues ("Hoochie Coochie Man"), and Mamie Smith ("You can't keep a good man down"), American songwriters and singers in the 20th century have seemed obsessed with seeing how much they can get away with (Arnett, 2002). Yet there is no question that lyrics have become more provocative and explicit in the past five decades (Hall, West, & Hill, 2011; Herd, 2009) (see Table 5.3).

Music has always been popular with teens, and to a great extent, teen music must be provocative, antiestablishment, and disliked by adults. Rock music (a term hereafter used for all popular teenage music, unless otherwise specified) is an important badge of identity for adolescents and an important activity for them (Council on Communications and Media, 2009; D. F. Roberts & Christenson, 2012). For 15- to 18-year-olds, only television remains a more important medium in terms of hours spent per day (4:22) than music (3:03) (Rideout et al., 2010). By age 18, the two are equal (see Figure 5.11). For many teenagers, music is the "soundtrack" of their lives, and they use it to regulate their moods, comfort themselves, and as a background for socializing, driving, and even doing homework (D. F. Roberts & Christenson, 2012). Of course, as Madison Avenue has nearly completely coopted mainstream rock music (see Table 5.4), adolescents have been pushed farther into rap, alternative rock, and heavy metal music.

Numerous content analyses document what every parent of a teenager already knows—contemporary rock music contains abundant sexual content. An analysis of the 279 most popular songs in 2005 showed that more than one-third contained sexual references, many of which were degrading to women. Rap music had the highest concentration of degrading sexual lyrics (64%), whereas country (45%) and rhythm and blues (28%) had sexual lyrics that were not degrading (Primack, Gold, Schwarz, & Dalton, 2008). A survey of *Billboard*'s top 100 year-end songs from the end of every decade from 1959 to 2009 found significant increases in sexy lyrics (Hall et al., 2011). The most recent study—an analysis of the lyrics from the 174 songs that made *Billboard*'s top 10 in 2009—found that 92% had a variety of

---

Table 5.3   Sample Rap Music Lyrics

"I Smoke, I Drank," Lil" Boosie, 2004
I smoke (Yea!), I drank (Yea!)
I'm supposed to stop but I can't (Uh-huh)
I'm a dog (Yea!), I love hoes (Yea!)
And I'm addicted to money, cars and clothes
Do it big then
I do it big nigga [3X].

"Livin' It Up," Ja Rule, 2001
Half the ho's hate me, half them love me
The ones that hate me
Only hate me 'cause they ain't fucked me
And they say I'm lucky
Do you think I've got time
To fuck all these ho's?

SOURCE: www.lyricsandsongs.com/song/503875.html and Ja Rule, *Pain Is Love*, Def Jam Recordings, New York.

Figure 5.11

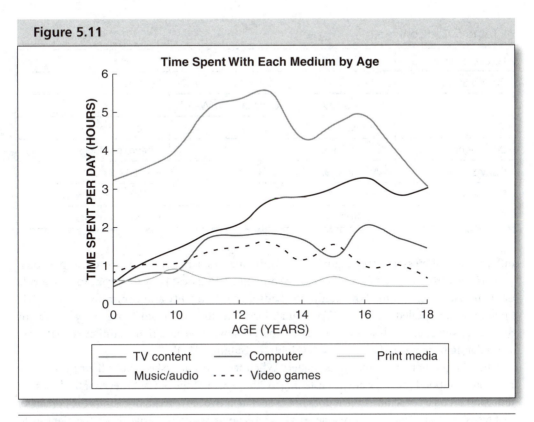

SOURCE: Rideout, Foehr, and Roberts (2010). Reprinted with permission.

Table 5.4   Madison Avenue and Mainstream Rock 'n' Roll

Artist/Group	Song	Used in Advertising for:
Aerosmith	"Dream On"	Buick
Bachman-Turner Overdrive	"Takin' Care of Business"	Office Depot
Beatles	"Help"	Ford Motor Company
	"Revolution"	Nike
	"Taxman"	H & R Block Tax Service
	"All You Need Is Love"	Luvs disposable diapers
Cat Stevens	"If You Want to Sing Out, Sing Out"	T-Mobile phones
Donovan	"Catch the Wind"	MassMutual insurance
Janis Joplin	"Mercedes Benz"	Mercedes Benz cars
Jefferson Airplane	"Volunteers"	Tommy Hilfiger
Kool and the Gang	"Jungle Boogie"	Capitol One credit cards

(Continued)

Table 5.4   (Continued)

Led Zeppelin	"Rock and Roll"	Cadillac
Rolling Stones	"Start Me Up"	Microsoft
	"You Can't Always Get What You Want"	Coke
	"Monkey Man"	Victoria's Secret
Bob Seger	"Like a Rock"	Chevrolet trucks
Carly Simon	"Anticipation"	Heinz ketchup
Donna Summer	"Hot Stuff"	DiGiorno Pizza
Styx	"Mr. Roboto"	Volkswagen cars

different sexual messages (see Figure 5.12), with an average of nearly 11 references per song. They ranged from explicit (e.g., "Let's have some fun / This beat is sick / I want to take a ride on your disco stick" from "Love Game" by Lady Gaga) to fidelity and commitment (e.g., "He knelt down and pulled out a ring / And said 'Marry Me, Juliette'" from "Love Story" by Taylor Swift). However, an analysis of opera arias and art songs revealed many similar sexual messages dating back more than 400 years (Hobbs & Gallup, 2011)!

The real question is, do the lyrics matter? When teenagers are asked about their music, they most often respond that they are just listening to "the beat," not the lyrics. Yet even if the lyrics are unimportant on a conscious level, it does not exonerate provocative lyrics or dismiss the possibility that teens can learn from them. As one set of experts notes, we do not drive down the highway to look at billboards, but we see them and often read them anyway (D. F. Roberts & Christenson, 2012). If there is "good news" about increasingly explicit lyrics in popular music, it is that teenagers do not typically even know the lyrics to their favorite songs or comprehend their intended meaning. For example, only 10% of 4th graders could correctly interpret a Madonna song, none could correctly interpret a Springsteen song, and nearly half of the college students studied thought that "Born in the USA" was a song of patriotism, not alienation (Greenfield et al., 1987). Of course, interpreting song lyrics can be problematic as well; considerable differences may exist, depending on race, ethnicity, age, experience, and personal values (D. F. Roberts & Christenson, 2012).

Behaviorally, music seems to have some impact but much less than other, visual media. In one interesting experiment, university students were exposed either to four "sexually charged" songs or four nonsexual songs and then asked to rate personal ads in an online dating service. Those exposed to the sexually provocative songs tended to place a much heavier emphasis on sex appeal (Carpentier, Knobloch-Westerwick, & Blumhoff, 2007). A meta-analysis of 23 mostly experimental studies also found support for the notion that music could have a significant impact on various beliefs and actions (Timmerman et al., 2008). In addition, a number of correlational studies have found that misogynistic lyrics increase negative attitudes toward women (Fischer & Greitemeyer, 2006; Hall et al., 2011; Ter Bogt, Engels, Bogers, & Kloosterman, 2010); but as with all correlational studies, it is entirely possible that males with more negative attitudes toward women seek out more misogynistic music. One study of 711 ninth graders also correlated exposure to sexually degrading lyrics (students averaged 14.7 hours per week with such songs) to a two times greater risk of sexual intercourse by 9th grade (Primack, Douglas, Fine, & Dalton, 2009).

Figure 5.12   Distribution of reproductive themes for 2009 songs as a function of song type.

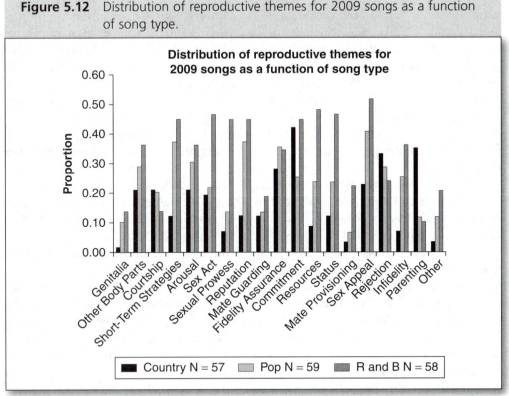

SOURCE: From Hobbs and Gallup (2011). Reprinted with permission.

Finally, a number of longitudinal studies have now incorporated music into their assessment of whether overall media consumption by teenagers leads to earlier sexual activity. In one that dealt exclusively with music—a national telephone survey of nearly 1,500 teenagers, ages 12 to 17, with a one- to three-year follow-up—teens who listened to music with sexually degrading lyrics were more likely to begin having sexual intercourse early or advance in their noncoital sexual activities than teens who listened to other music (Martino et al., 2006). This was true even after controlling for 18 other determinants of early intercourse. Degrading sexual lyrics are more likely to focus on casual sex, "boys being boys," and women's primary usefulness as objects for sexual pleasure (Martino et al., 2006). This study's findings are consistent with the theory that teens learn important cues about sexual behavior ("scripts") from media (Strasburger, 2012a; Ward & Friedman, 2006).

Music Videos. As Tennyson once wrote, "things seen are mightier than things heard." Although music lyrics may be ambiguous or difficult even to hear or understand, there is no mistaking a scene of graphic violence, drug use, or a couple cavorting in bed together (Ashby & Rich, 2005). When a particular song is heard, listeners tend to flash back to the associated music video (Greenfield & Beagles-Roos, 1988). Therefore, music videos would seem to have a greater potential to affect attitudes and behavior than music alone, just as television is behaviorally more potent than radio.

Music Television (MTV) turned 30 in 2011. In the beginning, MTV aired performance videos (the band playing), concept videos (telling a story), and advertising. Although the performance videos could often be outlandish (e.g., David Lee Roth's attire or his masturbating on stage with a huge inflatable phallus in the video "Yankee Rose"), there is no evidence that such videos had a demonstrable behavioral impact (Council on Communications and Media, 2009). They were roughly the equivalent of Elvis Presley gyrating his hips back in the 1950s. But concept videos do have effects: Numerous studies have shown that music videos frequently contain abundant sexual content (Ashby & Rich, 2005; Turner, 2011), and some have documented the effect of rap videos, particularly on male attitudes—objectification of women and turning them into sex objects, increased attitudes of sexual permissiveness, and even increased acceptance of date rape (Conrad, Dixon, & Zhang, 2009; Kaestle, Halpern, & Brown, 2007; Kistler & Lee, 2010; Ward, Hansbrough, & Walker, 2005; Zhang, Miller, & Harrison, 2008). In the only longitudinal study to date, 522 Black female adolescents with a median exposure to rap videos of 14 hours per week had engaged in a variety of risky sexual behaviors one year later, independent of other known factors (Wingood et al., 2003).

But as discussed above, MTV has morphed into more of a mainstream TV channel, having pioneered reality programs like *The Real World* and *MTV's Fear* (Martin, 2010). Currently, *Jersey Shore* is a major reality hit, and MTV also airs *Teen Mom 2*, *True Life*, and *Is She Really Going Out With Him?*. TRL (*Total Request Live*) last aired in 2008. MTV began in 1981 as a network devoted to airing music videos 24 hours a day, but music videos are now confined to 3 to 9 a.m., weekdays only (VH1 devotes only slightly more time to videos). That does not mean that music videos as a medium are dead, however. Lady Gaga and YouTube have resurrected the form. In 2010, "Bad Romance" had been viewed more than 244 million times, with Justin Bieber's "Baby" lagging just behind and Miley Cyrus's "Party in the U.S.A." having received 138 million views (Setoodeh, 2010). (As of this writing, "Bad Romance" has been viewed almost 500 million times.) Every time YouTube broadcasts a video, it is accompanied by a brief ad. For every 1,000 ads seen, YouTube's partner, Vevo, earns at least $25 (Setoodeh, 2010). Music videos are now being shared via Facebook, cell phones, and tweets.

New Technology

Many people feel that new technology (the Internet, social networking sites, cell phones and iPads, and Twitter) have revolutionized the way media are used. While new technology offers an interactivity not found in traditional media, it is also true that it has merely changed the platform that TV, movies, and videos are viewed on. For example, a 2009 Kaiser survey of two thousand 8- to 18-year-olds found that they spent an average of seven hours a day with a variety of different media, but TV remained predominant (Powers & Comstock, 2012; Rideout et al., 2010). TV viewing is actually at an all-time high, with Nielsen reporting that time spent watching TV and videos online rose 45% from 2010 to 2011 (Nielsen Company, 2011a). Although teenagers watch slightly less TV than children ages 2 to 11, total TV time still amounts to more than three hours per day (22:24 hours per week vs. 24:52 hours per week) (Nielsen Company, 2012).

New technology has allowed greater access to media 24/7, anytime, anywhere, as well as introduced new potential problems into the mix (e.g., displays of risky behavior on social networking sites, sexting, and Internet pornography) (Moreno & Whitehill, 2012). Although there is very little research other than content analyses, it is entirely possible that new media may be even more "potent" than traditional media when it comes to sex and sexuality (Collins, Martino, & Shaw, 2011). The Internet may be particularly appealing as a source of sex information for teenagers because it is readily available, anonymous, quick, and nonjudgmental. However, it is not always accurate: A review of 177 sexual health websites found below-average quality, with those sites that had the most complex or controversial topics containing the most inaccuracies (Buhi et al., 2010). An experiment with 210 first-year college students found that even heavy Internet users had difficulty finding accurate information about birth control (Mann, 2012).

Nevertheless, in the 2011 TECHsex USA survey of fifteen hundred 13- to 24-year-olds, the Internet was the leading source of information about a variety of sexual topics; and the media clearly outdistanced medical personnel, parents, and schools (Boyar, Levine, & Zensius, 2011) (see Figure 5.13). The bottom line here seems to be that the media—and particularly the Internet—may be replacing traditional sex education classes and parents as the primary source of sex education for young people. Another 2011 survey of two hundred 14- to 17-year-olds in Canada revealed that 40% rated the Internet more useful than parents for information about sex, and nearly one-quarter ranked it ahead of their high school sex ed classes (Tobin, 2011).

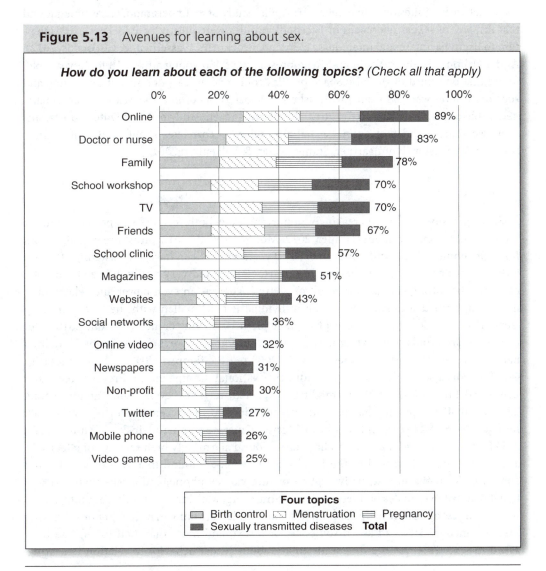

Figure 5.13   Avenues for learning about sex.

SOURCE: Boyar, Levine, and Zensius (2011).

Social Networking

A study of MySpace profiles found that nearly one-quarter of them referenced sexual behaviors (Moreno, Parks, Zimmerman, Brito, & Christakis, 2009). Adolescents who display explicit sexual references are also more likely to have online friends who do the same (Moreno, Brockman, Rogers, & Christakis, 2010). A smaller study examined 100 profiles posted by 16- to 18-year-olds and found that nearly half contained explicit or graphic language, and 16% contained references to sexual activity (A. L. Williams & Merten, 2008). A study of 752 publicly viewable profiles of teens 14 to 18 years old on a teen dating website found that 16% contained sexual content (Pujazon-Zazik, Manasse, & Orrell-Valente, 2012). Clearly, females who display sexual references on their social networking profiles may be influencing potential partners' sexual expectations and dating intentions (Moreno, Swanson, Royer, & Roberts, 2011). To date, only three studies have examined the impact of sexual displays on social networking sites on actual behavior: A pilot study of 85 undergraduate freshmen found that displays of sexual references in Facebook profiles were positively associated with intention to begin having sexual intercourse (Moreno, Brockman, Wasserheit, & Christakis, 2012). And a National Study of Youth and Religion survey of 560 young adults, 18 to 23 years old, found that one-third of their MySpace profiles contained at least one sexual disclosure, and such disclosures were associated with risky sexual behaviors offline, like sex with casual partners (Bobkowski, Brown, & Neffa, 2012). Similarly, a recent study of 1,762 Dutch adolescents over two years found that online sexual risk behavior correlates significantly with offline sexual risk behavior (Baumgartner, Sumter, Peter, & Valkenburg, 2012).

Sexting

Sexting has become an increasingly important issue, both for parents and teens and for schools and law enforcement (Draper, 2012; Moreno & Kolb, 2012; Strasburger et al., 2012). It is a phenomenon that did not even exist 10 years ago but can have a devastating effect on individuals, as evidenced by the rare but heartbreaking and very well publicized examples of teens committing suicide as a result of sexting. There is an even newer and related phenomenon, termed *sextortion*, where an individual is blackmailed with the threat of being "sexted" because of the existence of explicit pictures of him or her (Wilson, 2010). But recent research finds that sexting may not be as common as previously thought. Initially, a national survey of nearly 1,300 teenagers in 2008 put the figure at 20%—a figure that triggered major alarm and national headlines (National Campaign to Prevent Teen and Unwanted Pregnancy, 2008). As might be expected, rates are even higher among young adults, with 43% reporting having sent or received a sext in a recent survey of nearly 3,500 individuals 18 to 24 years olds (Gordon-Messer, Bauermeister, Grodzinski, & Zimmerman, 2012). Two recent regional surveys have again found alarmingly high rates among teens. In a single private high school in the Southwest, researchers found that 17% of females and 18% of males had sent a sexually explicit picture via cell phone, and a remarkable 31% of females and 50% of males had received one (Strassberg, McKinnon, Sustaita, & Rullo, 2012). And a survey of 948 Texas public high school students found that 28% reported having sexted someone, 31% had asked someone for a sext, and more than half (57%) had been asked to sext. This was the first study to ask about sexual behavior in relation to sexting, however, and adolescents who had engaged in sexting behavior were far more likely to have begun having sex and to have engaged in risky sexual behaviors (Temple et al., 2012). A second study has also found that teenagers who sext are more likely to report being sexually active (Rice et al., 2012).

However, a very recent national study of 1,560 Internet users, ages 10 to 17, puts the sexting figure at a more conservative 1% for youth reporting having sent sexual images of themselves and 5.9% for youth reporting having received sexual images (Mitchell, Finkelhor, Jones, & Wolak, 2012) (see Table 5.5). Clearly, results of studies will vary according to the time frame assessed (within the past year? ever?), the age of the subjects (older teenagers are more likely to be involved in any sexually related behavior), and definition (is it "sexting" if you receive a sexual image or just if you send one?) (Lounsbury, Mitchell, & Finkelhor, 2011).

Table 5.5 How Prevalent Is Sexting?

Study	Sample	Prevalence	Definition
Sex Tech Survey (National Campaign to Prevent Teen and Unwanted Pregnancy, 2008)	13- to 19-year-olds ($N = 653$) 20- to 26-year-olds ($N = 627$)	20%	Sent or posted nude or seminude photos or videos online
Harris/Teen Online (Cox Communications, 2009)	13- to 18-year-olds ($N = 655$)	19%	Received sexually suggestive text messages or emails with nude or nearly nude photos
		9%	Sent sexually suggestive messages or emails
AP-MTV Survey (Associated Press & MTV, 2009)	14- to 24-year-olds ($N = 1,247$)	45%	Sent or received nude photos of themselves or sexual partners via cell phone
South West Grid Survey (Phippen, 2009)	13- to 18-year-olds ($N = 535$)	40%	Knew friends who had shared "intimate" photos or videos
Pew Internet Project (Lenhart, 2009)	12- to 17-year-olds ($N = 800$)	4%	Sent a sexually suggestive nude or seminude photo or video via cell phone
		9%	Received a sexually suggestive nude or seminude photo or video via cell phone

(Continued)

Table 5.5. (Continued)

Study	Sample	Prevalence	Definition
Youth Internet Safety Survey 3 (YISS-3) (Mitchell, Finkelhor, Jones, & Wolak, 2012)	10- to 17-year-olds (N = 1,560)	6.9%	Created, appeared in, or received photos showing breasts, genitals, or bottom during the past year
Southwestern High School Survey (Strassberg, McKinnon, Sustaita, & Rullo, 2012)	Students at one private high school (N = 602)	17–18%	Sent a sexually explicit photo
		31–50%	Received a sexually explicit photo
Texas High Schools Survey (Temple et al., 2012)	14- to 19-year-olds (N = 948)	28%	Sent a sexually explicit photo (these teens also showed an increased rate of early sex and risky sexual behaviors)
		31%	Asked someone to send a sext
		57%	Were asked to send a sext
Los Angeles High Schools Survey (Rice et al., 2012)	12- to 18-year-olds (N = 1,839)	15%	Sent a sexually explicit photo or text message
Young Adults Survey (Gordon-Messer, Bauermeister, Grodzinski, & Zimmerman, 2012)	18- to 24-year-olds (N = 3,447)	57%	Nonsexters
		28%	Sent and received sexts
		13%	Received a sext
		2%	Sent a sext

Pornography

Estimates are that the pornography industry generates between $10 and $15 billion a year in the United States alone, more than Hollywood films ($10 billion a year) (Jensen, 2007). More than 13,000 adult videos are produced annually in the U.S. (Bridges, Wosnitzer, Scharrer, Sun, & Liberman, 2010). This is not your father's pornography, however. What is now available, whether online, on DVDs, or on premium cable channels, can be raw, explicit, and involve virtually any combination and permutation you can think of. *Playboy* magazine—which in one older study 92% of teenage males had seen or read (D. Brown & Bryant, 1989)—now looks as innocent as *Reader's Digest* by comparison. So one must view the research with a degree of caution: "Old" pornography research may not accurately reflect the impact of "new" pornography.

Pornography is easily available online, but trying to assess whether teenagers are accessing it voluntarily or accidentally is definitely problematic. Even in confidential surveys, are teenagers really going to admit to unknown researchers that they have been searching for porn? A 2001 Kaiser survey found that nearly 70% of teens had been "accidentally" exposed to pornography online (Rideout, 2001). In the second Youth Internet Safety Survey (YISS-2) from 2005, 42% of the national sample of 1,500 youth 10 to 17 years old reported exposure, with two-thirds saying it was "unwanted" (Wolak, Mitchell, & Finkelhor, 2007). The YISS-3 survey in 2010 found that the "unwanted" figure had decreased to 23% (Jones, Mitchell, & Finkelhor, 2012). Another large study found that 93% of males and 62% of females reported having viewed pornography online by age 18 (Sabina, Wolak, & Finkelhor, 2008). A 2006 Australian study found that 92% of boys and 61% of girls, ages 13 to 16, had been exposed to online pornography (Ryan, 2012). And in a 2007 Canadian study of 429 students in 17 urban and rural schools in Alberta, Canada, 74% reported having viewed pornography online. In addition, more than one-third of the male teenagers reported having viewed pornographic DVDs or videos "too many times to count" ("One in Three Boys," 2007). Pornography is viewed by teenagers worldwide and in similar numbers in Swedish, Italian, Taiwanese, and Australian studies (Flood, 2009). A very large Swiss study of more than 7,500 young people 16 to 20 years old found wanted exposure rates of 29% for males and, surprisingly, higher exposure rates for females at 36% (Luder et al., 2011). But, unfortunately, these rates were based on a 2002 survey and may not be accurate a decade later.

Most studies wanting to assess the impact of pornography on teenagers ask college students to recall their exposure. In a huge study of 16,799 college males and 11,338 college females, 82% of the males and 52% of the females said that they had been exposed to pornography by age 14 (Leahy, 2009). And pornography is becoming mainstream among young adults. For example, a study of 813 college students found that two-thirds of the males and half of the females thought that viewing pornography was acceptable (J. S. Carroll et al., 2008).

Is pornography now becoming more acceptable among teens as well? With rare exceptions, it is difficult to do such research (Strasburger, 2009). What has been done is based entirely on self-reports, and it is usually impossible to ask probing questions such as, "Exactly what sort of pornography have you seen online?" and "Do you enjoy what you've seen?" Similarly, most researchers shy away from asking about the extent of exposure, just as they rarely ask about the extent of sexual activity in general, so a full picture of adolescent pornography is unusual. Europeans have a more benign attitude toward sex in general and adolescent sex and sexuality specifically, and so the most comprehensive study of teen pornography use was conducted in Sweden, examining 2,015 eighteen-year-old males and asking the above questions and many more (Svedin, Akerman, & Priebe, 2011). Ten percent of the subjects viewed pornography daily, 30% of the frequent viewers watched violent pornography, and nearly half of the frequent users were preoccupied with sex.

Considerable research has been done in the past 30 years, almost exclusively with adults. Older research suggests that sexualized violence against women, as seen in R-rated videos that are less sexually explicit but often far more violent than X-rated ones, probably do have antisocial effects. These contains scenes of women being tortured, murdered, or mutilated in a sexual context and may be the most important category for teenagers because they are more "mainstream" and represent an important genre of Hollywood films—the "slice 'em and dice 'em" movies (e.g., *Halloween I–V*, *Friday the 13th I–VIII*). Such films are frequently available on cable TV, and often the title alone tells the tale: *Slaughter High*, *Splatter University*, *I Dismember Mama*, *Lunch Meat*, *Watch Me When I*

Kill, Chopping Mall, Deadtime Stories. A content analysis of popular porn videos found that 88% contained physical aggression (spanking, gagging, slapping), nearly half contained verbal aggression, and the perpetrators were almost always male, while the female targets often showed pleasure (Bridges et al., 2010).

Still, considerable controversy currently exists, and the newfound availability of pornography and the lack of new research have complicated the picture. But the latest research seems to suggest the following findings (Wright et al., 2012):

- Pornography is not necessarily "bad" for adults (Moyer, 2011). Many people report that they use pornography as a way of enhancing their sex lives (Hald & Malamuth, 2008).
- In general, pornography that is simply "erotica" (e.g., R- or X-rated material with implied or actual sexual contact but with no violence or coercion) probably has no or little antisocial effect on adults (Donnerstein, Linz, & Penrod, 1987; Malamuth & Huppin, 2005).
- However, the most recent meta-analysis of nine studies with more than 2,300 subjects did find that nonviolent pornography may affect a small number of predisposed individuals and tends to perpetuate the notion that women are sexually promiscuous and want to be dominated (Hald, Malamuth, & Yuen, 2010).
- Even for the very small number of men at risk for sexual aggression, the research suggests that large amounts of pornography—particularly violent pornography—must be consumed before behavioral effects become apparent (Wright et al., 2012). This may be true of juvenile sexual offenders as well (Alexy, Burgess, & Prentky, 2009).

Despite research constraints, several recent studies *have* examined the impact of pornography on teenagers' sexual attitudes and even their sexual behavior. Remember that teenagers' sexual attitudes and behaviors are a work in progress. All of these studies have found significant effects, particularly more callous sexual attitudes toward women (J. D. Brown & L'Engle, 2009; Peter & Valkenburg, 2006, 2008, 2009, 2011; Ybarra, Mitchell, et al., 2011). A study of 433 adolescents in New York City found that visiting sexually explicit websites was linked to a greater likelihood of having multiple lifetime sexual partners and having greater sexual permissiveness; but of course, this might be expected, given that it was a cross-sectional study (Braun-Courville & Rojas, 2009). A Swedish study also found a correlation between viewing pornography frequently and coercive sex, as well as risk taking behaviors like smoking, drinking, drug use, and even criminal behavior and buying sex; but it, too, was cross-sectional (Svedin et al., 2011).

Several longitudinal studies have included an assessment of X-rated media in their studies of teenagers' media diets and have found behavioral effects. One study found an increase in "sexual preoccupation" with exposure to Internet pornography (J. D. Brown & L'Engle, 2009). A second recent longitudinal study of more than fifteen hundred 10- to 15-year-olds found a nearly sixfold increase in the odds of self-reported sexually aggressive behavior with exposure to violent X-rated material over time, whereas exposure to nonviolent X-rated material and sexually aggressive behavior were not statistically related (Ybarra et al., 2011). And a third longitudinal study found that exposure to X-rated material, including magazines, movies, and Internet porn, increased the risk of early sexual intercourse or oral sex (Delgado et al., 2009).

What the Research Says

Unlike the violence research, studies of the impact of sexy media are, by necessity, considerably scarcer and more limited. Researchers cannot simply show a group of 13-year-olds several X-rated movies and then measure the attitudinal or behavioral changes that result. But a number of research modalities have yielded important data, and an increasing number of longitudinal studies have yielded data that potentially show cause and effect.

As previously discussed, content analyses simply assay the amount of sexual material in current programming, lyrics, movies, articles, or websites without addressing its effects. But analyses of every medium available show a strong trend toward increased sexual content, both suggestive and explicit. Simple common sense would tell us that this is not healthy for children and younger adolescents. But people want stronger evidence. Does all of this sexy content actually harm children, or is it merely fantasy and entertainment? Do teenagers who become sexually active at a younger age do so because of exposure to sexy media, or do they simply prefer to watch such programming?

Correlational Studies

Correlational studies can help to address some of these issues, but they do not and can not provide cause-and-effect answers. They are "static" studies: At one point in time, does a certain population exposed to more sexual content behave differently? If so, it could be that those who are more involved sexually simply choose to watch more sexual content in their media. This is the "chicken-and-egg" dilemma that has plagued correlational research for centuries, but such research is far easier to do than longitudinal studies and can provide important information if interpreted cautiously.

There is a long history of correlational research on this topic, dating back into the 1970s. Only studies done since 2000 will be discussed here, but older studies and newer studies are in agreement (a good, brief summary of older studies can be found in Wright et al., 2012):

- Teenagers who watch or read more sexual content are more likely than lighter viewers to have stereotypical ideas about sex. For example, TV viewing is positively correlated with the belief that females are sex objects (Ward, Gorbine, & Cytron, 2002), that sex should occur early in a relationship (Aubrey, Harrison, Kramer, & Yellin, 2003), that casual sex is acceptable (Chia, 2006), and that most teenagers are already sexually active (Ward et al., 2002). Reality TV dating shows (Zurbriggen & Morgan, 2006) and TV talk shows (Ward & Friedman, 2006) have similar effects. Heavier viewers of TV are generally less satisfied with their own sex lives and have higher expectations of their prospective partners (Chia, 2006; Martino et al., 2005).
- Exposure to women's magazines has been associated with stereotypical sexual beliefs, recreational attitudes toward sex, and a belief that birth control is unnecessary (Bleakley, Hennessy, Fishbein, & Jordan, 2009; Kim et al., 2007). Exposure to men's magazines has been associated with permissive sexual attitudes and objectification of women (Taylor, 2006; Ward, Merriwether, & Caruthers, 2006).
- Heavy viewers of music videos are more likely to demonstrate stereotypical sexual beliefs, permissive sexual attitudes, less use of birth control, and (for males) greater acceptance of date rape (Kaestle et al., 2007; Ward et al., 2005; Zhang et al., 2008).

- Getting sex information from movies is positively correlated with the belief that birth control is not needed when having sex (Bleakley et al., 2009) and that overweight women are not sexually appealing (Hatoum & Belle, 2004).
- One recent study from Canada—a cross-sectional sample of 8,215 youth in Grades 6 to 10 and a one-year longitudinal sample of 1,424 youth in Grades 9 to 10—examined TV, computer, and video game use and a variety of risky behaviors (smoking, drunkenness, marijuana use, other illicit drug use, nonuse of seatbelts, and nonuse of condoms). High computer use was the screen-time behavior most strongly and consistently associated with risky behaviors, including nonuse of condoms. Youth in the highest quartile were 53% more likely to engage in risky behaviors. For TV use, the risk was 30% higher (Carson, Pickett, & Janssen, 2011).
- Many cross-sectional studies have found an association between exposure to a variety of media and increased likelihood of earlier sexual intercourse (Fisher et al., 2009; Pardun, L'Engle, & Brown, 2005; Pazos et al., 2001; Ward & Friedman, 2006), oral sex (Fisher et al., 2009), failure to use condoms (Carson et al., 2011), and intention to begin having sex (Chia, 2006; L'Engle, Brown, & Kenneavy, 2006; Pardun et al., 2005). This is true of international studies as well; a study of more than seventeen thousand 15- to 24-year-olds in Asia found that exposure to sexual content is associated with earlier sexual activity (Cheng, Lou, Gao, & Zabin, 2013, in press). One American study found that African American female teens who had had greater exposure to rap music videos or X-rated movies were more likely to have had multiple sexual partners and test positive for a sexually transmitted disease (Wingood et al., 2001).

Overall, media exposure—particularly exposure to a lot of sexual content—clearly has an impact on teenagers' beliefs and attitudes about sex.

Experimental Studies

Several experimental studies have been done since 2000, mostly with young adults. Only two have specifically studied adolescents, and they have concluded that exposure to music videos (Ward et al., 2005) and to TV sitcoms and dramas (Ward & Friedman, 2006) enhances sexual stereotypes and objectification of women. At least nine studies have been conducted using young adults, and the findings have been very similar to those from the correlational studies discussed above (Emmers-Sommer, Pauley, Hanzal, & Triplett, 2006; Eyal & Kunkel, 2008; Farrar, 2006; Ferguson, Berlin, & Noles, 2005; Mazur & Emmers-Sommer, 2002; Nabi & Clark, 2008; Taylor, 2005a, 2005b). Experimental studies have frequently been criticized because of their "artificiality," but in this case, the fact that the findings are congruent with correlational and longitudinal studies means that they should not be summarily dismissed.

Longitudinal Studies

Up until the last decade, there were no substantial longitudinal studies that could implicate or absolve sexy media content in terms of leading to early teen sex. But that situation has recently changed. As stated at the beginning of the chapter, there are 18 studies that use longitudinal data (although, again, some of these studies reuse the same population sample to draw their conclusions) (see Table 5.6). In addition, a 19th study has found an association between viewing sexual content on TV and regret over having sex too early among males but not among females (Martino, Collins, Elliott, Kanouse, & Berry, 2009).

In the first study of its kind, California researchers found that teens exposed to sexy media were more likely to begin having intercourse at a younger age. Nearly 1,800 teens, ages 12 to 17, were studied initially and then a year later. Exposure to sexy media doubled the risk of their initiating sexual intercourse or advancing significantly in their noncoital sexual activity (Collins et al., 2004). Similar findings were reported using data from the National Longitudinal Study of Adolescent Health. In a study of nearly 5,000 teenagers younger than 16 who had not yet had sexual intercourse, researchers found that those who watched more than two hours of TV per day were nearly twice as likely to begin having sex within a year, compared with lighter viewers (Ashby et al., 2006). Finally, the "gold standard" study was done by J. D. Brown and her colleagues (2006) using a sexual media diet comprising not only TV but movies, music, and print media as well. Exposure to a heavier sexual media diet among one thousand 12- to 14-year-olds in North Carolina accelerated White adolescents' sexual activity and doubled their risk of early intercourse within two years (see Figure 5.14). The study was compelling and comprehensive in every way, except for omitting exposure to online pornography.

Table 5.6 Recent Studies of the Impact of Sexual Content on Sexual Behavior Using Longitudinal Data

Study	Participants	N	Media Type	Duration	Findings
Wingood et al. (2003)	14- to 18-year-old females	480	Rap videos	1 year	Exposure to sexual rap videos predicted multiple partners
Collins et al. (2004)	12- to 17-year-olds	1,792	TV	1 year	Sexual media exposure strongly predicted intercourse 1 year later
Martino, Collins, Kanouse, Elliott, and Berry (2005)	12- to 17-year-olds	1,292	TV	1 year	Exposure to popular teen shows with sexual content increased risk of intercourse 1 year later
Ashby, Arcari, and Edmonson (2006)	7th–12th graders	4,808	TV	1 year	>2 hours of TV per day increased risk of intercourse 1.35×

(Continued)

Table 5.6 (Continued)

Study	Participants	N	Media Type	Duration	Findings
J. D. Brown, L'Engle, et al. (2006)	12- to 14-year-olds	1,107	Sexual media diet (TV, movies, magazines, music)	2 years	2× increased risk of sexual intercourse for White teens with high sexual media diet
Martino et al. (2006)	12- to-17-year-olds	1,242	Music	3 years	Degrading sexual content predicted earlier intercourse
Bersamin et al. (2008)	12- to 16-year-olds	887	TV	1 year	Parental coviewing of TV was protective against early intercourse and oral sex
Bleakley, Hennessy, Fishbein, and Jordan (2008)	14- to 16-year-olds	501	TV, movies, magazines, music, video games	1 year	Positive and reciprocal relationship between media and intercourse
Chandra et al. (2008)	12- to 20-year-olds	744	TV	3 years	Sexual media exposure was a strong predictor of teen pregnancy
L'Engle and Jackson (2008)	12- to 14-year-olds	854	Sexual media diet, including Internet	2 years	Peer and media exposure increased risk of early sex; stronger connections to parents and schools were protective
Peter and Valkenburg (2008)	13- to 20-year-olds	962	Internet	1 year	Exposure to sexual content on the Internet increased sexual preoccupation
J. D. Brown and L'Engle (2009)	7th–8th graders	967	X-rated movies, magazines, Internet pornography	2 years	Early exposure to X-rated media predicted earlier onset of sexual intercourse and oral sex

Study	Participants	N	Media Type	Duration	Findings
Delgado, Austin, Rich, and Bickham (2009)	7- to 18-year-olds	754	TV, movies	5 years	Watching adult-targeted TV increased the risk of intercourse by 33% for every hour/day viewed at a young age
Hennessy, Bleakley, Fishbein, and Jordan (2009)	14- to 18-year-olds	506	TV, movies, magazines, music, video games	2 years	Exposure to sexual media content predicted sexual intercourse initiation for White teens
Bersamin, Bourdeau, Fisher, and Grube (2010)	14- to 18-year-olds	824	TV	1 year	Premium cable TV viewing was associated with casual sex
Gottfried, Vaala, Bleakley, Hennessy, and Jordan (2011)	14- to 16-year-olds	474	TV (varying genres)	1 year	Overall, sexual content had no impact on sexual intercourse, but exposure to sexual content in situation comedies was a significant predictor of sexual intercourse
Ybarra, Mitchell, Hamburger, Diener-West, and Leaf (2011)	10- to 15-year-olds	1,159	X-rated media (movies, magazines, Internet pornography)	3 years	Intentional exposure to violent X-rated material predicted a nearly 6× greater risk of sexually aggressive behavior
O'Hara, Gibbons, Gerrard, Li, and Sargent (2012)	12- to 14-year-olds	1,228	Movies	6 years	Exposure to sexual content in movies predicted age of first intercourse and risky sexual behaviors

Since the North Carolina study, the findings have been replicated and expanded to include a variety of different media, including the Internet. Only one of the 17 studies has failed to find an overall impact of sexual content on sexual behavior, but it did find that exposure to TV sitcoms was more likely to predict a history of sexual intercourse a year later

Figure 5.14 Sexual media diet (SMD) and risk of early sexual intercourse.

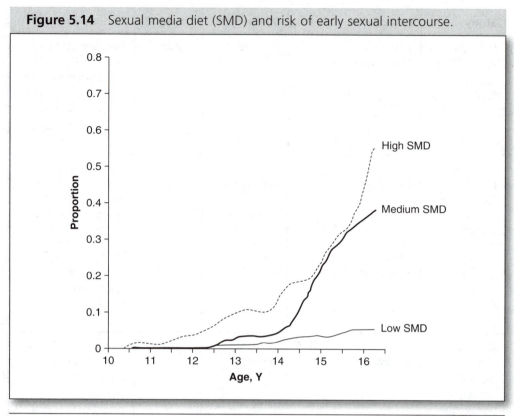

SOURCE: J. D. Brown, L'Engle, and colleagues (2006).

NOTE: New research has found a doubled risk of early sexual intercourse with exposure to more sexual content in a variety of different media.

compared with exposure to dramas (Gottfried et al., 2011). Several interesting findings have emerged from these longitudinal studies:

- As in other areas of media research (e.g., the relationship between advertisements and cigarette smoking), African Americans seem more resistant to being influenced by media than Whites do, perhaps because they do not see themselves portrayed in the media very often (Hennessy et al., 2009).
- Most of the studies involved sample sizes of 500 to 1,000 teenagers, but a few were quite large (e.g., Ashby et al., 2006; Collins et al., 2004). Similarly, most were relatively short term, one to two years, but one involved a five-year survey and examined children as young as 7 years old (Delgado et al., 2009).
- Several studies specifically included Internet pornography (J. D. Brown & L'Engle, 2009; L'Engle & Jackson, 2008; Peter & Valkenburg, 2008; Ybarra, Mitchell, et al., 2011).
- Several studies included music, including the most intriguing study, which studied more than twelve hundred 12- to 17-year-olds over a three-year period and found that listening to songs with degrading sexual lyrics predicted earlier intercourse (Martino et al., 2006).
- One three-year study actually found that exposure to sexual content on TV was a significant predictor of teen pregnancy (Chandra et al., 2008).

- Perhaps the greatest behavioral effect was found in the study of nearly twelve hundred 10- to 15-year-olds' exposure to X-rated media over a three-year period. The risk of sexually aggressive behavior increased nearly sixfold (Ybarra, Mitchell, et al., 2011).

How good is the research? Media research is difficult to do in general, but factor in the element of sex and it becomes extraordinarily difficult. Not only is funding generally unavailable, but schools and parents are reluctant to consent to any research dealing with children, adolescents, and sex and sexuality. Even with funding and access, institutional review boards at universities are reticent to approve such research. So the odds are stacked against media researchers, and consequently it is difficult to be overly critical of the 18 recent studies mentioned above. There are doubters (Steinberg & Monahan, 2011), but there always seem to be doubters of media research and media's impact on young people. It is almost as if there is a corollary to the third-person effect whereby society as a whole does not want to believe that the media can actually affect behavior.

So to answer the question of how good the research is, we have to ask, how large is the effect? Many studies find that exposure to sexual media content predicts between 10% and 20% of the variance, similar to media violence studies. And from a social science perspective, the ability to predict this much of the variance is highly significant. Defining the impact of media, when it is all around us, is like trying to assess the effect of pollution on the air we breathe—it may be subtle, but it is important to measure and control (Comstock & Strasburger, 1993). Taken together, the correlational, experimental, and longitudinal studies all speak to the power of the media to educate children and teens about sex and sexuality and to influence their attitudes, beliefs, and behaviors in a significant way.

Why Teenagers May Be Particularly Susceptible to Sexual Content in the Media

Teenagers sometimes seek to resemble actors and actresses as they experiment with different facets of their newly forming identities and try on different social "masks." In particular, the combined idiosyncrasies of adolescent psychology seem to conspire against successful use of contraception during early and middle adolescence (Strasburger et al., 2006). Teenagers often see themselves egocentrically as actors in their own "personal fable" (Elkind, 1993), in which the normal rules (e.g., having unprotected sexual intercourse may lead to pregnancy) are suspended—exactly as on television and in the movies. Even though 70% of teenagers, by age 16, have reached the final level of cognitive operational thinking described by Piaget (1972)—sequential logical thinking (formal operations)—they may still suffer from what Elkind (1984) calls "pseudostupidity": "The capacity to conceive many different alternatives is not immediately coupled with the ability to assign priorities and to decide which choice is more or less appropriate than others" (p. 384).

Although teenagers are probably not as susceptible as young children to media violence, they may be more susceptible to sexual content (Chia, 2006; Martino et al., 2005). Regular exposure to sexy media may alter teenagers' self-perceptions as well. In one study, two-thirds of sexually experienced teenagers in a three-year study of more than two thousand 12- to 17-year-olds said that they wished they had waited longer to have intercourse for the first time, and exposure to sexual content was positively associated with the likelihood of regret among males (Martino et al., 2009). Teenage girls frequently say that they want to be "in love" before they have sex, yet Hollywood movies portray very confusing images of what being in love actually means (K. R. Johnson & Holmes, 2009; Pardun, 2002). In short, the media may act as a kind of "super-peer" in exerting pressure on teenagers to begin having sex and making sexual activity seem like normative behavior for teens—a theory originally proposed by Strasburger (1995) and later supported by data from J. D. Brown, Halpern, and L'Engle (2005). Teenagers frequently cite their friends as being a major source of information about sex (Bleakley et al., 2009), but where do their friends get their information?

Teenagers typically overestimate the number of their peers who are engaging in sexual intercourse (National Campaign to Prevent Teen Pregnancy, 2004). Several studies document that teens who are avid consumers of media are more likely to overestimate the number of their peers and friends who are sexually active and to feel more pressure from the media to begin having sex than they feel from friends (Kaiser Family Foundation & Children Now, 1999; M. E. Tucker, 2000). In an anonymous survey of 1,015 *Seventeen* readers, ages 13 to 19, three-fourths believed that most teenagers were having sex, whereas only about half actually were (M. E. Tucker, 2000). Remarkably, in one survey of 2,100 preteen and teenage girls, only 11-year-olds said they did not feel pressure from the media to have sex (Haag, 1999). Early maturing girls are more likely to seek out sexual content in a variety of different media and to interpret that content as approving of teens having sex (J. D. Brown et al., 2005). This may represent a manifestation of the "cultivation hypothesis" as well—the notion that the more time viewers spend with media, the more their views of the world will be altered by what they see (Morgan, Shanahan, & Signorielli, 2009). Teenagers who are heavy users of media clearly get an eyeful and earful of sexual activity and therefore think that everyone is "doing it" except for them.

Interestingly, when teenagers are asked about the influence of media, they acknowledge media as an important source of information about sex but are equally quick to point out that the media have no influence on *their own* behavior. This is the well-known third-person effect— everyone is influenced by the media except oneself (Perloff, 2009). For teens, the very idea that something as simplistic and ordinary as the media could influence them is insulting; they are far more "sophisticated" than that. Yet they are willing to acknowledge peers as an influence, and who influences their peers (see Table 5.7). Similarly, when a Canadian survey asked nearly 1,200 teens ages 14 to 17 about their role models for healthy sexual behavior, 45% named their parents, 32% named their friends, and only 15% said that media celebrities influenced them (University of Montreal, 2011).

Table 5.7 Sources of Information About Sex for 14- to 16-Year-Olds (*N* = 458)

Sources	Total
Friends	75%
Teachers	62%
Mother	61%
Media	57%
Doctors	42%
Siblings	36%
Grandparent	14%
Religious leaders	12%

SOURCE: Adapted from Bleakley, Hennessy, Fishbein, and Jordan (2009).

Contraceptive Advertising

It's so hypocritical for any network in this culture to go all puritanical on the subject of condom use when their programming is so salacious. I mean, let's get real here. Fox and CBS and all of them are in the business of nonstop soft porn, but God forbid we should use a condom . . .

—Media critic Mark Crispin Miller
as quoted in *The New York Times* (Newman, 2007)

Failure to use contraception is an international problem. A recent survey of more than 6,000 young people in 29 countries, including Chile, Poland, and China, found that unsafe sex with a new partner had increased by 111% in France, 39% in the U.S., and 19% in Britain in the past three years (Bayer HealthCare Pharmaceuticals, 2011).

But the U.S. has the highest teenage pregnancy rate of 37 developed countries despite the fact that American teenagers are no more sexually active than French or Canadian or Belgian teens. There are only two possible hypotheses to explain why: Either American female teens are extremely fertile, or American teens do not use birth control as effectively as teens in other countries. In fact, these data confirm that American society limits access to birth control for teenagers in three vital ways—via their physicians (who are reluctant to prescribe it), their media (which are reluctant to mention it), and their school-based sex education programs (which are reluctant to talk about it) (Strasburger, 2012a, 2012b).

It seems odd, perhaps even hypocritical, that as American culture has become increasingly "sexualized" in the past 30 years, the one taboo remaining is the public mention of birth control. In 1985, the American College of Obstetricians and Gynecologists (ACOG) made headlines when its public service announcement about teen pregnancy, titled "I Intend," was banned from all three major networks. The one offensive line that had to be removed before the networks agreed to run the PSA said, "Unintended pregnancies have risks . . . greater risks than any of today's contraceptives" (Strasburger, 1989, p. 767). By 2006, contraceptive advertisements occasionally appeared in national network programming but were mostly for the "patch" or Ortho Tri-Cyclen and mentioned only ease of use or improvement in acne, not pregnancy prevention (see Figure 5.14) (Strasburger, 2012a; Strasburger & Council on Communications and Media, 2010). A year later, in another well-publicized incident, both FOX and CBS refused to air an ad for Trojan condoms ("Evolve. Use a condom every time.") because the two networks would air only condom ads that restricted their content to talking about preventing HIV and AIDS, not other sexually transmitted infections (STIs) or pregnancy (Brodesser-akner, 2007). Two of the six major networks refuse to air condom ads at all, and three others will air them only after 9 p.m. or 11 p.m. Several networks also refuse to air ads for birth control pills, and the ones that do permit them refuse to allow use of the words "prevent pregnancy" (Espey, Cosgrove, & Ogburn, 2007). Ads for emergency contraception are virtually nonexistent, yet every year American women have 3 million unplanned pregnancies, and less than half of teen mothers ages 15 to 19 years with unintended pregnancies report having used contraception (Centers for Disease Control and Prevention, 2012a) (see Figure 5.15). Advertising emergency contraception could be a major way to reduce the

1.3 million abortions that occur in the U.S. every year (Kristof, 2006). Yet network executives claim, without given any evidence for their assertions, that PSAs or advertisements for birth control products would offend many viewers.

The situation remains virtually the same as it did in 1985. However, birth control ads do air on many local TV stations around the United States (e.g., KABC-TV, Los Angeles) and on cable networks like Lifetime without complaints being registered. In addition, several national surveys of adults have found that a majority of Americans —including 62% of the Catholics surveyed—favor birth control advertising on television (Harris & Associates, 1987; Kaiser Family Foundation, 2001). In fact, more adults oppose beer ads (34%) than condom ads (25%) (Kaiser Family Foundation, 2001). By contrast, in the UK, a recent government decision allows condom ads—previously banned before 9 p.m.—to be aired at any time, provided that they are not shown during programs popular with children under age 10 and are tastefully done. The government advisory group that made the recommendation cited the fact that the UK has the highest teen pregnancy rate in Europe and rising rates of STIs (Hickman, 2010).

Meanwhile, two dramatic changes have occurred. In 2009, the Food and Drug Administration required Bayer HealthCare Pharmaceuticals to run a new $20 million advertising campaign for Yaz, the most popular birth control pill in the U.S., to correct the misperception from previous ads that women should take Yaz to cure their acne or their premenstrual syndrome symptoms (Singer, 2009). Unfortunately, the second change is not as

Figure 5.15 Percentage of teen mothers aged 15-19 years with unintended pregnancies resulting in live births who reported no contraceptive use before pregnancy —19 states* participating in Pregnancy Risk Assesment Monitoring System (PRAMS). 2004–2008

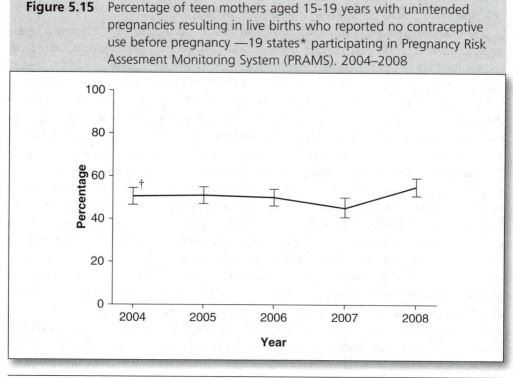

SOURCE: Centers for Disease Control and Prevention (2012a).

*Alaska, Arkansas, Colorado, Geogia, Hawaii, Illinois, Maryland, Maine, Michigan, Minnesota, Nebraska, New Jersey, New York, Oklahama, Oregon, Rhode Island, Utah, Washington, and West Virginia.

[†] 95% confidence interval.

proactive: Ads for Viagra, Cialis, and Levitra have now become ubiquitous and make sex seem like a recreational sport (see Figure 5.16). In 2006, $241 million was spent advertising erectile dysfunction (ED) drugs, which helped boost sales to $1.4 billion (Agovino, 2007). The apparent "disconnect" between the networks' willingness to air ads for ED drugs and their unwillingness to air ads for birth control products seems hypocritical at best (Strasburger & Council on Communications and Media, 2010). As one researcher notes,

> National sex surveys show that whether we're married or single, we're not having sex all the time. But these ads make us think we should be. The whole point of most ads is to make us feel inadequate. Without that as a motivation why would we buy something? (L. Carroll, 2010)

The only positive note is that in 2011, GlaxoSmithKline—the makers of Levitra—decided to suspend their advertising. GSK's president explained that while Glaxo believes erectile dysfunction is a legitimate medical condition, it "certainly is not a condition parents, aunts, uncles and grandparents want to explain to children while watching a football game on Thanksgiving" (Loftus, 2011).

Would advertising of condoms and birth control pills have an impact on the rates of teen pregnancy or acquisition of HIV? Considerable data seem to indicate that the answer is yes: European countries have far lower rates of teen pregnancy and far more widespread media discussion and advertising of birth control products (Advocates for Youth, 2011). Furthermore, according to Population Services International, when Zaire began advertising condoms, there was a 20-fold increase in the number of condoms sold in just three years—from 900,000 in

Figure 5.16

1988 to 18 million in 1991 (Alter, 1994). More recently, a study of condom advertising in Pakistan showed significant increases in discussion of family planning and use of condoms (Agha & Meekers, 2010). In a relevant "natural experiment," Earvin "Magic" Johnson's announcement of his HIV infection was associated with a decline in one-night stands and sex with multiple partners in the subsequent 14 weeks, according to a Maryland study (CDC, 1993). It also resulted in increased awareness about AIDS (Kalichman & Hunter, 1992).

On the other hand, would advertising birth control products make teenagers more sexually active than they already are? There is no evidence available indicating that allowing freer access to birth control encourages teenagers to become sexually active at a younger age (Farrar, 2006; Mueller, Gavin, & Kulkarni, 2008; Reichelt, 1978; Strasburger et al., 2006). In fact, the data indicate the exact opposite: There are now at least nine peer-reviewed, controlled clinical trials showing that giving teens freer access to condoms does not increase their sexual activity or push virginal teenagers into having sex, but does increase the use of condoms among those who are sexually active (Blake et al., 2003; Furstenberg, Geitz, Teitler, & Weiss, 1997; Guttmacher et al., 1997; Jemmott, Jemmott, & Fong, 1998; Kirby et al., 1999; Schuster, Bell, Berry, & Kanouse, 1998; Sellers, McGraw, & McKinlay, 1994; Wolk & Rosenbaum, 1995; Wretzel, Visintainer, & Koenigs, 2011). Typically, teenage females engage in unprotected intercourse for six months to a year before seeking medical attention for birth control (Strasburger et al., 2006). Organizations such as the American Academy of Pediatrics, ACOG, and the Society for Adolescent Medicine have all called for contraceptive advertising on American television (Espey et al., 2007; Society for Adolescent Medicine, 2000; Strasburger & Council on Communications and Media, 2010). Despite the hopes of many public health officials, the fear of AIDS may not be sufficient to increase teenagers' use of contraception. Thus, a major potential solution to a significant American health problem is being thwarted by the networks and the many people who misunderstand the "science" of teen pregnancy.

Prosocial Sexual Content on Television

One of the most appealing and practical approaches to address public health concerns about television has been dubbed "edutainment"—the practice of embedding socially responsible messages into mainstream programming (Brown & Strasburger, 2007; Kaiser Family Foundation, 2004). Although this occurs infrequently, the impact can be significant and speaks to the ability of some writers and producers to be extremely socially conscious:

- During the 1999 TV season, the Media Project (a partnership between Advocates for Youth and the Kaiser Family Foundation) worked with the producers of *Felicity* on a two-part episode about date rape. The Project encouraged the creation of a toll-free rape crisis hotline number to be displayed at the end of the episode, and the hotline received more than 1,000 calls directly after the show aired (Folb, 2000). In a small survey about a later episode that discussed birth control, more than one-fourth of 12- to 21-year-olds surveyed felt they had learned something new about birth control and safe sex.
- In 2002, *Friends* aired an episode about condoms, and 27% of a national sample of teens saw the program. Nearly half the teens watched the episode with an adult, and 10% talked about condom efficiency as a direct result of the episode (Collins, Elliott, Berry, Kanouse, & Hunter, 2003).

- Collaborative efforts between the Kaiser Family Foundation and the producers of the hit show *ER* resulted in successful storylines about the risks of human papillomavirus (HPV) and the usefulness of emergency contraception (Brodie et al., 2001) (see Figure 5.17).
- In England, one of the characters in the hit show *Coronation Street* died of cervical cancer, resulting in a 21% increase in Pap smears in the 19 weeks after the show aired (Howe et al., 2002).
- The Soap Opera Summit in Hollywood and international efforts to embed storylines in popular soap operas are other examples of prosocial efforts. For example, media giant Viacom and the Kaiser Family Foundation launched an ambitious project in 2003 to produce $120 million worth of public service announcements and print ads concerning HIV/AIDS and to encourage Viacom producers to include storylines in their TV shows that would raise AIDS awareness (Tannen, 2003).
- In 2008, a study showed that the viewers of a *Gray's Anatomy* episode learned that HIV-positive mothers could still have HIV-negative babies (Rideout, 2008). The media have actually played a major role in educating the public about HIV (DeJong, Wolf, & Austin, 2001; Romer et al., 2009).

Although these instances can probably still be counted on the fingers of two hands, they do demonstrate that the entertainment industry can be remarkably receptive to outside input and that healthier content can be introduced into mainstream television without government pressure or the threat of censorship.

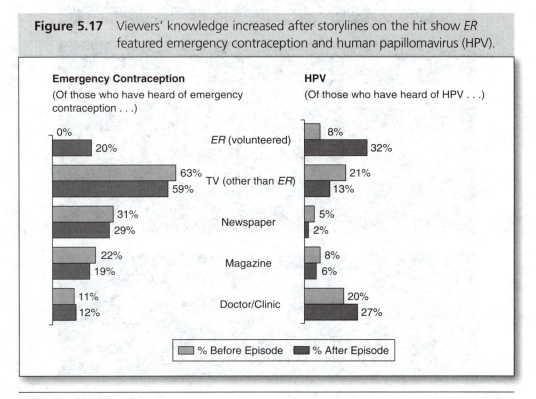

Figure 5.17 Viewers' knowledge increased after storylines on the hit show *ER* featured emergency contraception and human papillomavirus (HPV).

SOURCE: Brodie and colleagues (2001). Reprinted with permission from the Kaiser Family Foundation.

The mass media have also been used proactively to try to increase parent-child communication about sex. In North Carolina, a mass media campaign used billboards (see Figure 5.18) and radio and TV PSAs with the theme "Talk to your kids about sex. Everyone else is." The impact of the campaign was assessed via a post-exposure survey to 1,132 parents of adolescents living in the 32 counties covered by the campaign. Parents' exposure to a billboard message or PSA significantly correlated with talking to their child about sex during the following month (DuRant, Wolfson, LaFrance, Balkrishnan, & Altman, 2006; Evans, Davis, Umanzor, Patel, & Khan, 2011).

Meanwhile, new technology has resulted in an explosion of new and creative ways of reaching teenagers with prosocial health messages (Boyar et al., 2011; Bull, Levine, Black, Schmiege, & Santelli, 2012; Collins, Martino, & Shaw, 2011). Since teenagers are texters, a number of organizations have created text messaging services for information about sex (Hoffman, 2011b).

Figure 5.18   Billboards used in a North Carolina mass media campaign.

The San Francisco Department of Public Health has created "SexInfo," whereby a five-digit number links users to a menu of options about sexual health and referral options. In its first 25 weeks, the service received 4,500 texts (Levine, McCright, Dobkin, Woodruff, & Klausner, 2008). A statewide version of the program, titled "HookUp," allows users to access clinics in their area by texting "CLINIC" and their zip code. After nine months, nearly 3,000 subscribers had enrolled and one-third had obtained clinic appointments (Braun, Howard, & Madsen, 2010). Results of STI tests have been texted in a unique program in Washington, DC. Nearly 8,000 teens in 33 schools were introduced to the program, with 66% to 75% providing urine specimens for STI testing and a 5% to 9% receiving a positive test result (Winston, 2010).

As previously discussed, the Internet may be becoming the single greatest source of sex information for teens (Boyar et al., 2011). Many responsible online websites exist (e.g., Planned Parenthood, Go Ask Alice, Healthy Teen Network, Advocates for Youth, National Campaign to Prevent Teen and Unwanted Pregnancy). Some organizations have established very interactive websites for teens—for example, Boston Children's Hospital (http://www .youngwomenshealth.org/), American Social Health Association (http://www.iwannaknow .org/teens/index.html), the California Family Health Council (http://www.teensource.org/), and the Atlantic Health System (http://www.teenhealthfx.com/) (Borzekowski, McCarthy, & Rosenfeld, 2012). To date, none of these sites have been evaluated for their behavioral impact, but two older studies have examined content (Keller, LaBelle, Karimi, & Gupta, 2002; Noar, Clark, Cole, & Lustria, 2006). Of 21 Internet sites providing sex information specifically for teens, most advised the need for safe sex (95%), the use of condoms (95%), and abstinence as a primary prevention strategy (67%), but the sites surveyed seldom dealt with more difficult issues like sexual orientation (Noar et al., 2006).

Social networking sites on the Internet also have the potential to be used for prosocial purposes (Ralph, Berglas, Schwartz, & Brindis, 2011) and to teach young people about media literacy on the Internet. In one small but unique study, researchers sent an email from "Dr. Meg" to users who made three or more references in their profiles to sexual behaviors or drug use. The email warned that there are risks to disclosing such personal information online and encouraged the user to revise the profile. At follow-up, 13.7% of the sexual references and 26% of the drug references had been removed (Moreno, VanderStoep, et al., 2009). On the other hand, a social marketing campaign designed to increased condom use in 12 western U.S. neighborhoods failed (Bull et al., 2008). But a newer randomized controlled trial with 1,578 older teens and young adults used Facebook to deliver STI-prevention messages and resulted in significant increases in condom use after six months (Bull et al., 2012).

Finally, a variety of video games and programs have been developed that can be played either on cell phones or Internet platforms. *It's Your Game: Keep It Real* is a middle school sex ed program that includes computer components and was piloted in Texas with an urban, low-income 7th- to 8th-grade population. On follow-up of the students in 9th grade, one-third of the students in the control group had initiated sex compared with one-fourth of the students receiving the program (Tortolero et al., 2009). *What Could You Do?*, an interactive one-hour video that teaches about sexual decision making, was tested on 300 urban adolescent females in Pittsburgh. At six-month follow-up, more abstinence, better use of condoms, and less STIs were reported in comparison with controls (Downs et al., 2004). In Project Light, an interesting variation on the use of video games, researchers compared a computer-based program with an in-person training and found the former to be more effective (Lightfoot, Comulada,

& Stover, 2007). Many other creative uses for texting, social networking sites, and computer games are currently in development or have not yet been formally tested but potentially offer great promise for the future (Collins et al., 2011).

Solutions

Clearly, there is a strong case to be made for the impact of sexual content in a variety of media on young, impressionable preteens and teens (J. D. Brown, 2008; Escobar-Chaves et al., 2005; Strasburger, 2012a; Strasburger & Council on Communications and Media, 2010; Wright et al., 2012). In a society that limits access to sexual information, teenagers look to the media for answers to their questions. More important, the media may have a strong effect on teens without their even being aware of it, especially those whose parents do not inculcate in them a strong sense of "family values." Important questions get answered by the media: "When is it okay to have sex?" "How do I know if I'm in love?" "Is sex fun?" "Is sex risky?" Unfortunately, as we have seen, media answers to these questions are often not the healthiest or most accurate.

What changes in media would give American youth a healthier view of sex and sexuality? A number of possibilities come to mind:

1. *Widespread advertising of birth control in mainstream media (e.g., TV, magazines, radio).* Advertising birth control represents one means of increasing teenagers' access to it. Such advertising needs to address the risks of pregnancy, not merely the cosmetic difference that birth control pills can make if a teenager has acne. Unless new products such as the morning-after pill are widely advertised, teenagers will not know about them or use them (see Figure 5.19). Comparative studies between the United States and Europe make it clear that countries that promote the use of birth control via advertising, sex education classes, and programming are rewarded with lower rates of teen pregnancy (Advocates for Youth 2011; Mueller et al., 2008; Strasburger et al., 2006). Most national surveys have documented that adults favor birth control advertising (Mozes, 2001), yet the media remain resistant. Given that nine studies now indicate that making birth control available to teenagers does not increase the risk of early sexual intercourse, there is no longer any excuse to withhold access to it.

2. *Greater responsibility and accountability of mainstream media for producing healthy and accurate messages about sex and sexuality.* Entertainment industry executives need to realize that, like it or not, their product is educating American children and teenagers. Media have become one of the most important sources for sexual information for young people today (see Table 5.8) (J. D. Brown, L'Engle, et al., 2006; Levine, 2011; Strasburger, 2012a). Yet what they view on television and in the movies is almost counterproductive to healthy adolescence: frequent premarital sex and sex between unmarried partners, talk about infidelity on talk shows, graphic jokes and innuendoes in the movies, rape myths, and sexual violence. Where is the depiction of sexual responsibility? Where is the talk about the need for birth control or the risk of STDs? Where are the depictions of condom use when they are most needed in modern society? Why aren't topics such as abortion, date rape, and rape myths portrayed and examined in greater detail (Navarro, 2007)? When two-thirds of sexually experienced teenagers in

the U.S. say they wish they had waited longer to have intercourse for the first time, a more accurate portrayal of human sexuality in mainstream media would seem to be indicated (Martino et al., 2009). Clearly, as evidenced by the changing portrayal of sexual minorities in prime-time TV programming, Hollywood can be proactive and responsible.

In the new millennium, however, the answer is not a return to the "golden age" of the 1950s, when sex was rarely discussed and Laura and Rob Petrie slept in separate beds on *The Dick Van Dyke Show* despite being married. Nor should censorship be tolerated

Figure 5.19   Ads for emergency contraception.

SOURCE: The EC campaign is coordinated by the National Institute for Reproductive Health, the national research, education, and training arm of NARAL Pro-Choice New York. Mifeprex is a registered trademark of Danco Laboratories, LLC.

Table 5.8   Five Media Strategies for Sexual Health

1. Public service announcements

2. Social marketing (e.g., Trojan's "Evolve" campaign)

3. Entertainment-education (embedding social desirable behaviors and information into mainstream entertainment programming)

4. Media advocacy

5. Using new media technologies to reach adolescents

SOURCE: Adapted from J. D. Brown (2008).

in a free society. Voluntary restraint and good judgment on the part of Hollywood and television writers, producers, and directors, however, would go far in improving the current dismal state of programming (see Table 5.9).

A return to the "family hours" of protected programming between 7 p.m. and 9 p.m. would be one useful idea. *Boston Public*, which aired at 7 p.m Central and Mountain time, featured such storylines as a high school girl trading oral sex for a boy's agreement to withdraw from a student council race, a girl tossing her breast pads away in the hallway, and another high school girl's sexual affair with one of the teachers. Unfortunately, as one TV critic notes, "Almost anything goes in primetime . . . TV says get used to it" (Salamon, 2000, p. 6WK). Yet, in 2005, *Boston Public*'s writer-producer, David E. Kelley, handled the theme of emergency contraception being refused in a Catholic hospital emergency room extremely fairly and sensitively in a *Boston Legal* episode. Another positive development was the 2006 "Pause" public education campaign by FOX and the Kaiser Family Foundation that tried to teach teenagers to make wise decisions about difficult issues, including sex and teenage pregnancy (Kaiser Family Foundation, 2006). Clearly, Hollywood is capable of dealing with the theme of adolescent sexuality in a responsible way when it wants to, but such campaigns are often short-lived and their effectiveness has not been tested.

3. *Better taste in advertising* (see Exercises for a discussion of "taste"). When sex is used to sell products, it is cheapened and devalued. Manufacturers who pay for advertising and companies that produce it need to recognize that they, too, have a public health responsibility to produce ads that are not gratuitously provocative, suggestive, or demeaning (see Figure 5.20). Kilbourne's *Deadly Persuasion* (1999) should be a must-read for all account executives.

Table 5.9   Guide to Responsible Sexual Content in Media
Recognize sex as a healthy and natural part of life.
Parent and child conversations about sex are important and healthy and should be encouraged.
Demonstrate that not only the young, unmarried, and beautiful have sexual relationships.
Not all affection and touching must culminate in sex.
Portray couples having sexual relationships with feelings of affection, love, and respect for one another.
Consequences of unprotected sex should be discussed or shown.
Miscarriage should not be used as a dramatic convenience for resolving an unwanted pregnancy.
Use of contraceptives should be indicated as a normal part of a sexual relationship.
Avoid associating violence with sex or love.
Rape should be depicted as a crime of violence, not of passion.
The ability to say "no" should be recognized and respected.

SOURCE: Strasburger (1995). Modified from Haffner and Kelly (1987, pp. 9–11).

Figure 5.20   Inappropriate use of sexuality in ads.

4. *Using new media creatively to provide young people with accurate information about sex and sexuality.* Web-based outreach may help connect young people to the sexual health services they need (Ralph et al., 2011), and the Internet could prove invaluable as a source of reliable sex information, especially at a time when many schools are failing to provide comprehensive sex education (Guse et al., 2012; Martinez et al., 2010). A text messaging service that gives weekly messages relating to sexual health has been successfully piloted (Perry, Kayekjian, Braun, Sheoran, & Chung, 2012). The makers of Trojan condoms have partnered with HealthGuru.com to create online videos that answer more than 100 common questions about sex, STDs, and birth control (Fard, 2012). In Texas, which has the fifth highest teen pregnancy rate in the country and where 96% of the public schools still have abstinence-only sex ed curricula, a new initiative in Austin allows teens to text sex or reproductive health questions to experts and receive a response within 24 hours (Mulvaney, 2012). And MTV has actually pioneered an iPhone app that uses GPS to search for the nearest place that sells condoms (Sniderman, 2011). Using new technology may actually help clinicians prevent and treat STDs: In North Carolina, health department officials used social networking sites to locate 80% of at-risk individuals during an outbreak of syphilis (Clark-Flory, 2012).

5. *Incorporating the principles of media education into existing sex education programs.* Several studies seem to indicate that a media education approach may be effective in decreasing children's aggressive attitudes and behaviors, promoting better nutritional habits and decreasing their risk of obesity, decreasing their susceptibility to advertising, and reducing their use of alcohol and tobacco (J. D. Brown, 2006; Council on Communications and Media, 2010; Pinkleton, Austin, Chen, & Cohen, 2012) (see Chapter 12). There is no reason to think that helping children and teenagers decipher sexual content, the suggestiveness of advertising, and the conservatism of the broadcast industry regarding contraception would

have anything but positive outcomes. In fact, a recent media literacy curriculum conducted at 22 school sites in Washington state found that a five-lesson plan targeting 532 middle school students resulted in their being less likely to overestimate sexual activity among their peers and more aware of the truth about sex and sexual imagery in the media (Pinkleton, Austin, Cohen, Chen, & Fitzgerald, 2008). One group of Australian researchers is actually updating sex ed resources in that country to address the widespread availability of pornography and help teachers confront the issue (Ryan, 2012).

6. *More and better counteradvertising.* To date, only the National Campaign to Prevent Teen and Unwanted Pregnancy has engaged in long-term efforts to counterprogram through the national media (see Figure 5.21a). One organization has even taken on the abstinence movement (see Figure 5.21b). Although no data exist about their success, the communications literature about drugs and media does contain several successful efforts involving counteradvertising against tobacco and illicit drugs with teens as the primary target audience (see Chapter 6). On the other hand, scare tactics that exploit the fear of HIV/AIDS to try to prevent early teenage sexual activity are unethical and probably counterproductive (DeJong et al., 2001; Strasburger, 2012a).

Figure 5.21 Counteradvertising.

SOURCE: Grant Hill.

7. *Greater sensitivity of parents, schools, and society in general to the influence of the media on children and adolescents.* Many parents often seem to be "clueless" about the impact of media on their children and teenagers (Strasburger, 2006), although a 2007 survey of 1,008 parents nationwide found that two-thirds felt that they were "closely monitoring" their children's media use (Rideout, 2007). The most important steps that parents can take are to set rules about TV viewing, monitor what shows are being watched, and keep TV

sets out of the bedroom (Council on Communications and Media, 2010; Fisher et al., 2009). A national study of 1,762 teenagers found that having a TV in the bedroom and having no rules about viewing correlates with viewing more sexual content (Kim et al., 2006). Schools, too, need to be more sensitive to media in general and sex in the media specifically. Sex education programs should incorporate media literacy into their curricula, and schools need to teach and establish reasonable rules about online privacy, Internet use, and sexting (Strasburger, 2012b). Finally, law enforcement officials need to understand that sexting is a manifestation of poor judgment, not a crime (Draper, 2012; Hughes, 2011; Lithwick, 2009). A 2012 survey of more than 2,100 adults nationwide found great sympathy for a more rational approach to adolescents who sext (see Figure 5.22) (C. S. Mott Children's Hospital, National Poll on Children's Health, 2012).

Figure 5.22   Public support for youth sexting laws.

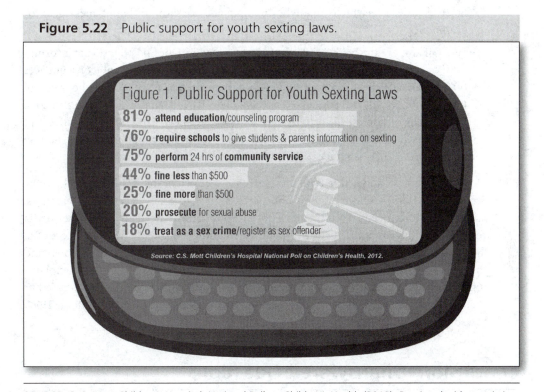

SOURCE: C. S. Mott Children's Hospital, National Poll on Children's Health (2012). Reprinted with permission.

8. *More research.* Many longitudinal studies now point to the media as one crucial factor in a teenager's decision of when to have sexual intercourse. But the amount of research on sex and the media pales in comparison to the 3,500 studies done on children and media violence. Considerably more research needs to be funded, and such research will need to be interdisciplinary, using a variety of methods and a variety of populations, and will need to take into account developmental, gender, and ethnic differences (Shafer, A., Bobkowski, P., & Brown, J. D., 2013). For example:

   ➢ How do different groups of children and teenagers view different sexual content? Do different groups use different types of media to find sexual content? Is that content interpreted differently? Are there developmental differences in how teens of different ages interpret sexual content? (A few preliminary studies of this kind have already been done [Aubrey et al., 2003; J. D. Brown & Schulze, 1990; Manganello et al., 2010; Rivadeneyra & Ward, 2005; Tolman, Kim, Schooler, & Sorsoli, 2007].)

➤ Do teens from different ethnic groups seek out programming unique to their own ethnic group (J. D. Brown & Pardun, 2004)?

➤ How do individuals negotiate sexual behavior in the media? What interpersonal contexts exist for sexual behavior? Do different media portray sexuality differently?

➤ How do current media change teens' knowledge about sex and sexuality, their emotions concerning sex, or their attitudes? Regular adolescent viewers of teen soap operas like *Gossip Girl* could be recruited and shown "future episodes" of their favorite program, which might be manipulated to show different messages, for example.

➤ What, if any, are the behavioral effects of new media? Does posting sexual information on one's social network profile or sexting have behavioral consequences (O'Sullivan, 2012)? For example, a new two-year study to be funded by the National Institutes of Health and conducted at the University of Dallas will capture and code the content of adolescent activity on Facebook (Nauert, 2012). Are the effects of Internet pornography the same as traditional ("tamer") pornography? (Guy, Patton, & Kaldor, 2012; Strasburger, 2012a; Wright et al., 2012).

The barriers to doing this type of research are considerable (Huston et al., 1998; Strasburger, 1998). School systems and parents need to grant access to researchers, and foundations need to fund such efforts. Foundations need to recognize media research as a new and much-needed priority. In addition, society needs to accept the fact that teenagers should be able to give consent for such research on their own and that parents can be informed "passively" about ongoing studies (e.g., a letter explaining the research, along with the opportunity to withdraw the child if need be) rather than "actively" (e.g., having to send back signed permission forms) (Santelli, 1997; Strasburger, 1998).

Conclusion: Unanswered Questions

Despite this discussion, not all media are unhealthy or irresponsible for young people. Some shows have dealt responsibly with the issue of teenage sexual activity and teenage pregnancy, from the original *Beverly Hills, 90210*, *Dawson's Creek*, *Felicity*, and *My So-Called Life* to the more contemporary *ER*, *Friday Night Lights*, and *Glee*. Made-for-TV movies such as *Babies Having Babies* and *Daddy* have used extremely frank language to good, educational effect. Historically, the 1980s cop drama *Cagney & Lacey* contained one of the first instances of a TV mother talking to her son about responsibility and birth control. On *St. Elsewhere*, the only known mention of a diaphragm on prime-time TV was aired during the 1987–1988 season, although accomplishing this required that the user be the chief of obstetrics and gynecology. The new threat of AIDS in the 1980s brought with it a superb episode of *L.A. Law* during the 1987–1988 season, which discussed the risk of

AIDS in heterosexual intercourse but also included good advice on birth control and limiting the number of sexual partners (see Strasburger, 1989). But these are all notable exceptions.

Sadly, as the years pass, the amount of suggestive and explicit sexual content on TV increases dramatically, but the amount of responsible sexual content does not. And, unfortunately, it has not been the tragedy of teenage pregnancy or the high rates of early adolescent sexual activity and STIs that have changed the network landscape, but paradoxically the apparent need to keep pace with the even sexier content on cable and premium channels and the Internet.

How do adolescents process the sexual content that they view? Do different ethnic groups interpret the same content differently? Can teenagers learn abstinence or the need to use birth control from what they view in the media? Would more widespread advertising of contraceptives and fewer ads for erectile dysfunction drugs make a significant dent in the U.S. teen pregnancy rate? Until the political and funding climate changes, and until adults understand that asking children and teenagers about sex will not provoke them into early sexual activity, we will simply have to rely on what research is available and speculate about many of these crucial issues. As one author notes,

> I've often wondered what it would be like if we taught young people swimming the same way we teach sexuality. If we told them that swimming was an important adult activity, one they will all have to be skilled at when they grow up, but we never talked with them about it. We never showed them the pool. We just allowed them to stand outside closed doors and listen to all the splashing. Occasionally, they might catch a glimpse of partially-clothed people going in and out of the door to the pool and maybe they'd find a hidden book on the art of swimming, but when they asked a question about how swimming felt or what it was about, they would be greeted with blank or embarrassed looks. Suddenly, when they turn 18 we would fling open the doors to the swimming pool and they would jump in. Miraculously, some might learn to tread water, but many would drown. (E. Roberts, 1983, p. 10)

Exercises

1. *Taste.* When we talk about "taste," whose taste do we mean? Ours? Yours? Hollywood's? This is a recurring problem in discussing the media and one we do not take lightly. In this volume, we have erred on the side of public health and psychology in discussing what is questionable taste and what represents "good" versus "bad" programming. Although we have tried to give examples, we have left the discussion purposefully vague because we acknowledge that taste can vary considerably. But when it comes to "bad" taste or "questionable" programming that is unhealthy, we would tend to agree with a paraphrase of Supreme Court Justice Potter Stewart's definition of pornography: "We know it when we see it."
   a. Should the media be criticized on grounds of taste?
   b. If so, whose taste should be used as the "gold standard"? Is an objective standard possible?
   c. In making judgments about taste, what sociocultural factors enter the discussion?
   d. "Push the envelope" seems to be the new guiding principle for Hollywood writers. The writer of the hit shows *2 Broke Girls* and *Whitney* is Whitney Cummings, who

half jokingly told a *New York Times* reporter, "If one day passes without me writing any more vagina jokes, my career is blown" and noted that "our tolerance for what is edgy is changing" (M. E. Williams, 2011). Is it? Is this a case of the media leading society or mirroring it?

2. *Prosocial content.* How would you go about making a prosocial soap opera that would appeal to teenagers and young adults and contain sexually responsible language, discussions, and behavior but not lose the audience with a "goody-two-shoes" program?

3. *Sex education.* For the first decade in the new millennium, the federal government only funded abstinence-only sex education. More than $1 billion has been spent on such sex education (Sexuality Information and Education Council of the United States, 2006), despite the lack of any convincing evidence that abstinence-only sex education actually works (Government Accountability Office, 2006; Santelli et al., 2006; Trenholm et al., 2007). Do you think abstinence-only sex ed is effective when the media are apparently *not* "abstinence only"?

4. *Media literacy.* Is there a media literacy approach to sex education that might work to decrease the impact of media on sexual attitudes and beliefs? What components would it have (see Chapter 12)? How would sex education teachers be able to avoid "family values" issues if they discussed programming with sexual content?

5. *Sexuality research.* How could research be sensitively designed to assess what children learn from sexual content in the media?

6. *Contraception and erectile dysfunction medication ads.* Figure 5.23 shows two actual print ads for condoms. Figure 5.19 shows two ads for emergency contraception. Is there a difference between advertising "regular" birth control and advertising emergency contraception? For which magazines would each be appropriate? Do the ads target different audiences? What other possibilities can you think of that might appeal specifically to all teenagers? To teenagers who are African American or Hispanic? To males? To females? How do these ads differ from other, "mainstream" ads? Are these ads effective?

Figure 5.23 Condom ads.

In June 2007, both CBS and FOX rejected an ad for Trojans because "advertising must stress health-related uses rather than the prevention of pregnancy," according to one network executive (Newman, 2007). The ad (http://www.youtube.com/watch?v=U6krr40mdHM) shows women at a bar, surrounded by pigs. One pig goes to use the bathroom, returns with a condom he's purchased, and is magically transformed into an attractive man. The tagline is "Evolve: Use a condom every time." Do you think this ad is creative? Offensive? Effective?

In December 2006, an ad for Viagra aired at around 9 p.m. during a G-rated movie, *Prancer*, about a young girl who nurses one of Santa's reindeers back to health; a Levitra ad appeared during an afternoon broadcast of *Pee-wee's Big Adventure*, and an ad for Cialis appeared during an early-evening showing of *Miracle on 34th Street* (A. Johnson, 2007). In 2009, Representative Jim Moran (D-Va.) introduced H.R. 2175, which would prohibit any ED ads from airing on broadcast radio or TV between 6 a.m. and 10 p.m. (Ruff, 2009). The American Academy of Pediatrics has called for a voluntary ban on erectile dysfunction ads during prime-time TV (Roan, 2010). If you were in Congress, would you vote for such legislation?

7. *HIV/AIDS prevention.* You are a school principal and are asked to view a sex ed video for possible inclusion in the curriculum. In it, a terminally ill AIDS patient, cachectic and stripped to the waist, stares straight at the camera and says, "Kids, if you have sex once, with the wrong person, you may die." Your brother died from AIDS a year ago, and this video affects you deeply. Should you approve it for use in the classroom?

8. *The Internet.* (1) In Shanghai, China, the government is providing sex education via the Internet (Lou, Zhao, Gao, & Shah, 2006). Is this a good idea? Can you see any drawbacks? (2) In one study of 1,500 Internet users, ages 10 to 17 years, 42% reported exposure to online pornography (two-thirds reported it was unwanted) (Wolak et al., 2007). What solutions exist to shield children and teens from online pornography? Effective December 6, 2011, the Internet's oversight agency instituted an ".xxx" domain for pornography on the Web. Domains are for sale for $60 each, but adult sites are not required to use the domain (Pachal, 2011). Will that work?

9. *Celebrities.* In March 2007, the Associated Press initiated a self-imposed week-long ban on reporting anything about Paris Hilton ("AP: We Ignored," 2007). Was that a reasonable thing to do? A month earlier, *Newsweek*'s cover story was "Girls Gone Wild: What Are Celebs Teaching Kids?" (Deveny & Kelley, 2007). Find the story and discuss it. Why are Paris Hilton and Kim Kardashian celebrities, and should they be? What do you think of Lady Gaga as a role model for children and teenagers? How does someone become famous in American culture?

10. *Young girls.* Recently, the American Psychological Association issued its report on the increasing sexualization of young girls (Zurbriggen et al., 2010). In covering the story, one news reporter wrote, "Ten-year-old girls can slide their low-cut jeans over 'eye-candy' panties. French maid costumes, garter belt included, are available in preteen sizes. Barbie now comes in a 'bling-bling' style, replete with halter top and go-go boots. . . . American girls, say experts, are increasingly being fed a cultural catnip of products and images that promote looking and acting sexy" (Weiner, 2007, p. HE01). Is this a relatively new problem or an ongoing one? Read the executive summary of the

report and see if you agree with the many recommendations (www.apa.org). How easy would it be to change the portrayal of sexuality in American society, and what will it take to do so?

11. *Teen pregnancy and abortion.* In 2006 and 2007, several movies seemed to portray teen pregnancy and single motherhood in a new light. According to one prominent columnist, "by some screenwriter consensus, abortion has become the right-to-choose that's never chosen. In *Knocked Up*, it was referred to as 'shmashmortion.' In *Juno*, the abortion clinic looks like a punk-rock tattoo parlor" (Goodman, 2008, January 5, p. A8). Other observers agree (Rickey, 2007, p. B8). Do you think this is a new trend? Is it "healthy," and will it have real-life repercussions?

12. *Preventing teen pregnancy.* In 2009, officials in Leicester, England (about 100 miles north of London), produced a gritty video simulation of a schoolyard birth (http://www.youtube.com/watch?v=frHOZn3tpdQ) in an attempt to decrease the teen pregnancy rate in the area, which was eight times the national average. The video was recorded on a cell phone and ends with the words, "Now what you expected? Being a teenage parent might not be either." Officials made no apologies for the graphic video. "Hairs on the back of my neck do stand up, but you know teenage pregnancy is a hard-hitting issue and we've got lots of teenage pregnancies in our city," one official was quoted as saying (Zuckerbrod, 2009). Was this a good idea? Do "scare tactics" work with adolescents? Can you think of alternative media approaches to the problem?

References

Abma, J. C., Martinez, G. M., & Copen, C. E. (2010). Teenagers in the United States: Sexual activity, contraceptive use, and childbearing, National Survey of Family Growth 2006–2008. *Vital Health Statistics, 23*(30), 1–47.

Advocates for Youth. (2011). *Adolescent sexual health in Europe and the U.S.* Retrieved from http://www.advocatesforyouth.org/publications/419?task=view

Agha, S., & Meekers, D. (2010). Impact of an advertising campaign on condom use in urban Pakistan. *Studies in Family Planning, 41,* 277–290.

Agovino, T. (2007, January 24). *Levitra, Viagra running new ad campaigns.* Retrieved from http://www.washingtonpost.com/wp-dyn/content/article/2006/05/02/AR2006050200857.html

Alexy, E. M., Burgess, A. W., & Prentky, R. A. (2009). Pornography use as a risk marker for an aggressive pattern of behavior among sexually reactive children and adolescents. *Journal of the American Psychiatric Nurses Association, 14,* 442–453.

Alter, J. (1994, January 17). The power to change what's "cool." *Newsweek,* p. 23.

American Pie 2: Editorial reviews [Product description]. (n.d.). Retrieved May 24, 2006, from http://www.amazon.com/gp/product/B00003CY6D

Ansen, D. (1999, September 13). A handful of tangos in Paris. *Newsweek,* p. 66.

AP: We ignored Paris Hilton. (2007, March 4). Retrieved from CNN.com

Armstrong, J. (2011, January 28). Gay teens on TV. *Entertainment Weekly, 1139,* 34-41.

Arnett, J. J. (2002). The sounds of sex: Sex in teens' music and music videos. In J. D. Brown, J. R. Steele, & K. Walsh-Childers (Eds.), *Sexual teens, sexual media* (pp. 253–264). Mahwah, NJ: Lawrence Erlbaum.

Ashby, S. L., Arcari, C. M., & Edmonson, M. B. (2006). Television viewing and risk of sexual initiation by young adolescents. *Archives of Pediatrics and Adolescent Medicine, 160,* 375–380.

Ashby, S. L., & Rich, M. (2005). Video killed the radio star: The effects of music videos on adolescent health. *Adolescent Medicine: State of the Art Reviews, 16,* 371–393.

Associated Press & MTV. (2009, September 23). AP-MTV digital abuse study [Executive summary]. Retrieved from http://www.athinline.org/MTV-AP_Digital_Abuse_Study_Executive_Summary.pdf

Aubrey, J. S., Behm-Morawitz, E., & Kim, K. (2013, in press). Understanding the effects of MTV's *16 and Pregnant* on adolescent girls' beliefs, attitudes, and behavioral intentions toward teen pregnancy. *Journal of Health Communication.*

Aubrey, J. S., Harrison, K., Kramer, L., & Yellin, J. (2003). Variety versus timing: Gender differences in college students' sexual expectations as predicted by exposure to sexually oriented television. *Communication Research, 30,* 432–460.

Bagdasarov, Z., Greene, K., Banerjee, S. C., Krcmar, M., Yanovitzky, I., & Ruginyte, D. (2010). I am what I watch: Voyeurism, sensation seeking, and television viewing patterns. *Journal of Broadcasting and Electronic Media, 54,* 299–315.

Baird, J. (2010, October 4). The shame of family films. *Newsweek.* Retrieved from http://www.thedailybeast.com/newsweek/2010/09/22/why-family-films-are-so-sexist.html

Ballam, S. M., & Granello, P. F. (2011). Confronting sex in the media: Implications and counseling recommendations. *Sex Roles, 19,* 421–426.

Batchelor, S. A., Kitzinger, J., & Burtney, E. (2004). Representing young people's sexuality in the "youth" media. *Health Education Research, 19,* 669–676.

Battaglio, S. (2010, October 10). The future of TV is now. *TV Guide,* pp. 22–23.

Baumgartner, S. E., Sumter, S. R., Peter, J., & Valkenburg, P. M. (2012). Identifying teens at risk: Developmental pathways of online and offline sexual risk behavior. *Pediatrics, 130,* 1–8.

Bayer HealthCare Pharmaceuticals. (2011). *"Clueless or clued up: Your right to be informed about contraception" media report.* Retrieved from http://www.ippf.org/NR/rdonlyres/BA30AEF4-2C7C-40F6-B8C7-BFFC882F8333/5706/CluelessOrCluedUpReport.pdf

Beckett, M. K., Elliott, M. N., Martino, S., Kanouse, D. E., Coronoa, R., Klein, D. J., & Schuster, M. A. (2010). Timing of parent and child communication about sexuality relative to children's sexual behaviors. *Pediatrics, 125,* 34-42.

Bennett, L. (2003). *TV commercials exploit, ridicule or sideline women* [Press release]. Retrieved from http://www.now.org/nnt/spring-2003/superbowl.html

Bersamin, M. M., Bourdeau, B., Fisher, D. A., & Grube, J. W. (2010). Television use, sexual behavior, and relationship status at last oral sex and vaginal intercourse. *Sexuality and Culture, 14,* 157–168.

Bersamin, M. M., Todd, M., Fisher, D. A., Hill, D. L., Grube, J. W., & Walker, S. (2008). Parenting practices and adolescent sexual behavior: A longitudinal study. *Journal of Marriage and Family, 70,* 97–112.

Blake, S. M., Ledsky, R., Goodenow, C., Sawyer, R., Lohrmann, D., & Windsor, R. (2003). Condom availability programs in Massachusetts high schools: Relationships with condom use and sexual behavior. *American Journal of Public Health, 93,* 955–962.

Bleakley, A., Hennessy, M., & Fishbein, M. (2006). Public opinion on sex education in US schools. *Archives of Pediatrics and Adolescent Medicine, 160,* 1151–1156.

Bleakley, A., Hennessy, M., & Fishbein, M. (2011). A model of adolescents' seeking of sexual content in their media choices. *Journal of Sex Research, 48,* 309–315.

Bleakley, A., Hennessy, M., Fishbein, M., & Jordan A. (2008). It works both ways: The relationship between exposure to sexual content in the media and adolescent sexual behavior. *Media Psychology, 11,* 443–461.

Bleakley, A., Hennessy, M., Fishbein, M., & Jordan, A. (2009). How sources of sexual information relate to adolescents' beliefs about sex. *American Journal of Health Behavior, 33,* 37–48.

Bleakley, A., Jamieson, P. E., & Romer, D. (2012). Trends in sexual and violent content by gender in top-grossing U.S. films, 1950–2006. *Journal of Adolescent Health, 51,* 73–79.

Bobkowski, P. S., Brown, J. D., & Neffa, D. R. (2012). "Hit me up and we can get down": US youths' risk behaviors and sexual self-disclosure in MySpace profiles. *Journal of Children and Media, 6,* 119–134.

Borzekowski, D. L. G., McCarthy, C., & Rosenfeld, W. (2012). Ten years of TeenHealthFX.com: A case study of an adolescent health website. *Pediatric Clinics of North America, 59,* 717–728.

Boyar, R., Levine, D., & Zensius, N. (2011). *TECHsex USA: Youth sexuality and reproductive health in the digital age.* Oakland, CA: ISIS.

Braun, R., Howard, H., & Madsen, A. (2010, February 26–27). *Implementing a text-message-based sexual health information and clinic referral service for California youth.* Paper presented at SexTech conference, San Francisco, CA.

Braun-Courville, D. K., & Rojas, M. (2009). Exposure to sexually explicit Web sites and adolescent sexual attitudes and behaviors. *Journal of Adolescent Health, 45,* 156–162.

Brenton, S., & Cohen, R. (2003). *Shooting people: Adventures in reality TV.* New York, NY: Verso.

Bridges, A. J., Wosnitzer, R., Scharrer, E., Sun, C., & Liberman, R. (2010). Aggression and sexual behavior in best-selling pornography videos: A content analysis update. *Violence Against Women, 16,* 1065–1085.

Brodesser-akner, C. (2007, September 17). Sex on TV is OK as long as it's not safe. *Advertising Age.* Retrieved from http://adage.com/article/news/sex-tv-long-safe/120489/

Brodie, M., Foehr, U., Rideout, V., Baer, N., Miller, C., Flournoy, R., & Altman, D. (2001). Communicating health information through the entertainment media. *Health Affairs, 20,* 1–8.

Brown, D., & Bryant, J. (1989). Uses of pornography. In D. Zillmann & J. Bryant (Eds.), *Pornography: Research advances and policy considerations* (pp. 3–24). Hillsdale, NJ: Lawrence Erlbaum.

Brown, J. D. (2006). Media literacy has potential to improve adolescents' health. *Journal of Adolescent Health, 39,* 459–460.

Brown, J. D. (Ed.). (2008). *Managing the media monster: The influence of media (from television to text messages) on teen sexual behavior and attitudes.* Washington, DC: National Campaign to Prevent Teen and Unplanned Pregnancy.

Brown, J. D., Halpern, C. T., & L'Engle, K. L. (2005). Mass media as a sexual super peer for early maturing girls. *Journal of Adolescent Health, 36,* 420–427.

Brown, J. D., & L'Engle, K. L. (2009). X-rated: Sexual attitudes and behaviors associated with U.S. early adolescents' exposure to sexually explicit media. *Communication Research, 36,* 129–151.

Brown, J. D., L'Engle, K. L., Pardun, C. H., Guo, G., Kenneavy, K., & Jackson, C. (2006). Sexy media matter: Exposure to sexual content in music, movies, television, and magazines predicts Black and White adolescents' sexual behavior. *Pediatrics, 117,* 1018–1027.

Brown, J. D., & Pardun, C. J. (2004). Little in common: Racial and gender differences in adolescents' television diets. *Journal of Broadcasting and Electronic Media, 48,* 266–278.

Brown, J. D., & Schulze, L. (1990). The effects of race, gender, and fandom on audience interpretations of Madonna's music videos. *Journal of Communication, 40,* 88–102.

Brown, J. D., & Steele, J. R. (1995). *Sex and the mass media.* Menlo Park, CA: Kaiser Family Foundation.

Brown, J. D., & Strasburger, V. C. (2007). From Calvin Klein, to Paris Hilton and MySpace: Adolescents, sex & the media. *Adolescent Medicine: State of the Art Reviews, 18,* 484–507.

Buhi, E. R., Daley, E. M., Oberne, A., Smith, S. A., Schneider, T., & Furhrmann, H. J. (2010). Quality and accuracy of sexual health information Web sites visited by young people. *Journal of Adolescent Health, 47,* 206–208.

Bull, S. S., Levine, D. K., Black, S. R., Schmiege, S. J., & Santelli, J. (2012). Social media–delivered sexual health intervention: A cluster randomized controlled trial. *American Journal of Preventive Medicine, 43,* 467–474.

Bull, S. S., Posner, S. F., Ortiz, C., Beaty, B., Benton, K., Lin, L., . . . Evans, T. (2008). POWER for reproductive health: Results from a social marketing campaign promoting female and male condoms. *Journal of Adolescent Health, 43,* 71–78.

Calzo, M. A., & Ward, L. M. (2009). Media exposure and viewers' attitudes toward homosexuality: Evidence for mainstreaming or resonance? *Journal of Broadcasting and Electronic Media, 53,* 280–299.

Carpentier, F. D., Knobloch-Westerwick, S., & Blumhoff, A. (2007). Naughty versus nice: Pop music influences on perceptions of romantic partners. *Media Psychology, 9,* 1–17.

Carroll, J. S., Padilla-Walker, L. M., Nelson, L. J., Olson, C. D., Barry, C. M., & Madsen, S. D. (2008). Generation XXX: Pornography acceptance and use among emerging adults. *Journal of Adolescent Research, 23,* 6–30.

Carroll, L. (2010, September 27). Erectile dysfunction ads too hot for primetime? *MSNBC.com.* Retrieved from http://www.msnbc.msn.com/id/39348004/ns/health-childrens_health/t/erectile-dysfunction-ads-too-hot-primetime/#

Carson, V., Pickett, W., & Janssen, I. (2011). Screen time and risk behaviors in 10- to 16-year-old Canadian youth. *Preventive Medicine, 52,* 99–103.

Carter, B. (2011a, September 21). This year's hot TV trend is anatomically correct. *New York Times.* Retrieved from http://www.nytimes.com/2011/09/22/arts/television/this-years-hot-tv-trend-is-a-word.html?pagewanted=all

Carter, B. (2010b, September 13). Tired of reality TV, but still tuning in. *New York Times.* Retrieved from http://www.nytimes.com/2010/09/13/business/media/13reality.html

Case, T. (2007, February 26). Trouble in teen land. *AllBusiness.com.* Retrieved from http://www.all business.com/services/business-services-miscellaneous-business/4845708-1.html

Cavazos-Rehg, P. A., Krauss, M. J., Spitznagel, E. L., Iguchi, M., Schootman, M., Cottler, L., . . . Bierut, L. J. (2012). Associations between sexuality education in schools and adolescent birthrates. *Archives of Pediatrics and Adolescent Medicine, 166,* 134–140.

Centers for Disease Control and Prevention. (1993). Sexual risk behaviors of STD clinic patients before and after Earvin "Magic" Johnson's HIV-infection announcement—Maryland, 1991–1992. *Morbidity and Mortality Weekly Report, 42,* 45–48.

Centers for Disease Control and Prevention. (2011a). *Sexually transmitted disease surveillance 2010.* Atlanta, GA: U.S. Department of Health and Human Services.

Centers for Disease Control and Prevention. (2011b). Vital signs: Teen pregnancy—United States, 1991–2009. *Morbidity and Mortality Weekly Report, 60*(13), 414–420.

Centers for Disease Control and Prevention. (2012a). Prepregnancy contraceptive use among teens with unintended pregnancies resulting in live births—Pregnancy Risk Assessment Monitoring System (PRAMS), 2004–2008. *Morbidity and Mortality Weekly Report, 61,* 25–29.

Centers for Disease Control and Prevention. (2012b). Youth Risk Behavior Surveillance—United States, 2011. *Morbidity and Mortality Weekly Report, 61*(SS-4), 1–162.

Chandra, A., Martino, S. C., Collins, R. L., Elliott, M. N., Berry, S. H., Kanouse, D. E., & Miu, A. (2008). Does watching sex on television predict teen pregnancy? Findings from a national longitudinal survey of youth. *Pediatrics, 122,* 1047–1054.

Chandra, A., Mosher, W. D., Copen, C., & Sionean, C. (2011). Sexual behavior, sexual attraction, and sexual identity in the United States: Data from the 2006–2008 National Survey of Family Growth. *National Health Statistic Reports, 36,* 1–36.

Cheng, Y., Lou, C., Gao, E., & Zabin, L. S. (2013, in press). Unmarried adolescents' and youth's sex-related knowledge, attitudes and behaviors in three Asian cities: The role of media variables. *Journal of Adolescent Health.*

Chia, S. C. (2006). How peers mediate media influence on adolescents' sexual attitudes and sexual behavior. *Journal of Communication, 56,* 585–606.

Christenson, P., & Ivancin, M. (2006). *The "reality" of health: Reality television and the public health.* Menlo Park, CA: Kaiser Family Foundation.

Clarke, J. N. (2010). The paradoxical portrayal of the risk of sexually transmitted infections and sexuality in US magazines *Glamour* and *Cosmopolitan* 2000–2007. *Health, Risk and Society, 12,* 560–574.

Clark-Flory, T. (2012, April 1). Facebook: The next tool in fighting STDs. *Salon.* Retrieved from http://www.salon.com/2012/04/01/facebook_the_next_tool_in_fighting_stds

Collins, R. L., Elliott, M. N., Berry, S. H., Kanouse, E., & Hunter, S. B. (2003). Entertainment television as a healthy sex educator: The impact of condom-efficacy information in an episode of *Friends. Pediatrics, 112,* 1115–1121.

Collins, R. L., Elliott, M. N., Berry, S. H., Kanouse, D. E., Kunkel, D., Hunter, S. B., & Miu, A. (2004). Watching sex on television predicts adolescent initiation of sexual behavior. *Pediatrics, 114,* e280–e289.

Collins, R. L., Martino, S. C., & Shaw, R. (2011). *Influence of new media on adolescent sexual health: Evidence and opportunities.* Santa Monica, CA: RAND.

Comstock, G., & Strasburger, V. C. (1993). Media violence: Q&A. *Adolescent Medicine: State of the Art Reviews, 4,* 495–510.

Conrad, M. A., Dixon, T. L., & Zhang, Y. (2009). Controversial rap themes, gender portrayals and skin tone distortion: A content analysis of rap music videos. *Journal of Broadcasting and Electronic Media, 53,* 134–156.

Cope-Farrar, K. M., & Kunkel, D. (2002). Sexual messages in teens' favorite prime-time TV programs. In J. D. Brown, J. R. Steele, & K. Walsh-Childers (Eds.), *Sexual teens, sexual media* (pp. 59–78). Mahwah, NJ: Lawrence Erlbaum.

Copen, C. E., Chandra, A., & Martinez, G. (2012). *Prevalence and timing of oral sex with opposite-sex partners among females and males aged 15-24 years: United States, 2007–2010* (National Health Statistics Report No. 56). Hyattsville, MD: National Center for Health Statistics.

Council on Communications and Media. (2009). Impact of music, music lyrics, and music videos on children and youth. *Pediatrics, 124,* 1488–1494.

Council on Communications and Media. (2010). Media education. *Pediatrics, 126,* 1012–1017.

Cox Communications, National Center for Missing & Exploited Children. (2009, May). *Teen online & wireless safety survey: Cyberbullying, sexting, and parental controls.* Atlanta, GA: Author.

Coy, M., & Horvath, M. A. H. (2011). Lads' mags, young men's attitudes towards women and acceptance of myths about sexual aggression. *Feminism and Psychology, 21,* 144–150.

Coyne, S. M., & Archer, J. (2004). Indirect aggression in the media: A content analysis of British television programs. *Aggressive Behavior, 30,* 254–271.

Coyne, S. M., Robinson, S. L., & Nelson, D. A. (2010). Does reality backbite? Physical, verbal, and relational aggression in reality television programs. *Journal of Broadcasting and Electronic Media, 54,* 282–298.

C. S. Mott Children's Hospital, National Poll on Children's Health. (2012). *For youth sexting: Public supports education, not criminal charges.* Retrieved from http://www.mottnpch.org/reports-surveys/youth-sexting-public-supports-education-not-criminal-charges

DeJong, W., Wolf, R. C., & Austin, S. B. (2001). U.S. federally funded television public service announcements (PSAs) to prevent HIV/AIDS: A content analysis. *Journal of Health Communication, 6,* 249–262.

Delgado, H., Austin, S. B., Rich, M., & Bickham, D. (2009, May 4). Exposure to adult-targeted television and movies during childhood increases risk of initiation of early intercourse [Abstract]. Presented at the Pediatric Academic Societies meeting, Baltimore, MD.

Deveny, K., & Kelley, R. (2007, February 12). Girls gone wild: What are celebs teaching kids? *Newsweek,* pp. 40–47.

Donnerstein, E., Linz, D., & Penrod, S. (1987). *The question of pornography: Research findings and policy implications.* New York, NY: Free Press.

Downs, J. S., Murray, P. J., Bruine de Bruin, W., Penrose, J., Palmgren, C., & Fischhoff, B. (2004). Interactive video behavioral intervention to reduce adolescent females' STD risk: A randomized controlled trial. *Social Science and Medicine, 59,* 1561–1572.

Doyle, S. (2010, September 20). *Easy A*: A teen sex comedy, minus the sex. *Atlantic.* Retrieved from http://www.theatlantic.com/entertainment/archive/2010/09/easy-a-a-teen-sex-comedy-minus-the-sex/63249/

Draper, N. R. A. (2012). Is your teen at risk? Discourses of adolescent sexting in United States television news. *Journal of Children and Media, 6,* 221–236.

Duffy, M., & Gotcher, J. M. (1996). Crucial advice on how to get the guy: The rhetorical vision of power and seduction in the teen magazine *YM. Journal of Communication, 20,* 32–48.

DuRant, R. H., Wolfson, M., LaFrance, B., Balkrishnan, R., & Altman, D. (2006). An evaluation of a mass media campaign to encourage parents of adolescents to talk to their children about sex. *Journal of Adolescent Health, 38,* 298e1–298e9.

Elkind, D. (1984, November/December). Teenage thinking: Implications for health care. *Pediatric Nursing,* pp. 383–385.

Elkind, D. (1993). *Parenting your teenager in the 90's.* Rosemont, NJ: Modern Learning Press.

Emmers-Sommer, T. M., Pauley, P., Hanzal, A., & Triplett, L. (2006). Love, suspense, sex, and violence: Men's and women's film predilections, exposure to sexually violent media, and their relationship to rape myth acceptance. *Sex Roles, 55,* 311–320.

Escobar-Chaves, S. L., Tortolero, S. R., Markham, C. M., Low, B. J., Eitel, P., & Thickstun, P. (2005). Impact of the media on adolescent sexual attitudes and behaviors. *Pediatrics, 116,* 303–326.

Espey, E., Cosgrove, E., & Ogburn, T. (2007). Family planning American style: Why it's so hard to control birth in the US. *Obstetrics and Gynecology Clinics of North America, 34,* 1–17.

Evans, W. D., Davis, K. C., Umanzor, C., Patel, K., & Khan, M. (2011). Evaluation of sexual communication message strategies. *Reproductive Health, 8,* 15.

Eyal, K., & Kunkel, D. (2008). The effects of sex in television drama shows on emerging adults' sexual attitudes and moral judgments. *Journal of Broadcasting and Electronic Media, 52,* 161–181.

Eyal, K., Kunkel, D., Biely, E. N., & Finnerty, K. L. (2007). Sexual socialization messages on television programs most popular among teens. *Journal of Broadcasting and Electronic Media, 51,* 316–336.

Fard, M. F. (2012, July 16). Web videos address questions on sex, birth control, sexually transmitted diseases. *Washington Post.* Retrieved from http://www.washingtonpost.com/national/health-science/web-videos-address-questions-on-sex-birth-control-sexually-transmitted-diseases/2012/07/16/gJQA6Oi5oW_story.html

Farrar, K. M. (2006). Sexual intercourse on television: Do safe sex messages matter? *Journal of Broadcasting and Electronic Media, 50,* 635–650.

Ferguson, C. J., Salmond, K., & Modi, K. (2013). Reality television predicts both positive and negative outcomes for adolescent girls. *Journal of Adolescent Health,* published online Jan. 7. DOI = 10.1016/j.jpeds.2012.11.037.

Ferguson, T., Berlin, J., & Noles, E. (2005). Variation in the application of the "promiscuous female" female stereotype and the nature of the application domain: Influences on sexual harassment judgments after exposure to *The Jerry Springer Show. Journal of Broadcasting and Electronic Media, 50,* 635–650.

Ferris, A. L., Smith, S. W., Greenberg, B. S., & Smith, S. L. (2007). The content of reality dating shows and viewer perceptions of dating. *Journal of Communication, 57,* 490–510.

Finer, L. B., & Kost, K. (2011). Unintended pregnancy rates at the state level. *Perspectives on Sexual and Reproductive Health, 43,* 78–87.

Fisher, D. A., Hill, D. L., Grube, J. W., Bersamin, M. M., Walker, S., & Gruber, E. L. (2009). Televised sexual content and parental mediation: Influences on adolescent sexuality. *Media Psychology, 12,* 121–147.

Fischer, P., & Greitemeyer, T. (2006). Music and aggression: The impact of sexual-aggressive song lyrics on aggression-related thoughts, emotions, and behavior toward the same and opposite sex. *Personality and Social Psychology Bulletin, 32,* 1165–1176.

Fisher, D. A., Hill, D. L., Grube, J. W., Bersamin, M. M., Walker, S., & Gruber, E. L. (2009). Televised sexual content and parental mediation: Influences on adolescent sexuality. *Media Psychology, 12,* 121–147.

Fisher, L. (2010, December 23). MTV airing teen abortion special, "No Easy Decision." *ABC News.* Retrieved from http://abcnews.go.com/Entertainment/mtv-airing-teen-abortion-special-easy-decison/story?id=12458576

Flood, M. (2009, July 11). The extent of exposure to pornography among children and young people. *XY Online.* Retrieved from http://www.xyonline.net/content/extent-exposure-pornography-among-children-and-young-people

Folb, K. L. (2000). "Don't touch that dial!" TV as a—what!?—positive influence. *SIECUS Report, 28,* 16–18.

Fouts, G., & Inch, R. (2005). Homosexuality in TV situation comedies. *Journal of Homosexuality, 49,* 35–45.

Furstenberg, F. F., Jr., Geitz, L. M., Teitler, J. O., & Weiss, C. C. (1997). Does condom availability make a difference? An evaluation of Philadelphia's health resource centers. *Family Planning Perspectives, 29,* 123–127.

Gay & Lesbian Alliance Against Defamation. (2011). *2011: Where are we on TV?* Los Angeles, CA: Author.

Glieberman, O. (1999, July 16). Virgin megascore. *Entertainment Weekly,* pp. 43–44.

Goodman, E. (2008, January 5). Real teen pregnancies don't have Hollywood ending. *Albuquerque Journal,* p. A8.

Gordon-Messer, D., Bauermeister, J.A., Grodzinski, A., & Zimmerman, M. (2012). Sexting among young adults. *Journal of Adolescent Health.* doi: 10.1016/j.jadohealth.2012.05.013

Gottfried, J. A., Vaala, S. E., Bleakley, A., Hennessy, M., & Jordan, A. (2011). Does the effect of exposure to TV sex on adolescent sexual behavior vary by genre? *Communication Research.* doi: 10.1177/0093650211415399

Government Accountability Office. (2006, October). Efforts to assess the accuracy and effectiveness of federally funded programs. *GAO Highlights.* Retrieved from http://www.gao.gov/cgi-bin/getrpt?GAO-07-87

Greenberg, B. S. (1994). Content trends in media sex. In D. Zillmann, J. Bryant, & A. C. Huston (Eds.), *Media, children, and the family: Social scientific, psychodynamic, and clinical perspectives* (pp. 165–182). Hillsdale, NJ: Lawrence Erlbaum.

Greenberg, B. S., & Busselle, R. W. (1994). *Soap operas and sexual activity.* Menlo Park, CA: Kaiser Family Foundation.

Greenberg, B. S., Siemicki, M., Dorfman, S., Heeter, C., & Stanley, C. (1993). Sex content in R-rated films viewed by adolescents. In B. S. Greenberg, J. D. Brown, & N. L. Buerkel-Rothfuss (Eds.), *Media, sex, and the adolescent* (pp. 45–58). Cresskill, NJ: Hampton.

Greenberg, B. S., Stanley, C., Siemicki, M., Heeter, C., Soderman, A., & Linsangan, R. (1993). Sex content on soaps and prime-time television series most viewed by adolescents. In B. S. Greenberg, J. D. Brown, & N. L. Buerkel-Rothfuss (Eds.), *Media, sex and the adolescent* (pp. 29–44). Cresskill, NJ: Hampton.

Greenfield, P., & Beagles-Roos, J. (1988). Television vs. radio: The cognitive impact on different socio-economic and ethnic groups. *Journal of Communication, 38,* 71–92.

Greenfield, P. M., Bruzzone, L., Koyamatsu, K., Satuloff, W., Nixon, K., Brodie, M., & Kingsdale, D. (1987). What is rock music doing to the minds of our youth? A first experimental look at the effects of rock music lyrics and music videos. *Journal of Early Adolescence, 7,* 315–329.

Guttmacher, S., Lieberman, L., Ward, D., Freudenberg, N., Radosh, A., & DesJarlais, D. (1997). Condom availability in New York City public high schools: Relationships to condom use and sexual behavior. *American Journal of Public Health, 87,* 1427–1433.

Gunasekera, H., Chapman, S., & Campbell, S. (2005). Sex and drugs in popular movies: An analysis of the top 200 films. *Journal of the Royal Society of Medicine, 9,* 464–470.

Guse, K., Levine, D., Martins, S., Lira, A., Gaarde, J., Westmorland, W., & Gilliam, M. (2012). Interventions using new digital media to improve adolescent sexual health: A systematic review. *Journal of Adolescent Health, 51,* 535–543.

Guy, R. J., Patton, G. C., & Kaldor, J. M. (2012). Internet pornography and adolescent health. *Medical Journal of Australia, 196,* 546–547.

Haag, P. (1999). *Voices of a generation: Teenage girls on sex, school, and self.* Washington, DC: American Association of University Women Educational Foundation.

Haffner, D. W., & Kelly, M. (1987, March/April). Adolescent sexuality in the media. *SIECUS Report,* pp. 9–12.

Hald, G. M., & Malamuth, N. M. (2008). Self-perceived effects of pornography consumption. *Archives of Sexual Behavior, 37,* 614–625.

Hald, G. M., Malamuth, N. M., & Yuen, C. (2010). Pornography and attitudes supporting violence against women: Revisiting the relationship in nonexperimental studies. *Aggressive Behavior, 36,* 14–20.

Hall, P. C., West, J. H., & Hill, S. (2011). Sexualization in lyrics of popular music from 1959 to 2009: Implications for sexuality educators. *Sexuality and Culture.* Retrieved from http://www.springer link.com/content/u777062808r5j228/

Halpern, C.T., & Haydon, A. A. (2012). Sexual timetables for oral-genital, vaginal, and anal intercourse: Sociodemographic comparisons in a nationally representative sample of adolescents. *American Journal of Public Health, 102,* 1221–1228.

Halpern-Felsher, B. L., Cornell, J. L., Kropp, R. Y., & Tschann, J. M. (2005). Oral versus vaginal sex among adolescents: Perceptions, attitudes, and behaviors. *Pediatrics, 115,* 845–851.

Hamilton, B. E., & Ventura, S. J. (2012). Birth rates for U.S. teenagers reach historic lows for all age and ethnic groups (*NCHS Data Brief* No. 89). Hyattsville, MD: National Center for Health Statistics.

Harris, L., & Associates. (1987). *Attitudes about television, sex and contraception advertising.* New York, NY: Planned Parenthood Federation of America.

Hatoum, I. J., & Belle, D. (2004). Mags and abs: Media consumption and bodily concerns in men. *Sex Roles, 7,* 397–407.

Heintz-Knowles, K. E. (1996). *Sexual activity on daytime soap operas: A content analysis of five weeks of television programming.* Menlo Park, CA: Kaiser Family Foundation.

Hennessy, M., Bleakley, A., Fishbein, M., & Jordan, A. (2009). Estimating the longitudinal association between adolescent sexual behavior and exposure to sexual media content. *Journal of Sex Research, 46,* 1–11.

Herd, D. A. (2009). Changes in the prevalence of violent rap song lyrics 1979–1997. *Journal of Public Health Policy, 30,* 395–406.

Hickman, M. (2010, March 17). Condom TV ads get prime-time all-clear. *Independent.* Retrieved from http://www.independent.co.uk/news/media/advertising/condom-tv-ads-get-primetime-allclear-1922379.html

Hill, A. (2005). *Reality TV: Audiences and popular factual television.* Oxford, UK: Routledge.

Hobbs, D. R., & Gallup, G. G., Jr. (2011). Songs as a medium for embedded reproductive messages. *Evolutionary Psychology, 9,* 390–416.

Hoffman, J. (2011a, April 10). Fighting teenage pregnancy with MTV stars as Exhibit A. *New York Times.* Retrieved from http://www.nytimes.com/2011/04/10/fashion/10TEEN.html?pagewanted=all

Hoffman, J. (2011b, December 31). Sex education gets directly to youths, via text. *New York Times.* Retrieved from http://www.nytimes.com/2011/12/31/us/sex-education-for-teenagers-online-and-in-texts.html

Howe, A., Owen-Smith, V., & Richardson, J. (2002). The impact of a television soap opera on the NHS Cervical Screening Programme in the north west of England. *Journal of Public Health Medicine, 24,* 299–304.

Hughes, S. A. (2011, June 6). Sexting teens need education, not jail, New York lawmakers say. *Washington Post.* Retrieved from http://www.washingtonpost.com/blogs/blogpost/post/sexting-teens-need-education-not-jail-new-york-lawmakers-say/2011/06/06/AGsayOKH_blog.html

Huntemann, N., & Morgan, M. (2012). Media and identity development. In D. G. Singer & J. L. Singer (Eds.), *Handbook of children and the media* (2nd ed., pp. 303–319). Thousand Oaks, CA: Sage.

Huston, A. C., Wartella, E., & Donnerstein, E. (1998). *Measuring the effects of sexual content in the media: A report to the Kaiser Family Foundation.* Menlo Park, CA: Kaiser Family Foundation.

Jacobs, A. J., & Shaw, J. (1999, April 2). Virgin spring. *Entertainment Weekly,* pp. 10–11.

Jemmott, J. B., Jemmott, L. S., & Fong, G. T. (2010). Efficacy of a theory-based abstinence-only intervention over 24 months. *Archives of Pediatrics and Adolescent Medicine, 164,* 152–159.

Jensen, R. (2007). *Getting off: Pornography and the end of masculinity.* Cambridge, MA: South End Press.

Johnson, A. (2007, February 16). New impotence ads draw fire—just like the old ones. *Wall Street Journal,* p. B1.

Johnson, K. R., & Holmes, B. M. (2009). Contradictory messages: A content analysis of Hollywood-produced romantic comedy feature films. *Communication Quarterly, 57,* 352–373.

Jones, L. M., Mitchell, K. J., & Finkelhor, D. (2012). Trends in youth Internet victimization: Findings from three Youth Internet Safety Surveys 2000–2010. *Journal of Adolescent Health 50,* 179–186.

Joshi, S. P., Peter, J., & Valkenburg, P. M. (2011). Scripts of sexual desire and danger in US and Dutch teen girl magazines: A cross-national content analysis. *Sex Roles, 64,* 463–474.

Kaestle, C. E., Halpern, C. T., & Brown, J. D. (2007). Music videos, pro wrestling, and acceptance of date rape among middle school males and females: An exploratory analysis. *Journal of Adolescent Health, 40,* 185–187.

Kaiser Family Foundation. (2001, June 19). Public and networks getting comfortable with condom advertising on TV [Press release]. Menlo Park, CA: Author.

Kaiser Family Foundation. (2004). *Entertainment education and health in the United States.* Menlo Park, CA: Author.

Kaiser Family Foundation. (2006, August 14). FOX Networks Group, Kaiser Family Foundation hit "Pause" [Press release]. Menlo Park, CA: Author.

Kaiser Family Foundation. (2011). *Sexual health of adolescents and young adults in the United States.* Menlo Park, CA: Author.

Kaiser Family Foundation & Children Now. (1999). *Talking with kids about tough issues: A national survey of parents and kids.* Menlo Park, CA: Kaiser Family Foundation.

Kalichman, S. C., & Hunter, T. L. (1992). The disclosure of celebrity HIV infection: Its effects on public attitudes. *American Journal of Public Health, 82,* 1374–1376.

Kann, L., Brener, N., McManus, T., & Wechsler, H. (2012). HIV, other STD, and pregnancy prevention education in public secondary schools—45 states, 2008–2010. *Morbidity and Mortality Weekly Report, 61,* 222–228.

Keller, S. N., LaBelle, H., Karimi, N., & Gupta, S. (2002). STD/HIV prevention for teenagers: A look at the Internet universe. *Journal of Health Communication, 7,* 341–353.

Kelly, C. (2005, October 17). Realities of teen sex ignored in mainstream films. *Seattle Times.* Retrieved from http://www.seattletimes.nwsource.com

Kelly, J., & Smith, S. L. (2006). *Where the girls aren't: Gender disparity saturates G-rated films.* Duluth, MN: Dads & Daughters.

Kilbourne, J. (1999). *Deadly persuasion: Why women and girls must fight the addictive power of advertising.* New York, NY: Free Press.

Kim, J. L., Collins, R. L., Kanouse, D. E., Elliott, M. N., Berry, S. H., Hunter, S., . . . Kunkel, D. (2006). Sexual readiness, household policies, and other predictors of adolescents' exposure to sexual content in mainstream entertainment television. *Media Psychology, 8,* 449–471.

Kim, J. L., Sorsoli, C. L., Collins, K., Zylbergold, B. A., Schooler, D., & Tolman, D. L. (2007). From sex to sexuality: Exposing the heterosexual script on primetime network television. *Journal of Sex Research, 44,* 145–157.

Kirby, D., & Laris, B. A. (2009). Effective curriculum-based sex and STD/HIV programs for adolescents. *Child Development Perspectives, 3,* 21–29.

Kirby, D., Brener, N. D., Brown, N. L., Peterfreund, N., Hillard, P., & Harrist, R. (1999). The impact of condom distribution in Seattle schools on sexual behavior and condom use. *American Journal of Public Health, 89,* 182–187.

Kistler, M. E., & Lee, M. J. (2010). Does exposure to sexual hip-hop music videos influence the sexual attitudes of college students? *Mass Communication and Society, 13,* 67–86.

Klein, J. D., Brown, J. D., Childers, K. W., Oliveri, J., Porter, C., & Dykers, C. (1993). Adolescents' risky behavior and mass media use. *Pediatrics, 92,* 24–31.

Kristof, N. (2006, May 2). Beyond chastity belts. *New York Times,* p. A25.

Kubey, R., Banerjee, S. C., & Donovan, B. W. (2012). Media and the family. In D. G. Singer & J. L. Singer (Eds.), *Handbook of children and the media* (2nd ed., pp. 341–361). Thousand Oaks, CA: Sage.

Kunkel, D., Cope, K. M., & Biely, E. (1999). Sexual messages on television: Comparing findings from three studies. *Journal of Sex Research, 36,* 230–236.

Kunkel, D., Cope, K. M., & Colvin, C. (1996). *Sexual messages on family hour television: Content and context.* Menlo Park, CA: Kaiser Family Foundation.

Kunkel, D., Eyal, K., Finnerty, K., Biely, E., & Donnerstein, E. (2005). *Sex on TV 4: A biennial report to the Kaiser Family Foundation.* Menlo Park, CA: Kaiser Family Foundation.

Lagus, K. A., Bernat, D. H., Bearinger, L. H., Resnick, M. D., & Eisenberg, M. E. (2011). Parental perspectives on sources of sex information for young people. *Journal of Adolescent Health, 49,* 87–89.

Lampman, C., Rolfe-Maloney, B., David, E. J., Yan, M., McCermott, N., Winters, S., . . . Lathrop, R. (2002). Messages about sex in the workplace: A content analysis of primetime television. *Sexuality and Culture, 6,* 3–21.

Leahy, M. (2009). *Porn University XXX: What college students are really saying about sex on campus.* Chicago, IL: Northfield.

L'Engle, K. L., Brown, J. D., & Kenneavy, K. (2006). The mass media are an important context for adolescents' sexual behavior. *Journal of Adolescent Health, 38,* 186–192.

L'Engle, K. L., & Jackson, C. (2008). Socialization influences on early adolescents' cognitive susceptibility and transition to sexual intercourse. *Journal of Research on Adolescence, 18,* 353–378.

Lenhart, A. (2009, December 15). *Teens and sexting.* Washington, DC: Pew Research Center, Pew Internet & American Life Project, Millennials: A Portrait of Generation Next.

Levin, D. E., & Kilbourne, J. (2009). *So sexy so soon: The new sexualized childhood and what parents can do to protect their kids.* New York, NY: Ballantine.

Levine, D. (2011, May 10). Pop culture sex ed: What media teaches us about sexual health. *Huffington Post.* Retrieved from http://www.huffingtonpost.com/deb-levine/sex-ed_b_859192.html

Levine, D., McCright, J., Dobkin, L., Woodruff, A. J., & Klausner, J. D. (2008). *SexInfo: A sexual health text messaging service for San Francisco youth. American Journal of Public Health, 98,* 1–3.

Lightfoot, M., Comulada, W. S., & Stover, G. (2007). Computerized HIV preventive intervention for adolescents: Implications of efficacy. *American Journal of Public Health, 97,* 1027–1030.

Lindberg, L. D., & Maddow-Zimet, I. (2012). Consequences of sex education on teen and young adult sexual behaviors and outcomes. *Journal of Adolescent Health.* doi:10.1016/j.jadohealth.2011.12.028

Lindberg, L. D., Santelli, J. S., & Singh, S. (2006). Changes in formal sex education: 1995–2002. *Journal of Adolescent Health, 38,* 182–189.

Lithwick , D. (2009, February 14). Textual misconduct: What to do about teens and their dumb naked photos of themselves. *Slate.com.* Retrieved from http://www.slate.com/articles/news_and_politics/jurisprudence/2009/02/textual_misconduct.html

Lo, D. (2011, March 24). Abercrombie is pushing push-up bikinis for 7-year old girls. *Racked.* Retrieved from http://racked.com/archives/2011/03/24/abercrombie-is-pushing-pushup-bikinis-for-7year-old-girls.php

Loftus, P. (2011, January 25). Glaxo pulls some ads, citing image. *Wall Street Journal.* Retrieved from http://online.wsj.com/article/SB10001424052748703555804576102113367709694.html

Lou, C.-H., Zhao, Q., Gao, E.-S., & Shah, I. H. (2006). Can the Internet be used effectively to provide sex education to young people in China? *Journal of Adolescent Health, 39,* 720–728.

Lounsbury, K., Mitchell, K. J., & Finkelhor, D. (2011). *The true prevalence of "sexting."* Retrieved from University of New Hampshire, Crimes Against Children Research Center website: http://www.unh.edu/ccrc/pdf/Sexting%20Fact%20Sheet%204_29_11.pdf

Luder, M-T., Pittet, I., Berchtold, A., Akre, C., Michaud, P. A., & Suris, J. C. (2011). Associations between online pornography and sexual behavior among adolescents: Myth or reality? *Archives of Sexual Behavior, 40,* 1027–1035.

Mager, J., & Helgeson, J. G. (2011). Fifty years of advertising images: Some changing perspectives on role portrayals along with enduring consistencies. *Sex Roles, 64,* 238–252.

Malamuth, N., & Huppin, M. (2005). Pornography and teenagers: The importance of individual differences. *Adolescent Medicine Clinics, 16,* 315–326.

Manganello, J. A., Henderson, V. R., Jordan, A., Trentacoste, N., Martin, S., Hennessy, M., & Fishbein, M. (2010). Adolescent judgment of sexual content on television: Implications for future content analysis research. *Journal of Sex Research, 47,* 364–373.

Mann, L. (2012, July 18). Credible online health information eludes collegians. *Chicago Tribune.* Retrieved from http://articles.chicagotribune.com/2012-07-18/health/ct-x-0718-birth-control-advice-20120718_1_emergency-contraception-abortion-pills-plan-b-one-step

Martin, D. (2010, February). MTV drops "Music Television" from the network logo. *Los Angeles Times.* Retrieved from http://latimesblogs.latimes.com/showtracker/2010/02/mtv-drops-music-television-from-its-logo.html

Martinez, G., Abma, J., & Copen, C. (2010). Educating teenagers about sex in the United States (NCHS Data Brief No. 44). Hyattsville, MD: National Center for Health Statistics.

Martinez, G., Copen, C. E., & Abma, J. C. (2011). Teenagers in the United States: Sexual activity, contraceptive use, and childbearing, 2006–2010 National Survey of Family Growth. *Vital Health Statistics, 23*(21), 1–44.

Martino, S. C., Collins, R. L., Elliott, M. N., Kanouse, D. E., & Berry, S. H. (2009). It's better on TV: Does television set teenagers up for regret following sexual initiation. *Perspectives on Sexual and Reproductive Health, 41,* 92–100.

Martino, S. C., Collins, R. L., Elliott, M. N., Strachman, A., Kanouse, D. E., & Berry, S. H. (2006). Exposure to degrading versus nondegrading music lyrics and sexual behavior among youth. *Pediatrics, 118,* e430–e441.

Martino, S. C., Collins, R. L., Kanouse, D. E., Elliott, M., & Berry, S. H. (2005). Social cognitive processes mediating the relationship between exposure to television's sexual content and adolescents' sexual behavior. *Journal of Personality and Social Psychology, 89,* 914–924.

Martino, S. C., Elliott, M. N., Corona, R., Kanouse, D. E., & Schuster, M. A. (2008). Beyond the "big talk": The roles of breadth and repetition in parent-adolescent communication about sexual topics. *Pediatrics, 121,* e612–e618.

Mazur, M. A., & Emmers-Sommer, T. M. (2002). The effect of movie portrayals on audience attitudes about nontraditional families and sexual orientation. *Journal of Homosexuality, 44,* 157–178.

Menard, A. D., & Kleinplatz, P. J. (2008). Twenty-one moves guaranteed to make his thighs go up in flames: Depictions of "great sex" in popular magazines. *Sexuality and Culture, 12,* 1–20.

Mitchell, K. J., Finkelhor, D., Jones, L. M., & Wolak, J. (2012). Prevalence and characteristics of youth sexting: A national study. *Pediatrics, 129,* 1–8.

Monea, E., & Thomas, A. (2011). Unintended pregnancy and taxpayer spending. *Perspectives on Sexual and Reproductive Health, 43,* 88–93.

Montemurro, B. (2003). Not a laughing matter: Sexual harassment as "material" on workplace-based situation comedies. *Sex Roles, 48,* 433–445.

Moreno, M. A., Brockman, L., Rogers, C. B., & Christakis, D. A. (2010). An evaluation of the distribution of sexual references among "top 8" MySpace friends. *Journal of Adolescent Health, 47,* 418–420.

Moreno, M. A., Brockman, L. N., Wasserheit, J. N., & Christakis, D. A. (2012, January 12). A pilot evaluation of older adolescents' sexual reference displays on Facebook®. *Journal of Sex Research.* doi: 10.1080/00224499.2011.642903

Moreno, M. A., & Kolb, J. (2012). Social networking sites and adolescent health. *Pediatric Clinics of North America, 59,* 601–612.

Moreno, M. A., Parks, M. R., Zimmerman, F. J., Brito, T. E., & Christakis, D. A. (2009). Display of health risk behavior on MySpace by adolescents. *Archives of Pediatrics and Adolescent Medicine, 163,* 27–34.

Moreno, M. A., Swanson, M. J., Royer, H., & Roberts, L. J. (2011). Sexpectations: Male college students' views about displayed sexual references on females' social networking Web sites. *Journal of Pediatric and Adolescent Gynecology, 24,* 85–89.

Moreno, M. A., VanderStoep, A., Parks, M. R., Zimmerman, F. J., Kurth, A., & Christakis, D. A. (2009). Reducing at-risk adolescents' display of risk behavior on a social networking Web site: A randomized controlled pilot intervention trial. *Archives of Pediatrics and Adolescent Medicine, 163,* 35–41.

Moreno, M. A., & Whitehill, J. M. (2012). New media, old risks. *Archives of Pediatrics and Adolescent Medicine.* doi:10.1001/archpediatrics.2012.1320

Morgan, M., Shanahan, J., & Signorielli, N. (2009). Growing up with television: Cultivation processes. In J. Bryant & M. B. Oliver (Eds.), *Media effects: Advances in theory and research* (3rd ed., pp. 34–49). New York, NY: Routledge.

Mosher, W. D., Chandra, A., & Jones, J. (2005). Sexual behavior and selected health measures: Men and women 15–44 years of age, United States, 2002. *Advance Data, 362,* 1–55.

Moyer, M. W. (2011, July/August). The sunny side of smut. *Scientific American Mind,* pp. 14–15.

Mozes, A. (2001, June 19). US TV viewers find condom ads acceptable. *Reuters Health.* Retrieved from www.reutershealth.com

Mueller, T. E., Gavin, L. E., & Kulkarni, A. (2008). The association between sex education and youth's engagement in sexual intercourse, age at first intercourse, and birth control use at first sex. *Journal of Adolescent Health, 42,* 89–96.

Mulvaney, E. (2012, April 5). Teens talk sex via text with new health initiative. *Houston Chronicle.* Retrieved from http://blog.chron.com/newswatch/2012/04/teens-talk-sex-via-text-with-new-health-initiative/

Murray, S., & Ouellette, L. (Eds.). (2004). *Reality TV: Remaking television culture.* New York, NY: New York University Press.

Nabi, R. L., & Clark, S. (2008). Exploring the limit of social cognitive theory: Why negatively reinforced behaviors on TV may be modeled anyway. *Journal of Communication, 58,* 407–427.

Nabi, R. L., Stitt, C. R., Halford, J., & Finnerty, K. L. (2006). Emotional and cognitive predictors of the enjoyment of reality-based and fictional television programming: An elaboration on the uses and gratifications perspective. *Media Psychology, 8,* 421–447.

National Campaign to Prevent Teen Pregnancy. (2004). *American opinion on teen pregnancy and related issues 2003.* Washington, DC: Author.

National Campaign to Prevent Teen and Unplanned Pregnancy. (2008). *Sex and tech.* Washington, DC: Author.

National Public Radio, Kaiser Family Foundation, & Kennedy School of Government. (2004). *Sex education in America: Principals survey.* Menlo Park, CA: Kaiser Family Foundation.

Nauert, R. (2012, April 17). Teen behaviors on Facebook focus of long-term study. *PsychCentral.* Retrieved from http://psychcentral.com/news/2012/04/17/teen-behaviors-on-facebook-focus-of-long-term-study/37445.html

Navarro, M. (2007, June 10). On abortion, Hollywood is no-choice. *New York Times*. Retrieved from http://www.nytimes.com/2007/06/10/fashion/10Knockedup.html?n=Top/Reference/Times Topics/People/N/Navarro, Mireya&adxnnl=1&adxnnlx=1325088846-LUljr0zFVs69XixNT5yg9w& pagewanted=print

Newman, A. A. (2007, June 18). Pigs with cellphones, but no condoms. *New York Times*. Retrieved from http://www.nytimes.com/2007/06/18/business/media/18adcol.html?_r=1&ref=media&oref=slogin

Nielsen Company. (2011a, March 10). *State of the media: TV usage trends: Q3 and Q4 2010*. Retrieved from http://blog.nielsen.com/nielsenwire/media_entertainment/tv-usage-trends-q3-and-q4-2010/

Nielsen Company. (2011b, June 8). *How the Class of 2011 engages with media*. Retrieved from http://blog.nielsen.com/nielsenwire/consumer/kids-today-how-the-class-of-2011-engages-with-media/

Nielsen Company. (2012, January 6). *State of the media: Consumer usage report 2011*. Retrieved from http://blog.nielsen.com/nielsenwire/mediauniverse/

Nielsen ratings, June 26–July 2. (2006). *USA Today*. Retrieved from http://www.usatoday.com/life/television/nielsenhtm.

Noar, S. M., Clark, A., Cole, C., & Lustria, M. L. A. (2006). Review of interactive safer sex Web sites: Practice and potential. *Health Communication, 20*, 233–241.

O'Hara, R. E., Gibbons, F. X., Gerrard, M., Li, Z., & Sargent J. D. (2012). Greater exposure to sexual content in popular movies predicts earlier sexual debut and increased sexual risk taking. *Psychological Science*. doi: 10.1177/0956797611435529

O'Sullivan, L. R. (2012). Open to the public: How adolescents blur the boundaries online between the private and public spheres of their lives. *Journal of Adolescent Health, 50*, 429–430.

One in three boys heavy porn users, study shows. (2007, February 23). *ScienceDaily*. Retrieved from http://www.sciencedaily.com/releases/2007/02/070223142813.htm

Pachal, P. (2011, December 6). New .xxx domain for porn debuts to mixed feelings. *USA Today*. Retrieved from http://www.usatoday.com/tech/news/story/2011-12-06/xxx-porn-domain/51680590/1

Pardun, C. (2002). Romancing the script: Identifying the romantic agenda in top-grossing movies. In J. D. Brown, J. R. Steele, & K. Walsh-Childers (Eds.), *Sexual teens, sexual media* (pp. 211–225). Mahwah, NJ: Lawrence Erlbaum.

Pardun, C. J., & Forde, K. R. (2006). Sexual content of television commercials watched by early adolescents. In T. Reichert & J. Lambiase (Eds.), *Sex in promotional culture: The erotic content of media and marketing* (pp. 125–139), Mahwah, NJ: Lawrence Earlbaum.

Pardun, C. J., L'Engle, K. L., & Brown, J. D. (2005). Linking exposures to outcomes: Early adolescents' consumption of sexual content in six media. *Mass Communication and Society, 8*, 75–91.

Parents Television Council. (2010). *Sexualized teen girls: Tinseltown's new target*. Retrieved from http://www.parentstv.org/FemaleSexualization/Study/Sexualized_Teen_Girls.pdf

Pazol, K., Zane, S. B., Parker, W. Y., Hall, L. R., Berg, C., & Cook, D. A. (2011). Abortion surveillance—United States, 2008. *Morbidity and Mortality Weekly Report, 60*(SS15), 1–41.

Pazos, B., Fullwood, E. U., Allan, M. J., Graff, C. A., Wilson, K. M., Laneri, H., & Klein, J. D. (2001, March 22). *Media use and sexual behaviors among Monroe County adolescents*. Paper presented at the annual meeting of the Society for Adolescent Medicine, San Diego, CA.

Perloff, R. M. (2009). Mass media, social perception, and the third-person effect. In J. Bryant & M. B. Oliver (Eds.), *Media effects: Advances in theory and research* (pp. 252–268). New York, NY: Routledge.

Perry, R. C., Kayekjian, K. C., Braun, R. A., Sheoran, B., & Chung, P. J. (2012). Adolescents' perspectives on the use of a text messaging service for preventive sexual health promotion. *Journal of Adolescent Health, 51*, 220–225.

Peter, J., & Valkenburg, P. M. (2006). Adolescents' exposure to sexually explicit online material and recreational attitudes toward sex. *Journal of Communication, 56*, 639–660.

Peter, J., & Valkenburg, P. M. (2008). Adolescents' exposure to sexually explicit Internet material and sexual preoccupancy: A three-wave panel study. *Media Psychology, 11,* 207–234.

Peter, J., & Valkenburg, P. M. (2009). Adolescents' exposure to sexually explicit Internet material and notions of women as sex objects: Assessing causality and underlying processes. *Journal of Communication, 59,* 407–433.

Peter, J., & Valkenburg, P. M. (2011). The influence of sexually explicit Internet material and peers on stereotypical beliefs about women's sexual roles: Similarities and differences between adolescents and adults. *Cyberpsychology, Behavior, and Social Networking, 14,* 511–517.

Phippen, A. (2009). *Sharing personal images and videos among young people.* South West Grid for Learning & University of Plymouth, UK. Retrieved from http://www.swgfl.org.uk/Staying-Safe/Sexting-Survey

Piaget, J. (1972). Intellectual evolution from adolescence to adulthood. *Human Development, 15,* 1–12.

Pinkleton, B. E., Austin, E. W., Cohen, M., Chen, Y.-C., & Fitzgerald, E. (2008). Effects of a peer-led media literacy curriculum on adolescents' knowledge and attitudes toward sexual behavior and media portrayals of sex. *Health Communication, 23,* 462–472.

Pinkleton, B. E., Austin, E. W., Chen, Y., & Cohen, M. (2012). The role of media literacy in shaping adolescents' understanding of and responses to sexual portrayals in mass media. *Journal of Health Communication, 17,* 460–476.

Pipher, M. (1997, February 1). Bland, beautiful, and boy-crazy. *TV Guide,* pp. 22–25.

Planned Parenthood Federation of America. (2006). *PPFA Maggie Awards: Ripped from the headlines.* Retrieved from http://www.plannedparenthood.org/pp2/portal/files

Powers, J., & Comstock, G. (2012). The rumors of television's demise have been greatly exaggerated: What the data say about the future of television content in a child's digital world. *Mass Communication and Journalism, 2,* 111.

Primack, B. A., Douglas, E. L., Fine, M. J., & Dalton, M. A. (2009). Exposure to sexual lyrics and sexual experience among urban adolescents. *American Journal of Preventive Medicine, 36,* 317–323.

Primack, B. A., Gold, M. A., Schwarz, E. B., & Dalton, M. A. (2008). Degrading and non-degrading sex in popular music: A content analysis. *Public Health Reports, 123,* 593–600.

Quindlen, A. (2009, March 16). Let's talk about sex. *Newsweek,* p. 62.

Pujazon-Zazik, M. A., Manasse, S. M., & Orrell-Valente, J. K. (2012). Adolescents' self-presentation on a teen dating Web site: A risk-content analysis. *Journal of Adolescent Health, 50,* 517–520.

Ralph, L. J., Berglas, N. F., Schwartz, S. L., & Brindis, C. D. (2011). Finding teens in TheirSpace: Using social networking sites to connect youth to sexual health services. *Sex Research and Social Policy, 8,* 38–49.

Reichelt, P. A. (1978). Changes in sexual behavior among unmarried teenage women utilizing oral contraception. *Journal of Population Behavior, 1,* 59–68.

Reichert, T., & Carpenter, C. (2004). An update on sex in magazine advertising: 1983 to 2003. *Journal of Mass Communication Quarterly, 81,* 823–837.

Rice, E., Rhoades, H., Winetrobe, H., Sanchez, M., Montoya, J., Plant, A., & Kordic, T. (2012). Sexually explicit cell phone messaging associated with sexual risk among adolescents. *Pediatrics, 130,* 667–673.

Rice, L. (2000, April 14). Ready to swear. *Entertainment Weekly,* pp. 20–21.

Rich, F. (2004, February 15). My hero, Janet Jackson. *New York Times,* section 2, p. 1.

Rich, M. (2008). Virtual sexuality: The influence of entertainment media on sexual attitudes and behavior. In J. D. Brown (Ed.), *Managing the media monster: The influence of media (from television to text messages) on teen sexual behavior and attitudes.* Washington, DC: National Campaign to Prevent Teen and Unplanned Pregnancy.

Rickey, C. (2007, December 7). The absent "a" word. *Albuquerque Journal,* p. B8.

Rideout, V. (2001). *Generation RX.com: How young people use the Internet for health information.* Menlo Park, CA: Kaiser Family Foundation.

Rideout, V. (2007). *Parents, children & media.* Menlo Park, CA: Kaiser Family Foundation.

Rideout, V. (2008). *Television as a health educator: A case study of* Grey's Anatomy. Menlo Park, CA: Kaiser Family Foundation.

Rideout, V. J., Foehr, U. G., & Roberts, D. F. (2010). *Generation M2: Media in the lives of 8- to 18-year-olds.* Menlo Park, CA: Kaiser Family Foundation.

Rivadeneyra, R., & Ward, L. M. (2005). From *Ally McBeal* to *Sabado Gigante:* Contributions of television viewing to the gender role attitudes of Latino adolescents. *Journal of Adolescent Research, 20,* 453–475.

Roan, S. (2010, August 29). Get erectile dysfunction ads out of prime time, nations' pediatricians say. *Los Angeles Times.* Retrieved from http://articles.latimes.com/2010/aug/29/news/la-heb-sex-20100829

Roberts, D. F., & Christenson, P. G. (2012). Popular music: The soundtrack of adolescence. In D. G. Singer & J. L. Singer (Eds.), *Handbook of children and the media* (2nd ed., pp. 479–500). Thousand Oaks, CA: Sage.

Roberts, D., Foehr, U., & Rideout, V. (2005). *Generation M: Media in the lives of 8-18 year olds.* Menlo Park, CA: Kaiser Family Foundation.

Roberts, E. (1983). Teens, sexuality and sex: Our mixed messages. *Television and Children, 6,* 9–12.

Romer, D., Sznitman, S., DiClemente, R., Salazar, L. F., Vanable, P. A., Carey, M. P., . . . Juzang, I. (2009). Mass media as an HIV-prevention strategy: using culturally sensitive messages to reduce HIV-associated sexual behavior of at-risk African American youth. *American Journal of Public Health, 99,* 2150–2159.

Ruff, B. (2009, May 7). Erectile dysfunction ads too hot for TV? *CNN.com.* Retrieved from http://am.blogs.cnn.com/2009/05/07/erectile-dysfunction-ads-too-hot-for-tv/

Ryan, D. (2012, February 13). Teachers urged to address porn factor. *Sydney Morning Herald.* Retrieved from http://www.smh.com.au/national/education/teachers-urged-to-address-porn-factor-20120211-1svr0.html

Sabina, C., Wolak, J., & Finkelhor, D. (2008). The nature and dynamics of Internet pornography exposure for youth. *CyberPsychology and Behavior, 11,* 1–2.

Salamon, J. (2000, December 10). Sex at 8: The Partridges don't live here anymore. *New York Times,* p. 6WK.

Santelli, J. (1997). Human subjects protection and parental permission in adolescent health research. *Journal of Adolescent Health, 21,* 384–387.

Santelli, J., Ott, M. A., Lyon, M., Rogers, J., Summers, D., & Schleifer, R. (2006). Abstinence and abstinence-only education: A review of U.S. policies and programs. *Journal of Adolescent Health, 38,* 72–81.

Schuster, M. A., Bell, R. M., Berry, S. H., & Kanouse, D. E. (1998). Impact of a high school condom availability program on sexual attitudes and behaviors. *Family Planning Perspectives, 30,* 67–72.

Sellers, D. E., McGraw, S. A., & McKinlay, J. B. (1994). Does the promotion and distribution of condoms increase sexual activity? Evidence from an HIV prevention program for Latino youth. *American Journal of Public Health, 84,* 1952–1959.

Setoodeh, R. (2010, July 26). I want my music videos! *Newsweek,* pp. 52–53.

Sexuality Information and Education Council of the United States. (2006, July 19). States and communities push back against abstinence-only-until-marriage dictates from Washington while proliferation of programs continues [Press release]. Retrieved from http://www.siecus.org/media/press/press0130.html

Shafer, A., Bobkowski, P., & Brown, J. D. (2013). Sexual media practice: How adolescents select, engage with, and are affected by sexual media (pp. 223–251). In K.E. Dill (Ed.). *The Oxford handbook of media psychology.* New York: Oxford University Press.

Signorielli, N. (2001). Television's gender role images and contribution to stereotyping. In D. G. Singer & J. L. Singer (Eds.), *Handbook of children and the media* (pp. 341–358). Thousand Oaks, CA: Sage.

Singer, N. (2009, February 10). A birth control pill that promised too much. *New York Times.* Retrieved from http://www.nytimes.com/2009/02/11/business/11pill.html

Smith, S., & Choueiti, M. (2010). *Gender disparity on screen and behind the camera in family films.* Los Angeles, CA: USC Annenberg School for Communications and Journalism.

Smith, S. L., Choueiti, M., Prescott, A., & Pieper, K. (2013). *Gender roles & occupations: a look at character attributes and job-related aspirations in film and television.* Los Angeles: Geena Davis Foundation.

Sniderman, Z. (2011, August 11). MTV app locates places to get condoms. *Mashable Social Media.* Retrieved from http://mashable.com/2011/08/09/mtv-condom-app/

Society for Adolescent Medicine. (2000). Media and contraception [Policy statement]. *Journal of Adolescent Health, 27,* 290–291.

Stankiewicz, J. M., & Rosselli, F. (2008). Women as sex objects and victims in print advertisements. *Sex Roles, 58,* 579–589.

Steele, J. R. (1999). Teenage sexuality and media practice: Factoring in the influence of family, friends, and school. *Journal of Sex Research, 36,* 331–341.

Steele, J. R. (2002). Teens and movies: Something to do, plenty to learn. In J. D. Brown, J. R. Steele, & K. Walsh-Childers (Eds.), *Sexual teens, sexual media* (pp. 227–251). Mahwah, NJ: Lawrence Erlbaum.

Steinberg, L., & Monahan, K. C. (2011). Adolescents' exposure to sexy media does not hasten the initiation of sexual intercourse. *Developmental Psychology, 47,* 562–576.

Stern, B. B., Russell, C. A., & Russell, D. W. (2005). Vulnerable women on screen and at home: Soap opera consumption. *Journal of Macromarketing, 25,* 222–225.

Strasburger, V. C. (1989). Adolescent sexuality and the media. *Pediatric Clinics of North America, 36,* 747–774.

Strasburger, V. C. (1995). *Adolescents and the media: Medical and psychological impact.* Newbury Park, CA: Sage.

Strasburger, V. C. (1998). Parental permission in adolescent health research [Letter]. *Journal of Adolescent Health, 22,* 362.

Strasburger, V. C. (2006). "Clueless": Why do pediatricians underestimate the influence of the media on children and adolescents? *Pediatrics, 117,* 1427–1431.

Strasburger, V. C. (2009). Why do adolescent health researchers ignore the impact of the media? *Journal of Adolescent Health, 44,* 203–205.

Strasburger, V. C. (2012a). Adolescents, sex, and the media. *Adolescent Medicine: State of the Art Reviews, 23,* 15–33.

Strasburger, V. C. (2012b). School daze: Why are teachers and schools missing the boat on media? *Pediatric Clinics of North America, 59,* 705–716.

Strasburger, V. C., Brown, R. T., Braverman, P. K., Rogers, P. D., Holland-Hall, C., & Coupey, S. M. (2006). *Adolescent medicine: A handbook for primary care.* Philadelphia, PA: Lippincott Williams & Wilkins.

Strasburger, V. C., & Council on Communications and Media. (2010). Sexuality, contraception, and the media [Policy statement]. *Pediatrics, 126,* 576–582.

Strasburger, V. C., Jordan, A. B., & Donnerstein, E. (2012). Children, adolescents, and the media: Health effects. *Pediatric Clinics of North America, 59,* 533–587.

Strassberg, D. S., McKinnon, R. K., Sustaita, M. A., & Rullo, J. (2012). Sexting by high school students: An exploratory and descriptive study. *Archives of Sexual Behavior.* doi: 10.1007/s10508-012-9969-8

Strauss, G. (2010, January 20). Sex on TV: Increasingly uncut—and unavoidable. *USA Today.* Retrieved from http://www.usatoday.com/life/television/news/2010-01-20-sexcov20_CV_N.htm

Suellentrop, K., Brown, J., & Ortiz, R. (2010). *Evaluating the impact of MTV's 16 and Pregnant on teen viewers' attitudes about teen pregnancy.* Washington, DC: National Campaign to Prevent Teen and Unplanned Pregnancy.

Svedin, C. G., Akerman, I., & Priebe, G. (2011). Frequent users of pornography: A population based epidemiological study of Swedish male adolescents. *Journal of Adolescence, 34,* 779–788.

Tannen, T. (2003). Media giant and foundation team up to fight HIV/AIDS. *The Lancet, 361,* 1440–1441.

Taylor, L. D. (2005a). All for him: Articles about sex in American lad magazines. *Sex Roles, 3,* 153–163.

Taylor, L. D. (2005b). Effects of visual and verbal sexual television content and perceived realism on attitudes and beliefs. *Journal of Sex Research, 42,* 130–137.

Taylor, L. D. (2006). College men, their magazines, and sex. *Sex Roles, 55,* 693–702.

Teens "borrow" babies to practice parenting on reality show. (2007, January 12). *ABC News.* Retrieved from http://www.abcnews.go.com/GMA/print?id=2789958

Temple, J. R., Paul, J. A., van den Berg, P., Le, V. D., McElhany, A., & Temple, B. W. (2012). Teen sexting and its association with sexual behaviors. *Archives of Pediatrics and Adolescent Medicine.* doi:10.1001/archpediatrics.2012.835

Ter Bogt, T. F. M., Engels, R. C. M. E., Bogers, S., & Kloosterman, M. (2010). "Shake it baby, shake it": Media preferences, sexual attitudes and gender stereotypes among adolescents. *Sex Roles, 63,* 844–859.

Timmerman, L. M., Allen, M., Jorgensen, J., Herrett-Skjellum, J., Kramer, M. R., & Ryan, D. J. (2008). A review and meta-analysis examining the relationship of music content with sex, race, priming, and attitudes. *Communication Quarterly, 56,* 303–324.

Tobin, A.-M. (2011, June 16). Internet more useful than parents in sex education, some teens report. *Canadian Press.* Retrieved from http://www.ctv.ca/CTVNews/Health/20110617/teens-sex-education-110617/

Tolman, D. L., Kim, J. L., Schooler, D., & Sorsoli, C. L. (2007). Rethinking the associations between television viewing and adolescent sexuality development: Bringing gender into focus. *Journal of Adolescent Health, 40,* 84e9–84e16.

Tomashoff, C. (2011, March 6). Are the kids all right? *TV Guide,* pp. 12–14.

Tortolero, S. R., Markham, C. M., Peskin, M. F., Shegog, R., Addy, R. C., Escobar-Chaves, S. L., & Baumler, E. R. (2009). *It's Your Game: Keep It Real:* Delaying sexual behavior with an effective middle school program. *Journal of Adolescent Health, 46,* 169–179.

Treise, D., & Gotthoffer, A. (2001). Stuff you couldn't ask your parents about: Teens talking about using magazines for sex information. In J. D. Brown, J. R. Steele, & K. Walsh-Childers (Eds.), *Sexual teens, sexual media* (pp. 173–189). Mahwah, NJ: Lawrence Erlbaum.

Trenholm, C., Devaney, B., Forston, K., Quay, L., Wheeler, J., & Clark, M. (2007). *Impacts of four Title V, Section 510 abstinence education programs.* Princeton, NJ: Mathematica Policy Research.

Tuck, L. (2011, January/February). Viewer discretion advised. *POZ.com.* Retrieved from http://www.poz.com/articles/Teens_HIV_TV_2557_19656.shtml

Tucker, K. (1999, December 17). Kids these days. *Entertainment Weekly,* pp. 62–63.

Tucker, M. E. (2000, April). Teen sex. *Pediatric News,* p. 5.

Turner, J. S. (2011). Sex and the spectacle of music videos: An examination of the portrayal of race and sexuality in music videos. *Sex Roles, 64,* 173–191.

United Nations Department of Economic and Social Affairs, Statistics Division. (2011). *Demographic yearbook 2008.* Retrieved from http://unstats.un.org/unsd/demographic/products/dyb/dyb2008.htm

University of Montreal. (2011, June 24). Teens look to parents as guide to healthy sexual behaviors [Press release]. Retrieved from http://www.nouvelles.umontreal.ca/udem-news/news/20110616-teens-look-to-parents-more-than-friends-for-sexual-role-models.html

Van Damme, E., & Van Bauwel, S. (2013, in press). Sex as spectacle: An overview of gender and sexual scripts in teen series popular with Flemish teenagers. *Journal of Children and Media.*

Wakefield, D. (1987, November 7). Teen sex and TV: How the medium has grown up. *TV Guide,* pp. 4–6.

Walsh-Childers, K. (1997). *A content analysis: Sexual health coverage in women's, men's, teen and other specialty magazines.* Menlo Park, CA: Kaiser Family Foundation.

Walsh-Childers, K., Gotthoffer, A., & Lepre, C. R. (2002). From "just the facts" to "downright salacious": Teens' and women's magazines' coverage of sex and sexual health. In J. D. Brown, J. R. Steele, & K. Walsh-Childers (Eds.), *Sexual teens, sexual media* (pp. 153–171). Mahwah, NJ: Lawrence Erlbaum.

Ward, L. M. (1995). Talking about sex: Common themes about sexuality in the prime-time television programs children and adolescents view most. *Journal of Youth and Adolescence, 24,* 595–615.

Ward, L. M., & Friedman, K. (2006). Using TV as a guide: Associations between television viewing and adolescents' sexual attitudes and behavior. *Journal of Research on Adolescence, 16,* 133–156.

Ward, L. M., Gorbine, B., & Cytron, A. (2002). Would that really happen? Adolescents' perceptions of sexual relationships according to prime-time television. In J. D. Brown, J. R. Steele, & K. Walsh-Childers (Eds.), *Sexual teens, sexual media* (pp. 95–123). Mahwah, NJ: Lawrence Erlbaum.

Ward, L. M., Hansbrough, E., & Walker, E. (2005). Contributions of music video exposure to Black adolescents' gender and sexual schemas. *Journal of Adolescent Research, 20,* 143–166.

Ward, L. M., Merriwether, A., & Caruthers, A. (2006). Breasts are for men: Media, masculinity ideologies, and men's beliefs about women's bodies. *Sex Roles, 55,* 703–714.

Weinberg, C. (2006). This is not a love story: Using soap opera to fight HIV in Nicaragua. *Gender and Development, 14,* 37–46.

Weiner, S. (2007, February 20). Goodbye to girlhood. *Washington Post,* p. HE01.

Williams, A. L., & Merten, M. J. (2008). A review of online social networking profiles by adolescents: Implications for future research and intervention. *Adolescence, 43,* 253–274.

Williams, M. E. (2011, September 26). Television's season of the vagina. *Salon.* Retrieved from http://www.salon.com/2011/09/26/vagina_sitcom_season/

Wilson, C. (2010, August 15). Feds: Online "sextortion" of teens on the rise. *Associated Press.* Retrieved from http://www.msnbc.msn.com/id/38714259/ns/technology_and_science-security/t/feds-online-sextortion-teens-rise/

Wingood, G. M., DiClemente, R. J., Bernhardt, J. M., Harrington, K., Davies, S. L., Robillard, A., & Hook, E. W. (2003). A prospective study of exposure to rap music videos and African American female adolescents' health. *American Journal of Public Health, 93,* 437–439.

Wingood, G. M., DiClemente, R. J., Harrington, K., Davies, S., Hook, E. W., & Oh, M. K. (2001). Exposure to X-rated movies and adolescents' sexual and contraceptive-related attitudes and behavior. *Pediatrics, 107,* 1116–1119.

Winston, L. (2010). *Good, better, best: school-based STD screening in Washington, DC.* Washington, DC: U.S. Department of Health.

Wolak, J., Mitchell, K., & Finkelhor, D. (2007). Unwanted and wanted exposure to online pornography in a national sample of youth Internet users. *Pediatrics, 119,* 247–257.

Wolfe, T. (2001). *Hooking Up.* New York: Picador. Quote available at: http://www.tomwolfe.com/HookingUp.html

Wolk, L. I., & Rosenbaum, R. (1995). The benefits of school-based condom availability: Cross-sectional analysis of a comprehensive high school-based program. *Journal of Adolescent Health, 17,* 184–188.

Worden, N. (2011, February 14). Online video viewing jumps, bolstering Netflix. *Wall Street Journal.* Retrieved from http://online.wsj.com/article/SB10001424052748703584804576144371093782778.html

Wray, J., & Steele, J. (2002). Girls in print: Figuring out what it means to be a girl. In J. D. Brown, J. R. Steele, & K. Walsh-Childers (Eds.), *Sexual teens, sexual media* (pp. 191–208). Mahwah, NJ: Lawrence Erlbaum.

Wretzel, S. R., Visintainer, P. F., & Koenigs, L. M. P. (2011). Condom availability program in an inner city public school: Effect on the rates of gonorrhea and chlamydia infection. *Journal of Adolescent Health, 49,* 324–326.

Wright, P. J. (2011). Mass media effects on youth sexual behavior: Assessing the claim for causality. *Communication Yearbook, 35,* 343–386.

Wright, P. J., Malamuth, N. M., & Donnerstein, E. (2012). Research on sex in the media: What do we know about effects on children and adolescents. In D. G. Singer & J. L. Singer (Eds.), *Handbook of children and the media* (2nd ed., pp. 273–302). Thousand Oaks, CA: Sage.

Ybarra, M. (2011, August 6). *Digital adolescence: Myths and truths about growing up with technology.* Paper presented at American Psychological Association meeting, Washington, DC.

Ybarra, M. L., Mitchell, K. J., Hamburger, M., Diener-West, M., & Leaf, P. J. (2011). X-rated material and perpetration of sexually aggressive behavior among children and adolescents: Is there a link? *Aggressive Behavior, 37,* 1–18.

Zhang, Y., Miller, L. E., & Harrison, K. (2008). The relationship between exposure to sexual music videos and young adults' sexual attitudes. *Journal of Broadcasting and Electronic Media, 52,* 368–386.

Zuckerbrod N. (2009, May 20). UK officials post shock video of "teen birth." *Associated Press.* Retrieved from http://www.pr-inside.com/uk-officials-post-shock-video-of-r1266117.htm

Zurbriggen, E. L., Collins, R. L., Lamb, S., Roberts, T.-A., Tolman, D. L., Ward, L. M., & Blake, J. (2010). *Report of the APA Task Force on the sexualization of girls.* Retrieved from http://www.apa.org/pi/women/programs/girls/report-full.pdf

Zurbriggen, E. L., & Morgan, E. M. (2006). Who wants to marry a millionaire? Reality dating television programs, attitudes toward sex, and sexual behaviors. *Sex Roles, 54,* 1–17.

CHAPTER 6

Drugs and the Media*

A cigarette in the hands of a Hollywood star onscreen is a gun aimed at a 12- or 14-year-old.

—Screenwriter Joe Eszterhas
Hollywood Animal (2004)

How about that powerful antidrug commercial paid for by the US government? It aired right between the seventh and eighth Budweiser commercials.

—David Letterman, on the 2002 Super Bowl commercials
on CBS's *Late Show* (as quoted in "Cheers & Jeers," 2002)

My 6 year-old daughter turned to me and said, "What's a 4-hour erection?" How do you explain it?

—Kelly Simmons, Executive Vice President
Tierney Communications, Philadelphia
as quoted in *The New York Times* (Elliott, 2004)

The Marlboro Man emanated in 1954 from the minds of Chicago admen Leo Burnett and John Benson, who were trying to devise a more macho pitch for Philip Morris' filter-tip cigarette and agreed that the "most masculine figure in America" was the cowboy. In the next 40 years, the smoking cowboy traveled the world (and 2 actors who played him died of lung cancer).

—Walter Nugent
Into the West (1999)

*An earlier version of this chapter, by Strasburger, appeared in Singer and Singer, 2012.

While the "War on Drugs" and "Just Say No" campaigns have been waged since the 1980s, children and teenagers have been exposed to more than $20 billion worth of cigarette, alcohol, and prescription drug advertising annually, which has worked very effectively to get them to "just say yes" to smoking, drinking, and other drugs (Federal Trade Commission, 2011; Strasburger & Council on Communications and Media, 2010a) (see Figure 6.1). In addition, content analyses show that television programs, movies, popular music, and certain Internet sites all contain appreciable drug content (Federal Trade Commission, 2011; Strasburger, 2013, in press) (see Figure 6.2). Until recently, many correlational studies had found a significant association between exposure to advertising and exposure to drug content, but no conclusions could be made about a cause-and-effect impact. However, increasing evidence now exists that exposure to drug advertising and scenes of smoking or drinking in movies may be one of the leading causes—if not *the* leading cause—of early adolescent experimentation with cigarettes and alcohol (Sargent, Tanski, & Stoolmiller, 2012; Sargent, Wills, Stoolmiller, Gibson, & Gibbons, 2006).

Adolescent Drug Use

Illegal drugs certainly take their toll on society, but tobacco and alcohol—two legal drugs—pose a far greater danger to children and teenagers. Every year, more than 400,000 Americans die from tobacco-related causes—more than from AIDS, car crashes, murder, and suicide

Figure 6.1

SOURCE: Copyright © Jim Borgman

Figure 6.2a   Substance appearance in popular movies and songs. Note that movies far exceed songs as a source of drug depictions.

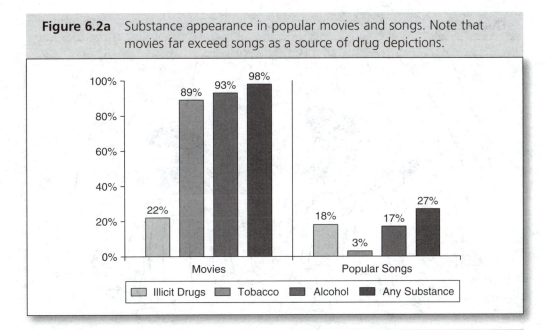

SOURCE: Christenson, Henriksen, and Roberts (2000).

Figure 6.2b   Substance use in television.

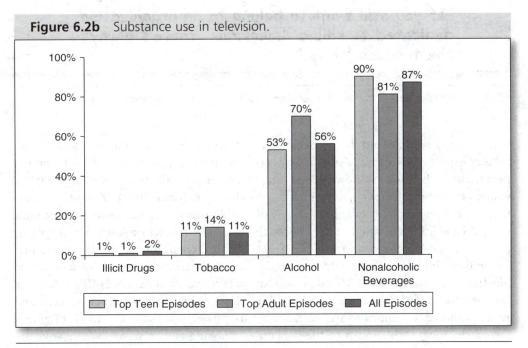

SOURCE: Christenson, Henriksen, and Roberts (2000).

combined (Strasburger & Council on Communications and Media, 2010a) (see Figure 6.3). Tobacco is the only known legal drug that kills when used as directed. And each day in the U.S., approximately 4,000 adolescents try their first cigarette (Centers for Disease Control and Prevention [CDC], 2008).

Figure 6.3

"If you still want to belong to an organization dedicated to killing Americans, there's always the tobacco lobby."

With increased globalization, concerns are emerging about the impact of American tobacco exports on worldwide smoking rates (Prokhorov et al., 2006). More than 1.1 billion people currently smoke worldwide, resulting in 4 million deaths per year. Nearly 100,000 young people begin smoking *daily* (Tanski, Prokhorov, & Klein, 2004). If this trend continues, a billion people will die prematurely of smoking-related causes during this century (World Health Organization, 2008). Secondhand smoke has also become an important problem in developing countries. The World Health Organization (WHO) reports that 700 million children are exposed to environmental smoke annually, especially in countries like India, China, Indonesia, Pakistan, and Russia (Prokhorov et al., 2006). The U.S. is the leading producer of cigarettes, exporting three times as many as any other country, and American tobacco companies are increasingly turning overseas as the U.S. market tightens (Womach, 2003). While most of the dangers of smoking and of secondhand smoke are well understood (lung cancer, other cancers, heart disease, respiratory illness, infertility, etc.), new research is finding additional concerns for young people (U.S. Department of Health and Human Services, 2012). Smoking may cause damage to lung cell DNA, producing physiological changes that persist despite quitting smoking (Wiencke et al., 1999).

Tobacco use may also be a marker for depression and anxiety disorders in adolescence (Sims & Committee on Substance Abuse, 2009).

Alcohol is the most commonly abused drug by young people ages 12 to 17 years (Committee on Substance Abuse, 2010) and may account for as many as 100,000 deaths annually, including 5,000 people under 21 years (U.S. Department of Health and Human Services, 2007; Williams & Ribisl, 2012). In the U.S. alone, alcohol accounts for 28,000 unintentional injury deaths, 17,000 traffic deaths, 300,000 traffic injuries, and 1.4 million injury visits to the emergency department annually (Hingson & Zha, 2009). In a large study of more than 44,000 fatally injured drivers between 1998 and 2009, 37% exceeded the legal limit for alcohol (Romano & Voas, 2011). The risk of an injury increases ninefold among patients who have consumed five to six drinks in the past few hours (Hingson & Zha, 2009). In the most recent survey of teen highway deaths, 20% of the 1,280 sixteen- to nineteen-year-old drivers had alcohol in their system. One in 10 students reports having driven after drinking during the past 30 days, and most students who drive after drinking have been binge drinking (CDC, 2012a; CDC, 2013).

In fact, underage drinkers account for about 20% of all alcohol consumption (Foster, Vaughan, Foster, & Califano, 2003) and for one-third of all alcohol industry revenues (Foster, Vaughan, Foster, & Califano, 2006). Underage drinking costs society an estimated $68 billion a year, however (National Center on Addiction and Substance Abuse, 2011a). Physicians who treat teenagers know that alcohol can contribute significantly to the three leading causes of death among teens—accidents, homicides, and suicides—which together account for 75% of their mortality rate (J. W. Kulig & Committee on Substance Abuse, 2005; Swahn, Bossarte, & Sullivent, 2008; Thompson, Sims, Kingree, & Windle, 2008). Research is increasingly discovering that alcoholism begins young; nearly half of all alcoholics are diagnosable before age 21(S. A. Brown et al., 2008; Hingson, Heeren, & Winter, 2006). Globally, alcohol consumption causes 1.8 million deaths (3.2%) annually and is the leading risk factor for morbidity in many developing countries (WHO, 2007).

Nine out of 10 Americans who meet the medical criteria for addiction started smoking, drinking, or using other drugs before the age of 18. In a cross-sectional study of more than ten thousand 13- to 18-year-olds, the median age at onset for alcohol and drug abuse was 14 to 15 years (Swendsen et al., 2012). Total costs of substance use for federal, state, and local governments are estimated to be at least $468 billion per year (National Center on Addiction and Substance Abuse, 2011a). The best data regarding adolescent drug use come from the University of Michigan's Monitoring the Future study (MTF), which surveys nearly 45,000 students annually in the 8th, 10th, and 12th grades at more than 430 public and private schools across the country (www.monitoringthefuture.org). Funded by the National Institute on Drug Abuse (NIDA), this study has been conducted annually since the mid-1970s (see Figure 6.4 and Tables 6.1 and 6.2). No data set is perfect, however. The MTF fails to capture high school dropouts—who may have very high rates of drug use—and depends on self-reporting by teens. But no other collection of data is so extensive over so long a period of time. The next best source of data is the Youth Risk Behavior Survey (YRBS), conducted by the CDC every two years in nearly every state (www.cdc.gov/mmwr/PDF/ss/ss5704.pdf) (see Figures 6.5 and 6.6). The 2009 survey included more than 13,000 students in 8th grade and more than 15,000 in 10th and 12th grades.

Figure 6.4 Trends in annual prevalence of 12th graders' use of illegal drugs, 1975–2011.

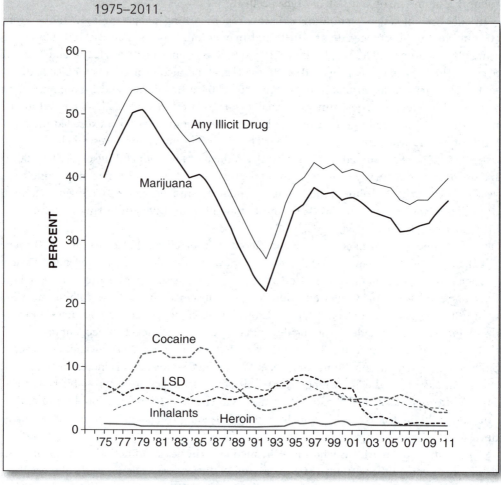

SOURCE: Data from the Monitoring the Future study, University of Michigan. Reprinted with permission.

Table 6.1 Adolescent Drug Use, 2012 (in percentages) (*N* = 13,700 Grade 12 students)

Drug	Used During Lifetime	Used During Past Year
Any illicit drug	49	40
Any illicit drug other than marijuana	24	17
Alcohol	69	64
Ever been drunk	54	45
Cigarettes	40	—

Drug	Used During Lifetime	Used During Past Year
Marijuana	45	36
Smokeless tobacco	17	—
Amphetamines	12	8
Inhalants	8	3
Hallucinogens	8	5
Ecstasy	7	4
Tranquilizers	9	5
Cocaine	5	3
Steroids	2	1
Heroin	1	1
OxyContin	—	4
Vicodin	—	8

SOURCE: Adapted from Johnston, O'Malley, Bachman, and Schulenberg (2013).

Table 6.2   Trends in 12th Graders' Perception of Drugs as Harmful (in percentages)

How much do you think people risk harming themselves if they . . .	1975	1990	2012
Try marijuana once or twice	15	23	15
Smoke marijuana occasionally	18	37	21
Smoke marijuana regularly	43	79	44
Try LSD once or twice	49	45	33
Try cocaine once or twice	43	59	52
Try MDMA once or twice	—	—	49
Try one or two drinks of an alcoholic beverage	5	8	9
Have five or more drinks once or twice each weekend	38	47	49
Smoke one or more packs of cigarettes per day	51	68	78

SOURCE: Adapted from Johnston, O'Malley, Bachman, and Schulenberg (2013).

Highlights of the 2011 MTF survey and the 2011 YRBS include the following (CDC, 2012b; Johnston et al., 2013; CDC, 2013):

- There have been continued decreases in smoking levels, which according to the MTF reached a peak in 1996 and 1997. Whereas in 1996, 49% of 8th graders had tried cigarettes at some point in their lives, in 2011, only 18% had. Those reporting cigarette use in the month prior to being surveyed had decreased from 21% of 8th graders in 1996 to 6% in 2011, from 30% of 10th graders in 1996 to 12% in 2011, and from 37% of 12th graders in 1996 to 19% in 2011. Interestingly, in 2011, more than 80% of 8th and 10th graders and 75% of 12th graders said they "would prefer to date people who don't smoke."
- At the same time, the YRBS found that nearly half of all teenagers had tried smoking cigarettes at some time, down from a high of 71% in 1995 but still an alarming figure. More than 10% had smoked a cigarette before age 13.

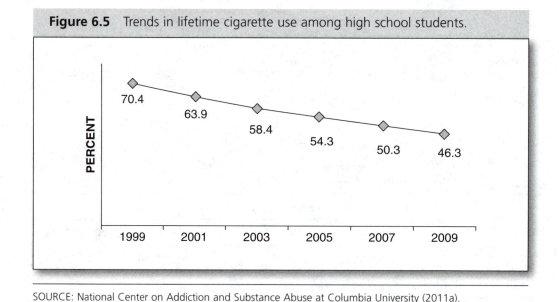

Figure 6.5   Trends in lifetime cigarette use among high school students.

SOURCE: National Center on Addiction and Substance Abuse at Columbia University (2011a).

- A leveling off in alcohol use rates has occurred. Nearly three-fourths of 12th graders have tried alcohol at least once, down from a peak of 88% in 1991. One-third of 8th graders have tried alcohol at least once. More worrisome are the figures for binge drinking and having ever being drunk. While only 6% percent of 8th graders reported having consumed five or more drinks of alcohol in the two weeks prior to being surveyed, 15% of 10th graders and nearly one-fourth of all high school seniors have engaged in binge drinking. About 17% of 8th graders, 36% of 10th graders, and half of 12th graders reported having been drunk at some point in their lives.

    In the YRBS, 39% of high school students reported having had at least one drink of alcohol in the 30 days prior to being surveyed, and 22% reported binge drinking during

Figure 6.6 Trends in alcohol use among high school students.

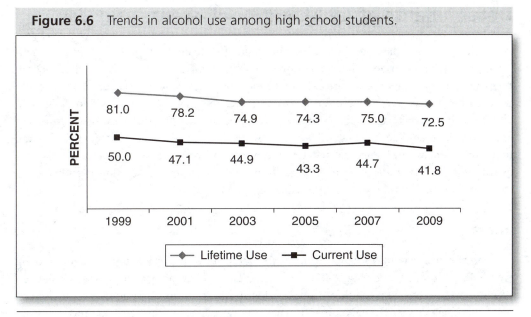

SOURCE: National Center on Addiction and Substance Abuse at Columbia University (2011a).

the previous 30 days. Although athletes are ordinarily less likely to use illicit drugs other than anabolic steroids (K. Kulig, Brener, & McManus, 2003), male athletes may be more likely to use alcohol (Fisher, Miles, Austin, Camargo, & Colditz, 2007).

- Levels of illicit drug use among teenagers have remained relatively stable over the past several years. Use peaked at 66% in 1981 and declined to a low of 41% in 1992. Currently, nearly half of all seniors, more than a third of sophomores, and one in five 8th graders report having used an illicit drug. One-fourth of seniors have used an illicit drug other than marijuana.
- A leveling off in marijuana use among teenagers has occurred. Marijuana use peaked in 1979, when 60% of high school seniors reported having tried it. Now, just over 45% of seniors say that they have tried marijuana.
- Marijuana, cocaine, heroin, and MDMA ("ecstasy") use bottomed out in the early 1990s, began rising in the mid to late 1990s, and now has slowly decreased again.
- For all drugs, it is important to understand that young adults and older adults have higher rates of smoking and alcohol use, and young adults have the highest rates of illicit drug use. But the onset of alcohol and tobacco use invariably occurs during adolescence.

The United States is not unique in having an adolescent drug problem. More than half of all female 15-year-olds in Greenland smoke daily, 85% of Scottish 11-year-olds have tried alcohol at least once, more than half of Welsh 15-year-olds consume alcohol at least weekly, and more than 70% of Danish 15-year-olds have been drunk at least twice (Currie, Hurrelmann, Settertobulte, Smith, & Todd, 2000). In the United Kingdom, 10% to 12% of 15-year-olds reported having used marijuana in the month prior to being surveyed (Brooks et al., 2009).

Determinants of Child and Adolescent Drug Use

Adolescent drug use is associated with a number of different factors, including poor self-image, low religiosity, poor school performance, alienation from parents, family dysfunction, physical and emotional abuse, and self-medication (Briones, Wilcox, Mateus, & Boudjenah, 2006; Fisher et al., 2007; Schydlower & Arredondo, 2006; Shrier, Harris, Kurland, & Knight, 2003). Media can play an important role as well, making substance use, especially smoking and drinking, seem like "normative" behavior. Reviews of adolescent substance use often fail to mention media influence as an etiologic agent for young people initiating drug use (Strasburger, 1998), and researchers typically neglect to ask media-related questions when they survey teens for substance use (Strasburger, 2009b).

Peers

Peer pressure may play one of the most important roles in early drug use among young teens (Bahr, Hoffmann, & Yang, 2005), but it may also be a key factor in teens abstaining from drugs as well. Teens who see their friends using drugs are more likely to do so themselves; teens who believe their friends are anti-drugs are more likely to abstain (Robin & Johnson, 1996). (Another possible and as-yet untested hypothesis is that teens prone to drug use or to abstaining search out like-minded peers.) Mapping the social networks of nearly 8,500 adolescents has shown that the likelihood of marijuana use may increase if "friends" are known to use drugs (Mednick, Christakis, & Fowler, 2010).

In many ways, the media can function as a "super-peer," making it seem as if "everyone" is using alcohol, tobacco, or other drugs (Strasburger, 1995). Because teens always want to be doing what is "normal" and "current" for their peer group (Olds, Thombs, & Tomasek, 2005), the media may represent one of the most powerful influences on their behavior. Media are also a leading source of health information for teens. One study of nearly 800 students in 5th to 12th grade found that television was the leading source of information about smoking (Kurtz, Kurtz, Johnson, & Cooper, 2001).

Family

Parents represent an important influence on whether teens use drugs or not. Depending on the circumstances, parents can be a significant risk factor or a significant protective factor (Bahr et al., 2005; Briones et al., 2006; Halpern-Felsher & Cornell, 2005). Abused children are at greater risk for drug use, for example. Similarly, a "coercive" parenting style can lead to greater substance use and even delinquency (McMahon, 1994). Genetically, alcoholic parents are two to nine times more likely to produce biological children who are alcoholic (Belcher & Shinitzky, 1998). This inherited risk may extend to other drug abuse as well (Comings, 1997). Alternatively, nurturing parents with good communication skills represent a major protective factor (Fisher et al., 2007). Interestingly enough, in a recent poll of parents of 13- to 17-year-olds, only 10% of the parents thought their teens had taken a drink in the past year, and only 5% thought their teens had used marijuana (Keeping, 2011).

Media have sometimes been called "electronic parents," and if parents and schools fail to give children appropriate information about drugs, the media may fill the void with unhealthy information or cues. For example, latchkey children are more prone to substance use, perhaps because they are unsupervised and have unrestrained access to a variety of potentially unhealthy media (Chilcoat & Anthony, 1996). Likewise, teens who have TV sets in their own bedrooms are more likely to watch more TV and to engage in risky behaviors like sex or using tobacco, marijuana, or alcohol (Gruber, Wang, Christensen, Grube, & Fisher, 2005).

Personality

Adolescents are notorious for being risk takers. Part of the explanation for this comes from new research on brain development that shows that the key areas of the frontal cortex (involved in judgment) do not mature until the early to mid 20s (Giedd, 2008; Walsh & Bennett, 2005). MRI studies of teens with alcohol problems show that areas of the brain involved in drug craving and reward (e.g., the limbic system) light up more in subjects who are being shown pictures of alcoholic beverages than they do in controls (Tapert et al., 2003). Areas of the brain involved in motivating behavior are also different in teenagers (Bjork et al., 2004; White & Swartzwelder, 2004). Both tobacco and alcohol can be considered "gateway drugs" as well, meaning that their use may lead to use of more worrisome drugs later. For example, teens who smoke are 3 times more likely to use alcohol than nonsmokers, 8 times more likely to use marijuana, and 22 times more likely to use cocaine (U.S. Department of Health and Human Services, 2004). Alcohol is often the first drug to be experimented with and may lead to lower grades and risk taking behaviors like premature sexual intercourse and experimentation with other drugs (S. A. Brown et al., 2008; Champion et al., 2004; Rehm, Shield, Joharchi, & Shuper, 2012).

Biology

Adolescents' developing brains may make them more susceptible to nicotine addiction and require fewer cigarettes smoked to establish addiction compared to adults (Prokhorov et al., 2006). New research shows that the nicotine in cigarettes can become addictive after only a few puffs (Sims & Committee on Substance Abuse, 2009). A small number of adolescents with psychiatric disorders may also use substances like marijuana or alcohol to try to regulate their mood disorders ("Teen 'Self Medication,'" 2008).

The Impact of Advertising on Children and Adolescents

Tobacco and alcohol represent two hugely profitable industries that require the constant recruitment of new users. With the death of 1,200 smokers a day and with thousands more trying to quit, the tobacco industry must recruit new smokers to remain profitable. Inevitably, these new smokers come from the ranks of children and adolescents, especially given the demographics of smoking (50% of smokers begin by age 13, and 80% before age 18 [CDC, 2010; Strasburger & Council on Communications and Media, 2010a]). Worldwide, this amounts to nearly 100,000 young people starting smoking daily (Strasburger & Council on

Figure 6.7   Ad from the 2007 Camel No. 9 campaign.

Communications and Media, 2010a). Big Tobacco has engaged in a systematic campaign to attract underage smokers for decades and then lied to Congress about it (Glantz, Slade, Bero, & Hanauer, 1998; Kessler, 2001). Specific age and ethnic groups are often targeted. For example, the Camel No. 9 advertising campaign in 2007 seemed custom made to attract young teenage girls and was very effective (Pierce et al., 2010) (see Figure 6.7). The industry continues to resist any congressional attempts to regulate it (Cruz & Deyton, 2010; "Tobacco Giants Suing," 2011).

Similarly, the alcohol industry has targeted minority groups and the young for years, particularly through promotion of sports, youth-oriented programming, and flavored alcohol drinks. Because 5% of drinkers consume 40% of all alcoholic beverages, and 20% account for 90% of all alcohol consumption (Greenfield & Rogers, 1999), new recruits—preferably heavy drinkers—are a must for the alcohol industry as well. For underage drinkers, more than 90% of the alcohol drunk is consumed as binge drinking (Jernigan, 2006). A recent study of 11 U.S. magazines with disproportionately adolescent readerships found more than 2,600 alcohol ads between 2003 and 2007, with one-quarter featuring risk, sexual activity, or sexism (Rhoades & Jernigan, 2013).

Celebrity endorsers are commonly used, and older children and teenagers may be particularly vulnerable to such ads (Committee on Communications, 2006; Gunter, Oates, & Blades, 2004). Many commercials for alcohol and ads for tobacco employ some combination of rock music, young attractive models, humor, or adventure (see Figure 6.8). "Beach babes," frogs, lizards, and dogs are all commonly seen in beer commercials. Sex and humor are particularly effective with adolescents (Salkin, 2007). Production values are extraordinary: Costs for a single 30-second commercial may easily exceed those for an entire half-hour of regular programming, and 30 seconds' worth of advertising during the 2012 Super Bowl cost $3.5 million ("Their Super Bowl Ads," 2012). In 2007, Anheuser-Busch bought five entire minutes of advertising during the Super Bowl (Sutel, 2007). Several years ago, a new form of alcoholic beverage was marketed—"hard" lemonades, containing 5% alcohol. These have been dubbed "learner drinks for kids." They, too, use fictitious cool guys such as "Doc" Otis and One-Eyed

Jack and "make a mockery of the industry's claim that it doesn't market to kids," according to one expert (Cowley & Underwood, 2001). Similarly, until they were banned in 2009, flavored cigarettes were marketed with names like "Beach Breezer," "Kuai Kolada," "Twista Lime," and "Mandarin Mints," despite the 1998 Master Settlement Agreement (see Table 6.3) that included a promise not to market to children (Harris, 2005).

A variety of studies have explored the impact of advertising on children and adolescents. Nearly all have shown advertising to be extremely effective in increasing youngsters' awareness of and emotional responses to alcohol products, their recognition of certain brands, their desire to own or use the products advertised, and their recognition of the advertisements themselves (Borzekowski & Strasburger, 2008). There are, however, some researchers who disagree and feel that children have become increasingly sophisticated about the intent of advertising in general and therefore more media resistant to alcohol advertising specifically. They cite the fact that older meta-analyses find a much larger effect size than more recent ones (Desmond & Carveth, 2007). Nevertheless, two recent studies confirm an association: One analysis involved seven prospective cohort studies involving 13,255 subjects and found at least modest effects (Smith & Foxcroft, 2009); a second analysis examined 13 longitudinal studies involving more than 38,000 young people and concluded that "alcohol advertising and promotion increases the likelihood that adolescents will start to use alcohol, and to drink more if they are already using alcohol" (P. Anderson, de Bruijn, Angus, Gordon, & Hastings, 2009, p. 229).

Although the research is not yet considered to be scientifically "beyond a reasonable doubt," there is a preponderance of evidence that cigarette and alcohol advertising is a significant factor in adolescents' use of these two drugs (Borzekowski & Strasburger, 2008; Federal Trade Commission, 1999; Grube & Waiters, 2005; Jernigan, 2006; Snyder, Milici, Slater, Sun, & Strizhakova, 2006; U.S. Department of Health and Human Services, 2012). The Federal Trade Commission (1999) report on the alcohol industry concluded, "While many factors may influence an underage person's drinking decisions, including among other things parents, peers and the media, there is reason to believe that advertising also plays a role." For alcohol, advertising

Table 6.3 Some Features of the 1998 Tobacco Master Settlement Agreement

Payment of $206.4 billion from the tobacco industry to the states over the next 25 years, including $1.5 billion to fund research to reduce teen smoking

A ban on the use of cartoon characters in the advertising, promotion, or labeling of tobacco products

A prohibition on targeting youth in advertising, promotions, or marketing

A ban on all outdoor advertising, including billboards and signs in stadiums

A ban on the sale of merchandise with brand-name logos, such as T-shirts or backpacks

A ban on payments to producers of TV and movies for product placements

SOURCE: Adapted from *AAP News, 15*(1): 4 January 1999.

Figure 6.8 Many commercials for alcohol and ads for tobacco employ attractive models, humor, and the promise of adventure.

may account for as much as 10% to 30% of the variance in adolescents' usage (Atkin, 1995). Interestingly, one study of students' use of cigarette promotional items found that a similar figure applies to cigarettes as well: Approximately one-third of adolescents' cigarette use could be predicted by their purchase or ownership of tobacco promotional gear (Pierce, Choi, Gilpin, Farkas, & Berry, 1998). Nevertheless, as one group of researchers notes,

To reduce the argument regarding the demonstrable effects of massive advertising campaigns to the level of individual behavior is absurdly simplistic. . . . Rather, what we are dealing with is the nature of advertising itself. Pepsi Cola, for example, could not convincingly prove, through any sort of defensible scientific study, that particular children or adolescents who consume their products do so because of exposure to any or all of their ads. (Orlandi, Lieberman, & Schinke, 1989, p. 90)

Although there is some legitimate debate about how much of an impact such advertising has on young people and their decisions regarding whether to use cigarettes or alcohol, advertising clearly works—or else companies would not spend millions of dollars a year on it (the U.S. spends $250 billion a year on advertising, more than any other country in the world by a factor of two). This leaves American society with a genuine moral, economic, and public health dilemma: Should advertising of unhealthy products be allowed, when society then has to pay for the disease, disability, and death that these products cause (Kunkel, 2007; Strasburger, 2012; 2013). Tobacco companies and beer manufacturers claim that they are simply influencing "brand choice," not increasing overall demand for their products. Moreover, they claim that because it is legal to sell their products, it should be legal to advertise them as well, and any ban represents an infringement on their First Amendment rights of commercial free speech. Recently, a conservative U.S. Supreme Court has seemed to agree with them (Bayer & Kelly, 2010; Gostin, 2009).

Public health advocates counter that tobacco companies and beer manufacturers are engaging in unfair and deceptive practices by specifically targeting young people, using attractive role models and youth-oriented messages in their ads, and making smoking and drinking seem like normative behavior (Borzekowski & Strasburger, 2008; A. Brown & Moodie, 2009; Grube & Waiters, 2005; U.S. Department of Health and Human Services, 1994). Teens are exposed to 48% more beer advertising, 20% more advertising for hard liquor, and 92% more ads for sweet alcoholic drinks in magazines than are adults of legal drinking age (Center on Alcohol Marketing and Youth, 2007; Garfield, Chung, & Rathouz, 2003). Teen girls are actually more likely to be exposed to alcohol advertising than women in their 20s or 30s (Jernigan, Ostroff, Ross, & O'Hara, 2004). The fact that alcohol and tobacco manufacturers are trying to get adolescents to "just say yes" to cigarettes and beer at a time when society is trying to get them to "just say no" to drugs seems like a situation straight out of *Alice in Wonderland* (Strasburger, 2010). As we shall see, the available data strongly support the public health viewpoint.

Cigarettes

The Impact of Cigarette Advertising

More money is spent on the advertising and promotion of tobacco—more than $15 billion in 2003 alone (see Figure 6.9)—than on alcohol ($5 billion/year) or prescription drugs ($4 billion/year) (Federal Trade Commission, 2011; Strasburger & Council on Communications and Media, 2010a).

Most youth in the U.S. are exposed to pro-tobacco messages in the media (see Figure 6.10). In a sample of as many as 33,000 students in 6th to 12th grade, 85% had seen tobacco ads in stores and half had seen ads in newspapers and magazines (Duke et al., 2009).

Figure 6.9 Tobacco company advertising and promotional spending, 1998–2008 (in billions).

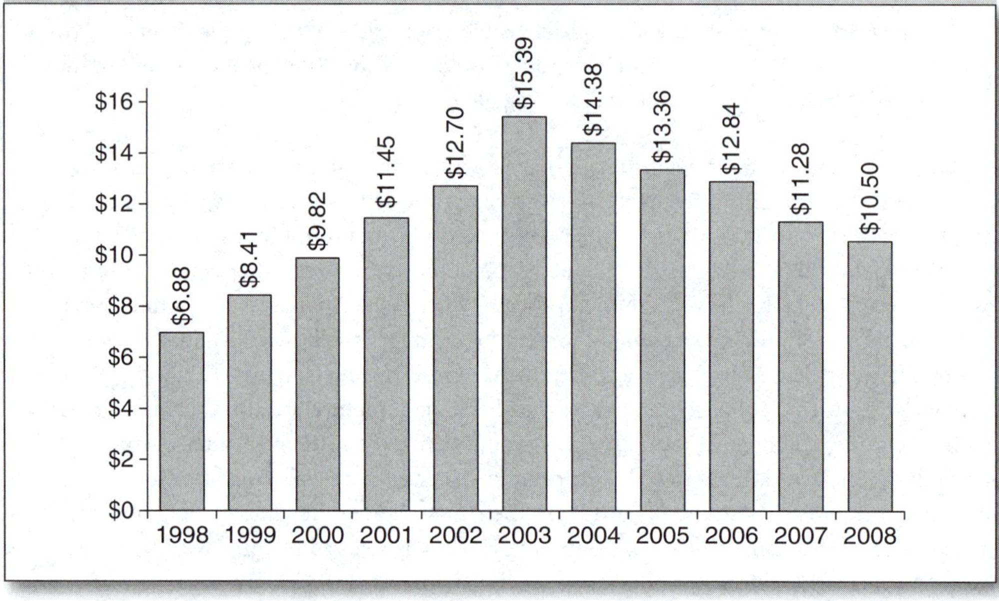

$16 – | $15.39 | $14.38 | $13.36 | $12.84 | $11.28 | $10.50

1998	$6.88
1999	$8.41
2000	$9.82
2001	$11.45
2002	$12.70
2003	$15.39
2004	$14.38
2005	$13.36
2006	$12.84
2007	$11.28
2008	$10.50

SOURCE: Federal Trade Commission (2011).

Figure 6.10 Most youth in the U.S. are exposed to pro-tobacco messages in the media.

NOTE: Joe Camel was outlawed by the 1998 Master Settlement Agreement but is alive and well in other parts of the world (e.g., Argentina, Spain, China, Japan).

Cigarette advertising appears to increase teenagers' risk of beginning to smoke by glamorizing both the act of smoking and smokers themselves (Borzekowski & Strasburger, 2008; Davis, Gilpin, Loken, Viswanath, & Wakefield, 2008). Attractive celebrities have seemingly always smoked (see Figure 6.11), and smokers are portrayed as being independent, healthy, youthful, unconventional, and adventurous. By contrast, the adverse consequences of smoking are almost never shown. Nearly 20 years ago, the U.S. Surgeon General concluded,

> Cigarette advertising appears to affect young people's perceptions of the pervasiveness, image, and function of smoking. Since misperceptions in these areas constitute psychosocial risk factors for the initiation of smoking, *cigarette advertising appears to increase young people's risk of smoking* [emphasis added]. (U.S. Department of Health & Human Services, 1994, p. 195)

The history of cigarette advertising on TV is one of the more remarkable public health stories on record. In June 1967, the Federal Communications Commission (FCC) ruled that the "fairness doctrine" applied to cigarette advertisements, which were being broadcast for 5 to 10 minutes per day. That meant that TV stations would be required to air antismoking ads for free, to provide a "balance" to the pro-tobacco "viewpoint" expressed by the cigarette ads. The FCC's decision was subsequently upheld by the courts. The industry volunteered to remove their ads from TV and radio, but Congress refused to permit tobacco companies to

Figure 6.11 Celebrities—and even doctors and babies—have been used to advertise cigarettes.

discuss it among themselves, claiming it would be a violation of antitrust law. Gradually, as the number of antismoking ads rose, the industry decided it was wise not to oppose the Public Health Cigarette Smoking Act of 1970, which then banned tobacco ads altogether. The upshot of supporting the legislation was that antismoking public service announcements (PSAs) then had to compete with all other PSAs and quickly—dramatically—diminished in quantity. In addition, the tobacco industry used the money saved on TV and radio ads for other forms of marketing and promotion (Fritschler & Hoefler, 2006; K. Warner, personal communication, 2010).

To this day, some of the industry's advertising strategies are nearly Orwellian in their sophistication. Litigation originally brought by the U.S. attorneys general uncovered the fact that tobacco companies have specifically targeted teenage smokers as young as age 13 in an attempt to regain market share (Weinstein, 1998), and a federal judge ruled in 2006 that the tobacco industry had been deceiving the public for five decades about the risks of smoking ("Big Tobacco's Promises," 2006). In November 2003, the tobacco industry did agree to cease advertising in school library editions of four magazines with a large youth readership (*Time, People, Sports Illustrated*, and *Newsweek*) ("Tobacco Ads," 2005)", but the industry continued for a while to target youth with ads in adult magazines with a high youth readership (Alpert, Koh, & Connolly, 2008). Recently, the two largest tobacco companies stopped advertising major brands in many magazines—Philip Morris (e.g., Marlboro) in 2005 and R. J. Reynolds (e.g., Camel) in 2008 (Newman, 2009). At the same time, the industry has begun publishing lifestyle magazines like *Unlimited* and *CML*, both of which feature "under-the-radar" strategies like attractive brand imagery that targets young adults (Cortese, Lewis, & Ling, 2009). New marketing strategies also include targeting teen girls and young women with new brands and packages—for example, Camel No. 9 that comes in shiny black boxes with hot pink and teal borders and is advertised with wording like "Light and luscious" or "Now available in stiletto" in women's magazines like *Vogue, Glamour*, and *Cosmopolitan* (Campaign for Tobacco-Free Kids, 2009a; Pierce et al., 2010). Researchers estimate that the Camel No. 9 campaign may have attracted as many as 170,000 new female teenage smokers in just a few years (Pierce et al., 2010). The few studies that have been published that do not find an association between tobacco marketing and teen use have been secretly underwritten by the industry itself (DiFranza et al., 2006). More recently, the industry has attempted to deflect criticism by introducing "youth smoking education and prevention" programs worldwide. The programs stress that smoking is an "adult choice," that children begin smoking because of peer pressure and lack of guidance from their parents, and that buying cigarettes is illegal for teens. The programs do *not* mention the fact that nicotine is addictive, that smoking causes disease, or that marketing increases smoking. In addition, the research done for such programs allows the tobacco industry to collect valuable demographic data on teenagers and their habits (Landman, Ling, & Glantz, 2002). Finally, Lewis Carroll might have admired the fact that in 2009 R. J. Reynolds acquired Niconovum, a Swedish company that makes nicotine gum and other nicotine replacement devices to wean smokers off of cigarettes (Gomstyn, 2009).

Perhaps as a result, one in five 8th graders believes that the harmful effects of cigarettes have been exaggerated (Johnston et al., 2012). Tobacco advertising may even undermine the impact of strong parenting practices (Pierce, Distefan, Jackson, White, & Gilpin, 2002).

In 2008, the magazine landscape changed. Yet ads for smokeless tobacco in magazines with a large youth readership have actually increased (Morrison, Krugman, & Park, 2008). Magazine advertising currently represents only about 1% of the almost $13 billion spent annually on marketing and promotion (Alpert et al., 2008). The major companies could decide to resume print advertising at any time, of course, depending on their business needs (Alpert et al., 2008), but the Family Smoking Prevention and Tobacco Control Act promoted by the Food and Drug Administration (FDA), passed in 2009, will put a crimp in future promotional efforts (Wilson, 2009) (see Table 6.4).

Beginning in the early 1990s, some classic research has more clearly delineated the impact of cigarette advertising on young people. In 1991, two studies examined the impact of the Old Joe the Camel advertising campaign. In one, 6-year-olds were as likely to recognize Old Joe as they were the famous Mouseketeer logo for the Disney Channel (Fischer, Schwartz, Richards, Goldstein, & Rojas, 1991). Even at age 3, 30% of children could make the association between the Old Joe Camel figure and a pack of cigarettes. In the second study, more than twice as many children as adults reported exposure to Old Joe. Not only were children able to recognize the association with Camel cigarettes, but they found the ads to be appealing as well (DiFranza et al., 1991). Not coincidentally, in the three years after the introduction of the Old Joe campaign, the preference for Camel cigarettes increased from 0.5% of adolescent smokers to 32%. During the same time period, the sale of Camels to minors increased from $6 million to $476 million, representing one-quarter of all Camel sales and one-third of all illegal cigarette sales to minors (DiFranza et al., 1991).

Since then, the research has been clear and convincing that tobacco marketing and promotion are highly effective in influencing young people to begin smoking. There are at least four dozen cross-sectional and longitudinal studies (see Table 6.5). The size of the effect remains a matter of discussion (see Table 6.5), although the Hill criteria for causality have been fulfilled (see Hill, 1965) (see Table 6.6).

Table 6.4   Some Provisions of the Tobacco Control Act

Tobacco Law (signed into law by the President on June 22, 2009)

- All advertising for cigarettes and smokeless tobacco must be black text on white background only (effective 6/22/10)
- No advertising in magazines with more than 15% or 2 million youth readers (effective 6/22/10)
- No outdoor advertising within 1,000 feet of schools, parks, or playgrounds (effective 6/22/10)
- No branded sponsorships of athletic or cultural events by cigarette manufacturers (effective 6/22/10)
- FDA must issue regulations to prevent the sale of tobacco products to youth via the Internet or mail-order (effective 10/1/12)
- FDA must issue regulations addressing the marketing and promotion of tobacco products on the Internet (effective 4/1/13)

SOURCE: American Academy of Pediatrics, Office of Government Affairs, Washington, DC, 2010.

Table 6.5 How Good Is the Research Linking Tobacco Marketing to Onset of Adolescent Smoking?

Research Question	# Of Studies	# Of Subjects
Are nonsmoking children exposed to and more aware of tobacco promotion?	4 prospective 12 cross-sectional	37,649
Does exposure to promotions increase the risk of initiation?	12 prospective 14 cross-sectional 2 time-series	349,306
Does a dose-response relationship exist?	2 prospective 7 cross-sectional	25,180

SOURCE: Adapted from DiFranza and colleagues (2006).

Table 6.6 Does the Research on Tobacco Marketing and Onset of Smoking Fulfill the Hill Criteria[a] for Causality?

YES.

1. Children are exposed to tobacco marketing before they begin smoking.

2. Exposure to marketing increases the risk for initiation of smoking.

3. A dose-response relationship dose exit: Increased exposure results in higher risk.

4. The association between exposure and increased risk is well substantiated with a variety of research methodologies and populations.

5. Cohesive theories can explain the relationship.

6. No other explanation other than causality can explain the relationship.

SOURCE: Adapted from DiFranza and colleagues (2006).

[a]Hill (1965).

Some of the most notable and recent research studies include the following:

- Numerous studies that show that children who pay closer attention to cigarette advertisements, who are able to recall such ads more readily, or who own promotional items are more likely to view smoking favorably and to become smokers themselves (Biener & Siegel, 2000; Hanewinkel, Isensee, Sargent, & Morgenstern, 2010, 2011; Sargent, Dalton, & Beach, 2000; Sargent, Gibson, & Heatherton, 2009) (see Figure 6.12). Teens who smoke are also more likely to believe messages in print ads for cigarettes

Figure 6.12 Crude association between exposure to advertisements and youth smoking.

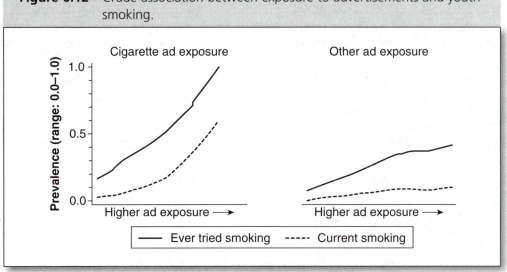

SOURCE: Hanewinkel, Isensee, Sargent, and Morgenstern (2010). Reprinted with permission.

(Hawkins & Hane, 2000). Among teenage girls, smoking rates increased dramatically around 1967, exactly the same time that women were being targeted by such new brands as Virginia Slims (Pierce, Lee, & Gilpin, 1994).

- Comprehensive three- and six-year longitudinal studies of 1,752 California adolescents who had never smoked that found that one-third of all smoking experimentation in California between 1993 and 1996 could be attributed to tobacco advertising and promotions (Gilpin, White, Messer, & Pierce, 2007; Pierce et al., 1998). These were the first studies to use longitudinal correlational data that could yield cause-and-effect conclusions. More recently, a longitudinal survey of 2,102 ten- to seventeen-year-olds found that high exposure to cigarette ads was a significant predictor of adolescent smoking initiation, even after controlling for many other, known contributing factors (Hanewinkel et al., 2011). At last count, there were 19 longitudinal studies, which consistently show that exposure to tobacco advertising and promotions increases the likelihood of adolescents' starting to smoke (Lovato, Watts, & Stead, 2011).

- Studies of adolescent brand preferences showing that they closely follow the amount of money that tobacco companies spend on advertising. Marlboro, Newport, and Camel are the brands of choice for 87% of high school smokers (CDC, 2009) (see Table 6.7). Similarly, in England, the most popular brands of cigarettes (Benson & Hedges, Silk Cut, Embassy, and Marlboro) are the mostly heavily advertised (Vickers, 1992).

- A study by Sargent and his colleagues (2000) that found a dose-response relationship between the number of cigarette promotional items owned by adolescents and their smoking behavior.

- A meta-analysis of 51 separate studies that found that exposure to tobacco marketing and advertising more than doubles the risk of a teenager's beginning to smoke (Wellman, Sugarman, DiFranza, & Winickoff, 2006).

Table 6.7 Is Cigarette Advertising Effective?

Advertising in $ Millions	Adolescent Brand Preference	Adult Brand Preference
1. Marlboro ($110)	1. Marlboro (52%)	1. Marlboro (34%)
2. Camel ($54)	2. Newport (21%)[a]	2. Newport (10%)
3. Newport ($48)	3. Camel (13%)	3. Camel (6%)

SOURCE: Data from Davis, Gilpin, Loken, Viswanath, and Wakefield (2008) and Centers for Disease Control and Prevention (2009). Data for advertising dollars are from 1993 to 2000; data for brand preference are from 2004 and 2006.

[a]Among African Americans, Newport is the brand of choice for 79%.

This is hardly an American phenomenon, however. In the United Kingdom, a survey of 1,450 students ages 11 and 12 years found that awareness of cigarette advertising correlated with smoking (While, Kelly, Huang, & Charlton, 1996), as did a survey of nearly 2,000 students who had been exposed to so-called passive cigarette advertising during an India–New Zealand cricket series televised in India. The message conveyed was "You become a better cricketer if you smoke," and the risk for initiation of smoking in nonsmoking youth tripled if they believed this message (Vaidya, Vaidya, & Naik, 1999). In Germany, a recent cross-sectional survey of 3,415 schoolchildren ages 10 to 17 years also found a two- to threefold higher risk of new-onset smoking with exposure to cigarette ads, as well as a dose-response relationship (Hanewinkel et al., 2010).

Unlike the United States, other countries have been more aggressive in banning cigarette advertising. In New Zealand, consumption fell after a complete ban on cigarette advertising (Vickers, 1992). In Norway, the prevalence of 13- to 15-year-old smokers decreased from 17% in 1975 to 10% in 1990 after an advertising ban was imposed (Vickers, 1992). In fact, an analysis of factors influencing tobacco consumption in 22 countries revealed that since 1973, advertising restrictions have resulted in much lower rates of smoking (Laugesen & Meads, 1991).

In 1998, the U.S. attorney general negotiated a remarkable settlement with the tobacco industry, calling for the payout of more than $206 billion to the states over the next 25 years, along with severe restrictions on marketing and advertising to children (see Table 6.3). Critics point to the fact that this figure represents a mere 8% of the $2.5 trillion that the federal government will lose over the same 25 years in health care costs related to smoking (D. Z. Jackson, 1998). In addition, according to the Federal Trade Commission, the tobacco industry actually spent more money on advertising and promotions immediately after the lawsuits were settled: $8.2 billion in 1999, a 22% increase from 1998 (Journal Wire Reports, 2001). Nevertheless, the now-substantial cigarette advertising research is hardly moot and may certainly have implications for alcohol advertising as well. For example, will there be future lawsuits by attorneys general to recover health care costs? In addition, the research may come back into play if the attorney general settlement is overturned by a federal court decision, or by a Congress that has traditionally been heavily influenced by tobacco money. What may replace concerns about advertising and promotion is increasing alarm over depictions of tobacco use in movies, music videos, and television programs—in a sense, the new "advertising" arena for tobacco companies.

Cigarettes in Television Programming, in Music and Music Videos, in Movies, and on the Internet

A report from the National Cancer Institute in 2008 concluded that "the total weight of evidence from cross-sectional, longitudinal, and experimental studies indicates a causal relationship between exposure to depictions of smoking in movies and youth smoking initiation" (Davis et al., 2008, p. 12). In 2011, the World Health Organization issued a report seconding this conclusion and calling for a comprehensive ban on tobacco advertising, promotion, and sponsorship and substantial reductions in smoking imagery in all film media (WHO, 2011). Although the amount of smoking in movies may now be decreasing, new research shows that it may be one of the leading factors in adolescents' decision of whether to smoke or not (Davis et al., 2008; Sargent, Gibson, et al., 2009; Titus-Ernstoff, Dalton, Adachi-Mejia, Longacre, & Beach, 2008).

Hollywood seems to use cigarette smoking as shorthand for troubled or antiestablishment characters, but the smoking or nonsmoking status of the actors themselves is also influential in whether their characters will smoke on screen (Shields, Carol, Balbach, & McGee, 1999). Until the Surgeon General's report on smoking in 1957, there was a long tradition of movie stars smoking onscreen and off (see Figures 6.11 and 6.13). Smoking among male characters is associated with violent behavior and dangerous acts; among females, it is associated with sexual affairs, illegal activities, and reckless driving (Heatherton & Sargent, 2009).

Figure 6.13   Hollywood stars in the 1940s and 1950s were often seen smoking onscreen and off. (Humphrey Bogart died from throat cancer; John Wayne died from lung cancer.)

Movie depictions also tend to be very pro-smoking, with only 14% of screen time dealing with adverse health effects (Stockwell & Glantz, 1997). Of the 100 top-grossing films of 2002, less than 1% of the smoking incidents depicted the fatal consequences of smoking (Dozier, Lauzen, Day, Payne, & Tafoya, 2005).

In previous decades, teenagers constituted 26% of the moviegoing audience but only 16% of the U.S. population (Rauzi, 1998). For many years, content analyses have found that a large proportion of American movies contain cigarette smoking. For example, in a study of the 100 top-grossing films from 1996 through 2004, researchers found that half of all R-rated movies (as well as 26% of PG-13 and 17% of PG movies) contained tobacco use (Tickle, Beach, & Dalton, 2009). From 1998 to 2004, nearly three-quarters of the top 100 box office hits contained smoking, and each movie had been seen by 25% of the 6,500 teenagers surveyed nationwide. That adds up to billions of smoking images overall and 665 per 10- to 14-year-old (Sargent, Tanski, & Gibson, 2007). Even G-rated movies can contain tobacco use (Goldstein, Sobel, & Newman, 1999; Yakota & Thompson, 2001) (see Table 6.8), although exposure to smoking in these films may not be as harmful (Lochbuehler, Sargent, Scholte, Pieters, & Engels, 2012).   However, three recent analyses—of the 25 top-grossing movies each year from 1990 to 2007, the 30 top-grossing movies from 1950 to 2006, and the 137 top-grossing movies from 2005 to 2010—have found that smoking occurrences have decreased significantly in the last few years (CDC, 2011; Jamieson & Romer, 2010; Sargent & Heatherton, 2009) (see Figure 6.14). In 2011, this downward trend may have ended: A study of the 134 top-grossing movies found that total tobacco incidents per movie rose 7% from 2010 to 2011.   Most alarming was the increase in tobacco incidents in G- and PG-rated movies (Glantz, Iaccopucci, Titus, & Polansky, 2012).

Table 6.8   Tobacco or Alcohol Content of G-Rated Children's Films

Film	Tobacco Use/Exposure (Seconds)	Alcohol Use/Exposure (Seconds)
The Three Caballeros	Yes (548)	Yes (8)
101 Dalmations	Yes (299)	Yes (51)
Pinocchio	Yes (22)	Yes (80)
James & the Giant Peach	Yes (206)	Yes (38)
All Dogs Go to Heaven	Yes (205)	Yes (73)
Alice in Wonderland	Yes (158)	No
Great Mouse Detective	Yes (165)	Yes (414)
The Aristocats	Yes (11)	Yes (142)
Beauty & the Beast	No	Yes (123)

SOURCE: Adapted from Goldstein, Sobel, and Newman (1999).

Figure 6.14   Number of tobacco incidents in top-grossing movies, by movie rating—United States, 1991–2010.

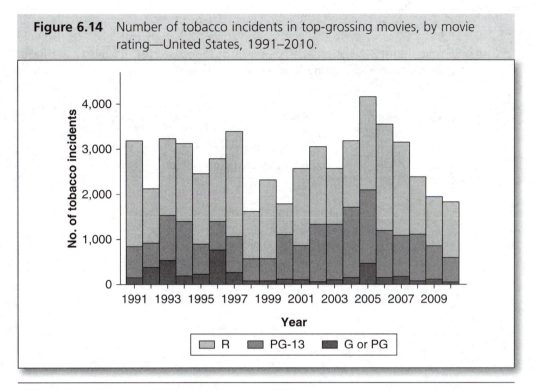

SOURCE: Centers for Disease Control and Prevention (2011).

As tobacco smoking in movies has decreased, so has the prevalence of smoking among adolescents (Sargent & Heatherton, 2009) (see Figure 6.15). Meanwhile, in Europe, tobacco imagery is still very common in popular films: A study of the most commercially successful films in six European countries between 2004 and 2009 found that 87% of "youth-rated" films contained smoking, compared with only 67% in the U.S. (Hanewinkel, Sargent, Karlsdottir, et al., 2012).

- A number of correlational and longitudinal studies have confirmed that exposure to smoking in the media is one of the key factors prompting teenagers to smoke. It may account for up to one-third of smoking initiation in young teenagers (Dalton et al., 2002). Public health advocates estimate that smoking portrayals in movies lead 300,000 adolescents to begin smoking each year, resulting in nearly $1 billion in profit for the tobacco industry (Alamar & Glantz, 2006; Charlesworth & Glantz, 2005). In fact, exposure to movie smoking may even trump parents' smoking status as being the key factor in adolescents' initiation of smoking (Titus-Ernstoff et al., 2008).
- Many large, recent European cross-sectional and cohort studies have found robust associations between onscreen smoking and adolescent smoking (S. J. Anderson, Millett, Polansky, & Glantz, 2010; Hanewinkel et al., 2010; Hunt, Henderson, Wight, & Sargent, 2011; Morgenstern, Poelen, et al., 2011; Waylen, Leary, Ness, & Tanski, 2011). European movies may actually contain more smoking than American movies; 85% of the 464 most commercially successful movies between 2004 and 2009 that portrayed smoking were

"youth" rated, compared with 59% in the U.S. (Hanewinkel, Sargent, Karlsdottir, et al., 2012). In India, a cross-sectional study of nearly 4,000 adolescents 12 to 16 years old found a significant association between exposure to tobacco use in Bollywood movies and onset of adolescent smoking (Arora et al., 2011).

Figure 6.15 Comparison of trends for adolescent smoking and smoking in movies, 1990–2007.

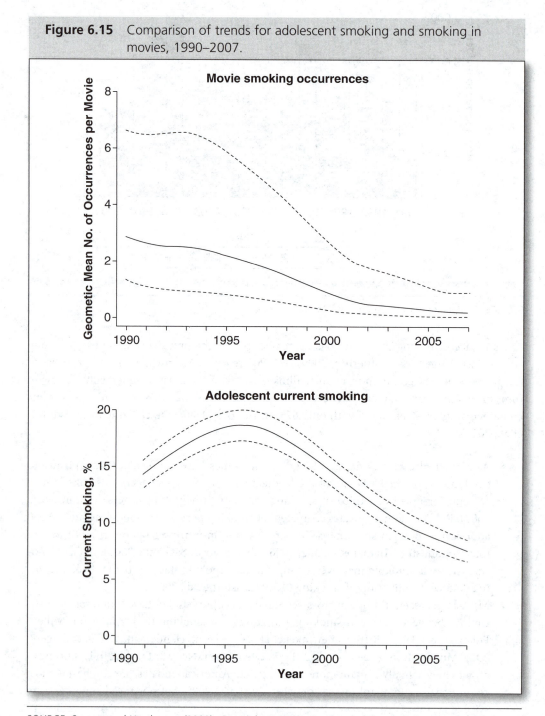

SOURCE: Sargent and Heatherton (2009). Copyright © AMA. Reprinted with permission.

- A prospective study of more than 3,500 teenagers found that exposure to R-rated movies doubles the risk of smoking, even when controlling for all other known factors (Dalton et al., 2002) (see Figure 6.16). Even exposure to movie trailers in movie theaters or on TV may increase the lure of cigarettes (Hanewinkel, 2009).

- A study of 735 adolescents 12 to 14 years old, with a two-year follow-up, found that exposure to R-rated movies and having a TV set in the bedroom significantly increased the risk of smoking initiation for White teens but not for Black teens (C. Jackson, Brown, & L'Engle, 2007). This is now the third longitudinal study documenting the risk of R-rated movies (Dalton et al., 2003; C. Jackson et al., 2007; Sargent et al., 2005).

- Five other longitudinal studies have documented the risk for youth of seeing smoking in movies of all ratings (Sargent, Stoolmiller, Worth, Gibson, & Gibbons, 2007; Sargent et al., 2012), including for German preteens and teens (Hanewinkel & Sargent, 2007, 2009) and elementary schoolchildren (Titus-Ernstoff et al., 2008). PG-13 movies—not R-rated movies—actually accounted for about two-thirds of the population effect in the most recent study (Sargent et al., 2012).

- A unique experimental study with 358 youth 11 to 14 years old found that preteens and teens exposed to movie scenes that depicted characters smoking for either social motives or relaxation were at particular risk for future smoking (Shadel et al., 2012).

Unfortunately, the most comprehensive content analyses that have examined substance use on television are now 10 years or more old and need updating (Christenson et al., 2000; DuRant et al., 1997). A study of the top-rated TV series for 12- to 17-year-olds found that 40% of episodes had at least one depiction of tobacco use, and shows rated TV-PG actually had more smoking incidents (50%) than those rated TV-14 (26%) (Cullen et al., 2011).

Figure 6.16   Does smoking in movies increase the risk of teen smoking?

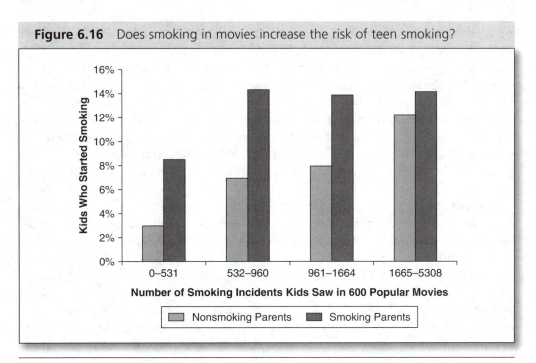

SOURCE: Charlesworth and Glantz (2005). Reproduced with permission from Stanton A. Glantz.

Self-reported exposure to pro-tobacco messages in various media have apparently declined from 2000 to 2004, except on the Internet. Still, 81% of 6th to 12th graders reported seeing images of smoking on TV or in movies (down from 90% previously) and 33% saw tobacco ads on the Internet (up from 22%) in three very large longitudinal samples (Duke et al., 2009). The first 18 seasons of *The Simpsons* contained an average of two smoking depictions per episode (Eslick & Eslick, 2009). Reality shows like *The Osbournes* frequently featured content endorsing tobacco use (Blair, Yue, Singh, & Bernhardt, 2005). On British TV, one content analysis found smoking-related scenes to occur at a rate of 3.4 instances per hour (Cumberbatch & Gauntlett, 2005). But generally, tobacco portrayals on TV are outnumbered by portrayals of alcohol and illicit drugs: On prime-time TV, 16% of all episodes studied in one analysis featured smoking and 29% illicit drug use, but one-third featured alcohol (Murphy, Hether, & Rideout, 2008).

Clearly, movies currently represent the greatest risk factor for teenagers, but a few studies have found a relationship between viewing smoking on TV and initiation of smoking. An older, two-year longitudinal study found a nearly sixfold risk of smoking initiation with more than five hours of TV viewing per day (Gidwani, Sobol, DeJong, Perrin, & Gortmaker, 2002). A more recent cross-sectional study found a similar dose-response relationship (Gutschoven & Van den Bulck, 2004). Nearly all children and teenagers have seen tobacco use on TV in the form of movie trailers (Healton, Watson-Stryker, & Allen, 2006), and one study found that such trailers increase the attractiveness of smoking for young people (Hanewinkel, 2009). Only a single study has examined the impact of TV on adult smoking—a unique 26-year longitudinal study in New Zealand that followed an unselected cohort of 1,000 individuals from birth. Researchers found that heavy TV viewing in childhood correlated with smoking at age 26 and that 17% of the variance in adult smoking might be attributable to the influence of excessive TV viewing during childhood (Hancox, Milne, & Poulton, 2004).

In music videos, smoking seems to have taken a backseat to more illicit substances (Gruber, Thau, Hill, Fisher, & Grube, 2005). Similarly, an analysis of the 279 most popular songs from 2005 found that only 3% mentioned tobacco use, whereas 24% mentioned alcohol use and 14% mentioned marijuana use (Primack, Dalton, Carroll, Agarwal, & Fine, 2008).

On the Internet, tobacco may not be as much of a problem currently—but that could change. A study involving 346 teenagers viewing 1.2 million webpages found that less than 1% of the pages contained tobacco content, much of which was anti-tobacco anyway. However, more than half of the content was from social networking sites, especially MySpace (Jenssen, Klein, Salazar, Daluga, & DiClemente, 2009). For many years teenagers could purchase cigarettes easily online (J. A. Bryant, Cody, & Murphy, 2002). The Preventing Illegal Internet Sales of Cigarettes and Smokeless Tobacco (PACT) Act would prevent that and was recently passed by Congress (Campaign for Tobacco-Free Kids, 2010; Cruz & Deyton, 2010). The Tobacco Control Act also contains provisions to address this by 2012 (see Table 6.4).

However, tobacco companies been spending more on Internet advertising; the figure increased from $125,000 in 1998 to $17.8 million in 2008 (Campaign for Tobacco-Free Kids, 2011). A 2010 study found that British American Tobacco employees were using social networking sites like Facebook to promote their products, especially in countries where advertising is banned (Freeman & Chapman, 2010). YouTube has also become a new source of pro-tobacco videos and tobacco imagery (Forsyth & Malone, 2010). One recent and interesting study of more than 1,000 teens found that teens who spend time every day on social networking sites are five times likelier to use tobacco than those who do not visit such sites (National Center on Addiction and Substance Abuse, 2011b) (see Figure 6.17).

Figure 6.17 Teen tobacco, alcohol, and marijuana use.

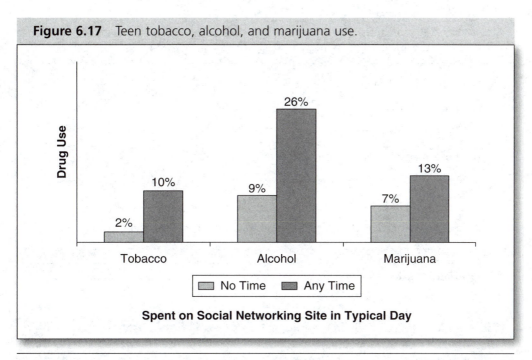

SOURCE: National Center on Addiction and Substance Abuse at Columbia University (2011b). Reprinted with permission.

Alcohol

Research on Alcohol Advertising

Although the research on alcohol advertising is not quite as compelling as that on tobacco advertising, children and teenagers are uniquely vulnerable audiences. Beer ads often seem custom made to appeal to preteens and teens, with images of fun-loving, sexy, successful young adults having the time of their lives (Borzekowski & Strasburger, 2008; Chen, Grube, Bersamin, Waiters, & Keefe, 2005). Who wouldn't want to indulge, especially when the ads make it seem as if everyone drinks (see Table 6.9)? Alcohol ads frequently feature sexual and social stereotypes that target teenagers (Austin & Hust, 2005) (see Figure 6.18). Youth ages 12 to 20 are 22 times more likely to see a product advertisement for alcohol than an alcohol-industry funded "responsibility" message (Center on Alcohol Marketing and Youth, 2010b).

The density of alcohol ads and the exposure of children and teens to them is a major concern: The average young person in the U.S. sees nearly 2,000 annually on TV alone (Jernigan, 2006; Strasburger & Council on Communications and Media, 2010a)—more than adults see and an increase of 71% from 2001 to 2009 (Center on Alcohol Marketing and Youth, 2010b). Similarly, in Australia, teens' overall exposure to alcohol advertising exceeds adults' exposure (Winter, Donovan, & Fielder, 2008). Often, this advertising is concentrated in teen shows or sports programming. All of the top 15 teens shows in the early 2000s contained alcohol ads (Center on Alcohol Marketing and Youth, 2004). Ads are also frequently embedded in sports programming—on banners, on scoreboards, or emblazoned on race cars (Nicholson & Hoye, 2009). Even hard liquor is now being advertised on TV for the first time in years (Semuels, 2009).

Table 6.9 Seven Myths That Alcohol Advertisers Want Children and Adolescents to Believe

1. Everyone drinks alcohol.

2. Drinking has no risks.

3. Drinking helps to solve problems.

4. Alcohol is magic potion that can transform you.

5. Sports and alcohol go together.

6. If alcohol were truly dangerous, we wouldn't be advertising it.

7. Alcoholic beverage companies promote drinking only in moderation.

SOURCE: Adapted from Kilbourne (1993).

Figure 6.18 Alcohol ads frequently feature sexual and social stereotypes that target teenagers.

For many years, alcoholic beverages popular with underage drinkers were disproportionately advertised in magazines with a higher youth readership (King et al., 2009). However, in recent years, magazine advertising may have been curtailed by the industry's voluntary standard that now restricts ads in media where the youth audience exceeds 30%. Consequently, youths' exposure has dropped significantly (CDC, 2007) (see Figure 6.19). From 2001 to 2008,

Figure 6.19 Trends in youth exposure to alcohol advertising in magazines and on television, 2001–2005.

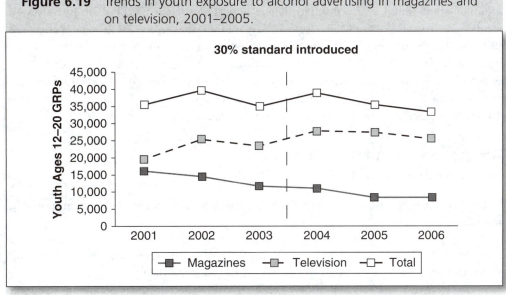

SOURCE: Center on Alcohol Marketing and Youth (2007). Reprinted with permission.

alcohol advertising in youth-oriented magazines decreased 48% (Center on Alcohol Marketing and Youth, 2010a). But on the radio—the second most popular medium for teenagers—young people often hear more alcohol ads than adults (Center on Alcohol Marketing and Youth, 2011b). A CDC study found that half of all the nearly 70,000 alcohol ads in 104 major markets around the country were airing on programming with a predominantly adolescent audience (CDC, 2007). A separate study of 75 local radio markets found that 9% of all alcohol ads were airing on programs with underage audiences, in violation of the industry's own 30% standard. Three brands (Bud Light, Coors Light, and Miller Lite) placed nearly half of the noncompliant ads (Center on Alcohol Marketing and Youth, 2011b).

Digital advertising and social networking sites have also come to the forefront (Montgomery & Chester, 2009; Moreno, Briner, Williams, Walker, & Christakis, 2009). In just a six-month period during 2003, teenagers made nearly 700,000 in-depth visits to 55 alcohol websites (Center on Alcohol Marketing and Youth, 2004). According to one survey, more than 3 million teens have a friend who has bought alcohol online, and more than half a million have done so themselves (Hitti, 2006).

Several studies have found significant associations between exposure to alcohol advertising and subsequent consumption (Borzekowski & Strasburger, 2008; Jernigan, 2006, 2009). At least eight cohort studies involving more than 13,000 young people have found modest associations (Gordon, MacKintosh, & Moodie, 2010; Smith & Foxcroft, 2009). Teenagers who obtain alcohol-branded merchandise are more likely to begin drinking (McClure, Stoolmiller, Tanski, Worth, & Sargent, 2009). Adolescents who engage in binge drinking are also more likely to name a favorite brand, which is usually one that is also heavily advertised (Tanski, McClure, Jernigan, & Sargent, 2011). In one large longitudinal study of more than a thousand 6th to 8th graders, those who had never tried alcohol but were receptive to alcohol marketing were 77% more likely to initiate drinking a year later than those who were unreceptive (Henriksen, Feighery, Schleicher, & Fortmann, 2008). Another recent longitudinal study found a 35% positive change in attitudes toward alcohol with exposure to alcohol advertising (Morgenstern, Isensee, Sargent, & Hanewinkel, 2011a), and a cross-sectional study of more than 3,400 sixth to eighth graders in Germany found a two- to threefold higher risk of drinking with frequent exposure to alcohol ads (Morgenstern, Isensee, Sargent, & Hanewinkel, 2011b). Finally, a 2013 longitudinal study of 3,890 students found that exposure to alcohol ads in 7th grade was predictive of alcohol use 4 years later, even when other known factors were controlled for (Grenard, Dent, & Stacy, 2013).

Alcohol on TV, in Music and Music Videos, in Movies, and Online

Several content analyses have been done recently that show that alcohol remains prevalent in mainstream American media:

- From 2004 to 2006, one-third of the top 10 prime-time shows featured alcohol, with only 6% showing negative consequences (Murphy et al., 2008).
- A recent analysis of 50 episodes of children's shows, 50 episodes of "tween" programs (with a 9- to 14-year-old target audience), 40 episodes of soap operas, and 50 episodes of prime-time shows during the 2003 season found as much alcohol content in the tween shows (37%) as in the soaps (33%) and the adult shows (38%) (Greenberg, Rosaen, Worrell, Salmon, & Volkman, 2009). On *The O.C.*, a show popular with preteens and teens, most of the drinking was done by adult women, but one-third did involve adolescents (Van den Bulck, Simons, & Van Gorp, 2008).
- In an analysis of 359 music videos broadcast in 2001, nearly half contained depictions of alcohol (Gruber, Thau, et al., 2005).
- Of the 279 most popular songs of 2005, nearly one-quarter contained references to alcohol use. Rap music had the most alcohol references, with 53% of the songs studied mentioning alcohol (Primack et al., 2008). And a study of the 793 most popular songs for teenagers between 2005 and 2007, according to *Billboard* magazine, found that 21% contained explicit alcohol references and that a typical teenager listening to an hour of popular music a day on the radio would hear three to four specific brand references (Primack, Nuzzo, Rice, & Sargent, 2012).
- In the UK, the top 10 programs watched by 10- to 15-year-olds in 2004 contained 12 alcohol-related scenes per hour (Cumberbatch & Gauntlett, 2005). In New Zealand, a study of 98 hours of prime-time TV programs from 2004 found one scene every nine minutes, with positive portrayals of alcohol outnumbering negative ones by a 12 to 1 margin (McGee, Ketchel, & Reeder, 2007).
- An analysis of the 100 top-grossing films for each year from 1996 through 2004 found that half of all R- and PG-13-rated movies and one-fourth of PG-rated movies contained alcohol use (Tickle et al., 2009). A 2006 study found that 92% of a random sample of 601 contemporary movies contained alcohol use (Sargent et al., 2006).

As with cigarette portrayals, alcohol portrayals seem to have an impact on actual use among adolescents (Sargent et al., 2006; Tanski, Dal Cin, Stoolmiller, & Sargent, 2010; Wills, Sargent, Gibbons, Gerrard, & Stoolmiller, 2009). A survey of more than 1,200 Pittsburgh high school students found that exposure to movies was independently associated with alcohol use (Primack, Kraemer, Fine, & Dalton, 2009). Similarly, a longitudinal study of more than 2,700 German students ages 10 to 16 years found that exposure to movie depictions of alcohol use was an independent predictor of alcohol initiation (Hanewinkel & Sargent, 2009). Most recently, a longitudinal study of 2,406 students in 5th to 8th grade who had never used alcohol found that exposure to R-rated movies tripled the likelihood of their having used alcohol when they were resurveyed one to two years later (see Figure 6.20) (Tanski et al., 2010).

A review of seven cohort studies involving more than 13,000 young people found modest but significant association between exposure to alcohol portrayals and subsequent consumption (Smith & Foxcroft, 2009). The most recent cohort sample involved 6,522 ten- to fourteen-year-olds, who were studied four times over a two-year period (Stoolmiller et al., 2012) (see Figure 6.21). An even larger study—of 13 longitudinal studies involving more than 38,000 young people—also concluded that exposure to media and commercial depictions involving alcohol is consistently associated with both an increased likelihood of starting to drink and increased alcohol consumption among teens already drinking (P. Anderson et al., 2009). In Europe, a cross-sectional survey of 16,551 students in six countries found a robust association between alcohol depictions in movies and adolescent binge drinking that was relatively unaffected by cultural contexts (Hanewinkel, Sargent, Poelen, et al., 2012). One creative lab experiment actually exposed young adults to various movies with and without alcohol depictions and observed what they drank while watching. Movies with alcohol content and alcohol commercials resulted in more alcohol being consumed during viewing (Engels, Hermans, van Baaren, Hollenstein, & Bot, 2009).

Social networking sites represent new ways of reaching teenagers and—intentionally or unintentionally—exerting peer pressure on them to begin drinking. The 10 leading alcohol

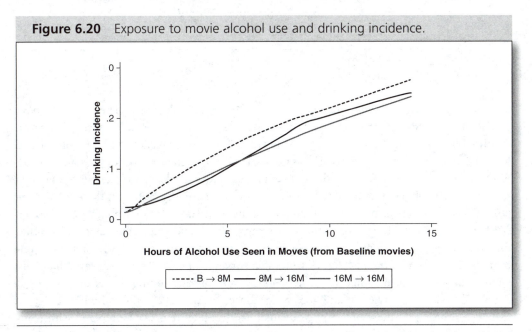

Figure 6.20   Exposure to movie alcohol use and drinking incidence.

Drinking Incidence

Hours of Alcohol Use Seen in Moves (from Baseline movies)

----- B → 8M —— 8M → 16M —— 16M → 16M

SOURCE: Data based on Sargent and colleagues (2005); Sargent, Worth, Beach, Gerrard, and Heatherton (2008).

Figure 6.21 Alcohol onset and progression to binge drinking.

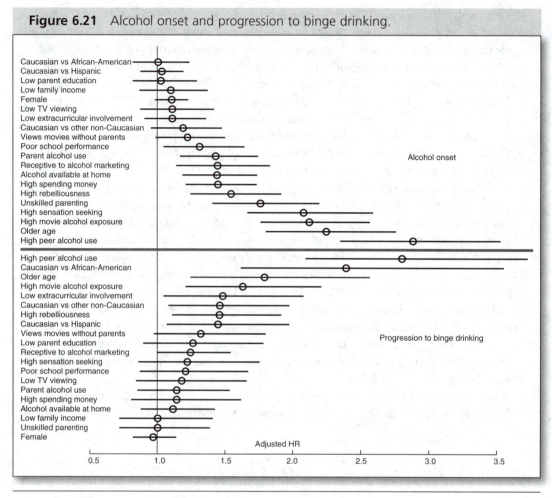

SOURCE: Stoolmiller and colleagues (2012). Reprinted with permission.

brands have nearly 7 million people "liking" their Facebook pages. These brands have uploaded more than 35,000 photos and 375 videos to their Facebook pages (Center on Alcohol Marketing and Youth, 2011a). A study of 500 MySpace profiles of 18-year-olds found that 41% referenced substance use (Moreno, Parks, Zimmerman, Brito, & Christakis, 2009). Another, similar study of four hundred 17- to 20-year-olds' profiles found that 56% contained references to alcohol (Moreno et al., 2010). Teens who reference alcohol on their profiles are more likely to engage in problem drinking (Moreno, Christakis, Egan, Brockman, & Becker, 2012; Moreno, Grant, Kacvinsky, Egan, & Fleming, 2012), and teens who see peers' profiles that describe alcohol adventures are more likely to view drinking as normative behavior (Litt & Stock, 2011). In two recent NCASA Columbia surveys, 40% of all teens surveyed had seen pictures on Facebook or other social networking sites of kids getting drunk or passed out (National Center on Addiction and Substance Abuse, 2011b, 2012). Often, these pictures are seen at a young (and therefore impressionable) age (see Figure 6.22). Compared with teens who did not access social networking sites in a typical day, teens who did were four times

Figure 6.22   Age of teens when they first saw pictures of kids drunk, passed out, or using drugs on a social networking site.

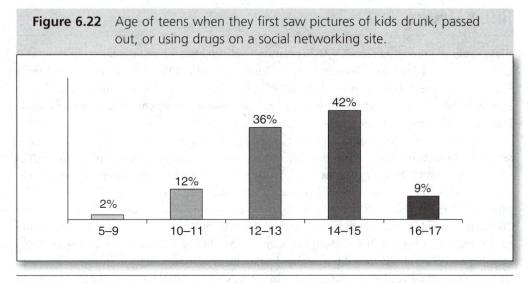

SOURCE: National Center on Addiction and Substance Abuse at Columbia University (2011b). Reprinted with permission.

likelier to have used marijuana, more than three times likelier to have used alcohol, and almost three times likelier to have used tobacco (National Center on Addiction and Substance Abuse, 2012) (see Figure 6.23). Note that these are cross-sectional data only, however. Finally, unlike cigarettes, alcohol can still be purchased illegally by teens online; of 100 orders placed online by underage buyers, 45% were successfully received (Williams & Ribisl, 2012).

Figure 6.23   Association between seeing pictures of teens using drugs, getting drunk or passed out and teen substance use.

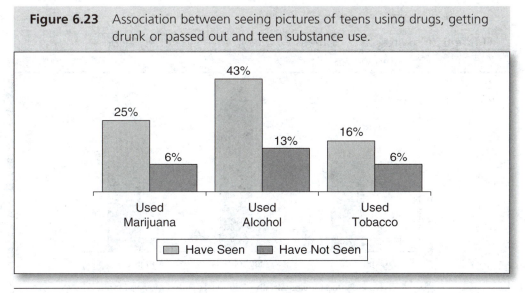

SOURCE: National Center on Addiction and Substance Abuse at Columbia University (2012). Reprinted with permission.

Illicit Drugs

Illicit drugs are rarely seen on TV (Christenson et al., 2000), with the exception of programs like Showtime's *Weeds* and *Shameless*, HBO's *Entourage*, and FOX's *That 70s Show*. But teens with a TV in their own bedroom have a far greater likelihood of engaging in risky health behaviors, such as sexual activity or using tobacco, marijuana, or alcohol (Gruber, Wang, et al., 2005; Hanewinkel & Sargent, 2009).

Drug scenes are more common in movies (22% of movies in one study contained drug scenes), where more than half of the time no harmful consequences are shown (Roberts & Christenson, 2000). Marijuana is the most frequent drug seen in movies and seems to be making a comeback in R-rated movies like the *Harold and Kumar* series, *Totally Baked* (2007), *Pineapple Express* (2008), *The Hangover Part II* (2011), and *Bad Teacher* (2011) (Halperin, 2008). A Columbia study found that viewing R-rated movies was associated with a sixfold higher risk of trying marijuana (National Center on Addiction and Substance Abuse, 2005) (see Figure 6.24). Hollywood filmmakers do not seem to understand that humor tends to undermine normal adolescent defenses against drugs and legitimizes their use (Borzekowski & Strasburger, 2008). Increased consumption of popular music is also associated with marijuana use (Primack, Kraemer, Fine, & Dalton, 2009; Primack, Douglas, & Kraemer, 2010).

In rap music, the prevalence of drug mentions and behavior has increased sixfold over the past several decades, with marijuana predominating (two-thirds of instances). Drug use in rap music has come to signify wealth and sociability, and attitudes toward drugs have changed from negative to positive (Herd, 2008). In one study, 77% of rap songs contained portrayals of substance use (Primack et al., 2008). Teens may hear as many as 84 drug references daily in popular songs (Primack et al., 2008) (see Figure 6.25). Music videos have paralleled this trend, with rap and hip-hop videos containing two to three times more alcohol and illicit substance mentions than other genres (Strasburger & Council on Communications and Media, 2010a).

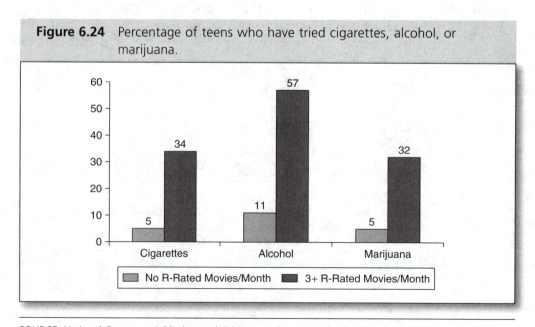

Figure 6.24 Percentage of teens who have tried cigarettes, alcohol, or marijuana.

SOURCE: National Center on Addiction and Substance Abuse at Columbia University (2005).

Figure 6.25

SOURCE: *Zits* © 1998 Zits Partnership. Dist. by King Features Syndicate.

Overall, nearly half of music videos examined in one study contained alcohol, tobacco, or other drugs of abuse, with alcohol present in 35%, tobacco in 10%, and illicit drugs in 13% (Gruber, Thau, et al., 2005).

Two new reports also implicate new media in teen drug use. A survey of more than a thousand 12- to 17-year-olds found that teens who spend time daily on social networking sites are twice as likely to use marijuana (National Center on Addiction and Substance Abuse, 2011b). In addition, there are more than 350 websites advertising or selling controlled prescription drugs, and 85% of the sites do not require a prescription (National Center on Addiction and Substance Abuse, 2008).

A Word About Prescription and Nonprescription Drugs

Currently, the only countries in the world that allow advertising of prescription drugs are the U.S. and New Zealand. In the U.S., nearly $30 billion is spent annually on promotion of a variety of prescription drugs, including $4.4 billion on advertising (Donohue, Cevasco, & Rosenthal, 2007; Rubin, 2009). In direct-to-consumer advertising, erectile dysfunction drugs lead the way; whereas statins and psychotropic drugs are most commonly marketed to healthcare professionals (Congressional Budget Office, 2009) (see Figure 6.26). The FDA has just 57 officials who are tasked with reviewing approximately 75,000 ads and marketing items a year. In 2010, they began a "Bad Ad" campaign to enlist doctors to help in spotting and reporting questionable ads or promotions (Heavey & Richwine, 2010).

In 2000, Merck spent more money advertising Vioxx ($161 million) than Dell, Budweiser, Pepsi, or Nike spent (Rosenthal, Berndt, Frank, Donohue, & Epstein 2002). Drug companies now spend more than twice as much money on marketing and promotion as they do on research and development, and studies show that these marketing efforts pay off (Rosenthal et al., 2002); a survey of physicians found that 92% of patients had requested an advertised drug (Thomaselli, 2003). Direct-to-consumer advertising has remained controversial since the FDA first approved of it in 1997 (Frosch, Grande, Tarn, & Kravitz, 2010; Gellad & Lyles, 2007). American TV viewers see as many as 16 hours of prescription drug ads per year (Frosch, Krueger, Hornik, Cronholm, & Barg, 2007). Emotional appeals are almost universal, and the

Figure 6.26 Spending for DTC advertising and detailing to health care professionals among the 10 drug classes in CBO's data set with the highest dtc spending, 2008.

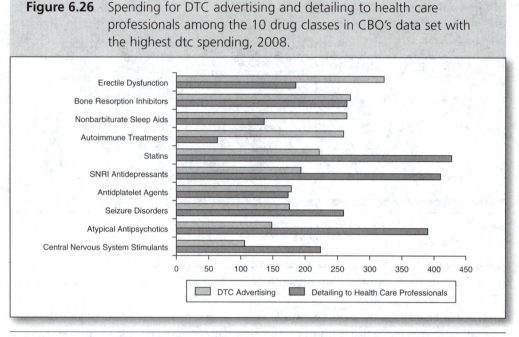

SOURCE: Congressional Budget Office Based on data from SDI Promotional Audits.

NOTES: Detailing refers to the practice in which pharmaceutical representatives make sales calls to physicians and other health care professionals to discuss the uses of a particular prescription drug and its benefits for patients
DTC = direct to consumer: SNRI = serotonin-norepinephrine reuptake inhibitors.

ads provide only limited educational information (Frosch et al., 2007). Children and teenagers get the message that there is a pill to cure all ills, and a drug for every occasion, including sexual intercourse (Borzekowski & Strasburger, 2008). In the first 10 months of 2004 alone, drug companies spent nearly half a billion dollars advertising Viagra, Levitra, and Cialis (Snowbeck, 2005) (see Figure 6.27). Yet the advertising of condoms, birth control pills, and emergency contraception is haphazard and rare and remains controversial (Strasburger and Council on Communications and Media, 2010b).

Figure 6.27 Drug companies spend billions of dollars advertising drugs for erectile dysfunction.

Solutions

In the past three decades, when "Just say no" has become the watchword for many parents, school-based drug prevention programs, and federal drug prevention efforts, unprecedented amounts of money are being spent to induce children and adolescents to "just say yes" to tobacco and alcohol. Perhaps, as one group of researchers has suggested, the "discussion [should] be *elevated* [emphasis added] from the scientific and legal arenas to the domain of ethics and social responsibility" (Orlandi et al., 1989, p. 92) (see Table 6.10). Below are eight possible approaches that could very well result in significant reductions in adolescent cigarette, alcohol, and drug use.

Table 6.10   Newspapers and Magazines That Refuse Cigarette Advertising (partial listing)

Newspapers	*The New Yorker* (does accept cigar ads)
The Christian Science Monitor	
The New York Times	*Parenting*
Parade	*Reader's Digest*
	Scientific American
Magazines (adult)	
American Baby	**Magazines (youth)**
Business Week	*Boy's Life*
Consumer Reports	*Mad*
Good Housekeeping	*Seventeen*

---

1. *A ban on cigarette advertising in all media and effective restrictions on alcohol advertising.* Any product as harmful as tobacco should have severe restrictions placed on it (Committee on Environmental Health, Community on Substance Abuse, Committee on Adolescence, and Committee on Native American Child Health, 2009; Kunkel, 2007; Strasburger and Council on Communications and Media, 2010a). An increasing number of countries are banning all tobacco advertising in all media (Prokhorov et al., 2006). Are such bans effective? One study of 30 developing countries found that partial bans reduced consumption 13.6%, while complete bans reduced consumption 23.5% (Blecher, 2008).

   On the other hand, a total ban on all alcohol advertising would be both impractical and unproductive, and probably illegal as well. Unlike cigarettes, alcohol may have legitimate uses when consumed in moderation. But restricting alcohol advertising in programming for youth audiences to less than 15% would be an easily achievable and significant step (Center on Alcohol Marketing and Youth, 2007), and it would result in a 20% reduction in teens' exposure to alcohol ads and would result in alcohol manufacturers being able to reduce their advertising costs by 8% (Jernigan, 2006; Jernigan, Ostroff, & Ross, 2005). In turn, reducing adolescents' exposure to alcohol ads could reduce their alcohol consumption by as much as 25% (Saffer & Dave, 2006). In 2007, a report by the U.S. Surgeon General supported reducing alcohol ads in venues popular with young people (U.S Department of Health and Human Services, 2007); and in 2011, 24 state attorneys general sent a letter to the Federal Trade Commission supporting the 15% standard (Join Together Staff, 2011).

Alternatively, beer and wine manufacturers could be restricted to so-called "tombstone ads" (an industry term for ads that show only the product, not the sexy beach babes or funny talking animals) (Chen et al., 2005; Strasburger & Council on Communications and Media, 2010a). A return to banning direct-to-consumer prescription drug marketing should be considered as well (Stange, 2007).

2. *Higher taxes on tobacco and alcohol products.* Taxes have a direct and immediate effect on the consumption of products, particularly by teenagers (U.S. Department of Health and Human Services, 1994). For cigarettes, every 10% increase in the price will reduce underage smokers by 6% to 7% (Campaign for Tobacco-Free Kids, 2009b).

3. *More aggressive counteradvertising.* Counteradvertising has been shown to be effective, but only if it is intensive, thoughtfully planned, and uses a variety of different media (Flynn et al., 2007; Ibrahim, & Glantz, 2007; Noar, 2006) (see Figure 6.28). For example, a four-year, $50 million campaign in Massachusetts resulted in a 50% reduction in the new onset of smoking by young teens (Siegel & Biener, 2000). Antismoking ads may be particularly effective for young children (Nixon, Mansfield, & Thoms, 2008). In 2011, the FDA announced that it will spend $600 million over the next five years on TV and print ads and via social media to try to educate the public about the dangers of tobacco use (Bacon, 2011). It has also revealed nine new large, graphic cigarette warning labels under the agency's new powers to regulate tobacco products (Young, 2011) (see Figure 6.29), but the tobacco industry is already challenging the constitutionality of the labels on First Amendment grounds (Outterson, 2010). In 2012, a U.S. court of appeals issued a two-to-one decision that the labels would violate corporate free speech rights—a ruling that

Figure 6.28   Examples of counteradvertising.

SOURCE: Partnership for a Drug-Free America and MADD.

Figure 6.29 Graphic cigarette pack warning labels proposed by the FDA.

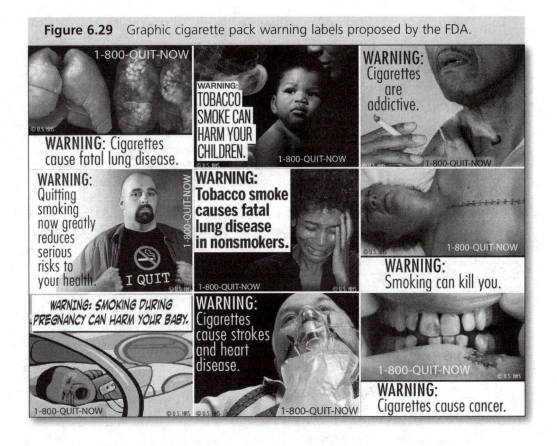

contradicted another appellate court decision and sets up the possibility that the U.S. Supreme Court will take the case (Bayer, Gostin, & Marcus-Toll, 2012; Reuters, 2012).

For current smokers, new brain imaging technology (functional magnetic resonance imaging) has found that low-key antismoking ads may actually be preferable to attention-grabbing ads (Langleben et al., 2009). By contrast, graphic warning labels may be effective (Strasser, Tang, Romer, Jepson, & Cappella, 2012). However, the biggest hurdle is that rarely, if ever, does the occurrence rate of counteradvertising come close to that of regular advertising and promotions and scenes of tobacco use on TV, in the movies, and online.

The three best-known counteradvertising efforts have done by the Partnership for a Drug-Free America (PDFA), the White House Office of National Drug Control Policy (ONCDP), and the Truth campaign:

- A study of PDFA ads found that more than 80% of nearly 1,000 public school students ages 11 to 19 could recall such ads, and half of the students who had tried drugs reported that the ads actually convinced them to decrease or stop using drugs (Reis, Duggan, Adger, & DeAngelis, 1992). However, a more recent study questioned the effectiveness of PDFA ads. A nationally representative sample of more than five thousand 9- to 18-year-olds was surveyed four times between 1999 and 2004. Although substantial exposure to antidrug advertising was achieved (94% of youths reported exposure to one or more ads per month, with a media frequency of about two to three per week), there was no change in prevalence of marijuana use and some evidence for a possible boomerang effect (Hornik, Jacobsohn, Orwin, Piesse, & Kalton, 2008).

Unfortunately, not a single PDFA ad has ever aired that targets either tobacco or alcohol. Similarly, Congress has given nearly $1 billion to the Office of National Drug Policy Control (ONDCP) for the National Youth Anti-Drug Media Campaign, which has included partnering with the PDFA (Hornik et al., 2008) (see Figure 6.30), but so far not a single ad has targeted tobacco or alcohol—a remarkable finding, given that tobacco and alcohol represent the two most significant drug threats to children and adolescents (Strasburger and Council on Communications and Media, 2010a). Effects of the 2002 "My Anti-Drug" campaign actually showed increased marijuana use among teenagers (Hornik et al., 2008). The ONDCP's new campaign, "*Above the Influence*," began in 2005 (see Figure 6.31), and two studies have shown some efficacy; exposure to the ads predicted reduced marijuana use among both male and female 8th graders in one study (Slater et al., 2011) but among only female 8th graders in a study of 8th-, 10th-, and 12th-grade males and females (Carpenter & Pechmann, 2011). Certainly, it may be unrealistic to expect antidrug advertising campaigns to have a major impact on teen use, given the multifactorial nature of adolescent drug use and the multitude of media influences (Terry-McElrath et al., 2010).

Figure 6.30   NYADMC and PDFA media campaigns.

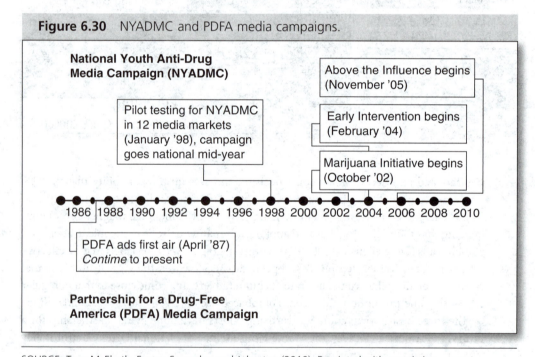

SOURCE: Terry-McElrath, Emery, Szczypka, and Johnston (2010). Reprinted with permission.

- As part of the tobacco industry's $246 billion Tobacco Master Settlement Agreement (see Table 6.3), the nonprofit American Legacy Foundation was established, which produces the "Truth" ads. Such ads often try to expose the tobacco industry as being manipulative and deceptive (see Figure 6.32). In one ad, two teenagers carry a lie detector into Philip Morris's New York headquarters and announce that they want to deliver it to the marketing department. In another, a group of teens in a large delivery truck pull up in front of headquarters and begin unloading body bags. One teen shouts through a megaphone, "Do you know how many people tobacco kills every day?" (A. Bryant, 2000). The ads are so hard-hitting that Philip Morris actually insisted that two be withdrawn. Yet in Florida, they accounted for one-fourth of the decline in the prevalence of teen smoking from 25% in 1999 to 18% in 2002 (Farrelly, Davis, Haviland, Messeri, & Healton, 2005). By contrast, ads made by Philip Morris as part of their $100 million campaign cautioning teens to "Think. Don't smoke" are ineffectual and may be a "sham" ("Big Tobacco's Promises," 2006; Henriksen, Dauphinee, Wang, & Fortmann, 2006; Paek & Gunther, 2007).

> *Citizens and policymakers should reject any "educational" programs by the tobacco industry. If the tobacco industry were sincere in its stated desire to contribute to reducing youth smoking, it would stop opposing policies and programs that have been demonstrated to be effective. (Landman et al., 2002, p. 925)*

A few years ago, the Motion Picture Association of America (MPAA) agreed

Figure 6.31 Ad from "Above the Influence" campaign.

Figure 6.32 "Truth" ad from the American Legacy Foundation.

to include an antismoking ad on all new DVDs (Serjeant, 2008). Airing antismoking ads just before showing big Hollywood movies that feature a lot of smoking would also be effective (Edwards, Harris, Cook, Bedford, & Zuo, 2004; Edwards, Oakes, & Bull, 2007), but this is not currently being done. The 15-minute period prior to movie previews is actually under the control of local theater owners, not Hollywood, so this would be feasible (Heatherton & Sargent, 2009). Hollywood filmmakers need to stop using smoking as a shorthand device for an evil or conflicted character, and film school students need to be educated about the health effects of what they produce (Chapman, 2008). In 2007, Disney actually vowed to discontinue all smoking in its movies ("Up in Smoke," 2007) (see Table 6.11).

4. *Increased sensitivity and awareness of the entertainment industry to the health-related issues of smoking, drinking, and other drug use in TV programming, movies, music and music videos, and video games.* Ideally, people in the entertainment industry would understand that with the billions of dollars they make each year comes a public health responsibility; sadly, most of the time they do not (Strasburger, 2009a). They are exceptions, however. The old *Beverly Hills, 90210* was conscientious in avoiding gratuitous drug use and showing the consequences instead. *Ferris Bueller's Day Off* was intentionally smoke-free in 1986, and so was *The Devil Wears Prada* in 2006. In the UK, old cartoons such as *Tom and Jerry*, *The Flintstones*, *The Jetsons*, and *Scooby-Doo* are now being edited to eliminate smoking scenes ("British Channel Bans," 2006). Prosocial content does not have to interfere with storylines, and it can contribute significantly to young people's notions about health (Hogan & Strasburger, 2008; Kaiser Family Foundation, 2004). The idea that being drunk is funny is a myth that needs to be seriously reexamined by the entertainment industry and could easily be contributing to the high rates of binge drinking among teens (Miller, Naimi, Brewer, & Jones, 2007) (see Figure 6.33). Rock music lyrics and music videos could avoid glamorizing drinking or getting drunk (Council on Communications and Media, 2009). Teen-oriented shows and channels like MTV and BET could lead the way by developing more prosocial

---

Table 6.11   Four Steps to Reducing Youth Exposure to Smoking in Movies

1. Give an R rating to all movies containing smoking (with exceptions for movies that depict the dangers of smoking or represent real historical figures). The World Health Organization, the American Heart Association, the American Medical Association, and the American Academy of Pediatrics all support this recommendation.

2. Certify that there are no payoffs from tobacco companies.

3. Show antismoking ads before showing movies that contain smoking.

4. Stop identifying tobacco brands in movies, including in background scenery such as billboards.

SOURCE: Bonnie, Stratton, and Wallace (2007); SmokeFreeMovies.ucsf.edu.

programming and by airing antismoking and anti-alcohol PSAs. Of course, according to one group of researchers, there may not be a problem to begin with—TV characters use drugs less often than the actual U.S. population does (Long, O'Connor, Gerbner, & Concato, 2002)!

Figure 6.33 Getting drunk isn't funny.

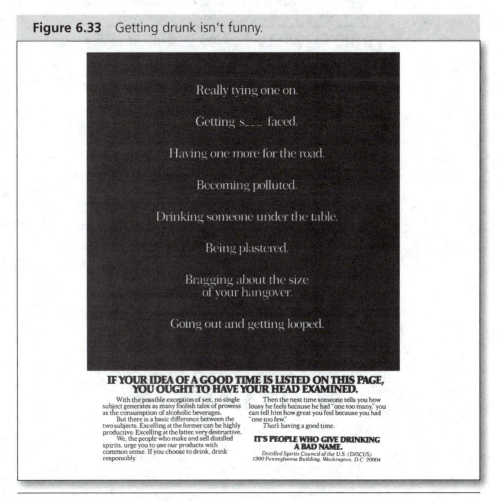

SOURCE: © Distilled Spirits Council of the United States.

5. *Revision of the ratings systems for both television and movies.* As discussed in Chapter 13, several studies show that parents would prefer a universal ratings system that would apply to movies, TV, and video games, one that would be more specific and content based (Greenberg, Rampoldi-Hnilo, & Mastro, 2000; Walsh & Gentile, 2001). A recent survey of more than 3,000 adults nationwide found that 70% support an R rating for movies that depict smoking (see Figure 6.34), and two-thirds would like to see antismoking PSAs before any film that depicts smoking (McMillen, Tanski, Winickoff, & Valentine, 2007). According to one recent study, an R rating for smoking

Figure 6.34 Americans support an R rating for movies that depict smoking.

SOURCE: SmokeFreeMovies.ucsf.edu. Reprinted with permission.

NOTE: Some critics have proposed that an R rating be given by the Motion Picture Association of America (MPAA) for tobacco use in films. An alternative solution would be to have all movie sets declared smoke-free because secondhand smoke is an occupational health hazard.

would reduce adolescent smoking onset by nearly 20%, since smoke-free PG-13 movies would come into the market (currently, PG-13 movies actually feature more smoking incidents than R-rated movies) (Sargent et al., 2012). In May 2007, the MPAA announced that it would consider cigarette smoking in their ratings scheme (MPAA, 2007), but it is unclear how exactly this will play out (Pupillo, 2007).

3. *Increased sensitivity to media effects and increased media literacy.* A century ago, to be "literate" meant that you could read and write. In the year 2013, to be literate means that you can read and write, text, download, tweet, and successfully understand and "decode" a dizzying array of different media and media messages (Rich & Bar-on, 2001). Ideally, parents need to begin this process early with their children and understand that a child who watches TV four hours or more a day has a fivefold increased risk of smoking, for example, compared to one who watches less than two hours per day (Gidwani et al., 2002). Similarly, young children exposed to PG-13- and R-rated movies at young ages are at increased risk for both smoking and drinking (Dalton et al., 2006; Dalton et al., 2009; Sargent et al., 2004; Tanski et al., 2009; Tanski et al., 2010; Thompson & Gunther, 2007). A study of more than 6,500 preteens and teens found that, on average, 12.5% of them had seen each of 40 R-rated movies (Worth, Chambers, Nassau, Rakhra, & Sargent, 2008). A four-wave longitudinal study of 6,522 preteens and teens found less smoking among teens whose parents had R-rated movie restrictions (de Leeuw et al., 2011). According to the American Academy of Pediatrics, parents need to avoid screen time for children younger than 2 years old, limit total entertainment screen time to less than 2 hours per day, co-view with their children, carefully monitor what media their children use and watch, and avoid letting young children see PG-13- and R-rated movies (Council on Communications and Media, 2010; Longacre et al., 2009).

Schools can help as well (Strasburger, 2012). Certain drug prevention programs— programs that incorporate media literacy—have been shown to be extremely effective in reducing levels of teen drug use (see Figure 6.35 and Chapter 12), but such programs must go far beyond the Drug Abuse Resistance Education (DARE) approach being used in 75% of public schools across the country (Botvin & Griffin, 2005). DARE tends to employ scare tactics, be very simplistic (see Figure 6.36), and may have boomerang effects (Lilienfeld, 2007). In 2001, the U.S. Surgeon General cited DARE as being ineffective (U.S. Department of Health and Human Services, 2001). A meta-analysis of 20 different studies and a 10-year follow-up study of 1,002 individuals who received the training in 6th grade both found the program to be ineffective as well (Lynam et al., 1999; Pan & Bai, 2009).

The U.S. is unique among Western nations in not requiring some form of media literacy for its students (J. D. Brown, 2007). Several studies now indicate that successful drug prevention may be possible through this unique route (Austin & Johnson, 1997; Austin, Pinkleton, Hust, & Cohen, 2005; Bickham & Slaby, 2012; Kupersmidt, Scull, & Austin, 2010; Pinkleton & Austin, 2013, in press; Potter, 2010; Primack, Fine, Yang, Wickett, & Zickmund, 2009; Primack, Gold, Land, & Fine, 2006; Primack & Hobbs, 2009; Primack, Sidani, Carroll, & Fine, 2009; Slater et al., 2006; Weichold, Brambosch, & Silbereisen, 2012) (see Chapter 12). In addition, there are now media education programs that can reduce adolescents' displays of risky behaviors on social networking websites (Moreno, VanderStoep, Parks, Zimmerman, Kurth, & Christakis, 2009).

Figure 6.35 Follow-up results from four published studies: 8th-grade drug use and 12th-grade polydrug use.

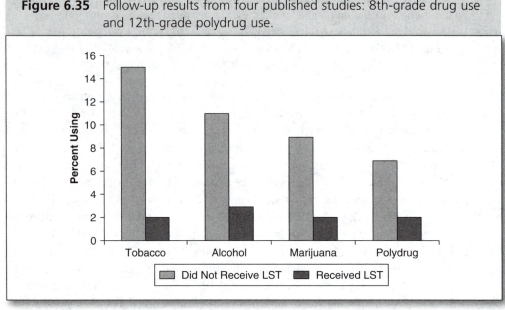

SOURCE: Copyright Princeton Health Press. Reprinted by permission.

NOTE: A LST (life skills training) approach to drug prevention has shown dramatic decreases in adolescents' use of a variety of drugs, yet has not been implemented in many communities because DARE (Drug Abuse Resistance Education) programs already exist. The LST approach is based on the work of Botvin (see Botvin & Griffin, 2005). By comparison, there is no evidence that the simplistic messages contained in the $226 million DARE program have had any impact (West & O'Neal, 2004), yet DARE has been used in 80% of school systems nationwide (Kalb, 2001). The DARE curriculum has undergone a revision to incorporate some of the LFT principles.

Figure 6.36 DARE advertising tends to be simplistic.

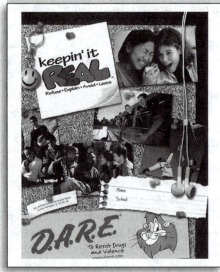

4. *More research.* Considering how significant the impact of the media is on young people, it seems astounding that more financial resources are not being devoted to media research (Christakis & Zimmerman 2006; Strasburger, Jordan, & Donnerstein, 2012). According to the most recent Kaiser report, children and teens spend more than seven hours per day with a variety of different media (Rideout, 2010), yet the federal government funds only a handful of studies. Currently no foundation funds any media research (the Kaiser Family Foundation announced in February 2010 that it was discontinuing its Program for the Study of Media and Health, which has produced some of the best media research in the past 15 years). New studies of how different teens process drug content in different media are

needed, as are continuing studies of the impact of the Internet and of social networking sites. Understanding how media affect audiences differently is critical to better focusing intervention efforts (Austin, Chen, & Grube, 2006; Ringel, Collins, & Ellickson, 2006; Ward, Day, & Thomas, 2010). For example, African American youth are known to be relatively resistant to tobacco advertising, but why this is true is unclear (CDC, 2006; West, Romero, & Trinidad, 2007). Existing research needs to be more widely disseminated as well. A new Surgeon General's report or National Institute of Mental Health (NIMH) report might prove to be extremely useful to researchers, health professionals, parents, and policymakers and could provide the impetus for increasing funding of research. The last NIMH report on children and media was published in 1982, well before the advent of the Internet, DVRs, cell phones, digital advertising, and social networking sites!

5. *Campaign finance reform in Congress.* This recommendation may seem strange in a chapter about the effects of media on young people, but four major groups arguably control much of what is media related in Congress—the National Rifle Association (NRA), beer and wine manufacturers, the tobacco industry, and the food industry—and not one has the best interests of the nation's children and adolescents at heart. Perhaps not coincidentally, violence, drug use, and obesity are three of the leading health problems facing children and adolescents. Congress can control the media and help to make them more healthful, but until they are liberated from their dependence to these special interest groups, American media will remain potentially unhealthy for young people.

Exercises

1. *Product placements.* You are the new owner of a baseball team in Milwaukee. The makers of Old Milwaukee Beer come to you, asking if they can help build you a new scoreboard out in center field. You drink Old Milwaukee Beer yourself, and you were born and raised in Milwaukee. They offer to pay for the new scoreboard ($2 million), plus give you an annual fee of $750,000. Should you accept their offer? If, instead, you are a member of the Milwaukee City Council, should you allow this to happen? Would it be legal to ban such advertising from public ballparks? If you were the director of sports broadcasting for a TV station, would it be ethical for you to instruct the camera operators to avoid showing advertising logos whenever possible?

2. *Drugs and the movies #1.* You are the heir apparent to Scorsese and Tarantino. A recent graduate of the USC School of Cinematic Arts and only 24 years old, you are being offered a directing assignment by a major studio: a big-budget action thriller with three major stars. But the film centers on an antihero. You, yourself, do not drink alcohol or smoke cigarettes, in part because your mother died from lung cancer and your father died from cirrhosis. How do you depict the antihero without showing him smoking or drinking and without consuming 10 extra pages of script? Will profanity alone accomplish your task?

3. *Drugs and the movies #2.* You are an Oscar-nominated film director in your 40s, but you have never made a film about the impact of drugs on society. You want this to be the overriding theme of your next film, which you will write, direct, and coproduce. You admired *Traffic* a great deal. On the other hand, you thought that *The Hangover Part II* and *Blow* glamorized cocaine more than they cautioned against its use (although you

would still very much like to work with Johnny Depp). Is it possible to make an "issue" film that shows a lot of drug use without glamorizing that use for certain audiences, such as teenagers?

4. *Drug advertising #1.* Over-the-counter remedies are legal, often useful, and frequently used. How should they be advertised in a way that is both fair and accurate? Try designing sample ads.

5. *Drug advertising #2.* How could a researcher design a study to determine if the advertising of nonprescription and prescription drugs makes teenagers more likely to use cigarettes, alcohol, or illicit drugs?

6. *Adolescents and alcohol.* According to national studies, more than 80% of teenagers have tried alcohol by the time they graduate from high school. If you are a filmmaker interested in doing a realistic film about contemporary adolescence, how do you deal with the issue of alcohol, remain socially responsible, attract an adolescent audience, and keep your artistic soul intact?

7. *Advertising alcohol and cigarettes.* (a) Try to create the most outrageous print ads you can think of for advertising alcohol and cigarettes. (b) Based on what you have learned in this chapter, analyze the two cigarette ads and two alcohol ads in Figure 6.8. Figure 6.37 shows an ad for an actual product called Bad Frog Beer. Does this ad target youth? If so, should restrictions be placed on where such ads can be displayed? (Note: This is based on an actual court case in New Jersey.)

Figure 6.37 Ad for Bad Frog Beer.

8. *Tobacco policy.* If tobacco is a legal product, how can a ban on all tobacco advertising be justified? Research the circumstances under which tobacco advertising was taken off TV by the early 1970s.

9. *Drug control policy.* You are the newly appointed head of the ONDCP in the White House. Your mission is to cut the use of drugs in the United States by 20% within the next four years. Where do you start? With which drugs? Should you engage in discussions with the entertainment industry regarding their portrayals of alcohol and cigarettes? Should you engage in discussions with the tobacco and alcohol industries regarding their use of advertising? Does counteradvertising work? Should the government be in the business of counteradvertising? If so, which media would you target?

References

Alamar, B., & Glantz, S. A. (2006). Tobacco industry profits from smoking images in the movies [Letter]. *Pediatrics, 117,* 1462.

Alpert, H. R., Koh, H. K., & Connolly, G. N. (2008). After the Master Settlement Agreement: Targeting and exposure of youth to magazine tobacco advertising. *Health Affairs, 27,* w503–w512.

Anderson, P., de Bruijn, A., Angus, K., Gordon, R., & Hastings, G. (2009). Impact of alcohol advertising and media exposure on adolescent alcohol use: A systematic review of longitudinal studies. *Alcohol and Alcoholism, 44,* 229–243.

Anderson, S. J., Millett, C., Polansky, J. R., & Glantz, S. A. (2010). Exposure to smoking in movies among British adolescents 2001–2006. *Tobacco Control, 19,* 197–200.

Arora, M., Mathur, N., Gupta, V. K., Nazar, G. P., Reddy, K. S., & Sargent, J. D. (2011). Tobacco use in Bollywood movies, tobacco promotional activities and their association with tobacco use among Indian adolescents. *Tobacco Control.* doi:10.1136/tc.2011.043539

Atkin, C. K. (1995). Survey and experimental research on effects of alcohol advertising. In S. Martin (Ed.), *Mass media and the use and abuse of alcohol* (pp. 39–68). Rockville, MD: National Institute on Alcohol Abuse and Alcoholism at Columbia University.

Austin, E. W., Chen, M. J., & Grube, J. W. (2006). How does alcohol advertising influence underage drinking? The role of desirability, identification and skepticism. *Journal of Adolescent Health, 38,* 376–384.

Austin, E. W., & Hust, S. J. T. (2005). Targeting adolescents? The content and frequency of alcoholic and nonalcoholic beverage ads in magazine and video formats November 1999–April 2000. *Journal of Health Communication, 10,* 769–785.

Austin, E. W., & Johnson, K. K. (1997). Effects of general and alcohol-specific media literacy training on children's decision making about alcohol. *Journal of Health Communication, 2,* 17–42.

Austin, E. W., Pinkleton, B. E., Hust, S. J. T., & Cohen, M. (2005). Evaluation of an American Legacy Foundation/Washington State Department of Health media literacy study. *Health Communication, 18,* 75–95.

Bacon, J. (2011, November 3). FDA unveils $600m anti-tobacco effort. *USA Today,* p. 3A.

Bahr, S. J., Hoffmann, J. P., & Yang, X. (2005). Parental and peer influences on the risk of adolescent drug use. *Journal of Primary Prevention, 26,* 529–551.

Bayer, R., Gostin, L., & Marcus-Toll, D. (2012). Repackaging cigarettes: Will the courts thwart the FDA? *New England Journal of Medicine, 367,* 2065–2065.

Bayer, R., & Kelly, M. (2010). Tobacco control and free speech—an American dilemma. *New England Journal of Medicine, 362,* 281–283.

Belcher, H. M. E., & Shinitzky, H. E. (1998). Substance abuse in children: Prediction, protection, and prevention. *Archives of Pediatrics and Adolescent Medicine, 152,* 952–960.

Bickham, D. S., & Slaby, R. G. (2012). Effects of a media literacy program in the US on children's critical evaluation of unhealthy media messages about violence, smoking, and food. *Journal of Children and Media, 6,* 255–271.

Biener, L., & Siegel, M. (2000). Tobacco marketing and adolescent smoking: More support for a causal inference. *American Journal of Public Health, 90,* 407–411.

Big Tobacco's promises to reform go up in smoke [Editorial]. (2006, September 12). *USA Today,* p. 14A.

Bjork, J. M., Knutson, B., Fong, G. W., Caggiano, D. M., Bennett, S. M., & Hommer, D. W. (2004). Incentive-elicited brain activation in adolescents: Similarities and differences from young adults. *Journal of Neuroscience, 24,* 1793–1802.

Blair, N. A., Yue, S. K., Singh, R., & Bernhardt, J. M. (2005). Sex, drugs, and rock and roll: Depictions of substance use in reality television: A content analysis of *The Osbournes. British Medical Journal, 331,* 1517–1519.

Blecher, E. (2008). The impact of tobacco advertising bans on consumption in developing countries. *Journal of Health Economics, 27,* 930–942.

Bonnie, R. J., Stratton, K., & Wallace, R. B. (Eds.). (2007). *Ending the tobacco problem: A blueprint for the nation.* Institute of Medicine of the National Academies. Retrieved from http://www.nap.edu/openbook .php?record_id=11795&page=R1

Borzekowski, D. L. G., & Strasburger, V. C. (2008). Tobacco, alcohol, and drug exposure. In S. Calvert & B. J. Wilson (Eds.), *Handbook of children and the media* (pp. 432–452). Boston, MA: Blackwell.

Botvin, G. J., & Griffin, K. W. (2005). Models of prevention: School-based programs. In J. H. Lowinson, P. Ruiz, R. B. Millman, & J. G. Langrod (Eds.), *Substance abuse: A comprehensive textbook* (4th ed., pp. 1211–1229). Philadelphia, PA: Lippincott Williams & Wilkins.

Briones, D. F., Wilcox, J. A., Mateus, B., & Boudjenah, D. (2006). Risk factors and prevention in adolescent substance abuse: A biopsychosocial approach. *Adolescent Medicine: State of the Art Reviews, 17,* 335–352.

British channel bans smoking cartoons. (2006, August 30). *Associated Press.* Retrieved from http://abcnews .go.com/Entertainment/print?id=2343123

Brooks, F., van der Sluijs, W., Klemera, E., Morgan, A., Magnusson, J., Gabhainn S. N., . . . Currie, C. (2009). *Young people's health in Great Britain and Ireland: Findings from the Health Behaviour in School-Aged Children (HBSC) survey, 2006.* Edinburgh, Scotland: University of Edinburgh.

Brown, A., & Moodie, C. (2009). The influence of tobacco marketing on adolescent smoking intentions via normative beliefs. *Health Education Research, 24,* 721–733.

Brown, J. D. (2007). Media literacy has potential to improve adolescents' health. *Journal of Adolescent Health, 39,* 459–460.

Brown, S. A., McGue, M., & Maggs, J., Schulenberg, J., Hingson, R., Swartzwelder, S., . . . Murphy, S. (2008). A developmental perspective on alcohol and youths 16 to 20 years of age. *Pediatrics, 121*(Suppl. 4), S290–S310.

Bryant, A. (2000, March 20). In tobacco's face. *Newsweek,* pp. 40–41.

Bryant, J. A., Cody, M. J., & Murphy, S. (2002). Online sales: Profit without question. *Tobacco Control, 11,* 226–227.

Campaign for Tobacco-Free Kids. (2009a). *Deadly in pink: Big Tobacco steps up its targeting of women and girls.* Retrieved from www.tobaccofreekids.org

Campaign for Tobacco-Free Kids. (2009b). *Raising cigarette taxes reduces smoking, especially among kids (and the cigarette companies know it).* Retrieved from http://tobaccofreekids.org/research/factsheets/ pdf/0146.pdf

Campaign for Tobacco-Free Kids. (2010, January 12). The PACT Act [Fact sheet]. Retrieved from www .tobaccofreekids.org

Campaign for Tobacco-Free Kids. (2011). *Tobacco product marketing on the Internet.* Retrieved from http://www.tobaccofreekids.org/research/factsheets/pdf/0081.pdf

Carpenter, C. S., & Pechmann, C. (2011). Exposure to the Above the Influence antidrug advertisements and adolescent marijuana use in the United States, 2006–2008. *American Journal of Public Health, 101,* 948–954.

Centers for Disease Control. (2013). Vital signs: binge drinking among women and high school girls, 2011. *Morbidity and Mortality Weekly Report, 62,* 9–13.

Center on Alcohol Marketing and Youth. (2004). *Clicking with kids: Alcohol marketing and youth on the Internet.* Washington, DC: Author.

Center on Alcohol Marketing and Youth. (2007). *Alcohol advertising and youth.* Washington, DC: Author.

Center on Alcohol Marketing and Youth. (2010a). *Youth exposure to alcohol advertising in national magazines, 2001–2008.* Washington, DC: Author.

Center on Alcohol Marketing and Youth. (2010b). *Youth exposure to alcohol advertising on television, 2001–2009.* Washington, DC: Author.

Center on Alcohol Marketing and Youth. (2011a). *Plugged in 24/7: Alcohol advertising & youth in the digital age.* Washington, DC: Author.

Center on Alcohol Marketing and Youth. (2011b). *Youth exposure to alcohol product advertising on local radio in 75 U.S. markets, 2009.* Washington, DC: Author.

Centers for Disease Control and Prevention. (2006). Racial/ethnic differences among youths in cigarette smoking and susceptibility to start smoking—United States, 2002–2004. *Morbidity and Mortality Weekly Reports, 55,* 1275–1277.

Centers for Disease Control and Prevention. (2007). Youth exposure to alcohol advertising in magazines—United States, 2001–2005. *Morbidity and Mortality Weekly Reports, 56,* 763–767.

Centers for Disease Control and Prevention. (2008). *Tobacco use and the health of young people.* Retrieved from http://www.cdc.gov/HealthyYouth/Tobacco/facts.htm

Centers for Disease Control and Prevention. (2009). Cigarette brand preference among middle and high school students who are established smokers—United States, 2004 and 2006. *Morbidity & Mortality Weekly Review, 58,* 112–115.

Centers for Disease Control and Prevention. (2010). Tobacco use among middle and high school students—United States, 2000–2009. *Morbidity and Mortality Weekly Report, 59,* 1063–1068.

Centers for Disease Control and Prevention. (2011). Smoking on top-grossing movies—United States, 2010. *Morbidity and Mortality Weekly Reports, 60,* 910–913.

Centers for Disease Control and Prevention. (2012a). Vital signs: Drinking and driving among high school students aged > 16 years—United States, 1991–2011. *Morbidity and Mortality Weekly Reports, 61,* 796–800.

Centers for Disease Control and Prevention. (2012b). Youth Risk Behavior Surveillance—United States, 2011. *Morbidity and Mortality Weekly Report, 61*(SS–4).

Champion, H. L., Foley, K. L., DuRant, R. H., Hensberry, R., Altman, D., & Wolfson, M. (2004). Adolescent sexual victimization, use of alcohol and other substances, and other health risk behaviors. *Journal of Adolescent Health, 35,* 321–328.

Chapman, S. (2008). What should be done about smoking in movies? *Tobacco Control, 17,* 363–367.

Charlesworth, A., & Glantz, S. A. (2005). Smoking in the movies increases adolescent smoking: A review. *Pediatrics, 116,* 1516–1528.

Cheers & jeers. (2002, February 23). *TV Guide.*

Chen, M. J., Grube, J. W., Bersamin, M., Waiters, E., & Keefe, D. B. (2005). Alcohol advertising: What makes it attractive to youth? *Journal of Health Communication, 10,* 553–565.

Chilcoat, H. D., & Anthony, J. C. (1996). Impact of parent monitoring on initiation of drug use through late childhood. *Journal of the American Academy of Child and Adolescent Psychiatry, 35,* 91–100.

Christakis, D. A., & Zimmerman, F. J. (2006). Media as a public health issue. *Archives of Pediatrics and Adolescent Medicine, 160,* 446–447.

Christenson, P. G., Henriksen, L., & Roberts, D. F. (2000). *Substance use in popular prime-time television.* Washington, DC: Office of National Drug Policy Control.

Comings, D. E. (1997). Genetic aspects of childhood behavioral disorders. *Child Psychiatry and Human Development, 27,* 139–150.

Committee on Communications. (2006). Children, adolescents, and advertising. *Pediatrics, 118,* 2563–2569.

Committee on Environmental Health, Committee on Substance Abuse, Committee on Adolescence, and Committee on Native American Child Health. (2009). *Pediatrics, 124,* 1474–1487.

Committee on Substance Abuse. (2010). Alcohol use by youth and adolescents: A pediatric concern. *Pediatrics, 125,* 1078–1087.

Congressional Budget Office. (2009). *Promotional spending for prescription drugs.* Washington, DC: Author.

Cortese, D. K., Lewis., M. J., & Ling, P. M. (2009). Tobacco industry lifestyle magazines targeted to young adults. *Journal of Adolescent Health Care, 45,* 268–280.

Council on Communications and Media. (2009). Impact of music, music lyrics, and music videos on children and youth. *Pediatrics, 124,* 1488–1494.

Council on Communications and Media. (2010). Media education. *Pediatrics, 126,* 1012–1017.

Cowley, G., & Underwood, A. (2001, February 19). Soda pop that packs a punch: Are the new alcoholic lemonades aimed at kids? *Newsweek,* p. 45.

Cruz, M. L., & Deyton, L. R. (2010). A new regulatory challenge: Youth and tobacco. *Pediatrics, 125,* 1066–1067.

Cullen, J., Sokol, N. A., Slawek, D., Allen, J. A., Vallone, D., & Healton, C. (2011). Depictions of tobacco use in 2007 broadcast television programming popular among US youth. *Archives of Pediatrics and Adolescent Medicine, 165,* 147–151.

Cumberbatch, G., & Gauntlett, S. (2005). *Smoking, alcohol and drugs on television: A content analysis.* Retrieved from http://www.ofcom.org.uk/research/radio/reports/bcr/smoking.pdf

Currie, C., Hurrelmann, K., Settertobulte, W., Smith, R., & Todd, J. (2000). *Health behaviour in school-aged children: A WHO cross-national Study.* Copenhagen, Denmark: Authors.

Dalton, M. A., Adachi-Mejia, A. M., Longacre, M. R., Gibson, J. J., Martin, S. K., Sargent, J. D., & Beach, M. L. (2006). Parental rules and monitoring of children's movie viewing associated with children's risk for smoking and drinking. *Pediatrics, 118,* 1932–1942.

Dalton, M. A., Ahrens, M. B., Sargent, J. D., Mott, L. A., Beach, M. L., Tickle, J. J., & Heatherton, T. F. (2002). Correlation between use of tobacco and alcohol in adolescents and parental restrictions on movies. *Effective Clinical Practice, 1,* 1–10.

Dalton, M. A., Beach, M. L., Adachi-Mejia, A. M., Longacre, M. R., Matzkin, A. L., Sargent, J.D., . . . Titus-Ernstoff, L. (2009). Early exposure to movie smoking predicts established smoking by older teens and young adults. *Pediatrics, 123,* e551–e558.

Dalton, M. A., Sargent, J. D., Beach., M. L., Titus-Ernstoff, L., Gibson, J. J., Ahrens, M. B., . . . Heatherton, T. F. (2003). Effect of viewing smoking in movies on adolescent smoking initiation: A cohort study. *Lancet, 362,* 281–285.

Davis, R. M., Gilpin, E. A., Loken, B., Viswanath, K., Wakefield, M. A. (Eds.). (2008). *The role of the media in promoting and reducing tobacco use* (National Cancer Institute Tobacco Control Monograph Series, No. 19, Pub No. 07-6242). Retrieved from http://cancercontrol.cancer.gov/tcrb/monographs/19/m19_complete.pdf

de Leeuw, R. N. H., Sargent, J. D., Stoolmiller, M., Scholte, R. H. J., Engels, R. C. M. E., & Tanski, S. E. (2011). Association of smoking onset with R-rated movie restrictions and adolescent sensation seeking. *Pediatrics, 127,* e96–e105.

Desmond, R., & Carveth, R. (2007). The effects of advertising on children and adolescents: A meta-analysis. In R. W. Preiss, B. M. Gayle, N. Burrell, M. Allen, & J. Bryant (Eds.), *Mass media effects research: Advances through meta-analysis* (pp. 169–179). Mahwah, NJ: Lawrence Erlbaum.

DiFranza, J. R., Richards, J. W., Paulman, P. M., Wolf-Gillespie, N., Fletcher, C., Jaffe, R. D., & Murray, D. (1991). RJR Nabisco's cartoon camel promotes Camel cigarettes to children. *Journal of the American Medical Association, 266,* 3149–3153.

DiFranza, J. R., Wellman, R. J., Sargent, J. D., Weitzman, M., Hipple, B. J., & Winickoff, J. P. (2006). Tobacco promotion and the initiation of tobacco use: Assessing the evidence for causality. *Pediatrics, 117,* e1237–e1248.

Donohue, J. M., Cevasco, M., & Rosenthal, M. B. (2007). A decade of direct-to-consumer advertising of prescription drugs. *New England Journal of Medicine, 357,* 673–681.

Dozier, D. M., Lauzen, M. M., Day, C. A., Payne, S. M., & Tafoya, M. R. (2005). Leaders and elites: Portrayals of smoking in popular films. *Tobacco Control, 14,* 7–9.

Duke, J. C., Allen, J. A., Pederson, L. L., Mowery, P. D., Xiao, H., & Sargent, J. D. (2009). Reported exposure to pro-tobacco messages in the media: Trends among youth in the United States, 2000–2004. *American Journal of Health Promotion, 23,* 195–202.

DuRant, R. H., Rome, E. S., Rich, M., Allred, E., Emans, S. J., & Woods, E. R. (1997). Tobacco and alcohol use behaviors portrayed in music videos: A content analysis. *American Journal of Public Health, 87,* 1131–1135.

Edwards, C. A., Harris, W. C., Cook, D. R., Bedford, K. F., & Zuo, Y. (2004). Out of the smokescreen: Does an anti-smoking advertisement affect young women's perception of smoking in movies and their intention to smoke? *Tobacco Control, 13,* 277–282.

Edwards, C., Oakes, W., & Bull, D. (2007). Out of the smokescreen II: Will an advertisement targeting the tobacco industry affect young people's perception of smoking in movies and their intention to smoke? *Tobacco Control, 16,* 177–181.

Elliott, S. (2004). Viagra and the battle of the awkward ads. *New York Times.* Retrieved from http://www.nytimes.com/2004/04/25/business/viagra-and-the-battle-of-the-awkward-ads.html?pagewanted=all

Engels, R. C. M. E., Herman, R., van Baaren, R. B., Hollenstein, T., & Bot, S. M. (2009). Alcohol portrayal on television affects actual drinking behaviour. *Alcohol and Alcoholism, 44,* 244–249.

Eslick, G. D., & Eslick, M. G. (2009). Smoking and *The Simpsons. Medical Journal of Australia, 190,* 637–639.

Eszterhas, J. (2004). *Hollywood animal.* New York, NY: Knopf.

Farrelly, M. C., Davis, K. C., Haviland, M. L., Messeri, P., & Healton, C. G. (2005). Evidence of a dose-response relationship between "truth" antismoking ads and youth smoking prevalence. *American Journal of Public Health, 95,* 425–431.

Federal Trade Commission. (1999). *Self-regulation in the alcohol industry: A review of industry efforts to avoid promoting alcohol to underage consumers.* Washington, DC: Author.

Federal Trade Commission. (2011). *Federal Trade Commission cigarette report for 2007 and 2008.* Retrieved from http://www.ftc.gov/os/2011/07/110729cigarettereport.pdf

Fischer, P. M., Schwartz, M. P., Richards, J. W., Goldstein, A. O., & Rojas, T. H. (1991). Brand logo recognition by children aged 3 to 6 years: Mickey Mouse and Old Joe the Camel. *Journal of the American Medical Association, 266,* 3145–3153.

Fisher, L. B., Miles, I. W., Austin, S. B., Camargo, C. A., Jr., & Colditz, G. A. (2007). Predictors of initiation of alcohol use among US adolescents: Findings from a prospective cohort study. *Archives of Pediatrics and Adolescent Medicine, 161,* 959–966.

Flynn, B. S., Worden, J. K., Bunn, J. Y., Dorwaldt, A. L., Connolly, S. W., & Ashikaga, T. (2007). Youth audience segmentation strategies for smoking-prevention mass media campaigns based on message appeal. *Health Education and Behavior, 34,* 578–593.

Forsyth, S. R., & Malone, R. E. (2010). "I'll be your cigarette—light me up and get on with it": Examining smoking imagery on YouTube. *Nicotine and Tobacco Research, 12,* 810–816.

Foster, S. E., Vaughan, R. D., Foster, W. H., & Califano, J. A., Jr. (2003). Alcohol consumption and expenditures for underage drinking and adult excessive drinking. *Journal of the American Medical Association, 289,* 989–995.

Foster, S. E., Vaughan, R. D., Foster, W. H., & Califano, J. A. Jr. (2006). Estimate of the commercial value of underage drinking and adult abusive and dependent drinking to the alcohol industry. *Archives of Pediatrics and Adolescent Medicine, 160,* 473–478.

Freeman, B., & Chapman, S. (2010). British American Tobacco on Facebook: Undermining Article 13 of the global World Health Organization Framework Convention on Tobacco Control. *Tobacco Control, 19,* e1–e9.

Fritschler, A. L., & Hoefler, J. M. (2006). *Smoking & politics: Policy making and the federal bureaucracy* (6th ed.). Upper Saddle River, NJ: Prentice Hall.

Frosch, D. L., Grande D., Tarn, D. M., & Kravitz, R. L. (2010). A decade of controversy: Balancing policy with evidence in the regulation of prescription drug advertising. *American Journal of Public Health, 100,* 24–32.

Frosch, D. L., Krueger, P. M., Hornik, R. C., Cronholm, P. F., & Barg, F. K. (2007). Creating a demand for prescription drugs: A content analysis of television direct-to-consumer advertising. *Annals of Family Medicine, 5,* 6–13.

Garfield, C. F., Chung, P. J., & Rathouz, P. J. (2003). Alcohol advertising in magazines and adolescent readership. *Journal of the American Medical Association, 289,* 2424–2429.

Gellad, Z. F., & Lyles, K. W. (2007). Direct-to-consumer advertising of pharmaceuticals. *American Journal of Medicine, 120,* 475–480.

Gidwani, P. P., Sobol, A., DeJong, W., Perrin, J. M., & Gortmaker, S. L. (2002). Television viewing and initiation of smoking among youth. *Pediatrics, 110,* 505–508.

Giedd, J. N. (2008). The teen brain: Insights from neuroimaging. *Journal of Adolescent Health, 42,* 335–343.

Gilpin, E. A., White, M. M., Messer, K., & Pierce, J. P. (2007). Receptivity to tobacco advertising and promotions among young adolescents as a predictor of established smoking in young adulthood. *American Journal of Public Health, 97,* 1489–1495.

Glantz, S. A., Iaccopucci, A., Titus, K., & Polansky, J. R. (2012). Smoking in top-grossing US movies, 2011. *Preventing Chronic Disease, 9,* 120170. Retrieved from http://www.cdc.gov/pcd/issues/2012/12_0170.htm

Glantz, S. A., Slade, J., Bero, L. A., & Hanauer, P. (1998). *The cigarette papers.* Berkeley: University of California Press.

Goldstein, A. O., Sobel, R. A., & Newman, G. R. (1999). Tobacco and alcohol use in G-rated children's animated films. *Journal of the American Medical Association, 281,* 1131–1136.

Gomstyn, A. (2009, November 12). Buying cigarettes and quit-smoking aids from the same company? *ABC News.* Retrieved from http://abcnews.go.com/print?id=9057261

Gordon, R., MacKintosh, A. M., & Moodie, C. (2010). The impact of alcohol marketing on youth drinking behavior: A two-stage cohort study. *Alcohol and Alcoholism, 45,* 470–480.

Gostin, L. O. (2009). FDA regulation of tobacco: Politics, law, and the public's health. *Journal of the American Medical Association, 302,* 1459–1460.

Greenberg, B. S., Rampoldi-Hnilo, L., & Mastro, D. (2000). *The alphabet soup of television program ratings.* Cresskill, NJ: Hampton Press.

Greenberg, B. S., Rosaen, S. F., Worrell, T. R., Salmon, C. T., & Volkman, J. E. (2009). A portrait of food and drink in commercial TV series. *Health Communication, 24,* 295–303.

Greenfield, T. K., & Rogers, J. D. (1999). Who drinks most of the alcohol in the U.S.? The policy implications. *Journal of Studies on Alcohol and Drugs, 60,* 78–89.

Grenard, J. L., Dent, C. W., & Stacy, A. W. (2013). Exposure to alcohol advertisements and teenage alcohol-related problems. *Pediatrics, 131,* e369–e379.

Grube, J. W., & Waiters, E. (2005). Alcohol in the media: Content and effects on drinking beliefs and behaviors among youth. *Adolescent Medicine: State of the Art Reviews, 16,* 327–343.

Gruber, E. L., Thau, H. M., Hill, D. L., Fisher, D. A., & Grube, J. W. (2005). Alcohol, tobacco and illicit substances in music videos: A content analysis of prevalence and genre. *Journal of Adolescent Health, 37,* 81–83.

Gruber, E. L., Wang, P. H., Christensen, J. S., Grube, J. W., & Fisher, D. A. (2005). Private television viewing, parental supervision, and sexual and substance use risk behaviors in adolescents [Abstract]. *Journal of Adolescent Health, 36,* 107.

Gunter, B., Oates, C., & Blades, M. (2004). *Advertising to children on TV.* Oxford, UK: Routledge.

Gutschoven, K., & Van den Bulck, J. (2004). Television viewing and smoking volume in adolescent smokers: A cross-sectional study. *Preventive Medicine, 39,* 1093–1098.

Halperin, S. (2008, April 18). Going to pot. *Entertainment Weekly,* pp. 38–41.

Halpern-Felsher, B. L., & Cornell, J. L. (2005). Preventing underage alcohol use: Where do we go from here? *Journal of Adolescent Health, 37,* 1–3.

Hancox, R. J., Milne, B. J., & Poulton, R. (2004). Association between child and adolescent television viewing and adult health: A longitudinal birth cohort study. *Lancet, 364,* 257–262.

Hanewinkel, R. (2009). Cigarette smoking and perception of a movie character in a film trailer. *Archives of Pediatrics and Adolescent Medicine, 163,* 15–18.

Hanewinkel, R., Isensee, B., Sargent, J. D., & Morgenstern, M. (2010). Cigarette advertising and adolescent smoking. *American Journal of Preventive Medicine, 38,* 359–366.

Hanewinkel, R., Isensee, B., Sargent, J. D., & Morgenstern, M. (2011). Cigarette advertising and teen smoking initiation. *Pediatrics, 127,* e271–e278.

Hanewinkel, R., & Sargent, J. D. (2007). Exposure to smoking in popular contemporary movies and youth smoking in Germany. *American Journal of Preventive Medicine, 32,* 466–473.

Hanewinkel, R., & Sargent, J. D. (2009). Longitudinal study of exposure to entertainment media and alcohol use among German adolescents. *Pediatrics, 123,* 989–995.

Hanewinkel, R., Sargent, J. D., Karlsdottir, S., Jonsson, S. H., Mathis, F., Faggiano, F., . . . Morgenstern, M. (2012). High youth access to movies that contain smoking in Europe compared with the USA. *Tobacco Control.* doi:10.1136/tobaccocontrol-2011-050050

Hanewinkel, R., Sargent, J. D., Poelen, E. A. P., Scholte, R., Florek, E., Sweeting, H., . . . Morgenstern, M. (2012). Alcohol consumption in movies and binge drinking in 6 European countries. *Pediatrics, 129,* 1–12.

Harris, D. (2005, November 2). Is big tobacco sweet-talking kids into smoking? *ABC News.* Retrieved from http://abcnews.go.com/WNT/QuitToLive/story?id=1274643

Hawkins, K., & Hane, A. C. (2000). Adolescents' perceptions of print cigarette advertising: a case for counteradvertising. *Journal of Health Communication, 5,* 83–96.

Healton, C. G., Watson-Stryker, E. S., & Allen, J. A. (2006). Televised movie trainers: Undermining restrictions on advertising tobacco to youth. *Archives of Pediatrics and Adolescent Medicine, 160,* 885–888.

Heatherton, T. F., & Sargent, J. D. (2009). Does watching smoking in movies promote teenage smoking? *Current Directions in Psychological Science, 18,* 63–67.

Heavey, S., & Richwine, L. (2010, September 3). Special report: Outgunned FDA tries to get tough with drug ads. *Reuters.* Retrieved from http://www.reuters.com/article/2010/09/03/us-drugs-advertising-idUSTRE6821PN20100903

Henriksen, L., Dauphinee, A. L., Wang, Y., & Fortmann, S. P. (2006). Industry sponsored anti-smoking ads and adolescent reactance: Test of a boomerang effect. *Tobacco Control, 15,* 13–18.

Henriksen, L., Feighery, E. C., Schleicher, N. C., & Fortmann, S. P. (2008). Receptivity to alcohol marketing predicts initiation of alcohol use. *Journal of Adolescent Health, 42,* 28–35.

Herd, D. (2008). Changes in drug use prevalence in rap music songs, 1979–1997. *Addiction Research and Theory, 16,* 167–180.

Hill, A. B. (1965). The environment and disease: Association or causality? *Proceedings of the Royal Society of Medicine, 58,* 295–300.

Hingson, R. W., Heeren, T., & Winter, M. R. (2006). Age at drinking onset and alcohol dependence. *Archives of Pediatrics and Adolescent Medicine, 160,* 739–747.

Hingson, R. W., & Zha, W. (2009). Age of drinking onset, alcohol use disorders, frequent heavy drinking, and unintentionally injuring oneself and others after drinking. *Pediatrics, 123,* 1477–1484.

Hitti, M. (2006, August 11). Teens buying alcohol online. *WebMD Medical News.* Retrieved from http://www.webmd.com/parenting/news/20060811/teens-buy-alcohol-online

Hogan, M. J., & Strasburger, V. C. (2008). Media and prosocial behavior in children and adolescents. In L. Nucci & D. Narvaez (Eds.), *Handbook of moral and character education* (pp. 537–553). Mahwah, NJ: Lawrence Erlbaum.

Hornik, R., Jacobsohn, L., Orwin, R., Piesse, A. N., & Kalton, G. (2008). Effects of the National Youth Anti-Drug Media Campaign on youths. *American Journal of Public Health, 98,* 2229–2236.

Hunt, K., Henderson, M., Wight, D., & Sargent, J. D. (2011). Exposure to smoking in films and own smoking among Scottish adolescents: A cross-sectional study. *Thorax, 66,* 866–874.

Ibrahim, J. K., & Glantz, S. A. (2007). The rise and fall of tobacco control media campaigns, 1967–2006. *American Journal of Public Health, 97,* 1383–1396.

Jackson, C., Brown J. D., & L'Engle, K. L. (2007). R-rated movies, bedroom televisions, and initiation of smoking by White and Black adolescents. *Archives of Pediatrics and Adolescent Medicine, 161,* 260–268.

Jackson, D. Z. (1998, November 23). Big tobacco's chump change. *Liberal Opinion Week,* p. 23.

Jamieson, P. E., & Romer, D. (2010). Trends in US movie tobacco portrayal since 1950: A historical analysis. *Tobacco Control.* Retrieved from http://tobaccocontrol.bmj.com/content/early/2010/04/14/tc.2009.034736.short?q=w_tobaccocontrol_ahead_tab

Jenssen, B. P., Klein, J. D., Salazar, L. R., Daluge, N. A., & DiClemente, R. J. (2009). Exposure to tobacco on the Internet: Content analysis of adolescents' Internet use. *Pediatrics, 124,* e180–e186.

Jernigan, D. H. (2006). Importance of reducing youth exposure to alcohol advertising. *Archives of Pediatrics and Adolescent Medicine, 160,* 100–102.

Jernigan, D. H. (2009). Alcohol-branded merchandise: The need for action. *Archives of Pediatrics and Adolescent Medicine, 163,* 278–279.

Jernigan, D. H., Ostroff, J., & Ross, C. (2005). Alcohol advertising and youth: A measured approach. *Journal of Public Health Policy, 26,* 312–325.

Jernigan, D. H., Ostroff, J., Ross, C., & O'Hara, J. A. (2004). Sex differences in adolescent exposure to alcohol advertising in magazines. *Archives of Pediatrics and Adolescent Medicine, 158,* 629–634.

Johnston, L. D., O'Malley, P. M., Bachman, J. G., & Schulenberg, J. E. (2013). *Monitoring the Future national results on adolescent drug use: Overview of key findings, 2012.* Ann Arbor: Institute for Social Research, The University of Michigan.

Join Together Staff. (2011, April 29). 24 attorneys general ask FTC to do more to keep alcohol advertising from teens. *Partnership at DrugFree.org.* Retrieved from http://www.drugfree.org/join-together/alcohol/24-attorneys-general-ask-ftc-to-do-more-to-keep-alcohol-advertising-from-teens

Journal Wire Reports. (2001, March 15). Advertising rose after tobacco suits. *Albuquerque Journal,* p. A4.

Kaiser Family Foundation. (2004). *Entertainment education and health in the United States.* Menlo Park, CA: Author.

Keeping, J. (2011, September 12). University of Michigan poll: Parents in the dark about teens' marijuana, alcohol use. *AnnArbor.com.* Retrieved from http://www.annarbor.com/news/university-of-michigan-poll-parents-in-the-dark-about-teens-marijuana-alcohol-use/

Kessler, D. (2001). *A question of intent: A great American battle with a deadly industry.* New York, NY: PublicAffairs.

Kilbourne, J. (1993). Killing us softly: Gender roles in advertising. *Adolescent Medicine: State of the Art Reviews, 4,* 635–649.

King, C., III, Siegel, M., Jernigan, D. H., Wulach, L., Ross, C., Dixon, K., & Ostroff, J. (2009). Adolescent exposure to alcohol advertising in magazines: An evaluation of advertising placement in relation to underage youth readership. *Journal of Adolescent Health, 45,* 626–633.

Kulig, J. W., & Committee on Substance Abuse. (2005). Tobacco, alcohol, and other drugs: The role of the pediatrician in prevention, identification, and management of substance abuse. *Pediatrics, 115,* 816–821.

Kulig, K., Brener, N. D., & McManus, T. (2003). Sexual activity and substance use among adolescents by category of physical activity plus team sports participation. *Archives of Pediatrics and Adolescent Medicine, 157,* 905–912.

Kunkel, D. (2007). Inching forward on tobacco advertising restrictions to prevent youth smoking. *Archives of Pediatrics and Adolescent Medicine, 161,* 515–516.

Kupersmidt, J. B., Scull, T. M., & Austin, E. W. (2010). Media literacy education for elementary school substance use prevention: Study of Media Detective. *Pediatrics, 126,* 525–531.

Kurtz, M. E., Kurtz, J. C., Johnson, S. M., & Cooper, W. (2001). Sources of information on the health effects of environmental tobacco smoke among African-American children and adolescents. *Journal of Adolescent Health, 28,* 458–464.

Landman, A., Ling, P. M., & Glantz, S. A. (2002). Tobacco industry youth smoking prevention programs: Protecting the industry and hurting tobacco control. *American Journal of Public Health, 92,* 917–930.

Langleben, D. D., Loughead, J. W., Ruparel, K., Hakun, J. G., Busch-Winokur, S., Holloway, M. B., . . . Lerman, C. (2009). Reduced prefrontal and temporal processing and recall of high "sensation value" ads. *NeuroImage, 46,* 219–225.

Laugesen, M., & Meads, C. (1991). Tobacco advertising restrictions, price, income and tobacco consumption in OECD countries, 1960–1986. *British Journal of Addiction, 86,* 1343–1354.

Lilienfeld, S. O. (2007). Psychological treatments that cause harm. *Perspectives on Psychological Science, 2,* 53–70.

Litt, D. M., & Stock, M. L. (2011). Adolescent alcohol-related risk cognitions: The roles of social norms and social networking sites. *Psychology of Addictive Behaviors, 25,* 708–713.

Lochbuehler, K., Sargent, J. D., Scholte, R. H. J., Pieters, S., & Engels, C. M. E. (2012). Influence of smoking cues in movies on children's beliefs about smoking. *Pediatrics, 130,* 1–7.

Long, J. A., O'Connor, P. G., Gerbner, G., & Concato, J. (2002). Use of alcohol, illicit drugs, and tobacco among characters on prime-time television. *Substance Abuse, 23,* 95–103.

Longacre, M. R., Adachi-Mejia, A. M., Titus-Ernstoff, L., Gibson, J. J., Beach, M. L., & Dalton, M. A. (2009). Parental attitudes about cigarette smoking and alcohol use in the Motion Picture Association of America rating system. *Archives of Pediatrics and Adolescent Medicine, 163,* 218–224.

Lovato, C., Watts, A., & Stead, L. F. (2011). Impact of tobacco advertising and promotion on increasing adolescent smoking behaviours (No. CD003439). *Cochrane Database System Reviews, 10.*

Lynam, D. R., Milich, R., Zimmerman, R., Novak, S. P., Logan, T. K., Martin, C., . . . Clayton, R. (1999). Project DARE: No effects at 10-year follow-up. *Journal of Consulting and Clinical Psychology, 67,* 590–593.

McClure, A. C., Stoolmiller, M., Tanski, S. E., Worth, K. A., & Sargent, J. D. (2009). Alcohol-branded merchandise and its association with drinking attitudes and outcomes in US adolescents. *Archives of Pediatrics and Adolescent Medicine, 163,* 211–217.

McGee, R., Ketchel, J., & Reeder, A. I. (2007). Alcohol imagery on New Zealand television. *Substance Abuse Treatment, Prevention, and Policy.* Retrieved from http://www.substanceabusepolicy.com/content/2/1/6

McMahon, R. L. (1994). Diagnosis, assessment and treatment of externalizing problems in children: The role of longitudinal data. *Journal of Consulting and Clinical Psychology, 62,* 901–917.

McMillen, R. C., Tanski, S., Winickoff, J., & Valentine, N. (2007). *Attitudes about smoking in the movies.* Retrieved from www.ssrc.msstate.edu/socialclimate

Mednick, S. C., Christakis, N. A., & Fowler, J. H. (2010). The spread of sleep loss influences drug use in adolescent social networks. *PloS One, 5,* e9775.

Miller, J. W., Naimi, T. S., Brewer, R. D., & Jones, S. E. (2007). Binge drinking and associated health risk behaviors among high school students. *Pediatrics, 119,* 76–85.

Montgomery, K. C., & Chester, J. (2009). Interactive food and beverage marketing: Targeting adolescents in the digital age. *Journal of Adolescent Health, 45,* S18–S29.

Moreno, M. A., Briner, L. R., Williams, A., Brockman, L., Walker, L., & Christakis, D. A. (2010). A content analysis of displayed alcohol references on a social networking Web site. *Journal of Adolescent Health.* Retrieved from http://download.journals.elsevierhealth.com/pdfs/journals/1054-139X/PIIS1054139X10000200.pdf

Moreno, M. A., Briner, L. R., Williams, A., Walker, L., & Christakis, D. A. (2009). Real use or "real cool": Adolescents speak out about displayed alcohol references on social networking sites. *Journal of Adolescent Health, 45,* 420–422.

Moreno, M. A., Grant, A., Kacvinsky, L., Egan, K. G., & Fleming, M. F. (2012). College students' alcohol displays on Facebook: Intervention considerations. *Journal of American College Health, 60,* 388–394.

Moreno, M. A., Parks, M. R., Zimmerman, F. J., Brito, T. E., & Christakis, D. A. (2009). Display of health risk behaviors on MySpace by adolescents. *Archives of Pediatrics and Adolescent Medicine, 163,* 27–34.

Moreno, M. A., VanderStoep, A., Parks, M. R., Zimmerman, F. J., Kurth, A., & Christakis, D. A. (2009). Reducing at-risk adolescents' display of risk behavior on a social networking Web site. *Archives of Pediatrics and Adolescent Medicine, 163,* 35–41.

Morgenstern, M., Isensee, B., Sargent J. D., & Hanewinkel, R. (2011a). Attitudes as mediators of the longitudinal association between alcohol advertising and youth drinking. *Archives of Pediatrics and Adolescent Medicine, 165,* 610–616.

Morgenstern, M., Isensee, B., Sargent J. D., & Hanewinkel, R. (2011b). Exposure to alcohol advertising and teen drinking. *Preventive Medicine, 52,* 146–151.

Morgenstern, M., Poelen, E. A. P., Scholte, R., Karlsdottir, S., Jonsson, S. H., Mathis, F., . . . Hanewinkel, R. (2011). Smoking in movies and adolescent smoking: Cross-cultural study in six European countries. *Thorax, 66,* 875–883.

Morrison, M. A., Krugman, D. M., & Park, P. (2008). Under the radar: Smokeless tobacco advertising in magazines with substantial youth readership. *American Journal of Public Health, 98,* 543–548.

Motion Picture Association of America. (2007, May 10). Film rating board to consider smoking as a factor [Press release]. Los Angeles, CA: Motion Picture Association of America.

Murphy, S. T., Hether, H. J., & Rideout, V. (2008). *How healthy is prime time? An analysis of health content in popular prime time television programs.* Menlo Park, CA: Kaiser Family Foundation.

National Center on Addiction and Substance Abuse at Columbia University. (2005). *National survey of American attitudes on substance abuse IX: Teens and parents.* New York, NY: Author.

National Center on Addiction and Substance Abuse at Columbia University. (2008). *"You've got drugs!" V.* New York, NY: Author.

National Center on Addiction and Substance Abuse at Columbia University. (2011a). *Adolescent substance use: America's #1 public health problem.* New York, NY: Author.

National Center on Addiction and Substance Abuse at Columbia University. (2011b). *National survey of American attitudes on substance abuse XVI: Teens and parents.* New York, NY: Author.

National Center on Addiction and Substance Abuse at Columbia University . (2012*). National survey of American attitudes on substance abuse XVII: Teens.* New York, NY: Author.

Newman, A. A. (2009, September 21). A different camel is back in the glossies. *New York Times.* Retrieved from http://www.nytimes.com/2009/09/22/business/media/22adco.html

Nicholson, M., & Hoye, R. (2009). Reducing adolescents' exposure to alcohol advertising and promotion during televised sports. *Journal of the American Medical Association, 301,* 1479–1482.

Nixon, C. L., Mansfield, P. M., & Thoms, P. (2008). Effectiveness of antismoking public service announcements on children's intent to smoke. *Psychology of Addictive Behaviors, 22,* 496–503.

Noar, S. M. (2006). A 10-year retrospective of research in health mass media campaigns: Where do we go from here? *Journal of Health Communication, 11,* 21–42.

Nugent, W. (1999). *Into the West.* New York, NY: Knopf.

Olds, R. S., Thombs, D. L., & Tomasek, J. R. (2005). Relations between normative beliefs and initiation intentions toward cigarette, alcohol and marijuana. *Journal of Adolescent Health, 37,* e75.

Orlandi, M. A., Lieberman, L. R., & Schinke, S. P. (1989). The effects of alcohol and tobacco advertising on adolescents. In M. A. Orlandi, L. R. Lieberman, & S. P. Schinke (Eds.), *Perspectives on adolescent drug use* (pp. 77–97). Binghamton, NY: Haworth Press.

Outterson, K. (2010). Smoking and the First Amendment. *New England Journal of Medicine, 365,* 2351–2353.

Paek, H.-J., & Gunther, A. C. (2007). How peer proximity moderates indirect media influence on adolescent smoking. *Communication Research, 34,* 407–432.

Pan, W., & Bai, H. (2009). A multivariate approach to a meta-analytic review of the effectiveness of the D.A.R.E. program. *International Journal of Environmental Research and Public Health, 6,* 267–277.

Pierce, J. P., Choi, W. S., Gilpin, E. A., Farkas, A. J., & Berry, C. (1998). Industry promotion of cigarettes and adolescent smoking. *Journal of the American Medical Association, 279,* 511–515.

Pierce, J. P., Distefan, J. M., Jackson, C., White, M. M., & Gilpin, E. A. (2002). Does tobacco marketing undermine the influence of recommended parenting in discouraging adolescents from smoking? *American Journal of Preventive Medicine, 23,* 73–81.

Pierce, J. P., Lee, L., & Gilpin, E. A. (1994). Smoking initiation by adolescent girls, 1944 through 1988: An association with targeted advertising. *Journal of the American Medical Association, 271,* 608–611.

Pierce, J. P., Messer, K., James, L. E., White, M. M., Kealey, S., Vallone, D. M., & Healton, C. G. (2010). Camel No. 9 cigarette-marketing campaign targeted young teenage girls. *Pediatrics, 125,* 619–626.

Pinkleton, B. E., & Austin, E. W. (2013, in press). Young people's attitudes and decision making concerning tobacco and tobacco-use prevention advertising. *Talking Tobacco.*

Potter, W. J. (2010). *Media literacy* (5th ed.). Thousand Oaks, CA: Sage.

Primack, B. A., Dalton, M. A., Carroll, M. V., Agarwal, A. A., & Fine, M. J. (2008). Content analysis of tobacco, alcohol, and other drugs in popular music. *Archives of Pediatrics and Adolescent Medicine, 162,* 169–175.

Primack, B. A., Douglas, E., & Kraemer, K. (2010). Exposure to cannabis in popular music and cannabis use among adolescents. *Addiction, 105,* 515–523.

Primack, B. A., Fine, D., Yang, C. K., Wickett, D., & Zickmund, S. (2009). Adolescents' impressions of antismoking media literacy education: Qualitative results from a randomized controlled trial. *Health Education Research, 24,* 608–621.

Primack, B. A., Gold, M. A., Land, S. R., & Fine, M. J. (2006). Association of cigarette smoking and media literacy about smoking among adolescents. *Journal of Adolescent Health, 39,* 465–472.

Primack, B. A., & Hobbs, R. (2009). Association of various components of media literacy and adolescent smoking. *American Journal of Health Behavior, 33,* 192–201.

Primack, B. A., Kraemer, K. L., Fine, M. J., & Dalton, M. A. (2009). Media exposure and marijuana and alcohol use among adolescents. *Substance Use and Misuse, 44,* 722–739.

Primack, B. A., Nuzzo, E., Rice, K. R., & Sargent, J. D. (2012). Alcohol brand appearances in US popular music. *Addiction, 107,* 557–566.

Primack, B. A., Sidani, J., Carroll, M. V., & Fine, M. J. (2009). Associations between smoking and media literacy in college students. *Journal of Health Communication, 14,* 541–555.

Prokhorov, A. V., Winickoff, J. P., Ahluwalia, J. S., Ossip-Klein, D., Tanski, S., Lando, H. A., . . . Ford, K.H. (2006). Youth tobacco use: A global perspective for child health care clinicians. *Pediatrics, 118,* e890–e902.

Pupillo, J. (2007). Hot air: AAP experts skeptical of movie industry's commitment to curb smoke-filled images in youth-rated films or add R-ratings. *AAP News, 28,* 16–17.

Rauzi, R. (1998, June 9). The teen factor: Today's media-savvy youths influence what others are seeing and hearing. *Los Angeles Times,* p. F1.

Rehm, J., Shield, K. D., Joharchi, N., & Shuper, P. A. (2012). Alcohol consumption and the intention to engage in unprotected sex: Systematic review and meta-analysis of experimental studies. *Addiction, 107,* 51–59.

Reis, E. C., Duggan, A. K., Adger, H., & DeAngelis, C. (1992). The impact of anti-drug advertising on youth substance abuse [Abstract]. *American Journal of Diseases of Children, 146,* 519.

Reuters. (2012, August 24). Appeals court blocks graphic warnings on cigarettes. *New York Times.* Retrieved from http://www.nytimes.com/2012/08/25/business/tobacco-groups-win-ruling-on-graphic-cigarette-warnings.html

Rhoades, E., & Jernigan, D. H. (2013). Risky messages in alcohol advertising, 2003–2007: Results from content analysis. *Journal of Adolescent Health, 52,* 116–121. doi:10.1016/j.jadohealth.2012.04.013

Rich, M., & Bar-on, M. (2001). Child health in the information age: Media education of pediatricians. *Pediatrics, 107,* 156–162.

Rideout, V. (2010). *Generation M2: Media in the lives of 8- to 18-year-olds.* Menlo Park, CA: Kaiser Family Foundation.

Ringel, J. S., Collins, R. L., & Ellickson, P. L. (2006). Time trends and demographic differences in youth exposure to alcohol advertising on television. *Journal of Adolescent Health, 39*(4), 473–480.

Roberts, D. F., & Christenson, P. G. (2000). *"Here's looking at you, kid": Alcohol, drugs and tobacco in entertainment media.* Menlo Park, CA: Kaiser Family Foundation.

Robin, S. S., & Johnson, E. O. (1996). Attitude and peer cross pressure: Adolescent drug and alcohol use. *Journal of Drug Education, 26,* 69–99.

Romano, E., & Voas, R. B. (2011). Drug and alcohol involvement in four types of fatal crashes. *Journal of Studies on Alcohol and Drugs, 72,* 567–576.

Rosenthal, M. B., Berndt, E. R., Frank, R. G., Donohue, J. M., & Epstein, A. M. (2002). Promotion of prescription drugs to consumers. *New England Journal of Medicine, 346,* 498–505.

Rubin, A. (2009, November 19). *Prescription drugs and the cost of advertising them.* Retrieved from http://www.therubins.com/geninfo/advertise2.htm

Saffer, H., & Dave, D. (2006). Alcohol advertising and alcohol consumption by adolescents. *Health Economics, 15,* 617–637.

Salkin, A. (2007, February 11). Noir lite: Beer's good-time humor turns black. *New York Times,* section WK, p. 3.

Sargent, J. D., Beach, M. L., Adachi-Mejia, A. M., Gibson, J. J., Titus-Ernstoff, L. T., Carusi, C. P., . . . Dalton, M.A. (2005). Exposure to movie smoking: Its relation to smoking initiation among US adolescents. *Pediatrics, 116,* 1183–1191.

Sargent, J. D., Dalton, M., & Beach, M. (2000). Exposure to cigarette promotions and smoking uptake in adolescents: Evidence of a dose-response relation. *Tobacco Control, 9,* 163–168.

Sargent, J. D., Dalton, M., Beach, M., Ernstoff, L. T., Gibson, J. J., Tickle, J. J., & Heatherton, T. F. (2004). Effect of parental R-rated movie restriction on adolescent smoking initiation. *Pediatrics, 2004,* 149–156.

Sargent, J. D., Gibson, J., & Heatherton, T. (2009). Comparing the effects of entertainment media and tobacco marketing on youth smoking. *Tobacco Control, 18,* 47–53.

Sargent, J. D., & Heatherton, T. F. (2009). Comparison of trends for adolescent smoking and smoking in movies, 1990–2007. *Journal of the American Medical Association, 301,* 2211–2213.

Sargent, J. D., Stoolmiller, M., Worth, K. A., Gibson, J., & Gibbons, F. X. (2007). Exposure to smoking depictions in movies: Its association with established adolescent smoking. *Archives of Pediatrics and Adolescent Medicine, 161,* 849–856.

Sargent, J. D., Tanski, S. E., & Gibson, J. (2007). Exposure to movie smoking among US adolescents aged 10 to 14 years: A population estimate. *Pediatrics, 119,* e1167–e1176.

Sargent, J. D., Tanski, S. E., & Stoolmiller, M. (2012). Influence of motion picture rating on adolescent response to movie smoking. *Pediatrics, 130,* 228–236.

Sargent, J. D., Wills, T. A., Stoolmiller, M., Gibson, J., & Gibbons, F. X. (2006). Alcohol use in motion pictures and its relation with early onset teen drinking. *Journal of Studies of Alcohol, 67,* 54–65.

Serjeant, J. (2008, July 11). Some U.S. DVDs to carry anti-smoking ads. *Reuters.* Retrieved from http://www.reuters.com/article/entertainmentNews/idUSN1134673320080711

Schydlower, M., & Arredondo, R. M. (Eds.). (2006). Substance abuse among adolescents. *Adolescent Medicine State of the Art Reviews, 17,* 259–504.

Semuels, A. (2009, February 13). Alcohol, sex ads get prime TV time. *Los Angeles Times.* Retrieved from http://articles.latimes.com/2009/feb/13/business/fi-ads13

Shadel, W. G., Martino, S., Setodji, C. M., Haviland, A. M., Primack, B. A., & Scharf, D. M. (2012). Motives for smoking in movies affect future smoking risk in middle school students: An experimental investigation. *Drug and Alcohol Dependence, 123,* 66–71.

Shields, D. L., Carol, J., Balbach, E. D., & McGee, S. (1999). Hollywood on tobacco: How the entertainment industry understands tobacco portrayal. *Tobacco Control, 8,* 378–386.

Shrier, L. A., Harris, S. K., Kurland, M., & Knight, J. R. (2003). Substance use problems and associated psychiatric symptoms among adolescents in primary care. *Pediatrics, 111,* e699– e705.

Siegel, M., & Biener, L. (2000). The impact of an antismoking media campaign on progression to established smoking: Results of a longitudinal youth study. *American Journal of Public Health, 90,* 380–386.

Sims, T. H., & Committee on Substance Abuse. (2009). Technical report: Tobacco as a substance of abuse. *Pediatrics, 124,* e1045–1053.

Singer, D. G., & Singer, J. L. (Eds.). (2012). *Handbook of children and media* (2nd ed., pp. 419–454). Thousand Oaks, CA: Sage.

Slater, M. D., Kelly, K. J., Edwards, R. W., Plested, B. A., Keefe, T. J., Lawrence, F. R., & Henry, K. L. (2006). Combining in-school and community-based media efforts: Reducing marijuana and alcohol uptake among younger adolescents. *Health Education Research, 21,* 157–167.

Slater, M. D., Kelly, K. J., Lawrence, F. R., Stanley, L. R., & Comello, M. L. G. (2011). Assessing media campaigns linking marijuana non-use with autonomy and aspirations: "Be Under Your Own Influence" and ONDCP's "Above the Influence." (2011). *Preventive Science, 12,* 12–22.

Smith, L. A., & Foxcroft, D. R. (2009). The effect of alcohol advertising, marketing and portrayal on drinking behaviour in young people: Systematic review of prospective cohort studies. *BMC Public Health, 9.* doi:10.1186/1471-2458-9-51

Snowbeck, C. (2005, April 19). FDA tells Levitra to cool it with ad. *Post-Gazette,* Business News section. Retrieved from http://www.postgazette.com/pg/05109/490334-28.stm

Snyder, L. B., Milici, F. F., Slater, M., Sun, H., & Strizhakova, Y. (2006). Effects of alcohol advertising exposure on drinking among youth. *Archives of Pediatrics and Adolescent Medicine, 160,* 18–24.

Stange, K. C. (2007). Time to ban direct-to-consumer prescription drug marketing. *Annals of Family Medicine, 5,* 101–104.

Stockwell, T. F., & Glantz, S. A. (1997). Tobacco use is increasing in popular films. *Tobacco Control, 6,* 282–284.

Stoolmiller, M., Wills, T. A., McClure, A. C., Tanski, S. E., Worth, K. A., Gerrard, M., & Sargent, J. D. (2012). Comparing media and family predictors of alcohol use: A cohort study of US adolescents. *BMJ Open, 2,* e000543. doi: 10.1136/bmjopen-2011-000543

Strasburger, V. C. (1995). *Adolescents and the media: Medical and psychological impact.* Newbury Park, CA: Sage.

Strasburger, V. C. (1998). Adolescents, drugs, and the media [Letter]. *Archives of Pediatrics and Adolescent Medicine, 153,* 313.

Strasburger, V. C. (2009a). Media and children: What needs to happen now? *Journal of the American Medical Association, 301,* 2265–2266.

Strasburger, V. C. (2009b). Why do adolescent health researchers ignore the impact of the media? *Journal of Adolescent Health, 44,* 203–205.

Strasburger, V. C. (2010, February 24). Is there a conspiracy against teenagers? *Liberal Opinion Week,* p. 26.

Strasburger, V. C. (2012). School daze: Why are teachers and schools missing the boat on media? *Pediatric Clinics of North America, 59,* 705–716.

Strasburger, V.C. (2013, in press). Whasssssssup? Adolescents, drugs, and the media. In A. B. Jordan & D. Romer (Eds.). *Media and the Well-Being of Children and Adolescents.* New York: Oxford University Press.

Strasburger, V. C., & Council on Communications and Media. (2010a). Children, adolescents, substance abuse, and the media. *Pediatrics, 126,* 791–799.

Strasburger, V. C., & Council on Communications and Media. (2010b). Sexuality, contraception, and the media. *Pediatrics, 126,* 576–582.

Strasburger, V. C., Jordan, A. B., & Donnerstein, E. (2012). Children, adolescents, and the media: Health effects. *Pediatric Clinics of North America, 59,* 533–587.

Strasser, A. A., Tang, K. Z., Romer, D., Jepson, C., & Cappella, J. N. (2012). Graphic warning labels in cigarette advertising. *American Journal of Preventive Medicine, 43,* 41–47.

Sutel, S. (2007, January 26). Watching the ads. *Albuquerque Journal* (Associated Press), p. B4.

Swahn, M. H., Bossarte, R. M., & Sullivent, E. E., 3rd. (2008). Age of alcohol use initiation, suicidal behavior, and peer and dating violence victimization and perpetration among high-risk, seventh-grade adolescents. *Pediatrics, 121,* 297–305.

Swendsen, J., Burstein, M., Case, B., Conway, K. P., Dierker, L., He, J., & Merikangas, K. R. (2012). Use and abuse of alcohol and illicit drugs in US adolescents. *Archives of General Psychiatry, 69,* 390–398.

Tanski, S. E., Dal Cin, S., Stoolmiller, M., & Sargent, J. D. (2010). Parental R-rated movie restriction and early onset alcohol use. *Journal of Studies of Alcohol and Drugs, 71,* 452–459.

Tanski, S. E., McClure, A. C., Jernigan, D. H., & Sargent, J. D. (2011). Alcohol brand preference and binge drinking among adolescents. *Archives of Pediatrics and Adolescent Medicine, 165,* 675–676.

Tanski, S. E., Prokhorov, A. V., & Klein, J. D. (2004). Youth and tobacco. *Minerva Pediatrica, 56,* 553–565.

Tanski, S. E., Stoolmiller, M., Dal Cin, S., Worth, K., Gibson, J., & Sargent, J. D. (2009). Movie character smoking and adolescent smoking: Who matters more, good guys or bad guys? *Pediatrics, 124,* 135–143.

Tapert, S. F., Cheung, E. H., Brown, G. G., Frank, L. R., Paulus, M. P., Schweinsburg, A. D., . . . Brown, S. A. (2003). Neural response to alcohol stimuli in adolescents with alcohol use disorder. *Archives of General Psychiatry, 60,* 727–735.

Teen "self medication" for depression leads to more serious mental illness, new report reveals. (2008, May 10). *Science Daily.* Retrieved from http://www.sciencedaily.com /releases/2008/05/080509105348.htm

Terry-McElrath, Y. M., Emery, S., Szczypka, G., & Johnston, L. D. (2010). Potential exposure to anti-drug advertising and drug-related attitudes, beliefs, and behaviors among United States youth, 1995–2006. *Addictive Behaviors, 36,* 116–124.

Their Super Bowl ads were a hit, but how did Chrysler, Groupon, others fare after the game? (2012, February 3). *Associated Press.* Retrieved from http://www.washingtonpost.com/sports/redskins/ theyre-super-bowl-ads-were-a-hit-but-how-did-chrysler-groupon-others-fare-after-the-game/2012/02/03/gIQAvZQbmQ_print.html

Thomaselli, R. (2003, January 14). 47% of doctors feel pressured by DTC drug advertising. *Advertising Age.* Retrieved from http://adage.com

Thompson, E. M., & Gunther, A. C. (2007). Cigarettes and cinema: Does parental restriction of R-rated movie viewing reduce adolescent smoking susceptibility? *Journal of Adolescent Health, 40,* e1–e6.

Thompson, M. P., Sims, L., Kingree, J. B., & Windle, M. (2008). Longitudinal associations between problem alcohol use and violent victimization in a national sample of adolescents. *Journal of Adolescent Health, 42,* 21–27.

Tickle, J. J., Beach, M. L., & Dalton, M. A. (2009). Tobacco, alcohol, and other risk behaviors in film: How well do MPAA ratings distinguish content? *Journal of Health Communication, 14,* 756–767.

Titus-Ernstoff, L., Dalton, M. A., Adachi-Mejia, A. M., Longacre, M. R., & Beach, M. L. (2008). Longitudinal study of viewing smoking in movies and initiation of smoking by children. *Pediatrics, 121,* 15–21.

Tobacco ads will be removed from school magazines. (2005, June 20). *Consumer Affairs.* Retrieved from http://www.consumeraffairs.com/news04/2005/tobacco_schools.html

Tobacco giants suing FDA over warning labels mandate. (2011, August 17). *CNN Health.* Retrieved from http://www.cnn.com/2011/HEALTH/08/17/cigarette.labels.lawsuit/index.html?hpt=hp_12

Up in smoke: Disney bans cigarettes. (2007, July 16). *ABC News.* Retrieved from http://abcnews.go.com/print?id=3416434

U.S. Department of Health and Human Services. (1994). *Preventing tobacco use among young people: Report of the surgeon general.* Washington, DC: U.S. Government Printing Office.

U.S. Department of Health and Human Services. (2001). *Youth violence: A report of the surgeon general.* Washington, DC: U.S. Government Printing Office.

U.S. Department of Health and Human Services. (2004). *The health consequences of smoking: A report of the surgeon general.* Rockville, MD: Author.

U.S. Department of Health and Human Services. (2007). *The surgeon general's call to action to prevent and reduce underage drinking.* Rockville, MD: Author.

U.S. Department of Health and Human Services. (2012). *Preventing tobacco use among youth and young adults: A report of the surgeon general.* Atlanta, GA: Author.

Vaidya, S. G., Vaidya, J. S., & Naik, U. D. (1999). Sports sponsorship by cigarette companies influences the adolescent children's mind and helps initiate smoking: Results of a national study in India. *Journal of the Indian Medical Association, 97,* 354–356.

Van den Bulck, H., Simons, N., & Van Gorp, B. (2008). Let's drink and be merry: The framing of alcohol in the prime-time American youth series *The OC. Journal of Studies of Alcohol and Drugs, 69,* 933–940.

Vickers, A. (1992). Why cigarette advertising should be banned. *British Medical Journal, 304,* 1195–1196.

Walsh, D., & Bennett, D. (2005). *WHY do they act that way? A survival guide to the adolescent brain for you and your teen.* New York, NY: Free Press.

Walsh, D., & Gentile, D. A. (2001). A validity test of movie, television, and video-game ratings. *Pediatrics, 107,* 1302–1308.

Ward, L. M., Day, K. M., & Thomas, K. A. (2010). Confronting the assumptions: Exploring the nature and predictors of Black adolescents' media use. *Journal of Broadcasting and Electronic Media, 54,* 69–86.

Waylen, A. E., Leary, S. D., Ness, A. R., & Tanski, S. E. (2011). Cross-sectional association between smoking depictions in films and adolescent tobacco use nested in a British cohort study. *Thorax, 66,* 856–861.

Weichold, K., Brambosch, A., & Silbereisen, R. K. (2012). Do girls profit more? Gender-specific effectiveness of a life skills program against alcohol consumption in early adolescence. *Journal of Early Adolescence, 32,* 200–225.

Weinstein, H. (1998, January 15). Papers: RJR went for teens. *Los Angeles Times,* p. A1.

Wellman, R. J., Sugarman, D. B., DiFranza, J., & Winickoff, J. P. (2006). The extent to which tobacco marketing and tobacco use in films contribute to children's use of tobacco. *Archives of Pediatrics and Adolescent Medicine, 160,* 1285–1296.

West, J. H., Romero, R. A., & Trinidad, D. R. (2007). Adolescent receptivity to tobacco marketing by racial/ethnic groups in California. *American Journal of Preventive Medicine, 33,* 121–123.

While, D., Kelly, S., Huang, W., & Charlton, A. (1996). Cigarette advertising and onset of smoking in children: Questionnaire survey. *British Medical Journal, 313,* 398–399.

White, A. M., & Swartzwelder, H. S. (2004). Hippocampal function during adolescence: A unique target of ethanol effects. *Annals of the New York Academy of Sciences, 1021*, 206–220.

Wiencke, J. K., Thurston, S. W., Kelsey, K. T., Varkonyi, A., Wain, J. C., Mark, E. J., & Christiani, D. C. (1999). Early age at smoking initiation and tobacco carcinogen DNA damage in the lung. *Journal of the National Cancer Institute, 91*, 614–619.

Williams, R. S., & Ribisl, K. M. (2012). Internet alcohol sales to minors. *Archives of Pediatrics and Adolescent Medicine, 166*, 808–813.

Wills, T. A., Sargent, J. D., Gibbons, F. X., Gerrard, M., & Stoolmiller, M. (2009). Movie exposure to alcohol cues and adolescent alcohol problems: A longitudinal analysis in a national sample. *Psychology of Addictive Behavior, 23*, 23–25.

Wilson, D. (2009, June 13). Congress passes measure on tobacco regulation. *New York Times.* Retrieved from http://www.nytimes.com/2009/06/13/business/13tobacco.html

Winter, M. V., Donovan, R. J., & Fielder, L. J. (2008). Exposure of children and adolescents to alcohol advertising on television in Australia. *Journal of Studies on Alcohol and Drugs, 69*, 676–683.

Womach, J. (2003). *U.S. tobacco production, consumption, and export trends: A report to Congress.* Washington, DC: Congressional Research Service, Library of Congress.

World Health Organization. (2007). *Alcohol and injury in emergency departments: Summary of the report from the WHO Collaborative Study on Alcohol and Injuries.* Retrieved from http://www.who.int/substance_abuse/publications/alcohol_injury_summary.pdf

World Health Organization. (2008). *WHO report on the global tobacco epidemic, 2008.* Geneva, Switzerland: Author.

World Health Organization. (2011). *Smoke-free movies: From evidence to action.* Geneva, Switzerland: Author.

Worth, K. A., Chambers, J. G., Nassau, D. H., Rakhra, B. K., & Sargent, J. D. (2008). Exposure of US adolescents to extremely violent movies. *Pediatrics, 122*, 306–312.

Yakota, F., & Thompson, K. M. (2001). Depiction of alcohol, tobacco, and other substances in G-rated animated films. *Pediatrics, 107*, 1369–1374.

Young, S. (2011, June 21). FDA reveals bigger, graphic warning labels for cigarette packages. *CNN Health.* Retrieved from http://www.cnn.com/2011/HEALTH/06/21/cigarette.labels/index.html

CHAPTER 7

Obesity, Eating Disorders, and the Media

Television presents viewers with two sets of conflicting messages. One suggests that we eat in ways almost guaranteed to make us fat; the other suggests that we strive to remain slim.

—Lois Kaufman
in *Journal of Communication* (1980, p. 45)

We're living in a food carnival, constantly bombarded by food cues, almost all of them unhealthy.

—Former FDA commissioner Dr. David Kessler
as quoted at *Reuters.com* (Begley, 2012)

Our kids didn't do this to themselves. They don't decide the sugar content in soda or the advertising content of a television show. Kids don't choose what's served to them for lunch at school, and shouldn't be deciding what's served to them for dinner at home. And they don't decide whether there's time in the day or room in the budget to learn about healthy eating or to spend time playing outside.

—Michelle Obama
Childhood Obesity Summit, April 9, 2010

First Lady Michelle Obama just launched a campaign to combat childhood obesity called "Let's Move." And this evening, obese children started their own program called "Let's Not."

—Comedian Jimmy Fallon
on NBC's *Late Night* ("Late Laughs," 2012)

While sex, drugs, rock 'n' roll, and violence grab the headlines, the media can have a major impact on other areas of young people's health as well. The modern world is facing an epidemic of obesity, spawned in the United States but now spreading all over the globe. As in other crucial areas of health, the media play a potentially important role; television in particular serves as an important source of information for children and teens about food and eating habits. Television nutrition—especially food advertising—and the image of women in programming and advertising are coming under increasing scrutiny as pediatricians and public health officials try to understand how and why children and teenagers are becoming obese or suffering from eating disorders. In the United States, childhood obesity now affects approximately 12.5 million children and teens (17%), with an additional 15% being overweight (J. Bell, Rogers, et al., 2011; Ogden, Carroll, Curtin, Lamb, & Flegal, 2010). Anorexia nervosa occurs in as many as 1 in 100 to 200 middle-class females (Strasburger et al., 2006) and bulimia in as many as 5% of young women (British Medical Association, 2000). All of which points to a new conundrum in American society: how to deal with the epidemic of obesity while, at the same time, avoiding scaring children and teenagers into abnormal eating behaviors and frank eating disorders.

The American food supply now furnishes 3,900 calories per capita per day, approximately twice what people actually need and 700 calories per day more than in 1980 (Nestle, 2006a, 2006b). When the producers of *Taking Woodstock* began casting for their movie about the 1969 concert, they had great difficulty finding extras who were as thin as the original concert-goers ("Obesity Rates Spin," 2011). Obesity has become a worldwide problem, however, with rates increasing dramatically in nearly every country (Guthold, Cowan, Autenrieth, Kahn, & Riley, 2010). Globally, diets are shifting toward higher intakes of animal and partially hydrogenated fats, with concomitant increases in the prevalence of obesity (Popkin, 2006). In Europe, as many as 20% to 35% of 10-year-olds in various countries are now overweight (Lang & Rayner, 2005; Preidt, 2008). Still, according to one recent international report, the U.S. is the fattest nation among 33 countries with advanced economies (Hellmich, 2010) (see Figure 7.1). The prevalence of childhood obesity slowly increased from the 1960s until the 1980s and 1990s, when the trajectory accelerated dramatically—tripling from nearly 5% to 15% (J. Bell, Rogers, et al., 2011) (see Figure 7.2).

For the first time in the history of the United States, there are now more overweight and obese adults than adults of normal weight (Ogden et al., 2006). Estimates are that by 2030, 51% of the entire population will be obese (Finkelstein et al., 2012). More than two-thirds of states have adult obesity rates over 25%, and eight states have childhood obesity rates that exceed 20% (Levi, Vintner, St. Laurent, & Segal, 2011).

Significant racial and ethnic differences exist (see Figure 7.3), there being an increased risk for Hispanic males and Black and Hispanic females. Prevalence by state also differs (see Figure 7.4). Interestingly, according to a recent poll of more than 2,100 parents nationwide, obesity has now moved to the top of parents' list of concerns (C. S. Mott Children's Hospital, 2011) (see Figure 7.5). Nearly three-fourths (72%) of parents think their children have too much access to junk food, and 40% are worried that their children will become obese; most interesting, however, is that 78% of parents believe that the fault lies with them (Mintel, 2009).

Obesity may be the single most serious health problem facing the world's children and teenagers in the new millennium. In the U.S., estimates put the medical costs of obesity at $168 billion a year, or 17% of all health costs (Cawley & Meyerhoefer, 2012). Overweight and obesity bring with them a whole host of medical problems and concerns, including metabolic syndrome—a collection of unhealthy factors that precedes diabetes (J. A. Morrison, Glueck,

Figure 7.1 Trends in obesity among children and adolescents: United States, 1963–2008.

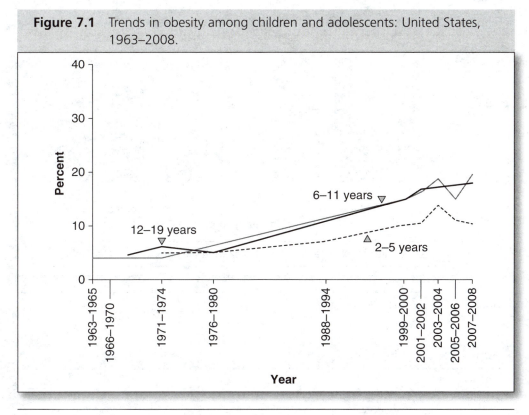

SOURCE: J. Bell, Rogers, and colleagues (2011).

Figure 7.2 Self-reported overweight and obesity in children aged 10–16 years.

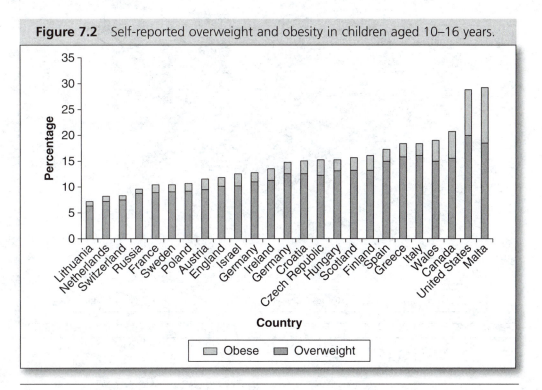

SOURCE: International Association for the Study of Obesity (IASO0). Data from the HSBC Survey 2005–2006.

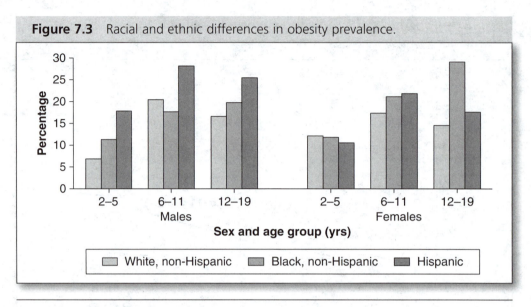

Figure 7.3 Racial and ethnic differences in obesity prevalence.

SOURCE: J. Bell, Rogers, and colleagues (2011).

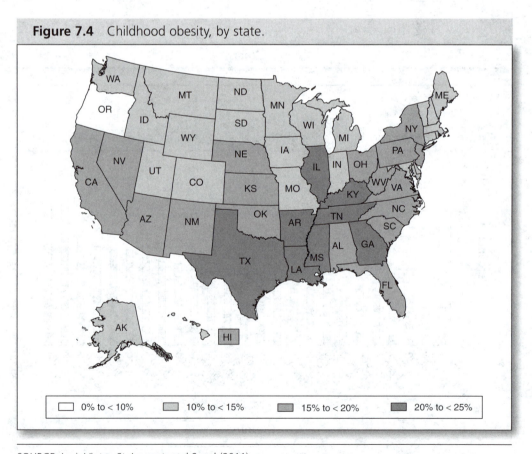

Figure 7.4 Childhood obesity, by state.

SOURCE: Levi, Vinter, St. Laurent, and Segal (2011).

Daniels, & Wang, 2010)—and Type 2 diabetes, the prevalence of which increased from 9% to 23% between 1999 and 2008 (May, Kuklina, & Yoon, 2012), as well as high blood pressure, asthma, sleep apnea, joint problems, fatty liver, and early mortality (Han, Lawlor, & Kimm, 2010; E. R. Sutherland, 2008; Flegal, Kit, Orpana, & Graubard, 2013). Current estimates are that by 2050, the prevalence of Type 1 diabetes among youth will have tripled and Type 2 diabetes will have doubled (Imperatore et al., 2012). Perhaps just as important, obese children and adolescents tend to suffer from discrimination and lower self-esteem than their peers (Franklin, Denyer, Steinbeck, Caterson, & Hill, 2006) and even face a higher risk of suicide (Swahn et al., 2009; Ul-Haq, Mackay, Fenwick, & Pell, 2013).

Figure 7.5 Parents' top child health concerns.

Child Health Concern, % Rated as "Big Problem" in 2011
1. Childhood obesity, 33%
2. Drug abuse, 33%
3. Smoking and tobacco use, 25%
4. Teen pregnancy, 24%
5. Bullying, 24%
6. Internet safety, 23%
7. Stress, 22%
8. Alcohol abuse, 20%
9. Driving accidents, 20%
10. Sexting, 20%

SOURCE: C. S. Mott Children's Hospital Poll an Children's Health (2011).

Are the Media a Cause of Obesity in Children and Adolescents?

Like other media research questions, whether or not the media cause obesity is a complicated issue and not completely understood; however, the American Academy of Pediatrics has taken the position that the media are clearly implicated as a significant contributor (Council on Communications and Media, 2011; Hingle & Kunkel, 2012; McKetta & Rich, 2011) (see Figure 7.6). In 2006, the Institute of Medicine identified more than 60 studies that show a statistically significant relationship between TV exposure and childhood obesity (Institute of Medicine, 2006). Since then, numerous large-scale studies have corroborated this relationship (e.g., Gable, Chang, & Krull, 2007; te Velde et al., 2007; Zimmerman & Bell, 2010). A recent review of 26 studies published between 1995 and 2010—15 cross-sectional and 11 prospective—shows that all but three found a positive association between hours of TV viewed and childhood adiposity (Cox, Skouteris, Rutherford, & Fuller-Tyszkiewicz, 2012).

The connection between media use and weight status was first established in the mid-1980s (Dietz & Gortmaker, 1985), but the difficulty is that even though researchers know the connection exists, they do not know exactly *why* it exists. Is it because of the 4,400 to 7,600 food advertisements that children and teens see every year on TV alone, most of them for junk food or fast food (Gantz, Schwartz, Angelini, & Rideout, 2007)? Is it the content of television shows, with all of its unhealthy nutrition, that teaches children bad eating habits? Is it because watching screen media is such a sedentary activity, and that the seven hours per day that children and

Figure 7.6

SOURCE: Reprinted with special permission of Universal Press Syndicate.

teens spend watching media displaces more vigorous activities? Is it because snacking increases in front of the TV set? Or is it because late-night media use interferes with sleep, and lack of sleep is a known risk factor for obesity? Epidemiologically, the answer is probably "all of the above," and one factor may predominate in any given individual.

As with other areas of media influence, the media are not the leading "cause" of obesity. But studies clearly show a significant contribution. Nearly every study controls for known correlates of obesity (e.g., socioeconomic status, race, ethnicity, maternal educational level). The most powerful evidence comes from longitudinal studies, and 12 of the 15 longitudinal studies have produced significant results (Institute of Medicine, 2006).

- Dietz and Gortmaker (1985) found that number of hours spent watching TV was a strong predictor of obesity among 6- to 11-year-olds and 12- to 17-year-olds. For every additional hour of TV viewing above the norm, the prevalence of obesity increased 2%. To exclude the possibility that children or teens watched more television because they were obese, the researchers studied only children and teens who were not obese at baseline (Dietz, 1993). The researchers concluded that nearly 30% of obesity could be prevented if children limited TV viewing to no more than one hour per day (Dietz & Gortmaker, 1993).
- A remarkable 30-year longitudinal study in the United Kingdom found that for each additional hour of TV watched per weekend day at age 5, the risk of adult obesity increased by 7% at age 30, even when adjustments were made for socioeconomic

status and parental weight status (Viner & Cole, 2005). Researchers from Dunedin, New Zealand, followed 1,000 people from birth to 26 years of age. Average weeknight TV viewing between the ages of 5 and 15 years was strongly correlated with higher body mass index (BMI) (Hancox, Milne, & Poulton, 2004; Hancox & Poulton, 2006). If the children had observed the American Academy of Pediatrics' recommendation of less than two hours of screen time per day, 17% of overweight, 15% of elevated serum cholesterol, 17% of smoking, and 15% of poor fitness would have been avoided.

- A study of 8,234 Scottish children found that viewing more than eight hours of TV per week at age 3 was associated with an increased risk of obesity at age 7 (Reilly et al., 2005). In a Japanese study of 8,170 children, heavier TV viewing at age 3 resulted in a higher risk of being overweight at age 6 (Sugimori et al., 2004). An Australian study of nearly 1,300 children ages 5 to 10 years with a three-year follow-up found that total screen time was positively associated with measures of obesity (Hesketh, Wake, Graham, & Waters, 2007).

- Longitudinal studies in the U.S. ranging up to 10 years have found very similar results (French, Mitchell, & Hannan, 2012; Kaur, Choi, Mayo, & Harris, 2003; Lumeng, Rahnama, Appugliese, Kaciroti, & Bradley, 2006; O'Brien et al., 2007; Proctor et al., 2003). In one study of 169 girls ages 7, 9, and 11 years, those who watched more than two hours of TV per day were 13 times more likely to be overweight at age 11 (Davison, Marshall, & Birch, 2006).

- Finally, a meta-analysis of 232 studies confirmed the association between TV viewing and unfavorable body composition and health outcomes (Tremblay et al., 2011).

Dozens of correlational studies have shown similar findings as well. More than 15 years ago, Gortmaker and his colleagues (1996) found a strong dose-response relationship between the prevalence of overweight and more than five hours of TV viewing per day compared with viewing zero to two hours per day in a national sample of 746 ten- to fifteen-year-olds. Some studies have found an association between screen time and obesity regardless of physical activity—for example, in a recent cross-sectional sample of 2,200 adolescents in 10 different European cities (Rey-López et al., 2012). Several studies have found a markedly increased risk of obesity with the presence of a TV set in the bedroom (Adachi-Mejia et al., 2007; Dennison, Erb, & Jenkins, 2002; Staiano, Harrington, Broyles, Gupta, & Katzmarzyk, 2013). Interestingly, children who have bedroom TVs are more likely to be overweight compared with those who watch the same amount of TV but do not have a TV set in their bedroom (Delmas et al., 2007). Teenagers with a bedroom TV spend more time watching TV, spend less time being physically active, eat fewer meals with their family, drink more sweetened beverages, and eat fewer vegetables than teenagers without a bedroom TV (Barr-Anderson, van den Berg, Neumark-Sztainer, & Story, 2008).

Studies have also found a strong association between time spent watching TV and hypertension (Martinez-Gomez, Tucker, Heelan, Welk, & Eisenmann, 2009; Pardee, Norman, Lustig, Preud'homme, & Schwimmer, 2007), high cholesterol levels in children (Fung et al., 2001), abnormal lipid levels in adolescents (Martinez-Gomez et al., 2010), Type 2 diabetes (Hu, Li, Colditz, Willett, & Manson, 2003), insulin resistance (Ford et al., 2010; Hardy, Denney-Wilson, Thrift, Okely, & Baur, 2010), metabolic syndrome (Mark & Janssen, 2008), and good glucose control in young people with diabetes (Margeirdottir, Larsen, Brunborg,

Sandvik, & Dahl-Jørgensen, 2007). At least four studies actually claim that TV viewing increases mortality—probably via metabolic risk factors—and one of the studies found that a person who spends a lifetime of viewing six hours per day reduces his or her life expectancy by nearly five years (Dunstan et al., 2010; Katzmarzyk & Lee, 2012; Stamatakis, Hamer, & Dunstan, 2011; Veerman et al., 2011).

What about other screens besides TV? The studies are either nonexistent (e.g., movies) or far less impressive (e.g., computer time, video games). One recent study found that length of play time, frequency of playing, and years of playing were each correlated with less exercise and higher BMI (Ballard, Gray, Reilly, & Noggle, 2009). A few other studies have also found an association between playing video games and obesity (McMurray et al., 2000; Vandewater, Shim, & Caplovitz, 2004), but several have not (Kautiainen, Koivusilta, Lintonen, Virtanen, & Rimpelä, 2005; Wake, Hesketh, & Waters, 2003). A 2008 meta-analysis of screen time and overweight found no relationship between video game playing and BMI but did find an excess of caloric intake in game players of about 92 calories per hour played (Sonneville & Gortmaker, 2008). Of course, playing video games may not be nearly as sedentary as watching TV, especially if games like *Wii Fit* and *Dance Dance Revolution* are being used (Daley, 2009; Graf, Pratt, Hester, & Short, 2009; Pate, 2008).

Similarly, computer screen time may contribute to obesity, but so far the studies are not nearly as numerous or as convincing (Kautiainen et al., 2005; Vandewater, Shim, & Caplovitz, 2004; Babey, Hastert, & Wolstein, 2013). One recent review did identify 22 separate studies that examined the combined impact of all screen time (TV, video, gaming, computer and Internet usage) and found strong evidence for a positive association between screen-based sedentary behavior and overweight status in adolescent girls (Costigan, Barnett, Plotnikoff, & Luvans, 2012). Computer content has not been examined closely, and that may be the key (McKetta & Rich, 2011). However, a recent study of more than 2,200 European teens did find that a combination of increased TV viewing, computer use, and Internet use (more than four hours per day) was associated with increased consumption of sweetened beverages and decreased fruit consumption (Santaliestra-Pasías et al., 2012). Two studies have examined cell phone use: One documented cell phones' interference with sleep, a known risk factor for obesity (Brunborg et al., 2011), and the other found that playing video games on cell phones was associated with higher BMIs (Yen et al., 2010).

One of the other most damaging pieces of evidence for the TV-obesity connection is the fact that when screen time is reduced, adiposity decreases. This was first documented in the 1990s with a randomized controlled trial that consisted of a series of 18 lessons (30 to 50 minutes each) taught by 3rd- and 4th-grade teachers over a period of six months. Significant reductions in screen time resulted, along with reductions in several measures of adiposity as well—without any significant change in physical activity (Robinson, 1999). Since then, several more studies have shown that reducing screen time can result in significant improvements in weight status (Dennison, Russo, Burdick, & Jenkins, 2004; Epstein, Paluch, Gordy, & Dorn, 2000; Epstein et al., 2008; Gortmaker et al., 1999; Robinson & Borzekowski, 2006). A recent meta-analysis has confirmed these findings, along with the fact that weight changes usually occur without any change in physical activity (Wahi, Parkin, Beyene, Uleryk, & Birken, 2011). This may be because decreasing TV use and computer/game use decreases consumption of soft drinks and unhealthy snacks (Gebremariam et al., 2013). Not all efforts have been entirely successful, however—preschoolers' screen time may be difficult to reduce when primary care practitioners counsel parents (Birken et al., 2012).

So what is it about screen time—especially television viewing—that seems to promote overweight and obesity?

The Role of Food Advertising and Marketing

In its comprehensive 2006 report, the Institute of Medicine concluded that "food and beverage marketing practices geared to children and youth are out of balance with healthful diets, and contribute to an environment that puts their health at risk" (2006, p. 374). They also found:

- Strong evidence that advertising influences the short-term food consumption of children 2 to 11 years old
- Strong evidence that exposure to advertising is associated with adiposity in children and teens
- Moderate evidence that advertising influences the regular diet of 2- to 5-year-olds and weaker evidence that advertising affects the regular diet of 6- to 11-year-olds

As seen in Chapter 2, advertising is ubiquitous in the U.S., with $250 billion being spent annually on it—more than twice what any other country in the world spends on advertising (Committee on Communications, 2006). Advertising is incredibly effective in increasing consumption; otherwise, why would companies spend so much on it? Young children are particularly susceptible. Remarkably, as long ago as 1981, the Federal Trade Commission (FTC) issued the following conclusion after reviewing the research:

The record . . . supports the following conclusions regarding child-oriented television advertising and young children six years and under: (1) they place indiscriminate trust in televised advertising messages; (2) they do not understand the persuasive bias in television advertising; and (3) the techniques, focus and themes used in child-oriented television advertising enhance the appeal of the advertising message and the advertised product. Consequently, *young children do not possess the cognitive ability to evaluate adequately child oriented television advertising* [emphasis added]. Despite the fact that these conclusions can be drawn from the evidence, *the record establishes that the only effective remedy would be a ban on all advertisements oriented towards young children, and such a ban, as a practical matter, cannot be implemented* [emphasis added]. (FTC, 1981, pp. 2–4)

This was the closest that the federal government has ever come to regulating junk food or fast food, specifically the advertising of sugared cereals to young children (which, at the time, arose from the concern over dental caries and not obesity). As noted in Chapter 13, the focus of policy related to advertising to children is on the amount of time rather than the type of content. This means that advertising is now considered more of a broadcasting issue, as time restrictions are enforced by the Federal Communications Commission (FCC), rather than an issue of corporate responsibility and public health. Many public health groups, like the American Academy of Pediatrics, continue to believe that advertising directed toward young children is inherently deceptive and exploitative (Committee on Communications, 2006) (see Figure 7.7). Yet as recently as 2012, the food industry has refused to engage in even considering the possibility of voluntary guidelines, not to mention regulations that would restrict the advertising of unhealthy foods to young children (J. L. Harris & Graff, 2012; Jacobson, 2012).

Figure 7.7

SOURCE: Berry's World: © by NEA, Inc. Jim Berry; reprinted by permission of Newspaper Enterprise Association, Inc.

This is not just an American problem, however. International studies show that children are exposed to high volumes of TV advertising for unhealthy foods worldwide (Kelly et al., 2010).

Fast Food

On any given day in the U.S., 30% of children and teens are eating fast food and therefore consuming an additional 187 calories (equaling 6 pounds per year) (Bowman, Gortmaker, Ebbeling, Pereira, & Ludwig, 2004; Brownell, 2004; Powell & Nguyen, 2013) (see Table 7.1).

Fast food is big business: Americans spend more than $110 billion on it annually, more than on higher education, computers, or cars (Schlosser, 2001). A recent study examined more than 3,000 possible meal combinations at a dozen restaurant chains and found only 12 meals that met nutritional standards for preschoolers. The same study found that 84% of parents had bought fast food for their children the previous week (J. L. Harris et al., 2010). Portion sizes have increased dramatically as well, by 100 to 400 calories for the average restaurant meal (Close & Schoeller, 2006; J. Schwartz & Byrd-Bredbrenner, 2006). The recent upsurge in obesity rates has been associated with an equivalent increase in fast food consumption (Niemeier, Raynor, Lloyd-Richardson, Rogers, & Wing, 2006) (see Figure 7.8).

Table 7.1 Fast Food and Kids

Kids ages 12 to 17:

spend $12.7 billion per year on fast food

eat 7% of all their meals at fast food restaurants

visit fast food restaurants an average of 2.13 times/week

46% say their favorite food is a hamburger

SOURCE: Adapted from Preboth and Wright (1999) and Brownell (2004).

Figure 7.8 Interesting new research shows a correlation between time spent eating and obesity rates worldwide and seems to implicate Americans' love of fast food as one causative factor in the new epidemic of obesity (Rampell, 2009).

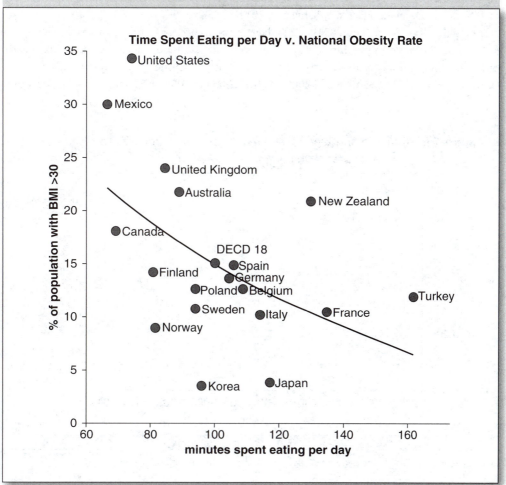

Junk Food

Contrary to popular belief, obese people are not obese because they constantly gorge themselves on food. Small increases in caloric intake (or decreases in activity) amount to large weight gains over time (Dietz, 1993). An extra pat of butter per day represents 50 calories per day and a weight gain of 5 pounds per year. Drinking a can of soda per day produces a weight gain of 15 pounds per year (Apovian, 2004). Movie popcorn is notorious for hidden calories. Nearly 40% of young people's caloric intake now comes from fats and added sugars, and soda and fruit drinks provide nearly 10% of total calories (Reedy & Krebs-Smith, 2010).

The Prevalence of Advertising

American children view an estimated 40,000 ads per year, and advertisers spend $10 billion annually trying to appeal to children (Committee on Communications, 2006). More than half of such ads are for food, especially sugared cereals, high-calorie snacks, and fast food (Institute of Medicine, 2006). Although children viewed 5% fewer food and beverage ads in 2011 compared with 2010 (see Figure 7.9), the average 2- to 11-year-old still sees nearly 13 ads per day on TV alone (Dembek, Harris, & Schwartz, 2012).

In children's programming, 83% of all advertisements are for fast food or snacks (Harrison & Marske, 2005). Young children may see more than 500 food references per week, nearly one-third being for empty-calorie snacks and another one-fourth for high-fat foods (Borzekowski, 2001). A sample of 50,000 ads from 2003 to 2004 on 170 top-rated shows found

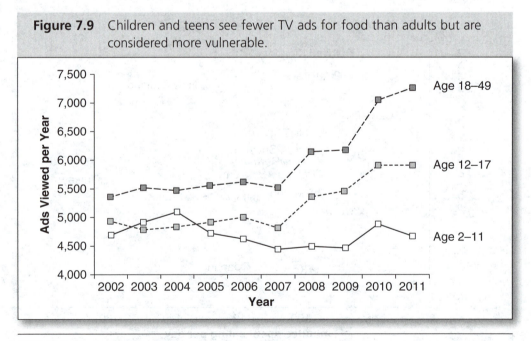

Figure 7.9 Children and teens see fewer TV ads for food than adults but are considered more vulnerable.

SOURCE: Dembek, Harris, and Schwartz (2012). Reprinted with permission.

that 98% of all food ads seen by children 2 to 11 years old and nearly 90% of ads seen by teens are for foods that are high in either fat, sugar, or sodium (Hingle & Kunkel, 2012; Powell, Szczypka, & Chaloupka, 2007) (see Figure 7.10).

A 2007 study of more than 1,600 hours of TV and nearly 9,000 food ads found that children and teens see an average of 12 to 21 food ads per day, for a total of 4,400 to 7,600 ads per year, yet they see fewer than 165 ads that promote fitness or good nutrition (Gantz et al., 2007) (see Figure 7.11). A 2007 FTC study had very similar findings (FTC, 2007). Even PBS, Disney, and Nickelodeon now target toddlers and preschoolers with ads in the form of "sponsorships" (Connor, 2006). African American children are particularly at risk, since they see 37% more ads than other children (J. L. Harris et al., 2010) and are more likely to be seen in commercials eating unhealthy food in fast food restaurants (Gilmore & Jordan, 2012).

Figure 7.10   Nutritional quality of foods advertised in 10 hours of children's programming.

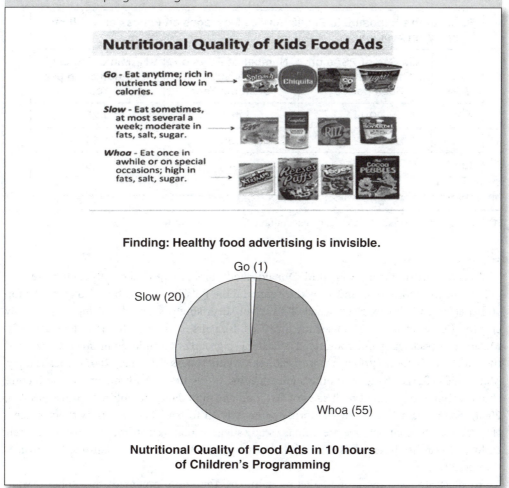

SOURCE: Kunkel, McKinley, and Wright (2009).

Figure 7.11 What nutritional messages do children receive on TV?

A. Children's Exposure to Food Advertising on TV, on Average:

AGE	Number of Food Ads Seen per Day	Number of Food Ads Seen per Year	Hr:Min of Food Ads Seen per Year
2–7	12	4,427	29:31
8–12	21	7,609	50:48
13–17	17	6,098	40:50

*This estimate of food ads seen per day has been rounded to the nearest whole number. For the calculation of the number of food ads seen per year, the more precise figure was used.

B. Children's Exposure to Public Service Messages on Fitness or Nutrition on TV, on Average:

AGE	Min:Sec of PSAs on Fitness/Nutrition Seen per Day	Number of PSAs on Fitness/Nutrition Seen per Year	Hr:Min of Fitness/Nutrition Seen per Year
2–7	0:14	164	1:25
8–12	0:12	158	1:15
13–17	0:04	47	0:25

SOURCE: Gantz, Schwartz, Angelini, and Rideout (2007).

As an advertising icon, Ronald McDonald rated number two in the 20th century, second only to the Marlboro Man; and Tony the Tiger and the Pillsbury Doughboy also made the top 10 list (Horgen, Choate, & Brownell, 2001). Not surprisingly, such advertising is incredibly effective (Keller et al., 2012). In a study that used five pairs of identical foods and beverages in McDonald's packaging and unbranded packaging, a group of 63 children uniformly preferred the McDonald's food (Robinson, Borzekowski, Matheson, & Kraemer, 2007). Increasingly, McDonald's, Burger King, and others are engaging in toy tie-ins with major motion picture studios, trying to augment both sales of fast food and attendance at children's movies (Sokol, 2000). Santa Clara County in California recently tried to ban such tie-ins, without success (Hess, 2012). By contrast, one preliminary study suggests that parents may be able to get their children to eat healthier foods if they ask, "What would Batman eat?" (Wansink, Shimizu, & Camps, 2012).

To illustrate the power of marketing, compare the commitment of the Robert Wood Johnson Foundation to spend $100 million *per year* to try to decrease childhood obesity with the fact that the food industry spends more than that *every month* marketing primarily junk food and fast food to children and teens (J. L. Harris, Pomeranz, Lobstein, & Brownell, 2009; Levi et al., 2011; FTC, 2012.).

New Technology

Advertisers are using a variety of online techniques to target very young children (Montgomery & Chester, 2012; Moore, 2006; Pempek & Calvert, 2009; Gearhardt & Brownell, 2013). A study of the most popular food and beverage brands found that all of them had Internet websites: 63% had advergames (games used to advertise the product), 50% used cartoon characters like Tony the Tiger or Chester Cheetah, and 58% had a designated children's area. Half of the websites urged children to ask their parents to buy the products, but only 17% contained any nutritional information (Weber, Story, & Harnack, 2006). Teens' cell phones can be accessed by fast food companies to offer a discount as the teens walk by a particular restaurant, and pizza ads on TV will soon offer a "click-and-order" feature (Montgomery & Chester, 2009).

Food Advertised in Schools

Advertisers are using any and all means possible to get messages in front of children and teens, including ads on schools buses, in gymnasiums, on book covers, on athletic teams' warm-up suits, and even on cafeteria tray liners and in bathroom stalls (Committee on Communications, 2006; Molnar, 2005). Major corporations contribute free curricula like Campbell Soup's "Prego Thickness Experiment," comparing the thickness of Prego and Ragu spaghetti sauces, and materials by Chevron challenging the existence of global warming (Kanner, 2008). More than 80% of American schools now engage in at least one type of advertising activity (Molnar, Garcia, Boninger, & Merrill, 2006).

A 2005 U.S. General Accountability Office report found that candy, soda, and snack food were crowding out nutritious foods in 90% of the schools surveyed (Quaid, 2005). When schools allow snacking and foods high in fat and calories, the BMI of their students increases, according to a study of more than 3,000 students in 16 different Minnesota middle schools (Kubik, Lytle, & Story, 2005). A recently published study that tracked 6,300 students in 40 states between 2004 and 2007 found that those who lived in states with strong policies banning or restricting junk food in schools gained less weight over that three-year period (Taber, Chriqui, Perna, Powell, & Chaloupka, 2012).

In 2004, former President Clinton and his foundation negotiated an agreement with the leading beverage companies to remove full-calorie soft drinks from schools and replace them with lower-calorie, smaller-portion beverages. As a result, as of 2010, an 88% reduction in calories from beverages shipped to schools had been achieved, according to the beverage industry (American Beverage Association, 2010; L. Turner & Chaloupka, 2012).

On the other hand, Channel One, which is 10 minutes of current-events programming along with 2 minutes of commercials, continues to be seen in 8,000 middle and high schools around the country and is seen by 40% of American teenagers (Kanner, 2008). Junk food ads are ubiquitous, and violent movies and prescription drugs are frequently advertised (Campaign for a Commercial-Free Childhood, 2012).

The Impact of Advertising

Research shows that advertising is extremely effective in getting children to request more junk food (high fat/low nutrition), eat less nutritious food, and to try to influence their parents' purchases (Andreyeva, Kelly, & Harris, 2011; Committee on Communications, 2006; J. L. Harris, Pomeranz, et al., 2009; Horgen, Harris, & Brownell, 2012; Institute of Medicine, 2006; Kunkel, McKinley, & Wright, 2009; McKetta & Rich, 2011; FTC, 2012). One might think that parents could "just say no," but studies show that parents often give in to their children's requests and that advertising seems to trump parental efforts (Ferguson, Munoz, & Medrano, 2011; O'Dougherty, Story, & Stang, 2006; G. Wilson & Wood, 2004). Numerous studies show that greater TV exposure leads to a greater likelihood that junk food will be judged to be nutritious, increased brand recognition, increased consumption of the foods being advertised, and poorer dietary choices (Borzekowski, 2013, in press; Hingle & Kunkel, 2012; Sisson, Shay, Broyles, & Leyva, 2012).

Meanwhile, a study of more than 21,000 children and teens nationwide found that the prevalence of snacking has increased dramatically in the past 20 years: By the mid-1990s, children were consuming 25% of their daily calories by snacking, compared with 18% in 1977, and teens consume 610 calories a day by snacking (Jahns, Siega-Riz, & Popkin, 2001). Numerous studies have demonstrated the impact of advertising on eating and food choices (and the advertising industry probably has many more, but they are considered proprietary):

- A study that followed 827 third-grade children for 20 months found that total TV time and total media screen time predicted future requests for foods and drinks that had been advertised (Chamberlain, Want, & Robinson, 2006).
- When watching cartoons, children consumed 45% more snacks when they were exposed to food advertising than they did when they were exposed to advertising for other products (J. L. Harris, Bargh, & Brownell, 2009).
- Children playing an online advergame that featured healthy foods were more likely to eat healthy snacks than those who played an advergame for junk food (Pempek & Calvert, 2009). Conversely, children playing unhealthy food advergames eat less nutritious foods and fewer fruits and vegetables (J. L. Harris, Speers, Schwartz, & Brownell, 2012).
- Even brief exposures to TV food ads—as little as 30 seconds—have been shown to influence children as young as preschool age in their choice of foods (Borzekowski & Robinson, 2001; Chamberlain et al., 2006; Story & French, 2004). African American children, who are at higher risk for overweight and obesity, are exposed to more food ads on channels that are popular with them (e.g., BET, WB, Disney) (Outley & Taddese, 2006).

Cross-cultural studies show similar problems vis-à-vis nutritional practices and advertising in Canada, Japan, Britain, New Zealand, and Australia (Dixon, Scully, Wakefield, White, & Crawford, 2007; Ishigaki, 1991; Lewis & Hill, 1998; Public Health Association of Australia, 1999; N. Wilson, Quigley, & Mansoor, 1999). Goldberg (1990) capitalized on the passage of a new law in Quebec banning advertising to children to find that Quebec children who viewed

American TV shows had more sugared cereal in their homes than those who watched only Canadian programming. In fact, there was a dose-response effect, with those who watched one hour per day of American programming having an average of 1.23 boxes of cereal at home, versus an average of 3.81 boxes in the homes of those who watched four hours per day.

Advertising is so highly connected to overweight and obesity that one study predicts that one-third of all obesity in childhood could be eliminated if food advertising were restricted (Veerman, Van Beeck, Barendregt, & Mackenbach, 2009). One of the most telling studies separated children's time spent watching commercial TV (with advertisements) from time spent watching public broadcasting and DVDs (without advertising). Time spent watching commercial TV was significantly correlated with BMI, while time spent watching noncommercial programming was not (Zimmerman & Bell, 2010).

Food on TV and in Movies

Only a handful of content analyses have been conducted to study the portrayal of food in TV programming or in movies. Perhaps this is because food advertising is such a powerful force on network and cable television and is therefore studied preferentially. Borzekowski (2001) conducted a content analysis of the 30 highest-rated programs among 2- to 5-year-olds. Of the top 30, 47% were on network TV, 30% were on Nickelodeon, and 23% were on PBS. Each episode had at least one reference to food, and one-third of the episodes contained 16 or more references. An average child would therefore see more than 500 food references per week during programming. Nearly one-third of the references were to empty-calorie foods high in fat, sugar, or salt. Another 25% of food references were to nutrient-rich foods that, however, were also high in fat, sugar, or salt. The most recent analysis of the most popular prime-time shows found that 2- to 11-year-olds see a health-related scene every four minutes, usually involving unhealthy foods or alcoholic beverages (Byrd-Bredbenner, Finckenor, & Grassno, 2003). Product placements are not rare on TV either. In 2005, the number one show, *American Idol*, had more than 3,000 instances of product placement (Edwards, 2006). With the advent of DVRs, commercials may be skipped, but product placements cannot be. In addition, while the FCC limits the number of advertising minutes per hour of TV, it sets no standards for the number or type of product placements (Jordan, 2008).

Borzekowski (2001) was surprised to find that many popular children's programs contained a wide array of food choices (e.g., one episode of PBS's *Arthur* mentioned milk, cookies, apple juice, steak, corn on the cob, peanut brittle, raisins, soup, pears, watermelon, grapes, a banana, chocolate cake, pasta, lettuce, cereal, and orange juice). Of course, the amount of PBS programming skewed the sample somewhat, as did choosing the youngest viewing population to study. Nevertheless, the authors of all of these content analyses concluded that the television diet is inconsistent with healthy nutritional guidelines. One unique study examined the four most popular sitcoms among Black audiences and among general audiences and found that the former contained 27% of actors who were overweight compared with only 2% of the latter. The study also found more food items displayed and a greater number of food commercials aired during the shows popular with African Americans—nearly 5 commercials per half hour, compared with 2.89 for the shows popular with general audiences (Jain & Tirodkar, 2001).

Only a few content analyses have been conducted on the portrayal of food in films. An analysis of 100 films from 1991 through 2000 found that food and drink appeared regularly, alcohol was the single most frequently portrayed food or drink, and fats and sweets were the most common foods depicted. In addition, product placements were shown an average of one to two times per movie, usually for a beer or soda (R. Bell, Berger, & Townsend, 2003). Similarly, a study of soft drinks in the 10 top-grossing movies from 1991 through 2000 found that branded soft drinks appeared in five times the number of movies as other nonalcoholic beverages did (Cassady, Townsend, Bell, & Watnik, 2006). In the 200 top movies from 1996 to 2005, a total of 1,180 product placements were identified; 70% of the movies contained them. Candy (26%) and salty snacks (21%) were the most prevalent foods, and sugar-sweetened beverages (76%) were the most prevalent drinks. Fast food restaurants made up two-thirds of the restaurant brand placements (L. S. Sutherland, MacKenzie, Purvis, & Dalton, 2010). And, finally, a study of food, beverage, and restaurant appearances in the top 20 movies each year from 1996 to 2005 found that preteens and teens potentially see billions of food images in movies, mostly in PG-13 films (Skatrud-Mickelson, Adachi-Mejia, MacKenzie, & Sutherland, 2012).

Do Media Displace Physical Activities?

Children spend more time with media than they do engaging in any other activity except sleeping—an average of more than seven hours a day (Rideout, 2010). A recent study of more than 72,000 schoolchildren from 34 countries found that nearly one-third are spending three hours a day or more on the computer or watching TV (Guthold et al., 2010; Kwon, Burns, Levy, & Janz, 2013). Intuitively, one would think that the *displacement effect* (seven hours a day spent in front of a screen is seven hours *not* spent playing outside, walking the dog, or doing intramural sports) would be a major factor in child and adolescent obesity. In fact, many studies have found that physical activity decreases as screen time increases (Babey, Hastert, & Wolstein, 2012; Hardy, Bass, & Booth, 2007; Nelson, Neumark-Sztainer, Hannan, Sirad, & Story, 2006; Sirard, Laska, Patnode, Farbakhsh, & Lytle, 2010; Sisson, Broyles, Baker, & Katzmarzyk, 2010), but surprisingly, nearly as many studies have not found an association (Burdette & Whitaker, 2005; Foley, Maddison, Jiang, Olds, & Ridley, 2011; Melkevik, Torsheim, Iannotti, & Wold, 2010; Taveras et al., 2007).

- One recent cross-sectional study of more than 53,000 six- to seventeen-year-olds found that boys and girls who are not physically active and engage in four hours or more of screen time are twice as likely to be overweight than more active, less sedentary children and teens (Sisson et al., 2010).
- Another cross-sectional study of 7,505 five-year-old children in the Netherlands found that children who eat breakfast fewer than seven days per week, drink more than two glasses of sweetened beverages per day, play outside less than one hour per day, and watch TV more than two hours per day are nearly twice as likely to be overweight or obese (Veldhuis, Vogel, et al., 2012).
- A longitudinal study of more than 1,300 Canadian children found that early childhood TV viewing compromises both muscular fitness and ideal waist circumference in children as they approach puberty (Fitzpatrick, Pagani, & Barnett, 2012). A two-year longitudinal study of more than 2,000 children 11 to 13 years old found decreased cardiovascular fitness in those who spent more time in front of the screen (Mitchell, Pate, & Blair, 2012).

- An Australian study of more than 2,300 adolescents who were resurveyed after five years found that regular physical activity was associated with higher quality of life and screen time was inversely associated with quality of life (Gopinath, Hardy, Baur, Burlutsky, & Mitchell, 2012).

In 2006, the Institute of Medicine reviewed 20 studies and found 14 that observed a significant relationship between physical activity and screen time (Institute of Medicine, 2006). In many studies, the number of children who are heavy TV viewers and are also less physically active is small. For example, a study of nearly 3,000 children ages 4 to 11 years found that only about one-fourth of boys and girls fit into this category. The challenge of establishing a relationship between heavy media use and physical activity is that (a) such children and teens may tend to be more sedentary in general, with or without screen time (Epstein, Roemmich, Cavanaugh, & Paluch, 2011; Jordan, 2010; Rey-López et al., 2012); (b) children's level of activity may vary significantly by country (Melkevik et al., 2010); and (c) researchers' measures of physical activity may be too imprecise, and self-reports of TV viewing or screen time may not always be accurate. Apparently, physical activity must be intense to have an effect (Hay et al., 2012).

One obesity researcher developed a "TV cycle," which is a bicycle hooked up electrically to a television set so that the set can work only when the bicycle is being ridden. Ten overweight 8- to 12-year-olds who enrolled in this study lost 1% of their total body fat in a pilot study and decreased average viewing time from 21 hours to 1.6 hours per week (Faith et al., 2001). Reducing total media time may trump increasing exercise time in reducing weight (Hingle & Kunkel, 2012; Robinson, 2000; Wahi et al., 2011; Washington, 2005). In addition, decreasing screen time, increasing exercise, and changing to better nutritional practices has been shown to prevent the onset of obesity, if not decrease existing obesity as well (Dietz, 2006a, 2006b; Epstein, Paluch, Consalvi, Riordan, & Scholl, 2002; Goldfield et al., 2006; Haerens et al., 2006; Washington, 2005). Clearly, if children and adolescents devoted just one of the three to five hours a day they spend watching screens to physical activities, their risk of obesity would diminish.

Media and Eating Behavior

Research strongly suggests that viewing screens leads to unhealthier eating behavior, both at the time of viewing and away from the screen.

In one of the most recent studies, television viewing was inversely related to the consumption of fruit and vegetables and positively related to the intake of candy and fast food among 12,642 students in Grades 5 through 10, even after adjusting for socioeconomic factors, computer use, and physical activity (Lipsky & Iannotti, 2012). Teenagers who watch more television tend to eat higher-fat diets (Blass et al., 2006; Wiecha et al., 2006), drink more sodas (Giammattei et al., 2003), and eat less fruit (Santaliestra-Pasías et al., 2012). A study of nearly 5,000 Midwest middle and high school students documented that high television use was associated with more snacking, more soft drink intake, and eating more fast food (Utter, Neumark-Sztainer, Jeffery, & Story, 2003). Similar studies of more than 162,000 preteens and teens in Europe and 10,000 Dutch teenagers found that snacking was correlated with TV viewing (Snoek, van Strien, Janssens, & Engels, 2006; Vereecken, Todd, Roberts, Mulvihill, & Maes, 2005). Similarly, two studies have found that both children and adolescents tend to consume higher-fat foods if they view a lot of television (Wiecha et al., 2006; Wong et al., 1992).

In a study of 548 students in five public schools near Boston, researchers found that each hour increase in daily TV viewing brought an additional 167 calories per day as the result of eating foods commonly advertised on TV (Wiecha et al., 2006).

One of the leading culprits in excess energy intake is sugar-sweetened beverages, especially sodas and fake fruit juices (Bawa, 2005; Dietz, 2006a; Jacobson, 2005; Malik, Schulze, & Hu, 2006) (see Table 7.2 and Figures 7.12 through 7.14). Half of the U.S. population consumes sugary drinks on any given day, and 25% consume at least 200 calories' worth (more than a 12-oz. can of soda) (Ogden, Kit, Carroll, & Park, 2011). There seems to be little disagreement—at least among physicians, nutritionists, and public health activists—that consumption of sugar-sweetened drinks is a major factor contributing to the new epidemic of childhood and adolescent obesity (Caprio, 2012; Kaiser Family Foundation, 2004a; Ogden et al., 2011).

Table 7.2 Sugar-Sweetened Drinks and Obesity

Sugar-sweetened drinks represent the largest single food source of calories in the American diet, providing 9% of daily calories[a,b]

Teenagers get 13% of their daily calories from soft drinks.[b]

The recent increase in Type 2 diabetes parallels the increase in sugar-sweetened drink consumption.[c,d]

The odds of becoming obese increase 1.6 times for every drink consumed per day.[e]

Enough soda pop is produced annually in the United States to provide 557 twelve-oz. cans to everyman, woman, and child.[b]

Soft drink companies spend approximately $700 million on advertising annually.[b]

One 12-oz. can of soda contains 150 kcal and 40 to 50 g of sugar. Drinking one can of soda per day will result in a 15-lb. weight gain over 1 year.[f]

There is now evidence of a causal connection between intake of sugar-sweetened beverages (soda and juice) and obesity.[f-j] A total of 30 studies have been done (15 cross-sectional, 10 prospective, 5 experimental), most of which find a significant connection.[i]

Of all beverages, soda consumption predicted BMI and poor calcium intake the best.[h]

Decreasing children's and teens' intake of sugar-sweetened beverages results in decreased measures of obesity.[k,l]

Colas contain caffeine and phosphoric acid that may also interfere with bone mineral density, according to the most recent findings of the Framingham Osteoporosis Study, which measured bone density in more than 3,000 adult subjects.[m]

---

a. Block (2004).
b. Jacobson (2005).
c. Schulze et al. (2004).
d. Bray, Nielson, and Popkin (2004).
e. Ludwig, Peterson, and Gortmaker (2001).
f. Apovian (2004).
g. Dietz (2006a).
h. Striegel-Moore et al. (2006).
i. Malik, Schulze, and Hu (2006).
j. Berkey, Rockett, Field, Gillman, and Colditz (2004).
k. James, Thomas, Cavan, and Kerr (2004).
l. Ebbeling et al. (2006).
m. Tucker et al. (2006).

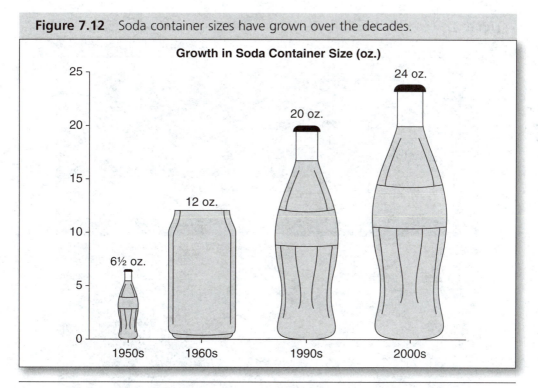

Figure 7.12   Soda container sizes have grown over the decades.

SOURCE: Horgen, Choate, and Brownell (2001).

Recently, many public health departments have tried using media campaigns to reduce consumption of sugar-sweetened beverages (Jordan, Piotrowski, Bleakley, & Mallya, 2012). Countermarketing strategies used in these campaigns have highlighted the amount of sugar in sodas, sports drinks, and fake juice drinks (see Figure 7.13) and have raised the public's awareness of the connection between the consumption of sugary beverages and obesity. New York City's health department has used particularly hard-hitting strategies (see Figure 7.14). One recent campaign featured an amputee, linking sugary beverage consumption with a complication of Type 2 diabetes (resulting from obesity).

Meanwhile, actual eating behavior in front of TV screens changes as well. A study of 91 parent-child pairs found that families who watch television during mealtimes tend to eat more pizzas, snack foods, and sodas and fewer fruits and vegetables (Coon, Goldberg, Rogers, & Tucker, 2001). TV viewing also predicts increased intake of less nutritious foods and decreased intake of fruits and vegetables in very young children (Harrison, Liechty, & STRONG Kids Program, 2012). Snacking on foods and beverages of low nutritional value while watching TV is extremely common (Pearson, Ball, & Crawford, 2011; Ranjit, Evans, Byrd-Williams, Evans, & Hoelscher, 2010). Even experimental studies have found that TV viewing is associated with increased snacking (Blass et al., 2006; Epstein et al., 2008; Temple, Giacomelli, Kent, Roemmich, & Epstein, 2007). In one study, college students consumed an additional 163 calories per day while watching TV (Stroebele & de Castro, 2004).

Food ads have the unique ability to increase food consumption *at the time of exposure* (Buijzen, Schuurman, & Bomhof, 2008; H. L. Harris, Bargh, & Brownell, 2009). A 2005 study in which obese teens were given camcorders to document their everyday life showed that they

Figure 7.13 Philadelphia Department of Public Health campaign to reduce sugar-sweetened beverages (posters appeared in mass transit).

SOURCE: FoodFitPhilly.org.

Figure 7.14 New York City Health Department campaign to reduce sugar-sweetened beverages (posters appear in mass transit).

SOURCE: www.nyc.gog/html/doh.

were not always aware of what they were eating in front of a TV set, or how much they were consuming. The study revealed that the teens often took entire containers of ice cream or bags of snacks and ate until the containers were empty (Rich, Patashnick, Huecker, & Ludwig, 2002). Experiments show that media may stimulate auditory and visual senses and lead to a disconnect from the physiologic cues of hunger and satiety (McKetta & Rich, 2011).

Media, Sleep, and Obesity

One of the newest and most exciting areas of research involves the impact of sleep on a variety of different health concerns, including obesity (Barlett, Gentile, Barlett, Eisenmann, & Walsh, 2012; J. F. Bell & Zimmerman, 2010; Garaulet et al., 2011; Lytle, Pasch, & Farbaksh, 2010). Screen media are known to disturb young people's sleep patterns (Cain & Gradisar, 2010; Dworak, Schierl, Bruns, & Strüder, 2007; Garrison & Christakis, 2012; Landhuis, Poulton, Welch, & Hancox, 2008; Ortega et al., 2010; Zimmerman, 2008) by affecting the amount and quality of sleep. A longitudinal study of New York adolescents found that teens who viewed three or more hours of TV per day doubled their risk of having difficulty falling asleep compared to teens watching less than one hour per day (Johnson, Cohen, Kasen, First, & Brook, 2004). A randomized controlled trial showed that both evening TV viewing and viewing of violent programming disrupted preschoolers' sleep patterns, but nonviolent daytime TV viewing did not (Garrison, Liekweg, & Christakis, 2011).

In turn, shorter sleep cycles and poorer quality of sleep may result in an increased risk of obesity. In one longitudinal study of young children in the United Kingdom, researchers found that shorter sleep duration at age 30 months predicted obesity at 7 years (Taheri, 2006). Another longitudinal study found a dose-response relationship between hours of sleep and later obesity, even after controlling for initial BMI and a variety of other known variables (Carter, Taylor, Williams, & Taylor, 2011). Later bedtimes and less sleep may be associated with a greater risk of obesity (J. F. Bell & Zimmerman, 2010; Taheri, 2006). Bedroom TVs, in particular, interfere with sleep and therefore are a risk factor for obesity (Delmas et al., 2007; Adachi-Mejia et al., 2007). Preteens and teens may use the TV as a sleep aid, but a study of 5th- through 10th-grade Dutch youth found that this actually decreased total number of hours of sleep (Eggermont & Van den Bulck, 2006). By contrast, preschool children who have limited screen media time, get adequate sleep, and eat meals with their family have a 40% lower risk of obesity than those who do not (Anderson & Whitaker, 2010). Again, the mechanisms are unclear: Sleep loss may lead to increased snacking (Wells & Cruess, 2006), fatigue and increased sedentary activity (Nelson & Gordon-Larsen, 2006), or metabolic changes (Van Cauter et al., 2007). It is also possible that the light of a bedroom TV screen at night may interfere with melatonin release, which, in turn, interferes with sleep (Higuchi, Motohashi, Liu, & Maeda, 2005).

The Impact of Media on Body Self-Image and Eating Disorders

A recent report on eating disorders found that hospitalizations surged 119% between 1999 and 2006 for children younger than 12 (Associated Press, 2010). The media may play a crucial role in the formation of young people's—especially girls'—body self-image; may be responsible for creating unrealistic expectations and body dissatisfaction; and may even contribute to the development of eating disorders (Anschutz, Sprijt-Metz, Van Strien, & Engels, 2011; Benowitz-Fredericks, Garcia, Massey, Vasagar, & Borzekowski, 2012; Field et al., 2008; Hayes & Tantleff-Dunn, 2010; Hogan & Strasburger, 2008; Levine & Murnen, 2009). In the past two decades, body self-image has become an increasingly major concern of preteens and teens, especially females, although body dissatisfaction has been observed in boys as well (McCable & Ricciardelli, 2004). Dissatisfaction seems to increase during adolescence (Bearman, Martinez, & Stice, 2006; Calzo et al., 2012). As many as half of normal-weight teenage girls consider themselves overweight and have tried to lose weight (Krowchuk, Kreiter, Woods, Sinal, & DuRant, 1998; Strauss, 1999).

One of the most important developments in communication research during the past two decades has been researchers' increased interest in examining the role that the media play in women's health, specifically women's self-image and eating disorders. In 2000, the British

Medical Association (2000) issued a landmark report on the subject, and many researchers, such as Borzekowski, Field, Kilbourne, Harrison, Levine, and Tiggemann, have added considerably to our knowledge (Benowitz-Fredericks et al., 2012; Field et al., 2008; Levin & Kilbourne, 2009; Levine & Harrison, 2003; Lopez-Guimera, Levine, Sanchez-Carracedo, & Fauquet, 2010; Slater, Tiggemann, Firth, & Hawkins, 2012).

Body Image in Media

Clearly, when it comes to body habitus, the world of television does not portray the real world accurately (Greenberg et al., 2003; van den Berg, 2012) (see Table 7.3). On both soap operas and sitcoms—both very popular with young female audiences—a disproportionate number of female characters are below average weight compared with the general population (White, Brown, & Ginsburg, 2010). Some researchers have suggested that the presence of so many TV commercials for food, combined with other ads' emphasis on female beauty, fosters the development of eating disorders (Botta, 1999; Lavine, Sweeney, & Wagner, 1999; Tiggemann, 2005). Others have suggested that situation comedies could play a role in eating disorders because thin characters receive significantly more positive verbal comments from male characters than heavier female characters do (R. Bell et al., 2003; Greenberg et al., 2003). There is little doubt that obese people are stigmatized in the media, not only on prime-time TV but also in movies (e.g., the *Nutty Professor* series), on YouTube, and in the news media (Ata & Thompson, 2010; Heuer, McClure, & Puhl, 2011; Hussin, Frazier, & Thompson, 2011; Pearl, Puhl, & Brownell, 2012).

Interestingly, as the number of diet food product commercials increased dramatically on network TV between 1973 and 1991, with a parallel rise in eating disorders (Wiseman, Gunning, & Gray, 1993). Similar research by Silverstein and Perlick (1995) found that as

Table 7.3   How Accurately Does TV Reflect Body Types in the Real World?
(N = 1,013 prime-time TV characters)

	On TV (%)	Real World (%)
Overweight/obese males	24	48
Overweight/obese females	14	28
Underweight females	33	5
Overweight characters	Nonrecurring	
	Fewer romances	
	Fewer friends	
	Less leadership	
	Less sex	
	Shown eating	

SOURCE: Greenberg, Eastin, Hofschire, Lachlan, and Brownell (2003).

thin models and actresses appeared more frequently in media from 1910 to 1930 and again from 1950 to 1980, eating disorders increased as well. In the 1990s, the diet industry tripled its revenues, from $10 billion a year to $36 billion (Kilbourne, 1999). Articles about dieting and exercise in women's magazines increased dramatically around the same time (Wiseman, Gray, Mosimann, & Ahrens, 1992) and far outnumber similar articles in men's magazines (Nemeroff, Stein, Diehl, & Smilack, 1994). From 1990 to 2000, the number of teen-oriented magazines more than tripled, from 5 to 19 (Kaiser Family Foundation, 2004b). Studies have found that girls who read fashion magazines often compare themselves with the models in the ads and the articles, resulting in more negative feelings about their own appearance (Clay, Vignoles, & Dittmar, 2005; Field et al., 2005; Hofschire & Greenberg, 2001; Pinhas, Toner, Ali, Garfinkel, & Stuckless, 1999). Interestingly, a magazine like *Ebony* with a pre-dominantly African American readership uses cover models that are more average in weight (76% of the time) versus underweight (5% of the time) (Thompson-Brenner, Boisseau, & St. Paul, 2011).

Whether this is cause and effect or simply correlational is arguable. As Kilbourne (1999) notes, there seems to be a very complicated connection between the diet industry and the real world. For example, a Weight Watchers ad shows a scrumptious piece of Boston cream pie, along with the caption, "Feel free to act on impulse." Why would Weight Watchers want to tempt people to indulge in high-calorie desserts? Could it be because it is actually in their best business interests for people to fatten up and then want to diet or to fail to lose weight, so that their revenues will continue to grow (Kilbourne, 1999)?

Teen Magazines

Magazines such as *Seventeen*, *Teen*, and *YM* were the top three teen magazines up until the late 1990s and enjoyed readerships of more than 6 million girls (Kaiser Family Foundation, 2004b). But then an explosion of teen magazines occurred, with *Teen People*, *CosmoGirl*, *Elle Girl*, *Teen Vogue*, and others entering the market. Today, only *Seventeen* remains in print, but many exist online. All practically dictate that thin is in, fat is out, and you are no one unless you are impossibly thin with big breasts and small hips. Several studies have found an association between reading popular teen or fashion magazines and the presence of weight concerns or symptoms of eating disorders in girls (Field, Cheung, et al., 1999; Hofschire & Greenberg, 2001; Jones, Vigfusdottir, & Lee, 2004; Stice & Shaw, 1994; Taylor et al., 1998). In a 1999 study of 548 girls in 5th to 12th grade, most were unhappy with their body weight and shape, and 69% reported that their ideal body was influenced by reading fashion magazines or other media (Field et al., 1999). Putting weight information labels on variously sized media models ("6-kg. underweight," "3-kg. underweight," "normal weight") actually decreased body dissatisfaction in one recent experiment with 184 preteen and teenage girls (Veldhuis, Konijn, & Seidell, 2012).

A fascinating experiment examining teenagers and magazines was performed by S. L. Turner, Hamilton, Jacobs, Angood, and Dwyer (1997). Young college women were randomly assigned to one or the other of two waiting rooms with two different sets of magazines before answering a survey about dieting and body image. They were exposed either to four fashion magazines or four news magazines. Those who chose a fashion magazine to read reported more dissatisfaction with their weight, more guilt associated with eating, and greater fear of getting fat. It is not surprising, then, that one ongoing meta-analysis of more than 20 experimental studies indicates that exposure to images of thin models causes an increase in a female's negative feelings about her body (Levine, 2000).

Many surveys have also found that adolescent females demonstrate exaggerated fears of obesity regardless of their actual body weight (Moses, Banilivy, & Lifshitz, 1989; Rome et al., 2003; Story & Larson, 2013). People trust the media, especially television (Horgen et al., 2001), but the image that the media display of the "ideal" woman is distorted. Aside from a few exceptions— for example, Roseanne Barr in the 1980s, Queen Latifah a decade later, and Melissa McCarthy most recently—there is a dearth of smart, successful, overweight female media role models. One notable exception was the outstanding 2002 movie portraying an overweight Hispanic teenager and her life, aptly named *Real Women Have Curves*. Another attempt to buck this trend has been the British Broadcasting Corporation's 1985 ban on tele-vising beauty pageants, labeling them "an anachronism in this day and age of equality and verging on the offensive" ("BBC Bans Beauty Contest," 1985).

Interestingly, the media themselves have taken up this concern as well, with a nearly over-bearing obsession with the fluctuation in weights of Snooki, Jennifer Love Hewitt, Lindsay Lohan, Mary-Kate Olsen, and female supermodels. Whether this degree of publicity about actresses' body weights is healthy or harmful remains to be empirically tested, although it is likely that a single-minded focus on women's bodies to the exclusion of all else results in intense self-objectification by female audiences (Hesse-Biber, Leavy, Quinn, & Zoino, 2006).

Definitions of Beauty

Meanwhile, the exact specifications for thinness continue to diminish, almost yearly. A classic study of body measurements of *Playboy* centerfolds and Miss America contestants over a 10-year period found that body weight averaged 13% to 19% below that expected for age (Wiseman et al., 1992). Among Miss America winners from 1922 to 1999, BMIs declined significantly from 22 to less than 18, which signifies undernutrition (Rubinstein & Caballero, 2000) (see Figure 7.15). Two decades ago, the average American model weighed 8% less than the average American woman; today, she weighs 23% less (Kilbourne, 1999). In one study, adolescent girls described the "ideal girl" as being 5 feet 7 inches tall, 100 pounds, size 5, with long blonde hair and blue eyes (Nichter & Nichter, 1991)—clearly a body shape that is both rare and close to impossible to achieve. For African American girls, the threshold at which they manifest body dissatisfaction appears to be higher than for Whites, which may explain why the prevalence of eating disorders is lower for them (van den Berg, 2012).

Evidence is increasing that there are tremendous sociocultural pressures on today's girls and young women to try to attain body shapes that are unhealthy, unnatural, and dictated by media norms (British Medical Association, 2000). Many researchers feel that this internaliza-tion of the thin-ideal body image has resulted in Western women's increasing dissatisfaction with their bodies and the subsequent increase in eating disorders (Field et al., 2001; Kilbourne, 2000; Levine & Harrison, 2003; Nishna, Ammon, Bellmore, & Graham, 2006; Stice & Whitenton, 2002; Thompson, 2003). Even young children's videos like *Cinderella* and *The Little Mermaid* have been shown to contain body image–related themes (Herbozo, Tantleff-Dunn, Gokee-Larose, & Thompson, 2004). A study of cartoons over nine decades found that

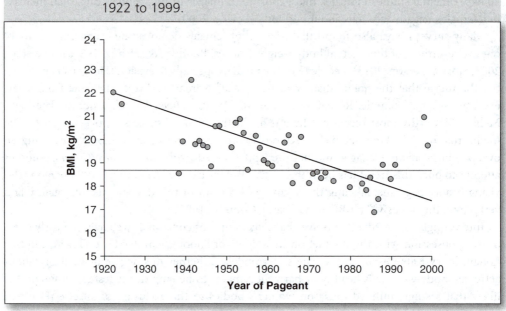

Figure 7.15 Trend in body mass index (BMI) of Miss America pageant winners, 1922 to 1999.

SOURCE: From the *Journal of the American Medical Association, 283,* p. 1569, 2000. Copyright © AMA

NOTE: The World Health Organization's BMI cutoff point for undernutrition is 18.5.

female characters' attractiveness was much more important than males' and that overweight characters were depicted as being less smart and less happy (Klein & Shiffman, 2006). In one startling study of 128 five- to eight-year-olds in Australia, many of them already wanted to be thinner by age 6 (Dohnt & Tiggemann, 2006). But, as always, the research does not yield a simplistic "yes or no" answer to the question of whether media exposure causes eating disorders. Probably the most conservative view is that there is now considerable evidence that the media influence body image and self-dissatisfaction among young girls and women.

Disordered Body Image

Television, movies, magazines, and music videos all display women with impossible bodies and put pressure on adolescent females to conform (B. T. Bell & Dittmar, 2011; Field et al., 2005; Field et al., 2001; Hofschire & Greenberg, 2001; Lawler & Nixon, 2011; Levine & Harrison, 2003; Tiggemann, Polivy, & Hargreaves, 2009) (see Figure 7.16). Sitcoms such as *Friends* and *Ally McBeal*, teen dramas like *Beverly Hills, 90210, Gossip Girl, and Pretty Little Liars*; soap operas; music videos; and films popular with teenagers may even expose young girls to potential role models who suffer from eating disorders themselves (Levine & Harrison, 2003). Overweight female characters on sitcoms are often criticized by male characters about their appearance (Fouts & Burggraf, 2000), whereas overweight male characters tend to make fun of themselves but receive no negative comments from female characters (Fouts & Vaughan, 2002).

Figure 7.16 Advertisements often feature women with impossibly thin bodies.

Research on Media and Body Self-Image

Dozens of studies have documented the impact of mainstream media on young girls' body self-image (Benowitz-Fredericks et al., 2012; Hogan & Strasburger, 2008):

- Young African American women who are dissatisfied with their body image may be at increased risk for unintended pregnancies and sexually transmitted infections (Wingood, DiClemente, Harrington, & Davies, 2002).
- In music videos, one study of 837 ninth-grade girls found that the number of hours spent watching videos was related to their assessment of the importance of appearance and their weight concerns (Borzekowski, Robinson, & Killen, 2000).

- A study of nearly 100 young women who were assigned to view either a music video that emphasized the importance of appearance or a neutral music video found that the former demonstrated increased comparisons and body dissatisfaction (Tiggemann & Slater, 2004).
- Similarly, exposing young girls to ultra-thin or even average-size magazine models lowers their body satisfaction and their self-esteem (Clay et al., 2005).
- Of the four meta-analyses performed, three have found a significant association between teenage girls' body dissatisfaction and their exposure to thin models in the media (Cafri, Yamamiya, Brannick, & Thompson, 2005; Groesz, Levine, & Murnen, 2002; Hausenblas et al., 2013) and one has not (Holmstrom, 2004).

A Sociocultural Theory

There are four key components to the theory that sociocultural factors play an important role in body image and, perhaps, eating disorders as well (Levine, Smolak, & Hayden, 1994) (see Table 7.4):

1. Although the "ideal" woman has gotten increasingly thinner since the 1990s, the real woman has actually gotten heavier (Levine & Smolak, 1996; Rubinstein & Caballero, 2000).

2. Thinness has become associated with social, personal, and professional success (Guillen & Barr, 1994; Signorielli, 1997).

3. For teen girls especially, the "thin look" has become normative (British Medical Association, 2000; Field, Cheung, et al., 1999; Signorielli, 1997).

4. Adolescent girls and grown women have been led to believe that thinness can actually be attained easily (British Medical Association, 2000; Field, Cheung, et al., 1999).

Women are often caught in the trap of living in a culture in which they are expected to be the objects of the male gaze but then feel the need to compare favorably with ultra-thin role

Table 7.4   *How Media Might Contribute to Eating Disorders*

Emphasis on importance of appearance

Narrow definition of physical beauty

Creation of thinness as the "gold standard"

Linking thinness to success and beauty

Abhorrence of fat and fat women

Emphasis on dieting and fashion

Establishment of gender roles based on unrealistic expectations

SOURCE: Adapted from Levine and Smolak (1996).

models (Jones et al., 2004). American media are notorious for this, whereas non-Western media focus more on the beauty of the face rather than the body (Frith, Shaw, & Cheng, 2005).

In one interesting experiment, college women concerned about their body shape judged thin celebrities to be thinner than they actually were, whereas women comfortable with their body shape judged them accurately (King, Touyz, & Charles, 2000). In another series of studies, girls who wanted to look like media figures on television, in the movies, or in magazines were twice as likely to be very concerned with their weight, become constant dieters, and engage in purging behavior (Field, Camargo, Taylor, Berkey, & Colditz, 1999; Field et al., 2001; Field, Cheung, et al., 1999). These ware large studies, with a one-year follow-up, of 6,770 girls ages 9 to 14 years in a national sample. Another longitudinal study of 257 preteen girls found that TV viewing predicted thinner body ideals and disordered eating a year later (Harrison & Hefner, 2006). Finally, in a large sample of nearly 11,000 male and female teens, males who wanted to look like media role models were significantly more likely to use anabolic steroids or unproven protein supplements (Field et al., 2005).

Anorexia Nervosa and Bulimia

Several cross-sectional studies have found an apparent link between level of media exposure and likelihood of having an eating disorder or eating disorder symptomatology (Field, Camargo, et al., 1999; Harrison, 2000a, 2000b; Levine et al., 1994; Martin & Kennedy, 1994; Murray, Touyz, & Beumont, 1996; Stice, Schupak- Neuberg, Shaw, & Stein, 1994). Body image disturbances seem to play an important role in anorexia nervosa and bulimia, according to a recent meta-analysis of 66 studies (Cash & Deagle, 1997).

How do such disturbances originate? Young women with eating disorders report that magazines influence their eating habits and their concept of beauty, for example (Murray et al., 1996). They tend to overestimate body sizes in experimental situations (Verri, Verticale, Vallero, Bellone, & Nespoli, 1997; Waller, Shaw, Hamilton, & Baldwin, 1994). A study of more than 11,000 males and females, ages 9 to 14, found that those who wanted to look like figures in the media were much more likely than their peers to be concerned about their weight (Field et al., 2001). The same research group found a greater likelihood of purging behaviors among teens subscribing to a "media ideal" of beauty. Wanting to look like actresses or models on television, in movies, or in magazines doubled the risk of beginning to purge at least monthly (Field, Camargo, et al., 1999). Another longitudinal study of more than 2,500 middle and high school students found that the prevalence of unhealthy behaviors such as purging and using laxatives doubled after five years for girls who were heavy readers of magazines containing dieting and weight loss articles (van den Berg, Neumark-Sztainer, Hannan, & Haines, 2007). Elementary and middle school girls whose devotion to fashion magazines leads them to compare their bodies with fashion models report greater levels of dissatisfaction with their bodies and higher numbers of eating disorder symptoms (Levine et al., 1994; Martin & Kennedy, 1994). Studies of college women find that those who most "internalize" the cultural bias toward thinness score higher on tests of body dissatisfaction and bulimia (Thompson, Heinberg, Altabe, & Tantleff-Dunn, 1999). And girls who decrease their exposure to fashion magazines and television exhibit less eating disorder symptomatology over time (Vaughan & Fouts, 2003). Finally, the Internet has become a source of support for continuing unhealthy eating behaviors: More than 100 pro-anorexia websites were identified in a 2010 study (Borzekowski, Schenk, Wilson, & Peebles, 2010).

Perhaps the most powerful link between media and eating disorders occurred in a naturalistic study (Becker, 2002). Three years after television was introduced on the Pacific isle of Fiji, 15% of teenage girls reported that they had vomited to control their weight. This contrasted with only 3% reporting this behavior prior to the introduction of TV. In addition, the proportion of teen girls scoring abnormally high on a test for disordered eating doubled. Three-fourths of girls reported feeling "too big or fat" after the introduction of TV, and those who watched TV at least three nights per week were 50% more likely to feel that way and 30% more likely to diet. Two other longitudinal studies are intriguing as well. A study of 315 preteens found that TV exposure significantly predicted disordered eating a year later for girls (Moriarty & Harrison, 2008). And in a study of nearly 3,000 Spanish 12- to 21-year-olds over a 19-month period, those who read girls' magazines doubled their risk of developing an eating disorder (Martinez-Gonzalez et al., 2003).

New Media

New media are contributing to this problem as well. There are now more than 100 pro-anorexia websites (pro-ana sites) that not only encourage disordered eating but offer specific advice on purging, severely restricting caloric intake, and excessive exercising (Borzekowski, Schenk, Wilson, & Peebles, 2010). Frequent use of pro-ana sites is predictive of having an eating disorder (Peebles et al., 2012). Female college students exposed to the sites for 1.5 hours showed a one-week post-exposure decrease in caloric intake of 2,500 calories and reportedly used techniques described in the websites (Jett, LaPorte, & Wanchisn, 2010). In another experiment with college students who were shown different websites (a pro-ana website, a female fashion website with normal-size models, and a home decor website), those who viewed the pro-ana website showed decreases in self-esteem and perceived attractiveness and an increase in perception of being overweight (Bardone-Cone & Cass, 2006). And a recent follow-up to the classic study in Fiji found that social network media exposure was associated with eating pathology in a sample of 523 young girls (Becker et al., 2011).

On YouTube, a study of videos about being fat found that women are often the ones being stigmatized by men for being fat (Hussin et al., 2011; Yoo & Kim, 2012). On the other hand, video games seem to offer the most realistic portrayal of body images: Females are depicted more accurately (except for breast size) (Martins, Williams, Harrison, & Ratan, 2009; Martins, Williams, Ratan, & Harrison, 2011).

Occasionally, studies do not find a correlation between eating disorders and exposure to fashion magazines (Cusumano & Thompson, 1997), television (Harrison & Cantor, 1997), or other media (Barrett, 1997; Cash, Ancis, & Strachan, 1997; Champion & Furnham, 1999). Sometimes a study may find that one medium has no correlation with dysfunctional symptoms (e.g., television), but other media (e.g., fashion magazines, music videos, soap operas, movies) do (Harrison & Cantor, 1997; Tiggemann & Pickering, 1996). These variable findings may result from researchers' reliance on self-reports of media exposure or from the fact that teens are notoriously susceptible to the "third-person effect" (i.e., the belief that the media affect everyone but oneself) (Eveland, Nathanson, Detenber, & McLeod, 1999). In addition, many "no effect" studies still report important findings. Harrison and Cantor's (1997) study found that reading "fitness" magazines and having an interest in dieting accounted for a significant amount of the variance in their subjects' Eating Attitudes Test (EAT) scores, but watching popular shows on television did not. Yet Harrison's (2000b) study of 300 children ages 6 to 8 years at two Midwest schools did find a correlation between television viewing and symptoms of eating disorders. Schooler and Trinh's (2011) longitudinal study of nearly 1,000 students in Grades 8 to 10 also found that girls who watched television frequently and indiscriminately at Time 1 had more severe body dissatisfaction two years later at Time 2 (whereas there was no association for boys).

Unfortunately, little research has been done on male body images and eating disorders (Field et al., 2001; Levine, 2000). One study of boys' action figures between 1964 and 1998 found that although waist sizes have remained constant, chest and biceps measurements have ballooned (Pope, 1999). In action movies that are so popular with males, three-fourths of the characters are hypermuscular and have greater success attracting women (T. G. Morrison & Halton, 2009). Mostly, boys want to bulk up, not slim down (Jones et al., 2004; Tiggemann, 2005). So boys and teenage males may possess sociocultural ideals that are completely opposite from those of girls and young women (Lawler & Nixon, 2011).

Media literacy interventions have been shown to be effective in "immunizing" young women against the image of impossibly thin role models in the media (see Chapter 12). In addition, seeing models with normal-size proportions can counteract negative role models and lower body self-image anxiety (Dittmar & Halliwell, 2008; Halliwell & Dittmar, 2008). "Warning labels" on fashion magazines have also been suggested and, in one experiment, shown to be effective (Slater et al., 2012).

Conclusion

Considerable data exist to justify the notion that the media have a significant impact on adolescents' eating habits, the occurrence of obesity during childhood and adolescence, and adolescents' and young women's self-images of their bodies and perhaps even contribute to the development of eating disorders. Exactly what role the media play remains open to conjecture. Clearly there is some cultivation effect at work here (Gerbner, Gross, Morgan, & Signorielli, 1994): Girls and young women view beautiful, thin characters in the media and are led to believe that these impossible ideals are "normative" and that they, themselves, are inadequate. But the research is certainly complex and incomplete at the present time, and considerably more work is needed (Hogan & Strasburger, 2008; Levine & Murnen, 2009).

Solutions

Solving the dual problems of obesity and eating disorders may be a mission impossible, and one fraught with potential danger: Stigmatizing obese people might tip vulnerable preteens and teens into eating disorders. Achieving a balance by warning people about the real dangers of obesity but not showing them impossibly thin role models seems an ideal solution, but it is impractical in today's society. However, if one thinks about all the public health–oriented changes that have occurred in society in the past few decades (attitudes about cigarette smoking, drunk driving, women in athletics, violence against women), perhaps changing society's attitudes about "impossibly thin" body imagery is not unrealistically naive (Levine & Harrison, 2003). And reducing the number of unhealthy food advertisements, particularly the ones targeting young children, would seem to be an easy and practical step. A recent survey of 2,454 parents with children ages 2 to 17 found that 69% rated the media as a negative influence on their children's eating habits, followed by the food industry (61%) and government (55%) (J. L. Harris, Milici, Sarda, & Schwartz, 2012).

Obesity

Some public health groups, such as the Center for Science in the Public Interest (CSPI), have been a thorn in the side of the food industry for many years and have successfully focused the public's attention on issues such as the fat content of movie popcorn and the poor nutritional choices available in fast food restaurants (Horgen, Choate, & Brownell, 2001). Several years ago, CSPI suggested a tax on junk food (Jacobson, 2000). A national 2-cent tax on every can of soda, for example, would raise $3 billion annually (Jacobson, 2005). Michael Jacobson, the director of CSPI, notes that the food industry spends more than $33 billion a year to encourage people to buy their products, many of which are high in fat, sugar, or salt. A tax on junk foods could even the score considerably (Jacobson, 2000). Clearly, according to many national experts, the food industry will need to be reined in (Brownell & Warner, 2009). Meanwhile, the industry is trying to deflect regulatory efforts by creative contributions and social responsibility campaigns (Dorfman, Cheyne, Friedman, Wadud, & Gottlieb, 2012). For example, the soft drink industry gave the Children's Hospital of Philadelphia a $10 million gift at a time when the city of Philadelphia was considering a soda tax (Brownell, 2012). Indeed, there are some remarkable parallels between the tactics used by the beverage industry and the tobacco industry (Brownell & Warner, 2009; Dorfman et al., 2012; Strom, 2012) (see Table 7.5).

Table 7.5 Tactics Used by the Food Industry

Is the food industry employing tactics similar to those the tobacco industry uses?

1. "If people eat unhealthy foods, it's their own fault" (personal responsibility).

2. "Government regulation hinders business and destroys personal freedom."

3. Label critics as "food fascists" and "nannies."

4. Discredit the research as being "junk science."

5. Emphasize that it is physical activity that is more important than diet.

6. "There are no good or bad foods; therefore, there is no need to pass regulations or legislation."

7. Whenever possible, plant doubt.

SOURCE: Adapted from Brownell and Warner (2009).

Since obesity is a multifactorial problem, many other solutions exist as well, including:

- Limiting or regulating the amount of advertising of snack foods, soda, and fast food on prime-time and children's TV (M. B. Schwartz & Ustjanauskas, 2012). Two recent studies show that a ban on fast food ads would reduce the number of overweight children and adolescents in the U.S. by an estimated 14% to 18% (Chou, Rashad, & Grossman, 2008; Veerman et al., 2009).
- Simply eliminating federal tax deductions for fast food ads, which would reduce childhood obesity by 5% to 7% (Chou et al., 2008). As noted in Chapter 13, many countries (Australia, the Netherlands, Sweden) already do this and have lower rates of childhood obesity (Hawkes, 2004; Nestle, 2006a). Taxing sugar-sweetened beverages might also be considered (Friedman & Brownell, 2012).
- Restrictions or a ban on the use of celebrities or cartoon characters in food advertising aimed at children (Nestle, 2006a).
- Restricting product placements. The FCC has the authority to do this for broadcast television, but has not yet considered the issue (Jordan, 2008).
- Increasing government funding for healthy nutrition public service announcements (PSAs) and expanding public education campaigns, such as recent efforts to reduce sugary beverage consumption (Jordan et al., 2012). The food industry should be encouraged to advertise more healthy foods (Glickman, Parker, Sim, Cook, & Miller, 2012). Children exposed to ads for healthy foods develop significantly more positive attitudes about nutrition than children viewing ads for junk food (Dixon et al., 2007).
- Encouraging parents to limit their children's current three to five hours per day of screen time to two hours or less (Council on Communications and Media, 2011; Rideout, 2010; Sigman, 2012), although recent research suggests that parents may have difficulty carrying this out if they are not given clear alternatives (C. A. Evans, Jordan, & Horner, 2011; Jordan, Hersey, McDivitt, & Heitzler, 2006; Pearson, Salmon, Crawford, Campbell, & Timperio, 2011). Reducing TV time may require different strategies than reducing computer time (Babey et al., 2012). In addition, parents need to be encouraged to turn off the TV during mealtimes (Jordan & Robinson, 2008). Currently, 40% of families have a TV set in the dining room or kitchen, and several studies suggest that the set is on during dinner (Jordan et al., 2006).
- Developing a set of fair marketing practices for digital marketing rather than trying to institute a ban (Montgomery, 2011).
- Increasing funding for research on the impact of advertising on children and adolescents, the impact of television on obesity, and creative solutions for protecting children and teens against harmful media effects (Strasburger, 2009). In particular, researchers interested in sedentary behavior need to take into account the use of mobile devices, including cell phone behaviors like viewing videos, texting, and instant messaging (Leatherdale, 2010). Racial and ethnic differences need to be researched as well (Durkin, Paxton, & Wertheim, 2005; Newman, Sontag, & Salvato, 2006; Nollen et al., 2006; Schooler, Ward, Merriwether, & Caruthers, 2004).

As discussed in Chapter 13, the real power—to date, virtually unused—lies with Congress and with the regulatory agencies of the federal government: the Federal Trade Commission, the Food and Drug Administration, and the U.S. Department of Agriculture (see Figure 7.17). The FCC and the FTC have the power to ban or regulate advertising, but, thus far, they have chosen not to do so (FTC, 2007). Despite the Institute of Medicine's 2006 report stating that "current food and beverage marketing practices put children's long-term health at risk," the federal government has "barely noticed this problem," and the FCC "decided last year that the food industry should police itself on marketing low-nutrient foods to increasingly fat children" ("Selling Junk Food," 2006). Many experts feel that self-regulation simply will not work (Hingle & Kunkel, 2012; Horgen, Harris, & Brownell, 2012; Koplan & Brownell, 2010; M. B. Schwartz & Ustjanauskas, 2012).

Currently, the FTC is empowered to regulate food advertising only if that advertising is deceptive, yet increasingly, that appears to be the case (Mello, Studdert, & Brennan, 2006; Pomeranz, 2012a). The food industry claims that it is protected by the First Amendment, but many public health law scholars disagree with that assertion (Graff, Kunkel, & Mermin, 2012; J. L. Harris & Graff, 2012; Pomeranz, 2012b). In 2001, the Department of Agriculture sent a report to Congress stating that it should have the legal authority to set nutritional standards for all foods and drinks sold in schools (Brasher, 2001). This would allow the Department of Agriculture to ban junk food in schools. However, it would take an act of Congress to give the department this discretionary power, and so far, Congress has been unwilling. In addition, a recent study of 6,900 students in 40 public schools nationwide

Figure 7.17 The Farm Bill and government subsidies provide billions of dollars to huge agribusinesses to produce feed for animals, resulting in a subsidy for meat and dairy production. By contrast, fruit and vegetable farmers receive less than 1% of total government subsidies from the Farm Bill.

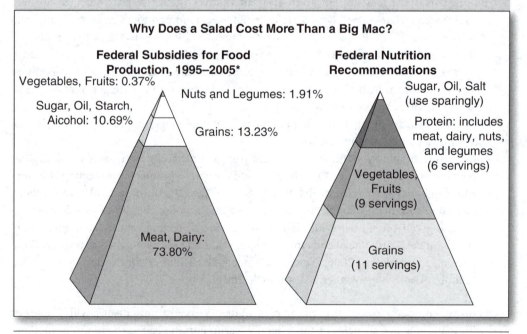

SOURCE: http://news.foodfacts.info/2012/02/why-is-big-mac-cheaper-than-salad.html.

found that banning the sale of sugar-sweetened beverages in schools reduced students' access while they were at school but did not reduce their overall consumption (Taber, Chriqui, Powell, & Chaloupka, 2012).

According to Jacobson (1999), the food industry may be even more difficult to deal with than the tobacco industry. It contains at least 78 different lobbying groups, ready to protect the industry's interests. The entire budget for the National Cancer Institute's "5 a Day" campaign for fruit and vegetable consumption is $3.5 million a year, compared to the $29 million spent annually for advertising Pringles, the $74 million for M&M's, the $209 million for Coke, and the $1.1 billion for McDonald's (Jacobson, 2000, 2005).

Certainly, more research is needed (Wilcox et al., 2004), but many new programs aimed at improving the weight status and nutritional practices of children and adolescents *are* showing significant results (Waters et al., 2011):

- A simple program to reduce the total amount of television viewed by children has resulted in decreased measures of adiposity (Robinson, 1999, 2000). This approach has been duplicated by a number of researchers (Dennison et al., 2004; Epstein et al., 2000; Epstein et al., 2008; Escobar-Chaves et al., 2010; Gortmaker et al., 1999, Robinson & Borzekowski, 2006; Wahi et al., 2011).
- A 12-week program that made TV viewing contingent on pedaling a stationary bicycle resulted in both less time spent viewing TV and reductions in total body fat (Faith et al., 2001).
- A similar experimental design using a pedometer to earn children TV time was also effective in increasing physical activity, decreasing TV time, and reducing BMI (Goldfield et al., 2006).
- A randomized controlled two-year trial of dance classes and reduced screen media time reduced lipid levels, hyperinsulinemia, and depressive symptoms in African American girls (but did not affect BMI) (Robinson et al., 2010).
- As few as seven sessions of a health curriculum for preschool children and their parents can successfully decrease total TV time (Dennison et al., 2004).
- Likewise, a mass media campaign to increase physical activity among "tweens" has been shown to be effective (Huhman et al., 2005). The VERB campaign spent $59 million on slick ads that portrayed exercise as being "cool." It resulted in a 30% increase in exercise among the preteens who saw it, but the campaign was cut by the Bush administration in 2006 (Neergaard, 2006).
- A recent meta-analysis of 33 intervention studies found that a number of programs have been successful in reducing both sedentary behavior and BMI (van Grieken, Ezendam, Paulis, van der Wouden, & Raat, 2012).
- Another recent meta-analysis of 47 studies found 29 that were successful in reducing screen media time in children by using electronic monitoring devices, counseling, or feedback systems (Schmidt et al., 2012).

New media are also increasingly being studied for their potential to prevent or decrease childhood obesity:

- So called "exergaming" can increase energy expenditure to moderate or even vigorous intensity levels (Bailey & McInnis, 2011; Durant, 2010), but there remains some skepticism about whether they will be used enough to make an impact (Baranowski et al., 2012). Video games such as *Dance Dance Revolution* have been used with overweight children and teenagers to encourage weight loss (Biddiss, & Irwin, 2010).

- A Web-based program that attempted to increase physical activity, decrease sedentary behavior, and promote healthy eating was tested on 883 twelve- to thirteen-year-olds in the Netherlands. The program was effective in improving diet but not in changing activity levels (Ezendam, Brug, & Oenema, 2012). However, the ability of Internet-based programs to change activity remains unclear (Davies, Spence, Vandelanotte, Caperchione, & Mummery, 2012).

- A social marketing campaign in Chicago called "5-4-3-2-1 Go!" is targeting parents with the message to encourage their children to increase consumption of fruits and vegetables, increase physical activity, and limit screen time to less than two hours per day (W. D. Evans, Christoffel, Necheles, & Becker, 2010).

- As of 2011, there were more than 2,000 cell phone apps available that would track caloric intake, physical activity, or fitness. Social networking sites also offer the potential for peer support for weight loss and physical fitness (Vandewater & Denis, 2011).

Increasing numbers of studies show that health information can be disseminated easily and effectively through TV shows (Brodie et al., 2001) or by linking plotlines to PSAs aired after the show (Kennedy, O'Leary, Beck, Pollard, & Simpson, 2004). Several years ago, a group of obesity experts and child advocates (including one of the authors of this textbook) asked Children's Television Workshop not to use sponsorship messages from McDonald's before or after *Sesame Street* (Public Citizen's Commercial Alert, 2003). The producers responded that removing such messages would also remove one of the most lucrative sources of funding for children's television (Kaiser Family Foundation, 2004a, 2004b). The solution? A dedicated source of public funding for children's programming that could be derived from the general federal budget; a tax on TV sets in the United States (Britain funds the BBC with a $75-per-set-per-year tax); or a 10% windfall profits tax on children's toy and food manufacturers who target children with their advertising. Public broadcasting in the United States, unlike other Western countries and Japan, is woefully underfunded (Palmer, 1988).

Eating Disorders

Rather than being part of the problem, the media could become part of the solution. Media are, after all, crucial sources of important information, some of it health related (British Medical Association, 2000; R. J. Harris, 1994). Media could be instrumental in raising awareness about eating disorders and providing information about where and when to seek help (British Medical Association, 2000). Some American companies, such as Lands' End and Dove, intentionally use models who are more "plus sized," and there are experimental data showing that teenagers' self-images can improve with more realistic advertising (see Figures 7.18 and 7.19). In 2006, the National Eating Disorders Association enlisted celebrities such as Jamie-Lynn Sigler from *The Sopranos* and Paula Abdul from *American Idol* to encourage young girls to "be comfortable in your genes" (see www.edap.org). Music videos can also buck the trend of showing beautiful women wholly subservient to men. One prime example of this is a video by TLC, "Unpretty." A young woman is shown going to a cosmetic surgery clinic at the urging of her

Figure 7.18

Figure 7.19

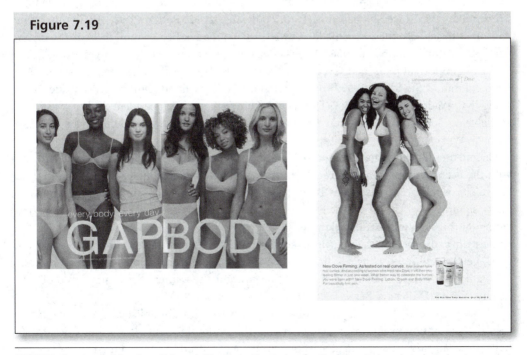

SOURCE: Courtesy of the Dove® brand. The Dove Campaign for Real Beauty is unique in trying to present realistic images of beauty and debunk the myth that only thin is beautiful.

boyfriend for a breast enlargement procedure, but at the last minute, she tears off the hospital gown, runs out, and dumps him. In a secondary storyline, a plump adolescent girl is shown gazing longingly at pictures of ultra-thin magazine models that she has pasted on her walls. She even cuts out a picture of her own face and tapes it over a model's face. But at the end of the video, she tears the pictures off the wall and decides to accept herself as she is (Arnett, 2001). This is powerful counterprogramming, indeed!

After the British Medical Association report was issued, the British government held a Body Image Seminar, a summit meeting attended by heads of the fashion industry and media. Editors of the leading women's and teen magazines in Britain announced that they would adopt a new voluntary code prohibiting pictures of ultra-thin models and celebrities in their publications (Frean, 2000). More recently, fashion houses in Spain, Brazil, and Milan have launched campaigns to ban ultra-skinny models from their shows, and the Council of Fashion Designers of America has emphasized the need for models with eating disorders to get treatment and for healthy food to be supplied backstage (Wulfhorst, 2007). Changing the way that various media portray beauty and thinness will take a true cultural shift and will not be easy to accomplish. But the reward of healthier young women, with healthier self-images, throughout the Western world would be astounding (British Medical Association, 2000).

Media Literacy

Media education classes can encourage young people to critically analyze and decode the images they view (see Chapter 13) (Council on Communications and Media, 2010; Hobbs, Broder, Pope, & Rowe, 2006; Jeong, Cho, & Hwang, 2012; Potter, 2012). If Channel One continues in schools, then a media literacy lesson about advertising could precede it (Austin, Chen, Pinkleton, & Johnson, 2006). Media education programs could also target eating disorders as an important issue, and several now exist (Gonzalez, Penelo, Gutierrez, & Raich, 2011; Levine, Piran, & Stoddard, 1999; Provencher et al., 2009; Wilksch, Durbridge, & Wade, 2008; Wilksch & Wade, 2009; Yager & O'Dea, 2008). One such program, Student Bodies, was made available to adolescents and their parents on the Internet and was found to be effective (Brown, Winzelberg, Abascal, & Taylor, 2004).

Sociocultural factors may be modifiable if they are recognized and discussed, particularly with the peer group present (Levine & Harrison, 2003; Levine & Smolak, 2001). At Stanford University, a college course titled "Body Traps: Perspectives on Body Image" resulted in students significantly decreasing their body dissatisfaction and their symptoms of disordered eating (Springer, Winzelberg, Perkins, & Taylor, 1999). Other experimental work with college students has also been successful in changing notions of body image (Levine & Harrison, 2003; Levine et al., 1999). Even at the high school level, media education courses can successfully alter students' perceptions of media images and their internalized standards of thin beauty (Irving, DuPen, & Berel, 1998; O'Dea & Abraham, 2000).

To date, there are more than 40 different published and unpublished reports of eating disorder prevention programs in elementary, middle, and high schools. Of these, two-thirds have shown positive changes in at least one measure of attitude or behavioral change (Levine & Smolak, 2001). A recent study of nearly three hundred 5th-grade students found that a health-focused media literacy program resulted in significant increases in students' understanding that advertising can make fast food look healthy and appealing (Bickham & Slaby, 2012). However, advertising is so pervasive and children's exposure to it so prolonged and intensive that even a child who has had media literacy training may not be sufficiently "immunized" against food advertising (Mehta et al., 2010).

Exercises

1. For one week, watch your normal television programs but keep a log of the commercials shown during the breaks. Try to show a link between the type of show and the type of advertising. What types of foods are being advertised? What types of body types are displayed in the advertising?

2. In 2003, the World Health Organization issued a report that concluded that obesity is a leading cause of death throughout the world and that diet and exercise are needed solutions. In addition, the report criticized the food industry for marketing unhealthy foods. As might be expected (Apovian, 2004), the food industry denounced the report as being inaccurate and unscientific. In turn, the federal government rejected the report in early 2004, saying that it was not evidence based (Dyer, 2004). In 2012, the Institute of Medicine issued a new report blasting the idea that obesity is largely the result of lack of willpower on the part of individuals. One of their suggested solutions to address the "obesogenic environment" was to impose a tax on sugar-sweetened beverages. A spokesperson for Coca-Cola immediately said, "I do not think in any way, shape or form that such punitive measures will change behaviors" (Begley, 2012).

   - Does the federal government have a responsibility to try to decrease obesity among its citizens?
   - Should federal limits be placed on food advertising?
   - Should warning labels or taxes be placed on heavily sugared cereals and drinks or on high-fat foods?
   - How much individual responsibility should obese and overweight people bear? How much responsibility should the food industry bear?
   - Can the problem of obesity ever be solved (Barry, Gollust, & Niederdeppe, 2012)?

3. Go online and watch the 2011 documentary *Miss Representation*, about how the media distort the representation of women and concentrate on sex and sexuality only (Grinberg, 2012). Are there any workable solutions to this problem? If the U.S. government were to convene a Body Image Seminar as the British government did, what would the result be?

4. Name your five favorite television actors. Would you still like/watch them if they weighed 30 pounds more than they currently weigh? Does being overweight or obese ever "help" an actor (hint: Renée Zellweger in *Bridget Jones's Diary*, Robert DeNiro/Jake LaMotta in *Raging Bull*, Melissa McCarthy/Molly Flynn on *Mike and Molly*)? Fat people are often depicted in comical ways on television and in movies. Are there ever any good traits attached to being fat?

5. Watch the movie *Real Women Have Curves*. From a public health point of view, there seems to be a very fine line between making people self-conscious about keeping a healthy weight and tipping them over into eating disorders. How does this movie deal with that? How should the media deal with it?

6. You are the new female editor-in-chief of *Sports Illustrated* magazine. The previous editor-in-chief (a male) was recently fired because revenues have been sagging during the past year. You know that the swimsuit issue is, by far, the leading revenue producer for your magazine, but you have two preteen daughters at home and are very familiar with the recent literature on body image and eating disorders. In fact, you had some bulimic symptoms in college for a year or two before getting counseling. How do you handle the swimsuit issue?

7. You are the president and CEO of the leading public health nonprofit association in the country. Your goal for this year is to devise a campaign that will inform parents and children about healthy nutritional practices and educate them about how unhealthy it is to eat at fast food restaurants frequently. What sort of public campaign do you envision? Take a look at the Children's Healthcare of Atlanta's 2012 media campaign (www .strong4life.com) (see Figure 7.20). Do you think it will be effective? Is it "ethical" (Crary, 2011)?

8. McDonald's is the leading producer of fast food in the world. It could be argued that McDonald's is also one of the leading causes of the new epidemic of obesity in the United States. At the same time, the Ronald McDonald House Charities contribute millions of dollars a year to children's hospitals around the country and provide funds for the housing of children and teens undergoing treatment for childhood cancers. Does McDonald's do more good than harm for American society? Could McDonald's do a better job of informing the public about healthier food choices it serves? Can a business that produces a product that is unhealthy compensate for it through its good deeds?

Figure 7.20   Children's Healthcare of Atlanta's 2012 media campaign.

9. If product placements are now viewed as unethical in the movie industry, should toy placements in fast food restaurants be allowed? What about movie advertisements on soft drink cups in fast food restaurants?

10. If the tobacco industry can be held liable for billions of dollars' worth of damages for the health-related illnesses that tobacco causes, should the fast food industry be held accountable as well?

11. As of 2007, there were approximately 500 websites providing advice on how to become anorexic or bulimic (Depowski & Hart, 2007). One study found that more than one-third of adolescents with eating disorders had visited a pro–eating disorder site on the Internet (J. L. Wilson, Peebles, Hardy, & Litt, 2006). Most pro-ana websites provide specific suggestions on how to engage in disordered eating behaviors (Borzekowski et al., 2010). What response, if any, should society give to such websites?

12. In February 2007, 18-year-old Uruguayan model Eliana Ramos was found dead from heart failure. Her sister, Luisel, had collapsed and died at a fashion show the previous year. In November 2006, Brazilian model Ana Carolina Reston died after eating only apples and tomatoes for months and letting her weight slip to 88 pounds (Watt, 2007). Should unnaturally thin models be banned from fashion runways and magazines? If so, how would that be accomplished?

References

Adachi-Mejia, A. M., Longacre, M. R., Gibson, J. J., Beach, M. L., Titus-Ernstoff, L. T., & Dalton, M. A. (2007). Children with a TV in their bedroom at higher risk for being overweight. *International Journal of Obesity, 31,* 644–651.

American Beverage Association. (2010, March 8). Beverage industry delivers on commitment to remove regular soft drinks in school, driving 88% decline in calories [News release]. Retrieved from http://www.ameribev.org/nutrition--science/school-beverage-guidelines/news-releases/more/183/

Anderson, S. E., & Whitaker, R. C. (2010). Household routines and obesity in US preschool-aged children. *Pediatrics, 125,* 420–428.

Andreyeva, T., Kelly, I. R., & Harris, J. L. (2011). Exposure to food advertising on television: Associations with children's fast food and soft drink consumption and obesity. *Economics and Human Biology, 9,* 221–233.

Anschutz, D. J., Spruijt-Metz, D., Van Strien, T., & Engels, R. C. (2011). The direct effect of thin ideal focused adult television on young girls' body figure. *Body Image, 8,* 26–33.

Apovian, C. M. (2004). Sugar-sweetened soft drinks, obesity, and Type 2 diabetes. *Journal of the American Medical Association, 292,* 978–979.

Arnett, J. J. (2001). The sounds of sex: Sex in teens' music and music videos. In J. D. Brown, J. R. Steele, & K. Walsh-Childers (Eds.), *Sexual teens, sexual media* (pp. 253–264). Mahwah, NJ: Lawrence Erlbaum.

Associated Press. (2010, November 30). More kids hospitalized for eating disorders. *USA Today.* Retrieved from http://www.usatoday.com/yourlife/health/medical/pediatrics/2010-11-30-eating-disorders_N.htm

Ata, R. N., & Thompson, J. K. (2010). Weight bias in the media: A review of recent research. *Obesity Facts, 3,* 41–46.

Austin, E. W., Chen, Y. Y., Pinkleton, B. E., & Johnson, J. Q. (2006). Benefits and costs of Channel One in a middle school setting and the role of media-literacy training. *Pediatrics, 117,* e423–e433.

Babey, S. H., Hastert, T. A., & Wolstein, J. (2013). Adolescent sedentary behaviors: Correlates differ for television viewing and computer use. *Journal of Adolescent Health, 52,* 70–76.

Bailey, B. W., & McInnis, K. (2011). Energy cost of exergaming. *Archives of Pediatrics and Adolescent Medicine, 165,* 597–602.

Ballard, M., Gray, M., Reilly, J., & Noggle, M. (2009). Correlates of video game screen time among males: Body mass, physical activity, and other media use. *Eating Behaviors, 10,* 161–167.

Baranowski, T., Abdelsamad, D., Baranowski, J., O'Connor, T. M., Thompson, D., Barnett, A., . . . Chen, T.-A. (2012). Impact of an active video game on healthy children's physical activity. *Pediatrics, 129,* e636–e642.

Bardone-Cone, A. M., & Cass, K. M. (2006). Investigating the impact of pro-anorexia websites: A pilot study. *European Eating Disorders Review, 14,* 256.

Barr-Anderson, D. J., van den Berg, P., Neumark-Sztainer, D., & Story, M. (2008). Characteristics associated with older adolescents who have a television in their bedrooms. *Pediatrics, 121,* 718–724.

Barlett, N. D., Gentile, D. A., Barlett, C. P., Eisenmann, J. C., & Walsh, D. A. (2012). Sleep as a mediator of screen time: Effects on US children's health outcomes—a prospective study. *Journal of Children and Media, 6,* 37–50.

Barrett, R. T. (1997). Making our own meanings: A critical review of media effects research in relation to the causation of aggression and social skills difficulties in children and anorexia nervosa in young women. *Journal of Psychiatric and Mental Health Nursing, 4,* 179–183.

Barry, C. L., Gollust, S. E., & Niederdeppe, J. (2012). Are Americans ready to solve the weight of the nation? *New England Journal of Medicine, 367,* 389–391.

Bawa, S. (2005). The role of the consumption of beverages in the obesity epidemic. *Journal of the Royal Society for the Promotion of Health, 125,* 124–128.

BBC bans beauty contest. (1985, June 30). *Parade Magazine,* 5.

Bearman, S. K., Martinez, E., & Stice, E. (2006). The skinny on body dissatisfaction: A longitudinal study of adolescent girls and boys. *Journal of Youth and Adolescence, 35,* 217–229.

Becker, A. E. (2002). Eating behaviours and attitudes following prolonged exposure to television among ethnic Fijian adolescent girls. *British Journal of Psychiatry, 180,* 509–514.

Becker, A. E., Fay, K. E., Agnew-Blaise, J., Khan, A. N., Striegel-Moore, R. H., & Gilman, S. E. (2011). Social network media exposure and adolescent eating pathology in Fiji. *British Journal of Psychiatry, 198,* 43–50.

Begley, S. (2012, May 8). Obesity fight must shift from personal blame—U.S. panel. *Reuters.* Retrieved from http://www.reuters.com/article/2012/05/08/us-usa-health-obesity-idUSBRE8470LC 20120508

Bell, B.T., & Dittmar, H. (2011). Does media type matter? The role of identification in adolescent girls' media consumption and the impact of different thin-ideal media on body image. *Sex Roles, 65,* 478–490.

Bell, J., Rogers, V. W., Dietz, W. H., Ogden, C. L., Schuler, C., & Popovic, T. (2011). CDC grand rounds: Childhood obesity in the United States. *Morbidity and Mortality Weekly Report, 60,* 42–46.

Bell, J. F., & Zimmerman, F. J. (2010). Shortened nighttime sleep duration in early life and subsequent childhood obesity. *Archives of Pediatrics and Adolescent Medicine, 164,* 840– 845.

Bell, R., Berger, C., & Townsend, M. (2003). *Portrayals of nutritional practices and exercise behavior in popular American films, 1991–2000.* Davis: University of California, Center for Advanced Studies of Nutrition and Social Marketing.

Benowitz-Fredericks, C. A., Garcia, K., Massey, M., Vasagar, B., & Borzekowski, D. L. G. (2012). Body image, eating disorders, and the relationship to adolescent media use. *Pediatric Clinics of North America, 59,* 693–704.

Berkey, C. S., Rockett, H. R. H., Field, A. E., Gillman, M. W., & Colditz, G. A. (2004). Sugar-added beverages and adolescent weight change. *Obesity Research, 12,* 778–788.

Bickham, D. S., & Slaby, R. G. (2012). Effects of a media literacy program in the US on children's critical evaluation of unhealthy media messages about violence, smoking, and food. *Journal of Children and Media, 6,* 255–271.

Biddiss, E., & Irwin, J. (2010). Active video games to promote physical activity in children and youth: A systematic review. *Archives of Pediatrics and Adolescent Medicine, 164,* 664–672.

Birken, C. S., Maguire, J., Mekky, M., Manlhiot, C., Beck, C. E., DeGroot, J., . . . Parkin, P. C. (2012). Office-based randomized controlled trial to reduce screen time in preschool children. *Pediatrics, 130,* 1–16.

Blass, E. M., Anderson, D. R., Kirkorian, H. L., Pempek, T. A., Price, I., & Koleini, M. F. (2006). On the road to obesity: Television viewing increases intake of high-density foods. *Physiology and Behavior, 88,* 597–604.

Block, G. (2004). Foods contributing to energy intake in the US: Data from NHANES III and NHANES 1999–2000. *Journal of Food Composition and Analysis, 17,* 439–447.

Borzekowski, D. (2013, in press). Examining media's impact on children's weight: Amount, content, and context. In A. Jordan & D. Romer (Eds.). *Media and the well-being of children and adolescents.* New York: Oxford University Press.

Borzekowski, D. L. G. (2001). *Watching what they eat: A content analysis of televised food references reaching preschool children.* Unpublished manuscript.

Borzekowski, D. L. G., & Robinson, T. N. (2001). The 30-second effect: An experiment revealing the impact of television commercials on food preferences of preschoolers. *Journal of the American Dietetic Association, 101,* 42–46.

Borzekowski, D. L. G., Robinson, T. N., & Killen, J. D. (2000). Does the camera add 10 pounds? Media use, perceived importance of appearance, and weight concerns among teenage girls. *Journal of Adolescent Health, 26,* 36–41.

Borzekowski, D. L. G., Schenk, S., Wilson, J. L., & Peebles, R. (2010). E-Ana and e-Mia: a content analysis of pro-eating disorder Web sites. *American Journal of Public Health, 100,* 1526–1534.

Botta, R. A. (1999). Television images and adolescent girls' body image disturbances. *Journal of Communication, 49,* 22–41.

Bowman, S. A., Gortmaker, S. L., Ebbeling, C. B., Pereira, M. A., & Ludwig, D. S. (2004). Effects of fast-food consumption on energy intake and diet quality among children in a national household survey. *Pediatrics, 113,* 112–118.

Brasher, P. (2001, February 7). USDA: Schools send mixed message. *ABC News.* Retrieved from http://abcnews.go.com/Health/story?id=117642&page=1

Bray, G. A., Nielsen, S. J., & Popkin, B. M. (2004). Consumption of high-fructose corn syrup in beverages may play a role in the epidemic of obesity. *American Journal of Clinical Nutrition, 79,* 537–543.

British Medical Association. (2000). *Eating disorders, body image & the media.* London: Author.

Brodie, M., Foehr, U., Rideout, V., Baer, N., Miller, C., Flournoy, R., & Altman, D. (2001). Communicating health information through the entertainment media. *Health Affairs, 20,* 192–199.

Brown, J. B., Winzelberg, A. J., Abascal, L. B., & Taylor, C. B. (2004). An evaluation of an Internet-delivered eating disorder prevention program for adolescents and their parents. *Journal of Adolescent Health, 35,* 290–296.

Brownell, K. D. (2004). Fast food and obesity in children. *Pediatrics, 113,* 132.

Brownell, K. D. (2012). Thinking forward: The quicksand of appeasing the food industry. *PLoS Medicine, 9,* e1001254.

Brownell, K. D., & Warner, K. E. (2009). The perils of ignoring history: Big Tobacco played dirty and millions died. How similar is Big Food? *Milbank Quarterly, 87,* 259–294.

Brunborg, G. S., Mentzoni, R. A., Molde, H., Myrseth, H., Mar Skouverøe, K. J., Bjorvatn, B., & Pallesen, S. (2011). The relationship between media use in the bedroom, sleep habits and symptoms of insomnia. *Journal of Sleep Research, 20,* 569–575.

Buijzen, M., Schuurman, J., & Bomhof, E. (2008). Associations between children's television advertising exposure and their food consumption patterns: A household diary-survey study. *Appetite, 50,* 231–239.

Burdette, H. L., & Whitaker, R. C. (2005). A national study of neighborhood safety, outdoor play, television viewing, and obesity in preschool children. *Pediatrics, 116,* 657– 662.

Byrd-Bredbenner, C., Finckenor, M., & Grasso, D. (2003). Health related content in prime-time television programming. *Journal of Health Communication, 8,* 329–341.

Cafri, G., Yamamiya, Y., Brannick, M., & Thompson, J. K. (2005). The influence of sociocultural factors on body image: A meta-analysis. *Clinical Psychology: Science and Practice, 12,* 421–433.

Cain, N., & Gradisar, M. (2010). Electronic media use and sleep in school-aged children and adolescents: A review. *Sleep Medicine, 11,* 735–742.

Calzo, J. P., Sonneville, K. R., Haines, J., Blood, E. A., Field, A. E., & Austin, S. B. (2012). The development of associations among body mass index, body dissatisfaction, and weight and shape concern in adolescent boys and girls. *Journal of Adolescent Health, 51*(5), 517–523.

Campaign for a Commercial-Free Childhood. (2012). *Let's stop Channel One.* Retrieved from http://www.commercialfreechildhood.org/actions/channelone.html

Caprio, S. (2012). Calories from soft drinks: Do they matter? *New England Journal of Medicine, 367,* 1462–1463.

Carter, P. J., Taylor, B. J., Williams, S. M., & Taylor, R. W. (2011). Longitudinal analysis of sleep in relation to BMI and body fat in children: The FLAME study. *British Medical Journal, 342,* d2712.

Cash, T. F., Ancis, J. R., & Strachan, M. D. (1997). Gender attitudes, feminist identity, and body images among young women. *Sex Roles, 36,* 433–447.

Cash, T. F., & Deagle, E. A., III. (1997). The nature and extent of body-image disturbances in anorexia nervosa and bulimia nervosa: A meta-analysis. *International Journal of Eating Disorders, 22,* 107–125.

Cassady, D., Townsend, M., Bell, R. A., & Watnik, M. (2006). Portrayals of branded soft drinks in popular American movies: A content analysis. *International Journal of Behavioral Nutrition and Physical Activity, 3,* 4.

Cawley, J., & Meyerhoefer, C. (2012). The medical care costs of obesity: An instrumental variables approach. *Journal of Health Economics, 31,* 219–230.

Chamberlain, L. J., Wang, Y., & Robinson, T. N. (2006). Does children's screen time predict requests for advertised products? *Archives of Pediatrics and Adolescent Medicine, 160,* 363–368.

Champion, H., & Furnham, A. (1999). The effect of the media on body satisfaction in adolescent girls. *European Eating Disorders Review, 7,* 213–228.

Chou, S. Y., Rashad, I., & Grossman, M. (2008). Fast-food restaurant advertising on television and its influence on childhood obesity. *Journal of Law and Economics, 51,* 599–618.

Clay, D., Vignoles, V. L., & Dittmar, H. (2005). Body image and self-esteem among adolescent girls: Testing the influence of sociocultural factors. *Journal of Research on Adolescence, 15,* 451–477.

Close, R. N., & Schoeller, D. A. (2006). The financial reality of overeating. *Journal of the American College of Nutrition, 25,* 203–209.

Committee on Communications. (2006). Children, adolescents, and advertising. *Pediatrics, 118,* 2563–2569.

Connor, S. M. (2006). Food-related advertising on preschool television: Building brand recognition in the youngest viewers. *Pediatrics, 118,* 1478–1485.

Coon, K. A., Goldberg, J., Rogers, B. L., & Tucker, K. L. (2001). Relationships between use of television during meals and children's food consumption patterns [Abstract]. *Pediatrics, 107,* 167.

Costigan, S. A., Barnett, L., Plotnikoff, R. C., & Lubans, D. R. (2012). The health indicators associated with screen-based sedentary behavior among adolescent girls: A systematic review. *Journal of Adolescent Health.* doi: 10.1016/j.jadohealth.2012.07.018

Council on Communications and Media. (2010). Media education [Policy statement]. *Pediatrics, 126,* 1012–1017.

Council on Communications and Media. (2011). Children, adolescents, obesity, and the media [Policy statement]. *Pediatrics, 128,* 201–208.

Cox, R., Skouteris, H., Rutherford, L., & Fuller-Tyszkiewicz, M. (2012). The association between television viewing and preschool child body mass index: A systematic review of English papers published from 1995 to 2010. *Journal of Children and Media, 6,* 198–220.

Crary, D. (2011, May 2). Obesity fight vs. battle over bullying. *Albuquerque Journal,* p. B5.

C. S. Mott Children's Hospital. (2011, August 15). Top 10 child health concerns: Exercise, obesity & smoking lead list. *National Poll on Children's Health, 13*(3). Retrieved from http://mottnpch.org/sites/default/files/documents/082012Top10report.pdf

Cusumano, D. L., & Thompson, J. K. (1997). Body image and body shape ideals in magazines: Exposure, awareness, and internalization. *Sex Roles, 37,* 701–721.

Daley, A. J. (2009). Can exergaming contribute to improving physical activity levels and health outcomes in children? *Pediatrics, 124,* 763–771.

Davies, C. A., Spence, J. C., Vandelanotte, C., Caperchione, C. M., & Mummery, W. K. (2012). Meta-analysis of Internet-delivered interventions to increase physical activity. *International Journal of Behavioral Nutrition and Physical Activity, 9,* 52.

Davison, K. K., Marshall, S. J., & Birch, L. L. (2006). Cross-sectional and longitudinal associations between TV viewing and girls' body mass index, overweight status, and percentage of body fat. *Journal of Pediatrics, 149,* 32–37.

Delmas, C., Platat, C., Schweitzer, B., Wagner, A., Oujaa, M., & Simon, C. (2007). Association between television in bedroom and adiposity throughout adolescence. *Obesity, 15,* 2495–2503.

Dembek, C., Harris, J. L., & Schwartz, M. B. (2012). *Trends in television food advertising to young people.* New Haven, CT: Yale Rudd Center.

Dennison, B. A., Erb, T. A., & Jenkins, P. L. (2002). Television viewing and television in bedroom associated with overweight risk among low-income preschool children. *Pediatrics, 109,* 1028–1035.

Dennison, B. A., Russo, T. J., Burdick, P. A., & Jenkins, P. L. (2004). An intervention to reduce television viewing by preschool children. *Archives of Pediatrics and Adolescent Medicine, 158,* 170–176.

Depowski, K., & Hart, K. (2007, February 25). "Pro-ana" Web sites glorify eating disorders. *ABC News.* Retrieved from http://abcnews.go.com/Health/print?id=2068728

Dietz, W. H., Jr. (1993). Television, obesity, and eating disorders. *Adolescent Medicine: State of the Art Reviews, 4,* 543–549.

Dietz, W. H. (2006a). Sugar-sweetened beverages, milk intake, and obesity in children and adolescents. *Journal of Pediatrics, 148,* 152–154.

Dietz, W. H. (2006b). What constitutes successful weight management in adolescents? *Annals of Internal Medicine, 145,* 145–146.

Dietz, W. H., Jr., & Gortmaker, S. L. (1985). Do we fatten our children at the television set? Obesity and television viewing in children and adolescents. *Pediatrics, 75,* 807–812.

Dietz, W. H., Jr., & Gortmaker, S. L. (1993). TV or not TV: Fat is the question. *Pediatrics, 91,* 499–501.

Dittmar, H., & Halliwell, E. (2008). Think "ideal" and feel bad? Using self-discrepancies to understand negative media effects. In H. Dittmar (Ed.), *Consumer culture, identity, and well-being: The search for the "good life" and the "body perfect"* (pp. 147–172). Hove, UK: Psychology Press.

Dixon, H. G., Scully, M. L., Wakefield, M. A., White, V. M., & Crawford, D. A. (2007). The effects of television advertisements for junk food versus nutritious food on children's food attitudes and preferences. *Social Science and Medicine, 65,* 1311–1323.

Dohnt, H. K., & Tiggemann, M. (2006). Body image concerns in young girls: The role of peers and media prior to adolescence. *Journal of Youth and Adolescence, 35,* 135–145.

Dorfman, L., Cheyne, A., Friedman, L. C., Wadud, A., & Gottlieb, M. (2012). Soda and tobacco industry corporate social responsibility campaigns: How do they compare? *PLoS Medicine, 9,* e1001241.

Dunstan, D. W., Barr, E. L., Healy, G. N., Salmon, J., Shaw, J. E., Balkau, B., . . . Zimmet, P. Z. (2010). Television viewing time and mortality: The Australian Diabetes, Obesity and Lifestyle Study (AusDiab). *Circulation, 121,* 384–391.

Durant, N. H. (2010). Not just fun and games: Harnessing technology to address childhood obesity. *Childhood Obesity, 6,* 283–284.

Durkin, S. J., Paxton, S. J., & Wertheim, E. H. (2005). How do adolescent girls evaluate body dissatisfaction prevention messages? *Journal of Adolescent Health, 37,* 381–390.

Dworak, M., Schierl, T., Bruns, T., & Strüder, H. K. (2007). Impact of singular excessive computer game and television exposure on sleep patterns and memory performance of school aged children. *Pediatrics, 120,* 978–985.

Dyer, O. (2004). US government rejects WHO's attempts to improve diet. *British Medical Journal, 328,* 185.

Ebbeling, C. B., Feldman, H. A., Osganian, S. K., Chomitz, V. R., Ellenbogen, S. J., & Ludwig, D. S. (2006). Effects of decreasing sugar-sweetened beverage consumption on body weight in adolescents: A randomized controlled pilot study. *Pediatrics, 117,* 673–680.

Edwards, J. (2006). On TV, kids and placements often show up together. *Brandweek, 47,* 43–45.

Eggermont, S., & Van den Bulck, J. (2006). Nodding off or switching off? The use of popular media as a sleep aid in secondary-school children. *Journal of Paediatrics and Child Health, 42,* 428–433.

Epstein, L. H., Paluch, R. A., Consalvi, A., Riordan, K., & Scholl, T. (2002). Effects of manipulating sedentary behavior on physical activity and food intake. *Journal of Pediatrics, 140,* 334–339.

Epstein, L. H., Paluch, R. A., Gordy, C. C., & Dorn, J. (2000). Decreasing sedentary behaviors in treating pediatric obesity. *Archives of Pediatrics and Adolescent Medicine, 154,* 220–226.

Epstein, L. H., Roemmich, J. N., Cavanaugh, M. D., & Paluch, R. A. (2011). The motivation to be sedentary predicts weight change when sedentary behaviors are reduced. *International Journal of Behavioral Nutrition and Physical Activity, 8,* 13.

Epstein, L. H., Roemmich, J. N., Robinson, J. L., Paluch, R. A., Winiewicz, D. D., Fuerch, J. H., & Robinson, T. N. (2008). A randomized trial of the effects of reducing television viewing and computer use on body mass index in young children. *Archives of Pediatrics and Adolescent Medicine, 162,* 239–245.

Escobar-Chaves, S. L., Markham, C. M., Addy, R. C., Greisinger, A., Murray, N. G., & Brehm, B. (2010). The Fun Families Study: Intervention to reduce children's TV viewing. *Obesity, 18*(Suppl. 1), S99–S101.

Evans, C. A., Jordan, A. B., & Horner, J. (2011). Only two hours? A qualitative study of the challenges parents perceive in restricting child television time. *Journal of Family Issues, 32,* 1223–1244.

Evans, W. D., Christoffel, K. K., Necheles, J. W., & Becker, A. B. (2010). Social marketing as a childhood obesity prevention strategy. *Obesity, 18*(Suppl. 1), S23–S26.

Eveland, W. P., Nathanson, A. I., Detenber, A. I., & McLeod, D. M. (1999). Rethinking the social distance corollary: Perceived likelihood of exposure and the third-person perception. *Communication Research, 26,* 275–302.

Ezendam, N. P. M., Brug, J., & Oenema, A. (2012). Evaluation of the Web-based computer-tailored FATaintPHAT intervention to promote energy balance among adolescents. *Archives of Pediatrics and Adolescent Medicine, 166,* 248–255.

Faith, M. S., Berman, N., Heo, M., Pietrobelli, A., Gallagher, D., Epstein, L. H., . . . Allison, D. B. (2001). Effects of contingent television on physical activity and television viewing in obese children. *Pediatrics, 107,* 1043–1048.

Federal Trade Commission. (1981). *In the matter of children's television advertising: FTC final staff report and recommendation.* Washington, DC: Government Printing Office.

Federal Trade Commission. (2007, June 1). *Children's exposure to TV advertising in 1977 and 2004: Information for the obesity debate.* Washington, DC: Author.

Federal Trade Commission (2012). *A review of food marketing to children and adolescents.* Washington, DC: FTC.

Ferguson, C. J., Munoz, M. E., & Medrano, M. R. (2011). Advertising influences on young children's food choices and parental influences. *Journal of Pediatrics, 160,* 452–455.

Field, A. E., Austin, S. B., Carmargo, C. A., Jr., Taylor, C. B., Striegel-Moore, R. H., Loud, K. J., . . . Colditz, G. A. (2005). Exposure to the mass media, body shape concerns, and use of supplements to improve weight and shape among male and female adolescents. *Pediatrics, 116,* e214–e220.

Field, A. E., Camargo, C. A., Jr., Taylor, C. B., Berkey, C. B., & Colditz, G. A. (1999). Relation of peers and media influences to the development of purging behaviors among preadolescent and adolescent girls. *Archives of Pediatrics and Adolescent Medicine, 153,* 1184.

Field, A. E., Camargo, C. A., Jr., Taylor, C. B., Berkey, C. S., Roberts, S. B., & Colditz, G. A. (2001). Peer, parent, and media influences on the development of weight concerns and frequent dieting among preadolescent and adolescent girls and boys. *Pediatrics, 107,* 54–60.

Field, A. E., Cheung, L., Wolf, A. M., Herzog, D. B., Gortmaker, S. L., & Colditz, G. A. (1999). Exposure to the mass media and weight concerns among girls. *Pediatrics, 103,* e36.

Field, A. E., Javaras, K. M., Aneja, P., Kitos, N., Camargo, C. A., Taylor, C. B., & Laird, N. M. (2008). Family, peer, and media predictors of becoming eating disordered. *Archives of Pediatrics and Adolescent Medicine, 162,* 574–579.

Finkelstein, E. A., Khavjou, O. A., Thompson, H., Trogdon, J. G., Pan, P., Sherry, B., & Dietz, W. (2012). Obesity and severe obesity forecasts through 2010. *American Journal of Preventive Medicine, 42,* 563–570.

Fitzpatrick, C., Pagani, L. S., & Barnett, T. A. (2012). Early childhood television viewing predicts explosive leg strength and waist circumference by middle childhood. *International Journal of Behavioral Nutrition and Physical Activity, 9,* 87.

Flegal, K. M., Kit, B. K., Orpana, H., & Graubard, B. I. (2013). Association of all-cause mortality with overweight and obesity using standard body mass index categories: A systematic review and meta-analysis. *Journal of the American Medical Association, 309,* 71–82.

Foley, L. S., Maddison, R., Jiang, Y., Olds, T., & Ridley, K. (2011). It's not just the television: Survey analysis of sedentary behavior in New Zealand young people. *International Journal of Behavioral Nutrition and Physical Activity, 8,* 132.

Ford, E. S., Li, C., Zhao, G., Pearson, W. S., Tsai, J., & Churilla, J. R. (2010). Sedentary behavior, physical activity, and concentrations of insulin among US adults. *Metabolism, 59,* 1268–1275.

Fouts, G., & Burggraf, K. (2000). Television situation-comedies: Female weight, male negative comments, and audience reactions. *Sex Roles, 42,* 925–932.

Fouts, G., & Vaughan, K. (2002). Television situation comedies: Male weight, negative references, and audience reactions. *Sex Roles, 46,* 439–442.

Franklin, J., Denyer, G., Steinbeck, K. S., Caterson, I. D., & Hill, A. J. (2006). Obesity and risk of low self-esteem: A statewide survey of Australian children. *Pediatrics, 118,* 2481–2487.

Frean, A. (2000, June 22). Magazines add weight to war on superwaif models. *London Times.*

French, S. A., Mitchell, N. R., & Hannan, P. J. (2012). Decrease in television viewing predicts lower body mass index at 1-year follow-up in adolescents, but not adults. *Journal of Nutrition Education and Behavior, 44,* 415–422.

Friedman, R. R., & Brownell, K. D. (2012). *Sugar-sweetened beverage taxes.* New Haven, CT: Yale Rudd Center.

Frith, K., Shaw, P., & Cheng, H. (2005). The construction of beauty: A cross-cultural analysis of women's magazine advertising. *Journal of Communication, 55,* 56–70.

Fung, T. T., Rimm, E. B., Spiegelman, D., Rifai, N., Tofler, G., Willett, W. C., & Hu, F. B. (2001). Association between dietary patterns and plasma biomarkers of obesity and cardiovascular disease risk. *American Journal of Clinical Nutrition, 73,* 61–67.

Gable, S., Chang, Y., & Krull, J. (2007). Television watching and frequency of family meals are predictive of overweight onset and persistence in a national sample of school-aged children. *Journal of the American Dietetic Association, 107,* 53–61.

Gantz, W., Schwartz, N., Angelini, J. R., & Rideout, V. (2007). *Food for thought: Television food advertising to children in the United States.* Menlo Park, CA: Kaiser Family Foundation.

Garaulet, M., Ortega, F. B., Ruiz, J. R., Rey-López, J. P., Béghin, L., Manios, Y., . . . Moreno, L. A. (2011). Short sleep duration is associated with increased obesity markers in European adolescents: Effect of physical activity and dietary habits. The HELENA study. *International Journal of Obesity.* Retrieved from http://www.nature.com/ijo/journal/vaop/ncurrent/full/ijo2011149a.html

Garrison, M. M., & Christakis, D. A. (2012). The impact of a healthy media use intervention on sleep in preschool children. *Pediatrics, 130,* 1–8.

Garrison, M. M., Liekweg, K., & Christakis, D. A. (2011). Media use and child sleep: The impact of content, timing, and environment. *Pediatrics, 128,* 29–35.

Gearhardt, A. N., & Brownell, K. D. (2013). The importance of understanding the impact of children's food marketing on the brain. Published online Jan. 10. DOI = 10.1016/j.jpeds.2012.11.068

Gebremariam, M. K., Bergh, I. H., Andersen, L. F., et al. (2013). Are screen-based sedentary behaviors longitudinally associated with dietary behaviors and leisure-time physical activity in the transition into adolescence? *International Journal of Behavioral Nutrition and Physical Activity, 10,* 9.

Gerbner, G., Gross, L., Morgan, M., & Signorielli, N. (1994). Growing up with television: The cultivation perspective. In J. Bryant & D. Zillmann (Eds.), *Media effects: Advances in theory and research* (pp. 17–41). Hillsdale, NJ: Lawrence Erlbaum.

Giammattei, J., Blix, G., Marshak, H. H., Wollitzer, A. O., & Pettitt, D. J. (2003). Television watching and soft drink consumption: Associations with obesity in 11- to 13-year-old schoolchildren. *Archives of Pediatrics and Adolescent Medicine, 157,* 882–886.

Gilmore, J. S., & Jordan, A. (2012). Burgers and basketball: Race and stereotypes in food and beverage advertising aimed at children in the US. *Journal of Children and Media, 6,* 317–332.

Glickman, D., Parker, L., Sim, L. J., Cook, H. D. V., & Miller, E. A. (Eds.). (2012). *Accelerating progress in obesity prevention: Solving the weight of the nation.* Washington, DC: National Academies Press.

Goldberg, M. E. (1990). A quasi-experiment assessing the effectiveness of TV advertising directed to children. *Journal of Marketing Research, 27,* 445–454.

Goldfield, G. S., Mallory, R., Parker, T., Cunningham, T., Legg, C., Lumb, A., . . . Adamo, K. B. (2006). Effects of open-loop feedback on physical activity and television viewing in overweight and obese children: A randomized, controlled trial. *Pediatrics, 118,* e157–e166.

Gonzalez, M., Penelo, E., Gutierrez, T., & Raich, R. M. (2011). Disordered eating prevention programme in schools: A 30-month follow-up. *European Eating Disorder Reviews, 19,* 349–356.

Gopinath, B., Hardy, L. L., Baur, L. A., Burlutsky, G., & Mitchell, P. (2012). Physical activity and sedentary behaviors and health-related quality of life in adolescents. *Pediatrics, 130,* e167–e174.

Gortmaker, S. L., Must, A., Sobol, A. M., Peterson, K., Colditz, G. A., & Dietz, W. H. (1996). Television viewing as a cause of increasing obesity among children in the United States, 1986–1990. *Archives of Pediatrics and Adolescent Medicine, 150,* 356–362.

Gortmaker, S. L., Peterson, K., Wiecha, J., Sobol, A. M., Dixit, S., Fox, M. K., & Laird, N. (1999). Reducing obesity via a school-based interdisciplinary intervention among youth: Planet Health. *Archives of Pediatrics and Adolescent Medicine, 153,* 409–418.

Graf, D. L., Pratt, L. V., Hester, C. N., & Short, K. R. (2009). Playing active video games increases energy expenditure in children. *Pediatrics, 124,* 534–540.

Graff, S., Kunkel, D., & Mermin, S. (2012). Government can regulate food advertising to children because cognitive research shows that it is inherently misleading. *Health Affairs, 31,* 392–398.

Greenberg, B. S., Eastin, M., Hofschire, L., Lachlan, K., & Brownell, K. (2003). Portrayals of overweight and obese individuals on commercial television. *American Journal of Public Health, 93,* 1342–1348.

Grinberg, E. (2012, March 9). Sex, lies, and media: New wave of activists challenge notions of beauty. *CNN.com.* Retrieved from http://articles.cnn.com/2012-03-09/living/living_beauty-media-miss-representation_1_social-media-natural-beauty-jennifer-siebel-newsom?_s=PM:LIVING

Groesz, L. M., Levine, M. P., & Murnen, S. K. (2002). The effect of experimental presentation of thin media images on body satisfaction: A meta-analytic review. *International Journal of Eating Disorders, 31,* 1–16.

Guillen, E. O., & Barr, S. I. (1994). Nutrition, dieting, and fitness messages in a magazine for adolescent women. *Journal of Adolescent Health, 15,* 464–472.

Guthold, R., Cowan, M. J., Autenrieth, C. S., Kahn, L., & Riley, L. M. (2010). Physical activity and sedentary behavior among schoolchildren: A 34-country comparison. *Journal of Pediatrics, 157,* 43–49.

Haerens, L., Deforche, B., Maes, L., Stevens, V., Cardon, G., & De Bourdeaudhuij, I. (2006). Body mass effects of a physical activity and healthy food intervention in middle schools. *Obesity, 14,* 847–854.

Halliwell, E., & Dittmar, H. (2008). Does size matter? The impact of ultra-thin media models on women's body image and on advertising effectiveness. In H. Dittmar (Ed.), *Consumer culture, identity, and well-being: The search for the "good life" and the "body perfect"* (pp. 121–146). Hove, UK: Psychology Press.

Han, J. C., Lawlor, D. A., & Kimm, S. Y. (2010). Childhood obesity. *Lancet, 375,* 1737–1748.

Hancox, R. J., Milne, B. J., & Poulton, R. (2004). Association between child and adolescent television viewing and adult health: A longitudinal birth cohort study. *Lancet, 364,* 257–262.

Hancox, R. J., & Poulton, R. (2006). Television is associated with childhood obesity: But is it clinically important? *International Journal of Obesity, 30,* 171–175.

Hardy, L. L., Bass, S. L., & Booth, M. L. (2007). Changes in sedentary behavior among adolescent girls: A 2.5-year prospective cohort study. *Journal of Adolescent Health, 40,* 158–165.

Hardy, L. L., Denney-Wilson, E., Thrift, A. P., Okely, A. D., & Baur, L. A. (2010). Screen time and metabolic risk factors among adolescents. *Archives of Pediatrics and Adolescent Medicine, 164,* 643–664.

Harris, J. L., Bargh, J. A., & Brownell, K. A. (2009). Priming effects of television food advertising on eating behavior. *Health and Psychology, 28,* 404–413.

Harris, J. L., & Graff, S. K. (2012). Protecting young people from junk food advertising: Implications of psychological research for First Amendment law. *American Journal of Public Health, 102,* 214–222.

Harris, J. L., Milici, F. F., Sarda, V., & Schwartz, M. B. (2012). *Food marketing to children and adolescents: What do parents think?* New Haven, CT: Yale Rudd Center.

Harris, J. L., Pomeranz, J. L., Lobstein, T., & Brownell, K. D. (2009). A crisis in the marketplace: How food marketing contributes to childhood obesity and what can be done. *Annual Reviews of Public Health, 30,* 211–225.

Harris, J. L., Speers, S. E., Schwartz, M. B., & Brownell, K. D. (2012). US food company branded advergames on the Internet: Children's exposure and effects on snack consumption. *Journal of Children and Media, 6,* 51–68.

Harris, J. L., Weinberg, M. E., Schwartz, M. B., Ross, C., Ostroff, J., & Brownell, K. D. (2010). *Rudd report: Trends in television food advertising.* New Haven, CT: Rudd Center for Food Policy & Obesity.

Harris, R. J. (1994). *A cognitive psychology of mass communication* (2nd ed.). Hillsdale, NJ: Lawrence Erlbaum.

Harrison, K. (2000a). The body electric: Thin-ideal media and eating disorders in adolescents. *Journal of Communication, 50,* 119–143.

Harrison, K. (2000b). Television viewing, fat stereotyping, body shape standards, and eating disorder symptomatology in grade school children. *Communication Research, 27,* 617–640.

Harrison, K., & Cantor J. (1997). The relationship between media consumption and eating disorders. *Journal of Communication, 47,* 40–67.

Harrison, K., & Hefner, V. (2006). Media exposure, current and future body ideals, and disordered eating among preadolescent girls: A longitudinal panel study. *Journal of Youth and Adolescence, 35,* 146–156.

Harrison, K., Liechty, J. M., & STRONG Kids Program. (2012). US preschoolers' media exposure and dietary habits: The primacy of television and the limits of parental mediation. *Journal of Children and Media, 6,* 18–36.

Harrison, K., & Marske, A. L. (2005). Nutritional content of foods advertised during the television programs children watch most. *American Journal of Public Health, 95,* 1568–1574.

Hausenblas, H. A., Campbell, A., Menzel, J. E., Doughty, J., Levine, M., & Thompson, J. K. (2013). Media effects of experimental presentation of the ideal physique on eating disorder symptoms: A meta-analysis of laboratory studies. *Clinical Psychology Review, 33,* 168–181.

Hawkes, C. (2004). *Marketing food to children: The global regulatory environment*. Geneva, Switzerland: World Health Organization.

Hay, J., Maximova, K., Durksen, A., Carson, V., Rinaldi, R. L., Torrance, B., . . . McGavock, J. (2012). Physical activity intensity and cardiometabolic risk in youth. *Archives of Pediatrics and Adolescent Medicine, 166*, 1022–1029.

Hayes, S., & Tantleff-Dunn, S. (2010). Am I too fat to be a princess? Examining the effects of popular children's media on young girls' body image. *British Journal of Developmental Psychology, 28*(Pt. 2), 413–426.

Hellmich, N. (2010, September 24). USA is fattest of 33 countries, report says. *USA Today.* Retrieved from http://www.usatoday.com/cleanprint/?1294413372342

Herbozo, S., Tantleff-Dunn, S., Gokee-Larose, J., & Thompson, J. (2004). Beauty and thinness messages in children's media: A content analysis. *Eating Disorders, 12*, 21–34.

Hesketh, K., Wake, M., Graham, M., & Waters, E. (2007). Stability of television viewing and electronic game/computer use in a prospective cohort study of Australian children: Relationship with body mass index. *International Journal of Behavioral Nutrition and Physical Activity, 4*, 60.

Hess, A. (2012, January 4). Does banning toys make fast food healthier? *Good Magazine.* Retrieved from http://www.good.is/post/does-banning-toys-make-fast-food-healthier/

Hesse-Biber, S., Leavy, P., Quinn, C. E., & Zoino, J. (2006). The mass marketing of disordered eating and eating disorders: The social psychology of women, thinness and culture. *Women's Studies International Forum, 29*, 208–224.

Heuer, C. A., McClure, K. J., & Puhl, R. M. (2011). Obesity stigma in online news: A visual content analysis. *Journal of Health Communications, 16*, 976–987.

Higuchi, S., Motohashi, Y., Liu, Y., & Maeda, A. (2005). Effects of playing a computer game using a bright display on presleep physiological variables, sleep latency, slow wave sleep and REM sleep. *Journal of Sleep Research, 14*, 267–273.

Hingle, M., & Kunkel, D. (2012). Childhood obesity and the media. *Pediatric Clinics of North America, 59*, 677–692.

Hobbs, R., Broder, S., Pope, H., & Rowe, J. (2006). How adolescent girls interpret weight-loss advertising. *Health Education Research, 21*, 719–730.

Hofschire, L. J., & Greenberg, B. S. (2001). Media's impact on adolescents' body dissatisfaction. In J. D. Brown, J. R. Steele, & K. Walsh-Childers (Eds.), *Sexual teens, sexual media* (pp. 125–149). Mahwah, NJ: Lawrence Erlbaum.

Hogan, M. J., & Strasburger, V. C. (2008). Body image, eating disorders, and the media. *Adolescent Medicine: State of the Art Reviews, 19*, 521–546.

Horgen, K. B., Choate, M., & Brownell, K. D. (2001). Television food advertising. In D. G. Singer & J. L. Singer (Eds.), *Handbook of children and media* (pp. 447–461). Thousand Oaks, CA: Sage.

Horgen, K. B., Harris, J. L., & Brownell, K. D. (2012). Food marketing: Targeting young people in a toxic environment. In D. G. Singer & J. L. Singer (Eds.), *Handbook of Children and Media* (2nd ed., pp. 455–478). Thousand Oaks, CA: Sage.

Holmstrom, A. J. (2004). The effects of the media on body image: A meta-analysis. *Journal of Broadcasting and Electronic Media, 48*, 196–217.

Hu, F. B., Li, T. Y., Colditz, G. A., Willett, W. C., & Manson, J. E. (2003). Television watching and other sedentary behaviors in relation to risk of obesity and Type 2 diabetes mellitus in women. *Journal of the American Medical Association, 289*, 1785–1791.

Huhman, M., Potter, L. D., Wong, F. L., Banspach, S. W., Duke, J. C., & Heitzler, C. D. (2005). Effects of a mass media campaign to increase physical activity among children: Year-1 results of the VERB campaign. *Pediatrics, 116*, e277–e284.

Hurley, J., & Liebman, B. (2009). BIG: Movie theaters fill buckets . . . and bellies. *Nutrition Action Healthletter, 36*, 1–4.

Hussin, M., Frazier, S., & Thompson, J. K. (2011). Fat stigmatization on YouTube: A content analysis. *Body Image, 8*, 90–92.

Imperatore, G., Boyle, J. P., Thompson, T. J., Case, D., Dabelea, D., Hamman, R. F., . . . Standiford, D. (2012). Projections of Type 1 and Type 2 diabetes burden in the U.S. population aged < 20 years through 2050: Dynamic modeling of incidence, mortality, and population growth. *Diabetes Care, 35*, 2515–2520.

Institute of Medicine. (2006). *Food marketing to children and youth: Threat or opportunity?* Washington, DC: National Academies Press.

Irving, L. M., DuPen, J., & Berel, S. (1998). A media literacy program for high school females. *Eating Disorders, 6*, 119–132.

Ishigaki, E. H. (1991). The health and eating habits of young children in Japan. *Early Child Development and Care, 74*, 141–148.

Jacobson, M. F. (1999). Diet & disease: Time to act. *Nutrition Action Healthletter, 26*, 2.

Jacobson, M. F. (2000, December). Tax junk foods. *Nutrition Action Healthletter, 27*, 2.

Jacobson, M. F. (2005). *Liquid candy: How soft drinks are harming Americans' health.* Washington, DC: Center for Science in the Public Interest.

Jacobson, M. F. (2012). True colors. *Nutrition Action Healthletter, 39*, p. 2.

Jahns, L., Siega-Riz, A. M., & Popkin, B. M. (2001). The increasing prevalence of snacking among US children from 1977 to 1996. *Journal of Pediatrics, 138*, 493–498.

Jain, A., & Tirodkar, M. (2001, April 30). *Food, obesity, and advertising and the African- American audience.* Paper presented at the annual meeting of the Ambulatory Pediatric Association/Society for Pediatric Research, Baltimore, MD.

James, J., Thomas, P., Cavan, D., & Kerr, D. (2004). Preventing childhood obesity by reducing consumption of carbonated drinks: Cluster randomised controlled trial. *British Medical Journal, 328*, 1237.

Jeong, S-H., Cho, H., & Hwang, Y. (2012). Media literacy interventions: A meta-analytic review. *Journal of Communication, 62*, 454–472.

Jett, S., LaPorte, D. J., & Wanchisn, J. (2010). Impact of exposure to pro–eating disorder websites on eating behavior in college women. *European Eating Disorder Reviews, 18*, 410–416.

Johnson, J. G., Cohen, P., Kasen, S., First, M. B., & Brook, J. S. (2004). Association between television and sleep problems during adolescence and early adulthood. *Archives of Pediatrics and Adolescent Medicine, 158*, 562–568.

Jones, D. C., Vigfusdottir, T. H., & Lee, Y. (2004). Body image and the appearance culture among adolescent girls and boys. *Journal of Adolescent Research, 19*, 323–339.

Jordan, A. B. (2008). Children's media policy. *Future of Children, 18*, 235–253.

Jordan, A. B. (2010). Children's television viewing and childhood obesity. *Pediatric Annals, 39*, 569–573.

Jordan, A. B., Hersey, J. C., McDivitt, J. A., & Heitzler, C. D. (2006). Reducing children's television-viewing time: A qualitative study of parents and their children. *Pediatrics, 118*, e1303–e1310.

Jordan, A., Piotrowski, J. T., Bleakley, A., & Mallya, G. (2012). Developing media interventions to reduce household sugar-sweetened beverage consumption. *Annals of the American Academy of Political and Social Science, 640*, 118–135.

Jordan, A. B., & Robinson, T. N. (2008). Children, television viewing, and weight status: Summary and recommendations from an expert panel meeting. *Annals of the American Academy of Political and Social Science, 615*, 119–132.

Kaiser Family Foundation. (2004a). *The role of media in childhood obesity.* Retrieved from http://www.kff.org

Kaiser Family Foundation. (2004b). *Tweens, teens, and magazines.* Retrieved from http://www.kff.org

Kanner, A. D. (2008, January/February). Today's class brought to you by. *Tikkun Magazine*, p. 245. Retrieved from http://www.commercialfreechildhood.org/articles/featured/todaysclass.pdf

Katzmarzyk, P. T., & Lee, I.-M. (2012). Sedentary behaviour and life expectancy in the USA: A cause-deleted life table analysis. *BMJ Open, 2*, e000828.

Kaufman, L. (1980). Prime-time nutrition. *Journal of Communication, 30,* 37–45.

Kaur, H., Choi, W. S., Mayo, M. S., & Harris, K. J. (2003). Duration of television watching is associated with increased body mass index. *Journal of Pediatrics, 143,* 506–511.

Kautiainen, S., Koivusilta, L., Lintonen, T., Virtanen, S. M., & Rimpelä, A. (2005). Use of information and communication technology and prevalence of overweight and obesity among adolescents. *International Journal of Obesity, 29,* 925–933.

Keller, K. L., Kuilema, L. G., Lee, N., Yoon, J., Mascaro, B., Combes, A.-L., . . . Halford, J. C. G. (2012). The impact of food branding on children's eating behavior and obesity. *Physiology and Behavior, 106,* 379–386.

Kelly, B., Halford, J. C., Boyland, E. J., Chapman, K., Bautista-Castaño, I., Berg, C., . . . Summerbell, C. (2010). Television food advertising to children: A global perspective. *American Journal of Public Health, 100,* 1730–1736.

Kennedy, M., O'Leary, A., Beck, V., Pollard, W., & Simpson, P. (2004). Increases in calls to the CDC National STD and AIDS Hotline following AIDS-related episodes in a soap opera. *Journal of Communication, 54,* 287–301.

Kilbourne, J. (1999). *Deadly persuasion: Why women and girls must fight the addictive power of advertising.* New York, NY: Free Press.

Kilbourne, J. (2000). *Can't buy my love: How advertising changes the way we think and feel.* New York, NY: Touchstone.

King, N., Touyz, S., & Charles, M. (2000). The effect of body dissatisfaction on women's perceptions of female celebrities. *International Journal of Eating Disorders, 27,* 341–347.

Klein, H., & Shiffman, K. S. (2006). Messages about physical attractiveness in animated cartoons. *Body Image, 3,* 353–363.

Koplan, J. P., & Brownell, K. D. (2010). Response of the food and beverage industry to the obesity threat. *Journal of the American Medical Association, 13,* 1487–1488.

Krowchuk, D. P., Kreiter, S. R., Woods, C. R., Sinal, S. H., & DuRant, R. H. (1998). Problem dieting behaviors among young adolescents. *Archives of Pediatrics and Adolescent Medicine, 152,* 884–888.

Kubik, M. Y., Lytle, L. A., & Story, M. (2005). Schoolwide food practices are associated with body mass index in middle school students. *Archives of Pediatrics and Adolescent Medicine, 159,* 1111–1114.

Kunkel, D., McKinley, C., & Wright, P. (2009). *The impact of industry self-regulation on the nutritional quality of foods advertised on television to children.* Oakland, CA: Children Now.

Kwon, S., Burns, T. L., Levy, S. M., & Janz, K. F. (2013). Which contributes more to childhood adiposity—high levels of sedentarism or low levels of moderate-through-vigorous physical activity? *Journal of Pediatrics,* published online Jan. 10. DOI = 10.1016/j.jpeds.2012.11.071

Landhuis, C. E., Poulton, R., Welch, D., & Hancox, R. J. (2008). Childhood sleep time and long- term risk for obesity: A 32-year prospective birth cohort study. *Pediatrics, 122,* 955–960.

Lang, T., & Rayner, G. (2005). Obesity: A growing issue for European policy? *Journal of European Social Policy, 15,* 301–327.

Late laughs: Week ending February 12. (2012). *TV Tabloid.* Retrieved from http://decoy.tvpassport.com/talk/late-laughs-week-ending-february-12

Lavine, H., Sweeney, D., & Wagner, S. H. (1999). Depicting women as sex objects in television advertising: Effects on body dissatisfaction. *Personality and Social Psychology Bulletin, 25,* 1049–1058.

Lawler, M., & Nixon, E. (2011). Body dissatisfaction among adolescent boys and girls: The effects of body mass, peer appearance culture and internalization of appearance ideals. *Journal of Youth and Adolescence, 40,* 59–71.

Leatherdale, S. T. (2010). Factors associated with communication-based sedentary behaviors among youth: Are talking on the phone, texting, and instant messaging new sedentary behaviors to be concerned about? *Journal of Adolescent Health, 47,* 315–318.

Levi, J., Vinter, S., St. Laurent, R., & Segal, L. M. (2011). *F as in Fat 2011: How obesity threatens America's future*. Princeton, NJ: Robert Wood Johnson Foundation.

Levin, D. E., & Kilbourne, J. (2009). *So sexy, so soon: The new sexualized childhood and what parents can do to protect their kids*. New York, NY: Random House.

Levine, M. P. (2000). Mass media and body image: A brief review of the research. *Health Weight Journal, 14*, 84–85, 95.

Levine, M. P., & Harrison, K. (2003). The role of mass media in the perpetuation and prevention of negative body image and disordered eating. In J. K. Thompson (Ed.), *Handbook of eating disorders and obesity* (pp. 695–717). New York, NY: John Wiley.

Levine, M. P., & Murnen, S. K. (2009). "Everybody knows that mass media are/are not [pick one] a cause of eating disorders": A critical review of evidence for a causal link between media, negative body image, and disordered eating in females. *Journal of Social and Clinical Psychology, 28*, 9–42.

Levine, M. P., Piran, N., & Stoddard, C. (1999). Mission more probable: Media literacy, activism, and advocacy as primary prevention. In N. Piran, M. P. Levine, & C. Steiner-Adair (Eds.), *Preventing eating disorders: A handbook of interventions and special challenges* (pp. 3–25). Philadelphia, PA: Brunner/Mazel.

Levine, M. P., & Smolak, L. (1996). Media as a context for the development of disordered eating. In L. Smolak, M. P. Levine, & R. Striegel-Moore (Eds.), *The developmental psychopathology of eating disorders* (pp. 235–257). Mahwah, NJ: Lawrence Erlbaum.

Levine, M. P., & Smolak, L. (2001). Primary prevention of body image disturbances and disordered eating in childhood and early adolescence. In J. K. Thompson & L. Smolak (Eds.), *Body image, eating disorders, and obesity in childhood and adolescence* (pp. 237–260). Washington, DC: American Psychological Association.

Levine, M. P., Smolak, L., & Hayden, H. (1994). The relation of sociocultural factors to eating attitudes and behaviors among middle school girls. *Journal of Early Adolescence, 14*, 471–490.

Lewis, M. K., & Hill, A. J. (1998). Food advertising on British children's television: A content analysis and experimental study with nine-year-olds. *International Journal of Obesity and Related Metabolic Disorders, 22*, 206–214.

Lipsky, L. M., & Iannotti, R. J. (2012). Associations of television viewing with eating behaviors in the 2009 Health Behaviour in School-Aged Children Study. *Archives of Pediatrics and Adolescent Medicine, 166*, 465–472.

Lopez-Guimera, G., Levine, M. P., Sanchez-Carracedo, D., & Fauquet, J. (2010). Influence of mass media on body image and eating disordered attitudes and behaviors in females: A review of effects and processes. *Media Psychology, 13*, 387–416.

Ludwig, D. S., Peterson, K. E., & Gortmaker, S. L. (2001). Relation between consumption of sugar-sweetened drinks and childhood obesity: A prospective, observational analysis. *Lancet, 357*, 505–508.

Lumeng, J. C., Rahnama, S., Appugliese, D., Kaciroti, N., & Bradley, R. H. (2006). Television exposure and overweight risk in preschoolers. *Archives of Pediatrics and Adolescent Medicine, 160*, 417–422.

Lytle, L. A., Pasch, K., & Farbaksh, K. (2010, May 2). Is sleep related to obesity in young adolescents? [Abstract]. Presented at the Pediatric Academic Societies meeting, Vancouver, British Columbia, Canada.

Malik, V. S., Schulze, M. B., & Hu, F. B. (2006). Intake of sugar-sweetened beverages and weight gain: A systematic review. *American Journal of Clinical Nutrition, 84*, 274–288.

Margeirdottir, H. D., Larsen, J. R., Brunborg, C., Sandvik, L., & Dahl-Jørgensen, K. (2007). Strong association between time watching television and blood glucose control in children and adolescents with Type I diabetes. *Diabetes Care, 30*, 1567–1570.

Mark, A. E., & Janssen, I. (2008). Relationship between screen time and metabolic syndrome in adolescents. *Journal of Public Health, 30*, 153–160.

Martin, M. C., & Kennedy, P. F. (1994). Social comparison and the beauty of advertising models: The role of motives for comparison. *Advances in Consumer Research, 21*, 365–371.

Martinez-Gomez, D., Rey-López, J.P., Chillón, P., Gómez-Martinez, S., Vincente-Ródriguez, G., Martin-Matillas, M., . . . AVENA Study Group. (2010). Excessive TV viewing and cardiovascular disease risk factors in adolescents: The AVENA cross-sectional study. *BMC Public Health, 10,* 274.

Martinez-Gomez, D., Tucker, J., Heelan, K. A.,Welk, G. J., & Eisenmann, J. C. (2009). Associations between sedentary behavior and blood pressure in children. *Archives of Pediatrics and Adolescent Medicine, 163,* 724–730.

Martinez-Gonzalez, M. A., Gual, P., Lahortiga, F., Alonso, Y., Irala-Esevez, J., & Cervera, S. (2003). Parental factors, mass media influences, and the onset of eating disorders in a prospective population-based cohort. *Pediatrics, 111,* 315–320.

Martins, N., Williams, D. C., Harrison, K., & Ratan, R. A. (2009). A content analysis of female body imagery in video games. *Sex Roles, 61,* 824–836.

Martins, N., Williams, D. C., Ratan, R. A., & Harrison, K. (2011). Virtual muscularity: A content analysis of male video game characters. *Body Image, 8,* 43–51.

May, A. L., Kuklina, E. V., & Yoon, P. W. (2012). Prevalence of cardiovascular disease risk factors among US adolescents, 1999–2008. *Pediatrics, 129,* 1035–1041.

McCable, M. P., & Ricciardelli, L. A. (2004). Body image dissatisfaction among males across the lifespan: A review of past literature. *Journal of Psychosomatic Research, 56,* 675–685.

McKetta, S., & Rich, M. (2011). The fault, dear viewer, lies not in the screens, but in ourselves: Relationships between screen media and childhood overweight/obesity. *Pediatric Clinics of North America, 58,* 1493–1508.

McMurray, R. G., Harrell, J. S., Deng, S., Bradley, C. B., Cox, L. M., & Bangdiwala, S. I. (2000). The influence of physical activity, socioeconomic status, and ethnicity on the weight status of adolescents. *Obesity Research, 8,* 130–139.

Mehta, K., Coveney, J., Ward, P., Magarey, A., Spurrier, N., & Udell, T. (2010). Australian children's views about food advertising on television. *Appetite, 55,* 49–55.

Melkevik, O., Torsheim, T., Iannotti, R. J., & Wold, B. (2010). Is spending time in screen-based sedentary behaviors associated with less physical activity: A cross national investigation. *International Journal of Behavioral Nutrition and Physical Activity, 7,* 46.

Mello, M. M., Studdert, D. M., & Brennan, T. A. (2006). Obesity—the new frontier of public health law. *New England Journal of Medicine, 354,* 2601–2610.

Mintel. (2009). *Marketing health to parents and children—US – March 2009.* Retrieved from http://oxygen .mintel.com/sinatra/reports/display/id=393524

Mitchell, J. A., Pate, R. R., & Blair, S. N. (2012). Screen-based sedentary behavior and cardiorespiratory fitness from age 11 to 13. *Medicine and Science in Sports and Exercise, 44,* 1302–1309.

Molnar, A. (2005). School commercialism and adolescent health. *Adolescent Medicine Clinics, 16,* 447–461.

Molnar, A., Garcia, D. R., Boninger, F., & Merrill, B. (2006). Advertising of foods of minimal nutritional value to children in schools. *Preventive Medicine, 47,* 504–507.

Montgomery, K. C. (2011). Balancing the needs of young people in the digital marketplace. *Journal of Children and Media, 5,* 334–337.

Montgomery, K. C., & Chester, J. (2009). Interactive food and beverage marketing targeting adolescents in the digital age. *Journal of Adolescent Health, 45*(Suppl. 3), S18–S29.

Montgomery, K. C., & Chester, J. (2012). The new threat of digital advertising. *Pediatric Clinics of North America, 59,* 659–676.

Moore, E. S. (2006). *It's child's play: Advergaming and the online marketing of food to children.* Menlo Park, CA: Kaiser Family Foundation.

Moriarty, C. M., & Harrison, K. (2008). Television exposure and disordered eating among children: A longitudinal panel study. *Journal of Communication, 58,* 361–381.

Morrison, J. A., Glueck, C. J., Daniels, S., & Wang, P. (2010). Determinants of persistent obesity and hyperinsulinemia in a biracial cohort: A 15-year prospective study of schoolgirls. *Journal of Pediatrics, 157,* 559–565.

Morrison, T. G., & Halton, M. (2009). Buff, tough, and rough: Representations of muscularity in action motion pictures. *Journal of Men's Studies, 17,* 57–74.

Moses, N., Banilivy, M. M., & Lifshitz, F. (1989). Fear of obesity among adolescent girls. *Pediatrics, 83,* 393–398.

Murray, S. H., Touyz, S. W., & Beumont, P. J. V. (1996). Awareness and perceived influence of body ideals in the media: A comparison of eating disorder patients and the general community. *Eating Disorders, 4,* 33–46.

Neergaard, L. (2006, September 14). Obese kids not getting right help. *Albuquerque Journal,* p. A6.

Nelson, M. C., & Gordon-Larsen, P. (2006). Physical activity and sedentary behavior patterns are associated with selected adolescent health risk behaviors. *Pediatrics, 117,* 1281–1290.

Nelson, M. C., Neumark-Sztainer, D., Hannan, P. J., Sirard, J. R., & Story, M. (2006). Longitudinal and secular trends in physical activity and sedentary behavior during adolescence. *Pediatrics, 118,* e1627–e1634.

Nemeroff, C. J., Stein, R. I., Diehl, N. S., & Smilack, K. M. (1994). From the Cleavers to the Clintons: Role choices and body orientation as reflected in magazine article content. *International Journal of Eating Disorders, 16,* 167–176.

Nestle, M. (2006a). Food marketing and childhood obesity—a matter of policy. *New England Journal of Medicine, 354,* 2527–2529.

Nestle, M. (2006b, September 11). One thing to do about food. *Nation,* p. 14.

Newman, D. L., Sontag, L. M., & Salvato, R. (2006). Psychosocial aspects of body mass and body image among rural American Indian adolescents. *Journal of Youth and Adolescence, 35,* 265–275.

Nichter, M., & Nichter, M. (1991). Hype and weight. *Medical Anthropology, 13,* 249–284.

Niemeier, H. M., Raynor, H. A., Lloyd-Richardson, E. E., Rogers, M. L., & Wing, R. R. (2006). Fast food consumption and breakfast skipping: Predictors of weight gain from adolescence to adulthood in a nationally representative sample. *Journal of Adolescent Health, 39,* 842–849.

Nishna, A., Ammon, N. Y., Bellmore, A. D., & Graham, S. (2006). Body dissatisfaction and physical development among ethnic minority adolescents. *Journal of Youth and Adolescence, 35,* 179–191.

Nollen, N., Kaur, H., Pulvers, K., Choi, W., Fitzgibbon, M., Li, C., . . . Ahluwalia, J. (2006). Correlates of ideal body size among Black and White adolescents. *Journal of Youth and Adolescence, 35,* 276–284.

Obesity rates spin out of control (Special feature). (2011). *Nutrition Action Healthletter,* p. 11.

O'Brien, M., Nader, P. R., Houts, R. M., Bradley, R., Friedman, S. L., Belsky, J., . . . NICHD Early Child Research Network. (2007). The ecology of childhood overweight: A 12-year longitudinal analysis. *International Journal of Obesity, 31,* 1469–1478.

O'Dea, J. A., & Abraham, S. (2000). Improving the body image, eating attitudes, and behaviors of young male and female adolescents: A new educational approach that focuses on self-esteem. *International Journal of Eating Disorders, 28,* 43–57.

O'Dougherty, M., Story, M., & Stang, J. (2006). Observations of parent-child co-shoppers in supermarkets: Children's involvement in food selections, parental yielding, and refusal strategies. *Journal of Nutrition Education and Behavior, 38,* 183–188.

Ogden, C. L., Carroll, M. D., Curtin, L. R., Lamb, M. M., & Flegal, K. M. (2010). Prevalence of high body mass index in US children and adolescents, 2007–2008. *Journal of the American Medical Association, 303,* 242–249.

Ogden, C. L., Carroll, M. D., Curtin, L. R., McDowell, M. A., Tabak, C. J., & Flegal, K. M. (2006). Prevalence of overweight and obesity in the United States, 1999–2004. *Journal of the American Medical Association, 295,* 1549–1555.

Ogden, C. L., Kit, B. K., Carroll, M. D., & Park, S. (2011). Consumption of sugar drinks in the United States, 2005–2008 (NCHS Data Brief No. 71). Retrieved from http://www.cdc.gov/nchs/data/databriefs/db71.htm

Oleck, J. (1994, July 20). Go ahead, make my lunch: Restaurant chains vying for school media market. *Restaurant Business Magazine,* p. 54.

Ortega, F. B., Chillón, P., Ruiz, J. R., Delgado, M., Albers, U., Álvarez-Granda, J., . . . Castillo, M. J. (2010). Sleep patterns in Spanish adolescents: Associations with TV watching and leisure-time physical activity. *European Journal of Applied Physiology, 110,* 563–573.

Outley, C. W., & Taddese, A. (2006). A content analysis of health and physical activity messages marketed to African American children during after-school television programming. *Archives of Pediatrics and Adolescent Medicine, 160,* 432–435.

Palmer, E. K. (1988). *Television and America's children.* New York:, NY Oxford University Press.

Pardee, P. E., Norman, G. H., Lustig, R. H., Preud'homme, D., & Schwimmer, J. B. (2007). Television viewing and hypertension in obese children. *American Journal of Preventive Medicine, 33,* 502–504.

Pate, R. R. (2008). Physically active video gaming: An effective strategy for obesity prevention? *Archives of Pediatrics and Adolescent Medicine, 162,* 895–896.

Pearl, R. L., Puhl, R. M., & Brownell, K. D. (2012). Positive media portrayals of obese persons: Impact on attitudes and image preferences. *Health Psychology, 31*(6), 821–829.

Pearson, N., Ball, K., & Crawford, D. (2011). Mediators of longitudinal associations between television viewing and eating behaviours in adolescents. *International Journal of Behavior, Nutrition, and Physical Activity, 8,* 23.

Pearson, N., Salmon, J., Crawford, D., Campbell, K., & Timperio, A. (2011). Are parental concerns for child TV viewing associated with child TV viewing and the home sedentary environment? *International Journal of Behavioral Nutrition and Physical Activity, 8,* 102.

Peebles, R., Wilson, J. L., Litt, I. F., Hardy, K. K., Lock, J. D., Mann, J. R., & Borzekowski, D. L. G. (2012). Disordered eating in a digital age: Eating behaviors, health and quality of life in users of websites with pro–eating disorder content. *Journal of Medical Internet Research, 14*(5), e148.

Pempek, T. A., & Calvert, S. L. (2009). Tipping the balance: Use of advergames to promote consumption of nutritious foods and beverages by low-income African American children. *Archives of Pediatrics and Adolescent Medicine, 163,* 633–637.

Pinhas, L., Toner, B. B., Ali, A., Garfinkel, P. E., & Stuckless, N. (1999). The effects of the ideal of female beauty on mood and body satisfaction. *International Journal of Eating Disorders, 25,* 223–226.

Pomeranz, J. L. (2012a). Extending the fantasy in the supermarket: Where unhealthy food promotions meet children and how the government can intervene. *Indiana Health Law Review, 9,* 117–185.

Pomeranz, J. L. (2012b). No need to break new ground: A response to the Supreme Court's threat to overhaul the commercial speech doctrine. *Loyola of Los Angeles Law Review, 45,* 389–434.

Pope, H. (1999, Summer). Toy muscles linked to harmful image of male body. *Harvard Medical Alumni Bulletin,* p. 13.

Popkin, B. M. (2006). Global nutrition dynamics: The world is shifting rapidly toward a diet linked with noncommunicable diseases. *American Journal of Clinical Nutrition, 84,* 289– 298.

Potter, W. J. (2012). *Media literacy* (6th ed.). Thousand Oaks, CA: Sage.

Powell, L. M., & Nguyen, B. T. (2013). Fast-food and full-service restaurant consumption among children and adolescents. *JAMA Pediatrics, 167,* 14–20.

Powell, L. M., Szczypka, G., & Chaloupka, F. J. (2007). Exposure to food advertising on television among US children. *Archives of Pediatrics and Adolescent Medicine, 161,* 553– 560.

Preboth, M. A., & Wright, S. (1999). Quantum sufficit. *American Family Physician, 59,* 1729.

Preidt, R. (2008). Overweight now a global problem. *ABC News.* Retrieved from http://abcnews.go.com/print?id=4509129

Proctor, M. H., Moore, L. L., Gao, D., Cupples, L. A., Bradlee, M. L., Hood, M. Y., & Ellison, R. C. (2003). Television viewing and change in body fat from preschool to early adolescence: The Framingham Children's Study. *International Journal of Obesity, 27,* 827–833.

Provencher, V., Bégin, C., Tremblay, A., Mongeau, L., Corneau, L., Dodin, S., . . . Lemieux, S. (2009). Health-at-Every-Size and eating behaviors: 1-year follow-up results of a size acceptance intervention. *Journal of the American Dietetic Association, 109,* 1854–1861.

Public Citizen's Commercial Alert. (2003, October 12). Obesity experts, child advocates ask *Sesame Street* not to advertise for McDonald's [Press release]. Retrieved from http://www.commercialalert .org/issues/health/childhood-obesity

Public Health Association of Australia. (1999). *Television food advertising during children's viewing times.* Retrieved from http://www.aeforum.org/aeforum.nsf/b6f532dc08e2a32e80256c5100355eab/840be ce6c51bb39180256c25005625d9/$FILE/PAUS0044.pdf

Quaid, L. (2005, September 7). Junk food more available in middle schools. *Associated Press.* Retrieved from http://news.google.com/newspapers?nid=1697&dat=20050907&id=MSUqAAAAIBAJ&sjid= TkgEAAAAIBAJ&pg=5520,794674

Rampell, C. (2009, May 15). Obesity and the fastness of food. *New York Times.* Retrieved from http:// economix.blogs.nytimes.com/2009/05/05/obesity-and-the-fastness-of-food

Ranjit, N., Evans, M. H., Byrd-Williams, C., Evans, A. E., & Hoelscher, D. M. (2010). Dietary and activity correlates of sugar-sweetened beverage consumption among adolescents. *Pediatrics, 126,* e754–e761.

Reedy, J., & Krebs-Smith, S. M. (2010). Dietary sources of energy, solid fats, and added sugars among children and adolescents in the United States. *Journal of the American Dietetic Association, 110,* 1477–1484.

Reilly, J. J., Armstrong, J., Dorosty, A. R., Emmett, P. M., Ness, A., Rogers, I., . . . Sherriff, A. (2005). Early life risk factors for obesity in childhood: Cohort study. *British Medical Journal, 330,* 1357.

Rey-López, J. P., Ruiz, J. R., Vicente-Rodríguez, G., Gracia-Marco, L., Manios, Y., Sjöström, M., . . . HELENA Study Group. (2012). Physical activity does not attenuate the obesity risk of TV viewing in youth. *Pediatric Obesity, 7,* 240–250.

Rich, M., Patashnick, J., Huecker, D., & Ludwig, D. (2002). Living with obesity: Visual narratives of overweight adolescents. *Journal of Adolescent Health, 30,* 100.

Rideout, V. (2010). *Generation M2: Media in the lives of 8- to 18-year-olds.* Menlo Park, CA: Kaiser Family Foundation.

Robinson, T. N. (1999). Reducing children's television viewing to prevent obesity: A randomized controlled trial. *Journal of the American Medical Association, 282,* 1561–1567.

Robinson, T. N. (2000). Can a school-based intervention to reduce television use decrease adiposity in children in Grades 3 and 4? *Western Journal of Medicine, 173,* 40.

Robinson, T. N., & Borzekowski, D. L. G. (2006). Effects of the SMART classroom curriculum to reduce child and family screen time. *Journal of Communication, 56,* 1–26.

Robinson, T. N., Borzekowski, D. L. G., Matheson, D. M., & Kraemer, H. C. (2007). Effects of fast food branding on young children's taste preferences. *Archives of Pediatrics and Adolescent Medicine, 161,* 792–797.

Robinson, T. N., Matheson, D. M., Kraemer, H. C., Wilson, D. M., Obarzanek, E., Thompson, N. S., . . . Killen, J. D. (2010). A randomized controlled trial of culturally tailored dance and reducing screen time to prevent weight gain in low-income African American girls: Stanford GEMS. *Archives of Pediatrics and Adolescent Medicine, 164,* 995–1004.

Rome, E. S., Ammerman, S., Rosen, D. S., Keller, R. J., Lock, J., Mammel, K. A., . . . Silber, T. J. (2003). Children and adolescents with eating disorders: The state of the art. *Pediatrics, 111,* e98–e108.

Rubinstein, S., & Caballero, B. (2000). Is Miss America an under-nourished role model? [Letter]. *Journal of the American Medical Association, 283,* 1569.

Santaliestra-Pasías, A. M., Mouratidou, T., Verbestel, V., Huybrechts, I., Gottrand, F., Le Donne, C., . . . Moreno, L. A. (2012). Food consumption and screen-based sedentary behaviors in European adolescents: The HELENA study. *Archives of Pediatrics and Adolescent Medicine, 166,* 1010–1020

Schlosser, E. (2001). *Fast food nation.* Boston, MA: Houghton Mifflin.

Schmidt, M. E., Haines, J., O'Brien, A., McDonald, J., Price, S., Sherry, B., & Taveras, E. M. (2012). Systematic review of effective strategies for reducing screen time in young children. *Obesity, 7,* 1338–1354.

Schooler, D., & Trinh, S. (2011). Longitudinal associations between television viewing patterns and adolescent body satisfaction. *Body Image, 8,* 34–42.

Schooler, D., Ward, L. M., Merriwether, A., & Caruthers, A. (2004). Who's that girl: Television's role in the body image development of young White and Black women. *Psychology of Women Quarterly, 28,* 38–47.

Schulze, M. B., Manson, J. E., Ludwig, D. S., Colditz, G. A., Stampfer, M. J., Willett, W. C., & Hu, F. B. (2004). Sugar-sweetened beverages, weight gain, and incidence of Type 2 diabetes in young and middle-aged women. *Journal of the American Medical Association, 292,* 927–934.

Schwartz, J., & Byrd-Bredbenner, C. (2006). Portion distortion: Typical portion sizes selected by young adults. *Journal of the American Dietetic Association, 106,* 1412–1418.

Schwartz, M. B., & Ustjanauskas, A. (2012). Food marketing to youth: Current threats and opportunities. *Child Obesity, 8,* 85–88.

Selling junk food to toddlers [Editorial]. (2006, February 23). *New York Times,* p. A26.

Sigman, A. (2012). Time for a view on screen time. *Archives of Disease in Childhood.* Retrieved from http://press.psprings.co.uk/adc/september/adc302196.pdf

Signorielli, N. (1997). *A content analysis: Reflections of girls in the media.* Menlo Park, CA: Kaiser Family Foundation.

Silverstein, B., & Perlick, D. (1995). *The cost of competence: Why inequality causes depression, eating disorders, and illness in women.* New York, NY: Oxford University Press.

Sirard, J. R., Laska, M. N., Patnode, C. D., Farbakhsh, K., & Lytle, L.A. (2010). Adolescent physical activity and screen time: Association with the physical home environment. *International Journal of Behavioral Nutrition and Physical Activity, 7,* 82.

Sisson, S. B., Broyles, S. T., Baker, B. L., & Katzmarzyk, P. T. (2010). Screen time, physical activity, and overweight in U.S. youth: National Survey of Children's Health, 2003. *Journal of Adolescent Health, 47,* 309–311.

Sisson, S. B., Shay, C. M., Broyles, S., & Leyva, M. (2012). Television-viewing time and dietary quality among U.S. children and adults. *American Journal of Preventive Medicine, 43,* 196–200.

Skatrud-Mickelson, M., Adachi-Mejia, A. M., MacKenzie, T. A., & Sutherland, L. A. (2011). Giving the wrong impression: Food and beverage brand impressions delivered to youth through popular movies. *Journal of Public Health, 34,* 245–252.

Slater, A., Tiggemann, M., Firth, B., & Hawkins, K. (2012). Reality check: An experimental investigation of the addition of warning labels to fashion magazine images on women's mood and body dissatisfaction. *Journal of Social and Clinical Psychology, 31,* 105–122.

Snoek, H. M., van Strien, T., Janssens, J., & Engels, R. (2006). The effect of television viewing on adolescents' snacking: Individual differences explained by external, restrained and emotional eating. *Journal of Adolescent Health, 39,* 448–451.

Sokol, R. J. (2000). The chronic disease of childhood obesity: The sleeping giant has awakened. *Journal of Pediatrics, 136,* 711–713.

Sonneville, K. R., & Gortmaker, S. L. (2008). Total energy intake, adolescent discretionary behaviors, and the energy gap. *International Journal of Obesity, 32(Suppl. 6),* S19–S27.

Springer, E. A., Winzelberg, A. J., Perkins, R., & Taylor, C. B. (1999). Effects of a body image curriculum for college students on improved body image. *International Journal of Eating Disorders, 26,* 13–20.

Staiano, A. E., Harrington, D. M., Broyles, S. T., Gupta, A. K., & Katzmarzyk, P. T. (2013). Television, adiposity, and cardiometabolic risk in children and adolescents. *American Journal of Preventive Medicine, 44,* 40–47.

Stamatakis, E., Hamer, M., & Dunstan, D.W. (2011). Screen-based entertainment time, all-cause mortality, and cardiovascular events. *Journal of the American College of Cardiology, 57,* 292–299.

Stice, E., & Shaw, H. E. (1994). Adverse effects of the media portrayed thin-ideal on women and linkages to bulimic symptomatology. *Journal of Social and Clinical Psychiatry, 13,* 288–308.

Stice, E., Schupak-Neuberg, E., Shaw, H. E., & Stein, R. I. (1994). Relation of media exposure to eating disorder symptomatology: An examination of mediating mechanisms. *Journal of Abnormal Psychology, 103,* 836–840.

Stice, E., & Whitenton, K. (2002). Risk factors for body dissatisfaction in adolescent girls: A longitudinal investigation. *Developmental Psychology, 38,* 669–678.

Story, M., & French, S. (2004). Food advertising and marketing directed at children and adolescents in the U.S. *International Journal of Behavioral Nutrition and Physical Activity, 1,* 3.

Story, M., & Larson, N. (Eds.). (2013, in press). Nutrition and physical activity. *Adolescent Medicine: State of the Art Reviews.*

Strasburger, V. C. (2009). Why do adolescent health researchers ignore the impact of the media? *Journal of Adolescent Health, 44,* 203–205.

Strasburger, V. C., Brown, R. T., Braverman, P. K., Rogers, P. D., Holland-Hall, C., & Coupey, S. (2006). *Adolescent medicine: A handbook for primary care.* Philadelphia, PA: Lippincott Williams & Wilkins.

Strauss, R. S. (1999). Self-reported weight status and dieting in a cross-sectional sample of young adolescents. *Archives of Pediatrics and Adolescent Medicine, 153,* 741–747.

Striegel-Moore, R. H., Thompson, D., Affenito, S. G., Franko, D. L., Obarzanek, E., Barton, B. A., . . . Crawford, P. B. (2006). Correlates of beverage intake in adolescent girls: The National Heart, Lung, and Blood Institute Growth and Health Study. *Journal of Pediatrics, 148,* 183–187.

Stroebele, N., & de Castro, J. M. (2004). Television viewing is associated with an increase in meal frequency in humans. *Appetite, 42,* 111–113.

Strom, S. (2012, August 18). Lawyers from suits against Big Tobacco target food makers. *New York Times.* Retrieved from http://www.nytimes.com/2012/08/19/business/lawyers-of-big-tobacco-lawsuits-take-aim-at-food-industry.html?pagewanted=all

Sugimori, H., Yoshida, K., Izuno, T., Miyakawa, M., Suka, M., Sekine, M., . . . Kagamimori, S. (2004). Analysis of factors that influence body mass index from ages 3 to 6 years: A study based on the Toyama Cohort Study. *Pediatrics International, 46,* 302–310.

Sutherland, E. R. (2008). Obesity and asthma. *Immunology and Allergy Clinics of North America, 28,* 589–602.

Sutherland, L. S., MacKenzie, T., Purvis, L. A., & Dalton, M. (2010). Prevalence of food and beverage brands in movies, 1996–2005. *Pediatrics, 125,* 468–474.

Swahn, M. H., Reynolds, M. R., Tice, M., Miranda-Pierangeli, M. C., Jones, C. R., & Jones, I. R. (2009). Perceived overweight, BMI, and risk for suicide attempts: Findings from the 2007 Youth Risk Behavior Survey. *Journal of Adolescent Health, 45,* 292–295.

Taber, D. R., Chriqui, J. F., Perna, F. M., Powell, L. M., & Chaloupka, F. J. (2012). Weight status among adolescents in states that govern competitive food content. *Pediatrics, 130,* 437–444.

Taber, D. R., Chriqui, J. F., Powell, L. M., & Chaloupka, F. J. (2012). Banning all sugar- sweetened beverages in middle schools. *Archives of Pediatrics and Adolescent Medicine, 166,* 256–262.

Taheri, S. (2006). The link between short sleep duration and obesity: We should recommend more sleep to prevent obesity. *Archives of Disease in Childhood, 91,* 881–884.

Taveras, E. M., Field, A. E., Berkey, C. S., Rifas-Shima, S. L., Frazier, A. L., Colditz, G. A., . . . Gillman, M. W. (2007). Longitudinal relationship between television viewing and leisure-time physical activity during adolescence. *Pediatrics, 119,* e314–e319.

Taylor, C. B., Sharpe, T., Shisslak, C., Bryson, S., Estes, L. S., Gray, N., . . . Killen, J. D. (1998). Factors associated with weight concerns in adolescent girls. *International Journal of Eating Disorders, 24,* 31–42.

Temple, J. L., Giacomelli, A. M., Kent, K. M., Roemmich, J. N., & Epstein, L. H. (2007). Television watching increases motivated responding for food and energy intake in children. *American Journal of Clinical Nutrition, 85,* 355–361.

te Velde, S., De Bourdeaudhuij, I., Thorsdottir, I., Rasmussen, M., Hagströmer, M., Klepp, K. L., & Brug, J. (2007). Patterns in sedentary and exercise behaviors and associations with overweight in 9-14-year-old boys and girls—a cross-sectional study. *BMC Public Health, 7,* 1–9.

Thompson, J. K. (Ed.). (2003). *Handbook of eating disorders and obesity.* New York, NY: John Wiley.

Thompson, J. K., Heinberg, L. J., Altabe, M., & Tantleff-Dunn, S. (1999). Exacting beauty: *Theory, assessment, and treatment of body image disturbance.* Washington, DC: American Psychological Association.

Thompson-Brenner, H., Boisseau, C. L., & St. Paul, M. S. (2011). Representation of ideal figure size in Ebony magazine: A content analysis. *Body Image, 8,* 373–378.

Tiggemann, M. (2005). Television and adolescent body image: The role of program content and viewing motivation. *Journal of Social and Clinical Psychology, 24,* 361–381.

Tiggemann, M., & Pickering, A. S. (1996). Role of television in adolescent women's body dissatisfaction and drive for thinness. *International Journal of Eating Disorders, 20,* 199– 203.

Tiggemann, M., Polivy, J., & Hargreaves, D. (2009). The processing of thin ideals in fashion magazines: A source of social comparison or fantasy? *Journal of Social and Clinical Psychology, 28,* 73–93.

Tiggemann, M., & Slater, A. (2004). Thin ideals in music television: A source of social comparison and body dissatisfaction. *International Journal of Eating Disorders, 35,* 48–58.

Tremblay, M. S., LeBlanc, A. G., Kho, M. E., Saunders, T. J., Larouche, R., Colley, R. C., . . . Connor Gorber, S. (2011). Systematic review of sedentary behaviour and health indicators in school-aged children and youth. *International Journal of Behavioral Nutrition and Physical Activity, 8,* 98.

Tucker, K. L., Morita, K., Qiao, N., Hannan, M. T., Cupples, L. A., & Kiel, D. P. (2006). Colas, but not other carbonated beverages, are associated with low bone mineral density in older women: The Framingham Osteoporosis Study. *American Journal of Clinical Nutrition, 84,* 936–942.

Turner, L., & Chaloupka, F. J. (2012). Encouraging trends in student access to competitive beverages in US public elementary schools, 2006–2007 to 2010–2011. *Archives of Pediatrics and Adolescent Medicine, 166,* 673–675.

Turner, S. L., Hamilton, H., Jacobs, M., Angood, L. M., & Dwyer, D. H. (1997). The influence of fashion magazines on the body image satisfaction of college women: An exploratory analysis. *Adolescence, 32,* 603–610.

Ul-Haq, Z., Mackay, D. F., Fenwick, E., & Pell, J. P. (2013). Meta-analysis of the association between body mass index and health-related quality of life among children and adolescents. *Journal of Pediatrics, 162,* 280–286.

Utter, J., Neumark-Sztainer, D., Jeffery, R., & Story, M. (2003). Couch potatoes or French fries: Are sedentary behaviors associated with body mass index, physical activity, and dietary behaviors among adolescents? *Journal of the American Dietetic Association, 103,* 1298– 1305.

Van Cauter, E., Holmback, U., Knutson, K., Leproult, R., Miller, A., Nedeltcheva, A., . . . Spiegel, K. (2007). Impact of sleep and sleep loss on neuroendocrine and metabolic function. *Hormone Research, 67(Suppl. 1),* 2–9.

van den Berg, P. (2012). Body weight and body image in children and adolescents. In T. F. Cash (Ed.), *Encyclopedia of body image and human appearance* (pp. 270–274). New York, NY: Academic Press.

van den Berg, P., Neumark-Sztainer, D., Hannan, P. J., & Haines, J. (2007). Is dieting advice from magazines helpful or harmful? Associations with weight-control behaviors and psychological outcomes in adolescents. *Pediatrics, 119,* e30–e37.

Vandewater, E. A., & Denis, L. M. (2011). Media, social networking, and pediatric obesity. *Pediatric Clinics of North America, 58,* 1509–1519.

Vandewater, E. A., Shim, M. S., & Caplovitz, A. G. (2004). Linking obesity and activity level with children's television and video game use. *Journal of Adolescence, 27,* 71–85.

van Grieken, A., Ezendam, N. P. M., Paulis, W. D., van der Wouden, J. C., & Raat, H. (2012). Primary prevention of overweight in children and adolescents: A meta-analysis of the effectiveness of interventions aiming to decrease sedentary behavior. *International Journal of Behavioral Nutrition and Physical Activity, 9,* 61.

Vaughan, K. K., & Fouts, G. T. (2003). Changes in television and magazine exposure and eating disorder symptomatology. *Sex Roles, 49,* 313–320.

Veerman, J. L., Healy, G. N., Cobiac, L. J., Vos, T., Winkler, E. A., Owen, N., & Dunstan, D. W. (2011). Television viewing time and reduced life expectancy: A life table analysis. *British Journal of Sports Medicine.* doi:10.1136/bjsm.2011.085662

Veerman, J. L., Van Beeck, E. F., Barendregt, J. J., & Mackenbach, J. P. (2009). By how much would limiting TV food advertising reduce childhood obesity? *European Journal of Public Health, 19,* 365–369.

Veldhuis, J., Konijn, E. A., & Seidell, J. C. (2012). Weight information labels on media models reduce body dissatisfaction in adolescent girls. *Journal of Adolescent Health, 50,* 600–606.

Veldhuis, L., Vogel, I., Renders C. M., van Rossem, L., Oenema, A., HiraSing, R. A., & Raat, H. (2012). Behavioral risk factors for overweight in early childhood: The "Be Active, Eat Right" Study. *International Journal of Behavioral Nutrition and Physical Activity, 9,* 74.

Vereecken, C. A., Todd, J., Roberts, C., Mulvihill, C., & Maes, L. (2005). Television viewing behaviour and associations with food habits in different countries. *Public Health Nutrition, 9,* 244–250.

Verri, A. P., Verticale, M. S., Vallero, E., Bellone, S., & Nespoli, L. (1997). Television and eating disorders: Study of adolescent eating behavior. *Minerva Pediatrica, 49,* 235–243.

Viner, R. M., & Cole, T. J. (2005). Television viewing in early childhood predicts adult body mass index. *Journal of Pediatrics, 147,* 429–435.

Wahi, G., Parkin, P. C., Beyene, J., Uleryk, E. M., & Birken, C. S. (2011). Effectiveness of interventions aimed at reducing screen time in children: A systematic review and meta-analysis of randomized controlled trials. *Archives of Pediatrics and Adolescent Medicine, 165,* 979–986.

Wake, M., Hesketh, K., & Waters, E. (2003). Television, computer use and body mass index in Australian primary school children. *Journal of Paediatrics and Child Health, 39,* 130–134.

Waller, G., Shaw, J., Hamilton, K., & Baldwin G. (1994). Beauty is in the eye of the beholder: Media influences on the psycho-pathology of eating problems. *Appetite, 23,* 287.

Wansink, B., Shimizu, M., & Camps, G. (2012). What would Batman eat? Priming children to make healthier fast food choices. *Pediatric Obesity, 7,* 121–123.

Washington, R. (2005). One way to decrease an obesogenic environment. *Journal of Pediatrics, 147,* 417–418.

Waters, E., de Silva-Sanigorski, A., Hall, B. J., Brown, T., Campbell, K. J., Gao, Y., . . . Summerbell, C. D. (2011). *Interventions for preventing obesity in children* [Review]. Available from Cochrane Database of Systematic Reviews. (CD001871)

Watt, N. (2007, February 28). Still skinny in Milan. *ABC News.* Retrieved from http://abcnews.go.com/Nightline/print?id=2908135

Weber, K., Story, M., & Harnack, L. (2006). Internet food marketing strategies aimed at children and adolescents: A content analysis of food and beverage brand Web sites. *Journal of the American Dietetic Association, 106,* 1463–1466.

Wells, T.T., & Cruess, D. G. (2006). Effects of partial sleep deprivation on food consumption and food choice. *Psychology and Health, 21,* 79–86.

White, S., Brown, N. J., & Ginsburg, S. L. (2010). Diversity of body types in network television programming: A content analysis. *Communication Research Reports, 16,* 386–392.

Wiecha, J. L., Peterson, K. E., Ludwig, D. S., Kim, J., Sobol, A., & Gortmaker, S. L. (2006). When children eat what they watch: Impact of television viewing on dietary intake in youth. *Archives of Pediatrics and Adolescent Medicine, 160,* 436–442.

Wilcox, B., Cantor, J., Dowrick, P., Kunkel, D., Linn, S., & Palmer, E. (2004). *Report of the APA Task Force on Advertising and Children.* Washington, DC: American Psychological Association.

Wilksch, S. M., Durbridge, M. R., & Wade, T. D. (2008). A preliminary controlled comparison of programs designed to reduce risk of eating disorders targeting perfectionism and media literacy. *Journal of the American Academy of Child and Adolescent Psychiatry, 47,* 937–947.

Wilksch, S. M., & Wade, T. D. (2009). Reduction of shape and weight concern in young adolescents: A 30-month controlled evaluation of a media literacy program. *Journal of the American Academy of Child and Adolescent Psychiatry, 48,* 652–661.

Wilson, J. L., Peebles, R., Hardy, K. K., & Litt, I. F. (2006). Surfing for thinness: A pilot study of pro–eating disorder Web site usage in adolescents with eating disorders. *Pediatrics, 118,* e1635–e1643.

Wilson, N., Quigley, R., & Mansoor, O. (1999). Food ads on TV: A health hazard for children? *Australia and New Zealand Journal of Public Health, 23,* 647–650.

Wilson, G., & Wood, K. (2004). The influence of children on parental purchases during supermarket shopping. *International Journal of Consumer Studies, 28,* 329–336.

Wingood, G. M., DiClemente, R. J., Harrington, K., & Davies, S. L. (2002). Body image and African American females' sexual health. *Journal of Women's Health and Gender-Based Medicine, 11,* 433–439.

Wiseman, C. V., Gray, J. J., Mosimann, J. E., & Ahrens, A. H. (1992). Cultural expectations of thinness in women: An update. *International Journal of Eating Disorders, 11,* 85–89.

Wiseman, C. V., Gunning, F. M., & Gray, J. J. (1993). Increasing pressure to be thin: 19 years of diet products in television commercials. *Eating Disorders, 1,* 52–61.

Wong, N. D., Hei, T. K., Qaqundah, P. Y., Davidson, D. M., Bassin, S. L., & Gold, K. V. (1992). Television viewing and pediatric hypercholesterolemia. *Pediatrics, 90,* 75–79.

Wulfhorst, E. (2007, January 12). NY fashionistas weigh in on thin model flap. *Reuters/ABC News.* Retrieved from http://abcnews.go.com/Entertainment/print?id=2790878

Yager, Z., & O'Dea, J. A. (2008). Prevention programs for body image and eating disorders on university campuses: A review of large, controlled interventions. *Health Promotion International, 23,* 173–189.

Yen, C.-F., Hsiao, R. C., Ko, C.-H., Yen, J.-Y., Huang, C.-F., Liu, S.-C., & Wang, S.-Y. (2010). The relationships between body mass index and television viewing, Internet use and cellular phone use. *International Journal of Eating Disorders, 43,* 565–571.

Yoo, J. H., & Kim, J. (2012). Obesity in the new media: A content analysis of obesity videos on YouTube. *Health Communication, 27,* 86–97.

Zimmerman, F. J. (2008). *Children's media use and sleep problems: Issues and unanswered questions.* Menlo Park, CA: Kaiser Family Foundation.

Zimmerman, F. J., & Bell, J. F. (2010). Associations of television content type and obesity in children. *American Journal of Public Health, 100,* 334–340.

CHAPTER 8

The Internet

Edward Donnerstein

Throughout this book, we have discussed the impact that various media have on children's and adolescents' behavior, values, and beliefs. We have seen the enormous ability of the media to transcend the influence of parents and peers in providing information (sometimes correct, but often not) about the world in which they live. The interesting thing about the research and findings we have discussed is that in many ways, it has dealt with fairly traditional media forms such as television, film, radio, music, and print. But the media have changed. Newer technologies—in particular, the Internet and interactive video games— have created a new dimension for researchers to consider when they examine the effects of both problematic content (violence and sex) and educational content. Just like video games (discussed in Chapter 10), the Internet is highly interactive, suggesting that the effects could be stronger than those of television or other traditional media (Donnerstein, 2011). There are some researchers (Livingstone, Ólafsson, O'Neill, & Donoso, 2012) who consider the Internet to be the most interactive of our current media.

Just think for a moment about the types of effects we have discussed. Many of these effects, particularly those of media violence, have been identified through research conducted in the 1960s or 1970s. If you take a look at Figure 8.1, there have been some interesting and fascinating changes. Going back to the 1960s, our media platforms were television, film, radio, and the press. Eventually cable and video games were added, and concerns about these new technologies drew the attention of researchers. In looking at today's media platforms, however, children and adolescents now have access to movies, print, radio, television, cable television, home video game consoles, portable music players, DVDs, home computers, portable handheld video game systems, the Internet, cell phones, MP3 players, DVRs, electronic interactive toys, Internet-connected smartphones, and tablet computers. Furthermore, the few television stations of the 1960s now number in the thousands. Does this change the impact? In many ways the answer is yes. Both this chapter and the next, on social media, take a look at these phenomenal changes in the media environment and their effect on how we view, process, and react to media.

Figure 8.1   Popular media platforms over time.

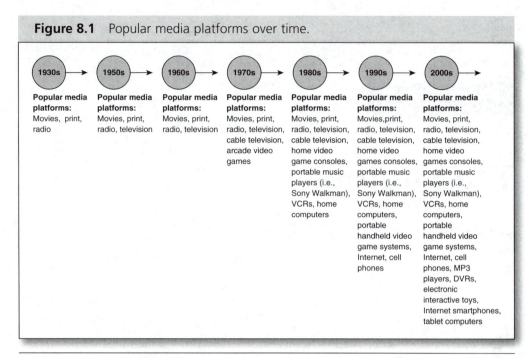

SOURCE: Adapted from Gutnick, A., Robb, M., Takeuchi, L., & Kotler, J. (2011). *Always connected: The new digital media habits of young children.* New York: Sesame Workshop.

Livingstone and her colleagues (2012) see these technological changes, particularly the Internet, as an increasing concern with respect to harm of children. They, like many others, argue that the Internet now contains content that is on TV or within other media, which we already know can influence children. Additionally, the Internet often takes the content out of context, creating more of a problem. Furthermore, the Internet makes available more extreme forms of content that can intentionally or unintentionally be accessed by children and adolescents. One reason for this concern is that content in traditional media like TV can be regulated or controlled, but this is difficult with respect to the Internet.

In Chapter 5, we discussed how sexual content on TV and in film can influence children and adolescents. In a recent review of the literature on sexual media, Wright, Malamuth, and Donnerstein (2012) noted the commentary of researchers about the potentially far-reaching influences of this newer technology on sexual behavior and attitudes. For example, Braun-Courville and Rojas stated, "Mass media play an important role in the sexual socialization of American youth, and given its expanding nature and accessibility, the Internet may be at the forefront of this education" (2009, p. 156).

The potential influences go beyond those of sexual content and can also have an impact in the areas of violence, obesity, stereotyping, fear, and all the areas we have discussed in this book (see Moreno & Kolb, 2012; O'Keeffe, 2012). As Donnerstein (2011, 2012) has noted, the Internet has become the medium in which traditional media like TV, film, and video games can be downloaded, viewed, and processed. The most recent survey by the Kaiser Family Foundation (2010) of child and adolescent media use in the United States indicates that the amount of time spent viewing TV content has increased over the last decade, but this increase is accounted for primarily by the viewing of such programming over the Internet and mobile devices. Adolescents now spend over 10 hours a day with some form of media.

Unlike traditional media such as TV, the Internet and other new technologies (e.g., mobile devices) give children and adolescents access to just about any form of content they can find (e.g., Donnerstein, 2011, 2012, 2013). Often with little effort, they are able to view almost any type of violence, advertising, or sexual behavior that has the potential to produce negative effects (Donnerstein, 2009; Strasburger, Jordan, & Donnerstein, 2010, 2012). Furthermore, this can be done in the privacy of their own room with little supervision from their parents (Moreno & Whitehill, 2012).

From a theoretical perspective, is there any reason to expect that the Internet or any of these newer technologies will have different effects than traditional media? Malamuth, Linz, and Yao (2005) have provided a perspective on Internet violence, but their theoretical stance applies equally to all forms of harmful materials. According to these authors, the Internet provides "Motivational," "Disinhibitory," and "Opportunity" aspects that make it somewhat different from traditional media in terms of its potential impact.

With regard to Motivation (the desire and drive to be online), the Internet is ubiquitous in that it is always on and can easily be accessed, thus leading to high levels of exposure. In the world of new technology, there is no "family viewing hour." Online content can be interactive and more engaging, which has the ability to inspire increased learning and certainly exposure time.

From a Disinhibitory perspective, the content is unregulated. Studies suggest that extreme forms of violent or sexual content are more prevalent on the Internet than in other popular media (e.g., Strasburger et al., 2010, 2012). Participation is private and anonymous, which allows for the searching of materials a child or adolescent would normally not encounter with traditional media. There is the suggestion that finding such materials (e.g., sites for bulimia or hate groups) could increase social support for these images and messages. Finally, online media exposure is much more difficult for parents to monitor than media exposure in traditional venues.

Opportunity aspects play a more important role in the area of cyberbullying and child sexual exploitation. Potential victims are readily available and reachable, and the identity of the aggressor can easily be disguised.

Are Children and Adolescents Using the Internet?

Figure 8.2

SOURCE: *Baby Blues* © 2007 Baby Blues Partnership. Dist. by King Features Syndicate.

Much of our discussion on the Internet would be meaningless if children and adolescents did not use it. This is not the case, however. Usage of the Internet and newer technologies by youth is substantial. Studies by the Pew Internet and American Life Project (Pew Foundation, 2010) revealed that 93% of youth ages 12 to 17 are online sometime during the day, and 71% have cell phones. Whether they are watching videos (57%), using social networking sites (65%), or playing video games (97%), children and adolescents have incorporated new technology into their daily lives. These frequencies are also observed across 21 different countries within Europe. The EU Kids Online Project found that in 2005, 70% of 6- to 17-year-olds used the Internet. By 2011, the figure was 87%, the largest increase being among younger children (Livingstone et al., 2012).

What about very young children, or even infants? A recent report on children under the age of 8 (Common Sense Media, 2011) found the following:

1. Twenty-seven percent of children under the age of 8 interact with new digital media (smartphones, iPads, etc.).

2. Fifty-two percent have access to smartphones, and 11% use them during a typical day.

3. Fifty-two percent of 2- to 4-year-olds have used a computer, and over 90% of 5- to 8-year-olds have used a computer.

4. Forty-four percent of 2- to 4-year-olds and 81% of 5- to 8-year-olds have played a video game.

The Technology Is Changing Fast

When Steve Jobs, the founder and CEO of Apple Inc., died in late 2011, it was interesting to think about his major achievements and how recently this technology has been brought to light. The iPod was introduced in 2001, the iTunes store in 2003, the first iPhone in 2007, and the iPad in 2010. Yet all of these are common, everyday technologies that have drastically altered how we receive and interact with the media—and with one another. Take a look at Figures 8.3 through 8.7, and think for a moment how rapidly our world has changed.

In the next chapter, we will look at the recent development of social networking sites and their influence. It seems hard to imagine that Facebook only started in 2006!

Are Parents Concerned?

For decades, parents and others have consistently been concerned about the potentially harmful influences of exposure to sexual and violent media content. A survey in Sweden (Carlsson, 2006) asked adults what they perceived to be the factors leading to violence in their society. While alcohol and drugs ranked the highest (90%), it is interesting to note that both TV and the Internet were identified by 60% of respondents as having a strong and significant influence. This was the first time the Internet was listed in this ongoing 10-year survey. Further, when respondents were asked their views on the extent to which sexual scenes in the media have a negative impact on children, Internet websites were considered more harmful than TV or music videos. In the most recent survey of parents in the European Union

Figure 8.3 In a short 10 years, Internet use has gone from 50% to almost 90%.

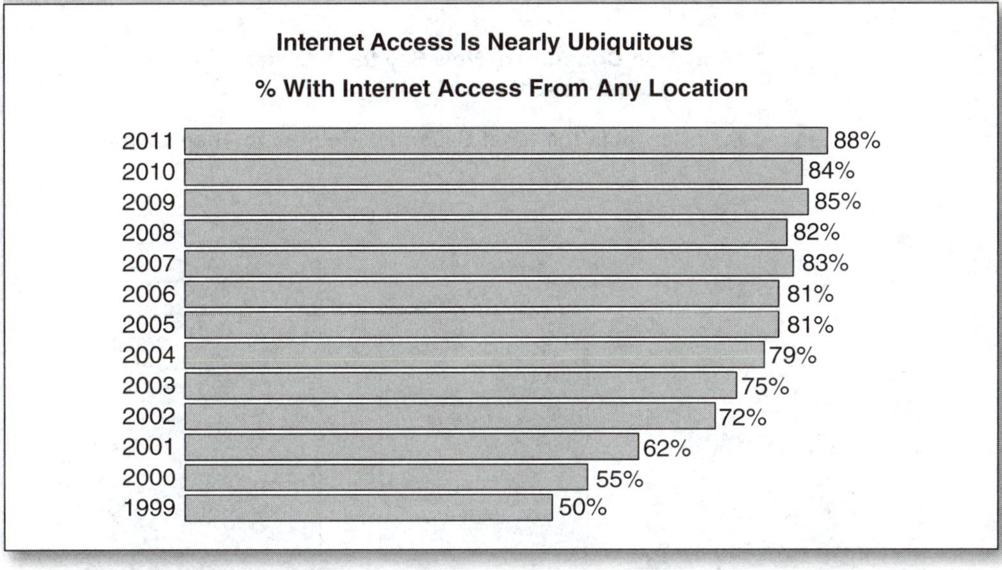

Internet Access Is Nearly Ubiquitous

% With Internet Access From Any Location

2011	88%
2010	84%
2009	85%
2008	82%
2007	83%
2006	81%
2005	81%
2004	79%
2003	75%
2002	72%
2001	62%
2000	55%
1999	50%

SOURCE: "The Infinite Dial 2011" (2011).

Figure 8.4 Most homes now have high-speed broadband access, allowing for rapid downloads of films and other content.

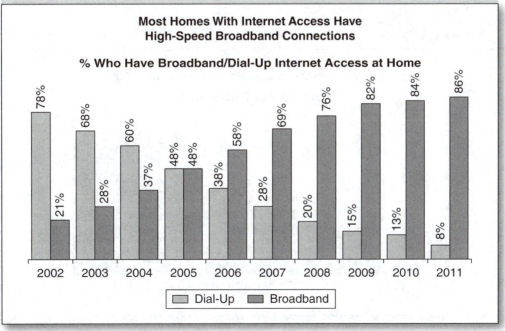

Most Homes With Internet Access Have High-Speed Broadband Connections

% Who Have Broadband/Dial-Up Internet Access at Home

Dial-Up   Broadband

SOURCE: "The Infinite Dial 2011" (2011).

Figure 8.5 The Internet has now become an essential medium in our lives.

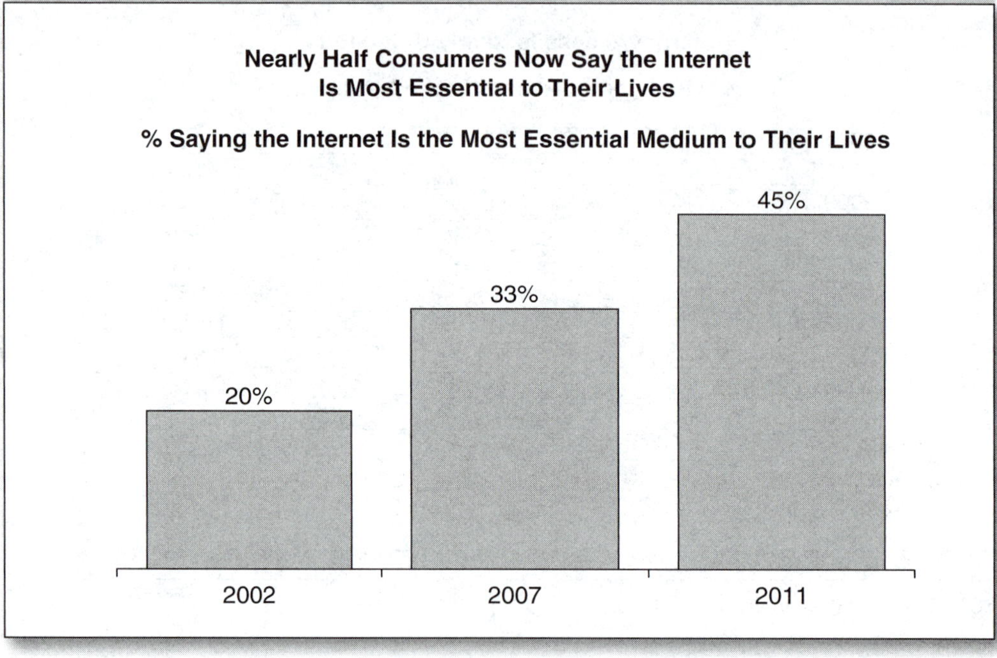

**Nearly Half Consumers Now Say the Internet
Is Most Essential to Their Lives**

% Saying the Internet Is the Most Essential Medium to Their Lives

Year	%
2002	20%
2007	33%
2011	45%

SOURCE: "The Infinite Dial 2011" (2011).

Figure 8.6 In a few years, smartphone use has tripled.

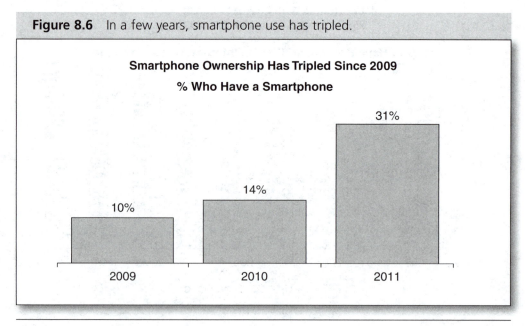

Smartphone Ownership Has Tripled Since 2009

% Who Have a Smartphone

Year	%
2009	10%
2010	14%
2011	31%

SOURCE: "The Infinite Dial 2011" (2011).

Figure 8.7   In just a few years, individuals with a social network profile have doubled.

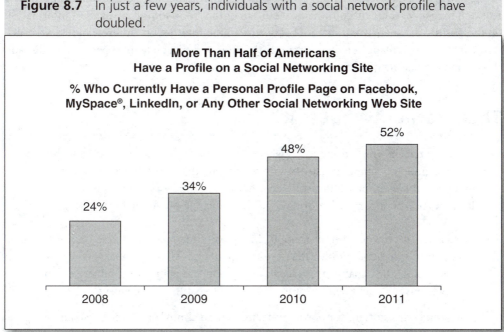

**More Than Half of Americans
Have a Profile on a Social Networking Site**

**% Who Currently Have a Personal Profile Page on Facebook,
MySpace®, LinkedIn, or Any Other Social Networking Web Site**

SOURCE: "The Infinite Dial 2011" (2011).

(Livingstone et al., 2012), parents rated online risks, such as being contacted by a stranger, as the fourth most concerning issue, ahead of worries about alcohol, drugs, getting into trouble with the police, and sexual activities.

These finding seem to reflect those in the United States. In a national poll of parents (Common Sense Media, 2011), over 92% considered the Internet a risk problem for their children and were supportive of laws to regulate access. Most concerning to parents were privacy issues.

The major difference in the concerns of today, compared to those of the past, is that children and adolescents are often more sophisticated and knowledgeable in their use of the technology than their parents are. Too often we hear of computer-phobic adults who possess little knowledge of expanding technology. Such resistance to the technology, combined with a limited knowledge base, makes solutions to potential problems (such as easy access to sexual images) even more difficult. Furthermore, when policy and advocacy groups attempt to inform parents about the Internet, we would argue that it does little good to tell them to contact "www.hereforhelp.com" if they are ignorant of these terms and World Wide Web usage.

Before discussing this new addition to our media world, it is important to point out a few differences in our knowledge base with regard to the Internet and more traditional media. First, the research on effects, both positive and negative, is limited. Not only is the technology new, but our research foundation is also. Second, content analysis is not only limited but, one may argue, also extremely challenging to conduct because of difficulties in determining a proper sample. Finally, solutions for dealing with harmful effects are further complicated by the global nature of this medium. In many ways, this is both a new medium and a new research focus. We can expect in the next edition of this book to find a wealth of information on the positive and negative impacts of exposure to the Internet on children and adolescents. In the interim, we will look at what we currently know and speculate from past knowledge and theory about what the outcomes may be.

The Internet: What Is It?

Very often we refer to the Internet more generally as the Web. This expanding technology is simply a vast group of computer networks linked around the world. It has a number of various components that are familiar (at least in terminology) to most of us, and they have the ability to deliver an enormous array of information. These include the following:

1. Email for electronic communication. Many would agree that this is one of the most popular forms of communication in today's society. Even this simple and everyday form of technology has changed in recent years, with the ability to send voice, video, and other forms of attachments around the world almost instantaneously.

2. Bulletin board systems for posting information on almost any topic one could imagine.

3. Chat groups and social media that can be used for real-time conversations, whether peer-to-peer or more public discussions on popular sites like Facebook. For many adolescents, this is the global equivalent of a free conference call. However, unlike the traditional conference call, you can choose your topic, person, and time in any manner you desire.

4. The World Wide Web, which combines visuals, sound, and text in a manner that allows linkages across many sites that deal with a particular topic. These topics obviously can be related to sex, violence, drugs, or any other subject about which we may have concerns.

And of course we have blogs and podcasting and other Internet-related activities, such as instant messaging, that have made the Internet *the* mass medium of choice.

The popularity and sophistication of the Internet are due to the increase in powerful search engines. A search engine, such as Google, is a server that searches other servers in a systematic manner and indexes its findings in a database. There is basically nothing on the Web that cannot be found by one of these engines. Interested in going to Disney World? Need a hotel? Just go to a search engine such as Google and type in the words "disney hotels," and, as shown in Figure 8.8, in less than a second you will have over 70 million websites where you can access more information than you could ever imagine. Only a few years ago, in the second edition of this book, that number was 21 million, and in the first edition a few years before that, it was 142,000. Take a virtual tour of your selection, book the room, and print out a map with explicit directions on how to get to your hotel from the airport. Of course, you also booked your travel (airline and car rental) with the same ease and speed.

It is important to note that we take the position that the Web and other Internet components are extremely informative and useful. This is one technology that we want our children to have access to and be knowledgeable about. It is exceedingly educational and almost indispensable in today's society. Like any technological advance, it will have some downsides, but

Figure 8.8   Google search on "disney hotels."

they should in no way be considered a barrier to continued advancement and to teaching children and adults about its vast usefulness and value. We strongly emphasize that in all respects, the Internet is a very powerful informational and instructional technology that we must continue to develop. We want the reader to keep this in mind, because many of the things discussed in this chapter deal with a small part of the Net that may be considered potentially harmful to children. While these materials comprise just a fraction of the total content available, they must be addressed because they can be found and accessed on the Internet much more easily than they could be accessed from other media in the past.

Concerns About the Internet

We can certainly see that the Internet is increasing in popularity. One of the issues of concern, however, is that this is a medium where youth are currently not only heavier users than their parents but also more sophisticated in their use of its applications. This is also a medium that parents often have little control over, provide few rules for using, and minimally supervise. Nevertheless, most parents believe that being online is more positive than watching TV. Perhaps they are unaware of the degree of unsolicited sexual materials on the Net, including violent pornography, which has increased over the years in both newsgroups and websites, or of drug advertising, hate group sites, and other risky content.

Even if parents were aware of these data, so much of the online activities carried out by children and adolescents is done alone, in an anonymous context, and without (as we have already noted) parental supervision. The messages of concern on the Internet do not differ from those of traditional media: those involving sex, violence, sexual violence, tobacco and alcohol, and more recently the advertising of unhealthy food products to children. We would expect the effects from exposure to be the same, if not enhanced. The interactive nature of the

Internet, which can lead to more arousal and more cognitive activity, suggests that influences such as those arising from media violence will be better facilitated (see Chapter 4). More important, easy access to materials that should be extremely limited to children and adolescents' view is now readily obtainable with the power of search engines and the Internet.

In thinking about the Internet and new media technologies, there are a number of concerns. This chapter will address four features of the Internet that put youth at risk:

1. Access to traditional media violence (both TV/film and video games)

2. Sexual exploitation, particularly of children

3. Exposure to explicit sexual materials, both intentional and accidental

4. Access to unhealthy food marketing

One of the more important risks is cyberbullying. Given its interface with social media and social networking sites, we will discuss this concern in more detail in the next chapter.

The Internet as a Medium for Media Violence

A number of chapters in this book examine the effects of media violence, both in traditional TV and film but also in video games. There is no question that newer technologies have not only expanded the realm of materials but also increased sources for viewing (e.g., Donnerstein, 2011, 2012). As the Kaiser Family Foundation (2010) survey found, TV content is more readily available on platforms other than traditional TV. We can see in Figure 8.9 how this might be conceptualized, in terms of both the Internet generally and the use of new technologies such as mobile phones, and the place of media violence in this conceptualization.

Figure 8.9   The Internet and violence.

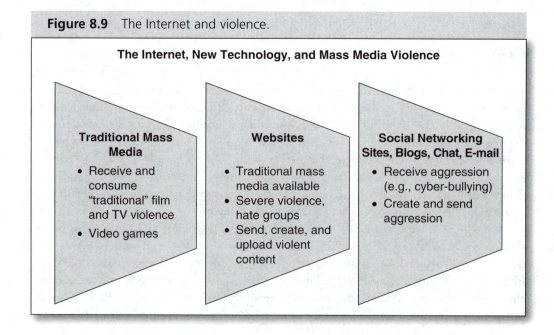

There are a number of theoretical reasons to expect even stronger effects from violence exposure with new technologies, given the interactive nature of the medium and opportunities for rehearsal, repetitiveness, and privacy. Websites offer not only the prospect of viewing more severe violence but also access to hate and terrorist groups messages and membership. Some online archives provide instructions for making bombs or other weapons. Since the events of September 11, terrorist groups have made extensive use of the Internet to recruit and spread propaganda. Hate speech and hate groups have also proliferated and become easily accessible on the Web. In an extensive survey of European countries, the EU Kids Online project (Livingston et al., 2012) found that approximately one-third of teenagers had seen graphic violent or hateful content, making this a high-level concern.

Recent research suggests that the types of materials found exclusively on the Internet may be related to aggressive behavior. In a national survey of youth, Ybarra and her colleagues (2008) found an association between the viewing of Internet violence and self-reported seriously aggressive behavior. While exposure to violence in the media overall was related to aggressive behavior, youth who reported that many or all of the websites they visited depicted real people fighting, shooting, or killing were five times more likely to report engaging in seriously violent behavior. This type of material seemed to be unique to the Internet and included (a) hate sites; (b) websites showing pictures of dead people or people dying, or "snuff" sites; (c) websites showing satanic rituals, (d) websites showing pictures of war, death, or terrorism; and (e) websites showing cartoons, such as stick people or animals, being beaten up, hurt, or killed. The authors suggested that the interactive environment of the Internet and the depiction of real people engaged in violence may explain the stronger association with reported seriously violent behavior.

Finally, an adolescent not only can view violence on the Internet but also can create and upload violent materials. The Internet (in particular social networking sites, blogs, chat rooms, and email) allows not only the creation of aggression, but also the ability to actually aggress against another in what has been termed *cyberbullying*. We will discuss this issue in the next chapter.

Sex on the Net: A Primary Concern

One of the most controversial Internet content categories is sexual material, which has raised concerns about child exploitation. Such material ranges from photographs to the Net equivalent of "phone sex," sometimes with a live video connection. The sending of sexual information over email or the posting of it on bulletin boards by those targeting children has been a long-term issue.

As researchers have noted (e.g., Mitchell, Finkelhor, Jones, & Wolak, 2010), children are more accessible to offenders through social networking sites, email, and texting because this is anonymous behavior and normally outside the supervision of parents. Children may also find the privacy and anonymity of this type of communication much more conducive to discussions of intimate relationships than face-to-face interaction. For the potential offender, there is certainly easier access to websites and other Internet groups that encourage and legitimize these types of behavior with children and adolescents.

Perhaps the most comprehensive series of studies on these issues has come from the Crimes Against Children Research Center at the University of New Hampshire. These studies (see Jones, Mitchell, & Finkelhor, 2011) involved a random national sample of 1,500 children ages 10 to 17 who were interviewed in 2000, and then an additional sample of 1,500 who were interviewed in 2005 and 2009. This procedure allowed the researchers to look at changes in youths' experiences with the Internet. The major findings from this study can be summarized as follows (see Figure 8.10):

1. Twenty-three percent of respondents reported exposure to unwanted sexual materials. This is down from 34% a few years earlier but essentially shows little change over the decade.

2. Nine percent of youth still reported sexual solicitations. Although this is down from 13% in 2005, it still reflects a significant number of children and adolescents at risk.

3. Internet harassment, or cyberbullying, has consistently increased.

We can look at these small percentages and say that broad claims of victimization may not seem justified. The problem with this interpretation is that these are large-scale national surveys, so even if the percentages are small, the number of youth impacted is actually quite substantial. There is also the issue of human trafficking for sex and the use of online services such as Backpage and Craigslist for this purpose. These are new research areas that are being explored in terms of both prevalence and intervention (see Latonero, 2011).

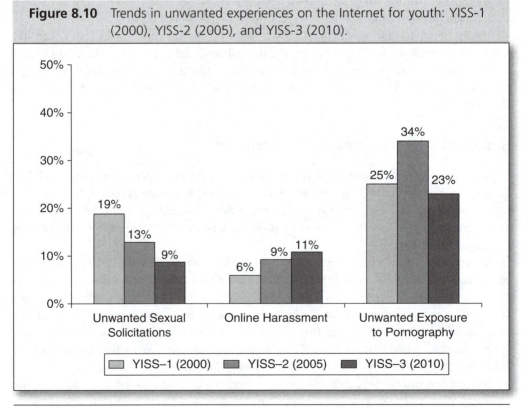

Figure 8.10 Trends in unwanted experiences on the Internet for youth: YISS-1 (2000), YISS-2 (2005), and YISS-3 (2010).

SOURCE: Jones, Mitchell, and Finkelhor (2011). Copyright © Elsevier. Reprinted by permission.

Viewing of Sexual Materials

More significant are findings that indicate substantial purposive viewing of sexually explicit materials by youth on the Internet (e.g., Wright et al., 2012). In one large-scale survey, Salazar, Fleischauer, Bernhardt, and DiClemente (2009) found that 17% of websites visited by teens were X rated (sexually explicit), and at least 6% contained sexual violence. Other studies have shown that between 25% and 65% of teens have experienced unwanted and accidental exposure (Braun-Courville & Rojas, 2009; Wolak, Mitchell, & Finkelhor, 2007). Given these data, there is ample reason to expect effects from Internet exposure. There are few studies, however, on the impact of Internet exposure. The few studies that have examined Internet websites strongly suggest an association between Internet exposure and sexual attitudes and behaviors. Two large-scale, longitudinal surveys of youth conducted in the Netherlands (Peter & Valkenburgh, 2008, 2009) found that more frequent intentional exposure to sexually explicit Internet material was associated with greater sexual uncertainty and more positive attitudes toward uncommitted sexual exploration (i.e., sexual relations with casual partners/friends or with sexual partners in one-night stands). Additionally, adolescents' exposure to Internet sex appeared to be both a cause and a consequence of their belief that women are sex objects. More frequent exposure predicted stronger beliefs that women are sex objects, while at the same time stronger beliefs that women are sex objects predicted more frequent exposure to such materials.

The above studies, while somewhat limited, do suggest that the Internet can influence adolescents' sexual attitudes and behaviors. Besides the fact that traditional media (which we have already acknowledged to be an influence) can easily be obtained via the Internet, more explicit and potentially riskier materials are readily available to youth online. In a longitudinal study of adolescents, Brown and L'Engle (2009) noted,

> By the end of middle school many teens have seen sexually explicit content not only on the Internet but in more traditional forms of media as well. Such exposure is related to early adolescents' developing sense of gender roles, sexual relationships, and sexual behavior, including perpetration of sexual harassment. (p. 148)

As children and adolescents move further away from traditional media channels to newer technologies, it will become increasingly important for researchers to explore the extent and nature of online sexual social influence.

As we know, the process of finding sexual material is quite easy. Search engines, such as Google, allow the user to type in words and word combinations that will ask the computer to search for any type of sexual content. If we consider for a moment the curiosity of a 12-year-old and let her or his fingers (and mouse) do the walking, one can see how easy the process can be. For example, if we use our search engine to type in the words "sex pictures," as we see in Figure 8.11, in less than a second we are given a list of 625 million sites that contain these words (and most likely the pictures that our 12-year-old is seeking). It is interesting to note that in the last edition of this book, only a few years ago, the number of sites was only 2 million.

Many times the material is found with just a slip in terminology. As we saw in Chapter 5, sexually violent material can have adverse effects on the viewer. The research on violence

Figure 8.11 Google search on "sex pictures."

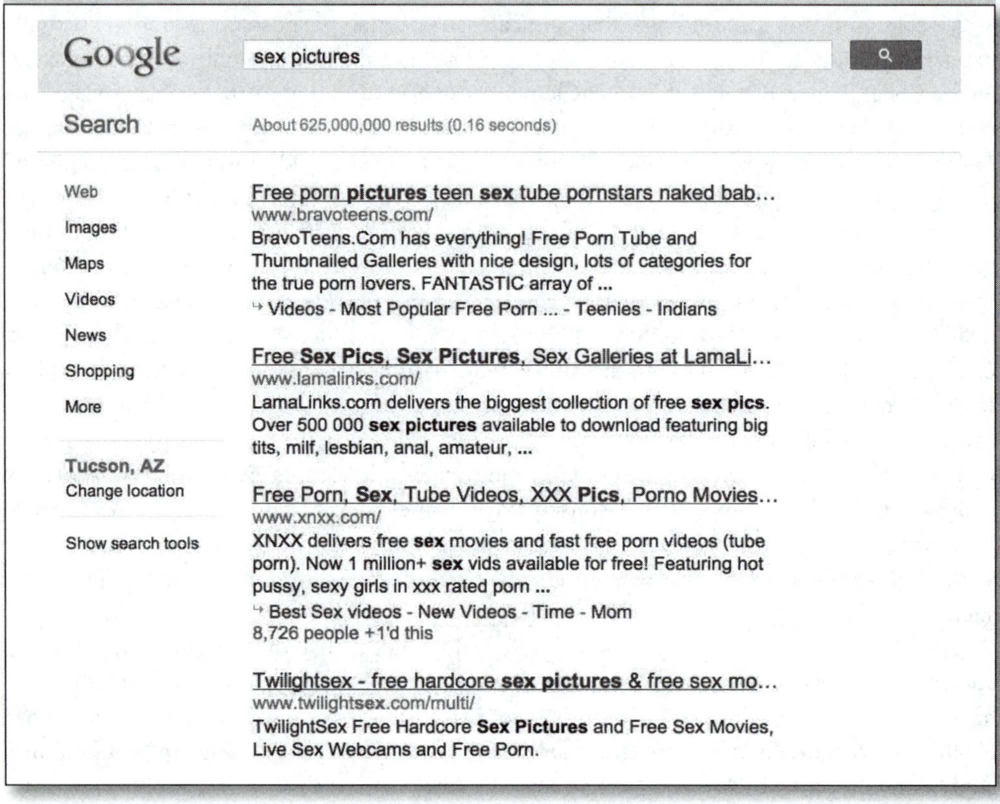

against women strongly suggests that aggressive pornography can have undesirable effects on rape-related attitudes (see Wright et al., 2012). If you were doing a research paper on the topic and typed in the words "aggressive pornography," your Google search would give you results like those shown in Figure 8.12. These are primarily research and scholarly papers. However, type in a shortcut like "aggressive porn," and you will find results like those in Figure 8.13. Needless to say, they are quite different.

If our 12-year-old then wanted to access one of these sites, it is not "officially blocked" to minors unless certain blocking software is implemented (which is often not entirely effective). Most sexually explicit adult sites will merely indicate that the site (a) contains sexually explicit pictures, (b) may be offensive to viewers, and (c) requires that the viewer be at least 18 years of age; if not, she or he must exit the site immediately. Needless to say, there are probably a high percentage of sexually curious adolescents, and even children, who will simply click their mouse and indicate they are of age and enter the adult site. Once within one of these sites, the viewer is able to link into other similar sites offering sample pictures, text, and video of a hardcore sexual nature, as shown in Figure 8.14. The great sophistication of search engines also allows for the searching of websites on (a) bestiality, (b) child pornography, (c) rape and bondage, and (d) teen sex.

Search engines exist to help, but the usual Internet user is not going to come in contact with inappropriate content without making a conscious decision to find these sites. However, in

Figure 8.12   Google search on "aggressive pornography."

Google | aggressive pornography

Search

About 8,870,000 results (0.27 seconds)

Web
Images
Maps
Videos
News
Shopping
Books
More

Tucson, AZ
Change location

Show search tools

[PDF] The Effects of **Aggressive Pornography** on Belie…
www.sscnet.ucla.edu/commstudies/faculty/malamuth/…/85Jrp19.pdf
File Format: PDF/Adobe Acrobat - Quick View
by JVP Check - 1985 - Cited by 163 - Related articles
sex portrayals (i.e., **aggressive pornography**) varying whether
the victim … In addition to assessing the impact of **aggressive
pornography** on beliefs in rape …

[PDF] The Effects of **Aggressive Pornographic Mass** …
www.sscnet.ucla.edu/commstudies/faculty/malamuth/…/82AESP15.p…
File Format: PDF/Adobe Acrobat - Quick View
by NM Malamuth - Cited by 99 - Related articles
The distinction between aggressive and nonaggressive
pornography is often … In the series of studies reported below,
aggressive pornography refers to …

[PDF] Repeated Exposure to Violent and Nonviolent **Por**…
www.apa.org/divisions/div46/articles/malamuth.pdf
File Format: PDF/Adobe Acrobat - Quick View
nonviolent pornography on males' laboratory aggression against
women. … **aggressive pornography** increases a person's
sexual responsiveness to such stimuli …

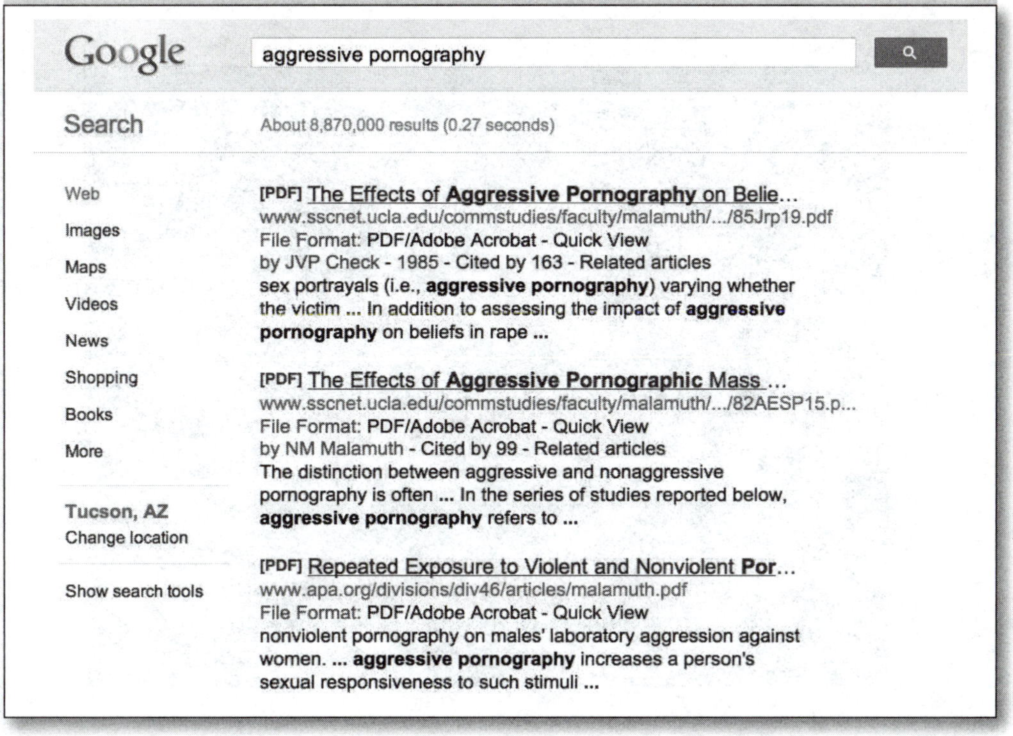

Figure 8.13   Google search on "aggressive porn."

Google | Aggressive Porn

Search

About 6,370,000 results (0.30 seconds)

Web
Images
Maps
Videos
News
Shopping
More

Tucson, AZ
Change location

Show search tools

Aggressive porn videos - Page 1 - at Epic Porn Tube
www.epic**porn**tube.com/categories/**aggressive**/1.html
Browse our **Aggressive porn** video archive. 1000's of hot sex
clips from biggest tube sites gathered in one place!

Aggressive videos on Hot-Sex-Tube.com - Free **porn** …
hot-sex-tube.com/categories/**aggressive**/1.html
Daily updated free **Aggressive porn** tube. … Tags: aggressive,
anal, beautiful ass, big cock, big tits, deepthroat, fat cock,
hardcore, latina, wife. Added: 5 months …

Aggressive videos on NastyVideoTube.com - Free **po**…
nastyvideotube.com/categories/**aggressive**1.html
Tags: **aggressive**, anal, beautiful ass, big cock, big tits,
deepthroat, hardcore, … Tags: **aggressive**, beautiful ass,
beautiful body, brunette, forced, from behind, …

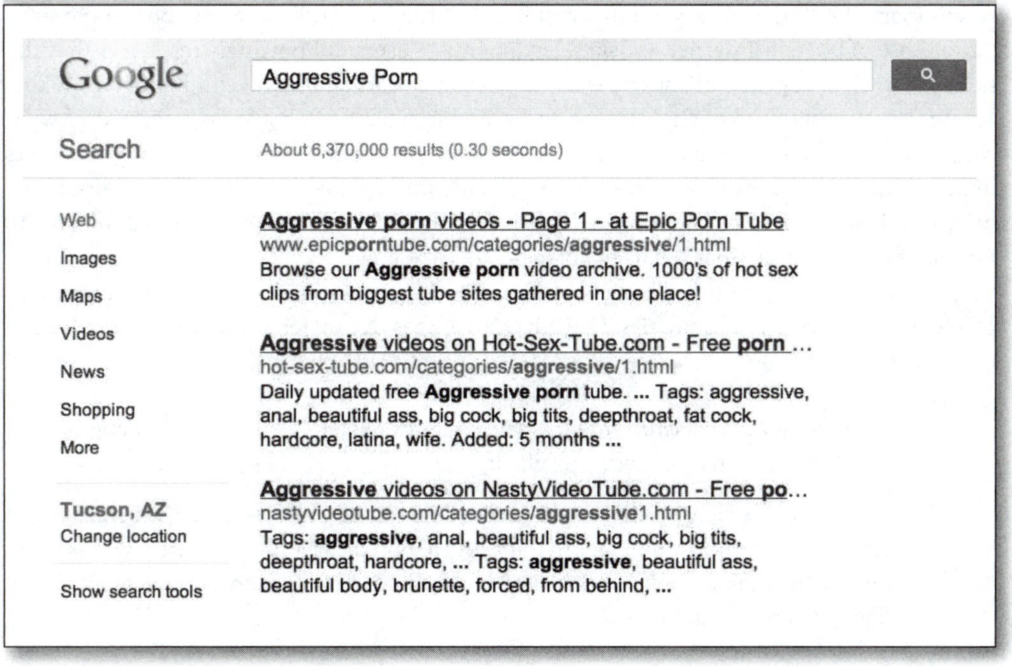

Figure 8.14 A hard-core website.

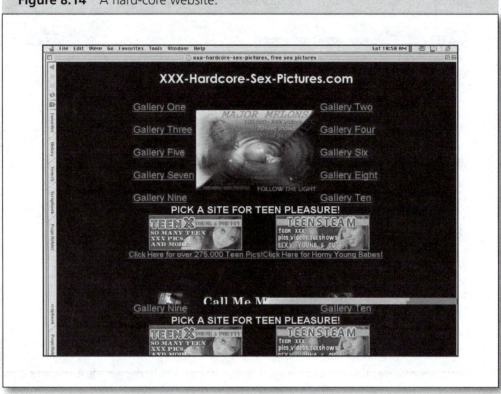

recent years, it has become known that certain adult sites have used address codes quite similar to those of popular Internet websites, leading many users unknowingly into areas they did not wish to visit. For example, it was well known some years ago that if children were looking for information about the White House and typed in www.whitehouse.com instead of www .whitehouse.gov (not an unlikely mistake in our dot-com world), they would find themselves linked to an adult site, as shown in Figure 8.15. This site has now been sold and changed. The price of this sale is hard to know, but it is estimated that the website Sex.Com sold for over 10 million. No one can say that sex does not sell.

The speed and anonymity of Internet technology has led users to a variety of ways to supplement traditional sexual activities. Griffiths (2010) sees five major areas of sex-related use of the Internet:

1. *The search for sexual educational materials.* Sites related to sex education and healthy sexual interactions are readily available.

2. *The buying or selling of sex-related goods.* This can be done at online sex shops in an atmosphere of almost total anonymity. As we noted earlier, sex industry websites are some of the most popular sites visited by adults and frequented by adolescents. Even Viagra can be bought online.

Figure 8.15   The website www.whitehouse.com.

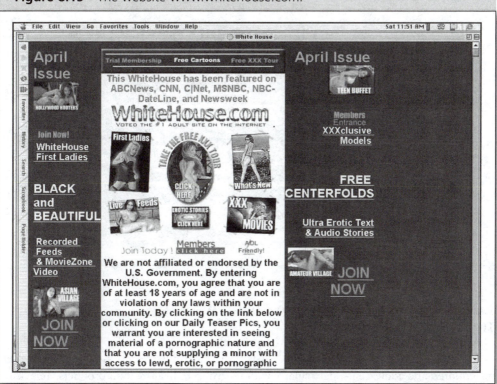

3. *The seeking out of materials for entertainment or masturbatory purposes.* Individuals can also digitally manipulate images in sophisticated programs. Virtual partners, including children, are now part of the interactive environment. Within a legal context, virtual child pornography will be difficult to manage, given the fact that no "real" underage child exists.

4. *The seeking out of sexual partners for long-term or short-term relationships and encounters.* Everything from dating and matchmaking services to prostitution is now available with the typing of a few words and the click of a mouse. In recent years, websites that provide information and reviews of prostitutes (escorts) have become more popular on the Web (see Figure 8.16).

5. Finally, there is the illegal seeking out of individuals for sex-related Internet crimes (e.g., sexual harassment, cyberstalking).

There is the possibility of some form of sexual addiction occurring with the proliferation and use of sex-related Internet sites. One argument is that the anonymity of the Internet could foster such addiction. However, the research does not demonstrate that such addiction occurs, and if it does it is a relatively small minority of users who are affected. There is no question, however, that this is one area that needs further examination.

Figure 8.16 Escort ads and review page.

Advertising Food Products to Children: The Latest Concern

In a number of chapters in this book, we have discussed the concern of advertising targeting children and adolescents, particularly with regard to unhealthy food products. Television has been the usual suspect in these concerns, and we have seen how federal regulations have helped in reducing both the amount and nature of food advertising to young audiences. But technology has changed, and so has the medium where much of the concern now resides. The Institute of Medicine of the National Academy of Science in the United States recently published a series of studies looking at childhood obesity as a major health problem among children today (Hingle & Kunkel, 2012; Kunkel & Castonguay, 2012). One concern was food marketing to children and the proliferation of advertisements that market unhealthy food choices. The research was quite clear on the negative impacts of marketing unhealthy foods to children, in terms of increased obesity and other health-related issues. While guidelines could be created for advertising in traditional media, such as television, the types of ads considered problematic have now crossed over to the Internet.

In a comprehensive overview of food advertising on the Internet, the Kaiser Family Foundation summarized the problem as follows:

> The world in which children encounter advertising is changing rapidly. While television and other more "traditional" forms of marketing to children still dominate, this study makes it clear that when it comes to targeting children, there is still a vast amount of food related content online, with the potential to significantly expand and deepen children's exposure to food marketing messages. (2006, p. 28)

The findings of this investigation were both fascinating and disturbing. The majority of companies that advertised to children on TV (85%) were also providing children with similar forms of advertising on the Internet. Of these companies, 75% maintained websites specifically created for children, and not surprisingly many mentioned their website on product packaging. A more recent analysis by Cai and Zhao (2010) found that:

1. Eighty-seven percent of children's most popular websites included some form of advertising.

2. Seventy-five percent of these websites offered children the ability to download logos, screensavers, or even wallpaper they could use for their computers.

3. Seventy-five percent of the sites featured advergames.

Given the interactive nature of the Internet, it was not surprising to find that around 75% of the sites had what are now called "advergames," in which a company's product or brand characters are featured in an online game format. Advergames are able to engage children in interesting activities while immersing them in a product-related environment. They also begin to blur the boundary between commercial and noncommercial content, something that is regulated in traditional media venues. Figure 8.17 gives some idea of the types of advergames children are exposed to online. The interactive nature of the Internet makes it easy for manufacturers to tout product "benefits" such as taste, fun, and popularity.

Making use of other technological advances, advertisers have begun employing what is now called "viral marketing." In this innovative technique, users are invited to send their friends emails or even e-cards containing news and entertainment features related to the product. The Kaiser Family Foundation (2006) study found that two-thirds used a brand character or a link to a game on the company's website.

Figure 8.17   Example of an advergame.

No different from traditional TV or print advertising, these Internet ads also try to attract children through contests, sweepstakes, and other promotional activities. In one such promotion, children gain points by watching what are basically TV ads online and sending the video on to their friends. More than half the sites in the Kaiser Family Foundation study (2006) made TV ads available for viewing, suggesting what we have already noted in many places in this book: the "blur" between traditional media and the Internet.

Many of the websites offered special memberships or clubs to keep children returning to them (Kaiser Family Foundation, 2006). These memberships might provide access to games, screensavers, or other incentives to maintain the viewer's interest and continual participation (see Figure 8.18). Even without memberships, many sites (75%) offered downloads of logos, screensavers, or computer desktop wallpaper. Many sites also offered children the opportunity to "customize" the site (e.g., with colors or characters) as a means of maintaining their loyalty.

Figure 8.18   Example of an interactive food product website.

One particular finding stands out in the Kaiser study (Kaiser Family Foundation, 2006). Almost 40% of the sites offered children promotions such as access to awards, games, and other prizes if they or their parents bought the product. This new venture into marketing to children raises a number of regulatory issues, which we will discuss later in the chapter. As others have noted (e.g., Montgomery, Chester, Grier, & Dorfman, 2012), new technologies, like the Internet, have changed the practice and regulation of children's advertising.

In a review of children's advertising, Kunkel and Castonguay (2012) came to the following conclusions with regard to new technology inroads:

1. The foods that are most heavily advertised on television are also strongly featured online.

2. The marketing of unhealthy foods to children that we have seen on television is now being replicated on the Internet.

3. A child's ability to discriminate an ad from other material on the Internet is much more difficult than it is in traditional media, such as television.

Other Areas of Concern

Concerns about children and adolescents' use of the Internet are not limited to those involving sexual content or food marketing. Other perceived dangers come from information on Satanism and religious proselytizing, as well as opportunities to glamorize drugs and gain access to gambling sites. Religious cults, which only a few years ago would have had a limited audience, can now reach out to a worldwide following. Offshore gambling is now a major e-business. We no longer need to go to Las Vegas to place a bet; offshore casinos do the same thing, as well as present online slots, craps, and poker. Poker has become one of the more popular activities for online gamers (see Figure 8.19). According to the Annenberg Public Policy Center (University

Figure 8.19 Example of an online poker site.

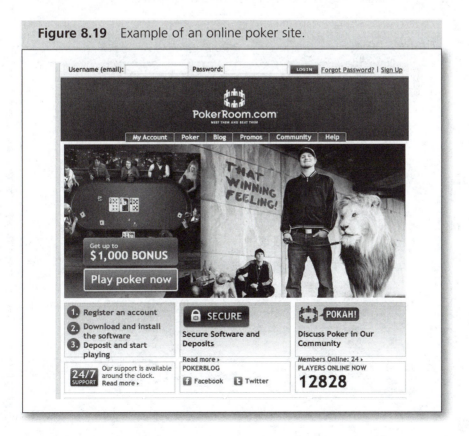

of Pennsylvania, 2010), weekly use of online gambling sites among young adults 18 to 22 years old doubled from 2005 to 2006 and increased from 4% to 16% in males between 2008 and 2010. Even among females, online sports gambling increased from 9% to 22% from 2008 to 2010. A credit card or a money order (something teenagers can purchase) allows access to any one of hundreds of offshore casinos (in spite of recent governmental intervention).

Alcohol and tobacco advertisements and websites dedicated to smoking and drinking are another problem. Many of these sites use promotional techniques that are considered quite attractive to adolescents. In previous chapters, we have seen the strong appeal of advertising to both children and adolescents. The enforcement of government regulations with respect to tobacco and alcohol has been of significant help in more traditional media such as television. This has not been the case with regard to the Internet and, as we discuss later, is not likely be an effective tool to combat advertising that exists within a global context. As we will discuss in Chapter 9, the mere depiction of smoking and drug use in social media can have attitudinal and behavioral effects on users.

Want to buy drugs? It's very easy on the Internet. With a simple money order you are on your way. In one report ("Teens Turn," 2006), it was noted that over 90% of sites that sell prescription drugs do not even require a doctor's note (see Figure 8.20). According to this report,

emergency department physicians are reporting an increasing number of adolescents who are overdosing on a bizarre combination of medications. And where are they getting them? More and more often they come from one of the hundreds of online pharmacies where there are no questions asked, no prescription necessary.

Figure 8.20 Example of an online pharmacy.

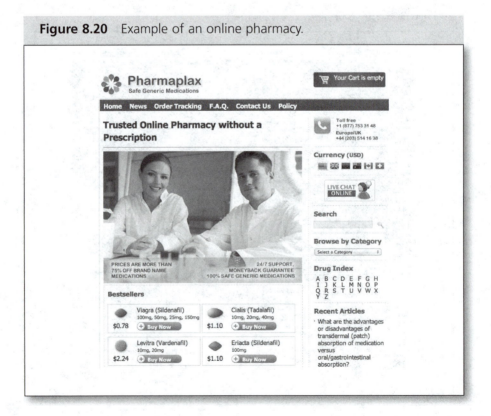

Children's privacy is another major issue. As discussed by Kunkel and Castonguay (2012), there is growing concern that many websites, even those aimed directly at children (under age 13), are requesting personal information without asking for parental permission. In fact, less than 25% asked children for their parents' permission to disclose information such as email addresses, phone numbers, home addresses, and information about their parents. The standard advertising techniques discussed in Chapter 2 seem to be just as appealing when children surf the Web. Recent governmental regulations have slowed this steady invasion of children's privacy, but concerns still exist. In fact, in one recent study (Cai & Zhao, 2010), 87% of children's websites were found to collect personal information, although this is forbidden by the Children's Online Privacy Protection Act (see Chapter 13).

We should not forget that the Internet also has the ability to promote prosocial efforts. According to Mares and Woodard (2001), it is a promising medium for three major reasons. First, it is not expensive for a small prosocial group to reach an audience on a global level. No other medium has this ability at the relative cost of the Internet. Second, it can target a specific, narrow audience. The ability of the Web to be selective and to gather information from users allows for the tailoring of specific webpages to a target audience. Finally, it is interactive, allowing for changes to be made in the site. The major problem is that few children are reaching these sites, and that the Internet is underused for prosocial purposes.

Solutions to Internet Concerns

In thinking about solutions to children and adolescents' access to inappropriate Internet content, there are three major approaches. The first is government regulation restricting the content. The second is technology, including blocking software and some form of rating system. Third, and we believe the most important, is media literacy for both parents and their children as to the benefits and problems of the Internet (see Figure 8.21). The issue of media literacy is discussed more in depth in Chapter 12.

Government Regulation

Within the United States, the First Amendment protects offensive "speech" from censorship, including sexually explicit materials. In general, the U.S. courts have struck down most content restrictions on books, magazines, and films. There are, of course, exceptions, such as "obscenity," child pornography, and certain types of indecent material, depending on the time, place, and manner of presentation. In 1996, Congress passed a bill to deal specifically with Internet content regulation, primarily in the area of pornography.

The bill took as its premise a number of questions regarding the protection of children. First, is access to pornography easy for children? The answer is probably yes, if the individual has some computer savvy. As discussed earlier, sophisticated search engines give rapid and extensive results. Second, is access to pornography accidental? Except in the case of typing errors, the answer is probably no. Finally, is access to this type of material harmful? This is difficult to assess and depends on many factors, as discussed in previous chapters. Nevertheless, most of us would agree that we should monitor the situation and protect children from these unwanted sites.

Figure 8.21

SOURCE: By permission of Mike Thompson and Creators Syndicate, Inc.

The Supreme Court of the United States ruled on the Communications Decency Act in 1998 and, as expected, held it to be unconstitutional and an infringement on freedom of speech. Other courts have noted that service providers, such as America Online, cannot be held liable for the sending of pornographic materials over the Internet. It is obvious that the courts are well aware that government regulation in this area would be difficult or nearly impossible to enforce, given not only the vastness of the materials available but also the global scope of the Internet.

In 2002, the Supreme Court overturned a law that banned virtual images of children, even those sexual in nature (*Ashcroft v. Free Speech Coalition* [122 S.Ct. 1389]). In other words, virtual child pornography is considered legal. These decisions, like many others from the Court, suggest the difficulty of federal legislation in confronting sex on the Internet. And more recently, the Court struck down a California law trying to restrict violent video games. In an age of convergence and mobile devices, it appears that attempts to "protect children" will move further and further away. As Jordan (2010) recently noted, "in a society where children have ownership over media devices and determine the content that appears on their screens, the 'protecting the children' argument for restricting mass media content may be difficult to achieve from afar."

With respect to online food marketing, the Kaiser Family Foundation (2006) noted the following:

To date, the primary regulatory concern regarding online marketing has been on protecting children's privacy, via the Children's Online Privacy Protection Act (COPPA). At the same time, the advertising industry's self-regulatory body, the Children's Advertising Review Unit (CARU), has instituted a set of general guidelines to advise advertisers on how to communicate with children in an age appropriate way on the Internet. At the time of this writing (June, 2006), more detailed guidelines regarding online marketing were expected soon from CARU. (p. 28)

Years later, regulations regarding advertising are still up in the air, in spite of the call for some form of governmental intervention (Montgomery et al., 2012).

Blocking Technology

One solution has been the development of software designed to block unwanted sites. This blocking software can block known adult sites, for instance, or any site containing predetermined words such as *sex*, *gambling*, or other unwanted content. A number of software programs are available that perform these and other functions.

But none of these blocking systems is completely effective. The Web changes quite rapidly, and software designed for today may not be entirely appropriate tomorrow. In 2005, *Consumer Reports* stated,

[The] latest tests of filtering software show that while Internet blockers have gotten better at blocking pornography, the best also tend to block many sites they shouldn't. In addition, *Consumer Reports* found the software to be less effective at blocking sites promoting hatred, illegal drugs or violence. ("Filtering Software," 2005, p. 70)
This report noted the following:

1. Filters kept out most, but not all, pornography. Well-informed teenagers could find their way around the blocks.

2. Informational sites could be blocked. The best software was also heavy-handed against sites dealing with health issues, sex education, civil rights, and politics.

3. The programs could make research more difficult, impeding older children in their attempts to write school reports.

4. Blocking software sometimes regulated more than websites. Some prevented the downloading of music and certain emails.

A recent comment from Carnegie Mellon University (2012) underscores the drawbacks of filters:

Many advocacy groups have raised concerns about the types of websites blocked by parental control software. Some of these applications block certain political, human rights, animal rights, artistic, gay/lesbian/bisexual issues, health and sex education websites. This is a serious issue because many libraries and schools are required to use this software as a result of the Children's Internet Protection Act.

Child-Friendly Sites

There are many "safe" places for children to surf the Internet that will protect them from much of the problematic content we have discussed in this chapter, such as sex, violence, and hate groups. While they are highly recommended, Figures 8.22 through 8.25 show one inter-esting concern that perhaps has been overlooked. Figure 8.22 shows a list of suggestions for child-friendly sites from Microsoft. Figures 8.23 and 8.24 show very well-known and certainly safe outlets that parents would welcome. But take a look at Figure 8.25. Do you note anything

Figure 8.22 A selection of sites that are "safe" for children.

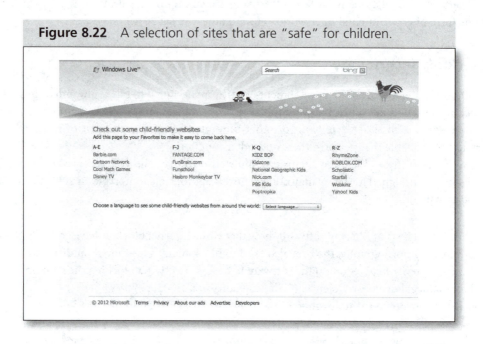

Figure 8.23 A Yahoo site for kids.

Figure 8.24   A National Geographic site for kids.

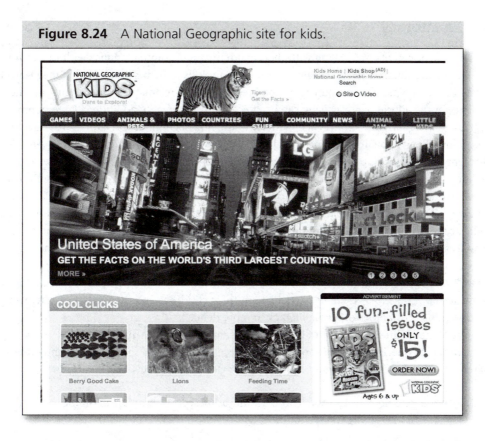

Figure 8.25   A Disney site for kids.

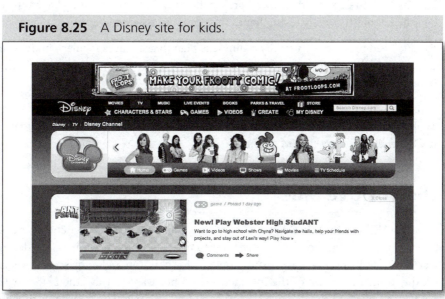

interesting? Look at the top banner, and if you were online and could click on the banner, you would get, once again, *advergames*, taking us directly back to Figure 8.17. I expect some might argue that this site is not entirely child friendly.

Media Literacy

The role of parents in working with their children and becoming familiar with this technology is critical. Children can be taught critical viewing skills in their schools so that they learn to better interpret what they encounter on the Web. The same techniques used to mitigate media violence or the appeal of advertising can be effective in this area. In addition, a large number of professional organizations concerned with the well-being of children and families have begun to take a more active role in reducing the impact of harmful Internet content (e.g., the American Academy of Pediatrics, the American Medical Association Alliance). Within this new arena of technology, we should take a lesson from our findings on media violence interventions. Research on intervention programs has indicated that we can reduce some of the impact of media violence by empowering parents in their role as monitors of children's television viewing. These studies indicate that parents who view programs with their children and discuss the realities of violence, as well as alternatives to aggressive behaviors in conflict situations, can actually reduce the negative impact of media violence (i.e., increased aggressiveness in children) (e.g., Donnerstein, Slaby, & Eron, 1994; Potter, 2012). It is likely that similar positive results will be obtained when parents begin to monitor, supervise, and participate in their children's Internet activities. Chapter 12 examines the possibilities of media literacy in more detail.

Part of media literacy is parental intervention and co-viewing. In terms of new technology solutions, the American Academy of Pediatrics recently released a set of recommendations for parents (O'Keeffe, Clarke-Pearson, & Council on Communications and Media, 2011):

1. Parents should talk to their children and adolescents about their online use and the specific issues facing today's online kids

2. Parents need to work on their own participation gap in their homes by becoming better educated about the many technologies their youngsters are using

3. Parents need to establish a family online-use plan that involves regular family meetings to discuss online topics, regular inspection of privacy settings, and regular checking of online profiles for inappropriate posts

4. Parents need to supervise online activities via active participation and communication, as opposed to remote monitoring with a Net Nanny program (software used to monitor the Internet in the absence of parents)

On the Positive Side

As we noted at the start of this chapter, the Internet can be extremely beneficial as both an educational teacher and a tool for positive development. Although we have alluded to the small fraction of websites that can create problems for children and adolescents, we cannot overlook the immense benefit of the Internet. We do not want to leave the reader with any feeling of hesitation about the positive aspects of this technology. The Internet is perhaps the greatest teaching tool we have ever encountered, and its impact on children and adolescents will enrich their lives in immeasurable ways. Therefore, it seems appropriate to end this chapter on a more positive note.

The American Academy of Pediatrics (AAP) suggests a number of activities for parents and children that can foster positive interaction and educational experiences. The AAP's website (see http://safetynet.aap.org) provides a lot of helpful information on cybersafety, parental discussions, and other topics.

The area of civic engagement for youth has taken on new excitement because of the Internet. In a report on this subject, Montgomery, Gottlieb-Robles, and Larson (2004) noted,

> Youth engagement in politics and community affairs has quietly been taking on new life and a dynamic new look, thanks to the Internet. Scarcely audible above the hubbub over piracy and pornography and the clamor of the media marketplace, a low-profile civic upsurge—created for and sometimes by young people—has taken root on the Net. Hundreds of websites have been created that encourage and facilitate youth civic engagement, contributing to an emerging genre on the Internet that could loosely be called "youth civic culture." (p. 14)

The popular Rock the Vote website is a good example of the Internet interacting with other media to encourage and engage youth (see Figure 8.26). In the State of Arizona, on a website called LawForKids.org, young people can ask questions about anything from child abuse to legal problems such as driving drunk or using drugs (see Figure 8.27). Attorneys within the State of Arizona provide feedback in an attempt to educate children and adolescents about the law, without giving actual advice. This endeavor has now expanded into other states.

Figure 8.26 RockTheVote.com.

Figure 8.27 LawForKids.org.

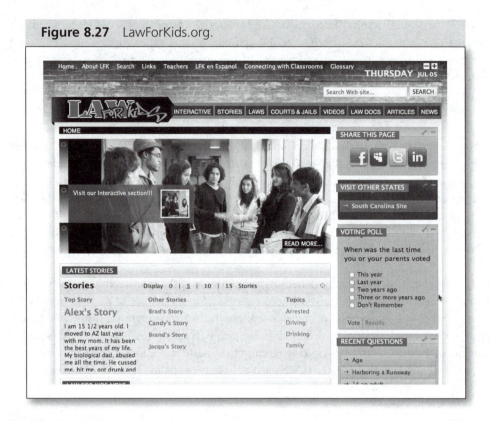

There are websites that foster creativity. For instance, MaMaMedia (see Figure 8.28) allows children to create their own digital stories, make digital drawings that include music and animation, and learn word meanings. There are websites that focus on social issues, and Sesame Workshop offers children an array of educational opportunities, including games and stories.

The Internet can also be an effective learning tool and facilitate academic achievement (Takeuchi & Levine, 2013, in press). Some years ago, Roschelle, Pea, Hoaddley, Gordin, and Means (2000) noted that learning is most effective when four fundamental characteristics are present. The first is active engagement. There is no question that computer-mediated teaching is highly effective in this area, and the Internet allows students to be anything but passive. The constantly interactive nature of the Internet makes it a highly efficient tool for positively engaging students in the learning process.

A second characteristic is learning through group participation. Although on one level, we may think of "surfing the Net" as an individual activity, many group-oriented activities are not only possible but highly engaging on the Internet. Many types of learning networks already developed have been shown to be effective teaching models in the classroom.

A third major characteristic is learning through frequent interaction and feedback. There should be no disagreement that computer-mediated learning is ideal for this form of instruction. The research in this area supports the position that children and adolescents' use of Internet-based activities can facilitate a deeper understanding of concepts and provide stronger motivation to engage in difficult assignments.

Figure 8.28   MaMaMedia.com.

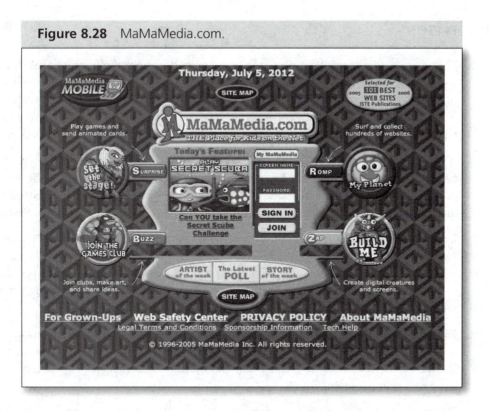

Finally, the Internet provides the ability to learn through connections to real-world contexts. The vast number of Internet websites allows students to explore almost any concept in an interactive multimedia context. Equally important, the Internet provides exposure to ideas and experiences that would normally be inaccessible with more traditional modes of learning.

There is general agreement that considerably more research is needed in all these areas, but the Internet is a technology with a rich array of possibilities. Its potential for positive impacts on learning, social and cognitive development, and the overall future of children and adolescents' lives is just emerging. We need to explore and continue our examination of all these possibilities as more and more children come online and the technology itself changes and expands.

Conclusion

The Internet is without question an innovative and exciting tool for information and education. It has become more accessible worldwide over the years and will only improve in its capacity to stimulate and enrich our lives. We need to understand its potential for increasing our children's educational opportunities while recognizing its limitations and dangers. These dangers, however, will not be easily remedied through traditional solutions such as governmental regulation. This technology necessitates parental involvement and leadership. With such involvement, it is very likely that both children and parents will experience the Internet as a new and enriching environment in which to interact.

Exercises

1. The Internet can be used for a wide array of activities, from the instructional to the entertaining. Consider an activity you normally do for which you have not yet used the Internet, such as taking a trip or buying tickets to a concert. Try doing the same activity with the help of the Internet. Was the process faster? Did you obtain more useful information? Was the Internet a better source for this activity than your normal procedure?

2. If you have blocking software or a service provider that allows you to restrict particular content, try the following: Select a topic that might be controversial, such as drugs or gambling. Perform a search on this topic with and without the blocking activated. Is there a significant difference in the quantity and quality of the information you find?

3. One suggestion for restricting children's access to inappropriate material on the Internet is a rating system similar to that applied to TV content. Could a system of this type be effective with the Internet? Given the global nature of the Internet, would it be possible to define a universal rating system for violence or sex? What might be an appropriate rating system?

4. We indicated in this chapter that the Internet should be used to facilitate learning in the classroom. Design a curriculum for high school students that relies entirely on the Internet. How does it differ from traditional modes of instruction? How might you evaluate its effectiveness?

5. Figures 8.23 and 8.24 provide examples of websites that have educational value for children. What other sites can you find? Why would you consider the sites you find to be particularly beneficial for children?

References

Braun-Courville, D., & Rojas, M. (2009). Exposure to sexually explicit Web sites and adolescent sexual attitudes and behaviors. *Journal of Adolescent Health, 45,* 156–162.

Brown, J. D., & L'Engle, K. L. (2009). X-rated: Sexual attitudes and behaviors associated with U.S. early adolescents' exposure to sexually explicit media. *Communication Research, 36,* 129–135.

Cai, X., & Zhao, X. (2010). Click here, kids! Online advertising practices on popular children's websites. *Journal of Children and Media, 4,* 134–154.

Carlsson, U. (2006). Violence and pornography in the media: Public views on the influence media violence and pornography exert on young people. In U. Carlsson & C. von Feilitzen (Eds.), *In the service of young people? Studies and reflections on media in the digital age.* Goteborg, Sweden: UNESCO.

Carnegie Mellon University. (2012). *Parental control software.* Retrieved from http://www.mysecure cyberspace.com/encyclopedia/index/parental-control-software.html

Common Sense Media. (2011). *Zero to eight: Children's media use in America.* Washington, DC: Author.

Donnerstein, E. (2009). The role of the Internet. In V. Strasburger, B. Wilson, & A. Jordan (Eds.), *Children, adolescents, and the media* (2nd ed.). Thousand Oaks, CA: Sage.

Donnerstein, E. (2011). The media and aggression: From TV to the Internet. In J. Forgas, A. Kruglanski, & K. Williams (Eds.), *The psychology of social conflict and aggression* (pp. 267–284). New York, NY: Psychology Press.

Donnerstein, E. (2012, June). Internet bullying. *Pediatric Clinics of North America, 59*(3), 623–634.

Donnerstein, E. (2013). Children and the Internet. (pp. 373–381). In K. Dill (Ed.), *The Oxford handbook of media psychology.* New York, NY: Oxford University Press.

Donnerstein, E., Slaby, R. G., & Eron, L. D., (1994). The mass media and youth aggression. In L. D. Eron, J. H. Gentry, & P. Schlegel (Eds.), *Reason to hope: A psychosocial perspective on violence and youth* (pp. 219–250). Washington DC: American Psychological Association.

Filtering software better, but still fallible. (2005). *Consumer Reports, 70*(6), 36–38.

Griffiths, M. D. (2010). Addicted to sex? *Psychology Review, 16*(1), 27–29.

Hingle, M., & Kunkel, D. (2012). Childhood obesity and the media. *Pediatric Clinics of North America, 59*(3), 677–692.

The infinite dial 2011: Navigating digital platforms. (n.d.). *Arbitron.* Retrieved from http://www.arbitron.com/study/digital_radio_study.asp

Jones, L. M., Mitchell, K. J., & Finkelhor, D. (2012). Trends in youth Internet victimization: Findings from three Youth Internet Safety Surveys 2000–2010. *Journal of Adolescent Health, 50,* 179–186.

Jordan A. (2010). Children's television viewing and childhood obesity. *Pediatric Annual, 39*(9), 569–573.

Kaiser Family Foundation. (2006). *It's child's play: Advergames and the online marketing of food to children.* Menlo Park, CA: Author.

Kaiser Family Foundation. (2010). *Generation M2: Media in the lives of 8- to 18-year-olds.* Menlo Park, CA: Author.

Kunkel, D., & Castonguay, J. (2012). Children and television advertising: Content, comprehension, and consequences. In D. Singer & J. Singer (Eds.), *Handbook of Children and the Media.* Thousand Oaks, CA: Sage.

Latonero, M. (2011, September). *Human trafficking online: The role of social networking sites and online classifieds.* University of Southern California, Annenberg School for Communication & Journalism, Center on Communication Leadership and Policy. Retrieved from http://technologyandtrafficking.usc.edu/report

Livingstone, S., Ólafsson, K., O'Neill, B., & Donoso, V. (2012). *Towards a better Internet for children: Findings and recommendations from EU Kids Online to inform the CEO coalition.* London, UK: London School of Economics and Political Science.

Malamuth, N., Linz, D., & Yao, M. Z. (2005). The Internet and aggression: Motivation, Disinhibitory and Opportunity aspects. In Y. Amichai-Hamburger (Ed.), *The social net: Human behavior in cyberspace* (pp. 163–191). New York, NY: Oxford University Press.

Mares, M., & Woodard, E. H. (2001). Prosocial effects on children's social interactions. In D. Singer & J. Singer (Eds.), *Handbook of children and the media* (pp. 183–205). Thousand Oaks, CA: Sage.

Mitchell, K., Finkelhor, D., Jones, L., & Wolak, J. (2010). Use of social networking sites in online sex crimes against minors: An examination of national incidence and means of utilization. *Journal of Adolescent Health, 47,* 183–190.

Montgomery, K. C., Chester, J., Grier, S. A., & Dorfman, L. (2012). The new threat of digital marketing. *Pediatric Clinics of North America, 59*(3), 659–676.

Montgomery, K., Gottlieb-Robles, B., & Larson, G. O. (2004). *Youth as e-citizens: Engaging the digital generation.* Retrieved from http://www.centerforsocialmedia.org/ecitizens/youthreport.pdf

Moreno, M. A., & Kolb, J. (2012). Social networking sites and adolescent health. *Pediatric Clinics of North America, 59*(3), 601–612.

Moreno, M. A., & Whitehill, J. M. (2012). New media, old risks: Toward an understanding of the relationships between online and offline health behavior. *Archives of Pediatrics and Adolescent Medicine, 166,* 1–2.

O'Keeffe, G. S. (2012). Overview: New media. *Pediatric Clinics of North America, 59*(3), 589–600.

O'Keeffe, G. S., Clarke-Pearson, K., & Council on Communications and Media. (2011). Clinical report: The impact of social media on children, adolescents, and families. *Pediatrics, 127*(4), 800–804.

Peter, J., & Valkenburg, P. M. (2008). Adolescents' exposure to sexually explicit Internet material, sexual uncertainty, and attitudes toward uncommitted sexual exploration: Is there a link? *Communication Research, 35,* 579–601.

Peter, J., & Valkenburg, P. M. (2009). Adolescents' exposure to sexually explicit Internet material and notions of women as sex objects: Assessing causality and underlying processes. *Journal of Communication, 59,* 407–433.

Pew Foundation. (2010). *The Pew Internet & American Life Project.* Philadelphia, PA: Pew Charitable Trusts.

Potter, J. (2012). *Media literacy.* Thousand Oaks, CA: Sage.

Roschelle, J., Pea, R., Hoaddley, C., Gordin, D., & Means, B. (2000). Changing how and what children learn in school with computer-based technologies. In *The future of children: Children and computer technology* (pp. 145–167). Los Altos, CA: David & Lucile Packard Foundation.

Salazar, L., Fleischauer, P. J., Bernhardt, J. M., & DiClemente, R. (2009). Sexually explicit content viewed by teens on the Internet. In A. Jordan, D. Kunkel, J. Manganello, & M. Fishbein (Eds.), *Media messages and public health: A decision approach to content analysis* (pp. 116–136). New York, NY: Routledge.

Strasburger, V. C., Jordan, A. B., & Donnerstein, E. (2010). Health effects of media on children and adolescents. *Pediatrics, 125,* 756–767.

Strasburger, V. C., Jordan, A. B., & Donnerstein, E. (2012). Children, adolescents, and the media: Health effects. *Pediatric Clinics of North America, 59*(3), 53–588.

Takeuchi, L., & Levine, M. (2013, in press). Learning in a digital age: Toward a new ecology of human development. In A. Jordan & D. Romer (Eds.), *Media and the well-being of children and adolescents.* New York: Oxford University Press.

Teens turn to Internet for prescription drugs. (2006). *NBC News.* Retrieved from http://www.msnbc.msn.com

University of Pennsylvania, Annenberg Public Policy Center. (2010). *Internet gambling grows among male youth ages 18 to 22; gambling also increases in high school age female youth, according to National Annenberg Survey of Youth.* Retrieved from http://www.annenbergpublicpolicycenter.org/newsdetails.aspx?myid=395

Wolak J., Mitchell K. J., & Finkelhor, D. (2007). Unwanted and wanted exposure to online pornography in a national sample of youth Internet users. *Pediatrics, 119,* 247–257.

Wright, P., Malamuth, N., & Donnerstein, E. (2012). Research on sex in the media: What do we know about effects on children and adolescents? In D. Singer & J. Singer (Eds.), *Handbook of children and the media.* Thousand Oaks, CA: Sage.

Ybarra, M. L., West, M. D., Markow, D., Leaf, P. J., Hamburger, M., & Boxer, P. (2008). Linkages between Internet and other media violence with seriously violent behavior by youth. *Pediatrics, 122,* 929–937.

CHAPTER 9

Social Media

Megan Moreno and Rajitha Kota

What is so "social" about social media? In short, social media are interactive media. These media are immensely popular among teens, as evidenced by the nearly ubiquitous use of Facebook and the growing popularity of Twitter. Through the capacity to both view and create content online, social media provide new risks and opportunities for adolescents. This chapter will review what makes social media unique and popular among teens, followed by a discussion of these risks and benefits. Our goal is to provide an understanding of social media as a set of tools, inherently neither good nor bad, whose outcome is determined by how they are used.

What Are Social Media?

The first version of the Internet, known as Web 1.0, allowed content to be viewed by a consumer. A typical Internet user could double-check the high school football team schedule or find the location of a movie theatre. In contrast, Web 2.0 allowed users to both read and write content. An Internet user could now blog a play-by-play of last night's football game or write a review of the movie seen last weekend. Social media represent a set of Web 2.0 tools that are centered on interaction and the sharing of content with others. The idea of interacting and sharing content via media is a remarkable concept in the area of media studies. In traditional media, such as television, a corporation created the content and the viewer consumed this content. Messages were unidirectional, a single arrow pointing from the corporation to the consumer. In the new world of social media, Internet users are both creators and consumers of content. Messages flow in all directions, from corporations to users, among users, and back to corporations through a seemingly endless array of potential paths. Today's adolescents have increased capacity to interact

Figure 9.1 The social media landscape.

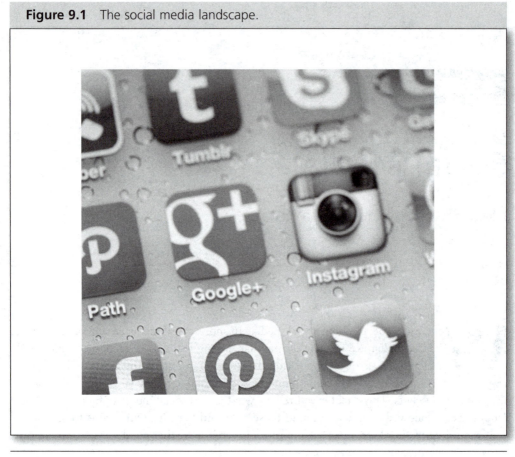

SOURCE: FredCavazza.net.

with one another and the larger world using media, enhanced opportunities to explore and experiment via media, and probably an increased likelihood of being influenced by media. Let us now consider the most popular social media sites used by teens.

Social Media Sites Popular Among Teens

Social media websites (SMWs) include social networking sites (SNSs), such as Facebook (www.facebook.com) and LinkedIn (www.linkedin.com). At present there are several different types of SNSs available, some with a more targeted audience and others aiming for more general appeal. Common SNSs used by adolescents include Facebook and Twitter.

Facebook originated in 2004, created by a Harvard University student, for students of that university to connect and communicate (Ahn, 2011). Since then, it has expanded to its current status, such that anyone over the age of 13 can register and create a profile page. While initially considered a social networking site only for elite college students, Facebook has significantly

Figure 9.2   Social Network Users by Race/Ethnicity

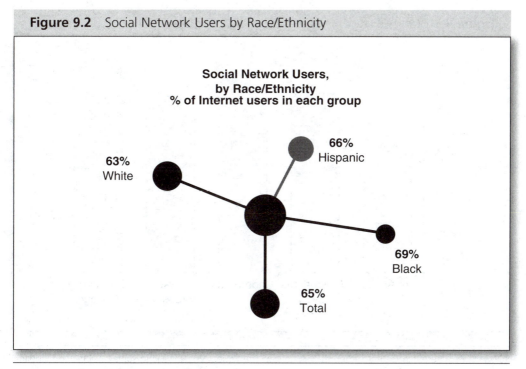

Social Network Users,
by Race/Ethnicity
% of Internet users in each group

66%
Hispanic

63%
White

69%
Black

65%
Total

SOURCE: Graphic by www.eMarketer.com based on data from Madden and Zickuhr (2011).

expanded into a site visited by nearly all ages and ethnicities (see Figure 9.2). Recently, the fastest growing age segment on Facebook was adults (Lenhart, 2009). The mission of Facebook, as posted on its website, is "to give people the power to share and make the world more open and connected" (http://www.facebook.com/facebook/info).

Facebook allows members to create an online profile, communicate with other profile owners, and build an online social network. Creating a profile allows members to display interests and hobbies, upload pictures and videos, and post comments, called status updates, about current events or emotions. Facebook users can also join groups about topics they are interested in, communicate with friends via email or instant messaging, and link their profiles with others in a process referred to as "friending" (Ahn, 2011; Moreno, 2010). Thus, SNSs are an important medium for self-expression, communication with friends, and peer feedback (Moreno, 2010).

Twitter (www.twitter.com) is an SMW in which short text comments, limited to 140 characters and also called microblogs or "tweets," are shared with users, creating an ongoing, continuously updated stream of information. Twitter began in 2006 as a site focusing on microblogging. In addition to generating tweets, Twitter users can "follow" the Twitter posts of other Twitter users. Followers are notified of and given the opportunity to view every tweet generated by the person they are following.

These sites are extremely popular (see Figure 9.3); Facebook recently surpassed Google for total number of daily hits (Childs, 2010). One study reported that 73% of teens between the ages of 12 and 17 owned an SNS profile, while another study found that

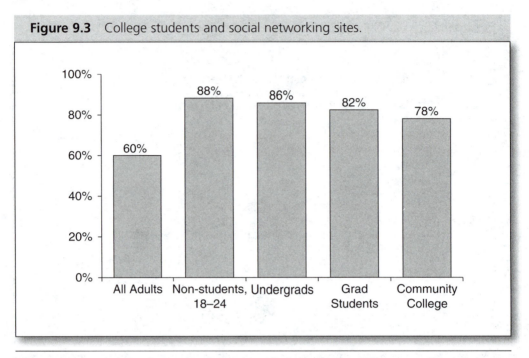

Figure 9.3   College students and social networking sites.

SOURCE: Pew Research Center's Internet & American Life Project 2010 tracking surveys. All include landline and cell phone interviews. N for all adults = 9,769; n for 18- to 24-year-old non-students = 717; n for four-year undergraduates = 246; n for graduate students = 112; n for community college students = 164.

22% of teenagers logged onto their favorite SNS more than 10 times per day (Lenhart & Madden, 2007b; Patchin & Hinduja, 2010). Facebook is used by over 90% of U.S. college students (Ellison, Steinfield, & Lampe, 2007). Even younger children are participating in SNS activities; one study found that 18% of 8- to 10-year-olds used an SNS daily (Rideout, Foehr, & Roberts, 2010).

Twitter's popularity grew more slowly than Facebook's (see Figure 9.4). Twitter was initially popular among young adults, but its popularity has filtered down to the college age group. It is likely that Twitter will continue to grow in popularity among the adolescent age group, particularly given the presence of teen stars such as Justin Bieber. As of December 2012, Twitter was the 10th most popular website in the world ("Top Sites," n.d.). Popular Twitter feeds, such as those created by Lady Gaga, can have as many as 20 million followers (Topping, 2012).

Like any other type of media, social media are not inherently good or bad. The impact of social media is dependent on the type and frequency of their use. Media reports as well as research have highlighted potential benefits and risks for adolescents interacting with social media. Among these concerns is the potential for social media to influence health behaviors. Adolescents are uniquely positioned to be particularly vulnerable to the effects of social media. They are early adopters of new media and highly susceptible to peer influences (Ellison et al., 2007; Lenhart & Madden, 2007a; Lenhart, Madden, & Hitlin, 2005; Lenhart, Purcell, Smith, & Zickuhr, 2010). The vast majority of adolescents go online every day, and many go online more than once a day (Lenhart et al., 2005; Sun et al., 2005).

Figure 9.4 Teen social network and Twitter use—trends over time.

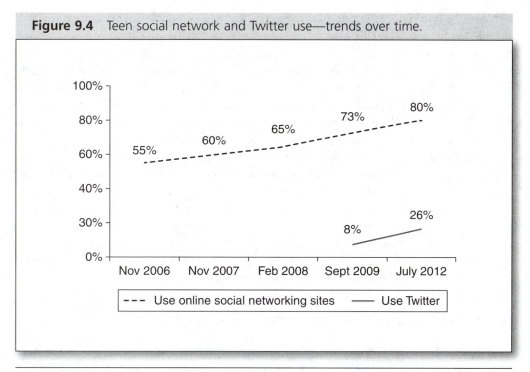

SOURCE: "Twitter Use 2012," Aaron Smith and Joanna Brenner, May 31, 2012. Reprinted with permission from Pew Internet, Pew Research Center. http://www.pewinternet.org/About-Us/Our-Research/Use-Policy .asps.

Risks Associated With Social Media Use

Influence

Previous research has shown strong links between what adolescents observe and how they behave (Bandura, 1986). This can apply to what adolescents observe in media as well as what they observe around them in their lives. The impact of this observation is particularly strong when it involves observing other adolescents, who can influence attitudes, intentions, and behaviors (Wood, Read, Mitchell, & Brand, 2004). For example, adolescents who perceive that their peers are sexually active are more likely to report the intention to become sexually active (Kinsman, Romer, Furstenberg, & Schwarz, 1998).

Another strong source of influence on adolescent attitudes, intentions, and behaviors is the media (Dalton et al., 2009; Dalton et al., 2003; Gidwani, Sobol, DeJong, Perrin, & Gortmaker, 2002; Titus-Ernstoff, Dalton, Adachi-Mejia, Longacre, & Beach, 2008). Many research studies conducted over the decades have consistently shown that exposure to risky behaviors (e.g., alcohol or tobacco use, sexual behaviors) through traditional media is associated with initiation of these behaviors (Dalton et al., 2009; Gidwani et al., 2002; Robinson, Chen, & Killen, 1998; Wichers et al., 2010). It is clear that adolescents can learn these behaviors through media and be influenced to try them themselves.

Given the influence of both peers and traditional media on adolescent behavior, it is worth considering how social media may influence teens. Social media are a form of media created by adolescents, and thus they combine both peer and media effects. Through a single website such as Facebook, millions of adolescents are now linked to millions of other adolescents online. Each of these ties represents a potential path of influence. Social media have been described as bringing together the power of interpersonal persuasion with the reach of mass media. Professor B. J. Fogg described "mass interpersonal persuasion" as "the most significant advance in persuasion since radio was invented in the 1890s" (Fogg, 2008).

Social media's potential influence on adolescent attitudes and behaviors is only beginning to be explored through research. In one study, adolescents who viewed alcohol references on their peers' Facebook profiles found them to be believable and influential sources of information (Moreno, Briner, Williams, Walker, & Christakis, 2009). Another study found that adolescents who perceived alcohol use to be normative based on others' Facebook profiles were more likely to report an interest in initiating alcohol use (Litt & Stock, 2011). Studies are beginning to illustrate social media as a widespread, available, and consistently accessed source of media for today's adolescents and young adults.

Displays of Health-Risk Behaviors on Social Media

The extensive and powerful influence that social media can exert leads to the question of which behaviors are being promoted via social media. Social media displays include photographs and text created and displayed by peers and viewed by peers. Are these social media displays typically health promoting, discussing fitness or adequate sleep? Or do they promote health-risk behaviors? Health-risk behaviors include any behaviors linked to morbidity and mortality among adolescents, such as substance use or risky sexual behavior. Several studies have illustrated that adolescents' displays on SNSs like MySpace and Facebook frequently include health-risk behaviors, such as alcohol use (see Table 9.1), substance use, or sexual behaviors (Aboujaoude, Koran, Gamel, Large, & Serpe, 2006; McGee & Begg, 2008; Moreno, Parks, & Richardson, 2007; Moreno, Parks, Zimmerman, Brito, & Christakis, 2009). It is interesting to note that these health-risk behaviors are commonly displayed in patterns consistent with studies of offline behavior, such as survey research. For example, adolescents who display references to religious commitment are less likely to display references to sexual behavior (Gannon & Moreno, 2013, in press). Additionally, an adolescent who displays one health-risk behavior, such as sexual activity, is more likely to display other such behaviors, such as alcohol or drug use (Moreno, Parks, et al., 2009). This suggests that patterns of adolescent behavior that have been researched and understood in offline life for decades are now being displayed publicly online by adolescents themselves.

The display of health-risk behaviors by a single adolescent can provide insight into that adolescent, but social media can tell us more. Social networking sites provide a visual depiction of an adolescent's social network, as well as the ability to understand how attitudes or behaviors are present or absent within particular peer groups. A 2010 study found that adolescents were more likely to display references to sexual behavior if a peer displayed similar references (Dunton, Liao, Intille, Spruijt-Metz, & Pentz, 2010). Research in this area is only beginning, but it is clear that social networking sites may provide a new lens through which we can better see how particular risk behaviors diffuse within and beyond peer groups.

Table 9.1 Categories and examples of alcohol use references.

N = 341 references to alcohol use from 400 adolescents' MySpace profiles

Explicit versus figurative use categories were applied to alcohol references without personal context provided, references with personal context provided were evaluated using SLT or CRAFFT criteria.

Category	Explanation	Examples
Explicit versus figurative use:		
Explicit Use N = 168 (49.3%)	Explicit text statements or photographs depicting profile owner drinking alcohol	*"I love drinking beer"*
Explicit Intoxication N = 58 (17%)	Explicit text statements referring to profile owner being intoxicated	*"I was so loaded on Friday"*
Figurative N = 39 (11.4%)	Statements that reference alcohol use but not use by the profile owner	*"Beer: breakfast of champions!"*
Social Learning Theory:		
Motivations:		
Peer pressure N = 16 (4.7%)	References to peer pressure as a reason to drink or use of peer pressure to motivate others to drink	*"I like to get drunk, if you like vodka then you are my friend"*
Associations:		
Sex N = 3 (0.9%)	References to alcohol use in association with sex	*"Beer and a cock, what more could you ask for?"*
Games N = 14 (4.1%)	Drinking games included beer pong, keg stands, and other drinking-related games and activities	*"Beer pong rematch this weekend!"*
Dancing/partying N = 75 (22%)	References to dancing or being at a party in association with alcohol use	*"My hobbies include drinking and partying"*
Consequences:		
Positive emotional consequences N = 2 (0.6%)	References that highlight positive mood, feeling, or emotion associated with alcohol use	*"A glass of wine and I'm just fine"*
Category	Explanation	Examples
Negative emotional consequences N = 2 (0.6%)	References that highlight negative mood, feeling, or emotion associated with alcohol use	*"I don't like the person I am when I'm drunk"*

(Continued)

Table 9.1 (Continued)

Positive Social consequences N = 6 (1.8%)	References that highlight perceived social gain associated with alcohol use	*"When I'm drunk I'm very outgoing"*
Negative social consequences N = 3 (0.9%)	References that highlight perceived poor social outcomes associated with alcohol use	*"I'm embarrassed that I drank Bailey's out of a shoe"*
Negative physical consequences N = 7 (2.1%)	References that describe adverse physical consequences or outcomes associated with alcohol use	*"I'm exhausted and hung over"*
CRAFFT:		
Problem drinking N = 11 (3.2%)	Text references that met the CRAFFT problem drinking criteria	*"Blacked out drunk at 7a.m."*

SOURCE: Moreno and colleagues (2010).

While health-risk behaviors are commonly displayed on SNSs, displays of the negative consequences of these behaviors are uncommonly noted. One study found that displays of negative consequences of alcohol use, such as hangovers or embarrassment, were rare (McGee & Begg, 2008). This is important because adolescents are more likely to mimic risky behaviors if they do not perceive that they have consequences. For example, seeing a peer skateboard down a steep hill without harm may lead another teen to try this stunt. While the complete picture is not yet known, it is reasonable to hypothesize that risky information that adolescents choose to display on social media may influence peers' attitudes and behaviors. These displays are prevalent, peer generated, and thus likely persuasive.

The displaying of health-risk or risqué behaviors may also have impact on an adolescent's future. Studies have shown numerous ways in which social media content can have negative impact. Such content may offend or confuse potential employers, college admissions personnel, adult role models, or romantic partners (Livingstone, 2008; Luscombe, 2010; Muise, Christofides, & Desmarais, 2009) (see Figure 9.5). While teens may post this information intending it for their friends, they may not realize that their audience of "friends" is over 1,000 people linked to their Facebook profile. An adolescent may not realize that the Facebook privacy settings have recently been reconfigured and that the content that was once digitally protected is now open to a global audience. Their every tweet is recorded and stored in the Library of Congress. Social media are social, and this often means that the concept of privacy in regard to what an adolescent displays is a constantly shifting illusion.

Cyberbullying

Bullying is a serious problem that has the potential to cause both mental distress and psychological harm to victims. The Internet and social media have provided new venues through which children and young adults can hurt their peers. This phenomenon has come to be

Figure 9.5

Signs of the social networking times.

known as cyberbullying, defined by Smith and his colleagues (2008) as "an aggressive, intentional act or behavior that is carried out by a group or an individual, using electronic forms of contact, repeatedly and over time against a victim who cannot easily defend him or herself" (p. 376). These electronic forms of contact seem to present endless opportunities, as they include social media websites such as Facebook and Twitter in addition to text messaging, email, blogs, online gaming, chat rooms, forums, instant messaging, video messaging, and picture messaging. Many people conceptualize cyberbullying as a particular entity or behavior. However, examples of online harassment include aggressive behavior, insults, denigration, impersonation, exclusion, outing others' sexual preferences, hacking, stealing information, breaking into accounts, and creating damaging websites or profiles to defame another person (Willard, 2006). Not all adolescents are aware of the scope of the definition of cyberbullying. If you ask an adolescent if he has ever been "cyberbullied," he may reply that he has not. But if you clarify by asking if he has ever had anyone hack into his Facebook account or impersonate him online, he may remember several such incidents.

Cyberbullying can be just as harmful, if not more harmful, than traditional "schoolyard" bullying (see Table 9.2). Traditional bullying occurs face-to-face, and there is often a physical component to the harassment. In contrast, online bullying offers perpetrators the advantage of anonymity. This can cause the perpetrator to act without regard for consequences, as well as reduce accountability and guilt for his or her behavior (Li, 2007). For victims, not knowing who their perpetrator is can lead to increased anxiety, especially if they fear encountering this person in their offline life (Shariff & Gouin, 2006).

Traditional bullying generally occurs at a specific time and place, such as on the playground during recess. In contrast, cyberbullying can occur anywhere and can potentially take place

Table 9.2 Cyberbullying versus traditional bullying.

Description	Cyberbullying	Bullying
General Characteristics		
Face-to-face, with a physical component		X
Can happen 24/7, anywhere	X	
Can rapidly, widely, and easily spread embarrassing info	X	
Repetitive, aggressive acts or behaviors	X	X
No direct feedback from victim	X	
Bully Characteristics		
Bully acts without regard for consequences	X	X
Bully feels less guilty because he or she does not have to face victim	X	
Bully can be anonymous	X	
Bully does not fear punishment	X	
Effects on Victim		
Harmful psychological effects	X	X
Anxiety and fear of encountering bully in "real life"	X	
Higher levels of depression and low self-esteem	X	X
Fewer friends and trouble adjusting socially	X	
Enforcement		
Hard to track down perpetrator	X	
Enforcement can be difficult (due to free speech rights)	X	

24 hours a day. Victims can therefore feel constantly harassed. Even if they remain offline, increased anxiety can occur if the victim continually worries about what is being posted without his or her knowledge. In addition, the nature of the Internet as a communication tool makes it easy to rapidly and widely spread embarrassing information (Raskauskas & Stolz, 2007).

Similar to offline bullying, cyberbullying can have substantial psychological effects on victims. Children and adolescents who are victims of cyberbullying often have higher levels of depression and lower self-esteem (Ybarra, Espelage, & Mitchell, 2007). Victims consistently report academic problems, such as falling grades and lower attendance, which is likely a result of the victim's preoccupation with the bully and the situation (Beran & Li, 2007). Problems such as emotional distress, anger, sadness, detachment, externalized hostility, and delinquency are also common among victims (Patchin & Hinduja, 2006). In addition, victims are less likely to be prosocial and are more likely to internalize their problems, which can prevent them from making friends and adjusting socially (Arseneault et al., 2006). Many of these effects have also been seen in victims of traditional bullying, supporting the idea that cyberbullying represents a serious problem.

A survey by the Pew Research Center found that 32% of adolescents reported having experienced some form of online harassment (Lenhart, 2007). Of these teens, girls ages 15 to 17 were most likely to have experienced cyberbullying, with 41% reporting having been harassed. Boys ages 12 to14 years were least likely to be victims, with 22% reporting that they had been the targets of online harassment. A study by Hinduja and Patchin (2009) found that 11% of respondents identified themselves as cyberbullies, while almost half of those surveyed reported having witnessed these behaviors online. The varied prevalence rates may be explained by definitions of cyberbullying that differ among studies. Despite this variation in prevalence, these numbers indicate that a sizable minority of students are involved in cyberbullying in some way, whether as bullies or as victims.

Since cyberbullying occurs online, it is often difficult if not impossible to restrict cyberbullying behaviors. Parents cannot constantly supervise their children, nor do they have knowledge about everything their children encounter online. For this reason, cyberbullies often do not fear punishment (Kowalski & Limber, 2007). Parents are not usually as technologically proficient as their children and are often unaware of how to regulate or monitor their child's Internet use (Ybarra et al., 2007). Free speech rights also make it difficult to remove offensive postings or websites made by cyberbullies. If the cyberbullying occurs anonymously, it can be nearly impossible to track down the perpetrator (Li, 2007).

School efforts to combat cyberbullying have been lukewarm at best. School administrators are often fearful of becoming involved in cyberbullying incidents for fear of legal repercussions surrounding First Amendment rights, especially because many instances of cyberbullying occur at home and after school hours. In addition, if school officials are unaware of the potential negative effects of cyberbullying, they may not view it as a problem that deserves immediate attention (Hinduja & Patchin, 2009). Hinduja and Patchin state that behavior or speech can be restricted if it "substantially or materially disrupts learning; interferes with the educational process or school discipline; utilizes school-owned technology to harass; or threatens other students or infringes on their civil rights" (p. 116). At the legislative level, cyberbullying is not explicitly included in criminal laws, which provide the guidelines for law enforcement responsibilities. However, 47 states have enacted laws that address electronic forms of harassment (National Conference of State Legislatures, 2012).

Sexting

The term *sexting* refers to sending, receiving, or forwarding sexually explicit messages or pictures. These messages can be sent over a cell phone via texting, or over the Internet via email or a social networking site. One 2011 survey found that 20% of teens had sent or posted nude or seminude photos or videos of themselves (National Campaign to Prevent Teen Pregnancy, 2008). Sexting does not typically represent a random or anonymous event; rather, it usually takes place in the context of existing offline relationships. A 2011 study found that in most cases of sexting, the sexual photos were intended to be viewed only by a romantic partner, such as a boyfriend or girlfriend (Dowdell, Burgess, & Flores, 2011). Two recent studies have deepened our understanding of sexting as more common than previously thought. In one study of high school students, 17% of females and 18% of males had sent a sext, and 31% of females and 50% of males had received one (Strassberg, McKinnon, Sustaita, & Rullo, 2012). A second 2012 study focusing on high school students found that 28% of teens had sent a sext, and 31% had asked someone else for a sext (Temple, Paul, van den Berg, McElhany, & Temple, 2012). This study was the first to note that sexting was associated with an increased likelihood of having engaged in sexual behavior.

Why would a teen want to engage in sexting? Social media are a form of identity exploration, and part of adolescence is developing a sexual identity. Adolescents may use sexting as a way to explore the boundaries of their own sexual identities, and doing this through media may give an illusion of safety or anonymity. This feeling of anonymity may be just enough to get a teen to do something through the Internet that he or she might not be ready to do in front of another person.

One controversy in the area of sexting is how it should be addressed at the school or legal level. Sending a nude or seminude photo of an underage person can be considered distribution of child pornography. If this occurs across state lines—for example, if one teen goes to school in Washington, DC, and sends a seminude photo as a sext to a teen in Baltimore, Maryland—this becomes distribution of child pornography across state lines, a federal felony. It is reasonable to suspect that most law enforcement officials would prefer to spend their time chasing adult sexual predators rather than teens who sext, but the laws remain unclear on how these cases should be handled. News reports have highlighted stories about adolescents who have been charged with felony child pornography or juvenile-law misdemeanors as a result of sexting messages that reached beyond the intended audience (O'Keeffe & Clarke-Pearson, 2011). Other consequences of sexting include emotional distress and school suspensions. (Sexting is covered in additional detail in Chapter 5, but here we place it in the context of the social media landscape.)

Online Solicitation

Given the anonymity of the Internet and the ease with which identity can be disguised on social media (see Figure 9.6), concerns have been raised about online solicitation of children using SNSs. One study assessed the online patterns of sexual offenders (both Internet and non-Internet offenders) from 2008 to 2009 and found that nearly three-quarters of past offenders were unwilling to answer questions about their use of SNSs (Dowdell et al., 2011). Past offenders who did admit to using SNSs named MySpace as the site they most commonly visited. Over half of the Internet offenders admitted to disguising their identity while on the Internet, and 63.3% reported that they initiated conversations about sexual activity during their first contact with a stranger online (Dowdell et al., 2011).

Although a previous study had demonstrated that youth were less likely to be solicited on an SNS than in a chat room, the danger is still

Figure 9.6

"On Facebook, 273 people know I'm a dog. The rest can only see my limited profile."

SOURCE: Cartoon by Rob Cottingham (RobCottingham.com).

present and measurable (see Ahn, 2011). A national survey of 10- to 15-year-olds who had used the Internet within the past half year found that 15% had experienced an unwanted sexual solicitation while online (Ybarra et al., 2007). However, despite concerns about adults soliciting adolescents for sexual activities, most recent studies have found that sexual solicitation most often occurs between two teenagers. Concerns that the anonymity of the Internet would give rise to an outbreak of adults preying on unknowing adolescents have not been borne out by the research. Rather, social media appear to provide new opportunities for adolescents to experiment with their identities, sometimes in ways that are harmful to themselves and others.

Benefits of Social Media

The Internet and social media can be beneficial for many reasons. Users can communicate with family and friends, create rewarding social connections, and even obtain information about academics, news, and other events. While many problems are associated with social media use, the fact remains that there are significant benefits of this emerging form of communication.

New Opportunities for Education and Prevention

Social media may present new opportunities for parents and pediatricians to discuss complex and challenging topics with their adolescents, such as sex, alcohol, and depression. Previous work has illustrated that references to health-risk behaviors, such as sexual behavior, alcohol consumption, and tobacco use, are commonly displayed by adolescents on social media (Moreno et al., 2010; Primack et al., 2011).

Preliminary evidence suggests that displays of sexual material on Facebook are associated with the reported intention to become sexually active (Connell, 2009). Adolescents who have engaged in sexting behaviors have been found to be more likely to report that they have begun dating and have engaged in sexual activity compared to those who have not sexted (Temple et al., 2012). In this 2012 study, sexting was also associated with risky sexual behaviors, but only among girls. Given these research findings, if parents notice sexual references on their adolescent's social media profile or displayed on his or her peers' profiles, they can take this as an opportunity to start a discussion. Such references may represent an interest in sexual behavior or an intention to become sexually active. If a parent finds a sext on a teen's cell phone, this represents an opportunity to discuss sexual identity and how to represent oneself using social media, as well as a chance to have "the talk" about sex overall. Using social media clues, parents may have a unique window in which to discuss sexual decision making or safe sex practices with their children prior to sexual initiation. Framing the discussion around a media representation of sex can pave the path to what can be a difficult conversation to initiate.

Other evidence suggests that displayed references to alcohol use on Facebook profiles are associated with alcohol use in real life. And it turns out that, just as discussions of alcohol use with teens in the clinical setting carry a different impact than some other kinds of talk regarding alcohol consumption, the context and content of the discussion matter. A 2011 study evaluated displays of alcohol use on the Facebook profiles of underage college students and found that Facebook displays that described problem drinking, such as driving while drinking or blacking out, were associated with higher scores on a problem drinking evaluation

(Moreno, Christakis, Egan, Brockman, & Becker, 2011). In comparison, displays of alcohol use on Facebook that did not include descriptions of intoxication or problem alcohol use were less likely to be associated with high scores on the problem drinking evaluation. Consider the teen who tells you in clinic that he had a beer at a party once: This patient is unlikely to trigger a flurry of referrals for alcohol abuse. Similarly, the Facebook display describing the "wine and book club night with the girls" is less worrisome than the "can't remember how I got home last night" status update. Physicians and parents can use common sense when reading adolescents' status updates that contain references to alcohol use, and consider both context and content. A concerning display about alcohol use should prompt a follow-up conversation. A 2012 study illustrated that older adolescents are open to discussing social media content with trusted adults, and that their preferred approach would be for the adult to "ask questions" rather than "make accusations" (Moreno, Grant, Kacvinsky, Egan, & Fleming, 2012).

Finally, one of the more prevalent and concerning illnesses among adolescents is depression. This problem is difficult to recognize and diagnose, and it is challenging for depressed adolescents to find ways to seek help (Eisenberg, Downs, Golberstein, & Zivin, 2009). Thus, it may be surprising that social media are places in which disclosures of depression symptoms are often displayed. A 2011 study found that approximately one-quarter of older adolescents displayed depression symptoms consistent with DSM-IV (*Diagnostic and Statistical Manual of Mental Disorders*, fourth edition [American Psychiatric Association, 2000]) criteria on their Facebook pages (Moreno, Jelenchick, et al., 2011). If you consider the date and time stamp on each of these disclosures, 2.5% of the profile met DSM-IV criteria for a current major depressive episode. Further, these comments were often noted and responded to by peers using the social media site. In this way, peers used social media to respond to these disclosures and provide support or encouragement (see Table 9.3). Social media may present new ways for peers to provide such support to friends when depression symptoms are present.

The follow-up study found that these displayed depression symptoms were associated with an increased likelihood of reporting depression symptoms during a clinical screening (Moreno, Christakis, Egan, Jelenchick, et al., 2011). These results are promising, although it is important to recognize that we do not advocate diagnosing depression formally using Facebook. A diagnosis of depression is based on symptom patterns over time and is best diagnosed in the clinical setting. However, social media may provide a new lens through which signs of depression can be recognized earlier and lead to improved treatment and outcomes.

The Media Practice Model identifies key factors in adolescents' use of media and hypothesizes that adolescents select and interact with media based on who they are—or who they want to be—at the moment. Thus, the model posits that behaviors and disclosures made through media reflect actual behaviors and traits, or behavioral intent (Brown, 2000). Indeed, sexting appears to be a media expression of adolescent sexual intent or behavior rather than a distinct phenomenon limited to the digital world. While further work is needed to understand how this knowledge can be translated into clinical practice or educational interventions, parents and physicians can use these social media displays to prompt important conversations.

Connection and Social Capital

Participation in social media offers individuals a form of social capital, which is an important feature of healthy, effective societies (Putnam & Goss, 2002). Social capital consists of

Table 9.3	Examples of Depression Symptom Displays and Comments; Responses From Online Peers

Example 1: 18-year-old female	
Status update	*"Feeling so bad today, like nothing is going to get better!"*
Responses from peers	*"Hang in there baby!"* *"It will get better, I promise"* *"Want to get coffee tomorrow?"*

Example 2: 19-year-old male	
Status update	*"Like a knife to my heart, like a bullet to the chest. . . . can't stop crying"*
Responses from peers	*"I'm coming over and I'm bringing the X box"* *"Are you ok?"*

Example 2: 20-year-old female	
Status update	*"Feel like I can't do anything right these days, sad and frustrated, blech."*
Responses from peers	*"But we love you!"* *"Yes, you are great!"* *"I agree"* *"Want us to take you out tonight?"*

SOURCE: Moreno, Jelenchick, and colleagues (2011).

the resources available to people through their social interactions, and researchers have postulated that individuals with greater social capital have large, diverse social networks, whereas people with smaller, less diverse networks have less social capital (Valenzuela, Park, & Kee, 2009) (see Figure 9.7).

Increasingly, these social networks have come to include online interactions—individuals consciously choose to invest in their social capital by engaging in social media and social networking websites. Internet communications, particularly through social media, are unique in that they combine aspects of mass media with interpersonal communication in order to build relationships between groups of individuals without a physical connection (Pasek, More, & Romer, 2009).

The term *social capital* has been used in many different ways and has a wide range of definitions. All of these definitions are based on the idea that social networks have value and that individuals can derive benefit from their interactions and relationships with others (Ahn, 2011). Given that SNSs allow individuals to create much larger social networks than they could offline, it seems logical that using an SNS could help adolescents build social capital. One 2007 study found that increased Facebook use was positively correlated with bridging and bonding in college students (see Ahn, 2011).

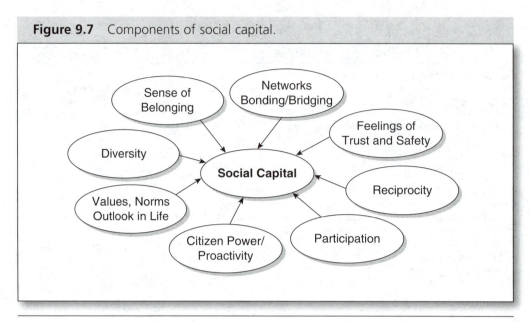

Figure 9.7 Components of social capital.

SOURCE: Boeck, Fleming, and Kemshall (2006).

There are several hypothesized ways in which online social networks could benefit adolescents. For instance, SNSs allow adolescents to access health information that they might be too uncomfortable to ask their pediatrician about, such as sexual health information. Further, they allow adolescents with chronic diseases to join online support groups to help them deal with new diagnoses or share stories with others who understand their situation in life (O'Keeffe & Clarke-Pearson, 2011). Additionally, SNSs give adolescents the benefit of being able to start and maintain relationships despite physical distance (Jent et al., 2011). This may be particularly salient for adolescents who move frequently or have family members who live abroad.

Civic and Political Engagement

Adolescents are increasingly using the Internet and social media to obtain information. According to a 2009 survey by the Pew Research Center, 62% of teens use the Internet to get information about current events and politics online (Lenhart et al., 2010). Many campaigns and organizations have used social media as a platform for fostering civic and political engagement among users, particularly adolescents and young adults. In a recent article on this subject, Valenzuela and his colleagues (2009) noted that "investment in social networks enables individuals to develop norms of trust and reciprocity, which are necessary for successful engagement in collective activities" (p. 877).

Some organizations have developed social networking aspects within their own websites to develop online communities through which users can learn about issues that are important to them and consequently participate in offline activities related to a certain cause. For example, TakingITGlobal is an organization that provides youth worldwide with an online community to facilitate education, social entrepreneurship, and civic engagement.

On this website (www.tigweb.org), users can find other individuals—locally or globally—who are interested in similar political and civic issues and with whom they can converse, develop projects, or promote events, campaigns, and causes ("About TIG," 2012). Another use of the social networking platform occurred during the 2008 presidential election, when the Obama campaign created the website my.barackobama.com to enlist volunteers to engage in campaign activities.

Other campaigns and causes have used existing social networking sites for promotion and engagement. For example, the human rights activism organization Amnesty International relies on Facebook to share news, promote events, facilitate discussion among followers, and even to organize major protests (Stirland, 2007). In terms of global impact, Facebook has been credited for contributing to the political revolution in Egypt in 2011. This social networking site was used to channel public sentiment, organize protests, and rapidly share information (Sutter, 2011).

Academic Work

Social media and social networking sites offer students collaborative environments in which they can interact with other students or teachers to enhance traditional classroom-based learning. The ubiquity of social media and social networking sites cannot be under-stated. A 2010 survey by the Kaiser Family Foundation found that 74% of all 7th to 12th graders had at least one profile on a social networking site, while another study found that 98% of college students had a Facebook profile (Egan & Moreno, 2011; Rideout et al., 2010). Using social media for educational purposes may offer schools a way to incorporate learning into a medium that students are familiar with and are already using (Strasburger, 2012).

Websites such as Edmodo, Wiggio, and Edublogs can be used in schools to facilitate learning and connect students to their peers and their teachers. For example, Edmodo (www .edmodo.com) is a microblogging platform set up similarly to Facebook ("Features," n.d.). It is safe and easy to use, in that students are not required to set up an account with their email address. Students can upload pictures and videos, take quizzes, create calendars, and share information with others. Teachers can send reminders, monitor their students' work, and even send text messages to students.

Some educators also believe that allowing and encouraging their students to post their school-work on social media websites provides them with motivation to perform higher-quality work, since their assignments and projects are shared with a broad audience. By using social media websites, students can collaborate on projects and receive feedback on their work from teachers and other students. Parents also have the opportunity to see their child's work and get a better sense of what is happening in the classroom (McMullen, 2012). A 2011 study by Pollara and Zhu examined the use of Facebook in a high school and university science-mentoring project to determine if the implementation of social networking would improve mentor-mentee relationships and increase student participation and dialogue. The researchers found that students and mentors who interacted regularly had a stronger relationship than those who did not. Students who were surveyed about their experience stated that they believed they had learned more by using the social media page, that it was helpful for achieving their project goals, and that they would like to use Facebook in the future for educational purposes (Pollara & Zhu, 2011).

An interesting application of the video chatting site Skype was implemented at Marquette University to connect Spanish language students in the United States with English-learning counterparts in South America. Students were able to receive weekly one-on-one tutoring with a native language speaker. College students have also been noted to use Facebook to reflect on the university experience and exchange practical and academic information, indicating that educators have the potential to share information on this platform (Selwyn, 2009). In addition to academic applications, educational institutions are using social media to communicate with students. For example, Twitter is used by many universities to relay important announcements to students (Silverman, 2012).

Conclusion

Throughout this chapter we have explored what makes social media "social," and which social media sites are currently most popular among adolescents. We fully expect that the popularity of these sites will change over time, and that new ones will arise. However, the driving forces of social media—interaction, connection, social capital—are likely to stand the test of time and be present in any popular social media site of the future. Thus, the inherent risks and opportunities presented by social media are likely to evolve over time but remain fundamentally constant.

Research in this area is still in its nascent stages, and much work remains to be done. Future research should explore how to translate what we have learned about social media and how adolescents use them into prevention messages and health education. Social media provide new opportunities to target health messages to groups at risk. Social media messages can also be distributed quickly and cheaply, resulting in an effective intervention that is easily scalable to the population level.

Research is needed on how to prevent the negative risks associated with social media, such as cyberbullying. On the positive side, future research can give us a better understanding of how to expand the "naturalistic" experiments that are already taking place on Facebook, such as peers providing support when depression symptoms are disclosed. There is much to be learned, but this new knowledge rests on a foundation of research around traditional media, adolescent behavior, and communication science. In many ways, social media provide us with a new lens through which we can view the ancient phenomenon of adolescent behavior.

Exercises

1. Should social media be monitored? If so, what group would be the best candidate to do so: law enforcement, health professionals, or school officials? For what ages would it be appropriate to monitor media behaviors?

2. Many adolescents feel constantly connected to media through smartphones and tablet computers. Is it possible for college students to take breaks from social media without compromising their educational and social experiences?

3. How do you feel when you are not online? Do you feel as if you are missing out on an important part of your social life?

4. Consider some ideas and strategies for providing education about the risks and benefits of media use to the next generation of adolescents.

References

Aboujaoude, E., Koran, L. M., Gamel, N., Large, M. D., & Serpe, R. T. (2006). Potential markers for problematic Internet use: A telephone survey of 2,513 adults. *CNS Spectrums, 11*(10), 750–755.

About TIG. (n.d.). Retrieved May 14, 2012, from http://www.tigweb.org/about/.

Ahn, J. (2011). The effect of social network sites on adolescents' social and academic development: Current theories and controversies. *Journal of the American Society for Information Science and Technology, 62*(8), 1435–1445. doi: 10.1002/asi.21540

American Psychological Association. (2000). *Diagnostic and statistical manual of mental disorders* (4th ed.). Washington, DC: Author.

Arseneault, L., Walsh, E., Trzesniewski, K., Newcombe, R., Caspi, A., & Moffitt, T. E. (2006). Bullying victimization uniquely contributes to adjustment problems in young children: A nationally representative cohort study. *Pediatrics, 118,* 130–138.

Bandura, A. (1986). *Social foundations of thought and action: A social cognitive theory.* Englewood Cliffs, NJ: Prentice Hall.

Beran, T., & Li, Q. (2007). The relationship between cyberbullying and school bullying. *Journal of Student Wellbeing, 1,* 15–33.

Boeck, T., Fleming, J., & Kemshall, H. (2006). The context of risk decisions: Does social capital make a difference? *Forum: Qualitative Social Research, 7*(17). Retrieved from http://www.qualitative-research.net/index.php/fqs/article/view/55

Brown, J. D. (2000). Adolescents' sexual media diets. *Journal of Adolescent Health, 27*(2, Suppl.), 35–40.

Childs, M. (2010). Facebook surpasses Google in weekly US hits for first time. *Business week.* Retrieved from http://www.businessweek.com/news/2010-03-17/facebook-surpasses-google-in-weekly-u-s-hits-for-first-time.html

Connell, R. S. (2009). Academic libraries, Facebook and MySpace, and student outreach: A survey of student opinion. *Portal: Libraries and the Academy, 9*(1), 25–36.

Dalton, M. A., Beach, M. L., Adachi-Mejia, A. M., Longacre, M. R., Matzkin, A. L., Sargent, J. D., . . . Titus-Ernstoff, L. (2009). Early exposure to movie smoking predicts established smoking by older teens and young adults. *Pediatrics, 123*(4), e551–558. doi: 10.1542/peds.2008-2102

Dalton, M. A., Sargent, J. D., Beach, M. L., Titus-Ernstoff, L., Gibson, J. J., Ahrens, M. B., . . . Heatherton, T. F. (2003). Effect of viewing smoking in movies on adolescent smoking initiation: A cohort study. *Lancet, 362*(9380), 281–285. doi: 10.1016/S0140-6736(03)13970-0

Dowdell, E. B., Burgess, A. W., & Flores, J. R. (2011). Online social networking patterns among adolescents, young adults, and sexual offenders. *American Journal of Nursing, 111*(7), 28–36. doi: 10.1097/01.naj.0000399310.83160.73

Dunton, G. F., Liao, Y., Intille, S. S., Spruijt-Metz, D., & Pentz, M. (2010). Investigating children's physical activity and sedentary behavior using ecological momentary assessment with mobile phones. *Obesity.* doi: 10.1038/oby.2010.302

Egan, K. G., & Moreno, M. A. (2011). Alcohol references on undergraduate males' Facebook profiles. *American Journal of Men's Health.* doi: 10.1177/1557988310394341

Eisenberg, D., Downs, M. F., Golberstein, E., & Zivin, K. (2009). Stigma and help seeking for mental health among college students. *Medical Care Research and Review, 66*(5), 522–541. doi: 10.1177/1077558709335173

Ellison, N. B., Steinfield, C., & Lampe, C. (2007). The benefits of Facebook "friends:" Social capitol and college students' use of online social network sites. *Journal of Computer-Mediated Communication, 12,* 1143–1168.

Features. (n.d.). Retrieved December 2, 2012, from http://www.edmodo.com/features

Fogg, B. J. (2008). *Mass interpersonal persuasion: An early view of a new phenomenon.* Paper presented at the Third International Conference on Persuasive Technology, Oulu, Finland.

Gannon, K. E., & Moreno, M. A. (2013, in press). Religion and sex among college freshmen: A longitudinal study using Facebook.

Gidwani, P. P., Sobol, A., DeJong, W., Perrin, J. M., & Gortmaker, S. L. (2002). Television viewing and initiation of smoking among youth. *Pediatrics, 110*(3), 505–508.

Hinduja, S., & Patchin, J. W. (2009). *Bullying beyond the schoolyard: Preventing and responding to cyberbullying.* Thousand Oaks, CA: Corwin.

Jent, J. F., Eaton, C. K., Merrick, M. T., Englebert, N. E., Dandes, S. K., Chapman, A. V., & Hershorin, E. R. (2011). The decision to access patient information from a social media Site: What would you do? *Journal of Adolescent Health, 49*(4), 414–420. doi: 10.1016/j.jadohealth.2011.02.004

Kinsman, S. B., Romer, D., Furstenberg, F. F., & Schwarz, D. F. (1998). Early sexual initiation: The role of peer norms. *Pediatrics, 102*(5), 1185–1192.

Kowalski, R. M., & Limber, S. P. (2007). Electronic bullying among middle school students. *Journal of Adolescent Health, 41*(6, Suppl. 1), S22–S30. doi: 10.1016/j.jadohealth.2007.08.017

Lenhart, A. (2007). *Cyberbullying.* Retrieved from Pew Internet & American Life Project website: http://pewinternet.org/Reports/2007/Cyberbullying.aspx

Lenhart, A. (2009). *Adults and social network websites.* Retrieved from Pew Internet & American Life Project website: http://www.pewinternet.org/Reports/2009/Adults-and-Social-Network-Websites.aspx

Lenhart, A., & Madden, M. (2007a). *Social networking websites and teens.* Retrieved from Pew Internet & American Life Project website: http://www.pewinternet.org/Reports/2007/Social-Networking-Websites-and-Teens.aspx

Lenhart, A., & Madden, M. (2007b). *Teens, privacy and online social networks.* Retrieved from Pew Internet & American Life Project website: http://www.pewinternet.org/Reports/2007/Teens-Privacy-and-Online-Social-Networks.aspx

Lenhart, A., Madden, M., & Hitlin, P. (2005). *Teens and technology: Youth are leading the transition to a fully wired and mobile nation.* Retrieved from Pew Internet & American Life Projec website: http://www.pewinternet.org/pdfs/PIP_Teens_Tech_July2005web.pdf

Lenhart, A., Purcell, K., Smith, A., & Zickuhr, K. (2010). *Social media and young adults.* Retrieved from Pew Internet & American Life Project website: http://www.pewinternet.org/Reports/2010/Social-Media-and-Young-Adults.aspx

Li, Q. (2007). New bottle but old wine: A research of cyberbullying in schools. *Computers and Human Behavior, 23,* 1777–1791.

Litt, D. M., & Stock, M. L. (2011). Adolescent alcohol-related risk cognitions: The roles of social norms and social networking sites. *Psychology of Addictive Behaviors, 25*(4), 708–713. doi: 10.1037/a0024226

Livingstone, S. (2008). Taking risky opportunities in youthful content creation: Teenagers' use of social networking sites for intimacy, privacy and self-expression. *New Media and Society, 10*(3), 393–411. doi: 10.1177/1461444808089415

Luscombe, B. (2010, August 21). Adoption 2.0: Finding mom on facebook. *Time, 176*(7), 45–46.

Madden, M., & Zickuhr, K. (2011, August 26). *65% of online adults use social networking sites.* Retrieved from Pew Interent & American Life Project website: http://www.pewinternet.org/Reports/2011/Social-Networking-Sites.aspx

McGee, J. B., & Begg, M. (2008). What medical educators need to know about "Web 2.0." *Medical Teacher, 30*(2), 164–169.

McMullen, L. (2012). Facebook, Edutopia collaborate on social media guide. *U.S. News and World Report.* Retrieved from http://www.usnews.com/education/blogs/high-school-notes/2012/05/14/facebook-edutopia-collaborate-on-social-media-guide

Moreno, M. A. (2010). Social networking sites and adolescents. *Pediatric Annals, 39*(9), 565–568. doi: 10.3928/00904481-20100825-07

Moreno, M. A., Briner, L. R., Williams, A., Walker, L., Brockman, L. N., & Christakis, D. A. (2010). A content analysis of displayed alcohol references on a social networking Web site. *Journal of Adolescent Health, 47*(2), 168–175.

Moreno, M. A., Briner, L. R., Williams, A., Walker, L., & Christakis, D. A. (2009). Real use or "real cool": Adolescents speak out about displayed alcohol references on social networking websites. *Journal of Adolescent Health, 45*(4), 420–422. doi: 10.1016/j.jadohealth.2009.04.015

Moreno, M. A., Christakis, D. A., Egan, K. G., Brockman, L. N., & Becker, T. (2011). Associations between displayed alcohol references on Facebook and problem drinking among college students. *Archives of Pediatrics and Adolescent Medicine, 166*(2), 157–163. doi: 10.1001/archpediatrics.2011.180

Moreno, M. A., Christakis, D. A., Egan, K. G., Jelenchick, L. A., Cox, E., Young, H., . . . Becker, T. (2011). A pilot evaluation of associations between displayed depression references on Facebook and self-reported depression using a clinical scale. *Journal of Behavioral Health Services and Research*. doi: 10.1007/s11414-011-9258-7

Moreno, M. A., Grant, A., Kacvinsky, L., Egan, K. G., & Fleming, M. F. (2012). College students' alcohol displays on Facebook: Intervention considerations. *Journal of American College Health, 60*(5), 388–394. doi: 10.1080/07448481.2012.663841

Moreno, M. A., Jelenchick, L. A., Egan, K. G., Cox, E., Young, H., Gannon, K. E., & Becker, T. (2011). Feeling bad on Facebook: Depression disclosures by college students on a social networking site. *Depression and Anxiety*. doi: 10.1002/da.20805

Moreno, M. A., Parks, M., & Richardson, L. P. (2007). What are adolescents showing the world about their health risk behaviors on MySpace? *Medscape General Medicine, 9*(4), 9.

Moreno, M. A., Parks, M. R., Zimmerman, F. J., Brito, T. E., & Christakis, D. A. (2009). Display of health risk behaviors on MySpace by adolescents: Prevalence and associations. *Archives of Pediatrics and Adolescent Medicine, 163*(1), 35–41.

Muise, A., Christofides, E., & Desmarais, S. (2009). More information than you ever wanted: Does Facebook bring out the green-eyed monster of jealousy? *CyberPsychology and Behavior*. doi: 10.1089/cpb.2008.0263

National Campaign to Prevent Teen Pregnancy. (2008). *Sex and tech: Results of a survey of teens and young adults*. Washington, DC: Author.

National Conference on State Legislatures. (2012). *State cyberstalking and cyberharassment laws*. Retrieved from http://www.ncsl.org/issues-research/telecom/cyberstalking-and-cyberharassment-laws.aspx

O'Keeffe, G. S., & Clarke-Pearson, K. (2011). Clinical report: The impact of social media on children, adolescents, and families. *Pediatrics, 127*(4), 800–804. doi: 10.1542/pecls.2011-0054

Pasek, J., More, E., & Romer, D. (2009). Realizing the social Internet? Online social networking meets offline civic engagement. *Journal of Information Technology and Politics, 6*(3), 197–215.

Patchin, J. W., & Hinduja, S. (2006). Bullies move beyond the schoolyard: A preliminary look at cyberbullying. *Youth Violence and Juvenile Justice, 4,* 148–169.

Patchin, J. W., & Hinduja, S. (2010). Changes in adolescent online social networking behaviors from 2006 to 2009. *Computers in Human Behavior, 26*(6), 1818–1821. doi: 10.1016/j.chb.2010.07.009

Pollara, P., & Zhu, J. (2011). *Social networking and education: Using Facebook as an edusocial space*. Paper presented at the Society for Information Technology and Teacher Education, Chesapeake, VA.

Primack, B. A., Silk, J. S., DeLozier, C. R., Shadel, W. G., Dillman Carpentier, F. R., Dahl, R. E., & Switzer, G. E. (2011). Using ecological momentary assessment to determine media use by individuals with and without major depressive disorder. *Archives of Pediatrics and Adolescent Medicine, 165*(4), 360–365. doi: 10.1001/archpediatrics.2011.27

Putnam, R. D., & Goss, K. A. (2002). Introduction. In R. D. Putnam (Ed.), *Democracies in flux: The evolution of social capital in contemporary society* (pp. 3–19). New York, NY: Oxford University Press.

Raskauskas, J., & Stolz, A. D. (2007). Involvement in traditional and electronic bullying among adolescents. *Developmental Psychology, 43,* 564–575.

Rideout, V. J., Foehr, U. G., & Roberts, D. (2010). *Generation M2: Media in the lives of 8 to 18 year olds*. Menlo Park: Kaiser Family Foundation.

Robinson, T. N., Chen, H. L., & Killen, J. D. (1998). Television and music video exposure and risk of adolescent alcohol use. *Pediatrics, 102*(5), E54.

Selwyn, N. (2009). Faceworking: Exploring students' education-related use of Facebook. *Learning, Media and Technology, 34*(2), 157–174.

Shariff, S., & Gouin, R. (2006). Cyber-dilemmas: Gendered hierarchies, new technologies and cyber-safety in schools. *Atlantis, 31*(1), 26–36.

Silverman, M. H. (2012). How higher education uses social media [Infographic]. *Mashable Social Media.* Retrieved from http://mashable.com/2012/02/03/higher-education-social-media/

Smith, P. K., Mahdavi, J., Carvalho, M., Fisher, S. M., Russell, S., & Tippett, N. (2008). Cyberbullying: Its nature and impact in secondary school pupils. *Journal of Child Psychology and Psychiatry, 49*(4), 376–385.

Stirland, S. L. (2007). "Open source politics" taps Facebook for Myanmar protests. *Wired.* Retrieved from http://www.wired.com/politics/onlinerights/news/2007/10/myanmarfacebook

Strasburger, V. C. (2012). School daze: Why are teachers and schools missing the boat on media? *Pediatric Clinics of North America, 59,* 705–716.

Strassberg, D. S., McKinnon, R. K., Sustaita, M. A., & Rullo, J. (2012). Sexting by high school students: An exploratory and descriptive study. *Archives of Sexual Behavior.* Retrieved from http://www.unboundmedicine.com/medline/citation/22674035/abstract/Sexting_by_High_School_Students:_An_Exploratory_and_Descriptive_Study_

Sun, P., Unger, J. B., Palmer, P. H., Gallaher, P., Chou, C. P., Baezconde-Garbanati, L., . . . Johnson, C. A. (2005). Internet accessibility and usage among urban adolescents in Southern California: Implications for Web-based health research. *CyberPsychology and Behavior, 8*(5), 441–453. doi: 10.1089/cpb.2005.8.441

Sutter, J. (2011). The faces of Egypt's "Revolution 2.0." *CNN Tech.* Retrieved from http://www.cnn.com/2011/TECH/innovation/02/21/egypt.internet.revolution/index.html

Temple, J. L., Paul, J. A., van den berg, P., D.L., V., McElhany, A., & Temple, B. W. (2012). Teen sexting and its association with sexual behaviors. *Archives of Pediatrics and Adolescent Medicine.* doi: 10.1001/archpediatrics.2012.835

Titus-Ernstoff, L., Dalton, M. A., Adachi-Mejia, A. M., Longacre, M. R., & Beach, M. L. (2008). Longitudinal study of viewing smoking in movies and initiation of smoking by children. *Pediatrics, 121*(1), 15–21. doi: 10.1542/peds.2007-0051

Top sites. (n.d.). Retrieved December 2, 2012, from http://www.alexa.com/topsites

Topping, A. (2012). Lady Gaga racks up 20 million Twitter followers. *UK Guardian.* Retrieved from http://www.guardian.co.uk/music/2012/mar/06/lady-gag-20-million-twitter-followers

Valenzuela, S., Park, N., & Kee, K. (2009). Is there social capital in a social network site? Facebook use and college students' life satisfaction, trust and participation. *Journal of Computer-Mediated Communication, 14,* 875–901.

Wichers, M., Peeters, F., Geschwind, N., Jacobs, N., Simons, C. J., Derom, C., . . . van Os, J. (2010). Unveiling patterns of affective responses in daily life may improve outcome prediction in depression: A momentary assessment study. *Journal of Affective Disorders, 124*(1–2), 191–195. doi: 10.1016/j.jad.2009.11.010

Willard, N. E. (Producer). (2006). *Cyberbullying and cyberthreats.*

Wood, M. D., Read, J. P., Mitchell, R. E., & Brand, N. H. (2004). Do parents still matter? Parent and peer influences on alcohol involvement among recent high school graduates. *Psychology of Addictive Behaviors, 18*(1), 19–30. doi: 10.1037/0893-164X.18.1.19

Ybarra, M. L., Espelage, D. L., & Mitchell, K. J. (2007). The co-occurrence of Internet harassment and unwanted sexual solicitation victimization and perpetration: Associations with psychosocial indicators. *Journal of Adolescent Health, 41*(6, Suppl. 1), S31–S41.

CHAPTER 10

Video Games

Jeanne Funk Brockmyer

V ideo games (including games played on dedicated systems, personal computers, and cell phones) are no longer the emerging phenomena they were in the 1990s. Instead, these games have established themselves as a permanent leisure choice for all age groups, and particularly for children and adolescents. This chapter will review the history of video games and describe current research in the following areas: time commitment, game preference, game ratings, the impact of violent games, physical and mental health risks, the potential for positive applications, public policy issues, and recommendations for parents. The term *video games* includes all electronic games played on any platform.

The Development of Video Games

The first video game was introduced about 40 years ago. In the early 1970s, adult consumers became fascinated with the first arcade version of Pong, which was basically a simple visual-motor exercise. Soon home systems and cartridge games became available, and video games became popular across all age groups. In the early 1980s, consumers became disenchanted with uninspiring copycat games, and sales dropped precipitously. At this point, video games were dismissed as just another vanishing toy fad.

The industry recovered in the second half of the 1980s, when special effects were improved, new game accessories were made available, and games with violent content were promoted. In addition, the industry introduced cross-media marketing, with game characters featured as action figures and in movies. At the same time, children became targeted consumers. Beginning with *Mortal Kombat*, violent games with ever more realistic graphics became an industry staple. The typical goal of violent games is to maim or kill one's opponent, and in many cases players can choose the level of realism of the battle, including very graphic portrayals of injuries. The introduction of "massively multiplayer online games" (MMOGs) and their most popular subset, "massively multiplayer online role-playing games" (MMORPGs), further strengthened the popularity of game-playing (see Figure 10.1). Spurred by the mega-hit *World of Warcraft*, MMORPGs gained wide acceptance in the early 2000s.

Figure 10.1   A massively multiplayer online game *(League of Legends)*.

"Casual games" are another category that has maintained gaming's popularity. These games are often free, typically have very simple rules, and do not require a lengthy time commitment or special skills. *Pac-Man* is considered the first casual game, debuting in 1980 as an arcade game. Most casual games are now played via the Internet, and women are the most frequent consumers of this game genre (Casual Games Association, 2011).

In 2006, gaming was again revolutionized via systems with wireless controllers, such as the Wii, which detect movement in three dimensions. Another feature allows the user to remain connected to the Internet while the console is on standby. Fueled by the success of multifunctional systems, wireless controllers, and the instant accessibility of embedded and Internet games via cell phones, sales of video games and related products now typically exceed several billion dollars annually worldwide (Entertainment Software Association, 2012).

Time Commitment

Video games are now well established as one of the most popular choices in the array of leisure activities available across childhood and adolescence. A 2010 report by the Kaiser Family Foundation indicated that, among 8- to 18-year-olds, "The transformation of the cell phone into a media content delivery platform, and the widespread adoption of the iPod and other MP3 devices, have facilitated an explosion in media consumption among American youth"

(Rideout, Foehr, & Roberts, 2010, p. 3). In another Kaiser study that included children ages 6 months to 6 years, 11% of children played video games on a typical day (Rideout & Hamel, 2006). In 2011, the Youth Risk Behavior Survey was conducted among students in Grades 9 through 12. Survey results were obtained nationally by the Centers for Disease Control and Prevention (CDC) and locally by state and local education and health agencies (CDC, 2012). Survey results indicated that nearly one-third (31.1%) of the sample played video or computer games for three or more hours on an average school day.

Gender differences in time commitment to game-playing are consistently reported, with boys playing more than girls at all ages (Hamlen, 2010). Understanding gender differences is critical to grasping the implications of some game-playing habits, so gender-specific information will be selectively highlighted throughout this chapter.

International studies also demonstrate the popularity of video games, as well as gender differences. For example, Gentile, Choo, Liau, Sim, and Li (2011) reported that most children in their sample of elementary and middle schoolers from Singapore played video games, with boys generally playing more than girls. In a study of German middle schoolers, only about 10% reported that they had never played video games, although, again, boys played more than girls (Krahe & Möller, 2011).

Most time-use studies identify a small group of players who spend considerable time playing each week. The possibility that some become addicted to video games has been debated for some time and will be discussed later in this chapter.

Why Are Video Games Popular?

The reason for the popularity of video games has received some scientific attention. Funk, Chan, Brouwer, and Curtiss (2006) used focus groups to directly examine the game-playing experiences of children and young adults. Pure entertainment value was mentioned by both groups. Children noted pride in game accomplishments as a primary motivator for play, while adults described relief from boredom and positive mood changes. Interacting with others was described as a social benefit of game-playing by both children and adults. Some adults reported that engaging in antisocial activities through the fantasy of video games is appealing. Both children and young adults noted becoming highly absorbed in game-playing; this experience was described in both positive and negative terms, with both children and adults noting that absorption in some games could be scary. These findings are generally consistent with those reported by other researchers (Olson, 2010; Przybylski, Weinstein, Murayama, Lynch, & Ryan, 2012; Ryan, Rigby, & Przybylski, 2006).

The experience of being psychologically engaged is an important aspect of game-playing for many (Brockmyer et al., 2009; Przybylski, Rigby, & Ryan, 2010). Because those who research this topic come from different research traditions, there is some definitional confusion. Terms such as *immersion* and *engagement* are used interchangeably by some, but have very specific meanings for others. Regardless of terminology, it is believed that becoming deeply involved in playing video games may precipitate an altered state of consciousness. When positive, this may be an example of the "flow" state described by Csikszentmihalyi and Csikszentmihalyi (1988). *Flow* is a term used to describe the intense feelings of enjoyment that occur when a balance between skill and challenge is attained in an activity that is intrinsically rewarding. It is believed that being in a flow state may enhance learning and make a person more susceptible to suggestion. It has been proposed that being deeply engaged in playing video games could impact how the effects of game content carry over into real-world behavior, which could be especially important in the case of violent content (Brockmyer et al., 2009; Przybylski et al., 2010).

In summary, some consistent themes emerge from research on reasons for playing video games. On the most basic level, video games are purely entertaining. Most research has been done with young adults, who seem to enjoy arousal, competition, and avoidance of boredom. Children also report that the competitive quality of game-playing is important. Both children and adults acknowledge the social interaction opportunities provided by playing video games and describe periods of intense involvement in game play, which seems to enhance the experience.

Game Ratings

As video games became a common leisure choice for children and adolescents, researchers and policymakers, as well as some members of the general public, became concerned about the increasing realism and graphic violence of many popular games. As a result, pressure was placed on the industry to self-regulate by the threat of government-imposed regulation. The Entertainment Software Rating Board (ESRB) was established in 1994 by the Entertainment Software Association (ESA) (see http://esrb.org).

The ESRB's system is age based and covers console games, PC software, and Internet games (Entertainment Software Rating Board, 2012). The age-based ESRB game classifications are presented in Table 10.1. Each game is rated independently by three trained raters. Raters come from a variety of occupational and ethnic backgrounds and are paid for their work. Because a solely age-based system did not seem adequate, content descriptors were added to highlight content in the following areas: violence, sexual themes, and language. Other specific descriptors such as the presence of alcohol and tobacco use may be added at the discretion of each individual rater. Rating information appears on game packaging (see Figure 10.2). Some researchers have found that the ratings provided by the ESRB do not correspond to content, particularly violent content, as perceived by consumers (see, e.g., Thompson, Tepichin, & Haninger, 2006).

The gaming industry asserts that violent games account for only a small percentage of sales and that the ultra-violent games are only bought by adults. In 2000, a Federal Trade Commission (FTC) investigation found that children were targeted consumers for violent video games as well as for other violent media. In a later report, however, the FTC noted that the video game industry had made great strides in restricting the marketing of violent M-rated games to children (FTC, 2009). In addition, the FTC noted that rating information was more prominently displayed and that retailers were doing a better job of restricting children's access to games rated for mature audiences.

In addition to possible inadequate capture of violent content, there are other concerns about the usability of the game ratings system. First, many parents are either not aware of or misperceive the ratings' descriptors (Becker-Olson & Norberg, 2010). One survey of 94 parents of children ages 5 and under found that even well-educated parents lacked familiarity

Table 10.1 Summary of Primary ESRB Rating Categories

Rating	Age Description
Early Childhood (EC)	Age 3 and older. No inappropriate content.
Everyone (E)	Age 6 and older. May have minimal violence and language.
Everyone 10 and older (E10+)	Age 10 and older. Mild violence, mild language, and minimally suggestive themes.
Teen (T)	Age 13 and older. Violence, suggestive themes, crude humor, minimal blood, infrequent strong language.
Mature (M)	Age 17 and older. Intense violence, blood and gore, sexual content, strong language.
Adults Only (AO)	Age 18 and older. Prolonged scenes of intense violence and/or graphic sexual content and nudity.
Rating Pending (RP)	Submitted to the ESRB, awaiting final rating.

SOURCE: Adapted from information presented at http://www.esrb.com.

Figure 10.2 ESRB rating information appears on video game packaging.

with video game ratings (Funk, Brouwer, Curtiss, & McBroom, 2009). In a recent survey, parents expressed a desire for one ratings system that could be applied to all entertainment media (Gentile, Maier, Hasson, & de Bonetti, 2011).

Another problem is that, for some, ratings appear to make mature content more desirable, a "forbidden fruit" effect. In research on the Pan European Game Information system (similar to the ESRB age-based system), Dutch youth ages 7 to 17 read descriptions of fictitious video games—some with age ratings, some with content ratings, and some with no rating—and then rated how much they would like to play the game. The more restrictive the age label, the more attractive the video games were judged to be. Labels had a stronger effect for boys than for girls, and there was no difference between age-based labels and violent-content labels: Both types of restrictive labels made video games forbidden fruits. The researchers suggested that parents need to be more directly involved in choosing and personally monitoring children's games (Bijvank, Konijn, Bushman, & Roelofsma, 2009).

In summary, the video game ratings provided by the ESRB do give information about game content and about the age appropriateness of this content from the perspective of the ESRB raters. There are continuing problems, however, including lack of agreement with consumer perceptions of content, failure to enforce ratings, lack of consumer familiarity with ratings, and the possibility that restrictive ratings actually make games with mature content seem more desirable to children and youth.

A Closer Look at Violent Video Games

The Appeal of Violent Video Games

One of the most interesting questions about violent video games is why they are so popular (see Figure 10.3). In addition to previously discussed reasons for the general popularity of video games, violent content seems to have unique appeal. The reasons behind the attraction to violent media have long been a subject of professional study and debate (Funk, 2000). Industry spokespersons often cite catharsis or tension release as a benefit of exposure to many forms of violent media, but this claim has been disproven in a sizable body of research (Bushman, Chandler, & Huesmann, 2010). Some have suggested that children and adolescents may seek out violent entertainment to meet their need for new experiences, and for pure physiological arousal (Raney, Smith, & Baker, 2006). For children and adolescents, it is most likely that media violence is appealing to different individuals for different reasons. Personal history seems to be a key variable, with callous children who have been overexposed to violence looking for continuing arousal, while anxious and emotionally reactive children may be trying to master anxiety-provoking experiences (Cantor, 1998).

There has been minimal research directed specifically to understanding the attraction of violent video games. In the focus groups described earlier, participants reported enjoying engaging in antisocial activity during game-playing, such as extreme defiance of authority and rule-breaking (Funk et al., 2006). Jansz (2005) suggests that the reason that violent video games are so appealing to adolescent males is because they provide the adolescent with the opportunity to choose to experience different emotions, some gender appropriate (anger) and some not as socially acceptable (fear).

The Importance of a Preference for Violent Video Games

Over the past several years, researchers have given considerable attention to the importance of the widespread preference for violent video games. Neuroimaging research shows that even brief exposure to violent media affects cortical networks that regulate behavior, possibly decreasing control over a variety of behaviors, including reactive aggression (Kelly, Grinband, & Hirsch, 2007). Behavioral research suggests that there may be a cumulative effect of long-term exposure to violent media (Prot, Anderson, Gentile, & Swing, 2013, in press; Krahe, B., 2013). For example, in research with American 3rd through 5th graders, children's consumption of media violence early in the school year predicted higher verbally, relationally, and physically aggressive behavior, as well as less prosocial behavior later in the school year (Gentile, Coyne, & Walsh, 2011).

Figure 10.3 Example of a violent video game (*Gears of War: Judgment*).

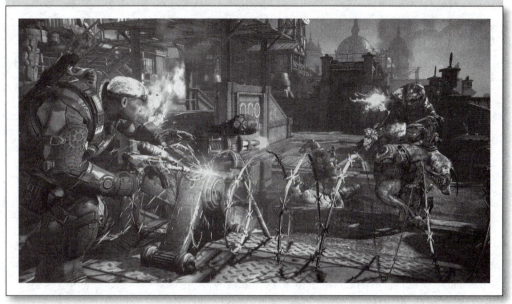

An Integrative Theoretical Model

Craig Anderson and his colleagues have proposed an integrative theoretical model to explain the occurrence of aggression: the General Aggression Model, or GAM (Swing & Anderson, 2010). They have applied this model to understand the possible effects of playing violent video games. In the GAM, there is continuous reciprocal interaction between the person and the environment. Three key elements contribute to this cycle: input variables related to both what the person brings to the situation and the current environment; the person's current internal state; and outcomes that result from decision processes. The continuous reciprocal interaction among these variables can influence both current and future cycles of aggression.

Mechanisms

Commonly recognized mechanisms for the effect of exposure to violent video games are summarized in Table 10.2. Short-term effects, either observable behavioral change or change in some specific aspect of thinking or emotion, are the immediate result of a specific game-playing experience. Short-term effects may be representative of real-life experience, and they may be long-lasting and cumulative; however this is not proven in the laboratory setting. Long-term effects are determined by examining relationships among certain behaviors, personality characteristics, cognitions, and game-playing habits, such as a preference for violent games. In some cases, long-term effects are examined by studying the same group of individuals over a period of time. Some studies examine both immediate (short-term) effects and longer-term relationships by combining experimental manipulations with surveys or longitudinal data collection.

Table 10.2   Mechanisms to Explain the Impact of Violent Video Games

Mechanism	Description	Time Span
Observational learning	After observation of the behavior of others, these behaviors are integrated into the individual's behavioral repertoire	Both short term and long term
Imitation	Learned behaviors are taken from the repertoire and exhibited	Short term
Schema development	Knowledge structures about the typical organization of daily experience develop as a way to manage information efficiently	Long term
Script development	Specific types of schemas for events develop to guide behavioral reactions	Long term
Priming	Violent media activate aggressive schemas	Short term
Automatization of aggressive schemas	Repetitive priming of aggressive schemas makes them chronically accessible	Long term
Arousal	Physiological arousal occurs in response to a particular stimuli; aggressive stimuli cause aggressive arousal	Short term
Excitation transfer	Misattribution of the source of aggressive arousal occurs; this could lead to aggression	Short term
Cognitive desensitization	The belief that violence is common and mundane decreases the likelihood that moral evaluation will inhibit aggression	Long term
Emotional desensitization	Numbing of the emotional response to violent actions or experiences decreases the likelihood that moral evaluation will inhibit aggression	Long term

NOTE: For a comprehensive discussion of these theoretical mechanisms, see Anderson and colleagues (2004).

Regarding the effect of exposure to violent video games in the short term, observational learning and imitation of game actions are possible. Increased aggressive arousal is a well-established short-term effect of playing violent video games. Misattribution of the source of aggressive arousal could lead to aggressive behavior (excitation transfer). In other words, a child who is shoved in a crowded school hallway could misinterpret this random and innocent act as being intentional and then deliberately shove someone else.

Over the longer term, game-playing has many characteristics of a powerful learning environment. In the case of violent video games, players experience repeated demonstrations of violent behavior, coupled with the reward of "winning" for choosing built-in violent strategies. Successful players will consistently choose the preprogrammed violent alternatives and receive cycles of positive reinforcement, which may increase the likelihood that these aggressive behaviors will be internalized and accessible later, outside the game-playing situation.

From another perspective, it is possible that the actual structure of experience could be affected by repeated exposure to violent video games (Bushman et al., 2010; Funk, 2006). Children learn general social rules and specific behaviors from observation, practice, and reinforcement. The development and internalization of behavioral scripts is one component of this process. A behavioral script is a set of situation-specific expectations and behavioral guidelines. A behavioral script helps an individual to predict what will happen in a certain situation and to implement a preprogrammed sequence of behaviors without really thinking about it. For example, most adults have driving scripts: Find the keys, walk to the car, open the door, get in the car, shut the door, put on the seat belt, turn on the ignition, and so forth. A restaurant script is another common example: Walk in the door, be seated, order, eat, pay, leave. Scripts may be triggered by internal or by situational cues, causing the individual to behave based on the previously internalized set of guidelines. Though they increase efficiency, scripts are not always entirely accurate and may cause an individual to misinterpret or disregard new information. Perceived experience may even be altered to conform to a script. This explains why it can be difficult to get used to a new car: Your driving script must be altered to accommodate differences in the location of the windshield wipers and other controls.

During childhood and adolescence, scripts are constantly being developed and revised in response to many different types of learning experiences. In theory, a person could develop and internalize scripts for aggression based in part on playing violent video games. Exposure to violent video games can also prime existing aggressive scripts; if this happens over and over, the scripts will become easily accessible to guide behavior. Games with more realistic story-lines may be even more likely to foster script development, as they have an added element of pseudocredibility.

Desensitization to Violence

Desensitization to violence is a possible outcome of exposure to media violence, as well as a mechanism that may explain the link between such exposure and aggressive behavior (Brockmyer, 2013). Desensitization may be one of the most important unintended consequences of exposure to media violence, as it could affect many social interactions, including a person's willingness to respond to others in need. Recent research has examined both psychophysiological and behavioral indicators of desensitization following exposure to violent video games. For example, Englehart, Bartholow, Kerr, and Bushman (2011) combined electroencephalographic and behavioral measures to examine the short-term impact of playing a violent or nonviolent video game. The primary physiological measure of interest was the P3 amplitude. A smaller P3 response to violent images indicates weaker activation of aversive motivation (motivation not to perform a behavior), in this case to the use of aggression. After game-playing, participants viewed violent and nonviolent pictures while their brain activity was measured, and then they completed a competitive reaction time task. Participants with low prior exposure who played a violent game had smaller P3 amplitudes than low-exposure participants who played a nonviolent game and demonstrated more aggressive responses during the reaction time task. The authors concluded that their results demonstrated short-term desensitization after playing a violent video game and that this desensitization explained increased aggression (Englehart et al., 2011). Bushman and Anderson (2009) measured behavioral responses after study participants had played either a violent or nonviolent video game or had viewed a violent or nonviolent movie. They found that individuals were less likely to aid someone in need after either playing a violent video game or viewing a violent movie (as opposed to the nonviolent alternative), suggesting short-term desensitization to the needs of others.

It is possible that long-term exposure to violent video games may result in a degree of permanent desensitization, as demonstrated by lower empathy. In research with children ages 5 to 12, more exposure to video game violence was related to lower scores on vignettes measuring empathy in everyday situations (Funk, Buchman, Jenks, & Bechtoldt, 2003). Krahe and Möller (2010) surveyed a large sample of 7th and 8th graders in Germany twice over a 12-month period. Self-reports of habitual violent media (including violent video games) usage were related to self-reports of lower empathy and more physical aggression at the end of the 12-month period. Analyses suggested that higher aggressive and lower prosocial behavior resulted from aggression becoming a normalized behavior, which could indicate desensitization. Similar findings were reported by Krahe, Möller, and their colleagues (2011). In addition, higher exposure to media violence was associated with greater enjoyment of the violent scenes presented during the experiment. In a 2010 meta-analysis (described in detail below), exposure to violent video games was significantly related to lower empathy (Anderson et al., 2010).

In summary, psychophysiological, behavioral, and survey data all indicate a need for additional research into the possible desensitizing effects of exposure to violent video games.

Evaluating Research on the Effects of Exposure to Violent Video Games

For over three decades researchers have been examining the effects of exposure to violent video games. In this research area, it is important to use multiple study methods and to examine both short- and long-term effects. Though there are still those who disagree, it must be recognized that most available research on violent video game effects does report some type of negative ramifications, ranging from immediate increases in aggression to longer-term effects, including desensitization to violence. But how much attention should be given to a minority of studies with different outcomes? Meta-analytic research (reanalysis that combines the results of many studies looking at the same question) has promise for resolving any remaining controversy.

In 2010, Anderson and his colleagues conducted meta-analyses of research from Japan and Western countries (Anderson et al., 2010). They included studies that met strict, well-established research criteria, such as those that used the amount of time spent playing *violent* video games (not all video games) as the measure of exposure to violent video games. Some unpublished studies were included (from, e.g., conference presentations) when they met these stringent criteria. Combining almost 400 studies, Anderson and his colleagues' sample included over 130,000 participants. As found in previous smaller-scale studies, exposure to video game violence was positively associated with aggressive behavior, aggressive cognition, and aggressive affect, as well as to desensitization, lower empathy, and less prosocial behavior.

Ferguson and Kilburn (2010), who had previously conducted more limited meta-analyses, criticized the 2010 paper by Anderson and his colleagues, stating that the work was biased and its conclusions based on misinterpretation. These concerns were subsequently addressed by three of the meta-analysis paper's authors (Bushman, Rothstein, & Anderson, 2010), who noted, "We rely on well-established methodological and statistical theory and on empirical data to show that claims of bias and misinterpretation on our part are simply wrong" (p. 182). An informed reader will find that Bushman and his colleagues' response is well reasoned and conclusive and their meta-analysis definitive. It seems clear that exposure to violent video games can lead to negative outcomes for some individuals. This conclusion is supported by the American Psychological Association's 2005 policy statement recommending the reduction of all violence in video games and interactive media marketed to children and youth.

High-Risk Players and a Relative Risk Model

Several researchers have attempted to determine what personality or other factors may explain or change the relationship between playing violent video games and various outcomes. Obviously not all players who play first-person shooter games actually kill someone (although there may be other more subtle effects for many players that are difficult to measure, such as desensitization). A relative risk model suggests that the more risk factors a person has, the more likely it is that there will be a negative outcome. Exposure to violent video games can be conceptualized as one potentially modifiable risk factor for aggressive behavior. First recognized in the mid-1990s, high-risk players are those who may be drawn to violent video games because of preexisting adjustment problems (Funk & Buchman, 1996b). Game-playing may then have a causal role in either perpetuating preexisting problems or in contributing to the development of new problems. For example, some children with academic problems may use video games as either an escape from schoolwork or as an area in which they can excel. Although there could be temporary benefits, such as an increase in self-esteem, over the long term academic problems may worsen because of this strategy, leading to a decrease in self-esteem (Funk & Buchman, 1996a).

Importantly, risk factors may be balanced by protective factors (Funk, 2003). Protective factors include such external factors as supportive and involved parents, socioeconomic stability, and individual characteristics such as an even temperament and cognitive strengths. Gentile and Bushman (2012) presented data to support a risk and resilience model to explain media violence effects in general. They surveyed 3rd through 4th graders (including self and peer reports), as well as their teachers and parents, at two different times over the course of a school year. The researchers examined both risk and protective factors known to be related to aggressive behavior, including gender (female gender is protective; male gender increases risk), prior physical victimization, hostile attribution bias (the tendency to interpret neutral behavior as aggressive), parental monitoring of child's media use, and previous child aggressive behavior. Increased risk at the first survey was associated with increased aggressive behavior at the time of the second survey. Having more protective factors at the beginning of the study was associated with less aggression at the end of the study. The greatest risk of aggression occurred with multiple risk factors. Important to the present topic, exposure to media violence seemed to have an impact similar to that of the other risk factors that were assessed, which was likewise moderated by protective factors.

Regarding violent video games specifically, two factors may be important risks for negative impact. The tendency for players to become deeply engaged in game play has already been discussed. Personality characteristics are another potentially important risk factor (Chory & Goodboy, 2011). Przybylski and his colleagues (2010) found that individuals high in trait aggression had a stronger preference for violent games than those without that characteristic. For such players, greater exposure to violent content may result in more impact, although this possibility needs further research. Hartmann, Toz, and Brandon (2010) examined relationships between empathy and justification of violence as these related to guilt in response to committing acts of virtual violence. They found that unjustified virtual violence triggered a stronger guilt response in players than when the violence was "justified," especially for players with stronger empathy. It is possible that individuals with lower trait empathy are more drawn to virtual violence, both justified and unjustified, and more susceptible to negative impact from this experience. Of interest, when shooting a virtual opponent was presented as being justified, even the more empathic players did not report feeling guilty.

Research on factors that may affect the impact of exposure to violent video games is intriguing and suggestive; however, much more work is needed to fully understand individual differences in the risk for negative outcomes from exposure to violent video games, as well as those characteristics that are protective. It is clear that a preponderance of research indicates that exposure to violent video games increases the relative risk of aggression and desensitization to violence.

Next we will consider other risks and benefits associated with playing video games.

The Negative Impact of Gender Stereotypes

The objectification, sexualization, and mistreatment of women in video games is another area of concern (see Figure 10.4). Women are often portrayed as helpless victims or brainless sex objects, and these stereotypes in video games are acknowledged even by those who do not regularly play video games (Dill & Thill, 2007). Although some recent games include powerful women, most of these are depicted with unrealistically sexualized body types. Brenick, Henning, Killen, O'Connor, and Collins (2007) found that males were more likely than females to find these stereotypic depictions to be acceptable. Yao, Mahood, and Linz (2010) examined the relationship between exposure to a sexually explicit video game with female objectification content and participants' subsequent willingness to sexually harass a female. Male college students first played either a sexually explicit video game or one of two control games. Then they were given a mixture of words and nonwords and asked to determine whether or not the stimulus was a word. How fast they made this decision was the variable of interest, with faster reaction time indicating greater accessibility to the ideas represented by the words. Two groups of stimuli were administered; each group contained two sets of words. The first group of stimuli was designed to compare participants' reaction time to either sexual words or neutral words. The second group included either words that described women as sex objects or words with nonobjectifying descriptions of women. Those who played the sexually oriented video game had faster reaction times in responding to sexual and sexually objectifying words compared to their response time for neutral words and nonwords, and compared to participants in the two control conditions. In addition, after finishing the reaction time task,

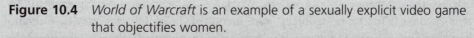

Figure 10.4 *World of Warcraft* is an example of a sexually explicit video game that objectifies women.

participants completed a scale that indicated their likelihood of sexually harassing a female coworker in several scenarios. Playing the sexually explicit video game was associated with a higher self-reported likelihood of sexually harassing a female. The authors concluded that exposure to sexually oriented video games with themes of female objectification may encourage men to view women as sex objects, as well as increase the possibility of inappropriate behavior toward women.

Video Games and Health Risks

Physical Injury

Since video games first became popular, there have been case reports of various types of negative health impact, primarily temporary musculoskeletal injury (see, e.g., Greene & Asher, 1982). The introduction of wireless gaming systems such as the Wii created new opportunities for injury. In addition to simply pushing buttons or moving levers, Wii players control games using physical gestures, resulting in a new category of video game–related musculoskeletal injuries. Sparks, Chase, and Coughlin (2009) reviewed all documented Wii injuries reported to the independently run website WiiHaveAProblem.com from November 2006 to November 2008. Nine types of injury were identified, including eye injuries, lacerations, bruises, fractures, dislocated knees ("Wii knee"), and tendonitis ("Wiitis"). Not surprisingly, hand laceration/bruising was the most common injury, and most injuries were associated with playing the Wii sports games. Similar findings were identified in a more recent follow-up (Sparks, Coughlin, & Chase, 2011). The authors suggest that injury is more likely to occur in players who are unfamiliar with or underestimate the Wii's unique user interface. Supervision of children's play seems important to minimize the occurrence of such injuries.

Excessive game play has resulted in serious injuries and even fatalities. There have been a few troubling reports of "eThrombosis" (a thrombosis is a blood clot) occurring in people who sit at a computers for long periods (Murrin, 2004; Ng, Khurana, Yeang, Hughes, & Manning, 2003). One recent fatality in a 20-year-old was reported following frequent online play for up to 12 hours at a time (Little, 2012). Researchers suspect that immobility and the sometimes odd positions associated with extensive game play could cause blood clots in susceptible individuals. They recommend regular leg exercises and periodic intermissions during prolonged game play.

Fife and her colleagues (2009) evaluated reports of carbon monoxide poisoning attributed to gasoline-powered electric generator use following a hurricane. Seventy-five percent of pediatric poisonings, including one death, were attributed to generators being used specifically to power video games or televisions.

Fortunately, extreme physical risks associated with video game play are all avoidable with good judgment.

Seizures

The risk of video or computer game–related seizures in photosensitive individuals, even those without a previous seizure history, is well established (Chuang et al., 2006). These seizures seem to be triggered by specific features, including the display flicker of the screen, screen brightness, distance from the screen, and the specific pattern of the images. Treatment alternatives include avoidance of video games, and medication for those whose seizures are persistent. It is important to note that researchers believe that individuals with epilepsy who do not have photosensitivity (estimated at greater than 95%) may safely play video games. Regarding online multiplayer games, reports are emerging of a variety of types of seizures in a small group of players (Chuang, 2006). Chuang suggests that factors such as anxiety, excitement, and stress may play a role in triggering seizures.

Cardiovascular Reactivity

Researchers have identified increases in the cardiovascular reactivity of children and adolescents during video game play (Borusiak, Bouikidis, Liersch, & Russell, 2008; Wang & Perry, 2006). This finding is important, as it has been suggested that cardiovascular reactivity may serve as either a marker or mechanism for the development of essential hypertension or coronary disease. Stamatakis and Hamer (2011) studied the relationship between all forms of screen time, cardiovascular disease, and death in Scottish adults. They found that higher screen time was associated with more cardiovascular disease. They speculate that this association results from metabolic disturbance and increased inflammation as a result of what they term "recreational sitting" (p. 298), but recommend additional research to confirm this finding and better understand the mechanisms.

Obesity

Like all media consumption, playing video games may contribute to a sedentary lifestyle, with its accompanying health risks. Obesity is a particular risk associated with a sedentary lifestyle. However, results of research examining relationships between playing video games and being overweight have been mixed. A meta-analysis done by Marshall, Biddle, Gorely, Cameron, and Murdey (2004) identified a small but significant relationship between being overweight and television viewing and video game play in 3- to 18-year-olds. However, the authors stated that the relationships between these types of sedentary behavior are complex and need to be considered in context with other contributing factors, such as consumption of high-calorie snacks during media involvement. Chaput and his colleagues (2011) studied how food intake might be affected by game play. They compared food intake in male adolescents following either an hour of playing a soccer video game play or an hour of sitting. More food was eaten after playing the video game, although hunger ratings were the same in both conditions. Even considering the additional caloric expenditure of game play, there was a significant calorie surplus in the video game condition, and players did not eat less than usual the rest of the day. The authors suggest that playing video games may impair sensations of being full and/or trigger a mental stress–induced need for a reward—in this case, food.

Attention Problems

Past research indicates that there is an association between television viewing and attention problems for some viewers. More recently, a similar association has been found with video game play (Swing, Gentile, Anderson, & Walsh, 2010). The reason for this relationship is still under study, but researchers hypothesize that the fast pace and immediate feedback inherent in video games makes it more difficult to focus on less exciting tasks. Impairment in cognitive control, which is the ability to maintain goal-directed information processing in the presence of distracters, may also be important. Bailey, West, and Anderson (2010) studied adults who were either high or low video game consumers using both behavioral (i.e., Stroop performance) and event-related brain potential (ERP) measures to examine the influence of video game experience on proactive cognitive control. Proactive control is a future-oriented form of control that enhances planning. Both behavioral and brain wave indicators showed that the gamers with more game experience did worse than low game consumers at tasks involving proactive control. Brain wave indicators of proactive control were relatively impaired in high game consumers. The researchers suggest that video game experience may have a specific negative effect on proactive cognitive control processes, resulting in attention problems.

Adjustment Disorders

There is some evidence that some individuals who play video games for excessive periods of time may have particular psychological problems. Van Rooij and his colleagues (2010) identified a small group of players who met their criteria for pathological game-playing. In other words, these players experienced a range of symptoms including withdrawal effects when game play was not possible, devoted inordinate resources to game-playing, and missed out on typical face-to-face social interactions because they preferred game-play. It has been suggested that playing video games is potentially damaging to mental health because it is a socially isolating activity. However, others believe that preexisting depression comes first and draws players, particularly to Internet multiplayer games (Weaver et al., 2009). Lemmens, Valkenburg, and Peter (2011) found that many indicators of lower psychosocial well-being were present before pathological gaming started, but by displacing social interactions, pathological gaming also contributed to increased loneliness in adolescents. Lemmens, Valkenburg, and Jochen also studied relationships between aggression and pathological gaming in adolescents. Across males and females, more violent game play was associated with more aggression. In addition, higher levels of pathological gaming with any content predicted an increase in physical aggression among boys. The authors suggest that excessive gaming leads to a variety of psychosocial problems, including conflict with parents about stopping excessive play. This, in turn, may lead to irritability and aggression.

Somewhat different findings were reported by Shen and Williams (2011), who examined the connections between online gaming and psychosocial well-being. They found that the associations between game use and adjustment were complicated, with some increase in positive social interactions via the Internet, although such interactions took time away from face-to-face social interactions, which were generally a better source of social support.

Addiction

It appears that most excessive video game play takes place online. Some have suggested that a diagnostic category named "Internet addiction" should be added to the upcoming revision of the *Diagnostic and Statistical Manual of Mental Disorders* (used to make mental health diagnoses). This designation would likely include other Internet activities in addition to gaming (e.g., social networking, shopping, gambling). It has been suggested, based on MRI and fMRI studies, that addiction to playing video games has a similar brain base as any other addiction (Han, Bolo, Daniels, & Arenellac, 2011). Small sample MRI studies suggest that medication that is effective for other addictions is also effective for video game addiction (Han, Hwang, & Renshaw, 2011). However, there is not yet consensus about whether or not addiction to Internet activities, or, in particular online gaming, is distinctive enough to warrant its own diagnosis (Pies, 2009; Gentile, D.A., Coyne, S. M., & Bricolo, F., 2013).

Deep psychological engagement has been identified as a primary reason for excessive game-playing. Billieux and his colleagues (2011) studied frequent players in a Swiss online café. Problematic use of MMORPGs was associated with the desire to play to experience immersion. The other predictor of problematic use was "urgency," a component of impulsivity defined as the tendency to act rashly when experiencing negative emotion. Interestingly, this aspect of impulsivity has also been found to play an important role in the occurrence of other addiction-related disorders.

In summary, there does appear to be a group of players whose video game play is excessive, leading to the life disruption seen in many addictions. Medication offers one treatment avenue, and specific psychotherapies are emerging (K. S. Young, 2011), but treatment may be difficult to access since this syndrome is not formally recognized by the primary diagnostic system that drives reimbursement for practitioners.

The Positive Potential of Video Games

Recent research suggests that exposure to prosocial video games can increase prosocial behavior (Grcitcmeyer & Osswald, 2010). There are a growing number of video games whose primary purpose goes beyond pure entertainment. Termed "serious games," these are designed for some purpose other than pure entertainment. This genre includes games with health and mental health applications, as well as games whose purpose may be educational, political, public policy related, or business oriented. Hundreds of serious games have been developed, and many are available through the Social Impact Games website (http://www.socialimpactgames.com). The Serious Games Initiative began formally in 2000, introduced by the Woodrow Wilson International Center for scholars with the goal of developing games to address policy and management issues. In 2004, subgroups of this movement were designated to help develop practice standards. These included Games for Health, focusing on games with health care applications, and Games for Change, focusing on social issues. Some applications of this genre are discussed below.

Skill Improvement

There is now a considerable body of experimental research that indicates that video games can be used to improve skills such as visual attention and visual-spatial skills, although the generalizability of such skills seems variable (Bavelier et al., 2011). For example, video games that use neurofeedback have been used to improve attention maintenance in children with attention deficit hyperactivity disorder (ADHD) (Lim et al., 2010). One system developed by SmartBrain Technologies, in conjunction with NASA, uses off-the-shelf video games from such popular platforms as Sony PlayStation and Microsoft Xbox (see http://www.smart braintech.com/gamelist/). Although the use of neurofeedback in the treatment of ADHD has general research support, published studies on the use of the video games as the agent of the feedback are just emerging.

There is also general agreement that video game play can improve visual-motor skills (Bavelier et al., 2011). This may be especially important for professions such as surgery (Lynch, Aughwane, & Hammond, 2011). Some researchers have used standard video games to enhance surgical skills, giving entertainment games a "serious" purpose. For example, Plerhoples, Zak, Hernandez-Boussard, and Lau (2011) demonstrated that playing *Monkey Ball* on an iPhone for just 10 minutes decreased subsequent errors on basic tasks performed on a laparoscopic surgery simulator by surgery residents with no prior laparoscopic experience. It should be noted that some believe that training on these types of action video games produces learning that transfers well beyond the training task (Green & Bavelier, 2012). This is one reason to support the judicious integration of video games into the classrooms of children and adolescents.

Video Games in Education

Video games have been called natural teachers (Gentile & Gentile, 2008). As previously noted, the game environment is a powerful combination of carefully graded challenge and immediate feedback and reward. These principles create an ideal learning environment, particularly when the playing environment is immersive (Krotoski, 2010).

Educational games are video games that are specifically designed to teach, while at the same time entertaining. Educational gaming systems are available for all age groups. Sometimes called "edutainment," this type of serious game delivers instruction or other messages packaged as entertainment. For example, the V.Smile system provides a "dynamic learning platform" for 3- to 9-year-olds, with games that address skill development in the areas of language, logic, and cognition. The LeapFrog family of games and devices is designed for players from early childhood through high school, with the line of products' stated goal being to instill a "lifelong love of learning." One of their most interesting products is the FLY Fusion. The student uses a special pen and notebook to take notes. The FLY Fusion Pentop is then connected to a computer and the writing is turned into typing. With additional software, this miniature computer can perform a range of tasks, including playing games for entertainment. Unfortunately, peer-reviewed research on the efficacy of these commercial systems is lacking.

Within the classroom, computer-assisted instruction, including games, has been an option for many years. However, there has been resistance to fully integrating games into the curriculum, despite the obvious fact that using video games as one teaching approach strengthens student engagement in the learning environment and is more adaptable to each student's changing mastery level than a lecture approach. Researchers blame this resistance on the negative beliefs about video games held by parents and teachers (Bourgonjon, Valcke, Soetaert, de Wever, & Schellens, 2011). M. F. Young and his colleagues (2012) reviewed over 300 studies evaluating the effectiveness of using video games to enhance student achievement. They found some evidence for effectiveness in language learning, history, and physical education, but not in science and math. They made several recommendations for future development of game-based learning, including developing partnerships among educators and game developers.

"Blended learning environments" take advantage of the latest advances in virtual and mixed-reality technologies (Kirkley & Kirkley, 2005). Virtual reality technology allows the individual to become immersed in a programmable synthetic environment where real-life physical limitations are not an issue. Mixed reality is the experience of a blended virtual and real world; in other words, some elements of the real world, such as physical space, are blended with digital objects. Although exciting, the applicability of these environments to classroom instruction continues to be limited by the nature of most current classrooms and by funding both for game development and for hardware.

"Location-based" games involve a variant of the blended learning environment (Avouris & Yiannoutsou, 2012). These games utilize all the current technologies available on which to play games, including mobile phones, computers, personal digital assistants, fax machines, television, and newspapers. Game play evolves and progresses via a player's location. Thus, location-based games almost always support some kind of localization technology—for example, satellite positioning such as GPS. "Urban gaming" or "street games" are typically multiplayer location-based games played out on city streets and built-up urban environments. The exciting potential of this emerging educational application (as well as ways to deal with its possible problems, such as invasion of privacy) is ready to be more fully developed and more widely used.

Video games are also used to create simulations designed to reproduce aspects of a real or fictional reality. This is another diverse group of games, with applications ranging from the military to the vehicular, the social, and the medical. M. F. Young and his colleagues (2012) suggest that there is a need to more clearly delineate the differences between video games and simulations, but the considerable overlap in definition and use make this difficult.

Games for Health

Games for Health includes serious games with a variety of health-related applications (see http://www.gamesforhealth.org). A new academic journal was launched in early 2012 to promote high-quality research on this genre (see http://www.liebertpub.com/overview/games-for-health-journal/588/).

Exergames

Although not specifically designed to improve health, popular exergames (also known as exertainment and active gaming), such as the series of *Dance, Dance Revolution* (DDR) games and the multitude of games available for the Wii system, appear to be having a positive impact on well-being and fitness. In January 2011, the American Heart Association and Nintendo of America cosponsored a conference to begin to examine the potential health benefits of active-play video games (Lieberman et al., 2011). At the conference, emerging research on physiological, academic, cognitive, and therapeutic applications was reviewed. Conference participants concluded that, at present, most games are active enough for only modest vigorous energy expenditure. Other exergaming benefits include positive social interactions, some improvement in academic performance, and increased effectiveness in rehabilitation for many disorders.

Brain Fitness Games

Brain fitness games have become popular with those who hope to avoid mental deterioration. The company MindFit has developed computer software that reputedly promotes brain fitness (http://www.mindfit.com). The player starts by doing a self-assessment that takes about one hour. The results of the assessment are compared to norms to determine the strengths and weakness of the user. The Individualized Training System (ITS) is an interactive system that "learns" about the users through their performance, offers an individualized training schedule, and responds to user performance both during and at the end of the training. As the training progresses, the ITS adjusts the level of difficulty of each task depending on the user's specific performance. Brain Age, published and developed by Nintendo (http://brainage.com), features a variety of puzzles, including Stroop tests, mathematical questions, and Sudoku puzzles, all designed to help keep certain parts of the brain active. Brain Age games have different levels but do not automatically adjust the degree of difficulty based on play success or failure. Unfortunately, peer-reviewed, published research on specific systems is lacking on this game genre, particularly in regard to possible applications for cognitive enhancement for children, although the theoretical arguments are logical (Baxter, 2011).

Games for Coping With Medical Conditions

Several video games have been developed specifically for children with serious or chronic medical conditions. For example, the *Diabetic Dog Game* demonstrates how managing Type 1 diabetes requires maintaining blood sugar at a normal level. In this game, the player's dog has Type 1 diabetes, and the goal of the game is to avoid letting the dog's blood sugar get too high or too low. The player is rewarded for stable levels with credits towards buying food for the dog or improving the dog's food bowl or doghouse. Unfortunately, despite the game's being developed and promoted by the official website of the Nobel Prize (see http://www.nobelprize.org/educational/medicine/insulin/about.html), no efficacy studies have been reported. A similar game developed to improve cancer knowledge does have some evidence of effectiveness. The efficacy of *Re-Mission* was investigated in a multisite, randomized controlled study with 375 adolescent and young adult cancer patients (Beale, Kato, Marin-Bowling, Guthrie, & Cole, 2007). Participants who played *Re-Mission* improved significantly in cancer knowledge compared with those who played a commercial (control) game. These encouraging results suggest that video games can be an effective medium for health education in adolescents and young adults with serious or chronic illnesses.

Psychotherapy

Several games have been developed specifically for use in psychotherapy. In the area of mental health, the game *Earthquake in Zipland* was developed to help 7- to 14-year-olds cope with divorce (see http://www.ziplandinteractive.com). The player goes on a quest to reunite a divided island. The game uses metaphor, music, and the game interface to help children examine difficult feelings within a therapeutic context.

The Journey to Wild Divine (see Figure 10.5) is a computer program that links biofeedback hardware with the computer (see http://www.wilddivine.com). Although the website states that the Wild Divine products are only for educational, entertainment, and leisure use, this game has become a very useful and kid-friendly way for psychotherapists to help children learn relaxation techniques.

Games have also been developed (most of them not thoroughly researched) to promote AIDS prevention, to relieve stress associated with cancer, to alert children to the dangers of child predators, to treat phobias and depression, to provide pain distraction, to aid rehabilitation, to promote relaxation, and to enhance self-esteem, among other things (see http://www.socialimpactgames.com for game descriptions and availability).

Games for Change

More and more games are being developed to address social issues. Many are available without cost, primarily over the Internet, or for a nominal fee. Although most have not

Figure 10.5 *The Journey to Wild Divine* is designed to help children deal with divorce.

been formally researched to determine the effectiveness of the message delivered, some have found a large audience, as demonstrated by the number of downloads. These games target the development of critical thinking about issues where there is no one right answer and difficult choices must be made—for example, regarding the pros and cons of various fuel sources. Designers believe that the games can raise public awareness and empower youth to work for positive social change, thus the designation "Games for Change" (see Figure 10.6). The group's website has many resources for players, designers,

Figure 10.6 New logo of Games for Change.

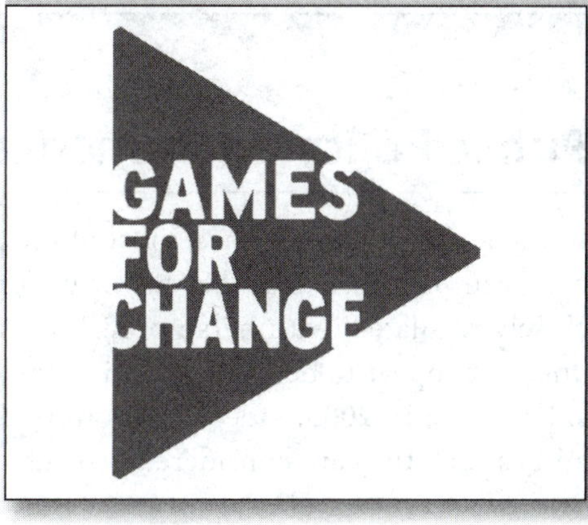

GAMES
FOR
CHANGE

and funders (see http://gamesforchange.org). Games for Change offers guidance to such diverse organizations as AARP and Heifer International on how to integrate gaming into various programmatic initiatives.

Half the Sky is one of the newest examples of how Games for Change works to address social issues, in this case the worldwide oppression of women, as part of a transmedia campaign (see Figure 10.7). Television, social and mobile games, the Web, and inspirational online videos are being used to bring awareness and drive engagement worldwide. Funding for the campaign is coming from the Ford Foundation, the United Nations Foundation, and USAID (the U.S. Agency for International Development, an independent agency that provides economic development and humanitarian assistance around the world in support of the foreign policy goals of the United States).

Figure 10.7   *Half the Sky* is part of a transmedia campaign that addresses the worldwide oppression of women.

Public Policy and Practical Recommendations

In the realm of video games, most of the public policy debate centers on violent games. It has been proposed that the sale of violent video games to minors be banned or at least closely regulated, with harsh punishments for retailers who violate this regulation. This does not appear to be a viable option for many reasons, especially First Amendment considerations. In 2003, video games were declared to be a medium for artistic expression, and as such they are considered protected speech (U.S. Court of Appeals, Eighth Circuit,

2003). However, some argue that exceptions to the First Amendment already exist for children. For example, children are restricted from exposure to various forms of what is deemed to be obscenity. Several communities and states have attempted to impose legal consequences on retailers who sell violent video games to minors, but all these laws have been overturned by the courts. Until recently, however, the Supreme Court had never agreed to hear a case with these issues (see Figure 10.8). Then in 2005, the State of California passed a law that prohibited the sale or rental of a defined class of violent video games to minors using a modification of an existing obscenity law, based on the premise that exposure to such games could cause psychological harm to children. The Ninth Circuit Court rejected this argument, refusing to recognize a violence-based notion of obscenity, and struck down the law because it violated the children's right to access the speech. In other words, the Court ruled that the law violated children's right to be exposed to extremely violent video games. When the State of California appealed the ruling, the Supreme Court agreed to hear the case. On June 27, 2011, the Supreme Court ruled in the case, called *Brown v. Entertainment Merchants Association*. In a seven-to-two decision, the court found that there is no compelling evidence that video games, even those with extreme, graphic, gratuitous violence, are more damaging to children than other forms of violent media with a long history of being protected speech (see http://www.supremecourt .gov/opinions/10pdf/08-1448.pdf).

Interestingly, opposing *amicus curiae* briefs had been submitted about the relevant scientific research, each with support from two different groups of researchers. Those claiming that violent games were not damaging had much weaker academic records with respect to relevant publications, according to an analysis by Sacks, Bushman, and Anderson (2011), published before the Supreme Court's decision was announced. For example, only 17% of the group claiming no harm had published at least one scientific article on violence or aggression, while 100% of the group expressing concern about the effects of violent video games had published such research. Scientifically speaking, it appears that the credibility of the experts who express concern about violent video games is stronger than those who deny that negative effects have been demonstrated.

In the majority decision written by Justice Scalia, it appears that the ruling was based in part on weighing the scientific evidence, and in part on considering precedent as well as constitutional issues. Justice Scalia appeared to agree with the "no harm" group in their belief that, even if behavioral changes are observed in experimental situations, such changes are not important in real life. It should be noted that many studies clearly indicate otherwise (see Anderson et al., 2010).

There are alternatives to imposed regulation. Children are attracted to violent games in part because of advertisement. As noted earlier, limiting the marketing of violent games to younger audiences has been a priority for the Federal Trade Commission, and there has been progress (FTC, 2009). Some believe that parents must take more responsibility for monitoring children's video game exposure. However, problems with game ratings have already been discussed, and many parents still do not realize that popular video games often have very violent content. Parents need to educate themselves about the content of their child's favorite games, preferably by playing the games themselves at all levels, as content may change dramatically over the course of a game. If this is not possible, then they can search on the name of the game on the Internet and look for game clips, often posted by fan groups called "clans." Parents

Figure 10.8   U.S. Supreme Court justices.

should become familiar with how the existing ratings system considers features such as violence and sexual material so they can use these guidelines to help them decide what games are consistent with their value system. The presence or absence of violence against humans, and especially against women and minorities, may be one way for parents to decide if a particular game is acceptable for their child to play.

Parents can at least partially insulate their children against possible negative violent video game effects by sensitizing them to the embedded messages about violence so that they can think about the validity of these messages. For example, is violence really fun? Older children and adolescents can be encouraged to watch news reports about current world conflicts and local violent crime and then discuss these with their parents. Parents can also counter the potentially desensitizing impact of embedded messages about violence by sharing their own ideas about conflict resolution and the use of violence to solve problems, and about the real-life consequences of violence.

Many of today's video games have strong potential for positive impact. There is a need for additional resources to be devoted to the development of games that can benefit society. In addition, promoting existing games that teach, develop skills, or deliver positive messages should be a priority for the game industry. Parents, educators, and health care providers also have a role in increasing children's access to games with constructive goals.

Conclusion

It is clear that video games have considerable positive potential, and it is vital that this potential continue to be developed. The "serious games" movement is an important step in this direction. However, at the present time, many of the most popular games require and reward violent actions. Given the preponderance of research findings on violent games, it is reasonable to be concerned about their potential impact on some children and adolescents. Game developers need support and encouragement to put in the additional effort necessary to develop interesting, commercially viable games whose appeal does not rely primarily on violent actions with unrealistic outcomes.

Exercises

1. Design a serious game in the Games for Change subgroup. Describe its purpose and action.

2. What do you think about the Supreme Court ruling? Should children be protected from exposure to ultra-violent video games? If so, what is the best way to protect them?

3. Do you think people can become addicted to video games? What is your evidence?

4. Design a media literacy program to counter the effects of a video game with justified and rewarded human violence. See Chapter 12 in this book for ideas and examples.

5. Look for clan clips on the Internet for five popular video games. Write down your reactions to what you view. Now look up the ESRB ratings for these games. Are the ratings consistent with what you saw?

References

American Psychological Association. (2005). *Resolution on violence in video games and interactive media.* Retrieved from http://www.apa.org/about/policy/interactive-media.pdf

Anderson, C. A., Carnagey, N. L., Flanagan, M., Benjamin, A. J., Eubanks, J., & Valentino, J. C. (2004). Violent video games: Specific effects of violent content on aggressive thoughts and behavior. *Advances in Experimental Social Psychology, 36,* 199–249.

Anderson, C. A., Shibuya, A., Ihori, N., Swing, E. L., Bushman, B. J., Sakamoto, A., Rothstein, H. R., & Saleem, M. (2010). Violent video game effects on aggression, empathy, and prosocial behavior in Eastern and Western Countries: A meta-analytic review. *Psychological Bulletin, 136,* 151–173.

Avouris N., & Yiannoutsou, N. (2012). A review of mobile location-based games for learning across physical and virtual spaces. *Journal of Universal Computer Science, 18*(Special issue). Retrieved from http://hci.ece.upatras.gr/index.php?option=com_content&view=article&id=431%3Aa-review-of-mobile-location-based-games-for-learning-across-physical-and-virtual-spaces&catid=116%3A2012&Itemid=115&lang=en

Bailey, K., West, R., & Anderson, C. A. (2010). A negative association between video game experience and proactive cognitive control. *Psychophysiology, 47,* 34–42.

Bavelier, D., Green, C. S., Han, D. H., Renshaw, P. F., Merzenich, M. M., & Gentile, D. A. (2011). Brains on video games. *Nature Reviews: Neuroscience, 12,* 763–768.

Baxter, M. (2011). Brain health and online gaming. *Generations, 35,* 107–109.

Beale, I. L., Kato, P. M., Marin-Bowling, V. M., Guthrie, N., & Cole, S. W. (2007). Improvement in cancer-related knowledge following use of a psychoeducational video game for adolescents and young adults with cancer. *Journal of Adolescent Health, 41,* 263–270.

Becker-Olson, K. L., & Norberg, P. A. (2010). Caution, animated violence: Assessing the efficacy of violent video game ratings. *Journal of Advertising, 39,* 83–94.

Bijvank, M. N., Konijn, E. A., Bushman, B. J., & Roelofsma, P. H. M. P. (2009). Age and violent-content labels make video games forbidden fruits for youth. *Pediatrics, 123,* 870–876.

Billieux, J., Chanal, J., Khazaal, Y., Rochat, L., Philippe, G., Zullino, D., & Van der Linden, M. (2011). Psychological predictors of problematic involvement in massively multiplayer online role-playing games: Illustration in a sample of male cybercafé players. *Psychopathology, 44,*165–171.

Borusiak, P., Bouikidis, A., Liersch, R., & Russell, J. B. (2008). Cardiovascular effects in adolescents while they are playing video games: A potential health risk factor? *Psychophysiology, 45,* 327–332.

Bourgonjon, J., Valcke, M., Soetaert, R., de Wever, B., & Schellens, T. (2011). Parental acceptance of digital game-based learning. *Computers and Education, 57,* 1434–1444.

Brenick, A., Henning, A., Killen, M., O'Connor, A., & Collins, M. (2007). Social evaluations of stereotypic images in video games: Unfair, legitimate, or "just entertainment"? *Youth and Society, 38,* 395–419.

Brockmyer, J. B. (2012). Media violence, desensitization, and psychological engagement. In K. E. Dill (Ed.), *The Oxford handbook of media psychology.* Cary, NC: Oxford University Press.

Brockmyer, J. B., Fox, C., McBroom, E., Curtiss, K., Burkhart, K., & Pidruzny, J. (2009). The development of the Game Experience Questionnaire: A measure of levels of engagement in video game-playing. *Journal of Experimental Social Psychology, 49,* 624–634.

Bushman, B. J., & Anderson, C. A. (2009). Comfortably numb: Desensitizing effects of violent media on helping others. *Psychological Science, 20,* 273–277.

Bushman, B. J., Chandler, J., & Huesmann, L. R. (2010). Do violent media numb our consciences? In W. Koops, D. Brugman, & T. J. Ferguson (Eds.), *The development and structure of conscience* (pp. 237–251). New York, NY: Psychology Press.

Bushman, B. J., Rothstein, H. R., & Anderson, C. A. (2010). Much ado about something: Violent video game effects and a school of red herring: Reply to Ferguson and Kilburn (2010). *Psychological Bulletin, 136,* 182–187.

Cantor, J. (1998). Children's attraction to violent television programming. In J. H. Goldstein (Ed.), *Why we watch: The attractions of violent entertainment* (pp. 88–115). New York, NY: Oxford University Press.

Casual Games Association. (2011). *F. A. Q.* Retrieved from http://www.casualgamesassociation.org/faq.php

Centers for Disease Control and Prevention. (2012). Youth risk behavior surveillance—United States, 2011. *Morbidity and Mortality Weekly Report, 61*(4), 1–162.

Chaput, J.-P., Visby, T., Nyby, S., Klingenberg, L., Gregersen, N. T., Tremblay, A., . . . Sjodin, A. (2011). Video game playing increases food intake in adolescents: A randomized crossover study. *American Journal of Clinical Nutrition, 93,* 1196–1203.

Chory, R. M., & Goodboy, A. K. (2011). Is basic personality related to violent and non-violent video game play and preferences? *Cyberpsychology, Behavior, and Social Networking, 14,* 191–198.

Chuang, Y.-C. (2006). Massively multiplayer online role-playing game-induced seizures: A neglected health problem in Internet addiction. *Cyberpsychology and Behavior, 9,* 451–456.

Chuang, Y.-C., Chang, W.-N., Lin, T.-K., Lu, C.-H., Chen, S.-D., & Huang, C.-R. (2006). Game-related seizures presenting with two types of clinical features. *Seizure: Journal of the British Epilepsy Association, 15,* 98–105.

Csikszentmihalyi, M., & Csikszentmihalyi, I. S. (1988). *Optimal experience: Psychological studies of flow in consciousness.* Cambridge, UK: Cambridge University Press.

Dill, K. E., & Thill, K. P. (2007). Video game characters and the socialization of gender roles: Young people's perceptions mirror sexist media depictions. *Sex Roles, 57,* 851–864.

Englehart, C. R., Bartholow, B. D., Kerr, G. T., & Bushman, B. J. (2011). This is your brain on violent video games: Neural desensitization to violence predicts increased aggression following violent video game exposure. *Journal of Experimental Social Psychology, 47,* 1033–1036.

Entertainment Software Association. (2012). *Games: Improving the economy.* Retrieved from http://www.theesa.com/games-improving-what-matters/economy.asp

Federal Trade Commission. (2009). *Marketing violent entertainment to children: A sixth follow-up review of industry practices in the motion picture, music recording & electronic game industries.* Retrieved from http://www.ftc.gov/bcp/edu/microsites/ratings/reports.htm

Ferguson, C., & Kilburn, J. (2010). Much ado about nothing: The misestimation and overinterpretation of violent video game effects in Eastern and Western nations: Comment on Anderson et al. (2010). *Psychological Bulletin, 136,* 174–178.

Fife, C. E., Smith, L. A., Maus, E. A., McCarthy, J. J., Koehler, M. Z., Hawkins, T., & Hampson, N. B. (2009). Dying to play video games: Carbon monoxide poisoning from electrical generators used after Hurricane Ike. *Pediatrics, 123,* e1035–e1038.

Funk, J. B. (2000). Why do we watch? A journey through our dark side. *Contemporary Psychology, 46,* 9–11.

Funk, J. B. (2003). Violent video games: Who's at risk? In D. Ravitch & J. Viteritti (Eds.), *Kid stuff: Marketing violence and vulgarity in the popular culture* (pp. 168–192). Baltimore, MD: Johns Hopkins University Press.

Funk, J. B. (2006). Script development. In J. J. Arnett (Ed.), *Encyclopedia of children, adolescents, and the media.* Thousand Oaks, CA: Sage.

Funk, J. B., Brouwer, J., Curtiss, K., & McBroom, E. (2009). Parents of preschoolers: Expert media recommendations and ratings knowledge, media effects beliefs, and monitoring practices. *Pediatrics, 123,* 981–988.

Funk, J. B., & Buchman, D. D. (1996a). Children's perceptions of gender differences in social approval for playing electronic games. *Sex Roles, 35,* 219–231.

Funk, J. B., & Buchman, D. D. (1996b). Playing violent video and computer games and adolescent self-concept. *Journal of Communication, 46,* 19–32.

Funk, J. B., Buchman, D. D., Jenks, J., & Bechtoldt, H. (2003). Playing violent video games, desensitization, and moral evaluation in children. *Journal of Applied Developmental Psychology, 24,* 413–436.

Funk, J. B., Chan, M., Brouwer, J., & Curtiss, K. (2006). A biopsychosocial analysis of the video game playing experience of children and adults in the United States. *Studies in Media Literacy and Information Education (SIMILE).* Retrieved from http://utpjournals.metapress.com/content/h2g0732025831q89/fulltext.pdf

Gentile, D. A., & Bushman, B. J. (2012). Reassessing media violence effects using a risk and resilience approach to understanding aggression. *Psychology of Popular Media Culture.*

Gentile, D. A., Choo, H., Liau, A., Sim, T., & Li, D. (2011). Pathological video game use among youths: A two-year longitudinal study. *Pediatrics, 127,* e319–e329.

Gentile, D. A., Coyne, S., & Walsh, D. A. (2011). Media violence, physical aggression, and relational aggression in school-age children: A short-term longitudinal study. *Aggressive Behavior, 37,* 193–206.

Gentile, D. A., Coyne, S.M., & Bricolo, F. (2013). Pathological technology addictions: What is scientifically known and what remains to be learned (pp. 382–402). In K. E. Dill (Ed.). *The Oxford handbook of media psychology.* New York: Oxford University Press.

Gentile, D. A., & Gentile, J. R. (2008). Violent video games as exemplary teachers: A conceptual analysis. *Journal of Youth and Adolescence, 9,* 127–141.

Gentile, D. A., Maier, J. A., Hasson, M. R., & de Bonetti, B. L. (2011). Parents' evaluation of media ratings a decade after the television ratings were introduced. *Pediatrics, 128,* 36–44.

Green, C. S., & Bavelier, D. (2012). Learning, attentional control, and action video games. *Current Biology, 22*(6), 197–206.

Greene, J. S., & Asher, I. (1982). Video games. *Journal of the American Medical Association, 248,* 1308.

Greitemeyer, T., & Osswald, S. (2010). Effects of prosocial video games on prosocial behavior. *Journal of Personality and Social Psychology, 98,* 211–221.

Hamlen, K. R. (2010). Re-examining gender differences in video game play. *Journal of Educational Computing Research, 43,* 293–308.

Han, D. H., Bolo, N., Daniels, M. A., & Arenellac, L. (2011). Brain activity and desire for Internet game play. *Comprehensive Psychiatry, 52,* 88–95.

Han, D., Hwang, D. W., & Renshaw, D. F. (2011). Bupropion sustained release treatment decreases craving for video games and cue-induced brain activity in patients with Internet video game addiction. *Psychology of Popular Media Culture, 1,* 108–117.

Hartmann, T., Toz, E., & Brandon, M. (2010). Just a game? Unjustified virtual violence produces guilt in empathetic players. *Media Psychology, 13,* 339–363.

Jansz, J. (2005). The emotional appeal of violent video games for adolescent males. *Communication Theory, 15,* 219–241.

Kelly, C. R., Grinband, J., & Hirsch, J. (2007). Repeated exposure to media violence is associated with diminished response in an inhibitory frontolimbic network. *PLoS ONE.* Retrieved from http://www.plosone.org/article/info%3Adoi%2F10.1371%2Fjournal.pone.0001268

Kirkley, S. E., & Kirkley, J. R. (2005). Creating next generation blended learning environments using mixed reality, video games and simulations. *TechTrends, 49,* 42–53, 89.

Krahe, B. (2013). Violent video games and aggression (pp. 352–372). In K. E. Dill (Ed.). *The Oxford handbook of media psychology.* New York: Oxford University Press.

Krahe, B., & Möller, I. (2010). Longitudinal effects of media violence on aggression and empathy among German adolescents. *Journal of Applied Developmental Psychology, 31,* 401–409.

Krahe, B., & Möller, I. (2011). Links between self-reported media violence exposure and teacher ratings of aggression and prosocial behavior among German adolescents. *Journal of Adolescence, 34,* 279–287.

Krahe, B., Möller, I., Huesmann, L. R., Kirwil, L., Felber, J., & Berger, A. (2011). Desensitization to media violence: Links with habitual media violence exposure, aggressive cognitions, and aggressive behavior. *Journal of Personality and Social Psychology, 100,* 630–646.

Krotoski, A. (2010). Serious fun with computer games. *Nature, 466*(7307), 695.

Lemmens, J. S., Valkenburg, P. M., & Jochen, P. (2011). The effects of pathological gaming on aggressive behavior. *Journal of Youth and Adolescence, 40,* 38–47.

Lemmens, J. S., Valkenburg, P. M., & Peter, J. (2011). Psychosocial causes and consequences of pathological gaming. *Computers in Human Behavior, 27,* 144–152.

Lieberman, D. A., Chamberlin, B., Medina, E., Franklin, B. A., Sanner, B. M., & Vafiadis, D. K. (2011). The power of play: Innovations in Getting Active Summit 2011: A Science Panel proceedings report from the American Heart Association. *Circulation, 123,* 2507–2516.

Lim, C. G., Lee, T. S., Guan, C., Sheng Fung, D. S., Cheung, Y. B., Teng, S. S., . . . Krishnan, K. R. (2010). Effectiveness of a brain-computer interface based programme for the treatment of ADHD: A pilot study. *Psychopharmacology Bulletin, 43,* 73–82.

Little, E. (2012, July 2). Xbox tragedy: Game addict, 20, killed by deep vein thrombosis. *Sun.* Retrieved from http://www.thesun.co.uk/sol/homepage/news/3723107/Lad-of-20-is-killed-by-blood-clot-caused-by-playing-his-Xbox-for-up-to-12-hours-at-a-time.html

Lynch, J., Aughwane, P., & Hammond, T. M. (2010). Video games and surgical ability: A literature review. *Journal of Surgical Education, 67,* 184–189.

Marshall, S. J., Biddle, S. J. H., Gorely, T., Cameron, N., & Murdey, I. (2004). Relationships between media use, body fatness and physical activity in children and youth: A metaanalysis. *International Journal of Obesity, 28,* 1238–1246.

Murrin, R. J. A. (2004). Is prolonged use of computer games a risk factor for deep venous thrombosis in children? *Clinical Medicine, 4,* 190–191.

Ng, S. M., Khurana, R. M., Yeang, H. A., Hughes, U. M., & Manning, D. J. (2003). Is prolonged use of computer games a risk factor for deep venous thrombosis in children? Case report. *Clinical Medicine, 3,* 593–594.

Olson, C. K. (2010). Children's motivations for video game play in the context of normal development. *Review of General Psychology, 14,* 180–197.

Pies, R. (2009). Should DSM-V designate "Internet addiction" a mental disorder? *Psychiatry, 6,* 31–37.

Plerhoples, T. A., Zak, Y., Hernandez-Boussard, T., & Lau, J. (2011). Another use of the mobile device: Warm-up for laparoscopic surgery. *Journal of Surgical Research, 170,* 185–188.

Prot, S., Anderson, C., Gentile, D., & Swing, E. (2013, in press). The positive and negative effects of video game play. In A. Jordan & D. Romer (Eds.), *Media and the well-being of children and adolescents.* New York: Oxford University Press.

Przybylski, A. K., Rigby, C. S., & Ryan, R. M. (2010). A motivational model of video game engagement. *Review of General Psychology, 14,* 154–166.

Przybylski, A. K., Weinstein, N., Murayama, K., Lynch, M. F., & Ryan, R. M. (2012). The ideal self at play: The appeal of video games that let you be all you can be. *Psychological Science, 23,* 69–76.

Raney, A. A., Smith, J. K., & Baker, K. (2006) Adolescents and the appeal of video games. In P. Vorderer & J. Bryant (Eds.), *Playing video games: Motives, responses, and consequences* (pp. 165–179). Mahwah, NJ: Lawrence Erlbaum.

Rideout, V. J., Foehr, U. G., & Roberts, D. F. (2010). *Generation M2: Media in the lives of 8- to 18-year-olds.* Menlo Park, CA: Kaiser Family Foundation.

Rideout, V. J., & Hamel, E. (2006). *Zero to six: Electronic media in the lives of infants, toddlers, and preschoolers.* Menlo Park, CA: Kaiser Family Foundation.

Ryan, R. M., Rigby, C. S., & Przybylski, A. (2006). The motivational pull of video games: A self-determination theory approach. *Motivation and Emotion, 30,* 347–363.

Sacks, D. P., Bushman, B. J., & Anderson, C. A. (2011). Do violent video games harm children? Comparing the scientific amicus curiae "experts" in *Brown v. Entertainment Merchants Association.* Retrieved from *Northwestern University Law Review* website: http://colloquy.law.northwestern.edu/main/2011/05/do-violent-video-games-harm-children-comparing-the-scientific-amicus-curiae-experts-in-brown-v-enter.html

Shen, C., & Williams, D. (2011). Unpacking time online: Connecting Internet and massively multiplayer online game use with psychosocial well-being. *Communication Research, 38,* 123–149.

Sparks, D., Chase, D., & Coughlin, L. (2009). Wii have a problem: A review of self-reported Wii related injuries. *Informatics in Primary Care, 17,* 55–57.

Sparks, D. A., Coughlin, L. M., & Chase, D. M. (2011). Did too much Wii cause your patient's injury? *Journal of Family Practice, 60,* 404–409.

Stamatakis, E., & Hamer, M. (2011). Screen-based entertainment time, all-cause mortality, and cardio-vascular events: Population-based study with ongoing mortality and hospital events follow-up. *American Journal of Cardiology, 57,* 292–299.

Staude-Müller, F., Bliesener, T., & Luthman, S. (2008). Hostile and hardened? An experimental study on (de-)sensitization to violence and suffering through playing video games. *Swiss Journal of Psychology, 67,* 41–50.

Swing, E. L., & Anderson, C. A. (2010). Media violence and the development of aggressive behavior. In M. DeLisi & K. M. Beaver (Eds.), *Criminological theory: A life-course approach* (pp. 87–108). Sudbury, MA: Jones & Bartlett.

Swing, E. L., Gentile, D. A., Anderson, C. A., & Walsh, D. A. (2010). Television and video game exposure and the development of attention problems. *Pediatrics, 126,* 214–221.

Thompson, K. N., Tepichin, K., & Haninger, K. (2006). Content and ratings of Mature-rated video games. *Archives of Pediatrics and Adolescent Medicine, 160,* 402–410.

U.S. Court of Appeals, Eighth Circuit. (2003). *Interactive Digital Software Association BFC v. St. Louis County Missouri* (No. 02–3010). Retrieved from http://caselaw.lp.findlaw.com/data2/circs/8th/023010p.pdf

van Rooij, A. J., Schoenmakers, T. M., Vermulst, A. A., van den Eijnden, R. J. J. M., & van de Mheen, D. (2010). Online video game addiction: Identification of addicted adolescent gamers. *Addiction, 106,* 205–212.

Wang, X., & Perry, A. C. (2006). Metabolic and physiologic responses to video game play in 7- to 10-year old boys. *Archives of Pediatrics and Adolescent Medicine, 160,* 411–415.

Weaver, J. B., Mays, D., Weaver, S. S., Kannenberg, W., Kannenberg, W., Hopkins, G. L., . . . Bernhardt, J. M. (2009). Health-risk correlates of video-game playing among adults. *American Journal of Preventive Medicine, 37,* 299–305.

Yao, M. Z., Mahood, C., & Linz, D. (2010). Sexual priming, gender stereotyping, and likelihood to sexually harass: Examining the cognitive effects of playing a sexually-explicit video game. *Sex Roles, 62,* 77–88.

Young, K. S. (2011). CBT-IA: The first treatment model for Internet addiction. *Journal of Cognitive Psychotherapy, 25,* 304–312.

Young, M. F., Slota, S., Cutter, A. B., Jalette, G., Mullin, G., Lai, B., . . . Yukhymenko, M. (2012). Our princess is in another castle: A review of trends in serious gaming for education. *Review of Educational Research, 82*(1), 61–89.

CHAPTER 11

The Family and Media

See, my son's the type you have to drag things out of him as far as what happened in school or, you know, what's going on. He never says anything. Now if we're watching a show or something and something comes up, you know, he may mention, oh, that happened, you know, the other day. So it kind of keeps me abreast of what's going on with that age group, you know.

—African American parent of a 10-year-old boy

It's really a very simple way to just get them to sit down and relax because, you know, my children are very active. [My son is] very active and to me, it's nice, it's very pleasant for me when he's sort of like fed, cleaned, you know, teeth are brushed, and he's going to just sit down for a while and watch TV. It's a calm, nice thing. Now, you know, I could do other things with him at that point.

—White mother of a 12-year-old boy

Oh, it's just a phenomenal babysitter. If everybody in the house needs to be doing things, it's just fabulous.

—White mother of a 9-year-old girl

The above quotes come from a study in which the researchers were exploring how to reduce children's TV time, a study that ultimately found that it would be very hard, given the integral role the medium plays in the lives of both children and parents (Jordan, Hersey, McDivitt, & Heitzler, 2006). To truly understand the role of the media in the lives of children and adolescents, we must simultaneously understand what media have come to mean to the family. As these quotes suggest, media are an important part of family life—part of the day-to-day lives of families, part of the resources parents draw on (e.g., to babysit, to stay connected), and part of the very structure of the modern household (Evans, Jordan, & Horner, 2011; Jordan et al., 2006). Media use not only shapes but also is shaped by what happens in the family setting (Garvis & Pendergast, 2011). What is more, children learn to use media in particular ways based on what they observe their parents and siblings doing with media.

In this chapter, we will (a) offer a picture of the current setup of the home environment as a multiple media environment, (b) examine research on parents' efforts to encourage and limit children's media use, (c) review four key theories that help inform research regarding how children make meaning of media in the context of family life, and (d) lay out what empirical studies suggests about "best practices" for making the most of media in the home.

The Home as a Multimedia Environment

Children who spend their days in environments filled with television sets, computers, and video games have greater opportunity to use media. Saelens and his colleagues (2002) explored home environment factors around TV access and their relation to children's overall TV watching. They followed 169 children from ages 6 to 12. Over time, mothers reported having more TVs and VCRs in the home, a higher frequency of children eating meals in front of the TV, and a higher percentage of children having TVs in their bedrooms (see Table 11.1 and Figures 11.1 and 11.2). In this study, home environment factors explained a significant amount of children's total TV time. Specifically, as the number of television sets increased in the house, so did the amount of children's viewing. Jordan and her colleagues found a similar pattern of television access and television time; however, their analyses revealed that children from different families responded differently to the availability of media. Specifically, their results showed that having a television set in the bedroom was the strongest predictor of TV time for White adolescents, while having more television sets in the home was the strongest predictor of TV time for Black adolescents (Jordan et al., 2010). While television is not, of course, the only medium in the home (see Chapter 1), in the context of the family it is the most heavily studied. Thus, many of the studies highlighted in this chapter will focus on the medium of television.

Television in the Bedroom

Children's own bedrooms are replete with media. In part, this is explained by the increased affordability and portability of technologies that are quite popular with children—for example, laptop computers, handheld video game players, and iPods. Indeed, several studies, including nationally representative studies from the Kaiser Family Foundation (Rideout, Roberts, & Foehr, 2005) and Common Sense Media (Rideout, 2011), suggest that the inclusion of media in children's sleeping spaces begins early on (see Figure 11.1). However, many experts have expressed concern about the consequences of multimedia bedrooms. Does bedroom access limit parents' ability to control media use? Do children spend more time with media as a result? Studies indicate that the answer to both questions is yes.

Table 11.1 Percentage of Children Ages 0 to 8 Who Have Selected Media Items in Their Bedroom

TV	42%
DVD/VCR player	29%
Video game console player	11%
Computer	4%

SOURCE: Rideout (2011).

Figure 11.1 Five profiles of shared activity during adolescence.

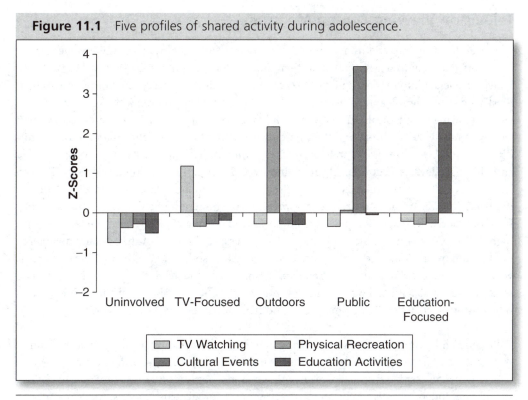

SOURCE: Crosnoe and Trinitapoli (2008).

Figure 11.2

SOURCE: *Baby Blues* © 2012 Baby Blues Partnership. Dist. by King Features Syndicate.

Children with bedroom TVs watch more programs that are inappropriate for their age (Woodard & Gridina, 2000), and they watch significantly more TV (Rideout et al., 2005). The presence of a bedroom television has also been found to be associated with sleep problems in preschool age children, particularly when it is used in the hours before bedtime (Garrison, Liekweg, Christakis, 2011). UCLA's Center on Everyday Lives of Families found that while parents say that they themselves engage in television viewing as a social activity, their children—especially those with bedroom TVs—are more likely to be solo viewers (Saxbe, Graesch, & Alvik, 2011).

Television Viewing During Mealtime

Generally speaking, children who live in families who regularly have dinner together are better off than children who consume their meals alone or on the go (Ray & Roos, 2012). However, Saelens and his colleagues (2002) found that children who consume their meals with the TV on spend significantly more time with the medium than children who do not. Television viewing during family meals affects what family members eat as well. A recent cross-sectional survey of nearly 800 children and their parents from 13 schools in California found that children whose TV was never or rarely on during family meals were less likely to consume soda and chips (Andaya, Arredondo, Alcaraz, Lindsay, & Elder, 2011). In Coon, Goldberg, Rogers, and Tucker's 2001 study—carried out with 91 parent-child pairs—parents were asked whether the television was usually on or off in the presence of children while they ate meals, and they filled out food diaries specifying what children ate and how much. Children from families with high television use during mealtime derived, on average, 6% more of their total daily energy intake from meats; 5% more from pizza, salty snacks, and soda; and nearly 5% less from fruits, vegetables, and juices than did children from families with low television use. In both of these studies, these associations hold despite controlling for other variables that might predict this relationship, such as family income. Coon and her colleagues (2001) argue that

> because children learn television-viewing habits, as well as eating habits, primarily from parents, the choices parents make about the use of television during meals may be associated with choices that they make regarding the foods they buy and make available to their children, independently of children's direct requests for advertised foods. (pp. e6–e7)

In addition to affecting what is eaten, mealtime TV may also affect family relationships. Jordan and her colleagues (2006) report that more than half of all families regularly eat dinner with the TV on; in their study, 4 in 10 families had a television in a room normally dedicated to eating (i.e., the kitchen or dining room). As Gentile and Walsh (2002) argue,

> this affects family interactions, in that this would be a time when family members would usually talk to one another. . . . Television use may both affect and be affected by family interactions. There is less verbal communication, less looking at each other, but more physical touching among family members when the TV is on. (p. 158)

The Constant TV Home

A 2005 survey of more than a thousand parents with young children (ages 6 months to 6 years) made national headlines when it was revealed that more than a third of these youngsters lived in homes where the television was on always or most of the time, even if no one was watching (Vandewater et al., 2005). Data from this study suggest that parental beliefs play a significant role in determining the role of television in the home. Children with parents who viewed educational television as a "very important" contributor to healthy development were more than twice as likely as other children to be from a "constant TV" household. Children whose parents used television as a babysitter and children with no siblings also had greater odds of being in heavy-television households.

But does background TV matter? Experiments conducted by researchers at the University of Massachusetts would suggest that it does. His research looked at the quality of children's play with and without the TV on, in an experimental lab setting where trained coders could carefully track babies' play. He found that children's play was less mature and of shorter duration when television was on in the background than when it was off (Schmidt, Pempek, Kirkorian, Lund, & Anderson, 2008). Background television has also been found to affect the quantity and quality of parent-child interactions. Using the same experimental design, the data showed not only that background TV reduced overall interactions, but that this effect was due to a reduction in parents' active engagement. In other words, because the parents' attention was on the television, they were less likely to talk to or play with their toddlers (Kirkorian, Pempek, Murphy, Schmidt, & Anderson, 2009).

Does the constant TV home environment of very young children affect their later patterns with media? First, children who live in heavy-television households use their time very differently than other children. According to Vandewater and her colleagues (2005), children who live with the television almost constantly on spend more time using electronic media than other children. Children from heavy-television households watch more television and videos than other children. They also spend less time reading books. These patterns appear to persist, moreover. Certain and Kahn's (2002) longitudinal analysis indicates that greater television viewing in early childhood is associated with greater viewing at school age. The persistence of this behavior pattern may reflect continuing environmental influences, the development of child preferences or habits, or, most likely, an interaction between the two.

Socialization to Media Use Within the Family Context

Beyond the media that parents bring into the home, invite to the dinner table, and put into children's bedrooms, families also use media in social ways. The "social uses of media," first described by Lull (1980), means that media are "handy expedients which can be exploited by individuals, coalitions, and family units to serve their personal needs, create practical relationships, and engage the social world" (p. 198). An important study by Crosnoe and Trinitapoli (2008), drawing from the time use data from the Child Development Supplement of the Panel Study of Income Dynamics (PSID), provides evidence that the time parents and children spend together is central to our understanding of how families function and how individual family members develop. Based on the PSID, it is observed that television watching is the primary activity that parents and children share. In more socioeconomically advantaged families, shared TV time is often coupled with other activities that take place outside the home, such as physical recreation and cultural events. In families with fewer resources, TV is often the sole shared activity. Moreover, the types of activities parents and children share have developmental implications. For example, adolescents who spend time with a parent by engaging in physical recreation as the dominant shared activity perform better in math.

The social uses of media generally fall along two dimensions. The first considers how media can structure the space and time of the home. The television set, for example, has been described as a kind of "electronic hearth" (Tichi, 1991) in the home, with furniture in the living room being arranged around the set in a way that was once reserved for a fireplace.

Others have considered the arrangement of media as facilitating multitasking—using several media at the same time or using media while doing chores, homework, or other activities. Media also serve to punctuate family time. Jordan (1992), for example, describes how in some families, books and videotapes are used to transition children from being awake to being asleep (with videotapes or DVDs replacing "story time" in many families). A second dimension to the social uses typology is "relational"—helping families build relationships or helping family members create a psychological distance. Considered in the context of the family, media may be a facilitator of communication (e.g., give family members common fodder for talking), may be a detriment to communication (e.g., when a parent tries to talk with a teen who is furiously instant messaging his friends), or may allow for physical connection (e.g., a father snuggling up with his infant daughter while she watches a Baby Einstein video).

Parental Mediation of Children's Media Use

Most parents say they have at least some rules about what media children can use or how much time they can devote to watching TV, playing video games, or surfing the Web (Scantlin & 2006); however, the extent to which such rules are validated by the children or consistently enforced is up for some debate (Kubey, Banerjee, & Donovan, 2012). In one large-scale longitudinal study of 9- to 13-year-olds, children from families in which the parent and child agreed on the presence of rules had the lowest prevalence of exceeding recommended screen time limits (two hours per day or less, as suggested by the American Academy of Pediatrics) (Carlson et al., 2010). Indeed, some of the earliest and most important parent-child negotiations that exist could be those in which parents attempt to regulate the flow of media content into the home. Such negotiations give parents an important opportunity not only to set boundaries but also to convey their personal values and cultural beliefs.

Three types of mediation styles—the ways in which parents try to buffer children's exposure to media content—typically dominate the research literature. First, "active mediation" involves the kinds of conversations that parents (or other adults, such as teachers) have with children about television. Talk about media may be initiated by parents, who aim to assist children in being more critical viewers. Talk may also be initiated by children, who have questions about character motivations or want to understand media conventions. Nathanson (2001) says that the tone of active mediation may be positive or negative, which will have different effects on children's reception of media content and beliefs about the media.

Second, many researchers have described a form of supervision typically labeled "restrictive mediation." This type of parental supervision involves the use of explicit rules about what games can be played, what channels can be watched, or how long a child can be on the Web. For example, parents who use restrictive mediation may use online filtering software to prohibit children from seeing content they feel may be harmful.

Finally, "co-viewing" has been explored as a strategy for parents to talk to children about content while watching along with them. Co-viewing has also been used to describe the simple act of sitting in the same room and watching a program with or without conversation.

Do the different mediation styles work to limit children's exposure to the "bad stuff" and enhance the potential benefits of the "good stuff"? Evaluations of media literacy programs, which typically focus on active mediation, suggest that adults can improve children's understanding of television (Hogan, 2012). One way is by involving them in formal media literacy programs (see Chapter 12). Another is to explore, clarify, or add to topics introduced by television (Nathanson, 2001), although, as Nathanson (2002) points out, such mediation must be handled with care lest it trigger reactance among adolescents. Scholars and activists have also argued that active mediation can reduce the negative effects of violent content in video games (see Chapter 10) and increase prosocial behavior (see Chapter 3).

Many positive correlations have been found for children whose parents restrict viewing, including decreased likelihood of engaging in sexual activity (Fischer et al., 2009) (see Figure 11.3), less aggressive behavior (Nathanson, 1999), and more physical activity (Vandebosch & Van Cleemput, 2007). Restrictive mediation appears to be most beneficial for younger children. When parents use this strategy for older children (primarily those in high school), at least with respect to television, restrictiveness can lead to unintended consequences. Nathanson (2002) found that "restrictive mediation was related to less positive attitudes toward parents and more viewing of the restricted content with friends, and was marginally related to more positive attitudes toward the restricted content" (p. 220). She hypothesizes that adolescents interpreted their parents' restrictive mediation efforts as evidence that they were not trusted to make good choices.

Parents who like to watch television themselves have been found to be more likely to engage in co-viewing with their children (Austin & Pinkleton, 1997; Bittman, Rutherford, Brown, & Unsworth, 2011). Indeed, when parents and children watch together, it is usually because children are watching the shows parents want to watch and not because parents are interested in

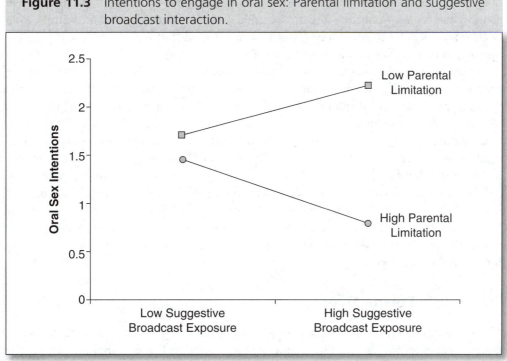

Figure 11.3 Intentions to engage in oral sex: Parental limitation and suggestive broadcast interaction.

SOURCE: Fischer and colleagues (2009).

sharing the experience of viewing children's shows (St. Peters, Fitch, Huston, Wright, & Eakins, 1991). Today, with the average household containing four television sets (Jordan et al., 2006), it is even less likely that parents will co-view with their children. Research on parents' co-viewing of infant-directed videos like Baby Mozart with young children suggests that children may learn more than children who watch alone (Barr, Zack, Garcia, & Muentener, 2008; Christakis, 2009; DeLoache & Chiong, 2009). However, it appears that parent-child co-viewing of adult programming has potentially detrimental outcomes, particularly if children infer that parents approve of certain kinds of depictions, such as violence (Nathanson, 2001).

Unlike what parents report, about half (53%) of all 8- to 18-year-olds say their families have no rules about TV watching (Rideout et al., 2005). The rest say their families do have some rules, but only 20% say their rules are enforced most of the time. The most common rule parents have is to complete homework or chores before watching TV (36%). Beyond that, parents appear to be most likely to regulate their children's computer use. For example, when it comes to setting rules about the media content their kids consume, 23% have rules about what their kids can do on the computer; only 16% set limits about the types of music their kids can listen to, 13% have rules about which TV shows children can watch, and 12% restrict the types of video games they can play.

Most research indicates that parents are more concerned about the kind of content to which children are exposed than to the amount of time they spend with a particular medium (Rideout et al., 2005; Woodard & Gridina, 2000). As discussed in Chapter 13, concern over content has led lawmakers to insist that media makers provide blocking technology and/or ratings. These regulations have met with only modest success, however. Parents are most likely to avail themselves of the tools to help them monitor their children's computer use: Twenty-five percent of 7th to 12th graders with a computer at home say it has a filter or parental controls on it. Fewer—only 6%—use the "parental control" technology for the TV (the V-chip or cable provider's blocking device). Advisories on music and video games are used by a small minority of parents, just 14% and 10%, respectively.

Given the widespread availability of content indicators and blocking devices, why are they not more widely used? Studies from the Annenberg Public Policy Center at the University of Pennsylvania and the Kaiser Family Foundation suggest that the industry's efforts to inform and empower parents are often confusing to parents. Very few parents understand that the rating TV-PG-D indicates that the program contains sexual innuendo (Stanger & Gridina, 1998). Similarly, the symbol used to denote educational programming for children on commercial broadcast stations is obtuse and idiosyncratic, as in ABC's lightbulb and voiceover that says "illuminating television." Today, most stations use the symbol *e/i* to indicate "educational and informational" programming. Moreover, the V-chip device, mandated by the Telecommunications Act of 1996 to be included in all television sets, is generally seen by parents as too complicated to program (Scantlin & Jordan, 2006) (see Figure 11.4).

Theoretical Perspectives

To understand how media fit into family life and parenting practices, it is useful to look at family theories for insight. Four family theories are highlighted here, as they are perhaps the most relevant to understanding why families use media differently and why parents supervise their children's media diets differently.

Figure 11.4

By Brian Duffy, The Des Moines Register, North America Syndicate

SOURCE: *Best & Wittiest* © 1986 North American Syndicate, Inc.

Ecological (Systems) Theory

Ecological systems theory, as well as its offshoot, family systems theory, has been used over the past two decades to situate children's media use where it most often occurs: in the home (see, e.g., Galvin, Dickson, & Marrow, 2006; Jordan, 2004). Ecological systems theory has also provided insight into how media shapes children's world views. For example, Shim, Serido, and Barber (2011) recently used ecological theory to argue the ways in which Internet technology, like the family, is a critical context of adolescence that shapes consumer ideology. This theory was born out of the belief that psychologists were not doing a very good job of measuring the many environmental contexts that shape children's development. Bronfenbrenner (1979) proposed that a child can be viewed as growing up in a set of nested systems, and he proposed four distinct subsystems (see Table 11.2). The *microsystem* contains the people (e.g., family, peers, or teachers) and the settings (e.g., the home, the neighborhood, or the school) that the child comes into contact with on a regular basis. A media-related example of this might be the family's habit of never turning the television set off, a microsystem component that offers children more opportunity to watch. The *mesosystem* lies at the intersection of microsystems and can be thought of as the relationships between them. For example, a mother's and a teacher's instructions to a child regarding which medium to use to research a school project may be contradictory or complementary within the meso-system. The *exosystems* are those social settings that influence a child's development but in which the child does not necessarily have a direct role. For example, parents' educational and occupational experiences shape their beliefs about time (that it is to be filled and is plentiful vs. something that needs to be managed and is a scarce resource). These beliefs then affect parents' rules about children's television viewing. In one study (Jordan, 1992), parents from a higher socioeconomic status (SES) were more likely to limit TV time, while lower-SES families were more likely to limit content. The likely reason? Parents who have been to college and who work in higher-prestige jobs have to learn to manage their time in ways that parents who live "by the bell" do not. Finally, the *macrosystem* is the broader cultural context that shapes attitudes, beliefs, and behaviors. If one thinks about the kinds of technological changes this generation of youth have experienced—cell phones with Internet access and handheld screens that play the latest TV shows, just to name a few—it is clear that the macrosystem has dramatically altered media use possibilities. Not only are media more ubiquitous, but they are also harder for parents to control.

What role do media play in the functioning of the family system? How do family members assimilate, accommodate, or reject media messages? How do parents or children use media to come together or maintain boundaries? Systems theory would suggest that to answer these questions, media cannot be isolated but rather must be seen as part of what makes up the rich and complex patterns of family life. Evans and her colleagues (2011) examined the challenges family systems perceive in restricting their children's TV time. As a feature of the family microsystem, television can be a kind of anchor for norms and habits for the people within the system. By introducing change to the system, such as by limiting screen media use, new stresses may be introduced. For example, this study found that one salient challenge to limiting TV time was the perception that there would be increased negativity within the family system. In interviews, children expressed defiance if they were told that parents would limit television. Parents also revealed increased family conflict as a result of limiting children's television. Similarly, Berge, Arikian, Doherty, and Neumark-Sztainer (2012) have written that it is necessary to recognize the importance of reciprocity inherent within the complex system of the family.

Table 11.2 Bronfenbrenner's Ecological Systems

Context	Definitions/Examples
Microsystems	Child's day-to-day setting: the places they inhabit, the people they live with, the things they do together. Examples: family, peers, teachers
Mesosystems	Relationships or intersections between microsystems. Examples: the congruence of family orientations and peer orientations
Exosystems	Social settings that influence a child's development but in which the child does not necessarily have a direct role. Examples: parents' workplace; media
Macrosystems	The broader cultural context that shapes attitudes, beliefs, and behaviors. Examples: ethnicity, historical setting

SOURCE: Jordan (2004).

Their research on healthful eating and physical activity within the home environment uses the family systems theory framework to understand barriers and opportunities related to youth obesity. Interviews with 26 families revealed that in order to be truly invested in a behavior, such as limiting the sedentary behavior of screen media use, the entire family must be "on board." Parents who want their child to spend less time with the media must model that behavior in their own leisure time activities, and must be invested in finding nonscreen alternatives for their children.

Within systems like families, it is necessary to identify critical patterns of behavior, including: how families typically communicate (Chaffee & McLeod's [1972] family communication patterns), the strategies parents typically use to bring up their children (Baumrind's [1978, 2012] taxonomy of parenting styles), and the decisions parents make about whether and how to mediate children's media use. Each of these theories is discussed in more detail below.

Baumrind's Taxonomy of Parenting Styles

What parents do around children's use of media is likely influenced by their general approaches to parenting and beliefs about how best to raise children. Baumrind (2012) has argued that children's well-being is impacted by how their parents assert power to control their child's behavior. How parents assert power, and whether they do so routinely, is, as Baumrind argues, "a defining component of their parenting style" (2012, p. 36). Over the years, three parenting styles have been explored—authoritarian, authoritative, and permissive (Baumrind, 1971, 1978, 1991). Later, a fourth parenting style, defined as uninvolved or neglectful, was developed out of the permissive parenting group. Two primary components to parenting style are (a) parental responsiveness and (b) parental demandingness. Parental responsiveness, or the warmth and support parents show their children, refers to the "extent to which parents intentionally foster individuality, self-regulation, and self-assertion by being attuned, supportive, and acquiescent to children's special needs and demands" (Baumrind, 1991, p. 62). Parental demandingness, or the control parents exert over their children's behavior, refers to the extent to which parents desire "children to become integrated into the family whole, by their maturity demands, supervision, disciplinary efforts and willingness to confront the child who disobeys" (Baumrind, 1991, p. 1062). Parenting style types are created by assessing parents as high or low on both parental demandingness and responsiveness dimensions (see Table 11.3).

Table 11.3 Parenting Styles

	High Expectation for Self-Control	**Low Expectation for Self-Control**
High Sensitivity	Authoritative: Respectful of child's opinions; maintains clear boundaries	Permissive: Indulgent without discipline
Low Sensitivity	Authoritarian: Strict disciplinarian	Neglectful: Emotionally uninvolved; does not set rules

SOURCE: Rhee, Lumeng, Appugliese, Kaciroti, and Bradley (2006).

Authoritative parenting, as contrasted with authoritarian, indulgent, or uninvolved styles, has been associated with positive outcomes among adolescents, including higher levels of psychological and cognitive development, mental health, self-esteem, academic performance, self-reliance, and socialization (Rhee, Lumeng, Appugliese, Kaciroti, & Bradley, 2006; Steinberg, Elmen, & Mounts, 1989). Baumrind argues that the authoritative parenting style is effective because it is a "synthesis of support and reasoning with power assertion" (p. 39). As might be expected, children with uninvolved parents consistently rate lower than those with parents using all other parenting styles across social, psychological, and behavioral outcomes. Although parenting style has been linked to many developmental and social outcomes within the psychology literature, how parenting styles correlate with parental mediation of media is relatively unknown. One notable exception to the gap is research by Eastin, Greenberg, and Hofschire (2006), who surveyed 520 parents with Internet access and a teenage child living at home and found that, with respect to the Internet, authoritative parents (those who are both warm and demanding) use evaluative and restrictive mediation techniques more often than authoritarian and neglectful parents do.

Health communication campaigns have recently used the parenting styles taxonomy as a strategy for reaching parents who might influence their adolescents' health behaviors. Stephenson and his colleagues (Stephenson & Quick, 2005; Stephenson, Quick, & Hirsch, 2010) assessed the differential effects of antidrug campaigns aimed at parents as a strategy for decreasing the risk of their adolescent's engaging in substance use. First, Stephenson and Quick evaluated antidrug print ads targeting parents and coded them for the types of messages, such as those that educated parents about risks or emphasized the importance of talking to kids about drugs, monitoring where children are and with whom, engaging in family activities, or limit setting. In a follow-up study testing the effects of these print public service announcements on adults, the researchers found that reaction to the ads was influenced by whether the parents were authoritarian or permissive (Stephenson et al., 2010). Specifically, the authors found that "authoritarian parenting tendencies can potentially be changed through exposure to antidrug ads that encourage nurturing practices, but the same cannot be said for permissive parents" (p. 91). Permissive parents, however, were more likely to respond to the antidrug ads encouraging monitoring (p. 88). (See Figure 11.5.)

Figure 11.5 Intention to use parenting technique depicted in ad.

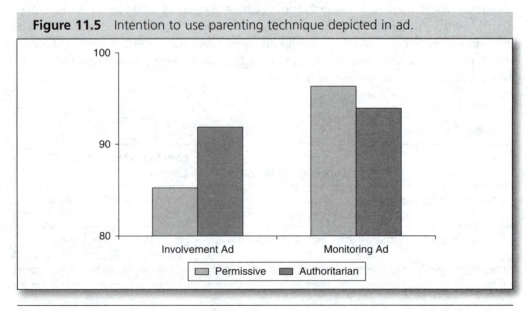

SOURCE: Stephenson, Quick, and Hirsch (2010).

Family Communication Patterns

Chaffee and McLeod (1972, 1973) developed the original model of family communication patterns (FCP) to describe families' tendencies to develop fairly stable and predictable ways of communicating with one another. As communication researchers, they were particularly interested in how information in the form of mass media messages was negotiated by families. The FCP paradigm has been adopted in several empirical studies, including examinations of new media technologies (Ledbetter, 2010) and other domains of family life (Ledbetter & Vik, 2012; Scott & Quick, 2012).

Chaffee and McLeod (1972, 1973) argue that family members typically communicate in two distinct ways. First, they can focus on other family members' evaluations of an object and adopt that evaluation. In other words, they aim for conformity and agreement (even if it is not genuine) between family members. Because this process emphasizes the relationships between family members, Chaffee and McLeod called this process "socio-orientation." Alternatively, families might focus on the object in the environment by discussing it and its attributes and arrive at a shared perception of the object. Because this process emphasizes how family members conceptualize the object, Chaffee and McLeod called this process "concept-orientation." Consequently, children are socialized differently in regard to the processing of information contained in media messages. Children of families that tend to use socio-orientation rely on others to interpret the meaning of media messages to them, mainly their parents or peers. Conversely, children of families that tend to use concept-orientation elaborate on the concepts and ideas contained in the messages to determine their meanings. In other words, the two strategies to achieve agreement in families are associated with different media uses and interpretations by children.

Several researchers have examined how FCP shapes interactions around media in the home. Krosnick, Anand, and Hartl (2003) and Austin (1993) found that children whose families emphasize obedience and social harmony (socio-orientation) in discussions are typically unusually heavy viewers, whereas children whose families emphasize open communication and exchange of ideas (concept-orientation) are, by comparison, light viewers. A more recent study by Hust, Wong, and Chen (2011) examined the factors associated with parents' intentions to allow children to view different types of television content (from educational to sexual to violent). Their results confirmed that two distinct family communication patterns exist (socio-orientation and concept-orientation), and they found that concept-oriented parents were more lenient in the type of content they would allow their children to watch.

Krcmar (1996) used FCP to explore children's reactions to parents' attempts to mediate television. Parents and children (in Grades K–1 and 4–5) were given a TV guidebook that described available programs in three time slots. Parent-child pairs were unobtrusively videotaped and observed, and family communication patterns were measured using the FCP inventory. Parent FCP scores were used to predict parents' attitudes and behaviors, and child FCP scores were used to test predictions involving children's attitudes and behaviors. One interesting finding of this study is that communication and control orientation may be perceived differently by parents and children and may differentially affect parents' and children's choices of discourse strategies (Krcmar, 1996, p. 269). The researcher found that children who perceived the family to exercise higher control (socio-orientation) were less likely to be compliant with their parents' wishes. Hust and her colleagues (2011) also looked at whether FCP could predict intention to allow viewing of different kinds of content (e.g., sexual innuendo, harsh language), and they found that mediation style (as described earlier in the chapter) is a better predictor of allowable viewing than FCP, but that it is likely that family communication patterns influence mediation styles. Ultimately, the authors write,

> These findings suggest that if practitioners want to help parents manage the media's potential effects on children, they may need to move beyond teaching parents how to generally communicate with their children, and instead teach parents how to talk with their children about television. (p. 397)

Social Cognitive Theory

Social cognitive theory is an important theory in communications research and has been used to explain the mechanism underlying the effects of media on children (see Chapters 4 and 5). Martins and Wilson (2011), for example, argue that different genres of television, particularly those that do not portray suffering as the result of aggression, may encourage children to learn from and model aggressive behavior.

Social cognitive theory (SCT) can also provide a useful framework for the study of family communication and children's uses of media within the home. Specifically, social cognitive theory argues that the models in children's lives powerfully shape their behavior (Bandura, 2009), so if parents model media behavior it will influence children's beliefs about the medium. Bandura (1977, 1986) believed that social learning occurs in four stages. In the first stage, the individual attends to the behavior of another—either directly via a live model or indirectly via a mediated source, such as television. In the second stage, the individual acquires and retains knowledge of the behavior. The third stage occurs when the individual can reproduce what he or she has seen or heard. In the final stage, the individual chooses whether to accept the model's behavior as a guide to performance, a decision that is determined largely by the perceived consequences of the behavior for the model (i.e., will something good or bad happen as a result of the behavior?).

Social cognitive theory has increasingly focused interest on the family as the social unit in which critical social learning occurs (Kunkel, Hummert, & Dennis, 2006). One example of this can be found in the research of James Lull (1990), who wrote extensively about how families provided contexts for learning how to use media (Stages 1 and 2), under what circumstances (Stage 3), and to what ends (Stage 4). From this perspective, it is perhaps not surprising that the best predictor of *children's* heavy television viewing is *parents'* heavy television viewing (see, e.g., Woodard & Gridina, 2000). A longitudinal study that tracked the question, "Which comes first: Parents' heavy viewing or children's heavy viewing?" found support for the notion that children learn to use television from their parents (rather than parents using more television because their children do) (Davison, Francis, & Birch, 2005).

Reducing Screen Time in the Home

Parents are told that they should limit the amount of time children spend with entertainment screen media to two hours per day or less (Bleakley, Piotrowski, Hennessy, & Jordan, 2013).

Recent studies suggest that most parents feel that this is a reasonable recommendation, but because of the integral role of the media in the day-to-day lives of children and families, parents have difficulty imagining how they can reduce screen time.

There are, however, several concrete suggestions that might be helpful for families trying to make the most of the media.

1. *Monitor children's time with all screen media.* Children report spending nearly five hours a day looking at a television, computer, or video game screen (Rideout et al., 2005; Woodard & Gridina, 2000). Parents, however, report that their children watch significantly less television than the children themselves report and acknowledge the difficulty of monitoring media time. In one study, parents questioned researchers about what "counted" as media use (e.g., co-viewing and background television) (Jordan et al., 2006). One important first step for reducing screen time is to get a clear sense of what that time amounts to and whether it is over the recommended two hours per day.

2. *Never put a television set in a child's bedroom.* Children with a television in their bedroom watch more television and have fewer rules about television than children without a television in their bedroom (Dennison, Erb, & Jenkins, 2002). National surveys show that most children have a television in their bedroom. Parents recognize that keeping televisions out of children's bedrooms is a means to control content exposure and time. Yet because of the difficulty the parents would face in trying to remove a bedroom TV, it seems much easier to simply never put it in there.

3. *Be aware of how media use is being modeled in the home.* Ecological systems theory highlights the ways in which family members' behaviors affect one another. Woodard and Gridina (2000) found that the best predictor of children's media use is parents' media use. A recent study by Bauer, Neumark-Sztainer, Fulkerson, Hannan, and Story (2011) found that parents' TV use was the *only* family environment variable significantly associated with adolescent girls' TV use.

4. *Eliminate background television.* An easy starting point for many families may be to turn the television off when it is on in the background or when it is not considered the primary activity. As we saw earlier in the chapter, there is a strong correlation between the prevalence of background television in the household and children's time spent viewing. In addition, research by the Kaiser Family Foundation (Rideout & Hamel, 2006) found a negative association between the use of television as "background" and children's time spent reading.

5. *Limit television on school days.* The parents quoted in Jordan and her colleagues' (2006) study at the beginning of the chapter were very focused on their child's school success. Indeed, this priority seemed to drive many of their decisions about television. Some parents restricted television use during the week to encourage homework completion and early bedtimes, and others took away television privileges when children did poorly in school.

6. *Identify nonscreen, in-home activities that are pleasurable to children.* Some parents may have trouble thinking of nonmedia activities that are safe and affordable. Parents may also worry that they will need to be the entertainers if they limit their children's television viewing. However, by restricting television viewing, parents can provide an opportunity for their children to develop their independent play skills (Schmidt et al., 2008) and could promote greater physical activity (Carlson et al., 2010).

Exercises

1. Think about the home in which you grew up. How many television sets were there? Where were they located? Do you think the number and placement of television sets had anything to do with your television viewing habits? In what way?

2. Imagine that you are answering a media use survey. How would you answer the following questions: How much time do you spend watching television on an average day? How much time do you spending using the computer on an average day? What about video games and music? Write your "average" times down. The next day, keep a "media use diary" in which you keep track of each medium you use and how long you use it. Include times when you "multitask." Add up the times at the end of the day. Does the diary show more time spent with media than you thought you were using?

3. Consider Lull's (1990) contention that media are implicitly and explicitly used to build family closeness and create personal space. Are there ways that family members in your home did this? Did your parents try to find common ground over a shared favorite TV show? Did your brother put up the sports page of the newspaper when he did not want to talk to anyone?

4. Baumrind (1991) lays out typologies of parenting styles. Go to Wikipedia.org or Google "*parenting styles*" to see the kinds of questions researchers ask to assess whether parents are authoritative, authoritarian, permissive, or neglectful. Where do your parents fall? Do you think their parenting style shaped the rules they made (or did not make) about media?

5. Using what you have learned from the chapter about how families use media, design a campaign that persuades parents to limit children's screen media use to bring it in line with the American Academy of Pediatrics' recommendations of two hours per day or less. Who would be the target audience? What would be the most persuasive messages? What obstacles would you need to overcome? How would you know if your campaign's message succeeded?

References

Andaya, A. A., Arredondo, E. M., Alcaraz, J. E., Lindsay, S. P., & Elder, J. P. (2011). The association between family meals, TV viewing during meals, and fruit, vegetables, soda, and chips intake among Latino children. *Journal of Nutrition Education and Behavior, 43*(5), 308–315.

Austin, E. W. (1993). Exploring the effects of active parental mediation of television content. *Journal of Broadcasting and Electronic Media, 37,* 147–158.

Austin, E. W., & Pinkelton, B. E. (1997, May). *Parental mediation as information source use: Political socialization effects.* Paper presented at the annual conference of the International Communication Association, Montreal, Quebec, Canada.

Bandura, A. (1977). *Social learning theory.* Englewood Cliffs, NJ: Prentice Hall.

Bandura, A. (1986). *Social foundations of thought and action: A social cognitive theory.* Englewood Cliffs, NJ: Prentice Hall.

Bandura, A. (2009). Social cognitive theory of mass communication. In J. Bryant & M. B. Oliver (Eds.), *Media effects: Advances in theory and research* (2nd ed., pp. 94–124). Mahwah, NJ: Lawrence Erlbaum.

Barr, R., Zack, E., Garcia, A., & Muentener, P. (2008). Infants' attention and responsiveness to television increases with prior exposure and parental interaction. *Infancy, 13,* 30–56.

Bauer, K. W., Neumark-Sztainer, D., Fulkerson, J. A., Hannan, P. J., & Story, M. (2011). Familial correlates of adolescent girls' physical activity, television use, dietary intake, weight, and body composition. *International Journal of Behavioral Nutrition and Physical Activity, 8,* 25. Retrieved from http://www.ncbi.nlm.nih.gov/pmc/articles/PMC3078831/

Baumrind, D. (1971). Current patterns of parental authority. *Developmental Psychology Monograph, 4*(1, Pt. 2), 1–103.

Baumrind, D. (1978). Parental disciplinary patterns and social competence in children. *Youth and Society, 9,* 238–276.

Baumrind, D. (1991). Effective parenting during the early adolescent transition. In P. E. Cowan & E. M. Heatherington (Eds.), *Advances in family research* (Vol. 2, pp. 111–163). Hillsdale, NJ: Lawrence Erlbaum.

Baumrind, D. (2012). Differentiating between confrontive and coercive kinds of parental *power-assertive* disciplinary practices. *Human Development, 55,* 35–51.

Berge, J. M., Arikian, A., Doherty, W. J., & Neumark-Sztainer, D. (2012). Healthful eating and physical activity in the home environment: Results from multifamily focus groups. *Journal of Nutrition Education and Behavior, 44,* 123–131.

Bittman, M., Rutherford, L., Brown, J., & Unsworth, L. (2011). Digital natives? New and old media and children's outcomes. *Australian Journal of Education, 55*(2), 161–175.

Bleakley, A., Piotrowski, J.T., Hennessy, M., & Jordan, A. (2013). Predictors of parents' intention to limit children's television viewing. Journal of Public Health; doi 10.1093/pubmed/fds104.

Bronfenbrenner, U. (1979). Contexts of child rearing: Problems and prospects. *American Psychologist, 34,* 844–850.

Carlson, S. A., Fulton, J. E., Lee, S. M., Foley, J. T., Heitzler, C., & Huhman, M. (2010). Influence of limit-setting and participation in physical activity on youth screen time. *Pediatrics, 126,* e89–e96.

Certain, L. K., & Kahn, R. S. (2002). Prevalence, correlates and trajectory of television viewing among infants and toddlers. *Pediatrics, 109,* 634–642.

Chaffee, S., & McLeod, J. (1972). Adolescent TV use in the family context. In G. A. Comstock & E. A. Rubenstein (Eds.), *Television and social behavior* (Vol. 3). Washington, DC: Government Printing Office.

Chaffee, S., & McLeod, J. (1973). Coorientation variables in family study. *American Behavioral Scientist, 16,* 513–535.

Christakis, D. (2009). The effects of infant media usage: What do we know and what should we learn? *Acta Paediatrica, 98,* 8–16.

Coon, K. A., Goldberg, J., Rogers, B., & Tucker, K. L. (2001). Relationships between use of television during meals and children's food consumption patterns. *Pediatrics, 107,* e6–e7.

Crosnoe, R., & Trinitapoli, J. (2008). Shared family activities and the transition from childhood into adolescence. *Journal of Research on Adolescence, 18*(1), 23–48.

Davison, K. K., Francis, L. A., & Birch, L. L. (2005). Links between parents' and girls' television viewing behaviors: A longitudinal examination. *Journal of Pediatrics, 147,* 436–442.

DeLoache, J. S., & Chiong, C. (2009). Babies and baby media. *American Behavioral Scientist, 52,* 1115–1135.

Dennison, B. A., Erb, T. A., & Jenkins, P. L. (2002). Television viewing and television in bedroom associated with overweight risk among low-income preschoolers. *Pediatrics, 109*, 1028–1035.

Eastin, M. S., Greenberg, B. S., & Hofschire, L. (2006). Parenting the Internet. *Journal of Communication, 56*, 486–504.

Evans, C., Jordan, A., & Horner, J. (2011). Only two hours? A qualitative study of the challenges parents perceive in restricting child television time. *Journal of Family Issues, 32*(9), 1223–1244.

Fischer, D. A., Hill, D. L., Grube, J. W., Bersamin, M. M., Walker, S., & Gruber, E. (2009). Televised sexual content and parental mediation: Influences on adolescent sexuality. *Media Psychology, 12*, 121–147.

Galvin, K. M., Dickson, F. C., & Marrow, S. R. (2006). Systems theory: Patterns and (w)holes in family communication. In D. O. Brathwaite & L. A. Baxter (Eds.), *Engaging theories in family communication: Multiple perspectives* (pp. 309–324). Thousand Oaks, CA: Sage.

Garrison, M. M., Liekweg, K., & Christakis, D. A. (2011). Media use and child sleep: The impact of content, timing, and environment. *Pediatrics, 128*(1), 29–35.

Garvis, S., & Pendergast, D. (2011). Warning – Television viewing may harm your child's health: Parent perceptions of early childhood viewing habits. *Australian Journal of Early Childhood, 36*(4), 22–28.

Gentile, D., & Walsh, D. (2002). A normative study of family media habits. *Applied Developmental Psychology, 23*, 157–178.

Hogan, M. (2012). Parents and other adults: Models and monitors of healthy media habits. In D. Singer & J. Singer (Eds.), *Handbook of children and the media* (2nd ed., pp. 661–680), Thousand Oaks, CA: Sage.

Hust, S. J. T., Wong, W. J., & Chen, Y.-C. Y. (2011). FCP and mediation styles: Factors associated with parents' intentions to let their children watch violent, sexual and family-oriented television content. *Journal of Broadcasting and Electronic Media, 55*, 380–399.

Jordan, A. (1992). Social class, temporal orientation and mass media use within the family system. *Critical Studies in Mass Communication, 9*, 374–386.

Jordan, A. (2004). The role of media in children's development: An ecological perspective. *Journal of Developmental and Behavioral Pediatrics, 25*(3), 196–207.

Jordan A., Bleakley, A., Manganello, J., Hennessy, M., Stevens, R., & Fishbein, M. (2010). The role of television access in the viewing time of U.S. adolescents. *Journal of Children and Media, 4*(4), 355–370.

Jordan, A., Hersey, J., McDivitt, J., & Heitzler, C. (2006). Reducing children's television-viewing time: A qualitative study of parents and their children. *Pediatrics, 18*, e1303–e1310.

Kirkorian, H. L., Pempek, T. A., Murphy, L. A., Schmidt, M. E., & Anderson, D. (2009). The impact of background television on parent-child interaction. *Child Development, 80*(5), 1350–1359.

Krcmar, M. (1996). Family communication patterns, discourse behavior, and child television viewing. *Human Communication Research, 23*(2), 251–277.

Krosnick, J. A., Anand, S. N., & Hartl, S. P. (2003). Psychosocial predictors of heavy television viewing among preadolescents and adolescents. *Basic and Applied Social Psychology, 25*(2), 87–110.

Kubey, R., Banerjee, S. C., & Donovan, B. W. (2012). Media and the family. In D. Singer & J. Singer (Eds.), *Handbook of children and the media* (pp. 341–361), Thousand Oaks, CA: Sage.

Kunkel, A., Hummert, M. L., & Dennis, M. R. (2006). Social learning theory: Modeling and communication in the family context. In D. O. Brathwaite & L. A. Baxter (Eds.), *Engaging theories in family communication: Multiple perspectives* (pp. 260–275). Thousand Oaks, CA: Sage.

Ledbetter, A. M. (2010). Family communication patterns and communication competence as predictors of online communication: Evaluating a dual pathway model. *Journal of Family Communication, 10*, 99–115.

Ledbetter, A. M. & Vik., T.A. (2012). Parental invasive behaviors and emerging adults' privacy defenses: Instrument development and validation. *Journal of Family Communication, 12*(3), 227–247.

Martins, N., & Wilson, B. J. (2011). Genre differences in the portrayal of social aggression in programs popular with children. *Communication Research Reports, 28*(2), 130–140.

Lull, J. (1980). The social uses of television. *Human Communication Research, 6*(3), 197–209.

Lull, J. (1990). *Inside family viewing: Ethnographic research on television's audience.* New York, NY: Routledge.

Nathanson, A. (1999). Identifying and explaining the relationship between parental mediation and children's aggression. *Communication Research, 26*, 124–143.

Nathanson, A. I. (2001). Mediation of children's television viewing: Working toward conceptual clarity and common understanding. *Communication Yearbook, 25*, 115–151.

Nathanson, A. I. (2002). The unintended effects of parental mediation of television on adolescents. *Media Psychology, 4*, 207–230.

Ray, C., & Roos, E. (2012). Family characteristics predicting favourable changes in 10 and 11-year-old children's lifestyle-related health behaviors during an 18-month follow up. *Appetite, 58*, 326–332.

Rhee, K. E., Lumeng, J. C., Appugliese, D. P., Kaciroti, N., & Bradley, R. H. (2006). Parenting styles and overweight status in first grade. *Pediatrics, 117*, 2047–2054.

Rideout, V. (2011). *Zero to eight: Children's media use in America.* Retrieved from http://www.commonsense media.org/sites/default/files/research/zerotoeightfinal2011.pdf

Rideout, V., & Hamel, E. (2006). *The media family: Electronic media in the lives of infants, toddlers, preschoolers, and their parents.* Menlo Park, CA: Kaiser Family Foundation.

Rideout, V., Roberts, D. F., & Foehr, U. G. (2005). *Generation M: Media in the lives of 8–18 year-olds.* Menlo Park, CA: Kaiser Family Foundation.

Saelens, B. E., Sallis, J. F., Nader, P. A., Broyles, S. L., Berry, C. C., & Taras, H. L. (2002). Home environment influences on children's television watching from early to middle childhood. *Developmental and Behavioral Pediatrics, 23*(3), 127–132.

Saxbe, D., Graesch, A., & Alvik, M. (2011). Television as a social or solo activity: Understanding families' everyday television viewing patterns. *Communication Research Reports, 28*(2), 180–189.

Scantlin, R., & Jordan, A. (2006). Families' experiences with the V-chip: An exploratory study. *Journal of Family Communication, 6*(2), 139–159.

Schmidt, M. E., Pempek, H. L., Kirkorian, H. L., Lund, A. F., & Anderson, D. R. (2008). The effects of background television on the toy play behavior of very young children. *Child Development, 79*(4), 1137–1151.

Scott, A. M., & Quick, B. (2012). Family communication patterns moderate the relationship between psychological reactance and willingness to talk about organ donation. *Health Communication, 27*(7), 702–711.

Shim, S., Serido, J., & Barber, B. (2011). A consumer way of thinking: Linking consumer socialization and consumption motivation perspectives to adolescent development. *Journal of Research on Adolescence, 21*(1), 290–299.

Stanger, J., & Gridina, N. (1998). *Media in the home: 1998.* Philadelphia: University of Pennsylvania, Annenberg Public Policy Center.

Steinberg, L., Elman, J., & Mounts, N. (1989). Authoritative parenting, psychosocial maturity, and academic success among adolescents. *Child Development, 60*, 1424–1436.

St. Peters, M., Fitch, M., Huston, A. C., Wright, J. C., & Eakins, D. J. (1991). Television and families: What do young children watch with their parents? *Child development, 62*, 1409–1423.

Stephenson, M. T., & Quick, B. L. (2005). Parent ads in the national youth anti-drug media campaign. *Journal of Health Communication, 10*, 701–710.

Stephenson, M. T., Quick, B. L., & Hirsch, H. A. (2010). Evidence in support of a strategy to target authoritarian and permissive parents in antidrug campaigns. *Communication Research, 37*, 73–104.

Tichi, C. (1991). *Electronic hearth: Creating an American television culture.* New York, NY: Oxford University Press.

Vandebosch, H., & Van Cleemput, K. (2007). Television viewing and obesity among pre-school children: The role of parents. *Communications, 32,* 417–446.

Vandewater, E. A., Bickham, D. S., Lee, J. H., Cummings, H. M., Wartella, E. A., & Rideout, V. J. (2005). When the television is always on: Heavy television exposure and young children's development. *American Behavioral Scientist, 48,* 562–577.

Woodard, E., & Gridina, N. (2000). *Media in the home: 2000.* Philadelphia: University of Pennsylvania, Annenberg Public Policy Center.

CHAPTER 12

Media Literacy/ Media Education

Robert McCannon

We say that we have no time. But we have lots of time, or every study wouldn't show that we watch three or four or five hours of television a day. . . . [T]ime the way it really works has come to bore us. Or at least make us nervous, the way that silence does, and so we need to shut it out. We fill time, instead of letting it fill us.

—Bill McKibben
The Age of Missing Information (1992, p. 72)

One result of this contemporary media landscape is that there exist incredible opportunities for learning, social connection, and individual enhancement in a wide variety of forms. . . . [N]ot having the skills to accurately assess the credibility of information can have serious social, personal, educational, relational, health, and financial consequences in today's networked world.

—Andrew J. Flanagin, Miriam J. Metzger, and Ethan Hartsell
Kids and Credibility: An Empirical Examination of Youth, Digital Media Use and Information Credibility (2010, p. 2)

The truth of it is that every singer out there with songs on the radio is raising the next generation. So make your words count.

—Taylor Swift
on *Sixty Minutes* (Finkelstein, 2012)

Teen sensation Taylor Swift summarizes today's media conundrum. Entertainment media are wonderful. Indeed, we are the most entertained culture in history, which is also a dangerous situation because not all media makers and consumers share the commendable responsibility of young Swift.

Bill McKibben and Andrew Flanagin and his colleagues augur that the siren song of today's ubiquitous media culture is a celebration. Who among us would abandon the addictive benefits of media: our big screens, small screens, smartphones, YouTube, DVRs, texting, 3-D movies and, sigh, Twitter? Who among us is smart enough to understand and brave enough to moderate the media matrix?

However, we celebrate at our peril; the costs of such gifts rival the wonders. Whatever one's position, values, or background, the empirical data on media's harms to our children, culture, and democracy call into question the enormous increases in centralization, power, and political influence of modern mainstream mass media (Big Media). *Concern about Big Media is the motivating force behind media literacy and media education*, yet a basic precept of media education is that *media are always good and bad*. Comprehending the former is easy; the latter, however, lurks in the misty confusion of propaganda, misinformation, false habits of mind, and overconfidence.

Starting with the U.S. Surgeon General's Report of 1971, which emphasized the dangers of media violence, health professionals, parents, teachers, researchers, and politicians have become concerned about the growing power of media. In an era of increasingly violent tragedies, observers are questioning the glorification of the gun and the role of shooting as a solution to problems. Never before has a society and its children been subjected to so much seductive violence.

Sex, advertising, materialism, negative role models, antisocial and unhealthy messages permeate the media that target everyone—from the very young to the elderly. Most important is the health of our democracy. Never before have electorates suffered so much indignity. Financed by huge donations that wind up in media corporations' coffers, negative and misleading political ads misinform, dishearten and subtract from the political debate.

Noted media scholar Robert McChesney (2004) calls today "the age of hyper-commercialism." It is an era in which the world's most dominant organizations are the media cartel and their major advertisers, driving relentlessly for profit, targeting children, and overwhelming busy parents, teachers, counselors, and preachers. Daily, we extend a historic and dangerous social experiment with the health of our children and democracy. It is the Wal-Martization of the world's information, with billion-dollar ad budgets mannedby lobbyists galore. Persuasion on such a scale can only be described as a new form of censorship.

Vested interests prefer the current system of advertiser-provided content, ineffectual rating systems, and weak regulation, deriding critics and stating that media "effects" research is flawed. Big Media defends its First Amendment right to artistic expression and suggests that if children or democracy has media-related problems, parents and citizens need to be more responsible. *It is always the consumers' problem*.

A caveat: No responsible media critic or educator thinks media are *completely* responsible for any problem, be it violence, poor grades, eating disorders, sexualized lifestyles, poor self-esteem, depression, attention deficit, obesity, drug use, social injustice, lack of faith, materialism, rampant debt, or the weakening of democracy. However, media harms, unlike sickness, poverty, racism, poor parenting, genetics, lack of education, and the like, which have proven difficult to remedy, *might be mitigated* with *media education*.

Demands for Change

The response to media abuses has included advocation of a wide range of proposed solutions, such as (a) *government censorship*, (b) increased *regulation*, (c) *reform* of the media system, and (d) *media education* or *media literacy* for children and adults. Thousands of organizations and programs exist that are dedicated to one or more. Real change will probably necessitate some measure of all four, and since the game is loaded in favor of Big Media, unprecedented citizen knowledge and involvement will be required.

Most controversial and unpopular, *censorship* runs straight into Big Media's demand for First Amendment rights to sell antisocial content. Such use of the First Amendment is ironic, as it was designed to protect citizens and minorities from more powerful political entities.

Regulation is complicated and politicized. The unprecedented political power given to corporations by the Supreme Court's *Citizen United* (Kennedy, 2010) decision looms large as vested interests typecast regulations as "wasteful" and part of "big government."

Reform depends on media education, because *only the media educated perceive the need for media reform*. In a media-educated culture, reform might be a natural process, meeting the needs of the public (Potter, 2004). Citizens who support prosocial issues (ecology, children, cancer research, etc.) often do not understand that without media reform, solving problems is hamstrung by those who control the news—that is, Big Media.

Media education and media literacy is an alternative to regulation and censorship (Bergsma & Carney, 2008; Byrne, 2009; Timmerman et al., 2008). It seems to generate the least controversy and most support from teachers, administrators, and researchers (Martens, 2010).

Defining Media Literacy

The standard definition of media literacy is the ability to access, analyze, evaluate, and communicate messages in a wide variety of forms (Aufderheide, 1992). Because *evaluate* can be confusing, and many believe it to be a subset of *analyze*, a less confusing definition is *the ability to analyze, access, and produce media in a variety of forms and contexts*. A more detailed definition comes from Silverblatt (2013):

Media literacy emphasizes:

1. A critical thinking skill that is applied to the source of much of our information: the channels of mass communication.

2. Furnishing individuals with the tools to make independent choices with regard to: 1) which media programming to select and 2) interpreting the information that they receive through the channels of mass communication.

3. Furnishing insight into the impact of various contexts on the construction of media messages.

4. Understanding the process of mass communication.

5. An awareness of the impact of the media on the individual and society.

6. An awareness of media content as a "text" that provides insight into our contemporary culture and ourselves.

7. The development of strategies with which to analyze and discuss media messages.

8. In the case of media communicators: the ability to produce effective and responsible media messages.

9. The cultivation of an enhanced enjoyment, understanding, and appreciation of media content.

10. The ability to comprehend, interpret, and construct messages, using the different "languages" of media.

11. Anticipating changes in the media landscape.

Use of the term *media literacy* is not universal: "For example, several scholars have coined the concept of digital or multiple media literacies" (Martens, 2010). *Visual literacy* is used, and educators concerned about commercialization and materialism can use the term *commercial literacy* for programs that concentrate on the burgeoning forms and content of advertising and credit and savings (Eagle, 2005). Primack, Sidani, Carroll, and Fine (2009) describe Big Media's political and financial *motives* and their ability to target groups as an *essential core concept* of media education.

A variety of similar literacies exist. *Internet literacy* was the subject of an extensive $1.8 million, three-year U.S. Department of Education study involving new ways to teach higher-level comprehension skills to 1,500 economically disadvantaged youth (Ascione, 2006). Literacies such as information literacy, computer literacy, business literacy, technology literacy, and health literacy overlap, often using similar methods. The National Forum on Information Literacy, supported by more than 90 education organizations, is attempting to provide definitions (see http://infolit.org/about-the-nfil/welcome/).[1]

Silverblatt (2001) suggests a *contextual* media literacy, one that emphasizes issues of production and consumption in addition to content. One can expand this to an analysis of information control and cultural ideologies (Kavoori & Matthews, 2004; Lewis & Jhally, 1998). As Jhally notes, "To appreciate the significance of contemporary media, we need to know why [messages] are produced, under what constraints and conditions, and by whom" (Lewis & Jhally, 1998, p. 111). As the number of literacies has expanded, such goals have multiplied, and philosophical underpinnings of media literacy are widely discussed and contested (Martens, 2010).

Defining Media Education

Another definitive but less recognized element of media literacy is the goal of "purpose" or *activism*. "The purpose of developing media literacy is to give the person greater control of exposures and the construction of meaning from the information encountered in these exposures" (Potter, 2004, p. 63).

Noted author Mary Pipher (2001), in *Reviving Ophelia*, suggests that one of the most valuable activities for an adolescent is to have a *cause*. To this end, a national media education organization, the Action Coalition for Media Education (ACME), was created to champion a more *independent* and *activist* solution to media conglomeration. At the first ACME conference, Robert McChesney (2002) stated this view:

The problem we face with a hyper-commercial, profit-obsessed media system is that it does a lousy job of producing citizens in a democracy. A solution is real media literacy education that doesn't just make people more informed consumers of commercial fare, but makes them understand how and why the media system works—so they may be critics, citizens and active participants. This is the type of media education ACME is committed to doing.

ACME is the only national media education organization that refuses to accept funding from Big Media and has a code of ethics.

The term *media education* has been common in Europe for decades. Drawing distinctions is difficult, and many use the terms *media education* and *media literacy* interchangeably, but media education is broader, more diverse, and more targeted toward solutions than media literacy. Media education includes a greater variety of media criticism and traditional scholarship.

Media literacy draws upon education, communication, media studies, psychology, cultural studies, literature, literacy studies, telecommunications, and library and information science (Hobbs, 2005). Media education adds health, medicine, science, religion, political science, history, justice studies, and technology. Media literacy tends to emphasize critical thinking for its own sake, whereas *media education is more concerned with using critical thinking methodologies to combat inequities and problems within cultures.*

Far more controversial but nonetheless important is the work of those who see media education in egalitarian terms. As Livingstone (2004) notes about media education, "crucially, it is the *relationship among textuality, competence, and power* [emphasis added] that sets those who see literacy as democratizing, empowering of ordinary people against those who see it as elitist, divisive, a source of inequality" (p. 13).

A United Nations Educational, Scientific, and Cultural Organization (UNESCO) study sums up the evolving definition of media education with an empowering vision of young media-educated adults: "The emerging new paradigms consider youth as protagonists who are capable of making decisions, exercising choices, and more important, as individuals who are active agents in promoting democratic processes and civic engagement" (Asthana, 2006, p. 6).

Thus, media education is a far-flung net. A "best" definition might be *the ability to analyze, access, and produce media in a variety of forms and contexts and a desire to act upon such abilities in a manner that benefits a healthy and democratic citizenship.*

This chapter will review most of the literature on programs that use the term *media literacy* and some that define themselves as *media education*. All use similar methods and skills for targeted purposes. After reviewing the results of these programs and curricula, this chapter will provide some of the basics of media literacy methodology, content, and skills, as well as examples and exercises.

Uses of Media Literacy

Some see media literacy as purely a subject for teaching media techniques and associated critical thinking skills. English teachers can view it as another aspect of teaching reading: People should learn how to "read" movies, television, the Internet, and other nontraditional screen-based "texts" (Arke, 2013; J. A. Brown, 2001; Potter, 2004; Tyner, 1998). Such practitioners can emphasize "creativity and authentic self-expression" (Hobbs, 2004b, p. 43). In the words of George Lucas:

> Most kids relate to each other through music or graphics. They are regularly bombarded with images and sound. Most of their awareness comes through the language of moving images and cinema. That's why it's so important that they learn the language of it. (as quoted in Daly, 2004)

While accepting such purposes, others see media education as a way to engage students in "exploring economic, political, social and cultural issues in contemporary society" (Hobbs, 2004b, p. 43). These educators teach the aforementioned techniques and skills but also use media content to investigate media-related topics, hopefully producing prosocial interests, attitudes, behaviors, and solutions. Frequently, profit motive, media monopoly, and producers' motives and biases are emphasized (Primack et al., 2009; Rosenbaum, Beentjes, & Konig, 2008).

Still others use media education *interventions*, which are "programs to help people, especially children, protect themselves from harmful effects of mass media" (Chen & Austin, 2013; Potter, 2010). Interventions are incorporated into everything from standard school disciplines to antidrug programs, smoking prohibition, antipoverty efforts, citizenship development, positive body image development, antiviolence efforts, sobriety efforts, nutrition education, fighting stereotyping and racism, and help-the-homeless curricula. Others are attempting, with some success, to use media education to control absenteeism, raise grades, promote self-esteem, reduce teacher-student-parent friction, and more.

Media education supporters can be found from the PTA to UNESCO (Asthana, 2006). Adherents are found in Japan, Canada, Australia, New Zealand, the United Kingdom, Sweden, Finland, Brazil, and every state in the United States (Beach & Baker, 2011; Kaiser Family Foundation, 2003; Yates, 2004). Major U.S. medical organizations support media education, especially the American Academy of Pediatrics (2012).

Media literacy programs and media education programs with media literacy components are being funded and implemented in most states (Martens, 2010). It is symbolic of this growth that Texas has instituted a wide-ranging media literacy program and includes media literacy on its mandatory high school graduation test (Hobbs & Frost, 2003).

Thus, while many stakeholders, definitions, and theories have created some confusion in a growing wealth of research areas, practitioners in these areas want to help youth and citizens become better able to deal with a hypermediated, hypercommercial future. Media literacy is only a small part of school curricula and social programs, but it is growing and also contributing content to other literacies.

Does Media Literacy Work? Reviewing the Literature

There are approximately 200 published media literacy studies, compared, for example, to thousands of studies about media effects. Allowing a caveat for the infancy of the field, one must note that the research is incredibly diverse and, as yet, only moderately impressive. The empirical data on the effectiveness of media literacy and media education indicate that *they can impart knowledge and change attitudes, as expressed on posttests, but only rarely change behavior.* Some respected scientists are not convinced they *can* change behavior. Noted University of Iowa media effects researcher Craig Anderson suggests that media literacy, at least in terms of violence reduction, is *not* effective:

To minimize observational learning, priming, automatization, and desensitization, an intervention must either reduce the child's exposure to violence or reduce the likelihood that the child will identify with the aggressive characters, perceive their actions as realistic and justified, and perceive aggression as acceptable. General media literacy programs do not specifically attempt to accomplish either of these two types of reductions; thus, it is not surprising that there is no valid research demonstrating effectiveness of general media literacy education. (Anderson et al., 2003, p. 103)

One needs to read the research carefully. For example, a well-known media literacy advocate conducted a careful and detailed review of 24 health-promoting media literacy education studies and concluded, "Media literacy education has the *potential* [emphasis added] to be a useful health-promoting strategy for *ameliorating* [emphasis added] a number of harmful health behaviors" (Bergsma & Carney, 2008). Such a conclusion can be misleading. An analysis of that review's statistics finds that 8 of the 24 studies that measured behavioral change failed to produce significant change, compared to only 1 that did.

The key weakness of media literacy and media education research is *the scarcity of funding*. Media literacy studies tend to treat *small samples*. They are frequently *survey based, simple in design, nonrandomized, short term*, and *not peer reviewed*. Longitudinal and replicated studies are almost nonexistent.

The lack of commonality of context, media literacy content, methodologies, skills taught, intervention length, and qualifications of trainers, as well as—and perhaps most important—the inability to measure the charisma and personality of the intervention leader's personality, makes coming to conclusions about research in this field a gamble at best. Careful quasi-experimental studies exist, but there are few longitudinal studies. Instead of day-to-day teachers, specially trained individuals or the researchers themselves usually perform the interventions. Frequently, there are no independent evaluators and the intervening groups do the evaluations. Despite a need for qualitative studies, quantitative studies dominate (Fox, 2005; Potter, 2004).

Nevertheless, there is room for enthusiasm. Many practitioners and researchers find that media literacy programs can successfully add knowledge, change attitudes, and, perhaps, affect behaviors. This research suggests that the content and skills of media literacy can be taught, and that media education might enhance childhood, culture, and democracy. When media literacy programs include parents, teachers, and students, as well as change students' habits of media consumption to a healthier media "diet," greater success in changing behavior seems likely.

Additionally, given that the field is in its infancy, one might suggest that students may gain benefits from media education long after their exposure. This writer has taught media education for decades, and I can say that some of the most resistant students became alumni who valued media education long after their courses; hence the need for longitudinal studies.

Teaching Media Literacy Skills

Research suggests that the content and skills of media analysis *can be taught*. Critical reading and viewing of multiple texts; the ability to recognize point of view, bias, commercial connections, target audience, text and subtexts of messages in multiple forms, and construction techniques; and the ability to express the related viewpoints and information omitted from media messages (i.e., the "untold stories" of media messages) were taught in one form or another and to varying degrees in many of the following studies. Most studies teach some version of the *basic principles of media education*:

1. All media messages are "constructed."

2. Media messages are created using a creative language with its own rules and production techniques.

3. Different people experience the same message differently.

4. Media messages have embedded values, stereotypes, myths, biases, values, lifestyles, and/or points of view.

5. Most media messages are constructed to gain profit and/or power. (Bergsma & Carney, 2008).

Quin and McMahon (1995) produced one of the first large-scale studies ($N = 1,500$) of media literacy skills in Australia. Students learned to identify the purpose, target audience, point of view, and qualities of representation of media messages. Hobbs and Frost (1999) demonstrated similar skills acquisition, as well as showing that media literacy that is integrated into existing curricula can be superior to prepackaged curricular units.

In one of the most innovative and carefully done studies of media literacy skills, Hobbs and Frost (2003) conducted a quasi-experimental measure in which 11th graders ($N = 293$) in one high school were compared to a random sample of 89 eleventh-grade students in a similar school. The teachers, with some expert aid, designed media literacy interventions that were integrated into a redesigned 11th-grade English curriculum.

The interventions varied somewhat from teacher to teacher and, in total, represent a useful list of the range of innovative possibilities for teaching media literacy. Most emphasized reading, listening, viewing, and writing comprehension, as well as identification of point of view, construction techniques, omissions, purpose, target audience, and comparison-contrast. Treatment students outperformed controls by varying amounts in all areas.

The study had a number of weaknesses: an unusually motivated faculty, an independent faculty who taught the lessons in differing styles, a mostly middle-class suburban student group, a nonrandomized treatment sample, and uncontrolled influences of other courses' media education that were not evaluated. Nonetheless, it showed that to varying degrees, students can learn media literacy skills and content. Equally interesting were the results concerning traditional English skills (Hobbs & Frost, 2003).

Hobbs (2004a) used a different evaluation of the aforementioned study's data (Hobbs & Frost, 2003) to analyze the effectiveness of a subset treatment of media literacy upon advertising's effect. The treatment resulted in increases in knowledge of advertising preproduction techniques, the ability to analyze a print ad, the identification of a target audience, the identification of attention manipulation techniques, and the ability to identify ad message subtexts.

Livingstone and Helsper (2006) added to the understanding of children's cognitive processing of ads, and they suggest that different treatments are effective for different ages. They use the term *advertising literacy*. Bergsma and Carney (2008) found that almost all of the 24 studies they analyzed were successful in teaching a wide variety of media education and analysis-based skills and knowledge.

Thus, media education encompasses many media-related analytic skills; it includes but is more than media criticism. Nonetheless, while appreciating increases in students' analytic abilities, many media educators believe that media literacy/media education can accomplish more than analytic skills. Can it make students more knowledgeable and healthier citizens (Phang & Schaefer, 2009)? Can it create a more functional democracy? Might it counter unhealthy advertising and entertainment? Could it create more involved parents? Might it achieve the mythical goal of education—causing students to become lifelong learners? One hopes that it can, because "children and teenagers spend more time engaged in various media than they do in any other activity except for sleeping" (Council on Communication and Media, 2010).

Media Literacy and Public Health

Tobacco, Alcohol, and Drugs

Most research has been done in the public health domain because (a) government agencies sponsoring grants see media literacy as a way to counter negative media effects (Huston et al., 1992); (b) it is easy for the public to understand relatively simple media problems, such as the targeting of children with tobacco and alcohol ads, inappropriate sex, and glorification of violent solutions to problems; and (c) much research supports the use of media education.

> Health behavior theory also supports the use of media literacy to prevent harmful health behaviors such as smoking. The Theory of Reasoned Action (TRA) is a well-accepted, broadly applied theory of health behavior that has been used to predict a variety of health behaviors. . . . According to the TRA, an individual's behavior (such as smoking) is determined by his or her *intention* to perform the behavior, which is in turn predicted by his or her *attitude* toward the behavior and sense of *normative beliefs* regarding it. (Primack et al., 2009, p. 543)

A subset of the TRA, the message interpretation processing (MIP) model, supported by a large body of research, accepts that people are *active* processors of media who, while not always logical, are *rational* decision makers. "Young people's identification with mediated portrayals associates with behavioral intentions and actual behavior" (Pinkleton, Austin, & Van de Vord, 2010, p. 4). According to MIP, "individuals' affect-based information processing strategies often override their logic-based thinking, which directly links to their behavioral intentions" (Pinkleton, Austin, Chen, & Cohen, 2011, p. 4).

The MIP increases critical thinking skills about media in an effort to reduce the influence of the media's role as a "super peer" (Scull, Kupersmidt, Parker, Elmore, & Benson, 2009) on students' intent to engage in risky behavior. *Media messages that possess similarities to the viewer, stir the emotions, make risky behavior seem cool, and are entertaining are likely to influence the viewer to engage in risky behavior.* The MIP model short-circuits that process, producing viewers with a higher level of cognitive power.

MIP advocates Austin and Johnson (1997) increased 3rd and 4th graders' understanding of the intent of alcohol advertising and decreased the treatment groups' desire to be like the ads' characters, all with just a single media literacy session. Even three months later, the study had decreased treatment group members' expectation of positive consequences from drinking alcohol and decreased their likelihood of choosing an alcoholic drink ($N = 225$).

Another study that used alcohol education and discussion of beer ads among 12- to 18-year-olds predicted cognitive resistance (counterarguing) after the treatment group viewed a 20-minute sports show with four beer ads. The effect lasted months after the intervention in many of the subjects (and years after in others) ($N = 83$) (Slater et al., 1996).

A large ($N = 789$ at 12 schools) and carefully done study based on a 10-lesson elementary school unit, *Media Detective*, successfully increased critical thinking skills, decreased intentions to use alcohol and tobacco, and increased self-efficacy to refuse future use in elementary students (Kupersmidt, Scull, & Austin, 2010). The interveners were teachers who received one day of training. The curriculum was professionally produced, and students looked for five "clues when shown an advertisement":

(1) the product being sold; (2) the target audience the advertisers are trying to attract; (3) the ad hook used to attract attention; (4) the hidden message, or what the ad is suggesting will happen if you use the product; and (5) the missing information about health consequences from using the product. (Kupersmidt et al., 2010, p. 528)

To reduce resistance, students were first guided in practicing deconstruction skills on ads other than those promoting alcohol and tobacco. The unit included attention to the benefits of being an active media consumer and concluded with the creation of a counter-ad. While short term, this experimental study created persuasive results.

A recent intervention exemplifies the growth of media education. Rona Zlokower and four colleagues attended a four-day workshop run by this writer in 2001. From that seed grew a successful organization, Media Power Youth. MPY conducted an impressive intervention designed to change the attitudes and intentions of 5th graders with respect to tobacco, violence, and nutrition ($N = 308$). The design of the study and corresponding curriculum (Bickham & Slaby, 2012) contains an impressive mix of protection, discussion, production, and critical thinking.

While some results were mixed, the program successfully taught that media glorify violence, magnify dubious "benefits" of nonnutritious food, and make smoking look cool. The program's *susceptibility reduction* strategy taught children to critically evaluate new media messages—ones not in the intervention—when they were presented with them. Students successfully applied critical media literacy skills that could help protect them from possible harms associated with unrealistic and misleading messages.

Media education has often been used in tobacco prevention and cessation efforts (Gonazales, Glik, Davoudi, & Ang, 2004). Failures aside, it seems to be effective at increasing knowledge about smoking, changing attitudes toward smoking and smoking advertising, and reducing smoking behavior (Bair et al., 2011; Pinkleton, Austin, Cohen, Miller, & Fitzgerald, 2007). Media education "has been shown to be strongly and independently associated with both reduced adolescent smoking and reduced susceptibility to future smoking" (Primack et al., 2009, p. 542).

A large-scale ($N = 1,372$) study by the New Mexico Media Literacy Project used a six-day intervention with three booster sessions and demonstrated a change in 8th graders' attitudes toward alcohol and tobacco advertising, engendered anger toward tobacco companies, created a greater awareness of the role of advertising, and increased students' desire to live a healthier lifestyle (McCannon, 2002, 2005).

Teen leaders, advised by adults, were effective in developing and teaching an anti-tobacco curriculum for high school students. The study (Pinkleton, Austin, Cohen, & Miller, 2003) notes that media literacy influenced tobacco use at various stages of the decision making process. Tobacco users and non–tobacco users gained knowledge of tobacco ads' techniques of persuasion, becoming better able to resist them. Non–tobacco users gained determination to dissuade peers from smoking. Some students became less likely to identify with people in ads who smoked, and overall the students felt they became less susceptible to peer pressure toward smoking.

The Importance of Emotion

Austin, Pinkleton, and Funabiki (2007) executed an impressive statewide six-day quasi-experimental anti-tobacco study ($N = 723$). A precise anti-tobacco media literacy program incorporating innovative tobacco information, media literacy skills, analysis, and media production, combined with an emotional activation/efficacy element, was used to increase students' comprehension of tobacco advertising methods and their desire to participate in tobacco prevention advocacy. This could be a good tobacco use prevention model.

Emotional activation techniques are contested within the media literacy field. Methods that create anticipation in advocacy work, anger at tobacco companies, mistrust of alcohol corporations, and the like are controversial. Some think media literacy should teach only critical thinking skills. Austin and her colleagues' treatment (Austin et al., 2007; Austin, Pinkleton, & Hust, 2005) represents a sophisticated and effective compromise between the two schools of thought.

Work by Austin and colleagues (2005), Scull and colleagues (2009), and *Kupersmidt* and colleagues (2010) augurs that media education inoculation treatments are effective in promoting resistance to persuasive appeals. More general media literacy approaches, for which data are rare, have been more adept at increasing knowledge, especially of media, than they have been at changing attitudes or decision making outcomes (Austin et al., 2005; Graham & Hernandez, 1993).

Media literacy that includes an emotional factor seems to overcome the seduction of modern advertising. However, some studies have noted an apparent paradox. While media education can create resistance to messages, *higher levels of perceived desirability of the ads' portrayals* have been found in some experimental groups (Austin, Chen, & Grube, 2006; Austin, Chen, Pinkleton, & Johnson, 2006).

Thus, participants need to understand media literacy concepts *and* have the *motivation* to apply this knowledge through logical decision making (Austin et al., 2002). Austin, Chen, Pinkleton, and Johnson (2006) provide an exhaustive analysis of the goal of this methodology— how media-literate students can enjoy, for example, emotion-filled beer advertising yet remain less susceptible to its persuasive subtexts. "Stated more simply, it is possible that participants in the media literacy training have learned to manage their response to enticing media portrayals while still recognizing that message creators produce messages that are highly desirable" (Austin, Chen, Pinkleton, et al., 2006, p. 426).

The Centers for Disease Control and Prevention (CDC) and other government entities have endorsed media literacy for drug prevention and have sponsored several curricula. Few have been seriously evaluated or independently replicated. One study using *Media Literacy for Drug Prevention*, done in conjunction with the *New York Times*, reported achieving a number of positive results, but it was evaluated by using surveys of teachers (Kaiser Family Foundation, 2003).

The large-scale and successful Florida *Truth* campaign, now the American Legacy Project, has set the standard for motivating students against tobacco companies. With a core of brilliant anti-ads, it provides a great model. The *Truth* campaign aggressively—and often humorously—lays blame for the tobacco problem at the doorstep of 40 years of tobacco company advertising. It makes smoking look "uncool" (see Figure 12.1).

A catch-all prevention program with a media education thread, Life Skills Training (LST) by Dr. Gilbert Botvin, is less aggressive in blaming tobacco companies and seems successful. LST began as an anti-tobacco program and has expanded to address other addictive behaviors. It consists of 20 or more lessons administered over three years. LST was first recommended by the CDC in 1997 (Mandel, Bialous, & Glantz, 2006) and is now recommended by the National Institute of Health. Recently, LST has been used for the prevention of HIV and even risky driving ("Resource Fact Sheet," n.d.).

One analysis of LST indicates that it improved youth knowledge of smoking's physiological effects but did not provide evidence of reduced youth smoking. "In fact, decision-making skills actually moved in the wrong direction" (Mandel et al., 2006). Since then, other researchers have given LST positive evaluations, but most of those studies have been done by LST's creator, Gilbert Botvin. Longitudinal studies do not exist.

LST is controversial, because Philip Morris spent millions of dollars on promotion, including hiring one of the world's largest public relations firms to popularize the LST program with

Figure 12.1 *Truth* ad from the American Legacy Project.

health professionals, administrators, teachers, and parents. Philip Morris even used third-party entities to disguise its financial support. Hundreds of thousands of students in more than 20 states have taken or are taking LST.

A standard media education question would be, "Why would Philip Morris go to such extremes to promote LST in this manner?" Philip Morris usually publicizes all its supposed prosocial programs. Perhaps Philip Morris is just a well-intentioned philanthropist, but its history would suggest otherwise. Mandel and his colleagues (2006) document many industry communications in which Philip Morris repeatedly related its opposition to programs that aggressively castigate the tobacco companies' 40 years of deceitful and irresponsible advertising to youth in magazines, television, and movies. Big Tobacco opposes such programs, saying they demonize the tobacco industry unjustly.

Relatively little of LST focuses on directly reducing tobacco use, and since there is controversy about its support and effectiveness, one wonders why the more media-intensive approaches, such as *Truth*, have not been more widely adopted. Could it be that LST diverts large amounts of resources away from other, more aggressive programs (Mandel et al., 2006)?

This situation presents a conundrum for media literacy/media education scholars. Organizations with vested interests see public relations value in working with media education organizations and financing media literacy curricula and research. They can even create "AstroTurf " organizations (fake grassroots groups), fake news reports, articles that attack opponents, and biased studies to aid their campaigns and lobbying for or against legislation (Stauber & Rampton, 1995).

Vested interests can produce curricula that put a positive light on the vested interest, avoiding legitimate criticism or deflecting attention from criticized activities. These activities are not confined to the tobacco industry. Other examples include Channel One, the cable television industry, the video game industry, alcohol companies, the movie industry, toy manufacturers, and food manufacturers targeting advertisements to the very young.

Some educators have gone to great lengths to avoid corporate bias. Utah has created its own long-term program. *Prevention Dimensions* utilizes a detailed, constantly evolving curriculum. The program contains over 200 lessons and covers Grades K through 12. It is innovative, comprehensive, and age appropriate.

Thus, use of media education suggests scrutinizing objectives and lessons carefully for industry support and looking for untold stories in the content.

Nutrition and Obesity

The obesity epidemic seems directly related to the food industry's advertising, which targets children as young as preschool age (Kunkel, 2005; McLellan, 2002). Five year-olds prefer food that comes in McDonalds wrappers to unbranded packages (Robinson, Borzekowski, Matheson, & Kraemer, 2007). Even though young people seem to have a very primitive understanding of ad techniques and can deconstruct ads in very basic ways, they still desire the highly advertised energy-dense, poor-nutrient foods (Mehta et al., 2010). This situation seems ripe for more media education.

A small after-school quasi-experimental study ($N = 19$) worked with kids and parents, changing the parents' and children's media awareness and, interestingly enough, the behavior of the parents, who provided more fruits and vegetables for their children. However, the children's consumption behavior did not change (Evans et al., 2006).

A number of industry-related programs exist in this area. The industry hopes to be seen as part of the solution to obesity and, perhaps, avoid advertising restrictions, particularly on advertising aimed toward young children and for food products that have little or negative nutritional value (Kleinman, 2003; Teinowitz, 2001). This is acknowledged by the industry itself (Cincotta, 2005). Furthermore, Hobbs (1998) suggests that industry-supported media literacy might reduce criticism of the potential negative effects of the media, which are supported by much advertising that can be interpreted as unhealthy.

Coca-Cola, McDonald's restaurants, Kellogg's, Nestlé, and others have operated Concerned Children's Advertisers (CCA) as a nonprofit organization in Canada since 1990 and have provided dietary media education for children through public service announcements (PSAs) as well as school and home media literacy resources on drug use, self-esteem, and bullying.

A similar European program, Media Smart, operating in 20% of the United Kingdom, aims to

> help people understand the distinctions between media services, critically appraise their content, use the tools which are increasingly available to navigate the electronic world, becoming empowered digital citizens. It also helps children learn how to maintain critical distinctions between fact and fiction (especially in interactive environments) or between reporting and advocacy, as well as how to assess commercial messages. ("Media Smart," 2003, p. 1)

Nonetheless, CCA's and Media Smart's stated objectives lack measurable specificity, and they have been evaluated by relatively superficial means (CCA, 2004). Rather than surveying changes in attitude or behavior, CCA surveys mass recall; for instance, 74% of Canadian children believe that the advertisements helped them to better understand television (Eagle, 2005). Media Smart uses teacher satisfaction to measure the program (Eagle, 2005; Muto, 2004). More rigorous evaluation is needed if the program is to be taken seriously. And, while these efforts might benefit youth, one wonders why these industries, with their tremendous resources, do not subsidize scientific research to evaluate these issues. Big Media is seldom willing to evaluate the effects of advertising on health. Few advertisers support efforts to create more media-literate consumers (Armstrong & Brucks, 1988; Eagle, 2005).

One of the best financed and most widespread interventions is a version of Media Smart's 10-lesson program, which is supported by the National Institute of Child Health and Human Development (NICHD). *Media-Smart Youth: Eat, Think and Be Active* is designed for adolescents 11 to 13 years old. It uses hands-on activities to evaluate media messages and teaches on media awareness, media production, nutrition, and physical activity ("For Your Information," 2006).[2] NICHD's evaluation of its program (Eunice Kennedy Shriver NICHD, 2009) found mixed and unimpressive results, with some changes in attitudes and none in behavioral intent—a disappointing outcome, especially for a high-profile government program.

A small Head Start intervention for parents succeeded in teaching nutrition and diet information as well as analysis skills, changing parents' TV behaviors (Hindin, Contento, & Gussow, 2004). Valkenburg (2005) reviews parental mediation techniques, suggesting that exposure to advertising predicts children's materialism and toy requests, which in turn affect parent-child conflict. Her study of 360 child-parent pairs found that discussion techniques were more effective than restrictive methods at reducing these effects. This reinforces other research suggesting that media education can work when parents are involved. A weakness of the study was its failure to include a technique of "enlightened" restriction (i.e., leading children to self-regulate and/or reduce their media diets).

Body Image

Media education as a treatment for body image and eating disorders is popular. Improvements in attitudes and knowledge can be had, but changes in behavior are elusive. A treatment reduced college women's perceptions of the reality and desirability of the thin stereotype, but did not improve body dissatisfaction (Irving & Berel, 2001). A review by Littleton and Ollendick (2003) suggests that school programs have little positive effect on body image satisfaction and disordered eating but can affect self-esteem, life skills, and awareness of media pressures.

The National Eating Disorders Association's "Go Girls" program of media literacy skills boosted high school girls' sense of empowerment and self-esteem regarding media images of women's bodies (Nirva, Levine, & Irving, 2000) and reduced their internalization of the slender media-constructed ideal and desire for thinness (Piran, Levine, & Irving, 2000).

A small study (Wade, Davidson, & O'Dea, 2003) compared a similar curriculum with a purely self-esteem-focused intervention, and the media literacy intervention had a more positive impact on weight *concern*, although *neither affected dietary restraint.* The authors thought the more collaborative methodology was a factor, but the study was very small.

Bergsma and Carney's review (2008) of seven mostly older studies showed some improvement in knowledge and attitudes about culture and media, but little change in diet, dieting, or other risk factors for eating problems. A small study *(N* = 10) treated women who were at high risk with a two-session media literacy treatment and succeeded in reducing some risk factors for eating disorders, including body dissatisfaction and drive for thinness, but it created no significant decreases in desire for perfection, appearance comparisons, or emphasis on beauty norms (Coughlin & Kalodner, 2006).

A substantial study (Steiner-Adair et al., 2002), organized by the Harvard Eating Disorders Center, evaluated 500 seventh-grade girls who took part in Full of Ourselves: Advancing Girl Power, Health, and Leadership. They were tested before the treatment, immediately after the treatment, and six months later. The treatment involved 10 sessions, including "Dieting Dilemma," "Claiming Our Strengths," and "The Power of Positive Action" (Giedrys, 1999, p. 1). Improvements in knowledge and weight-related body esteem were significant. Unfortunately, given the extent of dieting in young girls, behaviors such as skipping meals and dieting were unaffected.

Another study, a randomized controlled trial with 226 Girl Scouts, found that a six-lesson (90-minute, biweekly) unit improved "media-related attitudes and behaviors including internalization of sociocultural ideals, self-efficacy to impact weight-related social norms, and print media habits" (Neumark-Sztainer, Sherwood, Coller, & Hannan, 2000, p. 1466). Unfortunately, dieting behavior did not change.

A more hopeful note regarding behavior was sounded by Australian researchers Wilksch and Wade (2009), who did an eating disorder study with a large group (*N* = 540).

Twenty-four classes were randomly assigned to control or treatment groups at four schools. The intervention was evaluated immediately after the eight-session intervention and at four weeks, six months, *and 30 months*. The 50-minute program centered on media literacy, activism, and advocacy with carefully prepared lessons, activities, and a "take-home message." It treated shape and weight concern, body dissatisfaction, media internalization, perceived pressure and ineffectiveness, depression, self-esteem, and dieting. The treatment group was significantly better on *all risk factors* than the control group, which, interestingly enough, increased its risk factors over the 30 months (i.e., got worse). Most important, the treatment held up at 30 months.

Despite this success, the lack of consistent, positive behavioral results is unfortunate. While the research points in some positive directions, especially in the area of self-esteem and knowledge, more work remains in the area of behavior.

Media Education and Violence

As shown in previous chapters, all but a few experts accept that media violence can cause aggression, fear, desensitization, and other antisocial effects (see Chapter 4). And since media increasingly contain problematic content and are more and more marketed toward youth (Anderson & Bushman, 2001), researchers are attempting to combat the effects of media violence.

Using media literacy to reduce aggression is complex. Some treatments could be beneficial; others might accentuate the very effect they try to mitigate. An excellent review concludes,

> Studies show that adults' comments before or during media exposure can reduce the impact of violent programming on children's aggressiveness under some circumstances. Experiments involving more extensive media literacy curricula show that some approaches can alter attitudes toward media violence and, in a few cases, intervene in aggressive behavior. Studies of the impact of antiviolence media productions reveal that although such efforts can be effective, unanticipated "boomerang" effects are prevalent. (Cantor & Wilson, 2003, p. 363)

Students are learning about the techniques and nature of mass media (Dorr, Graves, & Phelps, 1980; Rapaczynski, Singer, & Singer, 1982; Singer, Zuckerman, & Singer, 1980), but many scholars would love to find a way to combat the violence in the media. One intervention is to *change or limit the media "diet"* of youth. It seems that restricting children's media consumption, if done right, can be beneficial, but it can also boomerang. Tom Robinson's careful work in this area (Robinson, 1999; Robinson, Saphir, Kraemer, Varady, & Haydel, 2001; Robinson, Wilde, Navracruz, Haydel, & Varady, 2000) crystallized the value of this approach by combining elements of limiting television and video games, working with parents, and teaching children to be wiser viewers. The experimental groups showed decreases in obesity, requests for toys, and, most impressive, aggressive behavior.

Two months of lessons by regular teachers (trained by the research staff) motivated children to monitor and reduce their screen watching habits. Then, a 10-day TV-turnoff period was followed by more lessons in an attempt to limit viewing to seven hours per week. Resources and instruction were provided for parents. After 20 weeks, the researchers achieved significant reductions in self-reported and observed physical aggression and verbal aggression in the experimental school, revealing the potential for this combination of media literacy strategies.

A program modeled on Robinson but with a shorter treatment, the 10-Day Challenge (Brodeur, 2005), emphasized limiting students' media diet as a form of *strike* against broadcasters, advertisers, and violent entertainment producers. It operated in 20 Quebec and Ontario elementary schools and was evaluated in one high school. Five hundred students participated, and evaluations surveyed students, teachers, and parents.

Students took the challenge, walking through the streets of their city at lunchtime, just like striking workers. Of the students, 78% participated, and 72% said that the challenge was very or quite useful and that they would do it again. Two-thirds of parents found the challenge very or quite useful, and 86.2% of the staff considered the process very or quite important.

The Challenge increased physical activities for half of the students; 45% reported increased time spent with friends, 25% reported increased time spent with parents and increased help with tasks at home, 32% reported decreased physical violence, and 27% reported decreased verbal violence. Verbal and physical violence at home decreased 38%. Sixty-five percent reported increased media awareness, and 60% of parents and 90% of teachers reported improvement in children's viewing skills (Brodeur, 2005). The study has a number of evaluation flaws, but this limited survey evaluation characterizes many simple, but possibly effective, media education programs.

Limitation can also produce negative results (Nathanson, 2002), as can rating systems. Both may increase youth desire to see forbidden programs (Bushman & Cantor, 2003; Bushman & Stack, 1996; Cantor, 1998). Parents and caregivers need to carefully observe the effects of limitations on children. *Giving children other enjoyable and valuable things to do*, especially teaching them to engage in self-directed creative play, rather than banning screens in a vacuum, is always a good strategy. More research is needed to discover if positive effects outweigh the value of proscriptions.

Another strategy is to watch with children. *Co-viewing* is relatively rare, as is actively watching or giving children *instruction* before, during, or after they experience media. Results are mixed, but co-viewing can be useful (Austin, 1993a, 1993b; Nathanson & Cantor, 2000; Nathanson & Yang, 2003; Potter, 2010).

In an important study with a fairly large group (N = 351 second through sixth graders), Nathanson and Cantor (2000) found that a brief introduction to a short cartoon clip, asking children to consider the victim and his feelings, caused young children, especially boys, to be more likely to identify with the victim. Children in the intervention group viewed the characters and the violence differently than the control group did and thought the violence was less justified. The intervention also reduced both boys' and girls' appreciation for the cartoon hero (Woody Woodpecker), whose comic treatment of violence was the essence of the plot.

Parents who use cartoons as a babysitter might take notice of Cantor and Wilson (2003), who suggest questioning the plight, consequences, and real-world suffering of cartoon victims, to avoid their children's imitation of, desensitization toward, and acceptance of violent solutions to problems.

Criticizing violent media content seems to reduce the inculcation of aggressive attitudes and behaviors. Praise may actually *promote* them (Austin, 2001; Bandura, 1986; Buerkel-Rothfuss & Buerkel, 2001).

Most important, co-viewing violence with parents who do not make comments or question media content may indicate to children and adolescents that the parents approve of the behavior (Chen & Austin, 2013; Buerkel-Rothfuss & Buerkel, 2001; Hicks, 1968; Horton & Santogrossi, 1978; Nathanson, 1999).

Several researchers report that giving youth information about violence causes them to devalue violence, but the available studies give conflicting results, do not measure behavior, or fail to affect behavior when the adult who gave the information is not present (Corder-Bolz, 1980; Hicks, 1968; Horton & Santogrossi, 1978).

Huesmann, Eron, Klein, Brice, and Fischer did two revealing studies in 1983. First, they taught 2nd and 4th graders in three hour-long training sessions over six to eight weeks about the difference between characters in violent shows and real people. They also revealed the production techniques that enabled these characters to do impossible things, and they showed that real people used different strategies to solve problems. The pretest was done nine months before the intervention. The posttest followed it by three months and revealed that *the intervention had no effect* on perceived realism of television shows, peer-assessed aggression, or reported viewing levels of television violence. The study suggests that teaching simple media literacy production techniques alone may not reduce children's vulnerability to violent media.

Huesmann and his colleagues (1983) later modified their intervention. Children made a film depicting students who were deceived, led to break rules, or harmed by violent media. They wrote papers about the negative violent media, videotaped their reading of the papers, watched the tapes, and discussed the messages. Control group children did the same procedures for an innocuous topic.

The results were significant. While rates of viewing TV violence for the two groups did not differ, treated students devalued television more and believed it less realistic. They were also assessed by peers as less aggressive than the comparison group four months after the intervention. Thus, it would seem that *active, carefully planned, and targeted media literacy content and production methodologies can reduce the harmful effects* of watching violent content, whereas *simplistic methods may cause the reverse.*

Nathanson (2004) compared value-neutral versus activist/media education strategies: in one group giving information about production and filming techniques, and in another giving negative information about violent characters, such as saying they were bullies, not cool, and probably had no friends. The value-neutral treatment was either ineffective or increased the chances of a negative effect, whereas giving negative information within an evaluative framework was a more effective strategy for promoting a positive outcome (a negative view of the violent characters), especially with younger children. It is important to note that critical analysis can also involve praise as well as disparagement. Regarding evaluation, Byrne (2009) notes, "Providing facts about the media, or media production, has been shown to be less effective than evaluative content."

Mediation interventions also can be effective (Nathanson, 2003; Nathanson & Yang, 2003), but it seems methodology is important. Nathanson and Yang (2003) found satisfactory results of mediation statements placed within violent programming; however, somewhat of a boomerang effect, whereby the intervention achieved the opposite of the desired result, occurred with older students (ages 9–12). It is possible that younger students (ages 5–8) had a need for the information whereas older students found it condescending. Both of these treatments were most effective with "heavy" viewers of media violence.

Doolittle (1980) showed one group how violent media were created and allowed another group to try producing programming. The former showed no effect, but the latter group self-reported perceived reality, arousal, and *increased* aggression—an important consequence when considering boomerang.

Vooijs and van der Voort (1993) tested the wisdom of media literacy based on the difference between fantasy and reality. Their five-week curriculum increased students' perceptions of the seriousness of TV violence and their knowledge of real violence. It reduced their approval of TV violence and their perceptions of TV's realism. Unfortunately, it demonstrated the *importance of continuing media literacy throughout the curriculum*, as some of the significant effects of their study had disappeared at the two-year follow-up posttest.

An innovative study was undertaken with children in Grades 1 through 3 ($N = 177$) by Rosenkoetter, Rosenkoetter, Ozretich, and Acock (2004). Thirty-one brief lessons revealed the many types of distortion in TV representations of violence. The intervention *reduced children's viewing of violent TV* and their identification with violent TV characters. While it was more successful with girls, boys were judged by their classmates to have *reduced their behavioral aggression* after treatment, an unusual result.

As we have seen, Robinson and his colleagues (2001) achieved significant *reduction in aggression* with a comprehensive 18-lesson media literacy curriculum that involved negotiated media limitation and parental involvement, suggesting the importance of a multipronged program or, at the very least, involving the parents. Interestingly enough, "it showed that reducing children's media exposure combined with negative parental mediation can reduce antisocial behavior even in the absence of instruction about media violence effects" (Cantor & Wilson, 2003, p. 387).

Byrne (2009) has concluded that successful treatments are evaluative, increase emotional involvement, are taught in a fun tone, and encourage participants to be active in the learning process. Her research, however, proves the complexity of trying to reduce aggression through media literacy. The 4th or 5th graders ($N = 156$) were divided into three groups: a control, one that received a lesson about media effects and how to evaluate violent characters, and one that experienced the same lesson, but then wrote a paragraph about their experience (which was videotaped). The latter group experienced *decreased* willingness to use aggression. However, the second group showed *increased* willingness to use aggression (i.e., a boomerang effect).

According to Byrne (2009), "The basic lesson may have increased attention to the violent clips used as examples in the media literacy lesson, while at the same time lacked the cognitive activity required to process and learn the critical concepts." Cantor and Wilson (2003) and Nathanson (2004) suggest similar explanations. In addition, while questioning and trying to elicit empathy for victims can also be effective, one must note that *making no comment or neutral comments produces an effect similar to praising the violence*.

Thus, media literacy used to reduce aggression can be useful, but one must consider the form, method, and age appropriateness of the intervention. Such interventions should be done very carefully and only in conjunction with detailed planning and precise evaluation (Cantor & Wilson, 2003).

Interveners should also recognize the limitations of these studies, which are diverse and short term, have not been replicated, and, of course, rely on parents' and caregivers' being present to co-view. Achieving co-viewing will also require a substantial change in the culture, since, as Muto (2004) indicates, up to 85% of children's viewing in multiset households is unsupervised and 58% of children ages 4 to 9 have televisions in their bedrooms.

So, for now, more research is needed on matching media literacy treatments, methods, appropriate content, and duration of intervention with different ages and types of students. Some treatments have worked with young children and some with older children. Some were failures, especially when methods were not age appropriate or precisely thought out. Until longitudinal studies with larger randomized samples and *other objectives* are done, practitioners need to remain cautious.

> One useful approach would be to assess other harmful outcomes of exposure to media violence, such as desensitization and fearful reactions. . . . the interventions generally failed to modify children's enjoyment of or exposure to violent programming (Huesmann et al., 1983; Rosenkoetter et al., 2002 [boys]; Sprafkin et al., 1987; Vooijs & van der Voort, 1993). Given the potential for desensitization, reducing children's preference for media violence is undoubtedly an important goal of media literacy. (Cantor & Wilson, 2003, p. 387)

A handful of studies suggest that use of *media productions* can be beneficial. Antirape productions, used in carefully planned curricula, can produce beneficial results among college students and older men (Intons-Peterson, Roskos-Ewoldsen, Thomas, Shirley, & Blut, 1989; Linz, Fuson, & Donnerstein, 1990). However, a similar objective produced mixed results among 15- to 16-year-olds (Winkel & DeKleuver, 1997).

Use of a made-for-TV movie about date rape with high school students, *No Means No*, followed by a discussion with two trained college students, produced some positive results but led some males (approaching significance) to a boomerang effect: perceptions of decreased responsibility of the perpetrators and decreased seriousness of the offense (Filotas, 1993).

In a larger study, Wilson, Linz, Donnerstein, and Stipp (1992) showed a critically acclaimed made-for-TV movie, *She Said No*, to a national sample of 1,038 participants the day before it played nationally. The telephone survey again revealed mixed results: positive feelings about the seriousness of the problem, but a negative effect among older males, who tended to blame the victim.

Antiviolence researchers have used TV programs to suggest alternatives to violent acts, using high-quality antiviolence PSAs with little effect (Biocca et al., 1997). A more carefully planned study used Court TV cases to form the core of a three-week curriculum that involved active deconstruction and role playing (Wilson et al., 1999). It showed *significant reductions in 513 randomized middle school students' verbal and physical aggression*, as well as increases in empathic skills and knowledge of the legal system.

These studies suggest that using powerful productions to achieve prosocial results is, at best, a risky business that can achieve positive results, but can also reinforce antisocial attitudes. Choice of media content is important, as is getting permission to show controversial media. Equally important is a careful strategy of previewing preparation and postviewing activities that *allow the participants to have ownership in the process.*[3]

In a related area, media literacy might be able to help at-risk youth. The New York State Office of Children and Family found benefits of media literacy for supporting decision making skills for young, at-risk students (Behson, 2002). The Massachusetts Juvenile Justice System developed Flashpoint, an innovative but very small media literacy program designed to deconstruct media and promote cognition about moments that might lead the students to risky actions. It relied upon intervention subjects' testifying to their changed behaviors (Budelmann, 2002; Moore, DeChillo, Nicholson, Genovese, & Sladen, 2000).

Responding to Sexual Portrayals

As noted in preceding chapters, the media are a universal sexual educator, giving children and adolescents an infinite number of cues for how to behave in romantic situations (J. D. Brown, Halpern, & L'Engle, 2005; Hust, Brown, & L'Engle, 2008). Only a small percentage of them portray the complexity, risks, and responsibilities of sexual relationships (Kunkel, 2005). Pinkleton and his colleagues (2011, p. 7) note how this situation correlates with ". . . increases in sexual knowledge [and] positive attitudes toward sexual behavior and actual teen pregnancy" (see also Chandra et al., 2008; Collins et al., 2004; Hust et al., 2008).

It is difficult to treat an issue as controversial as media sexuality in the United States; several states have laws against such interventions, and in other states, administrators and school boards are nervous, so the research base for U.S. media education interventions in this areas is meager.

It is different in other countries. Entertainment education is used to promote reproductive health in more than 20 countries. In India, Africa, and Latin America, mass media interventions, such as popular soap operas including plots about family planning and HIV prevention, have reportedly increased clinic visits and changed health behavior (Keller & Brown, 2002).

In some parts of the United States, safe-sex media campaigns have had some success, contributing to increased use of teen condoms (Alstead et al., 1999). Embedded messages in a number of programs, such as *Dawson's Creek*, have tried to present real information about teenage sexuality, violence against women, sexually transmitted diseases, death and dying, and assisted fertility. "Campaign for Our Children," designed to reduce teen pregnancy in Baltimore, Maryland, included dramatic billboards, television ads, and radio spots. It has been credited with contributing to a significant decrease in teen pregnancies (Keller & Brown, 2002).

The best U.S. study to date on this subject was done by media literacy research pioneers. Pinkleton and his colleagues (2011) conducted a large (N = 922 twelve- to eighteen-year-olds at 22 schools) quasi-experiment based on the MIP. According to MIP, "individuals' affect-based information processing strategies often override their logic-based thinking, which directly links to their behavioral intentions" (Pinkleton et al., 2011, p. 4). MIP increases critical thinking skills about media in an effort to reduce the influence of the media's role as a "super peer" (Scull et al., 2009). By short-circuiting that process, MIP produces viewers with a higher level of resistance.

Pinkleton and his colleagues (2011) discovered that well-trained students, leading their peers in five 45-minute lessons, increased participants' understanding of the media's influence over decision making about sex and the inaccuracy of glamorized media sex. Participants also reported a more realistic idea of how many teens practiced sex.

> Students were less likely to overestimate sexual activity among teens, more likely to think they could delay sexual activity, less likely to expect social benefits from sexual activity, more aware of myths about sex, and less likely to consider sexual media imagery desirable. (Pinkleton et al., 2011, p. 4)

The study lacked longitudinal components, randomness, and independent evaluation but was carefully planned, complex in its statistical evaluation, and thorough, giving rise to hopeful expectations in this controversial area of media education.

Channel One: The Largest Media Literacy Experiment

Approximately 35 million of the 42 million U.S. students are exposed to corporate advertising, mostly for foods of dubious nutrition (Molnar, Garcia, Boninger, & Merrill, 2006), and ever more youth-targeted advertising of a questionable nature. Schools used to be a sanctuary, but they are no more. As a Ralph Nader organization notes, "some things are too important to be for sale. Not our children. Not our health. Not our minds. Not our *schools* [emphasis added]" (Ruskin, 2006, p. 1).

Students have great buying power and are a captive audience that is vulnerable to advertising's effects. Schools seem to provide a "legitimizing" effect. The American Academy of Pediatrics posits that students may be more receptive to school ads (Brighouse, 2005; Buijzen & Valkenburg, 2003; Reid & Gedissman, 2000). In 1980, Consumer Reports counted 234 organizations marketing commercial products in schools, ranging from candy to sponsored educational materials (SEMs). SEMs are often biased toward the sponsoring company (Consumer Reports). And today there are a rush of companies from different sectors, led by News Corp., to get in on what is perceived to be a digital education boom (Grgurich, 2012).

Each day Channel One (C1) reaches nearly 6 million students in 7,809 schools with "news" stories and ads; some are violent and racy, some are for psychic readings, and some are ads for candy, gum, video games, skin care products, and the armed forces ("Channel One News," 2012). C1's ads are effective, perhaps more effective than the same ads when seen at home (Infante, Rancer, & Womack, 2003; Palmer & Carpenter, 2006). Interestingly, such corporate advertising adds little to school finances, and if it were removed, school programs would continue (Molnar et al., 2006).

In return for wiring and small television monitors, C1 gets students' eyeballs. Students *must* watch C1 for 12 minutes—2 minutes of ads and 10 minutes of "current events news." Twelve minutes per day equals *one full week of class time annually.* Frequently, the "news" stories feature commercial products.

Since studying product placement is a large part of media literacy, it is significant that C1 will not directly say whether it is paid for product placements ("Deconstructing Judy," 2006). If parents or school board members want to know about a product shown in this taxpayer-created environment, they cannot find out.

That teachers are not trained or motivated to teach the current history covered by C1 is a formula for dubious outcomes and a breach of commonly accepted educational principles.

Channel One's Media Literacy Curriculum

C1 suggests that teachers should use their ads and "news" for media education, and C1 provides a media literacy curriculum. Critics charge that C1's media education programs are like Big Tobacco's "education" programs: a public relations device to head off criticism.

In 2000, Renee Hobbs and Paul Folkemer wrote C1's media literacy curriculum, *Media Mastery* (Business Wire, 2008), which was to use C1's programs for content. It could have been called *Media Mystery*, because after several years, C1 removed it from websites that used to carry it.

Media Mastery was announced with fanfare and promoted for several years to convince doubtful teachers, parents, and school districts to adopt C1. The theory went like this: "We may have ads that could be bad for your kids, and your teachers may not be trained to do current events, but our media literacy program will fix those problems." Is there some irony here?

Millions of students using media literacy curricula: What an opportunity to study media literacy! People expected surveys and evaluations, but nothing significant was forthcoming. In 10 lessons there was *nothing* in *Media Mastery* about junk food, skin care products, rap music, sleazy movies, video games, and the other products C1 hawks.

Media Mastery is a key piece in the efficacy puzzle that media literacy/media education represents. It taught skills objectives, spending much of its time comparing the production techniques of different media. It did not use the emotive factor, and its level of complexity was over the heads of average high school students (not to mention millions of middle school children). It contained few examples that would have connected the student's concrete media world to the abstractions of media literacy, *which is the major strength of media education*. And it avoided any embarrassing or condemnatory questions about media corporations, particularly C1. As such, *Media Mastery* flew in the face of much previously mentioned effectiveness research.

This was a missed opportunity to study important questions. Could media literacy offset the effect of C1's slick youth programming cues, contexts, sophisticated advertising, Internet tie-ins, and target-keyed news content? Did the school environment add "legitimacy" to the ads?

While C1 did not study C1, there is research on it. Interestingly enough, students seem to enjoy C1 (Bachen, 1998; Johnston & Brzezinski, 1992; Johnston, Brzezinski, & Anderman, 1994). C1's benefit is unclear (Bachen, 1998; Ehman, 1993; Johnston et al., 1994). Students who discuss C1 with parents and older students exhibit a slight tendency to improve in their knowledge of current events (Anderman & Johnston, 1997; Bachen, 1998; Ehman, 1993; Johnston et al., 1994; Tiene & Whitmore, 1995; Whitmore & Tiene, 1994). A number of teachers feel they have no role in the adoption of C1 (Barrett, 1995; Knupfer & Hayes, 1994), and others feel unprepared to integrate C1's diverse content into their courses (Bachen, 1998). One study found that C1 increased students' perception of the truthfulness of ads (Krcmar, 2001).

Perhaps most important, *several studies found that C1 increased the desirability of the products advertised* (Bachen, 1998; Greenberg & Brand, 1993; Krcmar, 2001). As Austin noted in her excellent review (Austin, Pinkleton, Van de Vord, Arganbright, & Chen, 2006), "Bachen (1998) for example, found that >30% of adolescents who viewed *Channel One* believed that 'seeing the ads on Channel One made me want to go out and buy these products,' and 20% said that they actually did so." Seeing the ads increases materialism (Buijzen & Valkenburg, 2003).

Austin and her colleagues (Austin, Chen, Pinkleton, et al., 2006; Austin, Pinkleton, Van de Vord, et al., 2006) created posttest-only studies ($N = 239$) of randomized 7th and 8th graders who underwent media literacy treatment before or after seeing a C1 episode, with somewhat different expectations for the two studies. The basic treatment was a short media literacy lesson.

In each study, the media literacy treatment was divided—one treatment adding an emotive component *designed to make the students angry* at media companies that were "buying them."

Both studies concluded that the treatment with the *emotive component was more effective.* Austin, Pinkleton, Van de Vord, and their colleagues (2006) supported the value of media literacy for reducing the effects of television advertising. The treatment seemed to decrease materialistic values, a hopeful sign.

Austin, Chen, Pinkleton, and Johnson (2006) found that media literacy training increased recall of both news and advertisements and that the intervention increased skepticism toward advertisers, but the studies were unable to hypothesize about the effect of increased skepticism on future purchases. "Those who responded positively to the content and presentation style learned more from it but also tended to want things that they saw in the advertisements" (p. 429).

In addition, the studies give support to the "legitimizing" factor. The good news is that media education can perhaps buffer C1's ads, but the results also provide concern about the commercialization of the classroom, representing a significant pragmatic and ethical problem.

That C1 is a complex situation is a vast understatement. That it is of importance is obvious. Austin, Chen, Pinkleton, and Johnson (2006) conclude, "These results therefore suggest that schools that wish to use commercial programming such as Channel One should include *in-service training* for teachers on media-literacy education and should require that media literacy be taught with specific reference to the programming" (p. 431). Unfortunately, surveys have shown that teachers do not consistently discuss C1 content with their students, perhaps preferring to grade papers while it is being shown (Anderman & Johnston, 1997; Barrett, 1995, 1998; Johnston & Anderman, 1993; Knupfer & Hayes, 1994).[4]

Stakeholders need to consider the value and moral implications of annually devoting a *week* of school to C1, which seems to clearly add to the materialistic effects of advertising, thereby placing a burden on the schools to provide competent media literacy programs to counter the effect of the C1 ads. Millions of students are participating in this mandatory social experiment, which the multibillion-dollar corporation fails to research in a meaningful manner.

Teaching Media Literacy

While changing behavior is difficult, media education can certainly teach (a) information about the media, (b) media analysis skills, (c) techniques of media production, and (d) strategies of active involvement in media-related issues. What follows are suggestions for teaching media literacy and media education.

Teaching is an art, and giving advice is a risky business only attempted by the committed or the foolish. This writer undoubtedly falls into both categories; he has trained more than a thousand teachers in four-day workshops, 30 attendees at a time. Having seen many successes and failures, he offers some tips that come from 30-plus years of experience.

As indicated by the preceding review, *affect is more important than content.* A media education classroom should hold students' attention; they must feel they are central to the process of investigation. A multimedia-based workshop can be exciting and involving or as deadly as the plague, killing learning without regard for the educational corpus. What is more boring than a PowerPoint presentation in which the presenter reads quotations from the screen?

Emotion is crucial to media education. Most students are addicted to powerful entertainment media, so when dealing with media, classes must be *involving* and *entertaining.* Great teachers have a sense of drama and a sense of humor. They laugh *with* their students. They move around the room. They are not afraid to be enthusiastic. They notice when students are losing interest, and they are *flexible,* changing lesson plans and examples midclass to meet changes in students' levels of interest.

Asking questions about media examples is *the key method* of media education. A Socratic process involves students, honors their judgments and opinions, and creates guided discussion. Resonating with the group, listening to students' answers, and, often, letting their responses dictate the direction of the discussion are musts. Learning about media should become a lifelong process. Creating student lovers of media education is the objective, not pouring a finite set of concepts into them.

Insert information into the discussion in a way that seems natural. During discussions, many teachable moments arise, and at those times, *one should give students the information they need.* Research shows that "negative active mediation" of questionable content is possibly the most effective means of media education (Chen & Austin, 2013). The challenge is to time such moments correctly and avoid the universal tendency to lecture.

Media education must be fun. Even though much news is negative, one can present problems with a smile and an earnest desire to help, recognizing that every era has had huge problems to solve. People who motivate others create solutions. Do not smother students with a negative world view. Be sensitive to when a media message creates fear. If you try to scare today's kids, you will probably fail.

Credibility is crucial. Media criticism is not media education. One must not seem to disapprove of the students' media or indicate that students are passive objects of media manipulation. One's philosophy should be that *all media are good and bad.* An honest investigation of skills and principles *with* students will bring success.

Fascinate students with media's techniques. Media education unleashes great potential for teachers to interest students. The construction and power of media is interesting to the point of inspiration. Make it so.

Avoid continually using examples of what is wrong with the media we all watch. That creates guilt, and no one likes to feel guilty. Students will eventually dislike a person who makes them feel guilty. Encourage students to bring in their media examples.

Challenge students. Within the aforementioned context, students will accept media effects research. Use it; do not seek to only entertain. Some media educators cannot wait to toss out the video cameras and gush about the wonder of their students' videos. One should be a responsible and demanding *guide,* a model of intelligent investigation.

When choosing examples to deconstruct, be aware of student interest and appropriateness. What is appropriate for one age or one school may not be appropriate for another. *When in doubt, leave it out.* There is no shortage of media examples, and including some juicy media example is not worth creating a battle with administrators or parents.

The best tool for *providing examples* is a multimedia database that can be stored on a computer and projected in the classroom. The database can merely be a variety of examples stored in various folders on the computer's desktop. The objective is to allow quick access to an appropriate example in response to the flow of the group's discussion.

Buy *a good sound system* for the classroom; they're cheap. *Music is an integral* part of students' lives and media persuasion. Students love to analyze the musical forces in media and songs.

When deconstructing an example, *accept all honest interpretations as "correct."* If students feel free to disagree with the teacher, the classroom becomes a *safe*, enjoyable, and rewarding place for media learning. Providing safety is hard, but important.

The major goal is to leave the students or group *wanting more. Process is more important than content.* Remember, inspiring students works far better than trying to scare them. The teacher should be perceived as a mentor rather than one indulging pet peeves. Remember, we spend 12 years teaching kids to read, and as adults, they do not read. Try to beat the odds.

The Content of Media Literacy

Media literacy's body of content, or the information taught, varies widely, but some principles are fairly standard in media literacy programs. As previously noted, there are five traditionally accepted *basic principles* (or skills, or tools) of media literacy:

1. All media messages are "constructed."

2. Media messages are created using a creative language with its own rules and production techniques.

3. Different people experience the same message differently.

4. Media messages have embedded values, stereotypes, myths, biases, values, lifestyles, and/or points of view.

5. Most media messages are constructed to gain profit and/or power. (Bergsma & Carney, 2008)

Basic media literacy involves turning these principles into questions to be asked about a media example. It makes them into basic "tools of analysis." For example, in the case of the first principle (media messages are constructed), one could ask, "How is this message constructed?" Answers will reflect the age and experience of the students. Think about the difference between a 4th grader and someone in film school. Discussion will afford the leader many teachable moments.

What follows is an expanded list of skills or tools—the *advanced principles of media education*—that reflects this writer's experience, as well as the dramatically changing media landscape. Use it in the same manner as above, asking questions designed to draw students toward cognitive associations between media examples and the principles.

1. *Media construct "impressions of reality" which are not reality.* The deluge of media an individual experiences constructs her or his notion of reality. As George Gerbner, dean of the Annenberg School of Communication, was famous for saying, children's formative stories used to be told by people—family, friends, teachers, preachers (i.e., the natural world). Today's storytellers are television, movies, video games, the Internet, iPods, text messages, tweets, and magazines, mostly controlled by Gerbner's "handful" of corporations (i.e., Big Media). We are engaged in a huge social experiment with our kids' conceptions of reality and democracy.

This is not a Luddite-like position, but merely *recognizes* the importance of perceiving current social and antidemocratic trends—the extent and power of our relatively new and perhaps imprudent monopolized system of media and the political processes surrounding it. The classic work of Orwell and Huxley as well as modern scholars (Gentile, 2003; McChesney, 2004; McKibben, 1992) suggests that our democratic experiment may not survive the onslaught of Big Media. The first step toward a solution is to recognize the problem, and students will respect this information.

2. *Media messages affect our perceptions and decisions.* As Jean Kilbourne is famous for saying, and as third-person-effect research confirms, people do not think they are affected by advertising, but they are. We all are. So are our pocketbooks.

3. *Media monopoly threatens democracy.* Decision making in a democracy demands informed citizens. An increasingly small group of media-holding companies (five to seven) controls tens of thousands of media companies. They are dominated by a few global advertisers—the Fortune 40 corporations—that pay for most advertising. Hence, less people control more mainstream content, including the news.

4. *Monopoly is not capitalism.* Recent Supreme Court decisions allow corporations the same political rights as citizens, dramatically dominating our elections and relegating most people to the political margins. Some think media education and media reform are "liberal" issues. On the contrary, fighting monopoly is at the heart of free enterprise, supply, and demand (i.e., capitalism). If you fight Big Media, you are not a socialist; you are actually engaging the spirit of the Founding Fathers.

5. *Knowing and telling "untold stories" is an antidote for propaganda.* All communication is media. Media are always propaganda, because they are constructed by someone with a point of view, using techniques of persuasion. Most stories tell just one side of a story or a biased version of a story. What is not told, the "untold story," is *the related information left out* of a media message. Searching for untold stories is an empowering component of media education. Telling untold stories is activism. Production of such media is a beacon to those who search for truth.

6. *Fantasy differs from reality.* Media can create worlds of imagination that range from subtle disinformation to a reality that seems better than what is real, *causing people to want to live a particular lifestyle.* Some lifestyles cause children to strive to be doctors, scientists, or philanthropists and benefit humanity. Others are fantasies that can lead to wasted time, violence, and ill health. Today's advertising suggests that our highest calling is to shop. Media education helps individuals reconcile media's competing paradoxes, hopefully leading the individual to live an examined life.

7. *"The brands that create loyalty beyond reason bring premium profits* [italics added]" says Kevin Roberts, CEO of a large ad agency in *The Persuaders* (Goodman & Rushkoff, 2003). Be alert to the self-interestedness of media makers. It knows no bounds, and research shows that emotions sell better than logic. Is this cute, cuddly radio station, movie, YouTube video, or book created by a huge conglomerate seeking to advance its economic or political agenda? Often we don't know, but in a hypermediated world,

asking the question is an important mental exercise. Are they concerned about health? Addiction? Intelligent people or merely buyers?

8. *Individuals construct unique meanings from media.* Experiencing media is an *active* process. Different people comprehend different meanings from the same piece of media. Allowing students to gently increase their tolerance for others' interpretations is a key outcome of successful media education. Respecting everyone's honest interpretations broadens one's horizons.

9. *Media teach.* If media can sell psychic readings, media can sell anything, including the use of guns to solve problems, and they do. Media can instill standards, stereotypes, philosophies, morals, myths, values, ethics, biases, ideals, ideologies, principles, lifestyles, and points of view. Often, this process can be good *and* bad. Pat Robertson sells salvation; Miller's beer sells the high life. Shopping malls whisper that buying stuff solves problems. Cadillac fuels the human desire for status. A politician who says, "I refuse to bring up my opponents' troubles with the IRS" has just called his opponent a crook. Great entertainers are great salespeople.

10. *Emotion is primary.* Ever wonder why TV ads do not mention the product until the last second of the ad? *Emotional transfer* is the technique by which ads build emotion to cut through the "clutter," an advertising term for the thousands of ads we are exposed to each day. Once emotion is created, it transfers to the product *irrespective of any logical connection.* This is mostly a subconscious process.

11. *Studying media should include studying contexts.* The social, political, economic, historical, cultural, and psychological contributions to a piece of media aid understanding. For example, one can ask, "In this historical time, what makes this scene unusual?"

12. *Subliminalism exists.* Any part of a media message that one absorbs in an unconscious manner is subliminal. Since one "thinks about" so little of what one experiences, much remains in unconscious memory for a time—affecting individuals differently, but affecting them nonetheless. When a TV ad has 25 scenes in 30 seconds, many of the stimuli do not reach the level of conscious thought, leaving a good deal to the individual's subconscious. The same can be said for print-based media, but at least one has more time and can go back and experience it again.

13. *All human communication uses a "language of persuasion."* Communication is always created by someone with a point of view and, therefore, is biased—sometimes subtly and other times not so subtly. It tries to sway people for some purpose, usually to someone's benefit. Truth becomes subjective in a hypermediated culture, whether the medium is fiction or nonfiction or put out by an advertising agency, public relations firm, church, or scholarly journal. The good news is that everyone can learn the techniques and "deconstruct" media. The 20 or so techniques (e.g., flattery, repetition, fear, nostalgia, straw man, and humor) are simple and fun to learn. Understanding the language is a beneficial life skill for today's citizens.

14. *Media effects can be obvious or subtle.* Few people believe everything they see and hear in the media, but negative political ads reduce voter turnout. Few rush to buy beer after

a Budweiser ad, but viewing hundreds of thousands of sophisticated alcohol ads might impair the viewer. Experiencing violence will not turn one into a killer, but it could make it easier for one to lose one's temper, affecting family, friends, and community— a subtle difference. Thus, the effects of media are complex.

15. *Media include "texts" and "subtexts."* What "actually happens" in a media message is its *text*. It is objective. Anyone can figure it out. The *impression* imparted by the message is the *subtext*, and it is subjective. You can argue about subtext, but text is not negotiable. In Bill McKibben's famous example, the text of a McDonald's television ad showed a sad girl, moving away from her hometown and friends. Then, it showed her happy with her family in a McDonald's restaurant in her new town (McKibben, 1992). The subtext (which caused the ad to be banned in Sweden) was that McDonald's is just as important and satisfying as friendship. Do you think Sweden was right?

16. *Media education emphasizes the tension between the discourse-based culture of the past five centuries and the image-based culture of the last few decades.* The brain processes image-based media differently than text-based media. As often lectured by Neil Postman, images evoke emotions in the oldest and most powerful "reptilian" brain. Such reactions are more powerful than written language, which is processed in the most recently evolved part of the brain, the prefrontal cortex (Postman, 1985).

    Image-based media, such as movies, TV, and video, are more powerful and more quickly absorbed than text-based media because of their emotional effect, giving rise to enjoyment but also creating the potential for powerful propaganda, habituation, and, perhaps, a devaluation of more logic-based communication—for example, books. Thus, reading a book is different from watching a documentary. There are always trade-offs; one may reread text, but moving images leave an *impression* that can only be studied with difficulty.

17. *Composition techniques add effect.* By using effects, such as camera angles, close-ups, reaction shots, lighting, transitions, framing, graphics, sounds, computer-generated images (CGI), and music, media increase the emotive and persuasive power of their messages. Practice finding these techniques.

18. *Media education creates active "deconstructors" of media.* Constructions of media, especially high-speed electronic media, seek to create spontaneous consumers who accept products, lifestyles, or concepts without having much time for thought. *Deconstructing* media is a skill; the more it is practiced, the easier and more automatic it becomes. Media literacy helps people live life with more freedom, enjoying media but with a critical perspective, considering the message's purpose and, it is hoped, gaining more control over their own attitudes and behavior.

19. *Produce media and activists.* Creating activists requires making media. It does not have to be fancy. Word of mouth is valuable. Most of us influence a group of people, be it small or large, so everyone can *make* persuasive media. In Russia, Stalinist repression was brought down with word of mouth, copy machines, and videotape—a testament to the power of everyday people doing media education by telling untold stories. Today's students, armed with new technologies, can be powerful.

20. *Media education is a necessity for resolving social issues.* Only the media educated become *media reformers,* and only a reformed media will allow most social issues to gain wide publicity and, therefore achieve successful resolution (see Figure 12.2). As more people comprehend the current media system, people can take action to reform Big Media, creating new alternatives and, perhaps, more justice.

Figure 12.2

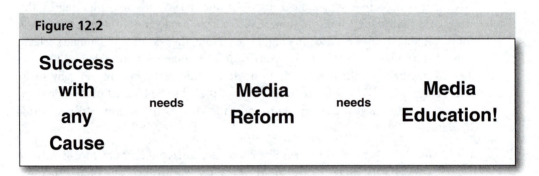

21. *Media education should not be left to Big Media.* Corporations frequently advertise their humanitarian endeavors and curricula. That is their right, but unfortunately, most of today's media literacy curricula are financed by the same corporations that control, trivialize, stereotype, and censor media content. We have curricula produced by Big Tobacco, Channel One, Big Energy, and other corporations. They exhibit the bias one would expect from conflicts of interest, so support for independent media organizations is critical.[5]

Another invaluable resource for media educators is the "language of persuasion." Often called the specific principles of media education, it entrances students and is used in thousands of media literacy curricula worldwide. Media makers, particularly advertisers, use it to persuade. People have used these techniques for centuries. For example, almost all of them can be found in Marc Anthony's funeral speech in Shakespeare's *Julius Caesar,* written over 400 years ago.

These rhetorical devices are still how we persuade one another. They are "specific tools" for *making and decoding* messages. They allow students to easily attain a skeptical attitude and a sense of control as they move through the media culture—defense mechanism that deflects cynicism. People of all ages gain an important baseline—a common language—for analyzing media. Any of the following devices may be used: symbols, emotional transfer, clutter, music, hyperbole, glittering generalities, humor, satire, beauty, action, special effects, the lie, stereotyping, stereotype breakers, name calling or ad hominem, scare tactics or fear, charisma, plain folks, testimonial, repetition, flattery, denial, warm and fuzzy, maybe, group dynamics, simple solutions, either/or, nostalgia, bandwagon, bribery, targeting children, non sequitur or red herring, scientific evidence, straw man. A teacher can use as many or as few as students' age and courses permit.

Using the language is a legitimate higher-level cognitive skill, and students' ability to recognize (analysis) or include (production) these tools greatly interests and empowers. Definitions and examples can be had by emailing this writer at mccannon@flash.net.

As noted above, *asking questions* about media examples is *the primary method of media education*. The Socratic process is based on the above principles and a commonly accepted group of questions such as the following:

1. Who made this message? Who paid for it? What was their purpose? Why did they need to do the ad?

2. Who is targeted by the message? What about the message leads you to that conclusion?

3. When was this made? Where or how was it shared with the public?

4. How might anyone benefit from it?

5. Who might be harmed by it? Does it depict a lifestyle that is healthy? Unhealthy?

6. What are the text and subtext of the message?

7. What ideas, values, information, and/or points of view are reinforced? Implied?

8. What is not told? What related stories are missing?

9. What kind of culture(s) does it create? Does it use stereotypes? "Break" stereotypes?

10. What techniques of persuasion are used to make it more effective?

11. How does the example try to move emotions? Is it simple or complex? Is it logical?

12. Is it closer to fantasy or reality? Why?

13. What different meanings might different people perceive?

14. Why might this message matter to me?

15. What kinds of actions might I take in response to this message?

16. What would a counter-message based on this message look like?

17. Is this an example of our "monopoly" media system?

18. Considering this example, what can I do to help reform our media system?

A valuable media education production technique is the counter-ad or anti-ad. Figure 12.3 is a scan of a real Camel ad and is followed by two counter-ads, one done by a 5th grader with pencils and tracing paper and another by a high school senior who used a scanner and Photoshop (see Figures 12.4 and 12.5).

While these two counter-ads vary in sophistication, both are effective at using the *power* of the advertiser's original ad campaign, which cost millions of dollars to create and disseminate, to send a reversed, equally powerful and more truthful story. Both cost little but added interest, insight, and impact to the students' experience.

When it comes to other content that can be investigated in media literacy and media education classes, the sky is the limit. The body of work on media production techniques, media criticism, and media lesson plans encompasses hundreds of books, videos, DVDs, websites, podcasts, and more. A good starting place might be the annotated bibliography at http://acmecoalition.org/essential_resources.

Figure 12.3   A Camel ad.

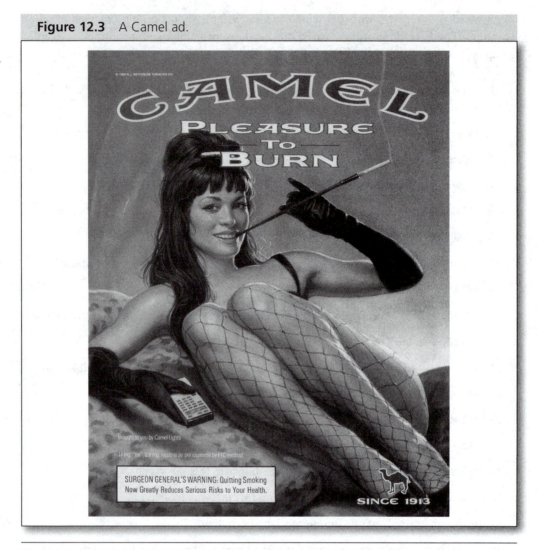

SOURCE: Camel Cigarettes®, ©R.J. Reynolds Tobacco Company. All rights reserved.

A Sample Deconstruction

"Deconstruction" develops important critical thinking skills. The preceding anti-ads utilized basic deconstruction. The following analysis of a typical alcohol ad exemplifies greater complexity (see Figure 12.6).

An alcohol company paid for the ad. Why? Alcohol is expensive, but costs little to make, producing substantial profit. No one needs it. In fact, it is *harmful*. Therefore, all alcohol companies *must* advertise and must use many persuasion techniques, including telling many lies, because if the truth were ever to become top of the mind, their industry would suffer.

The targets are young males; it's hard to tell, but they're probably Caucasian. The *text* compares relationships with girlfriends, drinking buddies, and Jim Beam whiskey. It shows the bottle and says, "Real friends. Real bourbon." In very small print, it names the company and alcohol percentage and says, "Real friends drink together responsibly."

Figure 12.4 Counter-ad by a 5th grader.

SOURCE: Copyright Bob McCannon.

Figure 12.5 Counter-ad by a high school senior.

SOURCE: Copyright Bob McCannon.

The *subtext* suggests that substituting whiskey for girlfriends is a good idea, because girls are frustrating. It suggests a cultural, media, and historical context for male drinking that is often found in our media and is similar to that of much media targeting men. The men are part of a cultural subgroup that drinks heavily, seeing it as a macho bonding ritual, possibly consisting of college men (a big market) or those who see such activities as being cool, perhaps young boys.

In this sense, the subtextual message is probably targeted at adolescent-minded males, who can be middle school, high school, college, and older males (once a Bud man, always a Bud man). Young adolescents often experience difficulty with relationships. Girls seem to be confusing and can cause anguish. In this world, girls can't be relied on, but Jim Beam will always be a buddy.

Alcohol companies have a problem similar to cigarette companies. They must create a culture that produces brand loyalty by ages 10 to 16 because that's the age when kids decide whether to drink or not, and during this age they usually develop some degree of brand loyalty. Suggesting a *fantasy* in which girls don't measure up is a technique that works well with adolescents and even older men, as they have yet to learn the *reality* of how to create satisfying relationships with the female sex in general and those they are dating in particular. In addition, adolescents near puberty are somewhat insecure, so this psychological ploy emphasizes the values of rugged independence and macho friendship in selling an addictive drug.

Other techniques include a variety of male symbols, card stacking, and straw men. The use of a black-and-white photo indicates casual fun down through history and, perhaps, helps to

Figure 12.6   A typical alcohol ad.

SOURCE: ©2008 James B. Beam Distilling Co., Clermont, KY.

spread the ethnicity. The glass is above the camera and foreshortened to add power to the drink. The dark colors add freshness and reality to the bottle, which is in brilliant color and has phallic power. The picture suggests in powerful terms that alcohol provides status, success, friendship, and dependability. The bottle suggests that such benefits originate from a warm and mystically powerful source.

It is not a healthy ad. Indeed, it glamorizes the *fantasy* that drinking makes one *happy* and the life of the party. This lifestyle must be repeated endlessly by alcohol companies and represents a Big Media *monopoly*, because we see the same message repeatedly in all media, including television, movies, and magazines.

The untold stories of alcohol may yield a far different reality. Those guys may have headaches, poor job performance, rocky relationships, and disintegrating livers, not to mention empty wallets. One often sees a tired movie hero come home or drop into a bar and get a double or two. How often does one see a tired movie hero come home and take a nap? Naps don't sell booze (or tickets).

Does the ad mention that about two-thirds of the population drink little or not at all? *Nondrinkers are just as happy, more successful, and better parents, and they think big drinkers are uncool, wasteful, and unattractive.* Drinkers are poorer, and after the high wears off, they feel bad and sad because alcohol is a depressant. Other disadvantages include, but are not limited to, hangovers, serious medical conditions, sexual mistakes, car accidents, rape, crime, and child abuse.

The average person sees 100,000 alcohol ads (in all media) by the time she or he is age 18. That is monopoly. It is a form of *censorship* in a hypermediated commercial culture, the power of which can be seen by asking, "Will the average child have heard 'I love you' a hundred thousand times before he or she is 18?"

Last, the teeny white print at the bottom of the page, hard to read, says, "Real friends drink together responsibly." The Big Lie rolls: One could imagine several reasons for that copy, but it is fun to ask kids to define responsible drinking and, then, carefully introduce the idea that *80% of the alcohol consumed is sold to problem drinkers* (Kleiman, 2009). Equally carefully (some parents are alcoholics), ask if problem drinkers drink *responsibly.*

When kids find out that problem drinkers consume *most* of the alcohol products produced, many students will ask, "Does Jim Beam make much money from irresponsible drinking?" Students also frequently ask, "Is Jim Beam serious about recommending responsible drinking?"

For those who value loving relationships and friendships based on respect, the ad is an unfortunate addition to youth culture. It is not a healthy message. Binge drinking among high school and college students, including women, is a major problem.

A counter-ad for a product like this might look something like this 6th grader's ad for an alcohol product (see Figure 12.7).

Figure 12.7 Counter-ad by a 6th grader.

SOURCE: Copyright Bob McCannon.

Media education skills are *true* skills. The more students practice, the better they become, and the more automatic the deconstruction process becomes, the more it empowers critically aware students and citizens. These are genuine and transferable critical thinking skills. When one asks, "How is this editorial an example of hyperbole?" a student must *apply an abstract principle to concrete data*, reinforcing both the principle and the process of higher-level cognition. The skill can also transfer to other media analysis or media production, and most important, it is *fun*.

Media Literacy Production

Much has been written about media production, but doing it with school kids can be either rewarding or, unfortunately, a waste of time. First, media production does not equal video production. Students can do much with pencil and paper, role playing, and skits. Computer word processing, drawing, animation, and music software enhance production, but low tech can also get high marks. In this writer's experience, 4th graders making cereal boxes can accomplish more than much 4th-grade video production.

Video is becoming easier and less expensive, but beware the tendency to spend inordinate amounts of time on the production process. One can never compete with professional production, and attempting to do so can take valuable time which could be spent *researching an issue* or learning more skills. Sometimes, media education classes have little time for production. In such cases, simple editing or even *no editing*, combined with a carefully researched script and storyboard, can produce interesting and valuable video.

Creating Counter-Ads

Anti-ads or counter-ads can be public service announcements, spoof ads, or ad satires. Creating counter-ads allows students to creatively talk back to deceptive or harmful messages and to experience some control over these powerful icons. Counter-ads can be parodies of advertisements and deliver untold information, yet use the same persuasion techniques as the original ads. Students can apply media literacy skills to production, communicating positive messages in a fun and engaging exercise.

The simplest way to create a counter-ad is to alter a real magazine or newspaper ad by changing the text or adding graphic elements. Young students can just write or draw over the original ad or paste new materials onto it. Note the examples in the figures above. Collage techniques work well. Older students can write scripts and read them to the class or Photoshop, record, or videotape their counter-ads. Here are some battle-tested tips for making effective counter-ads:

1. *Analyze.* Look at several real ads and figure out why they are effective. The best counter-ads use the same techniques to deliver a different message.

2. *Power.* Your message has to break through the clutter of all the real ads that people see or hear. Think about what makes an ad memorable. What techniques does it use to grab attention? Use them.

3. *Persuade.* Use the persuasion techniques found in real ads, such as humor, repetition, or flattery, to deliver an alternative message.

4. *Pictures.* Visual images are powerful. People often forget what they read or hear but tend to remember what they see. The best counter-ads, like the best ads, tell their stories through pictures.

5. *Rebellion.* Advertising targeted at young people often appeals to a sense of youthful rebellion. Effective counter-ads expose misleading and manipulative advertising methods and turn teens' rebellious spirits against the corporate sponsors who use these methods.

6. *KISS.* Keep it short and simple. Use only one idea for your main message. Focus everything on getting this message across.

7. *Plan.* Try to think of everything—words, images, and design—before you begin production. Make sketches, storyboards, and rough drafts.

8. *Practice.* If you are going to perform a radio or TV script, your cast and crew will need to rehearse until it works.

9. *Teamwork.* Working in a team can lighten your workload and spark creativity. Brainstorm ideas as a group. Make sure all members share responsibility.

10. *Revise.* When you think you are finished, show your counter-ad to uninvolved people for feedback. Do they understand it? Do they think it is funny? Effective? Use their responses to revise your work for maximum impact.

11. *Distribute.* Your ideas were meant to be seen! Make copies of your counter-ads and post them around your school. Get them published in your school newspaper. Show your videotape to other kids and adults. Your counter-ad can stimulate needed discussion and debate around media and health issues that get little coverage.

12. *Have fun!* Making a counter-ad is an enjoyable way to learn about media and health, to be creative, and to express your views.

Activism and Media Education

While media literacy purists do not agree, *prosocial activities* are included in many media education classes, interventions, and programs. Students and citizens can *become active* in hundreds of ways. Activism is important because it changes cynicism—that negative, depressing force—into skepticism, a positive, uplifting emotion based in knowledge of a problem and doing something to try to solve it. *Activist strategies should accompany all media literacy lessons.* What follows are a dozen suggestions for how to create activism.

1. *Question* by analyzing all media you consume. "Deconstruct" the values promoted by movies, television, magazines, and video games. Do they use flattery, emotion, censorship, or product placements?

2. *Research* information, sites, organizations, and goals. Do not be misled by AstroTurf (industry-supported public relations groups).

3. *Teach* by modeling critical media awareness for family and friends. *Share* ideas about media monopoly, media issues, and media reform. Be a "viral" cultural revolutionary; show exemplary clips/pictures/ads to friends.

4. *Get busy!* Get off the couch! Find activities that make you healthier, wealthier, and smarter. Don't take the flack; strike back!

5. *Boycott* by voting with your dollars. Make the worst offenders suffer.

6. *Communicate* with others; write letters to editors, sponsors, radio stations, and TV outlets about things you dislike and like. Look for images that denigrate people and cultures, are dishonest and unhealthy, and target the very young. Express yourself to store managers, billboard companies, advertising companies, politicians, and so on.

7. *Support* a position; investigate media's effects, find out what you believe, and develop an opinion. Find and work for a cause!

8. *Volunteer* your time and, perhaps, money for independent media, such as community cable, nonprofit campaigns, and so on. Start campaigns about ads, stories, or products. If you don't, who will?

9. *Produce* your own media (letters, stories, posters, essays, photos, performances, videos, music, murals); encourage others to do so. Make and share counter-ads.

10. *Establish* an independent media venue—blog, coffee house, zine, website, bulletin board—in your classroom or community.

11. *Think* about what makes you more feel more alive, more human, more natural, more loyal, more successful—now and (this is hard) in 30 years.

12. *Join* an activist group, media education, media reform, or issue-based organization, such as www.acmecoalition.org.

13. *Remember that activists* established democracy, abolished slavery, got the vote for women, fought for civil rights, and still are fighting for justice everywhere. You can be on a very important team.

Big Media: Part of the Solution?

Ironically, in this era in which a handful of conglomerates control almost all adult and children's media, the possibility exists that with relatively little effort, Big Media could institute prosocial change.

Just one example: An impressive body of research shows that smoking in the movies, especially PG-13 movies, is now *the major cause of smoking initiation* in children and adolescents, recruiting 390,000 kids per year (CDC, 2011; Charlesworth & Glantz, 2005; Sargent et al., 2001, 2002). Interestingly enough, a simple media literacy device, placing an effective antismoking ad (i.e., one not made by a tobacco company) before a movie, reduces the negative effect of the movie's smoking scenes (Charlesworth & Glantz, 2005).

The anti-ads would portray tobacco and tobacco companies in ways rarely seen in pro-tobacco movies. Many of the major studios in concert with Big Tobacco still resist such a simple and lifesaving innovation. Why? Perhaps it is the hundreds of nontobacco companies owned by Big Tobacco, companies that spend billions advertising in Big Media.

Thus, the present system of supply and demand, where supply (i.e., information) is controlled by conglomerates, promotes the profits of Big Media and its major advertisers by underreporting what is in the nation's best interests, helping to maintain the status quo (Straubhaar & LaRose, 2004) *even though it hurts children and costs society billions.* Such censorship by Big Media is common. Consider just a few of many underreported stories: violence, poverty, corporate corruption, information about food and drink, diets, alcohol, fashion, insurance fraud, credit abuses, mandatory arbitration clauses, lobbyists, banking, gambling, and political ads.

Parents, Media Literacy, and Corporate Funding

Parental involvement in media education is important (Anderson et al., 2003; Potter, 2010; Robinson et al., 2001). Many parents try to mitigate media's effects. A simple survey in pediatric offices of 1,831 parents of children (ages 2 to 11) from 27 states, Canada, and Puerto Rico indicated that 23% of parents restrict media viewing, 11% use more instructive techniques, and 59% use both of these methods. Only 7% indicated they provided no guidance for their children (Barkin et al., 2006). As more than half of children have televisions in their bedrooms, one wonders about the quality of these self-reported parental interventions; nevertheless, many parents say they are concerned.

Parents can reduce undesirable media effects, including media-induced aggression (Chen & Austin, 2013; Nathanson, 1999, 2004; Nathanson & Cantor, 2000). Parents can mitigate children's anxiety (Cantor & Wilson, 2003; Cantor, Sparks, & Hoffner, 1988; Wilson, 1989; Wilson & Weiss, 1991). The effect of ubiquitous alcohol portrayals can be moderated and may be reduced by parental reinforcement of positive and counter-reinforcement of negative messages (Austin & Johnson, 1997; Austin, Pinkleton, & Fujioka, 2000). Parental actions can also moderate children's materialism (Buijzen & Valkenburg, 2003; Valkenburg, 2005).

Parents can increase children's academic performance and learning. Much pragmatic advice for raising children in this hypermediated culture can be found online. One source is http://acmecoalition.org/raising_media_savvy_kids. General resources can be found at http://acmecoalition.org/essential_resources.

Parents and media education researchers are both concerned about *corporate funding* and whether to focus on behavioral/attitudinal outcomes or communication skills outcomes (Kubey & Hobbs, 2000). Those who want to focus predominantly on value-neutral communication skills tend to favor corporate involvement and funding, and those who distrust corporate aid tend to favor behavioral outcomes as a measure of success. Hobbs (1998) describes the issues from the procorporate point of view: ". . . the good that media organizations can do by contributing their funding outweighs the potential dangers of its use as part of a public relations campaign, or as a shield against government regulation" (Cowrie, 1995, p. 1). SEMs and *Media Mastery*–type curricula suggest the self-interestedness of corporate funding, but is teaching only basic media skills enough? One could argue that most of the research above calls for a more activist approach.

The question is not what skills of media comprehension does media literacy teach, but how it can positively affect behavior. Do we want media education to merely aid in creating more informed but more debt-laden, addicted, aggressive, sexualized, time-wasting, hedonistic consumers? Or do we want media education to help create a culture of more knowledgeable, thoughtful, concerned children and adults? Do we want media education to aid in producing better citizens, or only clever cynics who analyze media but participate minimally in their democracy?

Do we want media literacy to contribute to greater numbers of media-informed parents who will read, play, and talk with their children, or do we want to generate more glib, media-savvy moms and dads who increasingly consume media in one room while their children interact with screens in another?

Through their ads, powerful conglomerates own the media education of our children, benefiting their bottom lines. Should junk food companies, publishers, Wal-Mart, Exxon, Channel One, Philip Morris, Budweiser, purveyors of video games, creators of movie violence, and the cable television industries also be allowed to dominate the production of media education curricula?

They do now.

The most commonly accepted principle of media literacy is that media create culture. Corporate media literacy curricula also create culture. Another principle is that all media are commerce. Following the money is important. So, when Renee Hobbs (1998, p. 20) says, "The good that media organizations can do by contributing their funding outweighs the potential dangers of its use," one needs to ask, why is she saying that? Perhaps because she was paid to write the C1 *Media Mastery* curriculum, which was used to deflect attention from the negative aspects of a C1 program that was implemented in one of every four U.S. schools?

In today's hypermediated world, Channel One exemplifies the raw political power exerted by a billion-dollar corporation to gain entrance to schools. Politics means money and media. Understanding such connections should be a main objective of media education.

We now have emails, released by Congress, from infamous convicted felon and briber of congressional representatives Jack Abramoff, discussing how he conducted a public relations campaign on behalf of Channel One and how he attacked individuals who dared to fight C1's entry into U.S. schools. The campaign was to involve talk show hosts and tens of thousands of dollars' worth of articles to bash "loonies" and "weasels," such as Commercial Alert's Gary Ruskin and Obligation, Inc.'s Jim Metrock (U.S. Senate, Committee on Finance, 2006). In any other context Metrock would have been considered a hero. It is hard for parents and scholars to know what media corporation and what media literacy expert can be trusted with the welfare of their children.

One answer lies in pursuing an *active, independent, and activist* form of media education, one that attempts to lead students to investigate issues and take a position on the media-related problems of the day. That means taking on Big Media corporate power in our elections, the lawmaking process, and much more. Could this do anything but increase the health, education, and well-being of our children and democracy? Big Media will not support that kind of media literacy, and that is the biggest argument in favor of *independent* media education.

Summary

Empirical data on media literacy and media education are young and mixed. They are especially weak in the area of producing changes in behavior, but the possibility exists, especially if media education is combined with parental cooperation and changing and/or limiting students' media diets through nondraconian encouragement. Given the wide range of research results demonstrated to date, using media education to protect children from morbidities associated with media consumption is common and can be effective.

Media education holds out much promise for teaching about media-related issues, including media techniques, access, effects, skills, and production. Media literacy skills and content would seem to be genuine critical thinking skills, and they are worth teaching in their own right. Basic principles and methodological techniques of media literacy are widely agreed upon. At present, acceptance of media literacy is small, but growing.

Techniques for implementing media literacy are varied and complex. Instruction in media education is recommended for those embarking upon careers in education. Trainers of teachers should alert them to proper attitudes, philosophic stances, activities, and methods—ones that have been shown to avoid boomerang. Media production is complex and requires care in planning and preparation to avoid superficiality, wasted time, and the boomerang effect.

For teachers and caregivers, it is crucial to emphasize that *careful* negative active mediation is the most effective technique for reducing youth's positive attitudes toward questionable content and behavior. Expressing approval, limiting viewing, and unmediated coviewing usually create more negative outcomes than positive. In other words, the difficult fact is that if a parent or caregiver merely sits with the child and watches violent solutions to problems, drug and alcohol use, and so on, *the parent or caregiver is approving those behaviors* (Chen & Austin, 2013).

Activist strategies do not have a consensus, but they are numerous and being implemented. Students' freedom of choice and investigation is necessary for activism to be effective. An open, media-driven Socratic methodology is most likely to succeed. Many new and innovative classroom strategies are available, and media literacy/media education can, perhaps, be part of achieving the long-desired holy grail of educational reformers—facilitated, active classrooms emphasizing critical thinking and active methodologies that connect to the real world of students, producing a lifelong love of learning.

Exercises

1. Read an article, magazine ad, or view a video clip. Establish a spectrum of possible opinions about the example by writing down the names of a group of people who would have different reactions. Remember, people negotiate their own meanings from media. A reaction spectrum might include George W. Bush, Barack Obama, Pat Robertson, Al Gore, Ralph Nader, Hillary Clinton, Eminem, and Bart Simpson. You could also use local people or teachers and students from your school.

   When you have your list, think about the differing viewpoints of your group. If you are teaching in a classroom setting, assign a name to different students and have them write a paragraph that deconstructs the media *from that person's point of view*. Use the questions for deconstructing mentioned earlier in this chapter as your guide. This is a valuable exercise that circumvents the reluctance of students to express different points of view because of peer pressure. Interesting things can happen when a lover of Comedy Central has to deconstruct *South Park* from the point of view of Pat Robertson or has to role-play the television evangelist in a debate with a student who role-plays Bart Simpson.

2 Select a news article or story. Analyze 10 key words for bias. Then, change the words, and see if you can change the story. Make a list of the related ideas that the story did not mention (the untold stories). Discuss why that might be the case. Write a script for a news story that covers the omitted issues.

3. Establish a definition of news (perhaps "information useful to citizens who want to maintain/improve our democracy"). View a national network news program. List the stories. How long was each? How many stories fit the definition? How did each story make you feel? How many of the stories caused you to feel anxious? How many were "mayhem" (murders, disasters, typhoons, floods, tornadoes, repeat stories about older mayhem stories, etc.)? How many of these mayhem stories would actually be useful to the average person? How many of the other stories would be? What vital information did the stories leave out? Which were the most "enjoyable"? Were the enjoyable ones valuable for citizens in a democracy? Were any of the stories truly educational? How much of the half hour was advertising? What were the advertisements? Neil Postman's (1999) theory was that bad news makes people anxious, and anxious people buy more pain relievers, medications, insurance, and the other anxiety relievers advertised on the news. Make lists of the nation's and world's most pressing problems. Which did the program leave out? Were any addressed in meaningful detail? How many mentioned solutions to the problems they covered? What led the news (the first program, usually the most important)? Was it really the most important issue? If not, why was it first?

4. View a local news program. How many of the questions above also apply? How much of the half hour was local news? How much was repeated national news? Why was there national news on the local news (hint: It's cheaper—why)? How much mayhem? (Why do you have to see every car accident in your town?) How much was advertising? Was there more of it than there was national news? How much was sports? How much was weather? Was all of the weather information useful? Did the hosts spend some time in "chitchat"? How much? Were there any "fluff "stories (cute and emotional but useless "kitten rescued from tree" type stories)? Did any stories seem to benefit a corporation? (As much as 25% of local news stories are VNRs—video news releases—made by corporations for their benefit.) Make a list of the most important issues in your community for you, your school, or your neighbors. Were any of them addressed? Make your own news program that emphasizes your issues.

5. Visit a local television station and take a tour, or have a representative come to your class. Ask the news manager the questions listed in Exercise 3 regarding their programming. Ask about the station's profit. The local news is usually the most profitable local program. Ask about the experience and training of the field reporters (not the ones seen behind the desk on TV), who tend to be inexperienced and poorly paid. Compare the local television news story to an equivalent newspaper story for content, detail, variety, depth, and usefulness. Think about the process of reading a newspaper versus watching TV news. In which process do you think the individual consumer has more freedom? Learns more? Has more interest? Why would people rather watch than read? Is it the same for everyone? Which medium is better for creating informed voters? For democracy? Seek out some alternative sources of media (broadsheets, blogs, the Web,

community radio/TV, or tweets) and apply the same questions, making comparisons between the mainstream and independent media sources.

6. Bill McKibben (1992) insightfully and humorously observes the current explosion of information that has transformed our cultural landscape. He concludes that, despite our having access to more information than any other culture in history, "we also live in a moment of deep ignorance, when vital knowledge that humans have always possessed about who we are and where we live seems beyond our reach" (p. 9). McKibben refers to this condition as an *unenlightenment,* an age of missing information. One can test this theory in many ways, but here are a few. Watch a nature program with time-lapse photography of plants exploding before your very eyes, or view an SUV commercial that takes place in a natural setting. What meaning is sent about the natural world in these media messages? As the SUV chews its way across fields, climbs mountains, and blasts through forests, what is said about ecology, the delicate balances that maintain life? What message is sent about how to enjoy nature? Or the kind of stimulation that brings pleasure? Or conservation of resources? Or whether there should be any limits to man's enjoyment of nature? Research statistics on the world's loss of forests, species, habitats, and natural resources. Is the SUV ad reality or fantasy? How might that SUV ad be written in a more realistic way?

Next, grow a plant from a seed. Keep a detailed log. What *must* the plant have? What does growing a plant teach about *limits*? What happens if the plant does not get enough water or light or nutrients? Or too much? From what does it need to be protected? Which teaches the truer lesson about limits, the fantasy world of SUV advertising or the natural world of growing the plant?

Notes

1. *Business literacy:* The ability to use financial and business information to understand and make decisions that help an organization achieve success.

Computer literacy: The ability to use a computer and its software to accomplish practical tasks.

Health literacy: The degree to which individuals have the capacity to obtain, process, and understand basic health information and services needed to make appropriate health decisions.

Information literacy: The ability to know when there is a need for information and to identify, locate, evaluate, and effectively use that information for the issue or problem at hand.

Media literacy: The ability to decode, analyze, evaluate, and produce communication in a variety of forms.

Technology literacy: The ability to use media such as the Internet to effectively access and communicate information.

Visual literacy: The ability, through knowledge of the basic visual elements, to understand the meaning and components of the image.

2. The free program is available at www.nichd.nih.gov/msy.

3. Anecdotally, this writer showed the Media Education Foundation film *DreamWorlds II,* which is about music videos leading to attitudes that can demean or hurt women, to high school juniors and seniors each year for six years in a one-semester media literacy course. The first showing was a disaster, with males angry (boomerang effect) and females fearful. With the help of a psychologist, a strategy was developed that involved a structured previewing, preparation, and postviewing debriefing, which was

successful to the point that for the last two years, the students' evaluations unanimously rated the video as the number-one outside resource used in the course.

4.   This writer has provided workshops in hundreds of classrooms where C1 was shown and never saw a teacher-student discussion about C1's news.

5.   A gateway to such groups can be found at the Action Coalition for Media Education (ACME) website (www.acmecoalition.org).

References

Academy of Pediatrics. (2012). *Media and children.* Retrieved from http://www.aap.org/en-us/advocacy-and-policy/aap-health-initiatives/Pages/Media-and-Children.aspx

Alstead, M., Campsmith, M., Halley, C. S., Hartfield, K., Goldbaum, G., & Wood, R. W. (1999). Developing, implementing, and evaluating a condom promotion program targeting sexually active adolescents. *AIDS Education and Prevention, 11,* 97–512.

Anderman, E., & Johnston, J. (1997). Channel One: Television news in the middle school classroom. *Middle School Journal, 28,* 33–36.

Anderson, C. A., Berkowtiz, L., Donnerstein, E., Huesmann, L. R., Johnson, J. D., Linz, D., . . . Wartella, E. (2003). The influence of media violence on youth. *Psychological Science in the Public Interest, 4,* 103.

Anderson, C. A., & Bushman, B. J. (2001). Effects of violent video games on aggressive behavior, aggressive cognition, aggressive affect, physiological arousal, and prosocial behavior: A meta-analytic review of the scientific literature. *Psychological Science, 12,* 353–359.

Arke, E. T. (2013). Media literacy: History, progress, and future hopes. In K. E. Dill (Ed.), *The Oxford handbook of media psychology* (pp. 96–108). New York: Oxford University Press.

Armstrong, G. M., & Brucks, M. (1988). Dealing with children's advertising: Public policy issues and alternatives. *Journal of Public Policy and Marketing, 7,* 98–113.

Ascione, L. (2006). *eSchool news.* Retrieved from http://www.eschoolnews.com/news/showStory.cfm?ArticleID=6578

Asthana, S. (2006). *Innovative practices of youth participation in media: A research study on twelve initiatives from around the developing and underdeveloped regions of the world.* Retrieved from http://portal.unesco.org/ci/en/ev.php-URL_ID=22831&URL_DO=DO_TOPIC&URL_SECTION=201.htm

Aufderheide, P. (1992). *Media literacy: A report of the national leadership conference on media literacy.* Washington, DC: Aspen Institute.

Austin, E. W. (1993a). Exploring the effects of active parental mediation of television content. *Journal of Broadcasting and Electronic Media, 37,* 147–158.

Austin, E. W. (1993b). The importance of perspective in parent-child interpretations of family communication patterns. *Journalism Quarterly, 70,* 558–568.

Austin, E. W. (2001). Effects of family communication on children's interpretation of television. In J. Bryant & J. A. Bryant (Eds.), *Television and the American family* (2nd ed.). Mahwah, NJ: Lawrence Erlbaum.

Austin, E. W., Chen, M., & Grube, J. W. (2006). How does alcohol advertising influence underage drinking? The role of desirability, identification and skepticism. *Journal of Adolescent Health, 38,* 376–384.

Austin, E. W., Chen, Y., Pinkleton, B. E., & Johnson, J. Q. (2006). Benefits and costs of Channel One in a middle school setting and the role of media-literacy training. *Pediatrics, 117,* 423–433.

Austin, E. W., & Johnson, K. K. (1997). Effects of general and alcohol-specific media literacy training on children's decision making model about alcohol. *Journal of Health Communication, 2,* 17–42.

Austin, E. W., Miller, A. C.-R., Silva, J., Guerra, P., Geisler, N., Gamboa, L., . . . Kuechle, B. (2002). The effects of increased cognitive involvement on college students' interpretations of magazine advertisements for alcohol. *Communication Research, 29,* 155–179.

Austin, E. W., Pinkleton, B. E., & Fujioka, Y. (2000). The role of interpretation processes and parental discussion in the media's effects on adolescents' use of alcohol. *Pediatrics, 105,* 343–349.

Austin, E. W., Pinkleton, B. E., & Funabiki, R. P. (2007). The desirability paradox in the effects of media literacy training. *Communication Research, 34,* 483–506.

Austin, E. W., Pinkleton, B. E., & Hust, S. T. (2005). Evaluation of an American Legacy Foundation/ Washington State Department of Health media literacy pilot study. *Health Communications, 18,* 75–79.

Austin, E. W., Pinkleton, B. E., Van de Vord, R., Arganbright, M., & Chen, Y. (2006). Channel One and effectiveness of media literacy. *Academic Exchange Quarterly, 10,* 115–120.

Bachen, C. M. (1998). Channel One and the education of American youths. *Annals of the American Academy of Political and Social Science, 557,* 132–145.

Bair, M. C., Spring, J. S., Shields, D., Zwarun, L., Sherblom, S., Primack, B., Pulley, C. & Rucker, B. (2011). School-based smoking prevention with media literacy: A pilot study. *Journal of Media Literacy Education, 2,* 185–198.

Bandura, A. (1986). *Social foundations of thought and action: A social cognitive theory.* Englewood Cliffs, NJ: Prentice Hall.

Barkin, S., Ip, E., Richardson, I., Klinepeter, S., Finch, S., & Krcmar, M. (2006). Parental media mediation styles for children aged 2 to 11 years. *Archives of Pediatric Adolescent Medicine, 160,* 395–401.

Barrett, J. (1995, August). *Student and teacher perspectives on Channel One: A qualitative study of participants in Massachusetts and Florida schools.* Paper presented at the annual meeting of the Association for Education in Journalism and Mass Communication, Washington, DC.

Barrett, J. (1998). Participants provide mixed reports about learning from Channel One. *Journal of Mass Communication in Education, 53,* 54–68.

Beach, R., & Baker, F. (2011). Why core standards must embrace media literacy. *Education Week.* Retrieved from http://www.edweek.org/ew/articles/2011/06/22/36baker.h30.html

Behson, J. (2002). Media literacy for high-risk children and youth. *Telemedium: The Journal of Media Literacy, 48,* 38–40.

Bergsma, L. J., & Carney, M. E. (2008). Effectiveness of health-promoting media literacy education: A systematic review. *Oxford Journals, 23,* 522–542.

Bickham, G. S., & Slaby, R. G. (2012). Effects of a media literacy program in the U.S. on children's critical evaluation of unhealthy media messages about violence, smoking and food. *Journal of Children and Media.* Retrieved from http://www.tandfonline.com/loi/rchm20

Biocca, F., Brown, J. D., Shen, F., Bernhardt, J. M., Batista, L., Kemp, K., . . . Carbone, E. (1997). Assessment of television's anti-violence messages: University of North Carolina at Chapel Hill study. In *National television violence study* (Vol. 1, pp. 413–530). Thousand Oaks, CA: Sage.

Brighouse, H. (2005). Channel One, the anti-commercial principle, and the discontinuous ethos. *Educational Policy, 19,* 528–549.

Brodeur, J. (2005). *Preventing youth violence with media education, the 10-Day Challenge (TV and video-game free).* Retrieved from http://www.edupax.org/Assets/ divers/documentation/1_articles/ OCPVE%20Media%20Education%20For%20 Violence%20Prevention.htm

Brown, J. A. (2001). Media literacy and critical television viewing in education. In D. G. Singer & J. L. Singer (Eds.), *Handbook of children and the media* (pp. 572–573). Thousand Oaks, CA: Sage.

Brown, J. D., Halpern, C. T., & L'Engle, K. L. (2005). Mass media as a sexual super peer for early maturing girls. *Journal of Adolescent Health, 36,* 420–427.

Budelmann, R. (2002). Substance and flash: Media literacy meets juvenile justice. *Telemedium: The Journal of Media Literacy, 48,* 41–42.

Buerkel-Rothfuss, N. L., & Buerkel, R. A. (2001). Family mediation. In J. Bryant & J. A. Bryant (Eds.), *Television and the American family* (2nd ed., pp. 355–376). Mahwah, NJ: Lawrence Erlbaum.

Buijzen, M., & Valkenburg, P. M. (2003). The unintended effects of television advertising: A parent child survey. *Communication Research, 30,* 483–503.

Bushman, B. J., & Cantor, J. (2003). Media ratings for violence and sex: Implications for policy makers and parents. *American Psychologist, 58,* 130–141.

Bushman, B. J., & Stack, A. D. (1996). Forbidden fruit versus tainted fruit: Effects of warning labels on attraction to television violence. *Journal of Experimental Psychology: Applied, 2,* 207–226.

Business Wire. (2008). *Channel One appoints Dr. Paul Folkemer SVP, director of education.* Retrieved from http://biz.yahoo.com/bw/080124/20080124005179.html?.v=1

Byrne, S. (2009). Media literacy interventions: What makes them boom or boomerang? *Communication Education, 58,* 1–14.

Cantor, J. (1998). Ratings for program content: The role of research findings. *Annals of the American Academy of Political and Social Science, 557,* 54–69.

Cantor, J., Sparks, G. G., & Hoffner, C. (1988). Calming children's television fears: Mr. Rogers vs. the Incredible Hulk. *Journal of Broadcasting and Electronic Media, 32,* 271–288.

Cantor, J., & Wilson, B. J. (2003). Media and violence: Intervention strategies for reducing aggression. *Media Psychology, 5,* 363–403.

Centers for Disease Control and Prevention. (2011). Smoking in top-grossing movies—United States, 2010. *Morbidity and Mortality Weekly Report, 60,* 909–913.

Chandra, A., Martino, S. C., Collins, R. L., Elliott, M. N., Berry, S. H., Kanouse, D. E., & Miu, A. (2008). Does watching sex on television predict teen pregnancy? Findings from a national longitudinal survey of youth. *Pediatrics, 122,* 1047–1054.

Channel One news. (2012). Retrieved from http://www.obligation.org/category/alloy-channel-one-news

Charlesworth, A., & Glantz, S. A. (2005). Smoking in the movies increases adolescent smoking: A review. *Pediatrics, 116,* 1516–1528.

Chen, Y.-C., & Austin, E. W. (2013). The role of parental mediation in the development of media literacy and the prevention of substance use. *The International Encyclopedia of Media Studies.* Volume V, 33–51.

Cincotta, K. (2005). Accord gets kids to munch right. *B & T Magazine, 8,* 26. Retrieved from www.bandt.com.au

Collins, R. L., Elliott, M. N., Berry, S. H., Kanouse, D. E., Kunkel, D., Hunter, S. B., & Miu, A. (2004). Watching sex on television predicts adolescent initiation of sexual behavior. *Pediatrics, 114,* e280–e289.

Concerned Children's Advertisers. (2004). *2004 annual report.* Toronto, Ontario, Canada: Author.

Corder-Bolz, C. R. (1980). Mediation: The role of significant others. *Journal of Communication, 30,* 106–118.

Coughlin, J. W., & Kalodner, C. (2006). Media literacy as a prevention intervention for college women at low- or high-risk for eating disorders. *Body Image, 3,* 35–43.

Council on Communication and Media. (2010). Policy statement: Media education. *Pediatrics, 126,* 1012–1017.

Cowrie, N. (1995, Fall). Media literacy's new challenge. *Video and Learning,* p. 1.

Daly, J. (2004). Life on the screen: Visual literacy in education. *Edutopia.* Retrieved from http://www.edutopia.org/lucas-visual-literacy

Deconstructing Judy. (2006). Retrieved from http://www.obligation.org/article.php?recordID=44

Doolittle, J. C. (1980). Immunizing children against possible antisocial effects of viewing television violence: A curricular intervention. *Perceptual and Motor Skills, 51,* 498.

Dorr, A., Graves, S. B., & Phelps, E. (1980). Television literacy for young children. *Journal of Communication, 30,* 71–83.

Eagle, L. (2005). *Commercial media literacy: What does it do, to whom—and does it matter?* (Middlesex University Business School Discussion Paper Series). Retrieved from http://www.mubs.mdx.ac.uk/research/discussion_papers/marketing/dpap_mkt_no31.doc

Ehman, L. (1993, November). *Channel One in social studies: Three years later.* Paper presented at the annual meeting of the National Council for the Social Studies, Nashville, TN.

Eunice Kennedy Shriver National Institute of Child Health and Human Development. (2009). *Report on the evaluation of the media-smart youth curriculum.* Washington, DC: U.S. Government Printing Office. Retrieved from http://www.lifeskillstraining.com/resource_facts.php

Evans, A. E., Tanner, Dave, J., Duhe, S., Condrasky, M., Wilson, D., . . . Evans, M. (2006). Changing the home nutrition environment: Effects of a nutrition and media literacy pilot intervention. *Family Community Health, 29,* 43–54.

Filotas, D. Y. (1993). *Adolescents' rape attitudes: Effectiveness of rape prevention education in high school classrooms.* Unpublished master's thesis, University of California, Santa Barbara.

Finkelstein, S. (Producer). (2012, June 17). Taylor Swift. *Sixty Minutes.* CBS. Exact text retrieved from http://www.cbsnews.com/8301-18560_162-57451731/taylor-swift-a-young-singers-meteoric-rise/?pageNum=4&tag=contentMain;contentBody

Flanagin, A. J., & Metzger, M. J., & Hartsell, E. (2010). *Kids and credibility: An empirical examination of youth, digital media use and information credibility.* Cambridge, MA: MIT Press.

For your information: Media Smart youth program. (2006). *AAP News, 27,* 24.

Fox, R. F. (2005). Researching media literacy: Pitfalls and possibilities. *Yearbook of the National Society for the Study of Education, 104,* 251–259.

Gentile, D. A. (2003). *Media violence and children: A complete guide for parents and children.* Westport, CT: Praeger.

Giedrys, S. A. (1999). Creating a curriculum to help girls battle eating disorders. *Harvard Gazette Archive.* Retrieved from http://www.hno.harvard.edu/gazette/1999/02.11/eating.html

Goodman, B., & Rushkoff, D. (2003). The persuaders. *Nova.* Boston, MA: PBS. First aired November 9, 2003.

Gonazales, R., Glik, D., Davoudi, M., & Ang, A. (2004). Media literacy and public health: Integrating theory, research and practice for tobacco control. *American Behavioral Scientist, 48,* 189–201.

Graham, J. W., & Hernandez, R. (1993). *A pilot test of the AdSmarts curriculum: A report to the Scott Newman Center.* Los Angeles: University of Southern California, Department of Preventive Medicine, Institute for Health Promotion and Disease Prevention Research.

Greenberg, B. S., & Brand, J. E. (1993). Television news and advertising in schools: "Channel One" controversy. *Journal of Communication, 43,* 143–151.

Grgurich, J. (2012). News Corp. goes to school: Media giant sets sights on education biz. *Daily Finance.* Retrieved from http://www.dailyfinance.com/2012/07/26/news-corp-goes-to-school-media-giant-sets-sights-on-education

Hicks, D. J. (1968). Effects of co-observer's sanctions and adult presence on imitative aggression. *Child Development, 39,* 303–309.

Hindin, T. J., Contento, I. R., & Gussow, J. D. (2004). A media literacy nutrition education curriculum for Head Start parents about the effects of television advertising on their children's food requests. *Journal of the American Dietetic Association, 104,* 192–198.

Hobbs, R. (1998). The seven great debates in the media literacy movement. *Journal of Communication, 48,* 16–32.

Hobbs, R. (2004a). Does media literacy work? An empirical study of learning how to analyze advertisements. *Advertising Educational Foundation: Advertising and Society Review, 5,* 4.

Hobbs, R. (2004b). A review of school-based initiatives in media literacy education. *American Behavioral Scientist, 48,* 42–69.

Hobbs, R. (2005). The state of media literacy education. *Journal of Communication, 55,* 865–871.

Hobbs, R., & Frost, R. (1999). Instructional practices in media literacy education and their impact on students' learning. *New Jersey Journal of Communication, 6,* 123–148.

Hobbs, R., & Frost, R. (2003). Measuring the acquisition of media literacy skills. *Reading Research Quarterly, 38,* 330–355.

Horton, R. W., & Santogrossi, D. A. (1978). The effect of adult commentary on reducing the influence of televised violence. *Personality and Social Psychology Bulletin, 4,* 337–340.

Huesmann, L., Eron, L. D., Klein, R., Brice, P., & Fischer, P. (1983). Mitigating the imitation of aggressive behaviors by changing children's attitudes about media violence. *Journal of Personality and Social Psychology, 44,* 899–910.

Hust, S. J. T., Brown, J. D., & L'Engle, K. L. (2008). Boys will be boys and girls better be prepared: An analysis of the rare sexual health messages in young adolescents' media. *Mass Communication and Society, 11,* 1–21.

Huston, A. C., Donnerstein, E., Fairchild, H. H., Fesbach, N. D., Katz, P. A., Murray, J. P., . . . Zuckerman, D. (1992). *Big world, small screen: The role of television in American society.* Lincoln: University of Nebraska Press.

Infante, D. A., Rancer, A. S., & Womack, D. F. (2003). *Building communication theory.* Prospect Heights, IL: Waveland.

Intons-Peterson, M. J., Roskos-Ewoldsen, B., Thomas, L., Shirley, M., & Blut, D. (1989). Will educational materials reduce negative effects of exposure to sexual violence? *Journal of Social and Clinical Psychology, 8,* 256–275.

Irving, L. M., & Berel, S. R. (2001). Comparison of media-literacy programs to strengthen college women's resistance to media images. *Psychology of Women Quarterly, 25,* 103–111.

Johnston, J., & Anderman, E. (1993). *Channel One: The school factor.* Ann Arbor: University of Michigan Institute for Social Research.

Johnston, J., & Brzezinski, E. (1992). *Taking the measure of Channel One: The first year.* Ann Arbor: University of Michigan, Institute for Social Research.

Johnston, J., Brzezinski, E., & Anderman, E. (1994). *Taking the measure of Channel One: A three year perspective.* Ann Arbor: University of Michigan, Institute for Social Research.

Kaiser Family Foundation. (2003). *Media literacy fact sheet.* Retrieved from http://kaiserfamilyfoundation .org/entmedia/upload/Key-Facts-Media-Literacy.pdf

Kavoori, A., & Matthews, D. (2004). Critical media pedagogy: Lessons from the thinking television project. *Howard Journal of Communications, 15,* 99–114.

Keller, S. N., & Brown, J. D. (2002). Media interventions to promote responsible sexual behavior. *The Journal of Sex Research, 39,* 62–69.

Kennedy, A. (2010). Supreme Court of the United States: *Citizens United v. Federal Election Commission.* Retrieved from http://www.supremecourt.gov/opinions/09pdf/08-205.pdf

Kleiman, M. A. R. (2009). *When brute force fails: How to have less crime and less punishment.* Princeton, NJ: Princeton University Press.

Kleinman, M. (2003, October). Heinz fights food ad criticism with Media Smart link. *Marketing (UK),* p. 1.

Knupfer, N., & Hayes, P. (1994). The effects of the Channel One broadcast on students' knowledge of current events. In A. De Vaney (Ed.), *Watching Channel One: The convergence of students, technology and private business* (pp. 42–60). Albany: SUNY Press.

Krcmar, M. (2001, May). *Channel One: The effect of commercials in the classroom—a natural experiment.* Paper presented at the annual meeting of the International Communication Association, Chicago, IL.

Kubey, R., & Hobbs, R. (2000). *Setting research directions for media literacy and health education.* Retrieved from http://www.mediastudies.rutgers.edu/mh_ conference/index.html

Kunkel, D. (2005). Predicting a renaissance for children and advertising research. *International Journal of Advertising, 24,* 401–405.

Kupersmidt, J. B., Scull, T. M., & Austin, E. W. (2010). Media literacy education for elementary school substance use prevention: Study of media detective. *Pediatrics, 126,* 525–531.

Lewis, J., & Jhally, S. (1998). The struggle over media literacy. *Journal of Communication, 48,* 109–120.

Linz, D., Fuson, I. A., & Donnerstein, E. (1990). Mitigating the negative effects of sexually violent mass communications through preexposure briefings. *Communication Research, 17,* 641–674.

Littleton, H., & Ollendick, T. (2003). Negative body image and disordered eating behavior in children and adolescents: What places youth at risk and how can these problems be prevented? *Clinical Child and Family Psychology Review, 6,* 51–66.

Livingstone, S. (2004). Media literacy and the challenge of new information and communication technologies. *Communication Review, 7,* 3–14.

Livingstone, S., & Helsper, E. J. (2006). Does advertising literacy mediate the effects of advertising on children: A critical examination of two linked research literatures in relation to obesity and food choice. *Journal of Communication, 56,* 560–584.

Mandel, L. L., Bialous, S. A., & Glantz, S. A. (2006). Avoiding "truth": Tobacco industry promotion of life skills training. *Journal of Adolescent Health, 39,* 868–879.

Martens, H. (2010). Evaluating media literacy education: Concepts, theories and future directions. *Journal of Media Literacy Education, 2*(1), 1–22.

McCannon, R. (2002). Media literacy: What? Why? How? In V. Strasburger & B. Wilson (Eds.), *Children, adolescents, and the media* (pp. 322–367). Thousand Oaks, CA: Sage.

McCannon, R. (2005). Adolescents and media literacy. *Adolescent Medicine Clinics, 16,* 463–480.

McChesney, R. W. (2002, October). *Keynote.* Presented at the founding conference of the Action Coalition for Media Education, Albuquerque, NM. Recording available at http//www.acmeco alition.org

McChesney, R. W. (2004). *The problem of the media.* New York, NY: Monthly Review Press.

McKibben, B. (1992). *The age of missing information.* New York, NY: Plume.

McLellan, F. (2002). Marketing and advertising: Harmful to children's health. *Lancet, 360,* 1001.

Media Smart overview. (2003). Retrieved from http://www.mediasmart.org.uk/media_smart/ofcom.html

Mehta, K., Coveney, J., Ward, P., Megarey, A., Spurrier, N., & Udell, T. (2010). Australian children's views about food advertising on television. *Appetite, 55,* 49–55.

Molnar, A., Garcia, D. R., Boninger, F., & Merrill, B. (2006). *A national survey of the types and extent of the marketing of foods of minimal nutritional value in schools.* Arizona State University, Commercialism in Education Research Unit. Retrieved from http://www.asu.edu/educ/epsl/CERU/Documents/EPSL-0609-211-CERUexec.pdf

Moore, J., DeChillo, N., Nicholson, B., Genovese, A., & Sladen, S. (2000, Spring). Flashpoint: An innovative media literacy intervention for high-risk adolescents. *Juvenile and Family Court Journal,* pp. 23–33.

Muto, S. (2004). Children and media. *Young Consumers, 6,* 37–43.

Nathanson, A. I. (1999). Identifying and explaining the relationship between parental mediation and children's aggression. *Communication Research, 26,* 124–143.

Nathanson, A. I. (2002). The unintended effects of parental mediation of television on adolescents. *Media Psychology, 4,* 207–230.

Nathanson, A. I. (2003, October). *The effects of mediation content on children's responses to violent television: Comparing cognitive and affective approaches.* Paper presented at the International Communication Association Convention, San Diego, CA.

Nathanson, A. I. (2004). Factual and evaluative approaches to modifying children's responses to violent television. *Journal of Communication, 54,* 321–336.

Nathanson, A. I., & Cantor, J. (2000). Reducing the aggression-promoting effect of violent cartoons by increasing children's fictional involvement with the victim. *Journal of Broadcasting and Electronic Media, 44,* 125–142.

Nathanson, A. I., & Yang, M. (2003). The effects of mediation content and form on children's responses to violent television. *Human Communication Research, 29,* 111–134.

Neumark-Sztainer, D., Sherwood, N. E., Coller, T., & Hannan, P. J. (2000). Primary prevention of disordered eating among preadolescent girls: Feasibility and short-term effect of a community-based intervention. *Journal of the American Dietetic Association, 100,* 1466–1473.

Nirva, P., Levine, M., & Irving, L. (2000, November/December). Go girls! Media literacy, activism, and advocacy project. *Healthy Weight Journal,* pp. 89–90.

Palmer, E. L., & Carpenter, C. F. (2006). Food and beverage marketing to children and youth: Trends and issues. *Media Psychology, 8,* 165–290.

Phang, A., & Schaefer, D. J. (2009). Is ignorance bliss? Assessing Singaporean media literacy awareness in the era of globalization. *Journalism and Mass Communication Educator, 64,*156–172.

Pinkleton, B. E., Austin, E. W., Chen, Y. Y., & Cohen, M. (2011). The role of media literacy in shaping adolescents' understanding of and responses to sexual portrayals in the mass media. *Journal of Health Communication, 0,* 1–17.

Pinkleton, B., Austin, E. W., Cohen, M., & Miller, A. (2003, June). *Media literacy and smoking prevention among adolescents: A year-two evaluation of the American Legacy Foundation/Washington State Department of Health anti-tobacco campaign.* Paper presented at the International Communication Association, Health Communication Division, San Diego, CA.

Pinkleton, B. E., Austin, E. W., Cohen, M., Miller, A., & Fitzgerald, E. (2007). A statewide evaluation of the effectiveness of media literacy training to prevent tobacco use among adolescents. *Health Communication, 21,* 23–34.

Pinkleton, B. E., Austin, E., W., & Van de Vord, R. (2010). The role of realism, similarity and expectancies in adolescents' interpretation of abuse-prevention messages. *Health Communication, 25,* 258–265.

Pipher, M. (2001). *Reviving Ophelia: Saving the selves of adolescent girls* [Video]. Northhampton, MA: Media Education Foundation.

Piran, N., Levine, M., & Irving, L. (2000). GO GIRLS! Media literacy, activism, and advocacy project. *Healthy Weight Journal, 14,* 89–90.

Postman, N. (1985). *Amusing ourselves to death: Public discourse in the age of show business.* London, UK: Penguin.

Postman, N. (1999). *Building a bridge to the eighteenth century: How the past can improve the future.* New York, NY: Knopf.

Potter, W. J. (2004). *Theory of media literacy: A cognitive approach.* Thousand Oaks, CA: Sage.

Potter, W. J. (2010). The state of media literacy. *Journal of Broadcasting and Electronic Media, 55,* 675–696.

Primack, B. A., Sidani, J., Carroll, M. V., & Fine, M. J. (2009). Associations between smoking and media literacy in college students. *Journal of Health Communication, 14*(6), 541–555.

Quin, R., & McMahon, B. (1995). Evaluating standards in media education. *Canadian Journal of Educational Communication, 22,* 15–25.

Rapaczynski, W., Singer, D. G., & Singer, J. L. (1982). Teaching television: A curriculum for young children. *Journal of Communication, 32,* 46–55.

Reid, L., & Gedissman, A. (2000). Required TV program in schools encourages poor lifestyle choices. *AAP News.* Retrieved from www.aap.org/advocacy/reid1100.htm

Resource fact sheet. (n.d.). Retrieved August 23, 2006, from http://www.lifeskillstraining.com/resource_facts.php

Robinson, T. N. (1999). Reducing children's television viewing to prevent obesity: A randomized controlled trial. *Journal of the American Medical Association, 282,* 1561–1567.

Robinson, T. N., Borzekowski, D. L. G., Matheson, D. M., & Kraemer, H. C. (2007). Effects of fast food branding on young children's taste preferences. *Archives of Pediatric Adolescent Medicine, 161,* 792–797.

Robinson, T. N., Saphir, M. N., Kraemer, H. C., Varady, A., & Haydel, K. F. (2001). Effects of reducing television viewing on children's requests for toys: A randomized controlled trial. *Journal of Developmental and Behavioral Pediatrics, 22,* 179–184.

Robinson, T. N., Wilde, M. L., Navracruz, L. C., Haydel, K. F., & Varady, A. (2000). Effects of reducing children's television and video game use on aggressive behavior. *Archives of Pediatric and Adolescent Medicine, 156,* 17–23.

Rosenbaum, J. E., Beentjes, J. W. J., & Konig, R. P. (2008). Mapping media literacy: Key concepts and future directions. *Communication Yearbook, 32,* 313–353.

Rosenkoetter, L. I., Rosenkoetter, S. E., Ozretich, R. A., & Acock, A. C. (2004). Mitigating the harmful effects of violent television. *Journal of Applied Developmental Psychology, 25,* 25–47.

Ruskin, G. (2006). *Executive director of Commercial Alert.* Retrieved from http://www.commercialalert .org/issues/

Sargent, J. D., Beach, M. L., Dalton, M. A., Mott, L. A., Tickle, J. J., Ahrens, M. B., & Heatherton, T. F. (2001). Effect of seeing tobacco use in film on trying smoking among adolescents: Cross sectional study. *Behavior Medicine Journal, 323,* 1–16.

Sargent, J. D., Dalton, M. A., Beach, M. L., Mott, L. A., Tickle, J. J., Ahrens, M. B., & Heatherton, T. F. (2002). Viewing tobacco use in movies: Does it shape attitudes that mediate adolescent smoking? *American Journal of Preventive Medicine, 22,* 137–145.

Scull, T. M., Kupersmidt, J. B., Parker, A. E., Elmore, K. C., & Benson, J. W. (2009). Adolescents' media-related cognitions and substance use in the context of parental and peer influences. *Journal of Youth and Adolescence, 39,* 981–998.

Silverblatt, A. (2001). *Media literacy: Keys to interpreting media messages.* Westport, CT: Praeger.

Silverblatt, A. (Ed.). (2013). *The Praeger Handbook of Media Literacy.* Westport, CT: Praeger.

Singer, D. G., Zuckerman, D. M., & Singer, J. L. (1980). Critical TV viewing: Helping elementary school children learn about TV. *Journal of Communication, 30,* 84–93.

Slater, M., Rouner, D., Murphy, K., Beavais, F., Van Leuven, J., & Domenech-Rodriguez, M. (1996). Adolescent counterarguing of TV beer advertisements: Evidence for effectiveness of alcohol education and critical viewing discussions. *Journal of Drug Education, 26,* 143–158.

Stauber, J., & Rampton, S. (1995). *Toxic sludge is good for you: Lies, damn lies and the public relations industry.* Monroe, MA: Common Courage Press.

Steiner-Adair, C., Sjostrom, L., Franko, D., Pai, S., Tucker, R., Becker, A., & Herzog, D. B. (2002). Primary prevention of risk factors for eating disorders in adolescent girls: Learning from practice. *International Journal of Eating Disorders, 32,* 401–411.

Straubhaar, J., & LaRose, R. (2004). *Media now: Understanding media, culture, and technology.* Belmont, CA: Wadsworth/Thomson.

Teinowitz, I. (2001). World Ad Federation seeking consistency. *Advertising Age, 72,* 35.

Tiene, E., & Whitmore, D. (1995). Beyond "Channel One": How schools are using school-wide television networks. *Educational Technology, 33,* 38–42.

Timmerman, L. M., Allen, M., Jorgensen, J., Herrett-Skjellum, J., Kramer, M. R., & Ryan D. J. (2008). A review and meta-analysis examining the relationship of music content with sex, race, priming, and attitudes. *Communication Quarterly, 56,* 303–324.

Tyner, K. (1998). *Literacy in a digital world.* Mahwah, NJ: Lawrence Erlbaum.

U.S. Senate, Committee on Finance. (2006). *Minority report.* Retrieved from http://www.senate .gov/~finance/press/Bpress/2005press/prb101206.pdf

Valkenburg, P. M. (2005, June). Parental mediation of undesired advertising effects. *Journal of Broadcasting and Electronic Media, 49,* 153–165.

Vooijs, M. W., & van der Voort, T. H. A. (1993). Learning about television violence: The impact of a critical viewing curriculum on children's attitudinal judgments of crime series. *Journal of Research and Development in Education, 26,* 133–142.

Wade, T., Davidson, S., & O'Dea, J. (2003). A preliminary controlled evaluation of a school-based media literacy program and self-esteem program for reducing eating disorder risk factors. *International Journal of Eating Disorders, 33,* 371–383.

Whitmore, D., & Tiene, D. (1994). Viewing Channel One: Awareness of current events by teenagers. *Mass Communication Review, 21,* 67–75.

Wilksch, S. M., & Wade, T. D. (2009). Reduction of shape and weight concern in young adolescents: A 30-month controlled evaluation of a media literacy program. *Journal of the American Academy of Child and Adolescent Psychiatry, 48*(6), 652–661.

Wilson, B. J. (1989). The effects of two control strategies on children's emotional reactions to a frightening movie scene. *Journal of Broadcasting and Electronic Media, 33,* 397–418.

Wilson, B. J., Linz, D., Donnerstein, E., & Stipp, H. (1992). The impact of social issue television programming on attitudes toward rape. *Human Communication Research, 19,* 179–208.

Wilson, B. J., Linz, D., Federman, J., Smith, S., Paul, B., Nathanson, A., . . . Lingsweiler, R. (1999). *The choices and consequences evaluation: A study of Court TV's anti-violence curriculum.* Santa Barbara: Center for Communication and Social Policy, University of California.

Wilson, B. J., & Weiss, A. J. (1991). The effects of two reality explanations on children's reactions to a frightening movie scene. *Communication Monographs, 58,* 307–327.

Winkel, F. W., & DeKleuver, E. (1997). Communication aimed at changing cognitions about sexual intimidation: Comparing the impact of a perpetrator-focused versus a victim-focused persuasive strategy. *Journal of Interpersonal Violence, 12,* 513–529.

Yates, B. L. (2004). Applying diffusion theory: Adoption of media literacy programs in schools. *Studies in Media and Information Literacy Education, 4.* Retrieved from http://128.100.205.52/jour .ihtml?lp=simile/issue14/bradfordXfulltext.html

Children's Media Policy

This book has examined, in detail, the implications of media use for children's healthy development. As we conclude *Children, Adolescents, and the Media*, we consider the role of policy in shaping the media content that is available for and chosen by young audiences. Specifically, we consider the development, implementation, and impact of media policy designed to enhance the benefits and diminish the harms of media use. Chapter 13 covers both the "on the books" policies of federal regulatory agencies, as well the media and advertising industries' own self-regulatory efforts. The chapter concludes with a consideration of how audiences and consumers (including children and adults) can become active in ensuring a healthy media environment for all young people.

Philosophy of Regulation

In the U.S., much of the tension regarding how much say the government should have about media content stems from the Constitution's First Amendment protection clauses against government interference in free speech, including commercial speech. Courts have repeatedly found themselves balancing the rights of commercial entities to say what they please against the need to protect vulnerable citizens. In many instances, the Supreme Court has defined young people as "vulnerable citizens" and has restricted access to otherwise legal content. In *Ginsberg v. New York* (1968), for example, the Court held that children do not have the same constitutional right as adults to receive pornographic magazines. The Court argued: "Because of the State's exigent interest in preventing distribution of objectionable material, it can exercise its power to protect the health, safety, welfare and morals of its community by barring the distribution of books recognized as suitable for adults" (as quoted in Graff, 2008, p. 167).

The balancing act is even further complicated when it comes to nonprint media, particularly television and radio. In the latter case, broadcasters do not "own" the airwaves on which programs are disseminated; rather, networks like ABC and FOX are given licenses by the federal government to operate within a slice of the spectrum under the agreement that they will "serve the public interest, convenience, and necessity" established in 1934 with the Federal Communications

Act (Rice, 2008). Cable television networks have looser guidelines in some categories (e.g., foul language) but not others (e.g., advertising time on children's programming) (Napoli, 2001). Parents and other members of the public, moreover, often do not know the difference between a "broadcast" channel and a "cable" channel; to them it's all "television" (Schmitt, 2000). Evolving media technologies have further complicated regulatory efforts, particularly since policy has historically been made on the basis of the vehicle of delivery (e.g., a television set or a movie theatre) (Kunkel & Wilcox, 2012) rather than content. In a media environment in which vehicles or "platforms" have converged—so that one can watch episodes of *Saturday Night Live* on the Internet through Hulu or on the commercial broadcast station NBC—what was once "unavailable" to children through time restrictions is now easily available 24 hours a day, 7 days a week.

As technologies converge, evolve, and become more interactive, the desire to protect both the free-speech rights of media and special vulnerabilities of children has led to a fluid mix of federal mandates and industry self-regulation. In this chapter we explore the elements of this mix. But before we begin, it is necessary to ask: What triggers discourse about media policy or new regulatory activity?

Jordan (2008) argues that children's media policy is revisited under a variety of conditions and contexts. One is when an upwelling of serious public concern about the media comes to the attention of lawmakers—as, for example, when a national poll reveals that parents are worried about children revealing private information when they go online (Turow, 2003). Another is the discovery of new scientific evidence suggesting a connection between the media and a negative outcome—for example, the Institutes of Medicine (IOM) looked across studies and concluded that junk food advertising affected children's food preferences and intake (IOM, 2006). Yet another catalyst for policy change is when a focusing event occurs. The term *focusing event*, as used in the policy studies literature, refers to "those events that catapult an issue from relative obscurity on the systemic agenda to a place of prominence on the institutional or even the decision agenda" (Wood, 2006, p. 420). The Master Settlement Agreement (as described in Chapter 6) focused substantial attention on the topic of tobacco regulation and led to tighter restrictions on the marketing of cigarettes and similar products. Finally, advocacy groups have impacted policymaking by bringing constant and focused attention to an issue, as was the case when Action for Children's Television pressured broadcasters to "serve the public interest" by increasing the amount and quality of educational programming for children (Wilcox, 2003).

U.S. Agencies

Regulatory agencies overseeing media policy in the U.S. do not make laws; they implement them. The Children's Television Act of 1990 (see Chapter 3) was an act of Congress, but its implementation was ineffective until the Federal Communications Commission developed a set of "processing guidelines" that broadcasters were required to follow in order to receive expedited license renewal (Jordan, 2008). The agencies described below are what Napoli (2001) identifies as the "bureaucratic tier"—government agencies that serve a variety of constituents, including the White House (as commissioners are appointed by the executive branch), Congress (which makes the laws), and media/advertising industries (which both lobby for a level playing field and complain when they feel unfairly targeted). The government agencies are also, of course, beholden to the public, which will provide feedback through formal and informal channels.

The Federal Trade Commission

In the U.S., the Federal Trade Commission (FTC) is mandated to protect children from unfair and deceptive marketing practices. The five-member Commission's stated mission is "to prevent business practices that are anticompetitive or deceptive or unfair to consumers; to enhance informed consumer choice and public understanding of the competitive process; and to accomplish this without unduly burdening legitimate business activity" (http://www.ftc.gov/ftc/about .shtm). The FTC's enforcement activities related to children and youth have typically focused on *how* products are advertised, rather than *whether* they are advertised. For example, the Commission has brought cases challenging nutritional claims for foods that are likely to be appealing to children. In one case, it challenged a television ad for the Klondike Lite Ice Cream Bar for saying that it was 93% fat free (Beales, 2004). The FTC alleged that the claim was false because the entire bar included the chocolate coating and not just the "lite" ice cream; thus, when taken as a whole, it contained a substantial amount of fat and sugar and could not be fairly labeled "lite." From this vantage point, the FTC argued that the ad was misleading, since a reasonable consumer—especially a child consumer—would not eat the bar without its chocolate coating.

The Federal Trade Commission will take up cases of fraudulent claims but will also issue reports related to unethical advertising practices. As will be described, it issued a series of reports and called for voluntary self-regulations when it was brought to light that PG-13- and R-rated movies were being advertised to children. Additionally, it has looked into claims of unfair marketing of children's media directed to parents. In May 2006, the Campaign for a Commercial-Free Childhood filed a complaint with the FTC against the Baby Einstein Company, the Brainy Baby Company, and other companies that marketed videos and DVDs, saying that the companies made unsubstantiated claims about their educational value. The FTC did not take any enforcement action, but the advocacy group's efforts catalyzed changes in baby video marketing practices and spurred Disney (owner of the Baby Einstein series) to offer refunds or exchanges under a "customer satisfaction guarantee" (Lewin, 2009).

The Federal Communications Commission

The Federal Communications Commission (FCC) also has a role in regulating advertising to children over the broadcast and cable media. Like the FTC, the FCC is a five-member commission with members appointed by the president. Most FCC commissioners have background in the law, leading some scholars to complain that a lack of understanding of social science research has led to ill-informed or misinformed policy interpretation and implementation (Wartella, 2003; Wright, 2009).

Like the FTC, the FCC enforces laws passed by Congress. For example, the Children's Television Act of 1990 (CTA) limits the amount of advertising during children's programming to 10 and a half minutes on weekends and 12 minutes on weekdays (CTA, 2006). In addition, it requires commercial content to be separated from program content through what have come to be known as "bumpers" (in which there is a visual and/or auditory break), although the efficacy of these program separators is in dispute (An & Stern, 2011). The CTA also prohibits stations from including TV advertisements during the program or in spots adjacent to the beginning and end of the program in which the character appears (deemed "host selling"). If stations are found to violate the law, the FCC is the agency that levies the fines.

The FCC's mandate extends far beyond advertising, however. As will be discussed later in the chapter, the FCC enforces Congress's mandate that commercial broadcasters provide a minimum amount of educational programming for children (under the CTA) and responds to public complaints about indecent content by investigating and fining stations that violate the Broadcast Decency Enforcement Act of 2005.

Advocacy Groups

Action for Children's Television

Advocacy groups have long exerted pressure on federal regulatory agencies and the media industry. As early as 1968, Action for Children's Television (ACT), a grassroots advocacy group headed by a Boston mother and activist Peggy Charren, exerted influence on Congress and the Federal Communications Commission to increase the amount of educational programming for children and limit the amount of advertising directed at children. In 1992, ACT officially disbanded after the passage of the Children's Television Act of 1990 (Zoglin & Tynan, 1992), but founder Peggy Charren remained involved in advocacy and activism until the FCC processing guideline for educational television known as the "three-hour rule" was adopted. In 1996, she was given the Annenberg Public Policy Center's Award for Distinguished Lifetime Contribution to Children's Television (Jordan, 1996a).

The Parents Television Council

The conservative-leaning Parents Television Council (PTC), founded in 1995, states that its mission is to "promote and restore responsibility and decency to the entertainment industry in answer to America's demand for positive, family-oriented television programming" (http://www.parentstv.org/PTC/faqs/main.asp). Members of the PTC file complaints with the FTC and FCC and write letters, send emails, and make phone calls to corporations when they feel programming does not comport with family values. The PTC was a key influence on legislation to increase fines for broadcast indecency (see below) through its regular reports of sex, violence, and profanity in television and membership complaints to the FCC. The PTC has also advocated restrictions on the sales of violent video games, and continues to do so despite the Supreme Court decision in 2012 to strike down a California law prohibiting the sale of violent games to minors (for more detail about *Brown v. Entertainment Merchants Association*, see Chapter 10).

Campaign for a Commercial-Free Childhood

Another approach taken by advocacy groups has been to highlight the impact of consumer culture on children's media properties and on children themselves. The Campaign for a Commercial-Free Childhood (CCFC), noted above, is a national coalition of health care professionals, educators, advocacy groups, parents, and individuals that "supports parents' efforts to raise healthy families by limiting commercial access to children and ending the exploitive practice of child-targeted marketing" (http://www.commercialfreechildhood.org/). As mentioned earlier, CCFC played a key role in changing the marketing practices of the baby video industry. In another recent campaign they shed light on the irony of a Dr. Seuss book-turned-movie called *The Lorax*, which has a strong environmental message but has been used to promote a plethora of environmentally unfriendly products, including a Mazda sport-utility vehicle. In addition to raising public awareness, CCFC has pressured food manufacturers like Kellogg's to limit marketing using children's favorite characters and has worked to eliminate the presence of corporate marketing in the classroom.

The Center for Digital Democracy

A final example of an advocacy group is one that focuses on the challenges of new and interactive media technology. The Center for Digital Democracy (CDD) has been a leader in pressuring policymakers to ensure that children's privacy is protected and that their exposure to age-inappropriate and unhealthful product marketing is limited. The Children's Online Privacy Protection Act, passed in 1998, resulted in large part from a campaign led by CDD (http://www.democraticmedia.org/home) to raise awareness among policymakers about data collected from naive child Web surfers. As well, CDD has carefully tracked the variety of ways in which food marketers have used interactive media to reach children and adolescents, particularly as traditional marketing strategies, such as television advertising, have been under fire for contributing to the childhood obesity crisis in America (Montgomery, 2012).

Industry Self-Regulation

Self-regulatory practices are common in an industry that is wary of government intervention. Signs of potential governmental regulatory activity often stir the industry to preemptive self-censorship, as was the case with Disney's decision to offer refunds on its baby videos. If advertisers or media companies see new policymaking on the horizon, they will propose self-regulatory measures. Some scholars call this dynamic "regulation by raised eyebrow" (Kunkel, 1988; Starr, 2004).

The Children's Advertising Review Unit (CARU) of the Council of Better Business Bureaus is the advertising industry's self-monitoring group (Snyder, 2011). It seeks voluntary compliance from marketers by recommending a code of ethical practices to its members. In addition, CARU receives and acts upon complaints of deceptive or misleading advertising on a case-by-case basis. For example, in June 2011, CARU recommended that Reebok discontinue claims made in print advertising that suggested its Zigtech sneakers help children perform better in sports. Reebok responded by saying that it disagreed, but that the company supports "CARU's efforts to promote self-regulation" ("CARU Recommends," 2011).

Steps toward self-regulation have also been made in food marketing. Alarmed by a sharp rise in childhood obesity, policymakers, the public, and health professionals have challenged food industry marketing practices (Sharma, Teret, & Brownell, 2010). In response, the major food industry players have promised to change, and, since 2006, have issued a series of highly publicized pledges through CARU, including the promise to make significant shifts in what kinds of foods are promoted in children's television programming. At least two systematic content analyses have found that the landscape of food marketing has remained virtually unchanged, however (Kunkel, McKinley, & Wright, 2009; Yale Rudd Center for Food Policy & Obesity, 2011).

The media and advertising industries have adopted other self-regulatory practices. Strictly speaking, the ratings systems used for television, movies, video games, and music are voluntary. Like much self-regulation, however, ratings result in inconsistent and irregular application.

As well, the norms of the industry are such that certain products (e.g., condoms, birth control pills) are not advertised on major broadcast stations, leaving some observers to wonder about the rationale (for example, erectile dysfunction medication ads are common, as noted in Chapter 5).

In the sections below, we examine specific regulations and policies that shape what children see, hear, and read in the media. The policy landscape is expansive and constantly shifting; therefore, this chapter does not cover every policy or regulatory issue. Rather, it focuses on those topics that are most enduring or timely.

Advertising Policy

The ubiquity of advertisements and children's high exposure rates have generated concern about the effects of advertising on children. In the U.S., children are exposed to between 24,000 and 30,000 advertisements each year on television alone (Kunkel & Castonguay, 2012). As noted earlier, the constant barrage of marketing to children and the ever changing techniques used to reach young audiences have prompted advocacy groups like the Campaign for a Commercial-Free Childhood to consider what can be done to reduce exposure or inoculate children against its negative effects (Schor, 2004). As discussed earlier in the chapter, however, there are competing priorities at work.

Advertising to children is one domain in which debates have been quite contentious. On the one hand, children are rightly viewed as innocent, vulnerable, and in need of protection from marketing (Linn & Novosat, 2008; Schor, 2004). Research shows that children under 8 years old do not effectively comprehend persuasive marketing messages and that most children under 4 years old do not easily or consistently discriminate between television advertisements and programming (IOM, 2006). Findings like these have been used to justify limits on advertising to younger children (Caraher, Landon, & Dalmeny, 2006), and many countries around the world have set limits as to what can be advertised on television. On the other hand, however, media and advertising executives make the case that children are sophisticated and savvy consumers who deserve the right to engage in the market (Snyder, 2011). Furthermore, they argue that restrictions on advertising to children deny companies their right to inform children about their products and the right for children to receive information for purchase decision making.

Lobbyists for media and ad agencies are generously funded to fight potential new regulations, and they have a visible presence on the Hill (McIntyre, 2013). In 2011, the American Academy of Pediatrics called for a Federal ban on junk food advertising to children (Council on Communications and Media, 2011). That same year, the food industry spent $51 million lobbying against any federal regulation of its advertising (Sunlight Foundation, 2011). Also in 2011, a working group comprising the Centers for Disease Control and Prevention, the Food and Drug Administration, the U.S. Department of Agriculture, and the Federal Trade Commission was convened to establish voluntary guidelines for marketing food to children (FTC, 2011; Schwartz & Ustjanauskas, 2012). The guidelines produced cover a wide array of marketing, from television to toys in fast food meals to Internet sites and social media, and would severely limit advertising of foods exceeding limited amounts of added sugar, saturated or trans fats, or sodium (Layton, 2011). So far, food manufacturers have rejected the proposed guidelines in favor of their own, weaker guidelines (Layton, 2011). The counter-forces to restricting advertising directed at young children are so strong that it is unlikely that measurable changes can be made either voluntarily or through governmental intervention (Koplan & Brownell, 2010; Kunkel et al., 2009; Levi, 2010).

Privacy Policy

As noted earlier in the chapter, the Federal Trade Commission works to ensure that children do not disclose private information online. In 1999, pursuant to the Children's Online Privacy Protection Act (COPPA), the FTC issued its COPPA rule governing the online collection of personal information from children under the age of 13. The rule requires commercial websites and online services to obtain verifiable parental consent before collecting personal information (http://www.ftc.gov/ogc/coppa1.htm). For this reason, social networking sites such as Facebook do not allow children under 13 to register as users. Xanga, a social network site that was judged to "knowingly" collect information from children, was fined $1 million for violating COPPA (Jordan, 2008). The largest penalty to date issued for a violation of COPPA came in May 2011, when the Walt Disney Co. subsidiary Playdom agreed to pay $3 million to settle FTC charges that it "illegally collected and disclosed personal information from hundreds of thousands of children without parents' consent" (Troianovski, 2012). For this reason, social networking sites like Facebook have a requirement that users be age 13 or older in order to avoid violating COPPA rules.

COPPA has been criticized by some for not adapting to advances in Web technology and marketing (Troianovski, 2012). With the widespread use of smartphones and apps, the collection of personal information from children and adolescents is easier and, in many ways, more invisible to children and their parents. For example, when a user clicks the "like" button on Facebook, the user and his or her personal data are harvested. Additionally, researcher danah boyd has argued that COPPA actually undermines parents' decision making regarding children's Internet use. In a study conducted by boyd, Hargittai, Schultz, and Palfrey (2011), parents reported that they play a role in circumventing Facebook's "no users under 13" policy. Indeed, their research shows that about one-third of 11-year-olds and more than one-half of 12-year-olds have a Facebook account, and that parents often help children create these accounts. According to boyd and her colleagues, parents are sometimes confused about policies and regulations. Only one-half of the parents in their sample knew that Facebook had a minimum age, and only one-third understood that this is a requirement and not a recommendation. Moreover, boyd and her colleagues write,

> Given the frequency with which parents who knew there was a minimum age referenced issues of age appropriateness or maturity in an open-ended question—and given explanations we heard in qualitative work done as a pilot for this study—one explanation may be that parents see age restrictions as a form of maturity restriction or a type of maturity rating. (boyd et al., 2011)

Educational Media Policy

In 1961, FCC commissioner Newton Minow, in his first address as chair of the regulatory agency, famously stated to television executives that if they sat down to watch what was on their own networks they would see "a vast wasteland." In the ensuing years, television for children went from bad to worse. By 1990, after decades that saw the proliferation of toy-based programming and the diminution of educational content, Congress unanimously passed the Children's Television Act of 1990. The CTA reestablished the commercial time limits applicable to children's programming that had been eliminated during the Reagan administration. It also required broadcast stations like ABC, CBS, and NBC to significantly increase their educational offerings for children. What followed in the wake of this legislation, however, was the creative relabeling of existing shows as "educational" (for example, *The Jetsons* was listed as a show that could teach children about the future) (Kunkel & Canepa, 1994) and a juggling of the broadcast lineup so that the most valuable programs (e.g., *Bill Nye, the Science Guy*) aired at times when few children were likely to be awake and in the audience (for example, 5 a.m. on Saturday) (Jordan, 1996b).

The landscape of educational programming has improved since the 1990s for three reasons. First, groups like the Annenberg Public Policy Center and Children Now have called broadcasters out on their dubious educational claims, and policymakers have paid closer attention. In 1997, the FCC issued a processing guideline that provided stricter boundaries for what would count as "educational" and when such programs could air (Levi, 2010). Second, the widespread availability of cable and satellite, as well as the resulting need to program for niche audiences like preschoolers, led to the development of channels specifically designed for children and dayparts specifically programmed for distinct child audiences (Bryant, 2006; Pecora, 1997). Finally, the federal government stepped up its funding of television programming focused on specific content areas. For example, the National Science Foundation provided support for preschool programs to teach basic science principles, underwriting shows such as *Cyberchase* (see Figure 13.1) and *ZOOM*. As well, the Department of Education established a financial base for the development of programs that get children "ready to learn," including PBS programs like *Super Why* and *WordWorld*, and support for existing programs like *Sesame Street*.

Beyond television, Congress has also supported children's access to new media. In the Telecommunications Act of 1996, policymakers mandated the creation of the Schools and Libraries Program of the Universal Service Fund to provide discounts that would allow schools and libraries to obtain affordable Internet access. The provision, known as E-Rate (for "education rate"), is implemented by the FCC, with discounts varying depending on the percentage of students who qualify for the National School Lunch Program (Hudson, 2004). Additional funds to support connectivity were provided under the American Recovery and Reinvestment Act of 2009, which sought to expand broadband access and adoption in rural communities. Federal programs like E-Rate represent attempts to close the "digital divide"—the gap in access to computers and the Internet, based in large part on a family's socioeconomic status. Such programs reflect the recognition that children and families are educationally and economically disadvantaged if they do not have equal access to social networks (for job hunting) or information sources (for schoolwork). The Pew Internet and American Life Project, using a nationally representative survey, shows that more than three-quarters of adults use the Internet. While the "digital divide" has closed substantially, this is largely due to the widespread adoption of smartphones (Zickuhr & Smith, 2012). What has emerged in place of the digital access divide is the digital *use* divide. Those who access the Internet via a mobile device have different opportunities and use different skills than those who access it through a computer. Moreover, as Hudson (2004) has pointed out, "providing technology does not guarantee that it will be used effectively" (p. 320).

Figure 13.1 *Cyberchase* is a popular PBS program with a curriculum base and is supported in part by funds from the National Science Foundation.

Because schools and community libraries have accepted federal funding for providing Internet access, they have also been required to accept federal guidelines about restricting children's access to indecent or age-inappropriate material online. The Children's Internet Protection Act (CIPA) requires that libraries enable filters on all Internet-accessible computers in order to receive federal subsidies for Internet access and related computer equipment (Jordan, 2008). In *United States v. American Library Association*, the Supreme Court held that the act does not violate the First Amendment because libraries have the discretion to provide only filtered Internet access and Congress has the discretion to refuse subsidies to libraries with unfiltered access (Wu, 2004).

Age-Inappropriate Movie and Video Game Marketing and Sales

One of the greatest concerns about children and adolescents' use of media has to do with their exposure to content that is inappropriate for their age (Bushman & Cantor, 2003). When such content is deliberately marketed to youth, as has been found in the case of advertisements for violent movies and video games (American Academy of Pediatrics, 2006) and sexual content, the Federal Trade Commission will get involved.

In 1999, then-president Clinton requested a study of the marketing of violent entertainment products to youths. The objective of the $1 million study was to provide information to policymakers, the industry, parents, and the American public. A key finding of the report, based on data provided by more than 60 companies in the entertainment media industry, was that motion picture, recorded music, and electronic game companies had routinely marketed restricted products to children under 17 (Grier, 2001). Additionally, using a "mystery shopper" strategy in which child confederates were sent into stores and movie theaters, the FTC found that children under 17 years of age were able to buy tickets to R-rated motion pictures and purchase explicit-content-labeled music recordings and M-rated electronic games without an adult. The Commission recommended that all three industries enhance their regulatory efforts by (a) establishing or expanding codes that prohibit target marketing to children and imposing sanctions for violations, (b) increasing compliance at the retail level, and (c) increasing parental understanding of the ratings and labels (as reported in Grier, 2001, p. 126; for full FTC report, see Federal Trade Commission, 2000). The potential efficacy of the last recommendation is explored in the section on ratings.

As noted in Chapter 10, California passed legislation in 2005 that prohibited the sale or rental of violent video games to children under the age of 18, based on the argument that such games are developmentally harmful to youth (Sacks, Bushman, & Anderson, 2011). Retailers who violated the law would have been fined up to $1,000 for each infraction. The video game industry challenged the law all the way to the Supreme Court. In 2011, the high court upheld an earlier federal appeals court decision that ruled that the state law was unconstitutional because it violated minors' rights under the First Amendment (*Brown v. Entertainment Merchants Association*). Writing for the majority opinion, Justice Antonin Scalia argued:

> Like the protected books, plays and movies that preceded them, video games communicate ideas—and even social messages—through many familiar literary devices (such as characters, dialogue, plot, and music) and through features distinctive to the medium (such as the player's interaction with the virtual world). That suffices to confer First Amendment protection. (*Brown v. Entertainment Merchants Association*, p. 2)

The Court also questioned the claim of harmful effects, pointing out that the research does not prove definitively that violent video games *cause* minors to act aggressively. Clearly, the debate is not yet over. Responding to the ruling, California State Senator Leland Yee, who wrote the law, said "the Supreme Court once again put the interests of corporate America before the interests of our children" (Liptak, 2011).

Indecency

As noted earlier in the chapter, broadcasters are required to "serve the public interest, convenience, and necessity," which leaves room for a very broad and changing definition of what constitutes the "public interest" (Napoli, 2001). According to the FCC, it is a violation of the law to air obscene programming at any time. It is also a violation of federal law to broadcast indecent or profane programming during certain hours when children are likely to be in the audience (www.fcc.gov/encyclopedia/regulation-obscenity-indecency-and-profanity). Indecency is defined by the FCC as "language or material that depicts or describes, in terms patently offensive as measured by the contemporary community standards for the broadcast medium, sexual or excretory activities or organs" (Carter, Franklin, & Wright, 1999, p. 246).

One of the most important cases of broadcast indecency, *FCC v. Pacifica Foundation*, came in 1978, when broadcasters were fined for airing George Carlin's "Filthy Words" routine, in which he utters all the words that can't be said on radio or television. The FCC's right to prohibit indecency was upheld by the Supreme Court, which reasoned that the agency did not violate Pacifica Foundation's constitutional rights because it had created a "safe harbor," only enforcing the policy for those hours in which children are likely to be in the audience (6 a.m. to 10 p.m.). Over the next few decades, the FCC levied few fines for indecency when complaints were based on an isolated word or utterance (Kunkel & Wilcox, 2012). The position of the FCC signaled a change in priorities, however, when it began issuing fines for what have come to be known as "fleeting expletives." In response to a complaint from the advocacy group Parents Television Council, the FCC issued the opinion that Bono's declaration of delight at receiving an award ("f—ing brilliant") constituted profanity and signaled to broadcasters that they would issue fines over the "f" word and that they should implement a delay/bleeping system for live broadcasts (FCC, 2004). Moreover, the Janet Jackson "wardrobe malfunction" during the 2004 Super Bowl halftime show became a "focusing event" for policymakers. Congress determined that not only should the FCC issue fines for one-time indecent words or images, but it should also increase these fines tenfold. Thus, the Broadcast Decency Enforcement Act directed the FCC to fine stations $325,000 for violations (Jordan, 2008). As Kunkel and Wilcox (2012) note, the broadcasters predictably objected to the new policy and appealed in the courts to overturn it. In the 2009 decision *FCC v. Fox Television Stations*, the Supreme Court affirmed the constitutionality of the fines and remanded the case to the U.S. Second Circuit Court of Appeals. This court ruled that the fleeting expletive policy is too vague to be constitutional, a decision that was appealed to the Supreme Court. In a 2012 ruling, the high court reversed the FCC enforcement decisions in specific cases on administrative grounds, indicating that the agency did not provide stations with advance notice of its new policies. However, the Supreme Court did not address the First Amendment implications of the Commission's indecency policy (Richley, 2012).

Ratings Policy

One of the most important noncontroversial strategies for limiting children's access to adult content without unduly infringing on the First Amendment rights of media makers is to simply provide information about the content of the media property in advance. This is done through a voluntary, largely self-regulatory system.

Movie Ratings

The first ratings system, of movies, was created in 1968 as a joint venture between the Motion Picture Association of America (MPAA) and the National Association of Theatre Owners. Interestingly, it quickly followed two Supreme Court decisions that upheld the power of states to regulate children's access to media, otherwise protected by the First Amendment (*Ginsberg v. State of New York*, 1968; *Interstate Circuit v. Dallas*, 1968). Although the system is voluntary, most films are rated by the MPAA. Studies show that most parents are aware of the movie ratings system (Federman, 1996), and more than half routinely use them, although they do not always find them to be "very" useful (Rideout, 2007). It is possible that they are not always useful because, as one study found, parents often disagree with the ratings for particular movies (Walsh & Gentile, 2001). A recent national survey of nearly 1,000 parents nationwide found that parents favor ratings for media but do not think the existing ratings accurately provide the information they want, which is detailed content information (Gentile, Maier, Hasson, & Lopez de Bonetti, 2011). The current movie ratings are shown in Figure 13.2 and Table 13.1 and are available on the MPAA website (http://www.mpaa.org/ratings/what-each-rating-means).

There are several problems with the MPAA system. Initially, the ratings were evaluative only, not descriptive (see Table 13.2). Parents would be given only the "PG" or "PG-13" symbol without being told exactly what content was problematic (Harris, 2007). For certain parents, offensive language could be more of an issue than scenes with brief nudity, for example. In 2007, however, and with very little public fanfare, the MPAA added descriptive information below the symbols (e.g., the 2007 film *Hostel: Part II* is rated R for "sadistic scenes of torture and bloody violence, terror, nudity, sexual content, language, and some drug content"). But the descriptions do not always accompany the rating, nor is the print always large enough to be deciphered by the average parent with average eyesight. (Both Screenit.com and Common-SenseMedia.com do an excellent job of providing parents with descriptive information but are not nearly as widely known or accessible as the MPAA ratings are.)

Sometimes, decisions by the ratings board defy explanation (Ebert, 2010). The movie *Billy Elliot* was one that most parents would deem an acceptable film for children and teenagers,

Figure 13.2   MPAA movie ratings.

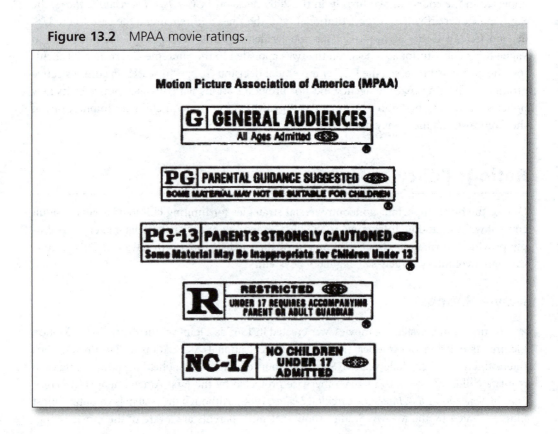

Table 13.1   MPAA Ratings Explained

G: General audiences (all ages admitted).

- Indicates that the film contains nothing that most parents would consider offensive, even for their youngest children. No scenes depicting language, nudity, sex, or drug use.
- Examples: *Finding Nemo*, *Toy Story* (1–3), *Alvin and the Chipmunks*, *Chipwrecked*, *Cars* (1 and 2), *Ratatouille*.

PG: Parental guidance suggested (some material may not be suitable for children).

- May contain some material that parents might not like their young children exposed to, but explicit sex scenes or scenes of drug use are absent. However, some profanity may be heard, nudity may be briefly seen, and horror and violence may be present at "moderate levels."
- Examples: *The Chronicles of Narnia*, *Alice in Wonderland* (2010), *Despicable Me*, Dr. Seuss's *The Lorax*, *Brave*, *Madagascar* (1–3).

PG-13: Parents strongly cautioned (some material may be inappropriate for children under 13).

- "Rough or persistent violence" is absent, as is sexually oriented nudity. There may be some scenes of drug use, and there may be a single use of a common sexually derived expletive.
- Examples: the *Harry Potter* series, the *Mission Impossible* series, *Avatar*, *The Hunger Games*, *The Avengers*, *The Dark Knight*.

R: Restricted (children under 17 require an accompanying parent or adult guardian).

- Contains some adult material. May contain "hard" language, "tough violence," sex or nudity, or drug use. Consequently, parents are urged to learn more about the film before taking their children to see it.
- Examples: *Saw* (I–VI), *Brokeback Mountain*, *The Hangover* (1 and 2), *Bridesmaids*, *Prometheus*.

NC-17: No one under 17 admitted.

- Contains material that the ratings board feels is "patently adult," and therefore children 17 and younger should not be viewing it. May contain explicit sex scenes, considerable sexually oriented language, and/or scenes of excessive violence.
- Recent examples: *Shame*, *Elles*, *This Film Is Not Yet Rated*. (Older examples: *Showgirls*, *Kids*)

except for repeated use of the "f" word. Despite the fact that the word was spoken in a northern English accent so thick that it was barely decipherable, the film received an R rating, putting it out of reach of many teens who would have enjoyed seeing it. More recently, the Oscar-winning

Table 13.2   Examples of Descriptive and Evaluative Ratings

Descriptive	Evaluative
Contains some violence	Parental discretion advised
Nudity/sex level 3	Teen: ages 13+
Violence: blood and gore	R: restricted
Language: mild expletives	Adults only
Contains extreme violence	Mature: ages 17+
BN: brief nudity	PG: parental guidance

SOURCE: Federman (1996). Reprinted with permission.

film *The King's Speech* suffered the same fate despite a single scene involving the use of the "f" word; and the movie *Bully* received an R rating for language even though the subject matter is extremely important for an adolescent audience to see. Conversely, *Hannibal*, a gory sequel to *Silence of the Lambs*, was rated R, not NC-17. As critic Roger Ebert noted in his review, "If it proves nothing else, it proves that if a man cutting off his face and feeding it to the dogs doesn't get the NC-17 rating for violence, nothing ever will" (Ebert, 2001, p. 4). The board is also notoriously susceptible to negotiation with the industry (Dick, 2006). Thus, the movie *South Park: Bigger, Longer & Uncut* received an R rating only after it was rated five times as NC-17. "God's the biggest bitch of them all" qualified the film for an R rating, whereas "God f—ing me up the a—" would have merited an NC-17 (Hochman, 1999). Even the makers of the film were surprised that their film escaped with just an R rating (Hochman, 1999).

Many observers and scholars have argued that the MPAA rates more harshly for sex than for violence, which is the reverse of what European countries do (Ebert, 2010; Nalkur, Jamieson, & Romer, 2010) (see Figure 13.3). Any depiction of sexual activity is likely to earn a picture an R rating, whereas a PG-13 movie can contain an appreciable amount of violence. Films that were extremely violent, such as *Natural Born Killers* and *Pulp Fiction*, received R ratings, whereas *Showgirls*, which had graphic sexuality and some nudity but only brief violence, received an NC-17 rating (Federman, 1996). A study of the 855 top-grossing movies from 1950 to 2006 found that the MPAA system has allowed increasingly violent content into PG-13 films while effectively screening out explicit sex (Nalkur et al., 2010). Even former members of the MPAA ratings board have serious problems with how the ratings are decided (Waxman, 2001a).

Another problem with the MPAA system is that, through the years, the industry has tolerated significant drug and violent content in G- and PG-rated movies, despite its own guidelines ("Are G-Rated Films," 2005). Of all the animated feature films produced in the United States between 1937 and 1999, 100% contained violence, and the portrayal of intentional violence increased during this 60-year period (Yokota & Thompson, 2000). Two studies of G-rated children's films released between 1937 and 1997 have found that nearly half displayed at least one scene of tobacco or alcohol use (Goldstein, Sobel, & Newman, 1999; Thompson & Yokota, 2001).

Figure 13.3

SOURCE: *Zits* © 2004 Zits Partnership. Dist. by King Features Syndicate.

Another significant problem is what has been labeled "ratings creep." Between 1992 and 2003, for example, the PG rating seemed to be turning into a G rating, the PG-13 rating into a PG rating, and the R rating into a PG-13 rating for many films (Thompson & Yokota, 2004). In particular, the amount of violence (PG and PG-13 films), sex (PG, PG-13, and R films), and profanity (PG-13 and R films) has been ratcheted up in the past decade. A quantitative study of 45 PG-13 films from 1988 to 1997 to 2006 found significant over-time increases in violent content within the PG-13 rating (Leone & Barowski, 2011). The MPAA rates more severely for sex or nudity than it does for violence, despite the fact that the research clearly finds violent content far more problematic than sexual content. Several studies have noticed that the age-based ratings simply encourage children, especially boys, to seek "older" fare (Cantor, 1998). When ratings are based on age rather than content, the "forbidden fruit theory" seems to become operational (Bushman & Stack, 1996).

There is some evidence that this trend may be changing, however. A 2001 study by an industry research firm found that films may lose as much as 40% of their potential opening-weekend earnings if they are rated R versus PG-13 or PG (Waxman, 2001b). Perhaps in response to the attention of the Federal Trade Commission, researchers found that after the 2000 report, more teens were being turned away at R-rated movies (Waxman, 2001b). In addition, of the top 20 films in 2011, only one (*Bridesmaids*) was rated R (James, 2011).

TV Ratings

The television industry has lagged far behind the motion picture industry in developing a ratings system. Nearly 30 years after the MPAA system was introduced, the television networks began rating their shows, but only after receiving considerable pressure from parents, advocacy groups, and the federal government (Hogan, 2012). In fact, it took congressional legislation to accomplish the final step of rating the programs. In 1996, the Telecommunications Act mandated that new television sets be manufactured with a V-chip and that television programs be rated so that the chip could be programmed by parents who wanted to block out inappropriate shows (see Figure 13.4). Congress indicated that if the television industry did not come up with a system for ratings, then it would be forced to take more deliberate actions and impose ratings (Jordan, 2008).

Figure 13.4 Illustration of the V-chip blocking device in U.S. television sets.

The TV ratings system, which is loosely based on the movie ratings system, has been criticized for similar problems (see Table 13.3). While the initial ratings, like movie ratings, were solely age based, advocacy groups and academic researchers successfully pressured for the inclusion of content descriptors (Cantor, 1998). However, even after descriptors were added, studies show that the system is still not working properly. For some observers, the current categories are not specific enough regarding content, and the contextual impact of violent or sexual references is completely ignored. For example, certain content becomes lost to the highest rating: A TV-MA program with an "S" for sexual content may contain violence at a TV-14 level but is not given a "V" for violent content. In addition, parents may be tempted to place inappropriate faith in the rating "FV" for fantasy violence,

Table 13.3 Current TV Ratings System

TV-Y (appropriate for all children)

TV-Y7 (directed to older children)

FV (fantasy violence—intense violence in children's programming)

TV-G (general audience)

TV-PG (parental guidance suggested)

   V (moderate violence)

   S (some sexual situations)

   L (infrequent coarse language)

   D (some suggestive dialogue)

TV-14 (parents strongly cautioned)

   V (intense violence)

   S (intense sexual situations)

   L (strong coarse language)

   D (intensely suggestive dialogue)

TV-MA (mature audiences only)

   V (graphic violence)

   S (explicit sexual activity)

SOURCE: Hogan (2001). Reprinted with permission.

even though research shows that this represents some of the most potentially detrimental programming for young children (Cantor, 1998; Federman, 1998). In fact, a study of more than 1,000 parents found that only 11% knew what FV stands for, and 9% actually thought it meant "Family Viewing" (Rideout, 2007).

Surveys conducted by the Kaiser Family Foundation have consistently shown that the V-chip device is used in less than 10% of households with children (Rideout, 2004, 2007). The Annenberg Public Policy Center conducted qualitative research on the reasons why parents do not use the V-chip and found that that while some parents admit to not understanding the ratings, others found the device awkward and difficult to program. Additionally, a substantial group of parents believe that they can do an adequate job of supervising their child's viewing without the assistance of technology (Scantlin & Jordan, 2006).

Unlike movie ratings, television ratings are applied on an episode-by-episode basis, usually by the producers of the program in consultation with the network. Two studies have revealed that producers are not always conscientious about rating their own programs (Greenberg, Rampoldi-Hnilo, & Mastro, 2000; Kunkel et al., 1998). In one early study of the implementation of the ratings system, nearly 80% of shows with violence and more than 90% of shows with sex did not receive the V or S content descriptors (Kunkel et al., 1998) (see Figure 13.5). For example, an episode of *Walker, Texas Ranger* featured the stabbing of two guards on a bus, an assault on a church by escaped convicts threatening to rape a nun, and a fight scene in which one escapee is shot and another is beaten unconscious. It did not receive a V descriptor. In addition, 80% of children's programs with violence do not receive the FV descriptor (Kunkel et al., 1998) (see Figure 13.6). More research is necessary to determine if the ratings applications have become more consistent between shows and across networks.

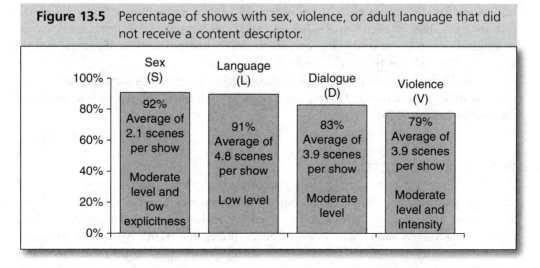

Figure 13.5 Percentage of shows with sex, violence, or adult language that did not receive a content descriptor.

SOURCE: Kunkel and colleagues (1998). Reprinted with permission.

Figure 13.6   Percentage of children's shows containing violence.

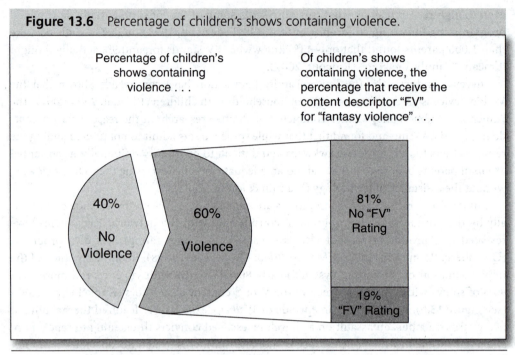

Percentage of children's shows containing violence . . .

Of children's shows containing violence, the percentage that receive the content descriptor "FV" for "fantasy violence" . . .

40% No Violence

60% Violence

81% No "FV" Rating

19% "FV" Rating

SOURCE: Kunkel and colleagues (1998). Reprinted with permission.

Video Game Ratings

As video game systems became more popular and game titles became more violent, the gaming industry initiated two different systems, one for video games and the other for computer games. The former won out, but it bears little resemblance to the movie and TV ratings systems (Gentile, Humphrey, & Walsh, 2005): a new EC rating (ages 3 and older), E (everyone), a new E10+ rating (everyone 10 and older), T (teen), M (mature), and AO (adults only). A study of the Entertainment Software Rating Board (ESRB) ratings found that more than half of all games are rated as containing violence, including more than 90% of games rated as appropriate for children 10 years and older (Gentile, 2008).

Finally, the music industry uses a single-rating system: "Parental Advisory: Explicit Lyrics." It, too, is voluntary and does not distinguish among lyrics that are explicitly violent, sexual, or profane (Federman, 1996).

Moving Forward

Although there are many ways in which communities can shield their children from problematic content and increase the availability of educational and prosocial content, the U.S. approach has been a fluid combination of public policy, self-regulatory mechanisms, and parental education. What follows are suggested strategies for improving the media landscape for children and adolescents.

Consistency in Ratings

The current "alphabet soup" of ratings systems is too confusing for parents to learn and apply and is even difficult for researchers to study (Greenberg et al., 2000). As can be seen in Figures 13.7 and 13.8, while the ratings are used by parents, they are often not seen as "very" useful. Many have argued that a single, uniform, content-based ratings system could and should be applied to all media that children and teenagers use (Gentile, 2010; Gentile et al., 2005; Greenberg & Rampoldi-Hnilo, 2012; Hogan, 2012). Consistency in ratings may improve parents' understanding of the ratings and lead to greater usage as a strategy for overseeing what children see, play, and listen to.

The voluntary nature of the current ratings systems is too easy for producers to exploit. The temptations are ever present to downcode a product to capture a larger audience (or, ironically, upcode it) or to depict increasingly edgy sexual, violent, or drug-taking behavior to attract attention and audiences (Gentile et al., 2005). An external ratings board, with representation from the various industries, along with parents, health professionals, and academics, would put the United States on par with many other Western countries (Federman, 1996). In addition, such a move would inevitably lead to a societal discussion of cultural values: What should we rate most heavily against? How do we define quality and "educational"? Such a dialogue, in and of itself, would be useful.

Figure 13.7   Percentage of parents who say they have ever used movie ratings, video game ratings, and music advisories.

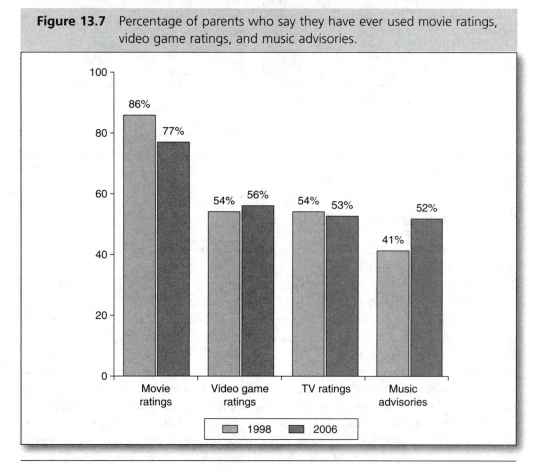

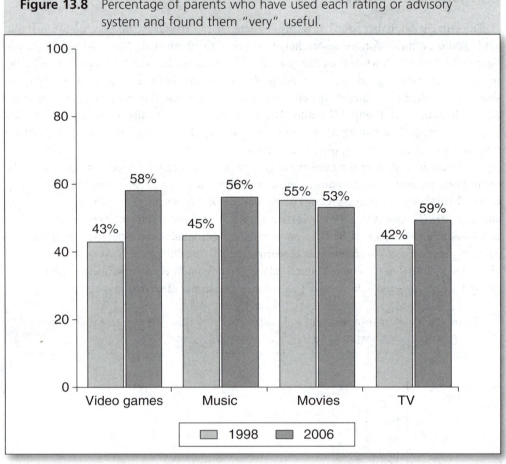

Figure 13.8   Percentage of parents who have used each rating or advisory system and found them "very" useful.

SOURCE: Rideout (2007). Used with permission.

Enforcement of Existing Rules

Many federal policies that are currently in place have been deemed ineffective, in large part because they are unenforced. One example of this lack of enforcement is the Children's Television Act of 1990. Seven years after passage of the act—after studies showed that the "vast wasteland" had not improved—the Federal Communications Commission developed a processing guideline informally known as the three-hour rule. Educational and informational (E/I) programming is defined by the FCC as content "that furthers the positive development of the child in any respect, including the child's cognitive/intellectual or social/emotional needs" (FCC, 1996). In addition, programming must be labeled educational on air, have education as a significant purpose, be specifically designed for children ages 16 and under, and air between the hours of 7 a.m. and 10 p.m. Broadcasters must specify the educational goal and target audience in quarterly reports to the FCC. Study after study has shown that despite these clear guidelines, as many as 20% of the programs that air as E/I are, in fact, devoid of educational content (Jordan, 1998, 2000; Wilson, Kunkel, & Drogos, 2009). Even when advocacy groups challenge the legitimacy of broadcasters' E/I claims, as happened in 2004, the FCC is slow and seemingly reluctant to act (Kunkel & Wilcox, 2012).

Greater Funding of Beneficial Media

Public policy has not dramatically changed the landscape of media for children. Broadcasters air the minimum number of hours of so-called E/I programs, but they do so reluctantly (Sullivan & Jordan, 1999). Levi (2010) has proposed that rather than being required to make room in their schedules for a child audience (which is less lucrative than an adult one), broadcasters can contribute to a fund for educational program development (a strategy Levi dubbed "pay or play"). Public broadcasting could surely benefit from such a scheme, as it is constantly faced with budget crises while attempting to stay on the cutting edge of new media. Funding is often cobbled together around a particular curricular goal (e.g., literacy or science) from agencies like the Department of Education and the National Science Foundation, which also function under the ever present threat of budget cuts. Consistent and sufficient funds are also necessary to study the impact of media that are designed to be educational. Historically, so much research focus has been on the problematic elements and outcomes of children's media use that we are only beginning to understand how media—particularly digital and interactive media—have the potential to advance the development of children and adolescents.

Parent Education

As the cartoon in Figure 13.9 illustrates, the generation of children who have grown up with new media technologies (dubbed "digital natives" by Marc Prensky in 2001) are often more savvy and sophisticated about the power of digital devices than their parents.

It is no longer reasonable to think that parents have the ultimate power over children's media use when, in fact, children have access to media content everywhere and all the time. An alternative way of thinking about parents' role in socializing their children comes from Ken Burns, the celebrated documentarian of *The Civil War* and *The National Parks: America's Best Idea.* Mr. Burns once said that the most important thing we can teach our children about media is a sense of aesthetics (K. Burns, personal communication, 1999). We must help children develop a sense of what is quality and what is garbage, and to give them tools to determine the best ways to deploy their media time in ways that will help them grow cognitively, emotionally, and socially.

Studies have shown that the best predictor of children's media use is parents' media use (e.g., Woodard, 2000). While we can exhort parents to take the TV out of children's bedrooms

Figure 13.9

SOURCE: *Dustin* © 2012 Steve Kelley & Jeff Parker. Dist. by King Features Syndicate, Inc.

or to block their access to Facebook until they are 13, what really shapes the way young people use media is what those around them are doing with media. Is it really surprising that we have a generation of children who cannot take their eyes off their smartphone screens when we have a generation of parents who do the same? Efforts to make media the best it can be in children's lives should start by asking parents to take stock of what they are doing with their time, and to reflect on whether they are providing what Hogan (2012) calls a "positive media role model."

Exercises

1. As regular viewers of *The Simpsons* know, "The Itchy & Scratchy Show" is a parody of violent children's cartoons. Like Wile E. Coyote and Roadrunner, Itchy and Scratchy do little more than pummel each other. After Marge Simpson writes a letter to the producer of the show, the tone of Itchy & Scratchy becomes much more prosocial—and dull. Kids begin turning off their TV sets and heading outdoors. However, as the episode proceeds, the advocates for change begin to protest other potentially offensive things, like a school field trip to the museum to see Michelango's statue *David*. Marge rethinks her position by saying that the experience proved to her that "one person *can* make a difference but most of the time they probably shouldn't." What do you think?

2. In 2007, the MPAA announced that it would allow filmmakers to appeal ratings based on what other films had been rated in the past. This move came after the success of the movie *This Film Is Not Yet Rated*, which is extremely critical of the MPAA. Should the MPAA ratings members be kept secret from the public? Should ratings be a negotiation between the MPAA and the filmmaker?

3. Why do you think parents take young children to see violent movies that are rated PG-13 or R and are clearly inappropriate for them? Is it because they cannot afford a babysitter? Or is it because they think such movies are harmless or will not affect their children? Should movie theaters bar young children from seeing such movies, even if their parents are accompanying them?

4. In some European countries, film ratings such as the "15" or "16" categories have legal force, such that children under those ages are not permitted by law to see such films. Would such laws effectively protect U.S. children from seeing age-inappropriate content? Why or why not?

5. In January 2000, news reports revealed that the White House Office of National Drug Control Policy (ONDCP) had been reviewing scripts from the networks' most popular shows, including *ER*, *Chicago Hope*, and *Beverly Hills, 90210*. Under an agreement involving a little-known $200 million government antidrug ad campaign, networks that accepted government PSAs had to include matching messages in their programming (Albiniak, 2000). Nearly $20 million in "credit" had been given to the networks. The ONDCP did not ask for prior approval of scripts but did help writers and producers with information about drugs or antidrug themes. (a) Did this agreement violate the First Amendment? (b) Should the government be involved in screening scripts for Hollywood? (c) Is there not a compelling public health interest in preventing drug use among citizens, especially children and teenagers? If so, what is wrong with the government aiding writers in creating antidrug messages in mainstream programming?

References

Albiniak, P. (2000, January 17). TV's drug deal: Networks exchange anti-drug programming for public service credits from White House. *Broadcasting and Cable*, p. 1.

American Academy of Pediatrics. (2006). Children, adolescents, and advertising. *Pediatrics, 118*, 2563.

An, S., & Stern, S. (2011). Mitigating the effects of advergames on children. *Journal of Advertising, 40*(1), 43–56.

Are G-rated films going too far? (2005, November 22). *Associated Press*. Retrieved from http://www .commonsensemedia.org/news/press-coverage.php?id=83

Beales, J. H. (2004). *Advertising to kids and the FTC: A regulatory retrospective that advises the present. Remarks before the George Mason Law Review 2004 Symposium on Antitrust and Consumer Protection, Competition, Advertising, and Health Claims: Legal and Practical Limits on Advertising Regulation.* Retrieved from http://www.ftc.gov/speeches/beales/040802adstokids.pdf

boyd, D., Hargittai, E., Schultz, J., & Palfrey, J. (2011, November). Why parents help their children lie to Facebook about age: Unintended consequences of the Children's Online Privacy Protection Act. *First Monday, 16*(11).

Brown v. Entertainment Merchants Association, Supreme Court No. 08-1448 (2010). Retrieved from http://www.law.cornell.edu/supct/html/08-1448.ZS.html

Bryant, A. (2006). *The children's television community.* London, UK: Routledge.

Bushman, B., & Cantor, J. (2003). Media ratings for violence and sex: Implications for policymakers and parents. *American Psychologist, 58*(2), 130–141.

Bushman, B. J., & Stack, A. D. (1996). Forbidden fruit versus tainted fruit: Effects of warning labels on attraction to television violence. *Journal of Experimental Psychology, 2*(3), 207–226.

Cantor, J. (1998). Ratings for program content: The role of research findings. *Annals of the American Academy of Political and Social Science, 557*, 54–69.

Caraher, M., Landon, J., & Dalmeny, K. (2006). Television advertising and children: Lessons from policy development. *Public Health Nutrition, 9*(5), 596.

Carter, T., Franklin, M., & Wright, J. (1999). *The First Amendment and the fifth estate: Regulation of electronic mass media* (5th ed.). New York, NY: Foundation Press.

CARU recommends Reebok discontinue certain claims for Zigtech sneakers; company agrees to do so. (2011, June 7). *CARU News.* Retrieved from http://www.caru.org/news/DocView.aspx?DocumentID=8637

Children's Television Act of 1990, Pub. L. No. 101–437, 104 Stat. 996 (codified at 47 U.S.C. 303a–303b (2006)).

Council on Communications and Media. (2011). Children, adolescents, obesity, and the media [Policy statement]. *Pediatrics, 128*, 201–208.

Dick, K. (2006). America's film rating system is a sham. *ABC News.* Retrieved from http://www.abcnews .go.com/Entertainment/print?id=2448557.

Ebert, R. (2001, February 9). A loose "Hannibal" loses power. *Albuquerque Journal*, p. 4.

Ebert, R. (2010, December 12). Getting real about movie ratings. *Wall Street Journal.* Retrieved from http://online.wsj.com/article/SB10001424052748703766704576009343432436296.html

Federal Communications Commission. (1996). In the matter of policies and rules concerning children's television programming: Report and order. *Federal Communications Commission, 11*, 10660–10778.

Federal Communications Commission. (2004). In the matter of complaints against various broadcast licensees regarding their airing of the "Golden Globe Awards" program. Memorandum Opinion and Order No. EB-03-IH-0110.

Federal Trade Commission. (2000). *Marketing violent entertainment to children: A review of self-regulation and industry practices in the motion picture, music recording and electronic game industries.* (Available from FTC Consumer Response Center, Room 130, 600 Pennsylvania Avenue NW, Washington, DC 20580)

Federal Trade Commission. (2011, April 28). *Interagency working group seeks input on proposed voluntary principles for marketing food to children.* Retrieved from http://www.ftc.gov/opa/2011/04/foodmarket.shtm

Federman, J. (1996). *Media ratings: Design, use and consequences.* Studio City, CA: Mediascope.

Federman, J. (Ed.). (1998). *National television violence study* (Vol. 3). Thousand Oaks, CA: Sage.

Gentile, D. A. (2008). The rating systems for media products. In S. Calvert & B. Wilson (Eds.), *The handbook of children, media and development*. Boston, MA: Blackwell.

Gentile, D. A. (2010). Are motion picture ratings reliable and valid? *Journal of Adolescent Health, 47,* 423–424.

Gentile, D. A., Humphrey, J., & Walsh, D. A. (2005). Media ratings for movies, music, video games, and television: A review of the research and recommendations for improvements. *Adolescent Medicine Clinics, 16,* 427–446.

Gentile, D. A., Maier, J. A., Hasson, M. R., & Lopez de Bonetti, B. (2011). Parents' evaluation of media ratings a decade after the television ratings were introduced. *Pediatrics, 128,* 36–44.

Ginsberg v. State of New York. (1968). 390 U.S. 629, 636.

Goldstein, A. O., Sobel, R. A., & Newman, G. R. (1999). Tobacco and alcohol use in G-rated children's animated films. *Journal of the American Medical Association, 281,* 1131–1136.

Graff, S. (2008). First Amendment implications of restricting food and beverage marketing in schools. *Annals of the American Academy of Political and Social Sciences, 615,* 158–177.

Greenberg, B. S., & Rampoldi-Hnilo, L. (2012). Child and parent responses to the age-based and content-based television ratings. In D. G. Singer & J. L. Singer (Eds.), *Handbook of children and the media* (2nd ed., pp. 615–630). Thousand Oaks, CA: Sage.

Greenberg, B. S., Rampoldi-Hnilo, L., & Mastro, D. (2000). *The alphabet soup of television program ratings.* Cresskill, NJ: Hampton.

Grier, S. (2001). The Federal Trade Commission's report on the marketing of violent entertainment to youths: Developing policy-tuned research. *Journal of Public Policy and Marketing, 20*(1), 123–132.

Harris, M. (2007, June 22). Hating the ratings. *Entertainment Weekly,* p. 76.

Hochman, D. (1999, July 9). Putting the "R" in "Park." *Entertainment Weekly,* pp. 15–16.

Hogan, M. J. (2012). Parents and other adults: Models and monitors of healthy media habits. In D. Singer & J. Singer (Eds.), *Handbook of children and the media* (2nd ed., pp. 661–680). Thousand Oaks, CA: Sage.

Hudson, H. (2004). Universal access: What have we learned from the E-Rate? *Telecommunications Policy, 28,* 309–321.

Institutes of Medicine. (2006). *Food marketing to children and youth: Threat or opportunity?* Washington, DC: National Academies Press.

Interstate Circuit, Inc. v. Dallas, Supreme Court (1968), 390 US 676.

James, K. (2011, December 30). 20 top grossing movies of 2011: THR year in review. *Hollywood Reporter.* Retrieved from http://www.hollywoodreporter.com/gallery/20-top-grossing-movies-2011-275348#1

Jordan, A. (1996a). *The state of children's television: An examination of quantity, quality, and industry beliefs* (Report No. 2). Philadelphia: University of Pennsylvania, Annenberg Public Policy Center.

Jordan, A. (1996b). *The first annual Annenberg Public Policy Center's Conference on Children and Television: A summary* (Report No. 6). Philadelphia: University of Pennsylvania, Annenberg Public Policy Center.

Jordan, A., & Woodard, E. (1998, May). Growing pains: Television for children in the new regulatory environment. *Annals of the American Academy of Political and Social Sciences, 557,* 83–95.

Jordan, A. (2000). *Is the three-hour rule living up to its potential?* (Report No. 34). Philadelphia: University of Pennsylvania, Annenberg Public Policy Center.

Jordan, A. (2008). Children's media policy. *Future of Children, 18*(1), 235–253.

Koplan, J. P., & Brownell, K. D. (2010). Response of the food and beverage industry to the obesity threat. *Journal of the American Medical Association, 13,* 1487–1488.

Kunkel, D. (1988). From a raised eyebrow to a turned back: The FCC and children's product-related programming. *Journal of Communication, 38*(4), 90–108.

Kunkel, D., & Canepa, J. (1994). Broadcasters' license renewal claims regarding children's educational programming. *Journal of Broadcasting and Electronic Media, 38,* 397–416.

Kunkel, D., & Castonguay, J. (2012). Children and advertising: Content, comprehension, and consequences. In D. Singer & J. Singer (Eds.), *Handbook of children and the media* (2nd ed., pp. 395). Thousand Oaks, CA: Sage.

Kunkel, D., Farinola, W. J. M., Cope, K. M., Donnerstein, E., Biely, E., & Zwarun, L. (1998). *Rating the TV ratings: One year out.* Menlo Park, CA: Kaiser Family Foundation.

Kunkel, D., McKinley, C., & Wright, P. (2009). *The impact of industry self-regulation on the nutritional quality of foods advertised on television to children. A report commissioned by Children Now.* Retrieved from http://www.childrennow.org/uploads/documents/adstudy_2009.pdf

Kunkel, D., & Wilcox, B. (2012). Children and media policy: Historical perspectives and current practices. In D. Singer & J. Singer (Eds.) *Handbook of children and the media* (2nd ed.). Thousand Oaks, CA: Sage.

Layton, L. (2011, May 24). Food makers resist lawmakers' proposal for guidelines in marketing to children. *Washington Post.* Retrieved from http://www.washingtonpost.com/politics/food-makers-resist-lawmakers-proposal-for-guidelines-in-marketing-to-children/2011/05/24/AFKf3mAH_story.html

Leone, R., & Barowski, L. (2011). MPAA ratings creep: A longitudinal analysis of the PG-13 rating category in US movies. *Journal of Children and Media, 5,* 53–68.

Levi, L. (2010, Spring). A "pay or play" experiment to improve children's educational television. *Federal Communications Law Journal,* p. 1.

Lewin, T. (October 23, 2009). No Einstein in your crib? Get a refund. *New York Times.* Retrieved from http://www.nytimes.com/2009/10/24/education/24baby.html?_r=1&em

Linn, S., & Novosat, C. L. (2008). Calories for sale: Food marketing to children in the twenty-first century. *Annals of the American Academy of Political and Social Science, 615,* 133.

Liptak, A. (June 27, 2011). Justices reject ban on violent video games for children. *New York Times.* Retrieved from http://www.nytimes.com/2011/06/28/us/28scotus.html?pagewanted=all

McIntyre, Jeff J. (2013). The political narrative of children's media research. In K. Dill (Ed.), *The Oxford Handbook of Media Psychology.* New York, NY: Oxford University Press, pp. 462–473.

Montgomery, K. (2012). Safeguards for youth in the digital marketing ecosystem. In D. Singer & J. Singer (Eds.), *Handbook of children and the media* (2nd ed., pp. 631–648). Thousand Oaks, CA: Sage.

Napoli, P. M. (2001). *Foundations of communications policy: Principles and process in the regulation of electronic media.* Cresskill, NJ: Hampton Press.

Nalkur, P. G., Jamieson, P. E., & Romer, D. (2010). The effectiveness of the Motion Picture Association of America's rating system in screening explicit violence and sex in top-ranked movies from 1950 to 2006. *Journal of Adolescent Health, 47,* 440–447.

Pecora, N. (1997). *The business of children's entertainment.* New York, NY: Guilford.

Prensky, M. (2001). Digital natives, digital immigrants. *On the Horizon, 9*(5), 1–5.

Rice, R. (2008). Central concepts in media ownership research and regulation. In R. Rice (Ed.), *Media ownership: Research and regulation.* Cresskill, NJ: Hampton Press.

Richley, W. (2012, June 21). Supreme Court says broadcast decency standards too vague. *Christian Science Monitor.* Retrieved from http://www.csmonitor.com/USA/Justice/2012/0621/Supreme-Court-says-broadcast-decency-standards-too-vague

Rideout, V. (2004). *Parents, media, and public policy: A Kaiser Family Foundation survey.* Menlo Park, CA: Kaiser Family Foundation.

Rideout, V. J. (2007). *Parents, children & media.* Menlo Park, CA: Kaiser Family Foundation.

Sacks, D. P., Bushman, B. J., & Anderson, C. A. (2011). Do violent video games harm children? Comparing the scientific amicus curiae "experts" in *Brown v. Entertainment Merchants Association. Northwestern University Law Review Colloquy, 106,* 1–12.

Scantlin, R., & Jordan, A. (2006). Families' experiences with the V-chip: An exploratory study. *Journal of Family Communication, 6*(2), 139–159.

Schmitt, K. (2000). *Public policy, family rules and children's media use in the home* (Report No. 35). Philadelphia: University of Pennsylvania, Annenberg Public Policy Center.

Schor, J. (2004). *Born to buy: The commercialized child and the new consumer culture.* New York, NY: Scribner.

Schwartz, M. B., & Ustjanauskas, A. (2012). Food marketing to youth: Current threats and opportunities. *Child Obesity, 8,* 85–88.

Sharma, L.L., Teret, S. P., & Brownell, K. D. (2010). The food industry and self-regulation: Standards to promote success and to avoid public health failures. *American Journal of Public Health, 100*(2), 240–246.

Snyder, W. (2011). Making the case for enhanced advertising ethics: How a new way of thinking about advertising ethnics may build consumer trust. *Journal of Advertising Research, 51*(3), 477–483.

Starr, P. (2004). *The creation of media: Political origins of modern communications.* New York, NY: Basic Books.

Sullivan, J., & Jordan, A. (1999). Playing by the rules: Impact and implementation of children's educational television regulations among local broadcasters. *Communication Law and Policy, 4*(4), 483–511.

Sunlight Foundation. (2011, December 7). *Food and media companies lobby to weaken guidelines on marketing food to children.* Retrieved from http://2012electioncontent.com/2011/12/07/the-sunlight-foundation-food-and-media-companies-lobby-to-weaken-guidelines-on-marketing-food-to-children/

Thompson, K. M., & Yokota, F. (2001). Depiction of alcohol, tobacco, and other substances in G-rated animated films. *Pediatrics, 107,* 1369–1374.

Thompson, K. M., & Yokota, F. (2004). *Violence, sex, and profanity in films: Correlation of movie ratings with content.* Retrieved from http://www.medscape.com/viewarticle/480900

Troianovski, A. (August 1, 2012). New rules on kids' Web ads. *Wall Street Journal,* Technology section.

Turow, J. (2003). *Americans and online privacy: The system is broken.* Philadelphia: University of Pennsylvania, Annenberg Public Policy Center. Retrieved from http://www.asc.upenn.edu/usr/jturow/internet-privacy-report/36-page-turow-version-9.pdf

Walsh, D. A., & Gentile, D. A. (2001). A validity test of movie, television, and video game ratings. *Pediatrics, 107,* 1302–1308.

Wartella, E. (2003). Communication research on children and public policy. In S. Braman (Ed.), *Communication researchers and policymaking* (pp. 359–373). Cambridge, MA: MIT Press Sourcebooks.

Waxman, S. (2001a, April 8). Rated S, for secret. *Washington Post,* p. G1.

Waxman, S. (2001b, May 31). Rating enforcement changes Hollywood's picture. *Washington Post,* p. C1.

Wilcox, B. L. (2003). The research/policy nexus: The Children's Television Act as case in point. *Applied Developmental Psychology, 24,* 367–373.

Wilson, B., Kunkel, D., & Drogos, K. (2009). *Educationally insufficient? An analysis of the availability and educational quality of children's E/I programming.* Oakland, CA: Children Now.

Wood, R. S. (2006). Tobacco's tipping point: The Master Settlement Agreement as a focusing event. *Policy Studies Journal, 34*(3), 419–436.

Woodard, E. (2000). *Media in the home—2000.* Philadelphia: University of Pennsylvania, Annenberg Public Policy Center.

Wright, P. J. (2009). An evaluation of the Federal Communications Commission's 2007 report on TV violence. *Communication Review, 12*(2), 174–186.

Wu, F. (2004). *United States v. American Library Ass'n: The Children's Internet Protection Act, library filtering, and institutional roles. Berkeley Technology Law Journal, 19,* 555–583.

Yale Rudd Center for Food Policy & Obesity. (2011). *Evaluating sugary drink nutrition and marketing to youth.* Retrieved from http://www.sugarydrinkfacts.org/resources/SugaryDrinkFACTS_Report.pdf

Yakota, F., & Thompson, K. M. (2000). Violence in G-rated animated films. *Journal of the American Medical Association, 283,* 1504–1506.

Zickuhr, K., & Smith, A. (2012). *Digital differences.* Washington, DC: Pew Research Center's Internet & American Life Project. Retrieved from http://pewinternet.org/~/media//Files/Reports/2012/PIP_Digital_differences_041312.pdf

Zoglin, R., & Tynan, W. (1992, January 20). Ms. Kidvid calls it quits. *Time* magazine. Retrieved from http://www.time.com/time/magazine/article/0,9171,974700,00.html

Author Index

Benton, K., 242
Beran, T., 444
Berchtold, A., 225
Berel, S., 376
Berel, S. R., 521
Berg, C., 198, 346
Berge, J. M., 496
Berger, A., 164, 466
Berger, C., 354, 361
Bergh, I. H., 344
Berglas, N. F., 241, 245
Bergsma, L. J., 509, 513, 514-515, 521, 532
Berk, L. E., 15
Berkey, C. B., 367
Berkey, C. S., 354, 356 (table), 363, 364, 367, 369
Berkowitz, L., 135, 151, 152, 156, 157, 158, 513, 545
Berlin, J., 228
Berlin, L., 142
Berman, A. L., 174
Berman, N., 355, 373
Bernat, D. H., 201
Berndt, E. R., 307
Berndt, T. J., 27, 33
Bernhardt, J. M., 197, 220, 229 (table), 298, 413, 472, 526
Bernstein, L., 104
Bero, L. A., 282
Berry, C., 284, 291
Berry, C. C., 490
Berry, M., 135, 140, 169
Berry, S. H., 120, 197, 219, 227, 229, 229 (table), 230 (table), 232, 233, 234, 238, 243, 247, 527
Bersamin, M., 299, 310
Bersamin, M. M., 197, 228, 230 (table), 231 (table), 247, 493, 493 (figure)
Beumont, P. J. V., 367
Bever, T. G., 62
Beyene, J., 344, 355, 373
Bharath-Kumar, U., 120
Bialous, S. A., 518, 519
Bichard, S., 67
Bickham, D., 197, 226, 231 (table), 232
Bickham, D. S., 31, 317, 377, 490, 491
Bickham, G. S., 516
Biddiss, E., 374
Biddle, S. J. H., 471
Biederman, J., 168
Biely, E., 196, 202, 204 (figure), 205, 206 (figure), 211, 575, 575 (figure), 576 (figure)
Biely, E. N., 202, 205
Biener, L., 290, 310
Bierut, L. J., 200
Bijvank, M. N., 461
Billieux, J., 472

Bingham, P. M., 118
Binswanger, I. A., 172
Biocca, F., 109, 526
Birch, L. L., 343, 500
Birch, S. H., 110
Birken, C. S., 344, 355, 373
Bittman, M., 493
Bjork, J. M., 281
Bjorvatn, B., 344
Black, S. R., 119, 240, 241
Blades, M., 82, 282
Blair, N. A., 298
Blair, S. N., 354
Blake, J., 208, 214, 215
Blake, S. M., 238
Blass, E. M., 355, 357
Blatt, J., 59, 60
Bleakley, A., 8, 139, 197, 198, 201, 213, 215, 227, 228, 230 (table), 231 (table), 232, 234, 234 (table), 357, 371, 488, 501
Blecher, E., 309
Bleijenberg, G., 119
Blix, G., 355
Block, G., 356 (table)
Block, M., 71
Blood, E. A., 360
Blum, R. W., 19, 172
Blumberg, F., 82
Blum-Dimaya, A., 123
Blumhoff, A., 218
Blut, D., 526
Bobkowski, P., 247
Bobkowski, P. S., 222
Boeck, T., 450 (figure)
Boerger, E. A., 26
Boersma, F. J., 24
Bogers, S., 218
Bohlin, G., 142
Bohn-Gettler, C., 27, 160
Boisseau, C. L., 362
Bolo, N., 472
Bomhof, E., 357
Bond, B. J., 76
Boninger, F., 84, 351, 528
Bonnie, R. J., 314 (table)
Booth, M. L., 354
Borusiak, P., 470
Borzekowski, D., 60
Borzekowski, D. L., 68
Borzekowski, D. L. G., 73, 241, 283, 285, 287, 299, 301, 306, 308, 344, 348, 350, 352, 353, 360, 361, 365, 367, 368, 373, 519
Bosker, B., 176
Bossarte, R. M., 275

Subject Index

About the Authors

Victor C. Strasburger is currently Chief of the Division of Adolescent Medicine, Distinguished Professor of Pediatrics, and Professor of Family & Community Medicine at the University of New Mexico. He graduated from Yale College (*summa cum laude* and *Phi Beta Kappa*), where he studied fiction writing with Robert Penn Warren, and from Harvard Medical School. He trained at the Children's Hospital in Seattle, St. Mary's Hospital Medical School in London, and the Boston Children's Hospital. Dr. Strasburger has authored more than 160 articles and papers and 13 books on the subject of adolescent medicine and the effects of television on children and adolescents, including *Getting Your Kids to Say No in the '90s When You Said Yes in the '60s* (1993), which has sold more than 15,000 copies to date; *Adolescent Medicine: A Practical Guide* (1991; 2nd edition, 1998); and *Adolescents and the Media* (1995). In the year 2000, he was named the recipient of the American Academy of Pediatrics' Adele Dellenbaugh Hofmann Award for outstanding lifetime achievement in adolescent medicine and the Holroyd-Sherry Award for outstanding achievement in public health and the media. He is a consultant to the American Academy of Pediatrics' Council on Communications and Media, has served as a consultant to the National PTA and the American Medical Association on the subject of children and television, and lectures frequently throughout the country.

Barbara J. Wilson is the Executive Vice Provost for Faculty and Academic Affairs at the University of Illinois at Urbana-Champaign (UIUC) and also the Kathryn Lee Baynes Dallenbach Professor in the Department of Communication at UIUC. Her research focuses on the social and psychological effects of the media on youth. She is coauthor of three book volumes of the National Television Violence Study (1997–1998). She also coedited the *Handbook of Children, Media, and Development* (Wiley-Blackwell, 2008) and has published over 100 articles, chapters, and technical reports on media effects and their implications for media policy.

Professor Wilson currently serves on the editorial boards of five academic journals, including *Media Psychology* and the *Journal of Media and Children*. In 2008, she was elected Fellow of the International Communication Association. She has served as a research consultant for Nickelodeon, the National Association of Television Program Executives, Discovery Channel Pictures, and the Centers for Disease Control and Prevention.

Amy B. Jordan is director of the Media and the Developing Child sector of the Annenberg Public Policy Center at the University of Pennsylvania, where she studies the impact of media policy on children and families. Her studies have examined the implementation and public reception of the educational television mandate known as the Three-Hour Rule, the V-Chip legislation. Her recent studies have focused on the contribution of children's heavy media use to the epidemic of overweight and obesity in America. In 2012, she joined Dafna Lemish as co-editor of *Journal of Children and Media*. She is the recipient of the International Communication Association's Best Applied/Policy Research Award and the National Communication Association's Stanley L. Saxon Applied Research Award.

About the Contributors

Jeanne Funk Brockmyer is a clinical child psychologist. She is Distinguished University Professor of Psychology, Emeritus, and past director of the Clinical Psychology doctoral training program in the University of Toledo's Department of Psychology in Toledo, Ohio. She is involved in teaching psychology to graduate and undergraduate students and conducting clinical research. Since 1990, Dr. Brockmyer's research team has been investigating relationships between playing violent video games and various personality and behavioral characteristics in children. In 2005, she was awarded the Outstanding Researcher award at the University of Toledo. Dr. Brockmyer and her team have developed and published measures of children's attitudes toward violence, empathy, and video game engagement, which are used in her research projects and by researchers worldwide. Using these measures, Dr. Brockmyer's team has worked on identifying characteristics that may be specific risk factors for negative impact from video game playing, including desensitization to violence and deep engagement in game playing. Dr. Brockmyer and her team have also examined parental perceptions and knowledge of game and other media ratings, particularly among parents of younger children. Dr. Brockmyer contributed to an amicus brief to the Supreme Court addressing the need to enforce the video game ratings system. She was a member of the International Society for Research on Aggression's Media Violence Commission that, in 2012, developed a public statement on the empirically established effects of media violence exposure.

Ed Donnerstein's major research interests are mass media violence and mass media policy. He has published over 240 scientific articles in these general areas and serves on the editorial boards of a number of academic journals in both psychology and communication. He was a member of the American Psychological Association's Commission on Violence and Youth as well as the APA Task Force on Television and Society. He served on the Surgeon General's Panel on Youth Violence as well as on the Advisory Council of the American Medical Association Alliance's violence prevention program. He is a past president of the International Society for Research on Aggression. In 2008 he received the American Psychological Association Media Psychology Division Award for Distinguished Scientific Contributions to Media Psychology. In addition, he was primary research site director for the National Cable Television Association's 3.5 million-dollar project on TV violence. He served as dean of the College of Social and Behavioral Sciences at the University of Arizona from 2002 to 2009. He was also Dean of Social

Sciences at the University of California–Santa Barbara as well as the Rupe Chair in the Social Effects of Mass Communication.

He has testified at numerous governmental hearings, both in the United States and abroad, regarding the effects and policy implications surrounding mass media violence and pornography, including testimony before the United States Senate on TV violence. He has served as a member of the United States Surgeon General's Panel on Pornography and the National Academy of Sciences' Subpanel on Child Pornography and Child Abuse.

Rajitha Kota graduated from the University of Wisconsin–Madison in 2011 with bachelor's degrees in biology and political science and in 2012 with a Master of Public Health (MPH) degree. She joined the Social Media and Adolescent Health Research Team (SMAHRT) in September of 2011 and has done research exploring the influence of Facebook and cyberbullying behaviors among college students. She is currently working as a researcher at Seattle Children's Research Institute. Her future plans involve pursuing a medical degree, where she hopes to further explore her interests in primary care and global health.

Robert McCannon is an independent media education consultant and cofounder and president of the Action Coalition for Media Education, the only independent national media education organization in the United States (http://www.acmecoalition.org). He was formerly executive director of the New Mexico Media Literacy Project (NMMLP), founded in 1993. From 1993 to 2005, it became the most successful media literacy project in the U.S.

Having studied psychology, history, and the cognition of education, Bob taught humanities, history, propaganda, advertising, and media education in middle, high, and graduate school. He is the only non-pediatrician to have been honored with the American Academy of Pediatrics' coveted Holroyd-Sherry award for quality media education and concern for the welfare of children.

Bob does workshops, keynotes, and presentations each year, having worked in every state and many countries. More than 1,000 people have taken his four-day Catalyst Institute—a train-the-trainers workshop. He has authored dozens of nationally recognized media education curricula in the fields of health, history, social studies, English, and civic education.

He can be reached at mccannon@flash.net.

Megan Moreno is an adolescent medicine physician at Seattle Children's Hospital and the University of Washington and is currently involved in patient care, medical education, and research. Dr. Moreno is the Principal Investigator for the Social Media and Adolescent Health Research Team (SMAHRT). The SMAHRT research team's focus includes ways in which technology can be used toward improving adolescent health, with a particular interest in new opportunities and challenges presented by social media.

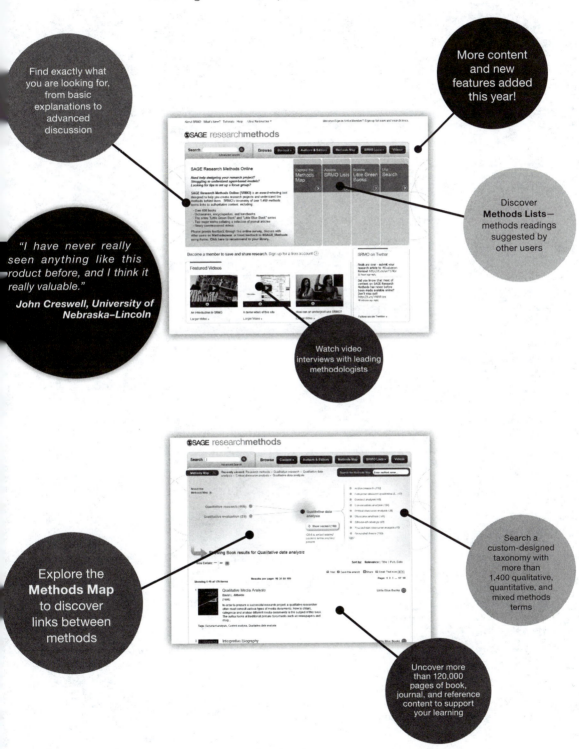

❍SAGE research**methods**

The essential online tool for researchers from the world's leading methods publisher

Find exactly what you are looking for, from basic explanations to advanced discussion

More content and new features added this year!

"I have never really seen anything like this product before, and I think it really valuable."

John Creswell, University of Nebraska–Lincoln

Discover **Methods Lists**— methods readings suggested by other users

Watch video interviews with leading methodologists

Explore the **Methods Map** to discover links between methods

Search a custom-designed taxonomy with more than 1,400 qualitative, quantitative, and mixed methods terms

Uncover more than 120,000 pages of book, journal, and reference content to support your learning

Find out more at
www.sageresearchmethods.com